The Exclusive Claims of Puseyite Episcopalians to the Christian Ministry Indefensible

THE EXCLUSIVE CLAIMS

OF

PUSEYITE EPISCOPALIANS

TO THE CHRISTIAN MINISTRY

INDEFENSIBLE:

WITH AN INQUIRY INTO THE DIVINE RIGHT OF

EPISCOPACY AND THE APOSTOLIC SUCCESSION:

IN A SERIES OF LETTERS TO THE REV. DR PUSEY

By JOHN BROWN, D.D.
MINISTER OF LANGTON, BERWICKSHIRE

TO WHICH IS PREFIXED

AN ARTICLE ON THE ANGLICAN REFORMATION

From the Edinburgh Presbyterian Review

PHILADELPHIA:
PRESBYTERIAN BOARD OF PUBLICATION.
Paul T Jones, Publishing Agent.
1844.

Wipf and Stock Publishers
199 W 8th Ave, Suite 3
Eugene, OR 97401

The Exclusive Claims of Puseyite Episcopalians
to the Christian Ministry Indefensible
With an Inquiry Into the Divine Right
of Episcopacy and the Apostolic Succession:
In a Series of Letters to the Rev. Dr. Pusey
By Brown, John
Softcover ISBN-13: 978-1-7252-9897-2
Hardcover ISBN-13: 978-1-7252-9898-9
eBook ISBN-13: 978-1-7252-9899-6
Publication date 1/29/2021
Previously published by
Presbyterian Board of Publication, 1844

This edition is a scanned facsimile
of the original edition published in 1844.

THE

ANGLICAN REFORMATION.*

THE origin of Puritan nonconformity,† its ample warrant, and complete justification, will be found in the character and proceedings of Queen Elizabeth, the principles on which the Anglican Church was at first based, and the means by which it was finally established.

Elizabeth was one of those persons whose character it is difficult to portray, because it consisted of elements apparently irreconcilable. She possessed the peculiar characteristics of both sexes in almost equal proportions. She had all the masculine energy and enlarged capacity of a strong-minded man, with all the caprice, vanity, and obstinacy of a weak-minded woman; while the circumstances in which she was placed had a direct tendency to develope and mature all the elements of her character. She was suspicious by nature, by education, and by necessity, and despotic by temperament, by habit, and by policy. Thoroughly and intensely selfish, she made all the means within her reach minister to her own interests; utterly insensible to the miseries she might occasion to the instruments of her will, or the objects of her

* The article on the Anglican Reformation is from the Presbyterian Review of January, 1843.

† Puritans and nonconformists were, at first, the common titles of those who were subsequently called Presbyterians, while Brownites, sectaries, and separatists, were the ordinary appellations of those who are now called Independents. See Pierce's Vindication of the Dissenters, pp. 147, 189, 205, 6, 213, 215, 223. Hanbury's Eccl. Memorials of Independents, i. 3, 5, *et passim*.

gave a reluctant assent to have them removed from the churches, she still retained a crucifix, with tapers burning before it, upon the altar in her own private chapel. Against this open idolatry, all her prelates, not even Cox excepted, remonstrated in a style of very unusual vehemence; and in terms the most obsequious, yet firm, they begged leave to decline officiating in her majesty's chapel until the abomination was removed. For the moment she seems to have given way to the storm. But she soon recovered her obstinate determination in favour of her crucifix and lighted tapers,—restored them to their former place upon the altar,*—and there they remained at least as late as 1572.† Nor were these badges of idolatry retained merely as ornaments. Strype informs us distinctly, that "she and her nobles used to give honour to them."‡ Nor could it be any ambi-

---

Martyr, (Burnet's Hist. Ref Records, Bk. vi. No. 60,) dated 4th Feb. 1560, beginning, "O my father, what shall I write thee?" in which he says, "That controversy about crosses (in Churches) is now hot amongst us You can scarcely believe in so silly a matter, how men, who seemed rational, play the fool. Of these the only one you know is Cox. To-morrow a disputation is appointed to take place upon this matter. Some members of parliament are chosen arbitrators. The disputants are, in favour of crosses, the Archbishop of Canterbury (Parker) and Cox; against them, Grindal (Bishop of London) and myself. The result lies at the mercy of our judges. However, I laugh when I think with what, and how grave and solid arguments they shall defend their paltry crosses. I shall write you the result, however it may go. At present the cause is in dependance. However, so far as I can divine, this is the last letter you shall receive from me as a bishop, for the matter is come to that pass, that we must either take back those crosses of silver and pewter, which we have broken, or resign our bishopricks."

* In 1570. Strype's Parker, ii. 35, 36.

† Strype, speaking of the year 1565, says, "The queen still, to this year, kept the crucifix in her chapel." Annals, i. ii. 198. Again, "I find the queen's chapel stood *in statu quo* seven years after" *Ibid.* 200. Cartwright also mentions the fact in his "Admonition to Parliament," published in 1570. Parker exerted himself strenuously, but in vain, against this nuisance. Strype's Parker, i 92. The encouragement which this attachment of the queen to some of the grossest errors of their system gave the papists, may be inferred from the fact, that a popish priest, in 1564, dedicated to her a work in defence of the crucifix being retained and worshipped as before. Strype's An. i. 260-2.

‡ Strype's An. i. 259, 260.

guous manifestation of popery and idolatry, which could extract from Cox that long and urgent declinature to officiate in her chapel, in which he says, "I most humbly sue unto your godly zeal, prostrate and with wet eyes, that ye will vouchsafe to peruse the considerations which move me, that I dare not minister in your grace's chapel, the lights and cross remaining."*

But although Elizabeth was thus obstinate in favour of these " dregs of Popery," and " relics of the Amorites," as Jewell termed them, she had not even the semblance of personal religion. Those members of the Church of England who are favourable to protestantism, and yet feel that their Church is identified with the Church of Elizabeth, may, as a matter of course, be expected to portray her both as Protestant and pious; and this has been done to an extent which, in our mind, has rendered every history of Elizabeth, by members of the Anglican Church, altogether unworthy of credit, except simply when they state facts, and give their authority for them. Even Strype, so favourably distinguished for veracity and candour, exerts himself to write a panegyric on Elizabeth, although the facts which he is too honest to conceal, jar oddly enough with his praises; and although also, occasional expressions drop unguardedly from his pen, which show how dissatisfied he was with the personal character and religion of that queen.

"And, indeed," he says, speaking of her religious character at her accession, "what to think of the queen at this time as to her religion, one might hesitate somewhat."† She seldom or never attended Church except during Lent, (which she observed, and compelled others to observe, with all the formality of Rome,) when the best pulpit orators from all parts of England were summoned up to preach before her.‡ She, indeed, held the preaching of the gospel not only in contempt, but in something bordering upon detesta-

* Strype's An. 1. 260, and Ap. Rec. No. 22.
† Annals, 1. 2.   ‡ Strype's Parker, 1. 401.

tion, and wished that all her subjects should follow her own example in absenting themselves from hearing sermons. While nine parishes out of every ten throughout the kingdom were destitute of a preaching ministry, she commanded Grindal, in 1576, to diminish still further the number of preachers, declaring that three or four were sufficient for a whole county—that preaching did more harm than good, and that, consequently, "it was good for the Church to have few preachers."* And because he would not obey, suppress "the prophesyings," and lessen the number of preachers, she suspended him from his functions, sequestered his revenues, and confined him a prisoner to his own house, and it was with some difficulty she was restrained from proceeding further against him. Grindal's firmness, however, under God, saved England; for had he yielded to her anti-christian tyranny, it is easy to perceive what the result must have been upon the moral and spiritual condition of the kingdom.

Nor were her morals more eminent than her piety. Without giving more attention than they deserve to the scandalous revelations of Lingard, or to the rumours which have descended to our own time in secret memoirs, in MSS., and by traditions, it is impossible to question that the "virgin queen" hardly deserved the epithet of which she was so ambitious.† She indulged freely in the pleasures of the table. During her annual "progresses," her prelates and nobles, aware of her taste for magnificent entertainments, rivalled one another in ministering to her gratification. After her return from these more than oriental *fêtes*, she was generally indisposed, nature exacting her usual tribute, not less from the queen, than from more

---

* Strype's Grindal, pp. 328, 329, and Appendix B. ii. No. 9, which we recommend to our readers to read throughout.

† Leicester, in a private letter to Walsingham, while ambassador at Paris, speaking of a mysterious illness, by which she was suddenly seized, says, "That, indeed, she had been troubled with a *spice or show of the mother*." And although he says that, "indeed, it was not so," he was too good a courtier, as well as too personally implicated, to be a trustworthy witness. Strype's An. iii. 319.

plebeian gourmands.* She swore most profanely, not only in her conversation, but also in her letters, and that not only to her profane men, but even to her prelates.†

As Elizabeth did not often attend church, she had the more time to desecrate the Sabbath; and while the puritans were persecuted for not honouring saints' day, she, her nobles and her prelates, profaned the day of the Lord. In one of her "progresses," in 1575, she spent three weeks at Kenilworth, one of the seats of her favourite, the Earl of Leicester. A contemporary chronicler gives the following account of the manner in which two of the Sabbaths spent there were desecrated. In the forenoon she went to the parish church. But "the afternoon" was spent " in excellent music of sundry sweet instruments, and in dancing of lords and ladies, and other worshipful degrees, with lively agility and commendable grace. At night, late after a warning or two," such as Jupiter's respects to the queen and other heathen masques and mummeries, there " were blazes of burning darts flying to and fro, beams of stars, coruscant streams, and hail of fiery sparks, lightning of wild-fire, in

* Thus, in 1571, after her return from one of these "progresses," "She was taken suddenly sick at her stomach, and as suddenly relieved by a vomit." Strype's An. III. 175.

† Sir John Harrington, giving a description of an interview he had with her in 1601, a year or two before her death, says, "She swears much at those that cause her griefs in such wise, to the no small discomfiture of all about her." *Nugae Antiquae*, i. 319. We owe the following anecdote to the same amusing gossip. Cox of Ely having refused to alienate some of the best houses and manors of his see to some of her courtiers, notwithstanding of a personal command from the queen, received from the indignant Elizabeth the following characteristic epistle. "Proud prelate, you know what you were before I made you what you are; if you do not immediately comply with my request, by G—d, I will unfrock you. ELIZABETH" However ludicrous to us, such a mandate must have been anything but laughable to the poor bishop of Ely. With a pertinacity, however, which would have been sublime, had it been displayed in a better cause, Cox preserved to the last the revenues of his see. After his death, however, Elizabeth was revenged She kept the diocese vacant for eighteen years, (as she kept Oxford for twenty-two years,) and before a succession was appointed, she stripped it so bare, that from having been one of the richest, it is now one of the poorest dioceses in England.

water and land, flight and shot of thunder-bolts—all with continuance, terror and vehemence, as though the heavens thundered, the water scourged, and the earth shook. This lasted till after midnight." Next Sabbath the same scene was repeated with sundry alterations. But, in addition, "this, by the kalendar," being "St. Kenelme's day," the genius or tutelary god of the place, there "was a solemn country bridal, with running at quintal, in honour of this Kenilworth Castle, and *of God* and St. Kenelme!"* When we bear in mind the manner in which the Sabbath has been desecrated in England down from the Reformation by princes, peers, and prelates, by "Book of Sports," by acts of parliament and convocation, and that the only friends of Sabbath observance have been the persecuted puritans, the wonder is, not that it should be so grievously desecrated, but that any veneration whatever should continue to be paid to it.

Among the manifold forms in which the queen's attachment to the "relics of Popery" displayed itself, few were so offensive to the clergy as her countenance of clerical celibacy and her opposition to the marriage of the priesthood. In her first parliament

* *Apud* Strype's An. ii. 1. 584, 585. It may be said in palliation of Elizabeth's desecration of the Sabbath, that she only followed the example set before her by the primate of all England. Parker having finished a princely dining hall in his palace at Canterbury, in 1565, gave several magnificent entertainments there. "The first," says his biographer, "was at Whitsuntide, and lasted three days, that is *Sunday*, Monday, and Tuesday." . . . "His second feast was on Trinity *Sunday* following. . . . The hall was set forth with much plate of silver and gold, adorned with rich tapestry of Flanders . . . There were dainties of all sorts, both meats and drinks, and in great plenty, and all things served in excellent order by none but the archbishop's servants." Strype's Parker, i. 376—380. It was Parker's ambition upon these occasions to rival the fêtes given by his predecessor Warham to the Emperor Charles V. and Henry VIII., and that such important matters might not be lost to posterity, he became their historian himself. *Ibid.* ii. 296, 297. Even when he retired to his smallest country residence, Parker's domestic establishment consisted of about a hundred retainers. *Ibid.* i. 277. Parker, however, was completely outshone by Whitgift, who rivalled Wolsey himself. See his Life by "Sir George Paule, comptroller of his Grace's household," in Wordsworth's Ecclesiastical Biography, iv. 387—9.

an attempt was made to pass an act to legalize the marriage of the clergy, as had been done in the reign of her brother, but she would not permit it.* Various efforts were made by Cecil, Parker (who was married himself) and others, to induce her, at subsequent periods, to yield; but their attempts only exasperated the vestal queen. In 1561, she issued an injunction forbidding married clergymen from living with their wives within the precincts of colleges or cathedral closes, and but for the importunity of Cecil, she would have absolutely forbidden the marriage of the clergy. When Parker shortly afterwards waited upon her, she scolded him with much "bitterness," and spoke in such terms not only against clerical matrimony, but the whole constitution of the Church of England, and threw out such hints of what it was her intention to do to remedy the evils she complained of, that, as he wrote to Cecil, he expected nothing short of an absolute order to restore things to the condition in which they stood in the reign of her sister, or, at all events, that she would restore so much of popery that 'he could not conform to the Church.† When she cooled, however, and saw that Protestantism was the only tenure by which she held her crown, she relented so far as not to compel a return to popery, but she issued orders imposing conditions upon the marriage of the priesthood, which he must have been not only uxorious indeed, but degraded in taste and spirit, who could comply with.‡ Never could she be got to give any thing more than a tacit connivance to clerical matrimony, while ever and anon she poured her contempt upon both the married clergy and their wives. That amusing gossip, Sir John Harrington, gives the following ludicrous instance of her treatment even of the primate's lady. Parker had given Elizabeth one of his sumptuous banquets at Lambeth. As the queen was retiring, she thus publicly addressed Mrs. Parker: "Madam"—(the usual title of mar-

* Strype's Ann. i. 118.   † Strype's Parker, i. 213—217.
‡ See the injunctions in Bishop Sparrow's Collections, 65, or in Dr. Cardwell's Documentary Annals of the Church of England, i. No. 43. pp. 178—209.

ried ladies)—"Madam I may not call you, Mistress" (the ordinary title of unmarried ladies) "I am loath to call you, but, however, I thank you for your good cheer." In 1594, she banished Bishop Fletcher, lately translated from Worcester to London, from her court for having married "a fine lady," (sister to Sir George Gifford, one of her gentlemen pensioners,) which she said "was a very indecent act for an elderly clergyman." Nor did her wrath end here. She commanded Whitgift to suspend him, and it was with considerable exertions on the part of Cecil that at the end of six months the suspension was removed. Still she would not suffer him for a twelvemonth afterward to appear in her presence. The poor court chaplain, who had hitherto basked in the sunshine of her smiles, pined away under her frowns, and died shortly afterwards of a broken heart,—a warning to all "elderly clergymen" not to be guilty of such "indecent acts" in future.* We shall show in the sequel that if Elizabeth had had any regard to the morals of the clergy, (which she had not,) she ought rather to have passed a law compelling them to marry, nor would it have militated against good morals had she set them the example.

Such having been Elizabeth's feelings against Protestantism and in favour of Popery, it must be matter of great surprise to ordinary readers that she should ever have become a Protestant at all. And, indeed, we are thoroughly persuaded that if she had not been necessitated, both by her personal and political position, to promote the reformed interest, she would have remained herself, and kept the kingdom too, in communion with the Church of Rome. Religion with Elizabeth was, all her life, a mere political engine. While she persecuted in her own kingdom all who opposed her ecclesiastical views, she aided by counsels, men, and money, the Protestants of Scotland, France, Geneva, and the Netherlands, who opposed the ecclesiastical supremacy of their civil governors.

* See the whole account in Strype's Whitgift, ii. 215—218.

The court of Rome had declared her father's marriage with her mother invalid, and herself consequently illegitimate, and incapable of inheriting the throne of England. On her accession, she despatched a notification of that event to Rome, and resolved in the meanwhile to do nothing in favour of the Reformation, lest she might alienate the Vatican. The pontiff, however, ignorant equally of his own impotency, and of the imperiousness of her whom he addressed, sent her back a haughty and arrogant answer, declared her illegitimate, commanded her to abandon the throne she had usurped, and resign herself entirely to the will of the holy see of which England was but a fief. Such language Elizabeth could little brook even from the assumed vicar of Christ. Had the energetic but wily and insinuating Sixtus V. then occupied the chair of Peter, from his avowed regard for the congenial character of Elizabeth, and from other politic considerations, the answer would assuredly have been different, and the result would as assuredly have been different also. Or had Elizabeth been a weak-minded Papist, as she was a strong-minded-one, she might have been terrified into compliance, and Mary of Scotland would have ascended the throne of England in her own person instead of that of her son. But God made the wrath of men to praise him, and human infirmities and folly to magnify his own wisdom and might. Elizabeth's courage could as little falter at the spiritual thunders of the Vatican as at the more formidable artillery of the Armada of Spain. She therefore at once determined to declare open war with the papacy, and to construct the Church of England after a model which, without banishing Popery in the splendour of its ornaments, the magnificence of its ritual, the mysticism of its sacraments, or the scholasticism of its dogmas, should be found more subservient to her own will, and more conducive to her personal aggrandizement, than if it held of Rome. She resolved to unite the *pontificale* with the *regale* in her own person, to incorporate the triple-storied tiara with the imperial

xiv   THE ANGLICAN REFORMATION.

diadem, and grasp the keys of Peter with the same hand which wielded the sword of Alfred. In one word, she determined to become to the Church of England what the Pope was to the Church of Rome; and she carried her determination into execution.

Elizabeth left neither her prelates nor her privy council at any loss to divine her intentions. She told Parker at the interview, at which, as already narrated, she had denounced the marriage of the clergy, that she meant to issue out injunctions in favour of Popery.* Had she been so disposed, the act of supremacy, to which we shall immediately allude, placed the entire constitutional power so to do in her hands. Political considerations, however, dissuaded her from seeking reconciliation with Rome. She valued her ecclesiastical supremacy at the very least as highly as her civil autocracy; and as a reconciliation with Rome could be purchased only by the surrender of the former, and most probably also of the latter, Elizabeth remained satisfied with the power to render the national religion Popish in every thing but a submission to the universal supremacy of the Pope. Parker, whose conscience was sufficiently elastic to enable him to remain in England during the reign of Mary, and whose nerves were not easily shaken, was in a "horror" at the determined manner in which she told him she was resolved to restore Popery; and he anticipated nothing else than that he should be one of the first victims of a new Popish persecution.† Even Cox, who, next to Cheney of Gloucester, was the most papistical of Elizabeth's first bishops, was so well aware of her inclinations to restore more of Popery than even he desired, that one of the arguments which he employed to urge Parker to a more vigorous persecution of the puritans, was an apprehension lest the opposition they gave to her ecclesiastical arrangements should provoke her to a total abandonment of Protestantism.‡ Indeed, so well established is this point by the clearest historic evi-

* Strype's Parker, i. 217, 218.
† Ibid. Ap. Records, No. 17.   ‡ Ibid. i. 456.

dence, that no man acquainted with the facts of the case now doubts it, except, perhaps, some Anglican evangelicals, who are retained in the bosom of the Church of England through a delusive idea that it had really been reformed by Elizabeth. The High Church party are perfectly aware that Elizabeth did prevent the reformation of the Church of England. "This arbitrary monarch," says one of that party, "had a tendency towards Rome almost in every thing but the doctrine of the papal supremacy. To the real presence she was understood to have no objection; the celibacy of the clergy she decidedly approved; the gorgeous rites of the ancient form of worship she admired, and in her own chapel retained."* The Puseyites gratefully acknowledge the service Elizabeth rendered to their cause. "Queen Elizabeth," says one of that school, "with her prejudices in favour of the old religion, was doubtless an instrument in the hand of God for stopping the progress of the Reformation."† Indeed, the only objections that party have to Elizabeth's measures is, that she kept the supremacy to herself instead of leaving it in the hands of the clergy.

Still with all her faults, and they are sufficiently numerous and aggravated, Elizabeth was a splendid monarch, and we can easily account for the admiration in which her memory is still held in England. To view her to advantage, or perhaps even to do her justice, we must forget her sex, overlook her religious opinions, bear in mind the unsettled form of the constitution, and judge her by the maxims of her own age. That assuredly could be no ordinary personage who could task the consummate sagacity and finished tact of Cecil, fix the volatile passions of Lei-

* Quarterly Review for June 1827, p. 31. See even the low church Burnet, the indiscriminate panegyrist of Elizabeth's measures, Hist. Ref. ed. 1839, ii. 582–3. Dr. Short, the present bishop of Sodor and Man, makes the same confession, Sketch of the Hist. of the Church of England, 2d ed. 313, et passim. And so, in short, as we have said, do all historians, except some evangelicals, to whose position it is essential to overlook the fact.

† British Critic for October 1842, p. 333. See also, p. 330—1.

cester, bend the stubborn spirit of Parker, outmanœuvre the Machiavellian policy of Montalto, and humble the genius, chivalry, and resources of Spain. In courage equal to Semiramis, in accomplishments to Zenobia, in policy and energy to Catharine, she possessed a combination of talents to which none of them could lay claim. Forget for the moment her creed, overlook her treatment of parliament and the Puritans, place yourself in her own age, and view her merely as a monarch, and even prejudice must acknowledge that she was the most magnificent sovereign that ever occupied the English throne.

The various steps by which the Church of England was brought to assume its present form, have been, as might well be expected, very keenly canvassed. We shall enable the reader, by a simple induction of facts, to form his own opinion both of the Church itself, and of the various means by which it was primarily established, and made to assume its present form.

The first act of Elizabeth's first Parliament restored to the crown the supremacy in matters spiritual which was possessed by Henry VIII. and Edward VI., but which Mary had resigned to the Pope. By this act

"Such jurisdictions, privileges, superiorities, and pre-eminences, spiritual and ecclesiastical, as by any spiritual or ecclesiastical power or authority hath heretofore been, or may lawfully be exercised or used for the visitation of the ecclesiastical state and persons, and for reformation, order, and correction of the same, and of all manner of errors, heresies, schisms, abuses, offences, contempts and enormities, shall for ever, by the authority of the present parliament, be united and annexed to the imperial crown of the realm."

By a clause in the act of uniformity, it was enacted, "That the Queen's Majesty, by advice of her ecclesiastical commissioners, may ordain and publish such ceremonies or rites as may be most for the advancement of God's glory, and the edifying of the church." So highly did Elizabeth esteem the authority thus conferred upon her that she told Parker she would never have consented to establish the Protestant religion at all but for the power with which she was thus invested to change it according to her own will. Nor let it be forgotten that our gracious sovereign Victoria, has, at this moment, the very same extent of power which the act of supremacy conferred upon Elizabeth.

In order to enable Elizabeth, and all her successors, to exercise this most exorbitant power, by a clause in the act of supremacy she was empowered to delegate her authority to any persons, being natural born subjects, whether lay or clerical, who, as commissioners from, and for the crown, were empowered to "visit, reform, redress, order, correct and amend all such errors, heresies, schisms, abuses, contempts and enormities whatsoever, which, by any manner of spiritual or ecclesiastical power, authority or jurisdiction, can or may lawfully be reformed, ordered, redressed, corrected, restrained or amended."

"Nothing," as a High Church historian has well observed, "can be more comprehensive than the terms of this clause. The whole compass of Church discipline seems (and not only seems, but in reality was) transferred upon the crown."* While all parties, except the most decided Erastians, low churchmen, and some also of the Evangelical body, have united in condemning, in the strongest terms, the spiritual powers thus conferred upon the crown, their indignation has been specially directed against that clause by which the whole ecclesiastical jurisdiction of the Church of England may be exercised by lay commissioners, acting by a warrant under the crown. Had the crown been restricted to employ only ecclesiastics in ecclesiastical causes, the evil would be practically redressed. But as the crown not only possessed, but exercised the power to place this jurisdiction in the hands of laymen, who, in virtue of their commission, were empowered to examine, censure,

* Collier's Ecclesiastical History, Barham's edition, vi. 224.

suspend, and even depose, not only the inferior clergy, but even the prelates and the primates, and did too, in manifold instances, execute their commission, it were strange, indeed, if any man who can distinguish the Church from the world, and things spiritual from things civil, could but deplore and condemn this foul invasion of the privileges of Christ's kingdom.

Such was the foundation of the high commission court, and of the star chamber, which in a subsequent age, proved so disastrous, not only to the liberties and the lives of the subject, but also to the stability of the altar and the throne. The authority of these courts was so undefined, their powers so despotic, that they could be perpetuated only by the destruction of all liberty, both civil and religious.

"Whoever," says a Romanist historian of high name, "will compare the powers given to this tribunal, (the high commission court) with those of the inquisition which Philip the Second endeavoured to establish in the Low Countries, will find that the chief difference between the two courts consisted in their names."*

And all that a learned and zealous advocate of the Church of England can say in her defence is, that "Dr. Lingard ought to have added, that though such commissions were not unknown in the time of Edward VI., the person who first brought into England the model attempted in the Low Countries was Queen Mary; . . . and that the same system was continued in the reign of Elizabeth, not because it was congenial with the spirit of Protestantism, but because the temper of the times had been trained and hardened in the school of Popery."† As if it were not admitted, even by this apologist himself, that the Church of England had the precedency of Philip in the institution of a court of inquisition under Edward, as if any man but an out-and-out apologist of the Church of England would identify

† Lingard's History of England, v. 316.
‡ Dr. Cardwell's Documentary Annals of the Church of England, i. 223.

THE ANGLICAN REFORMATION. xix

the actions of Elizabeth with the genuine manifestations of "the spirit of Protestantism," and as if, besides, the high commission court and the star chamber, as Dr. Cardwell's words would insinuate, had terminated with the reign of Elizabeth, or had been abolished by the Church of England, when he very well knows the horrors these courts perpetrated in subsequent reigns, and knows, too, that it was the rising power of the Puritans that demolished these infernal courts, which an increasing party in the Church of England, who fairly represent her genius, will ere long restore, if the old puritan spirit do not prevent such a national calamity.

Ample as the spiritual and ecclesiastical powers thus conferred upon Elizabeth were, she was not satisfied, until, by a clause in the act of supremacy, all persons holding public office, civil, juridical, municipal, military or ecclesiastical, were required to take an oath in recognition of the supremacy royal, binding themselves to defend the same, under pain of being deprived of their offices, and of being declared incapable of further employment. This oath, by the 36th canon, continues to be taken by all ecclesiastics down to this day.

Thus, by one disastrous stroke, the liberties of the Church of England were cloven down, and laid prostrate in the dust. All ecclesiastical jurisdiction, all spiritual power, were lodged in the crown, without respect to the sex, creed, or character of the party who, for the time, might happen to wear it. The prelates and pastors of that Church thus became, even in the discharge of their most sacred functions, the mere vicars and delegates of the supreme civil magistrate. Not one rite, even the most trivial, can they alter, not one canon, however necessary, can they pass, not one error, however gross, can they reform, not one omission, even the most important, can they supply. The civil magistrate enacts the creed they are bound to profess and inculcate, frames the prayers which they must offer at the throne of God, prescribes in number and form the sacraments they must administer, arranges the rites and vestments they must use, down to the colour, shape, and stuff of a cap or a tunicle, and takes discipline altogether out of their hand. The parish priest has no authority to exclude the most profligate sinner from communion, the lordliest prelate or primate cannot excommunicate the most abandoned sinner, or suspend the most immoral ecclesiastic from his functions, and should either the priest or the prelate attempt to exercise the discipline prescribed by the Lord Jesus in his house, he will speedily be made to understand, by the terrors of a *præmunire*, or the experience of a prison, that he is not appointed in the Church of England to administer the laws of Christ, but the statutes of the imperial parliament, or the injunctions of the crown.* Never was there so autocratical a despotism placed in the hands of a human being, as, by the Constitution of the Church of England, is reposed in the sovereign—never, on earth, was there so fettered and enthralled a community as the southern establishment. The muftis and other ecclesiastical functionaries (so to term them) have an indefinite authority by the constitution of Turkey to resist the jurisdiction of the Sultan—a general council, it is the prevalent opinion among Romanists, can control the authority of the pope, and in both cases the supreme functionaries are considered spiritual officers; but in the Church of England,

* It is only one or two years ago that a country clergyman wrote the editor of the Christian Observer for advice under the following circumstances. A married gentleman in his parish lived in a state of open adultery with the wife of another man. A child was the fruit of this unhallowed union. The guilty, but shameless mother, actuated by feelings which we are glad we cannot analyze, came to the minister, insisting upon being " churched," that is, that a particular office, appointed for the purpose, should be offered up next Sabbath, returning thanks to the God of all holiness for the safe delivery of this infant, born in double adultery. We know not what was the issue of the case, but our brethren of the Synod of Ulster, in one of their late admirable works in favour of presbytery (Presbyterianism Defended, pp. 183–4, 203–4,) mention an instance of a minister who was kept for years in prison for having refused the strumpet of a gentleman resident in his parish admission to the Lord's Supper The late case of the Dean of York shows the jurisdiction, or rather total want of jurisdiction, which the prelate possesses over the clergy.

priests, prelates, and primates, have no authority whatever, ecclesiastics though they be, to control, or even to modify, the spiritual supremacy of a lay and civil magistrate.

So anomalous a society was never witnessed, if society it can be called, which has not one single element of an organized community,—which consists of a mere congeries of individual atoms without laws enacted by themselves, without officers appointed by themselves, or powers lodged in themselves, which has no self-existing attributes, no self-regulating agency, which, in one word, has not one single element, even the most essential of a corporate body. Were we disposed to push our arguments, as far as we are warranted, we might deny that the Church of England is a Church at all. For let it be observed that, as from the nature of the case, spiritual power cannot be lodged in lay or civil hands, any more than authority to administer the sacraments, the Lord's Supper, as well as baptism, and to confer orders, can be possessed by a layman or a woman; and as all priestly powers, by the constitution of the Church of England, are placed in the sovereign—the prelates being his mere delegates, (and that, whether in the reign of Henry VIII., and of Edward VI., they are obliged to take out a commission to empower them to perform their functions, or submit, as they all must now do, to the 36th canon;) and as, moreover, every society must possess some species of organization, suited to its peculiar character, which the Church of England, *as a Church*, does not possess, it raises a serious question, whether that can be accounted a Church, if we are to take our ideas of a Church from the word of God. We certainly have no intention whatsoever to maintain, as so many of them do regarding us, that the individuals who compose that Church are cast out to the "uncovenanted mercies of God;" for we rejoice to know that the grace of God is not restrained by any external impediments; and we rejoice further to know, that there are many of God's chosen ones in communion with that Church, as we doubt not was also the case even in the Church of Rome, during the middle ages; but *as a Church*, or scripturally constituted society, we dare not but have considerable difficulty in recognizing it.*

The Erastian thraldom to which the Church of England has been reduced, cannot but be galling to all her rightly constituted clergy, and we so deeply sympathize with them, that we put the most favourable construction upon all their apologies for themselves. We cannot, however, lend the same indulgence to their attempts to prove that theirs is the best possible constitution, any more than we could listen with any patience to a West Indian slave, who should shake his fetters in our face as an evidence of the superior advantages of slavery. Even this, however, we might pass with a sigh for the degradation to which slavery reduces its victims, but we cannot extend the same tolerance to their libels upon other Churches for having had the manliness of spirit to assert their proper liberty, and the regard to the honour of Jesus to vindicate his sovereign exclusive supremacy in his own Church. And yet a member of the Church of England can never think of defend-

* When Henry VIII. was about to appoint a commission to examine the state of the religious houses, he, with one stroke of his pen, suspended all the prelates in England from the exercise of their jurisdictions. He afterwards, at the humble petition of each prelate separately presented, was graciously pleased to restore him to his functions by a commission, in which it was distinctly specified that he was to regard himself as the mere vicar of the crown. The terms of these commissions are sufficiently startling to any man who has not sounded the lowest depths of Erastianism. We may give a condensed summary of one clause of these singular instruments. "Since all authority, civil and ecclesiastical, flows from the crown, and since Cromwell," (a mere layman, but made vicar general *in spiritualibus* over all the clergy) " to whom (and not to the prelates) the ecclesiastical part has been committed," (*vices nostras* as the vicar of the crown) " is so occupied, that he cannot fully exercise it, we commit to you (each individual prelate) the license of *ordaining, granting institution and collation;* and, in short, of performing all other ecclesiastical acts, and we allow you to hold this authority during our pleasure, as you must answer to God and to us!" Similar commissions were granted by Edward VI. to his prelates. See the originals in Collier (fol.) ii rec. Nos 31, 41; or Barham's ed. ix. pp 123, 157; Burnet, i rec. b. iii. No. 14; and ii. No. 2; or London 8vo. ed. 1839; iv. pp. 104, 249.

ing his own Church, but he must at the same time attack the Churches of others, and especially the Church of Scotland.* Just notice the self-complacent absurdity of the following passage from the last page of the work noticed in the preceding note, by the present bishop of Sodor and Man: "Compare," says Dr. Short, addressing men who are too ignorant to be capable of instituting a comparison, or too prejudiced to be able to pass an impartial judgment, "compare what took place in Scotland with what took place in England, at the period of the Reformation;" and after showing some of those things which did take place in England, and stating that "the admirer of our Episcopal Church—our apostolic establishment" must thank the timid, if not the time-serving and Erastian Cranmer, that the Church of England was reformed precisely as she was, and that it did not happen there as it did happen among us—we have Dr. Short's word for it—"that the force of the multitude ... in Scotland (had) thrown down what the Episcopalians will consider as almost the Church itself."

And who, pray, composed that "multitude" of which Dr. Short speaks so very contemptuously? The Christian people of Scotland, who through "the unction of the Holy One," had, by an ordination higher than the Church of England can confer, been made a "royal priesthood;" and who, both by their position in the Church, and by their qualification, were thus entitled and bound by more authoritative "injunctions" than ever emanated from prince or prelate, to "try the spirits," and not accept of any man to be minister over them, unless, as his credentials, he brought with him, not "letters of orders," or an excerpt from a pretended apostolical genealogy, but the gifts, graces, and gospel of the living God. And, pray, what horrible acts did this same "multitude" commit, which should be so enormous as to

* See some specimens of this line of defence and attack, which would be amusing enough from their ludicrousness, if they were not pitiable from the perversity of judgment they display, in Dr Short's Sketch of the History of the Church of England, 104, 242-3, 198, and elsewhere.

lead "an episcopalian to consider that they had almost thrown down the Church itself?" Why, they just followed where their ministers led them—no great crime, one should suppose, in the eyes of a prelate; and also, in conformity with the prophetic enunciation of their God-commissioned apostle, they fancied, that the "best way to prevent the rooks from returning was to pull down their nests," a proceeding, the prophetic sagacity of which has been demonstrated by the history of the Church of England, in whose dark cloisters rooks have continued to roost ever since the Reformation, to which as their safe retreats they betake themselves whenever the moral effulgence of the truth becomes painful to their distempered optics, and from which, as at present, they come forth in darkening clouds whenever the fields seem ripe for their pillage But let us return to the history of the Anglican Reformation.

When Elizabeth ascended the throne, Popery, as restored by Mary, was the established religion. Those Protestants who had, in the words of Fuller, "contrived to weather out the storm" of Mary's persecutions at home in England, depending upon the protestantism of the daughter of Anne Boleyn, the early patroness of the Reformation, now ventured to celebrate public worship according to the liturgy of Edward VI. This was done with still more zeal by the exiles who had fled to the continent to avoid the persecution of Mary, and had now returned in the hope of enjoying liberty of conscience in their native land. Elizabeth, however, had hitherto done nothing to indicate that she was favourable to the reformed faith, but much to the contrary. She had been crowned according to the forms of the popish pontifical, of which a high mass was an essential part. The exiles, however, presuming at least upon a toleration, began to celebrate public worship according to the reformed ritual, and to preach to the people the unsearchable riches of Christ. Elizabeth, when apprized of this proceeding, issued a proclamation, forbidding all preaching, and the use of Edward's liturgy, and commanding that in public worship the missal in Latin should be employed, except the litany, the Lord's prayer, and the creed, which were tolerated in English. The only instruction to be given to the people consisted of the " gospel and the epistles of the day," with the ten commandments, which were allowed to be read in the English tongue. Religion, throughout this year (1558) continued precisely as it had been in the reign of Mary, and was celebrated by precisely the same priests, with the addition of so many of the exiles as had returned, and the few Protestants who had remained at home.*

Elizabeth, however, was aware that some alteration in religion must be made. Accordingly, about the period at which she summoned her first parliament, she appointed certain divines, under the presidency of Secretary Sir Thomas Smith, to prepare a liturgy which might be laid before the legislature. These divines were instructed to compare Edward's two liturgies with the popish offices, and to frame such a form of prayer as might suit the circumstances of the times. They were, however, to give a preference to Edward's first liturgy, which retained many popish dogmas and usages, in all matters to be very wary of innovations, and especially, to leave all matters in discussion between the Protestants and the Papists so undefined, and expressed in such general terms as not to offend the latter. Elizabeth's great desire in this, and, indeed, in all her measures, was to comprehend the Papists in any form of religion which might be established. She never seems to have entertained any desire to conciliate or concede any thing to her Protestant subjects.

The divines having finished their work, brought the draft of a liturgy to Cecil, in order to its being submitted to her majesty. Before presenting it to parliament Elizabeth made various important alterations on it, all for the express purpose of reducing it to a nearer conformity to the popish liturgies, and thus conciliating the Papists. It were altogether beyond

* Strype's Annals, i. 59, 74, 77, Burnet ii. 585, Collier vi.,200.

our present limits to give a minute enumeration of the various alterations introduced by Elizabeth into the draft presented to her by the divines, or to show in what, and how many particulars, her prayer-book, which (with a few verbal alterations since introduced) is the liturgy at present in use in the Church of England, is still more popish than even that which was in use at the death of Edward. A few, however, must be mentioned *

In the litany of Edward's second liturgy there was a prayer in the following terms:—" From the tyranny of the Bishop of Rome, and all his detestable enormities, good Lord deliver us." This was cancelled in the liturgy of Elizabeth,—we can be at no loss to divine for what reason. In the communion office of the former, when the minister delivered the bread to the communicant, he said, "Take, and eat this, in remembrance that Christ died for thee, and feed on him in thine heart by faith, with thanksgiving;" and when he delivered the cup, he said, "Drink this in remembrance that Christ's blood was shed for thee, and be thankful,"—clearly implying that it was merely an eucharistic commemoration, rendered efficacious only through faith. In the communion office of the latter, the priest, in handing the bread, said to the communicant, "The body of our Lord Jesus Christ, which was given for thee, preserve thy body and soul unto everlasting life. Take and eat this," &c. And when delivering the cup, "The blood of our Lord Jesus Christ, which was shed for thee, preserve thy body and soul unto everlasting life. Drink this," &c.—words that were expressly intended to imply the real presence, and an *opus operatum* efficacy, with-

* Those who desire fuller information, we recommend to study Dr. Cardwell's History of Conferences on the Book of Common Prayer; the two Liturgies of Edward VI. compared, by the same author; Dr. Short's Sketch of the History of the Church of England, 537—549; Collier's History, vi 248—250; and Records, No. 77, Strype's Annals, i. 98—123; see also Baillie's Parallel of the Liturgy with the Mass Book, the Breviary, and other Romish Rituals, 4to., 1641; Wheatley's Rationale of the Book of Common Prayer, and the other Ritualists, Palmer's Origines Liturgicæ. Burnet, Neal, and the other historians, all take up the subject, but very imperfectly.

THE ANGLICAN REFORMATION. xxvii

out any regard whatever to the faith or spiritual condition of the communicant. In order to prevent the idea that when kneeling was retained as the required posture at the communion, it was intended to imply that Christ was bodily present, or that any adoration was designed to be given to the elements, a rubric was added to the office in Edward's second prayer-book, which declared that the elements remained unchanged, and that no adoration was given them. This rubric was omitted in Elizabeth's prayer-book, and the communicant was left to believe and to adore as he had been accustomed to do. The divines who had drawn up Elizabeth's liturgy left it to the choice of the communicant himself to receive the communion kneeling or standing; Elizabeth made it imperative upon all to receive it kneeling. These divines, besides, had disapproved of any distinction being made between the vestments worn by the ministers while celebrating the eucharist, and those worn at other parts of the service; Elizabeth, however, made it imperative on the officiating priest to administer the sacrament in the old popish vestments, as was the case in Edward's first liturgy, but had been altered in the second; and in order that the benighted Papists might, by act of parliament, and of the supremacy royal, have every encouragement to continue in their idolatry, it was ordered that the bread should be changed into the *wafer* formerly used at private masses. Not satisfied with the popish innovations she had already made, and seemingly apprehensive that if she went at once so far as she felt inclined in her retrogression towards Rome, she might find some difficulty in carrying the prelates and the parliament along with her, Elizabeth introduced into the act of uniformity (to which we shall allude immediately) a clause by which she was empowered " to ordain and publish such further rites and ceremonies as should be most for the reverence of Christ's holy mysteries and sacraments;" words of ominous import; and, as we have already stated, she told Parker that if it had not been for the power thus conferred upon her, "she would not have agreed to divers orders of the book."*

The liturgy having been thus prepared was introduced into parliament, in a bill for "Uniformity of prayer, and administration of sacraments," and passed through the Commons, seemingly without opposition, in the short space of three days. It met with some opposition in the upper house from a few of the popish prelates and peers, but was carried, without one word being altered, by a most triumphant majority; and having received the royal assent, became law.

The population of England at this time consisted of two great parties, Puritans and Papists, with of course some neutrals, who were prepared to join either party according as their interests might seem to dictate. Both of these great parties differed, as in every thing else, so also in their estimation of the prayer-book. We now proceed to consider the opinions and the conduct of each of these parties in regard to the newly imposed liturgy.

The intrinsic character of the Anglican liturgy may be very safely inferred from the sources whence it was drawn, and the estimation in which it was held by Papists. In regard to the former, it is known to all in any measure conversant with the subject, that the book of common prayer was taken from the Romish service-book. "In our public services," says the present bishop of Sodor and Man, "the greater part of the book of common prayer is taken from the Roman ritual." Again,—"In giving an account of the common prayer book, it will be more correct to describe it as a work compiled from the services of the Church of Rome, or rather as a translation than as an original composition." Again, speaking of Edward's first prayer-book, of which, indeed, he spoke in both the preceding instances, he says, "almost the whole of it was taken from different Roman catholic

---

* Peirce's Vindic of Dis p. 47, Strype, Burnet, Collier, &c, fancy that some of these alterations were introduced by parliament, but Dr. Cardwell has shown that they were the work of Elizabeth; see Cardwell's History of Conf. pp. 21, 22.

services, particularly those after the use of Salisbury, which were then generally adopted in the south of England, and the principle on which the compilers proceeded in the work was to alter as little as possible what had been familiar to the people. Thus the litany is nearly the same as in the Salisbury hours." Speaking of the Anglican ordination office, he says, "its several parts are taken from that in use in the Church of Rome," with few exceptions, which he mentions. In a note, he states that those parts of the liturgy which were not taken from the service books of the Church of Rome were drawn from a prayer-book compiled about this time by Hærman, the popish bishop of Cologne.* Edward's second prayer-book was a revised edition of the first, omitting some of the grosser abominations of Popery which the first contained. The present prayer-book of the Church of England stands about half-way between the first and second of Edward, and was, as we have seen above, taken almost *verbatim* from the popish service book. Such, then, is the parentage of "our apostolic prayer-book—our incomparable liturgy—our inestimable service book," of which even evangelical members of the Church of England cannot speak in terms sufficiently expressive of their rapturous admiration.

Bearing all this in mind, we shall cease to feel any surprise at the fact mentioned by all historians of the period, that so well satisfied were the Papists with the Reformed (so termed) services, and so little difference did they discover between the modern and the ancient ritual, that for the first ten years of Elizabeth's reign they continued, "without doubt or scruple," as Heylin says, to attend public worship in the Church of England. Indeed, as all acknowledge, who know any thing of the subject, if the court of Rome had not altered its policy towards England, excommunicated Elizabeth, and forbidden her subjects to attend the Established Church, the Papists

* Sketch of the History, &c., 201, 537, 540, 541.

would have remained conscientiously convinced, that in worshipping in the Anglican establishment, they were still attending upon the Romish services; so imperceptible to their well-practised senses was the difference between the two, and so well did the compilers of the prayer-book or the revisers of their work accomplish the task prescribed to them by the queen, viz. to frame a liturgy which should not offend the Papists.* Nay, but what is more, when a copy of the prayer-book had been sent to the Pope, so well was he satisfied with it, that he offered, through his nuncio Parpalia, to ratify it for England, if the queen would only own the supremacy of the see of Rome.† Such was the estimation in which the Pope and his followers held the prayer-book, which Anglicans now can never mention without exhausting all the superlatives in the vocabulary of commendation to express their most unbounded admiration of " our inimitable, inestimable, incomparable, apostolic, (?) and all but inspired liturgy." Nothing strikes so painfully upon the ear as to hear a man of evangelical sentiments utter such hyperboles in laudation of a Popish compilation, which even antichrist offered to sanction. In attempting to account for so startling a phenomenon, we have heard men less charitable than ourselves surmise, that the only principle on which it can be accounted for is, that the less intrinsic merit any object possesses, the more loudly must it be praised, to secure for it popular acceptance. For our own parts we must say we rank the matter under the category *de gustibus*, &c., and say there is no

* Sir George Paule relates in his panegyric on Whitgift, that an Italian Papist, lately arrived in England, on seeing that ambitious primate in the cathedral of Canterbury one Sabbath, " attended upon by an hundred of his own servants at least, in livery, whereof there were forty gentlemen in chains of gold, also by the dean, prebendaries, and preachers, in their surplices and scarlet hoods, and heard the solemn music, with the voices and organs, cornets and sackbuts, he was overtaken with admiration, and told an English gentleman, that unless it were in the Pope's chapel, he never saw a more solemn sight, or heard a more heavenly sound."—Wordworth's Eccl. Biog., iv. 388—9.

† Strype's An., i. 340. Burnet, ii. 645. Collier, vi. 308—9.

disputing about taste. And if members of the Church of England were satisfied with enjoying it themselves, without thrusting it upon other people, and if moreover they did not, as some of them do, place it upon a level with the Bible, we should for our own part be as little disposed to deny them its use as we certainly are to envy them its possession.

The commendations bestowed by Papists upon the Anglican prayer-book might of itself lead us to infer that it did not satisfy the Reformers; and the conclusion thus arrived at is as much in accordance with historic facts as it is the result of logical accuracy. The continental Reformers to a man expressed both contempt and indignation towards the Anglican liturgy. Calvin* declared, that he found in it many *(tolerabiles ineptias)*, *i. e.*, "tolerable fooleries;" that is, tolerable for the moment, as children are allowed (to use quaint old Fuller's illustration) to "play with rattles to get them to part with knives." Knox† declared, that it contained "diabolical inventions, viz., crossing in baptism, kneeling at the Lord's table, mumbling or singing of the liturgy," &c., and "that the whole order of (the) book appeared rather to be devised for upholding of massing priests, than for any good instruction which the simple people can thereof receive." Beza,‡ writing to Bullinger about the state of England and the English Church, says, "I clearly perceive that Popery has not been ejected from that kingdom, but has been only transferred from the Pope to the queen; and the only aim of parties in power there is to bring back matters to the state in which they formerly stood. I at one time thought that the only subject of contention (between the Puritans and the Conformists) was about caps and external vestments; but I now, to my inexpressible sorrow, understand that it is about very differ-

* Epist. p. 28, t. ix. ed. 1667.
† Calderwood's History, (Wodrow ed.), i. 431. See the whole letter, pp. 425—434.
‡ Strype's An. ii. Rec. No. 29. The whole letter deserves a careful perusal.

ent matters indeed," even the most vital and fundamental elements of the Christian Church, as the sequel of the letter shows.* Beza concludes by saying, "such is the state of the Anglican Church, exceedingly miserable, and indeed, as it appears to me, intolerable." We might quote similar sentiments from other continental divines, such as Bullinger and Gualter, and may perhaps do so ere we close. But since the opinions of the Anglican Reformers themselves will be, in the circumstances, of more importance, and since we are very much hampered for want of space, we come at once to the recorded judgment which these great and good men passed upon the prayer-book and the Church of England.

The opinions of Grindal, successively bishop of London and archbishop of York and Canterbury; of Sandys, successively bishop of Worcester and London, and archbishop of York; of Parkhurst of Norwich, Pilkington of Durham, Jewell of Salisbury, and others, we need not refer to, as every one knows that they expressed themselves as strongly against the state of the Anglican Church as Sampson, Fox, Coverdale, or Humphreys. The only prelates of the first set appointed by Elizabeth who are claimed by Anglicans themselves, as having been in favour of the reformed condition of the Church of England, are Archbishop Parker, Cox of Ely, and Horne of Winchester, (as for Cheney of Gloucester and Bristol, we give him up an avowed Papist,) and if we show that these were dissatisfied with the condition of the Church of England, even her apologists must acknowledge that all Elizabeth's first prelates desired that that Church should be further reformed.

Parker was one of the compilers of the prayer-book, and we have already seen how much the first draft excelled the present liturgy. Even after it had been enjoined, both by parliament and the queen, that the

* The vicar of Leeds not only admits, but contends that Beza was correct in stating that the contention entered into the vital elements of Christianity. See Dr. Hook's Sermon, a Call to Union, &c., 2d ed., 74, 75.

THE ANGLICAN REFORMATION. xxxiii

communion should be received kneeling, Parker administered it in his own cathedral to the communicants standing.* At the very time when he was persecuting the Puritans for nonconformity, (1575,) he wrote Cecil, "Doth your lordship think that I care either for caps, tippets, surplices, or wafer bread or any such?"† And Strype says expressly, that his "pressing conformity to the queen's laws and injunctions, proceeded not out of fondness to the ceremonies themselves," which he would willingly see altered, "but for the laws establishing them he esteemed them."‡ "It may fairly be presumed," says Bishop Short, "that Parker himself entertained some doubts concerning the points which were afterwards disputed between the Puritans and the high church party; for in the questions prepared to be submitted to convocation in 1563, probably under his own direction, and certainly examined by himself," for his annotations stand yet upon the margin of the first scroll, "there are several which manifestly imply that such a difference of opinion might prevail."§ The questions here alluded to by Bishop Short embrace most of those matters which were at first disputed between the Puritans and conformists. In particular, "It was proposed that all vestments, caps, and surplices, should be taken away; that none but ministers should baptize; that the table for the sacrament should not stand altar-wise; that organs and curious singing should be removed; that godfathers and godmothers should not answer in the child's name;" and several other matters, which were then loudly complained of, but which remain in the Church of England till this day.‖ It was only after he had been scolded into irritation by the queen, after his morose and sullen disposition and despotic temper had been chafed and inflamed by the resistance of the Puritans, and he felt or fancied that his character and the honour of his primacy were in

* McCrie's Life of Knox, 6th ed., p. 64, note
† Strype's Parker, ii. 424.   ‡ Ibid. p. 528.
§ Sketch, &c , p. 250
‖ Burnet, iii. 457, 458. Strype's Parker, i. 386. Rec. No. 39.

C

jeopardy, that Parker committed himself to that course of persecution which has "damned his name to everlasting infamy." Had he even the inquisitor's plea of conscience, however unenlightened, to urge in his own defence, some apology, how inadequate soever, might be made for him. But Parker was a persecutor only from passion, or at best from policy.* Parker himself then was inclined to a further reformation of the Church of England.

As to Cox again: in a letter to Bullinger, in 1551, we find him writing thus:—"I think all things in the Church ought to be pure and simple, removed at the greatest distance from the pomp and elements of the world. But in this our Church what can I do in so low a station?" (he was then, if we rightly remember, only archdeacon of Ely:) "I can only endeavour to persuade our bishops to be of the same mind with myself. This I wish truly, and I commit to God the care and conduct of his own work."† In the following year we find him complaining bitterly of the opposition of the courtiers to the introduction of ecclesiastical discipline, and predicting that if it were not adopted, "the kingdom of God would be taken away from them."‡ After his return from exile, he joined with Grindal (whose scruples in accepting a bishopric were hushed only by all the counsels and exhortations of Peter Martyr, Bullinger, and Gualter)§ and the other bishops elect in employing the most strenuous efforts to effect a more thorough reformation in the Church of England, before they should accept of dioceses in it. When they found that they could not succeed, they seriously deliberated whether they could accept preferments in so popish a Church. At last they were induced to yield to the counsels of Bul-

---

* Bishop Short candidly acknowledges, that "when Parker and the other bishops had begun to execute the laws against nonconformists, they must have been more than men," or less, "if they could divest their own minds of that personality which every one must feel when engaged in a controversy in which the question really is, whether he shall be able to succeed in carrying his plans into execution." Sketch, &c, p. 251.
† Burnet, iii. 303—4.   ‡ Strype's Mem. Ref. ii. 366.
§ Strype's Grindal, 41—44, Ap. No. 11.

THE ANGLICAN REFORMATION.   XXXV

linger and Gualter, and other continental divines whom they consulted, because the rites imposed were not in themselves necessarily sinful; because they anticipated that when elevated to the mitre, they should have power to effect the reformation they desired, and because, moreover, by occupying the sees they might exclude Lutherans and Papists, who would not only not reform, but would bring back the Church still further towards Rome.* Even Cox, then, desired further reformation in the Church of England, and was so dissatisfied with its condition, that notwithstanding of the gold and power it would bestow, (and both of them he loved dearly) he scrupled to accept a bishopric within its pale. When we bear in mind his conduct at Frankfort, and his subsequent career in England, we may safely conclude that the Church that was too popish for Cox had certainly but few pretensions to the name either of Reformed or Protestant.

And finally, as to Horne, he not only had scruples at first, like the rest, as to accepting a bishopric, but when he found that the reformation he anticipated he should be able to effect after his elevation could not be accomplished, he deliberated with himself, and consulted with the continental divines, whether it did not become his duty to resign his preferments. In conjunction with Grindal, he wrote for advice to Gualter, asking, whether, under the circumstances, he thought they could with a safe conscience continue in their sees. Gualter induced Bullinger, whose influence was greater, to answer the question submitted to him. Bullinger accordingly replied, that if, upon a conscientious conviction, it should appear that, upon the whole, and all things considered, it were better to remain, then it became their duty to occupy their places, but if the reverse, then it was as clearly their duty to renounce them. He cautions them, however, against imagining, that because he gives this counsel, he therefore, in any manner, approved of the conduct of those who were for retaining "Papistical

* Strype's An. ii. 263.   Strype's Grindal, 41—49, 438.

dregs." On the contrary, he urges, with the greatest warmth, that the queen and the rulers of the nation should be importuned to proceed further with the Reformation, and that, among other reasons, lest the Church of England should remain "polluted with Popish dregs and offscourings, or afford any ground of complaint to the neighbour Churches of Scotland and France." Further information on this subject will be found in the note below.*

* Since attempts have been, and are still made, to represent the divines of Zurich as having been satisfied with the length to which reformation was carried in the Church of England, it is necessary to show that the very reverse is the truth. Those who have access to the work, and can read the language, we would recommend to peruse in full the letters sent by Grindal and Horne to Bullinger and Gualter, and the answers returned by these divines, as they appear in Burnet's Records, B. vi. Nos. 75, 76, 82, 83, 87. Those who cannot read the original, may form some idea of their contents from the translated Summary, iii. pp. 462—476.

Grindal, whose scruples were never removed, and who therefore wrote frequently and anxiously to foreign divines to obtain their sanction to the course he was pursuing, had, in conjunction with Horne, written to Bullinger and Gualter, requesting further counsel regarding the propriety of their remaining in the Church of England. Perceiving, most probably, the wounded state of the consciences of their brethren in the Lord, Bullinger and Gualter wrote a soothing reply, saying as much as they conscientiously could in favour of remaining in their cures When the Anglican prelates received this answer, they at once saw that the judgment of those eminent foreign divines would go far to stop the censures which the Puritans pronounced against their conforming brethren; and although the letter was strictly private, they published it. As soon as Bullinger and Gualter were apprised of this act, they wrote a letter to the Earl of Bedford, one of the leaders of the Puritan party, complaining of the breach of confidence of which Grindal and Horne had been guilty, and explaining the circumstances in which their letter had been written, deploring that it had been made the occasion of further persecution against their dear brethren in Christ (the Puritans,) and urging upon the good Earl to proceed strenuously in purifying the Church of England of the dregs of Popery, which, to their bitter grief, they found were still retained within her. When Horn and Grindal learned the feelings of their continental correspondents, they sent them a most submissive and penitential apology In reply, Bullinger and Gualter mentioned several of those errors still existing in the Church of England, which they urged all her prelates to reform; such as subscriptions to new articles of faith and discipline, theatrical singing in churches, accompanied by the "crash of organs," baptism by women, the interrogations of sponsors, the cross, and other superstitious ceremonies in baptism, kneeling at the communion, and the use of wafer bread (which Strype informs us was made like the

Such, then, was the judgment deliberately formed and often repeated, even of those Anglican High Church prelates, regarding the constitution and usages

" singing cakes" formerly used in private masses, Life of Parker, ii. 32—5,) the venal dispensations for pluralities, and for eating flesh meat in Lent, and on " fish days," (which dispensations were sold in the archbishop's court,) the impediments thrown in the way of the marriage of the clergy, the prohibition to testify against, to oppose or refuse conformity to those abuses, the restricting all ecclesiastical power to the prelates; and conclude by imploring them, " in the bowels of Jesus Christ," to purge the temple of God from such Popish abominations. In reply to this faithful appeal, poor Grindal and Horne write a very penitent and submissive letter, which we cannot read over at this day without the most painful emotion at the condition to which these men of God were reduced between their desire to serve God in the gospel of his Son, and their scruples of conscience against the antichristian impositions to which they were subjected. The drift of their letter was to show that they had no power to reform the evils complained of, (and which they condemn and deplore as much as their correspondents,) and that either they must remain as they are, or abandon their benefices, and see them filled by Papists, who would destroy the flock of Christ. In conclusion, they promise— but we must give their promise in a literal translation—" We shall do the utmost that in us lies, as already we have done, in the last sessions of parliament and of convocation, and that, even although our future exertions should be as fruitless as the past, that all the errors and abuses which yet remain in the Church of England shall be corrected, expurgated and removed, according to the rule and standard of the word of God." In a preceding part of their letter they had said, that " although they might not be able to effect all they desired, they should not yet cease their exertions until they had thrust down into hell, whence they had arisen," certain abuses which they mention. And are these, then, the men who are to be regarded as approving of the extent to which reformation had been carried in the Church of England ?

We have given the sentiments of the divines of Zurich at the greater length, because some of their letters are, till this day, perverted, as they were at the time when they were written. Had this been done only by Collier, Heylin, and their school, we should not take any notice of it in our present sadly limited space. But when such writers as Strype, Cardwell, and Short, lend their names to palm such impositions upon the public mind, it is necessary at once to show what was the real state of the case. Dr. McCrie (Life of Knox, note R.) has charged the Anglican prelates with having given " partial representations" to the foreign divines for the purpose of obtaining their sanction to the state of matters in England and any man of competent knowledge of the subject, who reads over their letters, must be painfully aware, that, although they may not have designed it, yet, as was so very natural in their circumstances, they did write in a manner which could not but lead their correspondents into the grossest mistakes.

of the Church of England. We should much deepen the impression we desire to produce upon our readers, had we space also to give the sentiments of the more evangelical prelates; of Parkhurst, for example, who, in a letter to Gualter in 1573, fervently exclaims,— "Oh, would to God, would to God, that now at last the people of England would in good earnest propound to themselves to follow the Church of Zurich as the most perfect pattern;"* or of his scholar and fellow-prelate Jewell, who calls the habits enjoined upon the ministers of the Church of England, " theatrical vestments—ridiculous trifles and relics of the Amorites," and satirizes those who submitted to wear them as men " without mind, sound doctrine or morals, by which to secure the approbation of the people, and who, therefore, wished to gain their plaudits by wearing a comical stage dress."† But it is unnecessary. The following passage from a High Church writer of the present day concedes all we desire to establish. After having condemned the Erastianism of Cranmer, and the want of what he terms " catholic" feeling and spirit in his coadjutors, and having denounced Hooper as " an obstinate Puritan—a mere dogged Genevan preacher," (the most opprobrious epithets the writer can bestow,) and Coverdale as " a thorough Puritan and Genevan, who officiated at the consecration of Archbishop Parker in his *black gown*," (in *italics*, to indicate the sacrilegious profanation of the act—we wonder whether it invalidated his share, or the whole of the proceeding,) the writer proceeds thus:—

"The immediate successors, however, of the Reformers, as often happens in such cases, went further than their predecessors did, and were more deeply imbued with the feelings of the day. The Episcopate, in the first part of Queen Elizabeth's reign, were successors of Hooper and Coverdale, almost more than they were of Cranmer and Ridley; indeed, it was

* Strype's An. ii. 286–342.
† See many such passages in Dr. McCrie's note last referred to, and the letters in Burnet's Records.

only her strong Tudor arm that kept them within decent bounds," (that is, that kept them from assimilating the Church of England to the other Reformed Churches.) "The greater part of them positively objected to the surplice—including Sandys, Grindal, Pilkington, Jewell, Horne, Parkhurst, Bentham, and all the leading men who were for simplifying our Church ceremonial in that and other respects, according to the Genevan, (that is, Presbyterian) model; Archbishop Parker almost standing alone with the queen in her determination to uphold the former." (And we have already seen that he was about as little enamoured of them as his coadjutors.)

After having referred to some of Jewell's letters to the foreign divines written against the Anglican ceremonies, the writer makes an observation which ought to be ever present to the minds of those who read the censures of Jewell and his contemporaries. "It was no Roman Catholic ritual, we repeat, of which he thus expressed himself, but our own doubly reformed prayer-book—the divine service as *now performed.*"* Who now are the lineal descendants and proper representatives of the Anglican Reformers?—the Puritans who desired further reformation, or those who so loudly praise our "Catholic Church, our apostolic establishment," and vigorously resist every attempt to amend the most glaring corruptions in the Church of England? We wish the evangelical party would ponder the answer that question must receive;—we say, the evangelical party, for we are aware that high churchmen, if they moved at all, would move in the direction of Rome.

Having thus shown the opinions of the prelates regarding the constitution and ceremonies of the Church of England, let us now show the opinions of the inferior clergy: And here one fact may stand for all. In the year 1562, a petition was presented to the lower house of convocation, signed by thirty-two members, most of them exiles, and the best men

* British Critic for October 1842, 330, 331.

in the kingdom, praying for the following alterations in the service of the Church of England. 1. That organs might be disused, responses in the "reading psalms" discontinued, and the people allowed to sing the psalms in metre, as was the custom on the continent, and had also been practised by the English exiles, not only when there, but after they had returned to their native land, and as was also the case among the Puritans when they non-conformed to (for they never seceded or dissented from) the Church of England, of which they could never be said to have been *bona fide* members. 2. That none but ministers should be allowed to baptize, and that the sign of the cross should be abolished. 3. That the imposition of kneeling at the communion should be left to the discretion of each bishop in his own diocese; and one reason assigned for this part of the petition, was, that this posture was abused to idolatry by the ignorant and superstitious populace. 4. That copes and surplices should be disused, and the ministers made to wear some comely and decent garment, (such as the Geneva gown, which all the early Puritans wore.) 5. That, as they expressed it themselves, "The ministers of the word and sacrament be not compelled to wear such gowns and caps as the enemies of Christ's gospel have chosen to be the special array of their priesthood." 6. That certain words in Article 33, be mitigated, which have since been omitted altogether. 7. That saints' days might be abolished, or kept only for public worship, (and not as was then the case for feasting, jollity, superstition, and sin,) after which ordinary labour might be carried on.

This petition was eventually withdrawn, and another very much to the same purpose substituted for it. This second petition prayed for the following alterations:—1. That saints' days be abolished, but all Sundays, and the principal feasts of Christ be kept holy. 2. That the liturgy be read audibly, and not mumbled over inaudibly, as had been done by the massing priests. 3. That the sign of the cross in baptism be abolished as tending to superstition. 4. That kneeling at the communion be left to the discretion of the ordinary. 5. That ministers may use only a surplice, or other decent garment in public worship, and the administration of the sacraments. 6. That organs be removed from churches.

After a protracted and vigorous debate, these articles were put to the vote, when forty-three, most of them exiles, voted that the petition be granted, and only thirty-five against it; thus leaving a clear majority of eight in favour of a further reformation. When, however, proxies were called for, only fifteen appeared for, while twenty-four appeared against the petition, being, on the whole, fifty-eight for, and fifty-nine against, leaving a majority of one for rejecting the prayer of the petition.*

There is one point mentioned in the minutes of convocation, an extract from which is given, both by Burnet and Cardwell, which must be kept in view, to enable us to arrive at a correct conception of the sentiments of those who voted against the above articles. In the minute, it is distinctly mentioned, that the most of those who voted against granting the prayer of the petition, did so, not upon the merits, but only from a feeling that since the matters in debate had been imposed by public authority of parliament and the queen, it was not competent for convocation to take up the subject at all. Thus, the motion for which they really voted was, not that the abuses complained of should be continued, but that the convocation had no power to alter them. A second section of those who voted against the articles, was composed of those who had held cures under Edward, and had a hand in the public affairs of his reign, and, who having remained in England during the reign of Mary, had not seen the purer churches on the continent, and regarded the reformation of Edward as sufficiently perfect. A third section of the majority consisted of those who held benefices under Mary, and who were of course Papists in their

* Strype's An i. 500—6. Burnet iii. 454, 455. Records, Bk. vi No. 74. Collier, vi. 371—3. Cardwell's Hist. of Conf. 117—120.

hearts, and would therefore vote against any further reformation. After we have thus analyzed the parties, and weighed, instead of numbering, the votes, and when, besides, we bear in mind that a majority of those who heard the reasoning upon the matters in dispute, voted for further reformation, it is easy to see on whose side truth and justice lay.

There is, besides, another point to which Dr. Cardwell has called our attention,* which we regard of the very highest importance, and to which, consequently, we call the special attention of our readers. It is this, that although, since the time of Burnet and Strype, it has been always said that the number of those who voted for the Articles was fifty-eight, yet, when we count them fairly, they are fifty-nine, precisely the number who voted against them. Now, if we give the prolocutor (the same as our moderator,) a casting vote, Nowell, dean of St Paul's, who was prolocutor of that convocation and voted in favour of the Articles, and would of course give his casting vote on the same side, this would give a majority in favour of further reformation.

But how are we to account for the fact that, if thus the numbers were equal, that fact should not be known to the members? We should be glad to hear of any other way of solving the difficulty, but the only mode of doing so that occurs to us, is to suppose that Parker or the queen had recourse to the artifice employed by Charles I. in the Scottish parliament, viz., concealed the roll and declared that the majority was in their favour, while it was against them, as was clearly seen when the original came into the hands of the public. That Parker was capable of the manœuvre, no man who knows his character can for one moment question : And that Elizabeth would feel at the least as little scruple in doing so as Charles I., he that doubts may consult the note at the foot of the page.†

* *Ut supra*, p. 120, note.
† In 1559 a bill passed through parliament authorizing the queen to restore to their former cures, such of the returned exiles as had been unlawfully deprived; that is, by Mary on account of their Protes-

From this induction of facts it is most abundantly manifest that the prelates and the great majority of the leading members of the lower house of convocation, were decidedly in favour of a further reformation. It only further remains to finish this branch of our argument, that we show the feelings of the leading statesmen of the kingdom. This may be done in the following passage from one who is certainly a competent enough witness so far as knowledge is concerned, and whom no one will accuse of any partiality towards the Puritans. After stating that several of the bishops were in favour of the Puritans, Hallam* goes on to say,

"They," the Puritans, "had still more effectual

tantism. "Yet," says Strype, (Annals i. 99,) "I do not find it was enacted and passed into law." It must therefore have been clandestinely suppressed by Elizabeth, who both hated and feared the Protestantism of the exiles. She acted very much in the same way in regard to the re enacting of Edward's statute in favour of clerical marriages, (Ibid. 118.) The convocation of 1575, among other articles of reformation, breathing the spirit of Grindal who was just then raised to the primacy, passed the following, that none but ministers lawfully ordained should baptize, and that it should be lawful to marry at any period of the year: but Elizabeth cancelled both. (Strype's Grindal, 290—1) We need not, however, multiply instances in which Elizabeth exercised this power, as it is admitted on all hands that she both claimed and exercised it. (Cardwell's Documentary Annals, ii 171—2, note.) The case most in point is the following, along with the liberty we have already seen she took with the first draft of the liturgy Our readers are aware of the controversy as to how the celebrated clause, ("the Church hath power to decree rites and ceremonies, and authority in controversies of faith,") crept into the Twentieth Article of the Church of England, when it occurs neither in the first printed edition of the Articles, nor in the draft of them which was passed by convocation, and which is still in existence, with the autograph signatures of the members. It is now the universal belief that Elizabeth inserted this clause, as well as cancelled the whole of the Thirty-ninth Article, whose title sufficiently indicates its contents, viz. "the ungodly (*impii*) do not eat the body of Christ in the sacrament of the supper," a dogma which Elizabeth, who believed in transubstantiation, could not admit. (See Lamb's Historical and Critical Essay on the thirty-nine Articles, p 35, &c. Cardwell's Hist. of Conf. 21, 22, note. Cardwell's Synodalia, i 38, 39, note. Cardwell's Doc. An. ii. 171, note. Bishop Short's Sketch, &c., 327, note.) The person who could thus act was certainly capable of falsifying the votes of convocation, 1562.

* Constitutional Hist. of England, i. 256, 257.

xliv   THE ANGLICAN REFORMATION.

support in the Queen's council. The Earl of Leicester, who possessed more power than any one, to sway her wavering and capricious temper, the Earls of Bedford, Huntington, and Warwick, regarded as the steadiest Protestants among the aristocracy, the wise and grave Lord Keeper Bacon, the sagacious Walsingham, the experienced Sadler, the zealous Knollys, considered these objects of Parker's severity (the Puritans) either as demanding a purer worship than had been established in the Church, or at least as worthy, by their virtues, of more indulgent treatment. Cecil himself, though on intimate terms with the archbishop, and concurring generally in his measures, was not far removed from the latter way of thinking, if his natural caution and extreme dread, at this juncture, of losing the Queen's favour, had permitted him more unequivocally to express it."

Mr. Hallam by no means does full justice to the sentiments of Cecil. No one can read his correspondence with the Puritans, and his private letters to the prelates, without being satisfied that that great statesman fully concurred in all the general principles of the former.

In regard again to

" The upper ranks among the laity, setting aside courtiers and such as took little interest in the disputes," these, says Mr. Hallam, " were chiefly divided between those attached to the ancient Church, and those who wished for further reformation in the new. I conceive the Church of England party, that is, the party adverse to any species of ecclesiastical change, to have been the least numerous of the three, (that is, Puritan, Popish, and Anglican,) during this reign, still excepting, as I have said, the neutrals who commonly make a numerical majority, and are counted along with the dominant religion. . . . The Puritans, or at least, those who rather favoured them, had a majority among the Protestant gentry in the Queen's days. It is agreed on all hands (and is quite manifest) that they predominated in the House of Commons. But that house was (then) composed, as it has ever been, of the principal landed proprietors, and as much represented the general wish of the community when it demanded a further reform in religious matters, as on any other subjects. One would imagine by the manner in which some (that is unscrupulous high churchmen) express themselves, that the discontented were a small fraction, who, by some unaccountable means, in despite of the government and the nation, formed a majority of all the parliaments under Elizabeth and her two successors."

Who now then constituted the real Church of England party? Elizabeth chiefly—a host in herself—aided by all the Popish, immoral and irreligious persons in the kingdom, whether lay or clerical.

Lest our readers should fancy that we have been all this time describing merely the transition state of the Church of England before she became fully organized as she is now established,—a state which is interesting in the present day only as it serves to indicate to a philosophic inquirer, in the same manner as a fossil does to a comparative anatomist the bygone condition of some primeval state of society;—in order to prevent such a mistake, we beg leave to remind our readers that we are describing the present constitution of the Church of England as by law established. The acts of supremacy and uniformity are still in operation, and the Anglican Church, in all the principles on which it was based, and in all points of practical importance, continues as it stood at the death of Elizabeth. Nay, we hesitate not to assert, that it is now nearer to the Church of Rome than it was then. Of all the alterations demanded by the Puritans, the only one of any practical moment was made at the Hampton court conference, when the "royal theologian," certainly not to please the Puritans, forbade any but ministers to administer baptism. But this improvement is more than counterbalanced by the anti-protestant alterations made upon the prayer-book by the convocation of 1661, and that for the express purpose of rendering it for ever impossible for the Presbyterians to think of entering the

Church of England. Of these alterations, one may be mentioned as showing the *animus* of that convocation, next to that of 1689, the most infamous, not even excepting that of 1640, that ever assembled in England. Down to that period there was comparatively but little of the apocrypha prescribed in the calendar, and even that little, by an "admonition" prefixed to the Second Book of Homilies in 1564, the officiating clergyman was not only authorized to omit and substitute in its place some more suitable portion of canonical Scripture, but he was recommended to do so.* The convocation of 1661, however, and the act of uniformity based upon their proceedings, not only introduced other portions of the apocrypha into the daily lessons, but rendered it imperative upon every clergyman to read them.† We have paid some little attention to the subject, and have no fear that we shall be contradicted by any competent judge, when we affirm that the constitution and formularies of the Church of England are now less Protestant than they were left by Parker, Whitgift, and Elizabeth. The progress of enlightened opinions, and the influence of a close contact with the evangelism of the Anglican non-conformists, and of the Church of Scotland, have, it must not be concealed, to some extent, practically modified the constitutional influence of the Anglican formularies. But how slight the influence of these disturbing causes upon the minds of Anglican churchmen are, in comparison with the intense *momentum* of their own constitution, may be estimated by any man who will study the history of Laud and his times, the history of the Restoration, of the Revolution, and in our own times, ponder over the unparalelled rapidity with which Puseyism has circulated, the wide spread ramification, and the all but universal reception to which it has already attained; a circumstance that must be unaccountable to those who are

---

* Cardwell's Hist. of Conf. 21, 22, note.

† Cardwell's Hist. of Conf. 378—392, where the various alterations then made in the liturgy may be read at large, or the "Synodalia" by the same writer, ii. 633—686, where copious extracts from the original minute may be seen.

unacquainted with the constitution and history of the Church of England, but of the easiest possible solution to those who are. Challenging contradiction, we once more affirm that, without altering one single canon, injunction, or rubric, or displacing one clause in her constitution, nay, only honestly and constitutionally carrying them out to their legitimate consequences and practical results, the Church of England might be made so to approximate to the Chuich of Rome, that it might matter little to a real Bible Protestant into which of them he might be required, under pain of persecution, to incorporate himself. Had the Puseyite leaders, instead of moving forward as they have avowedly done to take their stand upon the principles of the Church of Rome, contented themselves with working out the constitutional though partially dormant principles of the Chuich of England, their success would be all but certain. If they are ever defeated, it must be through the consequences to which this false movement must inevitably lead. The once all dominant cry, "No popery," is not yet so powerless, despite of all that has happened, but that many men who would blindly embrace whatever was proved to be *bona fide* Church-of-Englandism, will be shocked when required openly to embrace undisguised Romanism.

We have found, then, that without a single exception, all the first prelates of Elizabeth were dissatisfied with the constitution of the Church of England; that the most of them deliberated long and painfully before they could be induced to accept preferments within her pale; and that the motive which principally induced them to conform was a hope that they might thus be able to complete the Reformation.* There

---

* So little was Cranmer satisfied with the state of the Church of England in his day, that he "had drawn up a book of prayers an hundred times more perfect than that which was then in being," (Edward's second liturgy,) and if the king had been spared a little longer, it is agreed on all hands it would have been introduced along with many other alterations. See Dr. Cardwell's Two Prayer-Books, &c. Compared, preface, 34–6. And yet the present prayer-book, as we have seen, is more Popish than that which Cranmer would reform.

were others, however, still more enlightened, who saw further into the intentions of Elizabeth, and who would not accept of any benefice in the Anglican Church until they saw her further reformed. Among these, not to speak of those who are known as avowed Puritans, may be mentioned Bishop Coverdale,* and Fox the martyrologist. Parker used every means to induce Fox to conform, in order that the great influence of his name might prevail upon others to follow his example. "But the old man, producing the New Testament in Greek, 'To this,' saith he, 'I will subscribe.' But when a subscription to the canons was required of him, he refused, saying, 'I have nothing in the Church save a prebend at Salisbury, and much good may it do you if you will take it away.' "† The best part of the inferior clergy again, who conformed, did so in the hope that the prelates whom they knew to be of their own sentiments would, now that they were elevated to places of power, be able to accomplish the further reformation which all so very ardently desired. Of all the true Protestants, not one would have consented to accept a preferment in the Anglican Church, if he had been at the outset aware that no further reformation was to be accomplished. What, then, it may be asked, continued to retain them in her communion, when they found that they could not reform that Church? It is a delicate question, but we have no hesitation in rendering an answer.

The deteriorating influence of high stations of honour, power, and wealth, has been rendered proverbial by the experience of mankind; but never was it more disastrously manifested than by Elizabeth's first bishops.‡ Not one of them had escaped the cor-

---

* Strype's Ann. ii. 43; Life of Parker, i. 295, 297.
† Fuller's Ch. Hist. ii 475.
‡ Cecil, writing to Whitgift about filling up some bishoprics then vacant, says, " he saw such worldliness in many that were otherwise affected before they came to cathedral churches, that he feared the places altered the men." Strype's Whitgift, i. 338. He makes very much the same complaint to Grindal in 1575. Strype's Grindal, 281.

rupting influence of their stations.* Having so far overcome the scruples they at first entertained against conformity, not it must be feared without doing violence to their convictions, it was but natural that they should entertain not the most kindly feelings towards those whose consistency of conduct not only would degrade them in their own eyes, but open up afresh the wounds yet raw in their consciences. The apostate is ever the most vindictive persecutor of his former brethren. Besides, no one can fail to have noticed that when a man has irretrievably committed himself to a cause which he formerly opposed, he is compelled, by the necessity of his position, to become more stringent and inflexible in his proceedings than the man who is now pursuing only the course on which he first embarked. Bishop Short, in a passage already quoted, has candidly admitted, that "when Parker and the other bishops had begun to execute the laws against non-conformists, they must have been more than men if they could divest their own minds of that personality which every one must feel when engaged in a controversy in which the question really is, whether he shall be able to succeed in carrying his plans into execution." We could assign other reasons for the conduct of Elizabeth's first bishops, but we entertain too high a regard for what they had been, to take any pleasure in exposing their faults.

What now would these great and good men do were they, with their avowed principles, when they returned from exile, to appear in our day? Would they praise the Church of England as "our primitive and apostolic Church,—the bulwark of the Reformation,—the safeguard of Protestantism, and the glory of Christendom?" as some who boast of being their successors continue to do. Would they even accept cures in the Church of England, knowing, as all her ministers now do, that no further reformation is so much as to be mooted,—nay, that it must not be

* See a painful letter on this subject from Sampson to Grindal. Strype's Parker, ii. 376, 377.

so much as acknowledged that it is required? He knows neither the constitution of the Church of England, nor the character of the reformers, who hesitates for one moment to answer, and with the most marked emphasis, *they would* NOT.

And what a lesson of solemn warning do the consequences of a compromise of principles, as seen in the subsequent history of the Church of England, read to our own ministers in their present arduous struggle. The second set of bishops appointed by Elizabeth were, without a single exception, men of more Erastian sentiments, of more lax theology, of more Popish tendencies, than their predecessors. The first prelates had been trained amid the advancing reformation of Edward, and among the Presbyterians on the continent, and had imbibed the sentiments of their associates. But their successors had been trained in the Church of England, and bore the impress of her character. And such would also be the case in our own Church, were our ministers, by an unhallowed submission, to yield to the antichristian invasion of the Church's rights and liberties now attempted. To these our ministers, God has committed a glorious cause. May they be found worthy to maintain it. Their deeds are before men and angels. Future historians shall record their acts, and inscribe their names in the glorious muster-roll of martyrs and confessors, or denounce them to eternal infamy. We shall watch their proceedings with an interest which the shock of armed empires would not excite in our bosoms, and, by God's grace, shall lend our aid to make known to posterity how they have fought the good fight and kept the faith. The arena of their struggle may appear obscure and contracted. But it is the Thermopylæ of Christendom. On them, and on their success, under God, it depends, whether worse than Asiatic barbarism and despotism are to overwhelm Europe, or light, and life, and liberty, to become the birthright of the nations. May the Captain of the host of Israel ever march forward at their head. May the blue banner of the covenant, unstained by one blot, be victorious in their hands, as it was of yore. May the sword of the Lord, and of Gideon, now unsheathed, never return to its scabbard, until the Church of Scotland shall have vindicated her rights, and established her liberties on an immovable basis. No surrender! No compromise! Better the mountain side, like our fathers, and freedom of communion with our God, than an Erastian establishment, which would no longer be a Church,—than a sepulchral temple, from which the living God had fled.

We return from this digression, (for which we make no apology,—we would despise the man that would require it,) to relate the internal condition of the Church of England at and after the accession of Elizabeth.

One fact will prove, to every man who regards " Christ crucified as the power of God and the wisdom of God unto salvation," that the Church of England was at this time in the most wretched condition imaginable, both moral and spiritual. Of nine thousand four hundred clergymen, of all grades, then beneficed in that Church, and all, of course, Papists, being the incumbents of Mary's reign, only one hundred and ninety-two, of whom only eighty were parochial, resigned their livings; the rest, as much Papists as ever, and now, in addition, unblushing hypocrites, who subscribed what they did not believe, and submitted to what they could not approve, remained in their cures, and became the ministers of the Protestant (?) Church of England.* We should do these nine thousand two hundred and eight who remained in their cures, an honour to which they have no claim, were we to compare them to the most ignorant, scandalous, and profligate priesthood at present in Europe. Many of them did not understand the offices they had been accustomed to "mumble" at the altar. Some

* The following is Strype's list of those who resigned,—viz, 14 bishops, 18 deans, 14 archdeacons, 15 heads of colleges, 50 prebendaries, 80 rectors, 6 abbots, priors, and abbesses, in all 192. Annals, i. 106. Burnet, ii. 620, makes them only 189. Collier, vi. p 252, following, as is his wont, Popish authorities, when they can add credit to their own Church, makes them about 250.

of them could not sign their names, or even read the English liturgy. Yet into the hands of these men did Elizabeth and her prelates commit the immortal souls of the people of England. And if at any time the people, shocked at the immoralities and Papistry of their parish priest, attended ordinances under some more Protestant minister in the neighbourhood, they were compelled, by fines and imprisonment, to return to their own parish church.

When, in the course of a few years, several of these papistico-protestant priests had died, and others of them had fled out of the kingdom, there were no properly qualified ministers to replace them. Patrons sold the benefices to laymen, retaining the best part of the fruits in their own hands. Thus the parishes remained vacant. Strype, speaking of the state of the diocese of Bangor in 1565, says, "As for Bangor, that diocese was much out of order, there being no preaching used." And two years afterwards the bishop wrote to Parker, that "he had but two preachers in his whole diocese," the livings being in the hands of laymen.* In 1562 Parkhurst of Norwich wrote Parker, in answer to the inquiries of the privy council, that in his diocese there were 434 parish churches vacant, and that many chapels of ease had fallen into ruins.† Cox of Ely, in 1560, wrote the archbishop, that in his diocese there were 150 cures of all sorts, of which only "52 were duly served,"— many of them, of course, only by readers,—34 were vacant, 13 had neither rector nor vicar, and 57 were possessed by non-residents. "So pitiable and to be lamented," exclaims Cox, "is the face of this diocese; and if, in other places, it be so too," (and so it was,) "most miserable indeed is the condition of the Church of England."‡ We never can think of the condition of England,—when thus darkness covered the earth, and thick darkness the people, and when, emphatically, the blind led the blind,—without admiring grati-

* Strype's Parker, i. 404, 509. ‡ Strype's Parker, i. 143, 144.
† Strype's An i. 539, 540.

THE ANGLICAN REFORMATION. liii

tude to that God who did not altogether remove his candlestick, and leave the whole nation to perish, through the crimes of their rulers, civil and ecclesiastical.

In order to keep the churches open, and afford even the semblance of public worship to the people, the prelates were compelled to license, as readers, a set of illiterate mechanics, who were able to read through the prayers without spelling the hard words.* The people, however, could not endure these immoral, base-born, illiterate readers; and then, as if the mere act of ordination could confer upon them all the requisite qualifications, "not a few mechanics, altogether as unlearned as the most objectionable of those ejected, were preferred to dignities and livings."† The scheme, however politic, failed, through the indecorous manners, and the immoral lives, and the gross ignorance, of these upstart priests.‡ And then an order was issued to the bishop of London to ordain no more mechanics, because of the scandals they had brought upon religion;§ but the necessity of the case compelled the provincial bishops still to employ lay readers, and ordain mechanics to read the prayers.

Such was the condition of England when Parker, partly goaded on by the queen, and partly by his own sullen despotism, commenced a course of persecutions, suspensions, and silencing against the Puritans, who were the only preachers in the kingdom. In January 1564, eight were suspended in the diocese of London. It was hoped that this example would overawe the rest, and three months afterwards the London clergy were summoned again to subscribe to the canons, and conform to all the usages of the Church of England; but thirty refused, and were, of course, suspended.‖ A respite of eight months was given to the rest; and then in January 1656 they were cited, and 37 having refused to subscribe, were suspended.¶ These, as we

* Strype's An. i. 202, 203. ‖ Strype's Grindal, 144, 146.
† Collier, vi. 264. ¶ Ibid. 154.
‡ Strype's Parker, i 180.
§ Strype's Grindal, 60. Collier, vi. 313.

THE ANGLICAN REFORMATION.

may well believe, were, even in the estimation of Parker himself, and, indeed, as he acknowledged, the best men and the ablest preachers in the diocese.* The insults offered, and the cruelties inflicted upon these men, would, had we space to detail them, intensate the indignation of our readers against their ruthless persecutors.

The silencing of such preachers, and the consequent desolation in the Church excited the attention of the nation. All men who had any regard for the ordinances of God, were shocked at the proceedings of the primate, and bitter complaints were made of him to the privy council. Elizabeth herself ordered Cecil to write him on the subject. Parker sullenly replied, that this was nothing more than he had foreseen from the first, and that when the queen had ordered him to press uniformity, "he had told her, that these precise folks would offer their goods, and even their bodies to prison, rather than they would relent."† And yet Parker, who could anticipate their conduct, could neither appreciate their conscientiousness, nor respect their firmness.

The persecutions commenced in London soon spread over the whole kingdom. We have already seen the most destitute condition of the diocese of Norwich, in which four hundred and thirty-four parish churches were vacant, and many chapels of ease fallen into ruins. Will it be credited, that in these circumstances thirty-six ministers, almost the whole preaching ministers in the diocese, were, in one day, suspended, for refusing subscription to the anti-christian impositions of the prelates?‡ This is but a specimen of what took place throughout the kingdom. And when the people, having no pastor to teach them, met together to read the Scriptures, forthwith a thundering edict came down from the primate, threatening them with fines and imprisonment if they dared to pray together or read the word of God. In a certain small village a revival took place, under the ministrations of a reader,

* Strype's Parker, i. 429.   † Strype's Parker, i 448.   ‡ Ibid ii 341.

so illiterate that he could not sign his own name. As always happens under such circumstances, the people formed fellowship meetings. No sooner was this known than they were summoned to answer for such violations of canonical order. In a simple memorial, which would melt a heart of stone, these pious peasants stated to the inquisitors, that they only met together in the evenings, after the work of the day was over, to devote the time they formerly misspent in drinking and sin, to the worship of God, and the reading of his word. Their judges were deaf to their petitions and representations, and forbade them absolutely to meet any longer for such purposes, leaving it to be inferred, by no far-fetched deductions, that a man might violate the laws of God, without impunity; but wo be unto him that should break the injunctions of the prelates.*

And what was the crime for which these Puritans were suspended, sequestered, fined, imprisoned, and some of them put to death? Simply because they would not acknowledge that man, whether prelate, primate, or prince, has authority to alter the constitution of God's church, to prescribe rites and modes of "will-worship," and administration of sacraments, different from what He had appointed in his word. Nothing but gross ignorance, or grosser dishonesty, will lead any man to say, as has been said, and continues to be said down to this day, and that not by ministers of the Church of England alone, but by others of whom better things might be expected,† that the Puritans refused to remain in their ministry merely because of the imposition of " square caps, copes, and surplices;" or even, which are of higher moment, because of the " cross in baptism," and kneeling at the communion; these things being considered simply in themselves. What they condemned and resisted was the principle, that man has authority to alter the economy of God's house. " Considering, therefore," said the ministers of London in 1565, in a defence

* Strype's Parker, 381-5.
† See Orme's Life of Owen, commented on by Dr. McCrie in his Miscellaneous Works, pp. 465, 466.

they published of their own conduct, "considering, therefore, that at this time, by admitting the outward apparel, and ministering garments of the Pope's church, not only the Christian liberty should be manifestly infringed, but the whole religion of Christ would be brought to be esteemed no other thing than the pleasure of princes, they (the London ministers) thought it their duty, being ministers of God's word and sacraments, utterly to refuse" to submit to the required impositions. But if the prelates were determined to proceed in their infatuated career, then these enlightened servants of God professed their willingness " to submit themselves to any punishment the laws did appoint, that so they might teach by their example true obedience both to God and man, and yet to keep the Christian liberty sound, and show the Christian religion to be such, that no prince or potentate might alter the same."*

When Sampson and Humphreys were required to subscribe and submit to the prescribed impositions, they refused upon the following, among other accounts:—" If," they said, " we should grant to wear priests' apparel, then it might and would be required at our hands to have shaven crowns, and to receive more Papistical abuses. Therefore it is best, at the first, not to wear priests' apparel."† It was the principle involved in these impositions they opposed. And well are we assured, that had it not been for the resistance to the first attempts to enslave the conscience, which were made by these glorious confessors and martyrs, other and still more hateful abuses of Popery would have been perpetuated in the Anglican church. Only grant the principle, that man has the right to make such impositions, and where is the application of the principle to find its limit?

And as to the stale objection, that these men relinquished their ministry for frivolous rites and habits, it is enough to reply, that the objection is not founded upon truth.

* *Apud* Strype's An. ii. 166, 167.   † Strype's Parker, i. 340.

"As touching that point," (the habits,) says Cartwright, "whether the minister should wear it, although it be inconvenient; the truth is, that I dare not be author to any to forsake his pastoral charge for the inconvenience thereof, considering that this charge (the ministry) being an absolute commandment of the Lord, ought not to be laid aside for a simple inconvenience or uncomeliness of a thing which, in its own nature, is indifferent. . . . When it is laid in the scales with the preaching of the word of God, which is so necessary to him who is called thereunto, that a woe hangeth on his head if he do not preach it; it is of less importance than for the refusal of it we should let go so necessary a duty."*

We might challenge their accusers, whether Brownist or Prelatist, to show us sentiments more enlightened or more consistently maintained, since the world began.

We have said so much upon this point, because we do not mean at present to enter upon a formal defence of the Puritans, although we may, perchance, do so elsewhere, and at greater length, hereafter, if God spare us. We have done this also to prevent our readers from being carried away by the oft-repeated libels of pert pretenders to liberality, or of servile conformists to hierarchical impositions, against the best men that England has ever produced.

The universities did little or nothing to provide ministers for the necessities of the times. The condition of Oxford at the accession of Elizabeth was deplorable in the extreme.† In 1563 Sampson, Humphreys, and Kingsmill, three Puritans, were the only ministers who could preach, resident in Oxford;‡ and as if to deliver over that university to the unrestrained sway of Popery, the two former were ejected, while Papists swarmed in all the colleges. In one college, (Exeter,) in 1578, out of eighty resident members,

* Rest of Second Replie to Whitgift, ed. 1577, p. 262.
† See Jewell's Letters to Bullinger and Peter Martyr on the State of Oxford; Burnet's Records, bk. vi. 48, 56.
‡ Strype's Parker, i. 313.

there were only four professed Protestants.* Whenever a Puritan was discovered, he was instantly expelled; but never,—so far as we could discover, and we paid attention to the point,—never, for mere Popery, was one Papist ejected, from either cure or college, throughout the whole reign of Elizabeth. Oxford continued thus the stronghold of Popery; and instead of providing ministers for the Church of England, it provided members for Popish colleges "beyond the seas."† It is instructive, not less to the statesman and the philosopher, than to the divine, to find the self-propagating power of error, and the tendency to conserve corruption, which has been manifested in that celebrated seat of learning. Whenever Popery is assailed, it uniformly finds a safe retreat in Oxford.

In the reign of Edward, Cambridge had received a larger diffusion of the gospel than the rival university. Almost all the first prelates of Elizabeth had been educated on the banks of the Cam, and all the principal preachers of the same period had been trained in the same place. Cambridge, in fact, along with London, was the head quarters of Puritanism, not less among the undergraduates, than the heads and members. From a faculty which had been granted by the Pope to that university, to license twelve preachers annually, who might officiate in any part of the kingdom, without having their licences countersigned by the prelates, Cambridge seemed destined to be the salvation of England. The Protestant prelates, however, could not tolerate a licence to preach, which even their Popish predecessors had patronized, and never ceased until they had deprived Cambridge of its privilege. Not satisfied with this prevention of preaching, Parker and his successor determined to root out Puritanism from its stronghold; and as they had silenced its preachers in London, so they silenced its professors at Cambridge. Cartwright, Johnson, Dering, Brown, Wilcox, and their fellows, were expelled, some of

* Strype's An. ii. 196, 197.   † Ibid. 390, 391.

them imprisoned, and some of them driven into banishment. The salt being thus removed, the body sunk into partial corruption. Of Cambridge, however, it is right that it should be recorded, that whatever of Protestantism England possesses, it owes to that university. How singular it is, that after the lapse of three centuries, the two English universities should, at this day, retain the distinguishing features which characterized them at the Reformation.

In order to supply as much as they possibly could some instructors for their parishes, the Anglican prelates established in their dioceses what was called " prophesyings," or "exercises," that is, monthly or weekly meetings of the clergy for mutual instruction in theology and pulpit ministrations; and the plan was found to work so admirably, that, as Grindal told the queen in 1576, when she commanded him to suppress the prophesyings, and diminish the number of preachers, " where afore were not three able preachers, now are thirty meet to preach at Paul's Cross, and forty or fifty besides able to instruct their own cures."*
The prophesyings, however, were suppressed, and the people left to perish for lack of knowledge. On a survey of the condition of England at the time, nothing can more strongly convince a pious mind of the superintendence of a gracious Providence, than that the kingdom did not sink into heathenism, or at least remain altogether Popish.

The moral character of the Anglican priesthood was of a piece with their ignorance and Popish tendencies. This subject is so disgusting, and the disclosures we could make so shocking, that we hesitate whether it were not better to pass by the subject in total silence. We may give an instance or two, however, as a specimen of what was the almost universal condition of this clergy, and our specimens are by no means the worst we could adduce. Sandys of Worcester, in his first visitation in 1560, found in the city

* Strype's Grindal, Rec. B. ii. No. 9, p. 568. We recommend to our readers to peruse the whole of that noble letter, the noblest that was ever addressed to Elizabeth.

of Worcester, five or six priests, "who kept five or six whores a-piece."* And were they suspended? Our author gives not one single hint that they were. But had they preached the gospel at uncanonical hours, or saved sinners in uncanonical garments, they would not only have been deposed, but fined, imprisoned, and perhaps banished or even put to death. The laws of God might be violated with impunity, but wo unto him who broke the laws of Elizabeth and Parker. Again, in 1559, at a commission appointed to visit the province of York, comprising the whole of the north and east of England, with the diocese of Chester, which includes Lancashire, "the presentments," that is, the informations lodged against the incumbents "were most frequent, almost in every parish, about fornication, and keeping other women besides their wives, and for having bastard children."†
"As to Bangor, that diocese was much out of order, there being no preaching used, and pensionary concubinacy openly continued, which was an allowance of concubinacy to the clergy by paying a pension (to the bishop, or his court,) notwithstanding the liberty of marriage granted." And Parker himself was openly charged with having "such a commissioner there as openly kept three concubines."‡ This, let it be noticed, was not a libel by "Martin Marprelate," but an official report from a royal commission presented to the privy council. While Puritans crowded every pestiferous jail in the kingdom for merely preaching the truth as it is in Jesus, these infamous priests filled every parish in England. Let any man assert that we have given the only, or the most scandalous instances we could rake up from the polluted sewer of the early Anglican church history, and we shall give him references to fifty times as many more; for we decline polluting our pages with such abandoned profligacy.

One of the most fruitful sources of those enormous

* Strype's Parker, i. 156. † Strype's An. i. 246.
‡ Strype's Parker, i 404

evils under which the Church of England at this time groaned, was that prolific mother of all corruption, *patronage*, which has never existed in a Church without corrupting it, and which threatens, if God interpose not, to destroy our own beloved Zion. In 1584, "a person of eminency in the Church" gives a fearful picture of the evils which "the devil and corrupt patrons" had occasioned to the Anglican establishment. "For patrons now-a-days," he says, "search not the universities for most fit pastors, but they post up and down the country for a most gainful chapman; he that hath the biggest purse to pay largely, not he that hath the best gifts to preach learnedly is presented."* And what is the difference between this state of matters and what has existed among ourselves, but that the patron, instead of selling his presentations for money, has bestowed them in return for votes for his nominee to parliament, for support in gaining the lieutenancy of a county, or (as now seems the current price) for support in "swamping" the present majority in our General Assembly?

The bishops were just as corrupt in the disposal of the benefices in their gift as the lay patrons. Curtes of Chichester, for example, was charged by several gentlemen and justices of peace of his diocese, among other malversations of office, with keeping benefices in his gift long vacant, that he might himself pocket the fruits, and selling his advowsons to the highest bidder.† After a visitation of his province, Parker writes Lady Bacon, that "to sell and to buy benefices, to fleece parsonages and vicarages, was come to that pass, that *omnia sunt venalia;*" that all ranks were guilty of the practice, "so far, that some one knight had four or five, and others, seven or eight benefices clouted together," and retained in their own hands, the parishes all the while being vacant; while others again set boys and servants "to bear the names of such livings," and others again bargained them away

* Strype's An. ii. 146. Ibid. Whitgift, i. 368. † Ibid. 117.

at a fixed sum per year. And," he adds, "this kind of doing was common in all the country."*

When the Simonists came for orders or institution, they sometimes were rejected by the more conscientious prelates, on account, not indeed of their Simony, which, so far as we have noticed, never happened, but on account of their gross ignorance and scandalous lives. But the patrons, and these dutiful sons of the Church, anticipating by three centuries, the practices with which we are, alas, but too familiar in our own day, were not thus to be defrauded of their "vested rights" and "patrimonial interests." They commenced suits in the civil courts, and harassed the bishops with the terrors of a *quare impedit*, and of a *præmunire*. They did not always, however, put themselves to that trouble. Some of the presentees at once took possession of their benefices without waiting for orders, (as we shall bye and bye show,) and set themselves to read prayers, and administer *quasi* sacraments, or what was much more congenial to their tastes, to cultivate their glebes; varying the monotony of attending "farmers' dinners" by occasional other indulgences much less "moderate;" an example this, which (barring the last part,) we take leave most humbly to commend to those unpopular presentees who are not fortunate enough to get presentations to parishes within that paradise of moderatism, the synod of Aberdeen, or the presbytery of Meigle.

In consequence of this state of matters, pluralities and non-residence became universal. Nor could it well be otherwise when the prelates set such examples as that we are about to adduce before men by no means disinclined to follow them. We could show

---

* Strype's Parker, i. 495–8. By the 22d apostolical canon, the 2d council of Chalcedon, and the 22d Trullan canon, Simonists, if prelates, or priests, or deacons, were to be deposed and excommunicated. Pray, what becomes of the "apostolical succession" in the Church of England, if these canons are held valid? And if the canons are rejected, pray, on what other foundation does the Church of England stand?

several examples of pluralism such as never, we are persuaded, was witnessed in any other Church. The case of the following *Jacobus de Voragine*, however, may stand for all. From the frequency and the urgency of the complaints that came up to the privy council regarding the state of the diocese of St. Asaph, a commission was appointed in 1587 to visit it. The visitors, on their return, laid the following report before the high commission court, viz., that "most of the great livings within the diocese, some with cure of souls and some without cure, are either holden by the bishop (Hughes) himself in *commendam*," or by non-residents, the most of whom were laymen, civilians, or lawyers in the archbishop's court, through which dispensations to hold *commendams* were obtained. The prelate kept to his own share sixteen of the richest benefices. Fourteen of the same class were held by the civil lawyers, of course as fees for granting him dispensations to hold the rest. There was not a single preacher within the diocese, the "lord bishop only excepted," but three. One of the resident pluralists holding three benefices, two of them among the richest in the diocese, kept neither "house nor hospitality," but lived in an ale house. The prelate also sold (some on behoof of his wife, some on that of his children, and some on his own) most, if not all, the livings in his gift, besides those reserved in his own hands. He would grant the tithes of any living to any person who would pay for them, reserving for the support of an incumbent what would not maintain a mechanic; in consequence of which the parishes remained vacant. In his visitations he would compel the clergy, besides the customary "procurations," as they are called, (that is, an assessment upon the clergy to pay the ordinary expenses of a prelate during a visitation through his diocese,) to pay also for all his train.*

Our readers will not be surprised to hear that this wholesale dealer in tithes and benefices was amassing

* Strype's An. iii. 435, 436, and iv. Ap. No. 32.

a handsome fortune and purchasing large estates, besides dealing in mortgages and other profitable speculations. But they will be surprised to hear that no *commendam* could be held without a dispensation from the archbishop's court, and that while hundreds of parishes throughout England were vacant for want of ministers to supply them, and while hundreds more were so poor that they could not support a minister,* Parker was accustomed to grant dispensations to prelates to hold *commendams*, for the purpose of being able to maintain what he so much loved and commended to others, viz., "the port of a bishop;"† and they may also be surprised, that is to say if they are not so well acquainted with the primate as we happen to be, when we tell them that Parker was paid a sort of per centage upon all these dispensations; not that we insinuate that this had any share in inducing him to grant them, although his own maintenance of the "port of a bishop" entailed upon him no trifling expense.‡

Our readers will now be prepared to receive the

* There are in England 4543 livings, if *livings* they can be called, under L 10. See an extract from a document from the state paper office on the value of all the benefices in England in Collier ix. Rec. No. 99. "The Church of England probably stands alone," says Bishop Short, "in latter times as exhibiting instances of ecclesiastical offices unprovided with any temporal support." Sketch, &c. p 188. "The extreme poverty which has been entailed on many of our livings," he says again, "is one of the greatest evils which afflicts our Church property," p 509. And he says elsewhere, that if it were not for the number of persons of independent fortune who take orders in the Church of England, (allured of course by the higher prizes,) many of the cures must remain vacant. The manner in which the Church of England, and our own Church also, were pillaged at the Reformation by our benevolent friends the patrons, is an inviting subject for a dissertation, but we must not enter upon it here.

† For this purpose, he granted to Cheney a dispensation to hold Bristol in *commendam* with Gloucester. And for precisely the same purpose, he granted Blethyn of Landaff a dispensation to hold the archdeaconry of Brecon, the rectory of Roget, a prebend in Landaff, the rectory of Sunningwell, and in addition, "to hold *alia quæcunque, quotcunque, qualiacunque*, not exceeding L. 100 per an." Strype's Parker, ii 421, 422.

‡ As a specimen of the manner in which Parker maintained the "port of a bishop," the reader may consult Strype's Parker, i 378—380, 253, 254; ii 278, 296, 297, &c.

THE ANGLICAN REFORMATION. lxv

following account of the state of the Church and kingdom of England, drawn up by the industrious Strype* from the papers of Cecil:—

"The state of the Church and religion at this time (1572) was but low and sadly neglected. . . . The churchmen heaped up many benefices upon themselves and resided upon none, neglecting their cures. Many of them alienated their lands; made unreasonable leases and wastes of their woods; granted reversions and advowsons to their wives and children, or to others for their use. Churches ran greatly into dilapidation and decay, and were kept nasty and filthy, and indecent for God's worship. . . . Among the laity there was little devotion; the Lord's day greatly profaned and little observed; the common prayers not frequented; some lived without any service of God at all; many were mere heathens and atheists; the queen's own court an harbour for epicures and atheists, and a kind of lawless place because it stood in no parish;—which things made good men fear some bad judgments impending over the nation."

And yet ministers of the Church of England can find no terms sufficiently strong in which to praise the reformation in their own Church, or dispraise that in the other Protestant churches.

It may not be improper, although we have scrupulously confined ourselves to Church of England authorities, to give the testimony of a contemporary Puritan as to the condition of that Church about 1570:—

"I could rehearse by name," says our author, "a bishop's boy, ruffianly both in behaviour and apparel, at every word swearing and staring, having ecclesiastical promotions—a worthy prebend (prebendary?) no doubt. I could name whoremongers being taken, and also confessing their lechery, and yet both enjoying their livings and also having their mouths open, and not stopped nor forbidden to preach. I know

* Life of Parker, ii. 204, 205.

also some that have said mass diverse years since it was prohibited, and upon their examination confessed the same, yet are in quiet possession of their ecclesiastical promotions. I know double beneficed men that do nothing but eat, drink, sleep, play at dice tables, bowls, and read service in the Church,—but these infect not their flocks with false doctrine, for they teach nothing at all."*

Where is the man who ponders over these statements that will not sympathize with the bishop of Sodor and Man, in the reflection with which he closes his history of the reign of Elizabeth?—"The feeling which the more attentive study of these times is calculated to inspire," says Dr. Short,† "is the conviction of the superintendence of Providence over the Church of Christ." Assuredly but for the watchful providence of the God of all grace, the Church of Christ in England could never have survived the reign of Elizabeth.

There is just one subject more to which we must allude before we bring the lengthened sketch of the Anglican Reformation to a close; and we do so in order to show our readers that if "apostolical succes-

---

* Parte of a Register, p. 8. See also *passim*, the first of the Mar Prelate Tracts, just reprinted by Mr. John Petheram, bookseller, 71 Chancery Lane, London. The Mar Prelate Tracts having been written in a satirical style, were disclaimed by the stern and severe Puritans of the times, but so far as facts are concerned, we hold them perfectly trustworthy. We have read through Martin's Epistle, just published, and will at any time, at five minutes' warning, undertake to establish by positive or presumptive evidence the substantial, and in the great majority of cases the verbal, truth of any important fact it contains. Mr. Petheram intends, should he receive sufficient encouragement, to reprint by subscription, in a neat cheap form, several of the old Puritan tracts, such as The Troubles at Frankfort, Admonition to Parliament, Parte of a Register, and others exceedingly valuable, but so exceedingly rare, that not one in a hundred of our readers can ever have seen them. Mr. Petheram illustrates these tracts by judicious antiquarian notes, that add greatly to their value. We recommend our readers in the strongest terms to possess themselves of these curious and valuable productions, and trust Mr. Petheram may receive such encouragement in his spirited enterprise as may induce him to reprint even larger works of the old Puritan divines

† Sketch, &c. p. 318.

sion," or an uninterrupted succession of ministers canonically baptized, and prelatically ordained and consecrated, be essential to the being of a Church, then the Church of England not only cannot prove that she has this essential qualification, but we can prove that she has lost it, at least to an extent that invalidates all her pretensions to its possession.

We have some time ago shown, that, on canonical principles, baptism is valid only when it is administered by a minister canonically, that is, as it is commonly understood, prelatically ordained; and that without such baptism a man's orders, however canonically conferred, are null and void, inasmuch as he wanted a qualification which is essential as a substratum for orders subsequently received. Ministers of the Church of England, if they would prove that they possess an apostolical succession, must first prove that all through whom baptism and orders have descended to them have themselves been canonically baptized and ordained. But how can this be proved in the presence of such facts as the following? Midwives, about the period of the Reformation, were, it would appear, frequently guilty of changing infants at birth, strangling and beheading them, and baptizing them in what were called 'cases of necessity, with perfumed and artificial water, and "odd and profane words" and ceremonies. On these accounts it was deemed necessary not only to bind them over to keep the peace towards these "innocents," but to grant them a species of orders, by which they might be admitted among the subaltern grades of the hierarchy. Parker, for example, in 1567, grants to Eleanor Pead, a license to administer baptism, (having first exacted of her an oath of canonical obedience) of the following tenor,—" Also, that in the ministration of the sacrament of baptism, I will use apt, and the accustomed words of the same sacrament, that is to say, these words following, or the like in effect, 'I christen thee in the name of the Father, the Son, and the Holy Ghost,' and none other profane words."*

* Strype's An 1. ii. 242—3.

THE ANGLICAN REFORMATION.

Now, without being so hypercritical as to maintain that, Parker, in calling the words "I christen thee," &c. "profane words," as in the above sentence he necessarily does, seems himself to acknowledge the invalidity of such pretended sacrament; and without maintaining that the omission of the scriptural term "I baptize," and the substitution of the unscriptural and heretical term "I christen," invalidates the whole act, (even had it been performed by Parker himself) but granting that these irregularities derogate nothing from the validity of the ordinance, as performed by the said Eleanor, we yet beg leave to demand of every pretender to the apostolical succession in the Anglican Church, to prove to our satisfaction that some of his ghostly fathers were not "christened" by Eleanor Pead, or some of her "sage" sisterhood; and if they were, then to show us any authority whatever that such "sage femme" has to administer baptism any more than the Lord's Supper; and finally, if he contends that Eleanor Pead did, or could possess such authority, then we ask on what ground could she be inhibited from performing the other acts of the ministry, or why deacons, priests, and prelates are at all necessary, seeing an apostolical succession of midwives is just as sufficient as that of prelates or Popes? We trust these remarks may not be considered *very* unreasonable.

But we possess ample evidence that midwives were not the only uncanonical administrators of sacraments during the Anglican Reformation. We have already shown that the bishops were persecuted, both by patrons and presentees, when ordination and institution were refused to unqualified candidates.* But we have now to show that many of those whose only objects in getting a "living," was what the term so expressively signifies, on meeting with patrons, whose only desire was to make the most of their "patrimonial rights, and vested interests," not, indeed, in the patriotic form of "swamping" a noble-minded majority, who will neither be bullied nor bribed into

* See for example Strype's Parker, ii. 84—87.

a sacrifice of the rights and liberties of Christ and his people, (that plan was reserved for Scottish patrons in the nineteenth century) but in the more substantial, though not more offensive shape, of getting a good price for the presentation, or a long lease, or fee-simple possession of the best part of the benefice, had recourse to a plan which we again beg leave to recommend to those of our unpopular "moderate" preachers who may happen to have got into the good graces of our Dukes of Richmond, our Earls of Kinnoul, and our Sir James Grahams; that is, in plain terms, these Anglican intrusionist presentees, without troubling prelate or primate for orders, at once, in simple virtue of their civil presentations, not only took possession of the temporalities, but set themselves to perform all clerical acts, as ministers of the parishes. Are we wrong in thinking, as we really do, it were more manly and rational for those who maintain that a presentation, in ordinary circumstances, necessarily leads to ordination, at once to take possession of their benefices, in virtue of a warrant from the Court of Session, rather than trouble themselves and others for ordinations (so termed) from men who have no power to confer orders but in virtue of warrants from the civil courts? If, when the Church hath withdrawn the orders she conferred, the Court of Session can confer orders of its own (for that is the true state of the case,) why not remain satisfied with a civil title to a civil right, or with orders from the civil court rather than an unmeaning ceremonial at the hands of its nominees? But leaving these suggestions to be pondered on by those whom they may concern, we return to the history of "unordained ministers" in the Church of England.

Let us just present a sample of the numerous cases we could refer to by simply searching through the notes extracted by our own hand from the works of the "industrious Strype." In 1567, in a visitation of the cathedral of Norwich, it was discovered that one of the archdeacons (a part of whose functions it is to institute, or as we call it, to induct, into benefices) and a prebendary were not in orders at all.* In 1568, the bishop of Gloucester wrote Parker that he had discovered in his diocese two men who had "administered the communion, christened infants, and married people, and done other spiritual offices in the Church, and yet never took holy orders. One of them had counterfeited that bishop's seal, and the other was perjured."† In 1574 there was "one Lowth, of Carlisle side, who, though he had for fifteen or sixteen years exercised the function, yet he proved to be ordered neither priest nor minister."‡ He was discovered in consequence of some irregularity in his conformity, which led to his examination, and in consequence of which he was discovered to be a mere layman. Had he conformed, like so many more who were in similar circumstances, he might perhaps, layman though he was, have risen to the bench. In 1832, the bishop of St. David's wrote to Walsingham that he found in his diocese "divers that pretended to be ministers, and had counterfeited divers bishops' seals, as Gloucester, Hereford, Landaff and his predecessors, being not called at all to the ministry." There must have been at least four of them, and they had been in their cures " by the space of eight, ten, twelve, and some fourteen years."§ "But among the scandalous churchmen in these days (1571,) the greatest surely," says Strype,‖ who, however, knew far too much to be very confident in his assertion,— "the greatest surely was one Blackall..... He had four wives alive .... He had intruded himself into the ministry for the space of twelve years, and yet was never lawfully called, nor made minister by any bishop.... He was a chopper and changer of benefices," (that is, he was successful in getting a variety of presentations to benefices in various parts of the country, into which he intruded himself, without asking the leave or concurrence of any prelate—a very frequent occurrence at the time,) "little caring by

* Strype's Parker, i. 492. † Ibid. i 534.
‡ Ibid, ii 400. Life of Grindal, 275—6.
§ Strype's Life of Grindal, 401. ‖ Annals, iii. 144—5.

what ways or means so (as) he might get money from any man. He would run from country to country, and from town to town, leading about with him naughty women, as in Gloucestershire he led a naughty strumpet about the country, (nick) named *Green Apron*. He altered his name wherever he went, going by these several surnames, Blackall, Barthall, Dorel, Barkly, Baker!!"

Was there ever a church upon the earth in which such a monster as this could exist, in which such atrocious irregularities, and not only irregularities, but criminalities, could be openly perpetrated for the space of twelve years, without censure or detection, but the Church of England alone? And are we now, in blind unenquiring submission to " bulls" from Oxford, or London or Lambeth, in spite of such infamous facts open to the whole world,—are we, renouncing the characteristic attributes of man, and resigning the direction' of our judgments, and the interests of our souls into the hands of the successors, not of the apostles, but of such miscreants as Blackall, to receive, as the only commissioned messengers of Heaven to our land, the ministers of the Church of England? So common in fact was the practice of taking possession of benefices without orders, and when the right of possession was at any time questioned, to forge letters of orders, that in 1575, that is, seventeen years after the Anglican Church was settled under Elizabeth, the matter was brought before convocation, and it was enacted, that "diligent inquisition should be made for such as forged letters of orders," and " that bishops certify one another of counterfeit ministers."* The reason of this last enactment was, that when one of these "counterfeit ministers" was detected in one diocese, he fled into another, and so little unity of action was there, or can there ever be, in a prelatic regimen, (unlike our Church courts) that the same course of "counterfeit ministry" might be gone through in succession in all the dioceses in England.

* Strype's Grindal, 290. One of these was *e g.* summoned before the convocation of 1584. Strype's Whitgift, 1. 398.

What now, we repeat, becomes of the claim to the apostolical succession, so confidently and offensively put forth by ministers of the Church of England? "Even in the memory of persons living," says archbishop Whately,* "there existed a bishop, concerning whom there was so much mystery and uncertainty prevailing, as to when, and where, and by whom he had been ordained, that doubts existed in the minds of many persons whether he had ever been ordained at all," . . and from the circumstances of the case, and from the fact that such doubts did prevail in the minds of well-informed persons, it is certain "that the circumstances of the case were such as to make manifest the *possibility* of such an irregularity occurring under such circumstances." Such an irregularity, then, as a man not only officiating in the lower grades of the ministry, but even rising to the primacy of the Church of England, without ever having been in orders, or rather such a subversion of the very first elements of an apostolical constitution, was not confined to the dark and troublous period of the Reformation, when the whole framework of society was dissolved into its first rudiments, and every species of irregularity not only might, but as we know did occur, but the very same "unchurching" irregularities have existed in the Church of England down through every age of its history, "till within the memory of persons now living." Any one who will look at a "genealogical tree," and observe how many wide spreading and far distant branches may spring from one stem, will easily perceive how a very few such unordained or "counterfeit ministers" as we have referred to, and shown to have existed in the Church of England, were amply enough to have destroyed all apostolical succession in the kingdom. Such withered branches could not transmit any portion of the "sacred deposit." All who have succeeded to them are no successors of the apostles; and we challenge any, and every minister in the Church of England to prove to us that he has not received all the orders he ever possessed, through some of these Eleanor Peads, Lowths of Carlisle side,

* On the Kingdom of Christ, p. 178.

or Blackalls—a glorious parentage, certainly, of which they have great reason to be vain.

We have not, for our own part, been very much addicted to boast of our ancestry, albeit it contains names of whose call and commission from Heaven we have no more doubt than we have of those of the apostle Paul. We have commonly found, in *private* life, that such boasting is very much a characteristic of upstart *parvenus*, and we have yet to learn that it is greatly different in regard to *official* descent. Should occasion, however, demand, we have no great dislike to pay a visit to the Herald's College, and demonstrate to our Southern neighbours that we have no such bar sinister in ours as defaces their clerical escutcheon. May we therefore drop a hint to certain parties, that, however they may do it in private, where no one may mark their confusion, they should be specially chary how, in public, they turn up any ecclesiastical " Debrett." Much as they decry, and often as they twit our Wesleyan friends, he must have a peculiarly constituted taste, indeed, who would not prefer even genuine " Brumagem orders" to such as have been forged by such ghostly progenitors as they boast of.

We had purposed to show multifarious and other irregularities in the organization of the Church of England. We have, however, more than exhausted our present space. But should God grant us health we-may soon return to the subject, for we can assure our readers we have only broken ground, and simply tested the range and capabilities of our ordnance. It is assuredly in itself no grateful task to rake up the errors of the dead, and expose the defects in our neighbours' ecclesiastical constitution. But it has become necessary. We have now no option. The Church of England has now, for years, unprovoked, unresisted, poured upon us such torrents of abuse, from her lordliest prelates to her obscurest curates,— she has vilified all we held sacred, insulted all we held dear, and we must either tamely submit to see our beloved Church covered with infamy, or hurl back the foul missiles upon the aggressors.

An observation or two in conclusion. We have, upon this occasion, confined our remarks to the history of Elizabeth's first prelates. The second set became much less pious and Protestant, and consequently we have selected the period most favourable to the Church of England. This is clearly implied in a passage we have given from the British Critic, and we may hereafter prove it, should any call it in question. Our authorities have been exclusively from Church of England writers; not certainly because we deemed them more trustworthy than others, for no man of any pretensions to candour will dispute, as Bishop Short has remarked,[*] that members of other communions cannot be supposed to be more prejudiced against her than her own members are in her favour. We have selected this course, because we have found her own writers establish all that we desire in order to accomplish our end. When they write against the Church of Scotland, will they follow our example? If they do, it will present a new phasis in the controversy. Hitherto they have taken as their authorities works written by non-jurors, and Scottish prelatic sectaries, the most unscrupulous controversialists that ever disgraced a cause that had little indeed to commend it. We have said that the Church of England, in every thing of importance, stands now precisely where she stood at the demise of Elizabeth. This may be called in question by those who know not the facts of the case. We therefore appeal to the following testimony of one of her living prelates. "The kingdom," says Bishop Short,[†] "has, for the last two hundred years, been making rapid strides in every species of improvement, and a corresponding altera-

[*] Sketch, &c. sect. 419.

[†] Sketch of the History of the Church of England, 2d edit. pp. 436–7. Note. This is a work which we recommend to our readers. That we do not agree with Dr. Short in many of his statements we have not concealed But we should do him injustice if we did not say, that although his work is brief, too brief, and not free from faults, from which we never expect to see a history of the Church of England, by one of her own ministers, altogether exempt, still it is incomparably the best work on the subject which an Anglican clergyman has ever produced.

tion in the laws on every subject has taken place; *during this period nothing has been remedied in the church,"* (the *italics* are ours.) So grievous are the abuses which the anomalous constitution of the Anglican church has entailed upon her, that Dr. Short hesitates not to say, (with his usually interjected " perhaps," whenever he gives utterance to an unpalatable sentiment) that "the temporal advantages which the establishment possesses, are, perhaps, more than counterbalanced by the total inability of the church to regulate any thing within herself, and the great want of discipline over the clergy ; . . . . while the absurd nature of our ecclesiastical laws renders every species of discipline over the laity not only nugatory, but when it is exercised, frequently unchristian, ridiculous, and in many cases very oppressive," as in the case of excommunication, by which a man is deprived, not only of all ecclesiastical privileges, but even of civil, yea, of all social rights.

Some of our readers may be inclined to ask, if all these things be in reality so, how does it happen that good, pious, enlightened men remain in the communion of the Church of England? Now this is a question that ought not to be asked, and being asked, ought not to be answered. We judge no man. To his own master he standeth or falleth. We can, however, assign one reason, which, besides the all-powerful one of the prejudices of education, is sufficient to account to our own mind, and that without any imputation against them, for such men remaining in the Anglican church, and that is, total ignorance of her character and constitution. Let not this insinuation startle our readers. We shall prove that such ignorance exists. Dr. Short, in the preface to his work, (p. 1) assigns as the reason that led him to commence his history, that he " discovered after he was admitted into orders," and when engaged as tutor in his college, " that the knowledge of English ecclesiastical history which he possessed was very deficient. . . . . He was distressed that his knowledge of the sects among the philosophers of Athens was greater than his information on questions which affect the Church of England." Dr. Short's is no singular case. The ignorance of Anglican ministers upon the history and constitution of their own church would astonish our readers. A memorable instance of this has recently come to light in this city, and we allude to it because the well-known conscientiousness and high character of the party concerned give the instance all the greater authority. The Rev. D. T. K. Drummond, for whom personally we entertain the very highest respect, has shown, in one of his recent tracts, that he never, till within the last few days, had examined, or at least understood, the canons of that sect of which he was a minister; or at all events, that he was ignorant of what it regards as by far the most important part of its services, —the communion office. Mr. Drummond was, for years, a minister in that body, and it does not appear that a shadow of suspicion ever crossed his mind that its constitution contained anything either positively erroneous, or sinfully defective; indeed his character is a sufficient guarantee that no such thought ever found harbourage in his breast, for had he but entertained the suspicion, he would not have remained one day in that communion. And yet in the constitution and liturgical offices of that sect there existed all the while a plague-spot so deadly, that, on its discovery, Mr. Drummond is compelled, as he values his own soul, to come out of Babylon, that he be not a partaker of her sins and punishment. Such will also be the result to which pious ministers in the Church of England will be brought, should they ever unprejudicedly and dispassionately examine her constitution. And should Mr. Drummond, as we doubt not he will, continue his investigations in the spirit in which he has commenced them, we shall be astonished, indeed, if his love of truth, and of Him who is the truth, does not lead him to renounce all communion with the Church of England, as he has already done with the Scottish prelatic sectaries. A sifting time is at hand; and when the breath of the living God has blown over the thrashing floor of the Church, we confidently anticipate that only the chaff shall remain in the Church of England.

The Exclusive Claims of Puseyite Episcopalians to the Christian Ministry Indefensible

THE EXCLUSIVE CLAIMS

OF

PUSEYITE EPISCOPALIANS

TO THE CHRISTIAN MINISTRY

INDEFENSIBLE:

WITH AN INQUIRY INTO THE DIVINE RIGHT OF

EPISCOPACY AND THE APOSTOLIC SUCCESSION

IN A SERIES OF LETTERS TO THE REV DR PUSEY

By JOHN BROWN, D.D.

"Nothing has so effectually thrown contempt upon a regular succession of the ministry, as the calling no succession regular but what was uninterrupted, and the making the eternal salvation of Christians to depend upon that uninterrupted succession, of which the most learned can have the least assurance, and the unlearned can have no notion, but through ignorance and credulity." HOADLY.

"They who would reduce the Church to the form of government thereof in the primitive times would be found pecking towards the Presbytery of Scotland Which, for my part, I believe in point of government cometh nearer than either yours (the Popish) or ours of Episcopacy to the first age of Christ's Church." LORD DIGBY.

CONTENTS.

LETTER I.

Ungenerous and unprovoked attack by Puseyite Episcopalians on Presbyterian Churches.—Alarming view presented by the former, of the spiritual condition of the latter.—Necessity imposed on Presbyterians to defend their principles., ... 17

LETTER II.

Exclusive claims of Puseyite Episcopalians to the Christian ministry by no means of recent origin.—Saravia not the author of them, but Laud.—Account of the principal individuals in the Church of England who have brought them forward at different periods, when they considered her to be in danger.—Their doctrines proved to be contrary to her principles, from the Thirty-nine Articles, the writings of the Bishops who composed her Formularies, and their immediate successors, their conduct towards Presbyterian Churches, the Charter granted by Edward the Sixth to these Churches in London, and the establishment of Presbytery by Elizabeth in Jersey and Guernsey,. 21

LETTER III.

These doctrines condemned in the strongest terms by the most distinguished Protestant Statesmen after the Reformation; Cecil, the Lord President of Queen Elizabeth's Council, Sir Francis Knollys, and Lord Bacon, and denounced as "a Popish conceit," by the leading bishops and clergy.—Dissimilarity between the Church of England, beyond whose pale, and that of the Church of Rome, Puseyites deny that there is any hope of salvation, and the Apostolic Church, in the extent of its bishoprics, the civil power exercised by its prelates, the multitude of its ceremonies, and "its want," according to its own acknowledgment, "of a godly discipline,". . . 38

LETTER IV.

Extracts from the Oxford Tracts asserting the doctrines of Puseyite Episcopacy to be the doctrines of Scripture.—A contrary opinion avowed by the whole of the bishops and clergy who were zealous for the spiritual improvement of the Church for five hundred years before the Reformation, by the whole of the Protestant Churches at that memorable period, and by eight thousand Protestant ministers, who subscribed the Articles of Smalkald, which declare that bishops are not superior to presbyters by divine right.—Improbability that these distinguished individuals and the whole Protestant Churches were wrong, and Puseyite Episcopalians right,............ ...61

LETTER V.

Presumptive evidence that diocesan bishops have not been appointed by God, because the only bishops mentioned in Scripture among the standing ministers of the Church are presbyters, and no passage can be produced specifying the qualifications required in bishops as distinct from presbyters.—This inexplicable, if there was to be an order of ministers, denominated bishops, superior to presbyters. —Presbyter, a name of higher honour than bishop. No minister of an inferior order distinguished by the name of a minister of a superior order.—Deacons never called presbyters, but presbyters always represented as bishops —The powers of ordination and government ascribed in Scripture to presbyters.—Wickliffe held the principles of Presbytery, and maintained that Scripture gave no countenance to diocesan Episcopacy,......................71

LETTER VI.

Additional evidence that the principal Reformers of the Church of England rejected the divine right of Episcopacy, and pleaded for that form of ecclesiastical polity, chiefly on the ground that they considered it as better adapted to absolute monarchy.—Testimonies against the divine right of Episcopacy, and acknowledging that Presbyterianism is sanctioned by Scripture, from the writings of Tindal, Barnes, Lambert, Cranmer, Tonstall, Stokesly, Jewel, Redman, Robertson, George Cranmer, Willet, Bedel, and Lord Digby,...85

LETTER VII.

The argument for diocesan Episcopacy, from the different orders in the ministry under the Jewish dispensation, examined, and proved to be more favourable to Popery than to Prelacy.—As far as it establishes the latter, it furnishes a precedent merely for a *single* bishop in a nation, with far more limited powers than those of any modern bishop.—No resemblance between the powers and functions of the Jewish priests and Levites, and those of priests and deacons in Episcopalian Churches —Argument acknowledged to be inconclusive by some of the leading defenders of Episcopacy,...93

LETTER VIII.

The argument of Dr. Brett and Bishop Gleig for diocesan Episcopacy from the different orders in the ministry, during our Lord's ministry, inconclusive.—The Old Testament Church had not then ceased to exist, nor was the New Testament Church established —Their account of the ministry which was instituted at that time not supported by Scripture, contrary to the representations of it given by the Fathers, and so far as it furnishes a pattern of the Gospel ministry, would warrant the appointment of a single bishop over the Universal Church.—Archbishop Potter's hypothesis equally unsatisfactory, and would lead to a similar conclusion,..............102

LETTER IX.

The same argument, as stated by Bishop Bilson, Mr. Jones, and Bishop Skinner, invalid —Upon their hypothesis there would be no deacons in the Church.—No higher powers were possessed at that time by the Apostles than by the Seventy; and the different circumstances mentioned by Archbishop Potter, to prove the superiority of the former, do not establish it.—The office of the Seventy seems to have terminated with their mission, or, at furthest, at the death of the Saviour, and consequently they could not be an order in the Christian Church, ...111

LETTER X.

The argument of Archdeacon Daubeny and Bishop Gleig, for the order of bishops, from the extraordinary office assigned to the Apostles in the New Testament Church, proved to be fallacious —It no more follows from what is said in Matthew xxviii. 20, that there are to be Apostles till the end of the world, than from what is said in Ephesians iv. 11–13, that there are to be New Testament Prophets and Evangelists till that time.—That office proved to have ceased as to its peculiar powers with those who were first invested with it, because no one since their death has possessed the qualifications which it required, nor has been called to it in the way in which they were appointed, nor has been instructed by inspiration like them in the truths which he was to deliver, nor could perform miracles.—Sutclive, Willet, Barrow, and others, deny that bishops succeed Apostles in their peculiar powers, ... .121

LETTER XI.

As presbyters can perform the work of "discipling the nations" by preaching and baptizing till the end of the world, and are the highest order of standing ministers mentioned in the New Testament, they are entitled to be considered as the successors of the Apostles —This acknowledged by Willet.—The report that the Apostles divided the world into different parts, and that each of them laboured in one of them as its bishop, proved to be fabulous, though repeated by Bishop Gleig.—It cannot be inferred from the application of the name Apostles by the Fathers to some of the bishops that the latter succeed the Apostles, for they give it also to presbyters, and even females.—Refutation of the argument for Episcopacy from the appointment of James to the Bishopric of Jerusalem.—Quotations from spurious writings of the Fathers, in support of this fiction, by Bishop Gleig and the present Curate of Derry exposed, ... 133

LETTER XII.

Bishop Bilson represents the argument for Episcopacy, from the powers conferred on Timothy and Titus, as "the main erection of the Episcopal cause;" and Bishop Hall declares, that if it fails, "he will yield the cause, and confess that he has lost his senses."—None of the Fathers during *the first three centuries* represent them as diocesan bishops, and Willet, Stillingfleet, and Bishop Bridges acknowledge them to have been extraordinary ministers, or Evangelists.—Nature of the office of Evangelists, as illustrated by Scripture and the writings of the Fathers.—Different from that of diocesan bishops, and superior to it.—Diocesan bishops never said to have been associated with Evangelists or Apostles in any act of jurisdiction or government, though Presbyters repeatedly took part with them in such acts.—No notice of diocesan bishops as an order existing in their days —The argument in every point of view inconclusive,. 156

LETTER XIII.

Examination of the argument for diocesan Episcopacy, from the Angels of the seven Asiatic Churches —Refutation of it as stated by Milner, who would restrict the superintendence exercised by bishops to ten or twelve congregations, a plan which would create in England a thousand diocesan bishops.—Refutation of it as stated by Bishop Gleig, who represents these Angels as single individuals and prelates.—The name Angel borrowed from one of the ministers of the Jewish synagogue, who had *no authority over other syna-*

CONTENTS. 11

gogues, and was not the sole or chief ruler of his own synagogue.—
Remarkable blunder of Bishop Russel respecting the Angel of the
synagogue and its other officers, *for which he is praised by the Rev
Mr. Sinclair.*—If the Angels of the Churches were single persons,
no evidence that they were diocesan bishops.—Three arguments to
prove that they were not single individuals, but representatives of
the whole ministers of the different Churches, *as each of the stars
mentioned in* Rev. 1 *represented the whole of the ministers of each
of the Churches,* who shed their united light on the members.—
Striking remarks of Lord Bacon on the unprecedented powers
vested in bishops, and on their being allowed to exercise some of
them, without any appeal, by lay-chancellors, ... 178

LETTER XIV.

Apostolical succession.—If the Apostles were neither diocesan bishops
themselves, nor ordained such bishops, the apostolical succession,
as explained and claimed by Puseyite Episcopalians, *never began.*—
Waving that objection, as far as there was a succession, it was preserved to Presbyterian Churches before the Reformation, as uninterrupted as to Episcopalian Churches , and since that time it has
been preserved as regularly in the former, by Presbyterian ordinations, as in the latter by Episcopal.—Unfounded allegation by
Spottiswood and others, that the adoption of Presbytery at Geneva
originated in a wish *to assimilate the government of the Church to
that of the State,* and that this led to the adoption of that form of
ecclesiastical polity in other countries.—The contrary proved from
the reasoning of Farel with Furbiti, who preceded Calvin, and is
considered by many as the modern father or reviver of Presbytery.—
Eusebius acknowledges that he could not trace the succession in
many of the early Churches.—Jewel and Stillingfleet confess that
it cannot be traced in the Church of Rome, from which many
of the ministers of the Church of England have derived their
orders, ... 199

LETTER XV.

The succession destroyed in all those instances in which individuals
who had only Presbyterian baptism, and were not rebaptized,
joined Episcopalian Churches, and were made presbyters and
bishops.—Confirmation cannot remedy this defect, because, as
Cranmer admits, "it was not instituted by Christ," nor was *the
Redeemer himself, or any individual mentioned in the New Testament, confirmed,* and because, as some of the leading English Reformers acknowledged, "it is a domme ceremony," and "*has no
promise of grace connected with it*"—Butler, who had only Presbyterian baptism, and was not rebaptized, made a bishop, baptized
many, who were afterwards ministers, and made a number of
bishops,—Secker, who had only the same baptism, made Primate

of England, ordained many presbyters, and a number of bishops, and baptized two kings, who for a long time were heads of the Church.—Tillotson, though the son of a Baptist, and though there is no evidence that he was ever baptized, or ordained a deacon, made Archbishop of Canterbury.—Succession destroyed for more than two hundred years in the important Church of Alexandria, and in the early Church of Scotland, in consequence of the ordinations by the Culdee presbyters —Account of the presbyters of Iona, their evangelical doctrine, their Presbyterian government, and the acknowledgment of their ecclesiastical authority by the Clergy of Scotland, ...216

LETTER XVI.

The succession destroyed in the early Church of England, in consequence of the ordination of its first bishops by Scottish presbyters.— Scottish missionaries who were ordained by presbyters, acknowledged by Usher to have Christianized the greater part of England.— The Presbyterian Culdean Scottish Church asserted in the twelfth century, before an assembly of English bishops and nobles, to be the Mother Church of the Church of England, and not contradicted — An Archbishop of Canterbury in that century never consecrated, and a Bishop of Norwich consecrated by a presbyter who was an archdeacon.—Succession destroyed in the Church of Ireland through the ordination of many of its clergy by the Scottish Culdee presbyters.—Eight individuals who never had any orders, Archbishops of Armagh, and Primates of all Ireland.—Succession destroyed among the Scottish Episcopalians, who, according to Dr. Pusey, are not a Christian Church.—Their first prelates in 1610 never baptized, and their orders irregular —The orders of their next bishops in 1661 uncanonical, and those of the usage bishops, from whom their present bishops derive their orders, pronounced by the college bishops in 1727 to be null and void, ...246

LETTER XVII.

The Church of Denmark, as its first superintendents were only presbyters, and after the Reformation received imposition of hands only from Bugenhagen, a single Lutheran presbyter, without the succession, and upon the principles of Dr. Pusey, not a Christian Church —The same, too, the condition of the Church of Sweden, and of all the foreign Protestant Churches which have only superintendents —Superintendents both among Lutherans and Calvinists, when appointed to their office not ordained anew, but appointed merely the chairmen or moderators of presbyters, by whom they may be deposed —Their Churches, of course, not Christian Churches.—Account of the ancient Scottish superintendents, whose office is misrepresented by Episcopalians.—The Church of Prussia not a Church, nor the Protestant Churches of France, Geneva, Switzerland, Holland, America and Scotland.—The Presbyterians in Ire-

CONTENTS. 13

land and Great Britain, with the Methodists and Independents, not Churches, and their members without any covenanted title to salvation.—The succession destroyed in the Church of Rome—Pagans baptized some who became ministers—laymen ordained to be bishops—bishops often ordained to Sees which were not vacant—This the case with Augustine, Bishop of Hippo,. 272

LETTER XVIII.

Additional evidence that the succession has been lost in the Church of Rome—Boys ordained to be Bishops, and striplings made Popes—Atheists and avowed infidels raised to the Popedom—Papal canon, that "if a Pope should carry with him innumerable souls to hell, no man must presume to find fault with him."—Simoniacal ordinations declared void by the canons of many Councils, and yet for eight hundred years there were many such ordinations, both in the Western and Eastern Churches.—Idiots, and persons, "who, when they read, prayed, or sang, knew not whether they blessed God or blasphemed him," ordained to be bishops—Multitudes of the most immoral individuals, some of whom " drank wine in honour of the devil," made Popes and Bishops,.......286

LETTER XIX.

The Bible the only standard by which we are to regulate our opinions respecting faith and practice, the orders in the ministry, and the rites and ordinances of the Christian Church.—This the doctrine of the Bible itself, and of the early Fathers, each of whom rejected the opinions of the other Fathers on every subject when not supported by Scripture, or contrary to its statements.—This the doctrine, too, of Luther, and of the most eminent Reformers of the Church of England.—The Fathers not safe guides respecting the meaning of Scripture on other subjects besides Church government.—Numerous instances of the gross misinterpretation of the plainest passages in the writings of Barnabas, Justin Martyr, Irenaeus, Clemens Alexandrinus, Tertullian, Origen, Cyprian, and Jerome—Numerous instances also of their departing from the doctrine of the Apostles on some of the leading points of evangelical belief, and of their introducing into the Church superstitious rites and idolatrous observances.—This acknowledged by Whitgift and Cox.—Presumptive proof which it presents that they might depart as far from the original form of ecclesiastical government which was appointed for the Church,. 305

LETTER XX.

Extraordinary opinion of the Oxford Tractarians, that the Scriptures, though a rule of faith, are not a rule of discipline and practice, and that the latter is to be found in the traditions of the Fathers, along with the Scriptures.—This an impeachment of the perfection of the Scriptures in opposition to their own explicit statements, and a mean of virtually adding to the institutions which they prescribe to the Church, in opposition to their express and solemn warnings.— The traditions of the Fathers not a safe guide, because those who deliver them were weak, inexperienced, and fallible men, though they lived near to the Apostles, and if the Scriptures, which were written by men who were inspired, are not sufficient to direct us, we can have no assurance that when we are following these traditions we are not embracing error.—As much danger of our doing this, and of our making void the institutions of Christ, by our not trusting in the Scriptures exclusively, but adopting what is recommended by the traditions of the Fathers, as there was to the Jews of making void the law of God by following the traditions of the elders, because they lived near to the prophets, instead of trusting exclusively in the writings of the prophets.—Eusebius and Socrates condemn some of the traditions of the Fathers, and others of them such as even Puseyites would reject,................324

LETTER XXI.

If the reasoning employed in the two preceding letters be well founded, it will not follow that diocesan Episcopacy received the approbation of the Apostles, though it could be proved that it existed in the age next to the apostolic, unless it could be demonstrated that they had expressed their approbation of it in their writings, but it cannot be proved that it existed in that early age.—The mere catalogues of bishops, to which Episcopalians appeal, will not establish this, unless they can show that these bishops had the same powers which belong exclusively to their prelates.—This, however, they have never yet done; and Jerome declares, that even toward the end of the fourth century the power of ordination alone distinguished a bishop from a presbyter.—In his Commentary on Titus, and his Epistle to Evagrius, he represents bishops and presbyters as the same, not only in name, but in authority, and diocesan Episcopacy as a mere human institution, introduced by the Church to prevent schism.—He describes it farther as adopted *by degrees, as divisions arose in different Churches or nations,* by a decree of each of the Churches, and not of any general council, and as having commenced, not at the time of the schism in the Church of Corinth, referred to by Paul in his first Epistle to that Church, but after the writing of the third Epistle of John, and the death of the Apostles —This represented as the opinion of Jerome, as stated in his writings, by Luther, Melancthon, Calvin, and the most eminent foreign Reformers, by the Wirtemburg Confession and the Articles of Smalkald, and by Jewel, Willet, Whitaker, and many other learned and distinguished divines of the Church of England,.. ...339

LETTER XXII.

While the constitution of the Church, as settled by the Apostles, is acknowledged by Jerome to have been Presbyterian, he seems to

CONTENTS. 15

have approved of a modified Episcopacy as a human arrangement for the prevention of schism.—This remedy acknowledged by Gratius to have increased, in place of repressing the evil.—Invalidity of the objection to Presbyterian principles, that they were held by Arius, who denied the divinity of Christ, inasmuch, as though he might err on the latter point, it would not follow that he erred on every other, for he agreed in many things with Episcopalians, and especially with those of them who condemn prayers for the dead.—Hilary, Augustine and Chrysostom admit the identity of presbyters and bishops —Clemens Romanus mentions only two orders of ministers, and never refers to diocesan bishops.—No reference to them in the Epistle of Polycarp.—The short Epistles of Ignatius proved to be corrupted, so that no dependence can be placed on their statements respecting the orders in the ministry; and even admitting them to be genuine, no such powers are ascribed in them to bishops as are possessed by modern diocesan bishops,..363

LETTER XXIII.

No allusion to the powers of diocesan bishops in the writings of Hermas.—Nor any notice of such ministers, or of the sign of the cross in baptism, or of confirmation, by Justin Martyr.—No reference to them by Irenaeus, who speaks of the ministers who maintained a succession of sound doctrine from the time of the Apostles in the different Churches, alternately as presbyters and bishops.—The Churches of Gaul describe him as a presbyter, nine years after he was Bishop of Lyons, in the Epistle which they sent with him to the Bishop of Rome, considering it as the most honourable name which they could give him.—Irenaeus represents Polycarp as a presbyter.—No such powers as those of diocesan bishops ascribed to bishops in the writings of Clemens of Alexandria, or Tertullian, or Origen.—Examination of the writings of Cyprian, whose language respecting the dignity of bishops is frequently extravagant.—Proofs of his erring grievously on other subjects, so that it would not be wonderful if he had erred also on this —Evidence, however, even from his Epistles and other writings of the early Christians, that presbyters, both in his day, and for some time afterwards, could not only ordain, but sit in councils and even preside in them.—Passages in Cyprian's writings, which furnish more plausible arguments, not only for bishops, but for a Pope, than any which are to be found in the preceding Fathers,....................389

LETTER XXIV.

Reply to the argument for Episcopacy, that there was always imparity among the orders in the ministry under the preceding dispensations, and there ought still to be imparity under the New Testament Dispensation.—This proved to be a begging of the question, and that we must learn from the Scriptures themselves whether imparity was to continue among the ministers of the Gospel.—Dr. Raynolds acknowledges, that " those who had been most zealous for the Reformation of the Church for five hundred years before that event," did not believe in the divine institution of Episcopacy.— Dr. Raynolds and Hooker admit this to have been the doctrine of the Waldensian Churches, and of Huss and his followers, who had no minister superior to presbyters.—This proved to be the highest order of their ministers by the testimony of their own pastors, and other authorities.—Calvin and Beza, according to Dr. Raynolds, Hooker, and Heylin, denied the divine right of Episcopacy, and this confirmed by their writings.—The rest of the leading foreign Reformers rejected it, though Melancthon would have submitted to bishops, and even a Pope, for the sake of peace.—Zanchius unfairly claimed by Episcopalians as approving of the powers possessed by their bishops.—The foreign Protestant Churches without bishops, not from necessity, as Episcopalians allege, but from principle.— This proved by Jeremy Taylor, ... 412

LETTERS

ON

PUSEYITE EPISCOPACY.

LETTER I.

Ungenerous and unprovoked attack by Puseyite Episcopalians on Presbyterian Churches—Alarming view presented by the former, of the spiritual condition of the latter—Necessity imposed on Presbyterians to defend their principles

REVEREND SIR,—You cannot feel surprised, that, as a minister of the Presbyterian Church, I should address you on a subject of paramount importance to Presbyterians in general, and especially to the clergy of the Church of Scotland, namely, the validity of our orders, the efficacy of the sacraments, as we administer them to our people, and the covenanted title of the pious individuals who belong to our communion to the blessings of salvation. You concede the character of a true Church to the Church of Rome, though it is stated in your homilies, that, "for the space of nine hundred years, it has been so far aside from the nature of the true Church, *that nothing can be more;*" and yet you deny it to us and our Presbyterian brethren. And the least offensive terms in which you are accustomed to speak of us, are like those employed by the late Archbishop Magee, when he said of us, as compared to the Papists, that, "while they had a church without a religion, we had a religion *without a Church.*"

I have waited with anxiety to see whether these charges would be repelled by any of your leading dignitaries, and whether they would speak of us in the same terms of brotherly kindness in which Cranmer spake of Knox, when he recommended him to be one of King Edward's preachers, for spreading the true religion in England; or in which Parker, Grindal, Whitgift, and Hooker spake of the orthodox Presbyterian Churches in their day; or whether they would evince the same spirit which was displayed by Bishop Hall, Dr. Carlton, and Dr. Ward, when they sat as the representatives of the Church of England in the Synod of Dort, of which the president was a Presbyterian, and the majority of the members were ministers and elders of Presbyterian Churches. But I have unhappily been disappointed; and while no friendly voice has been raised on our behalf by any of your bishops or your superior clergy, we continue to be denounced as destitute of any right to the honourable character of Christian ministers, because we have not derived our orders from diocesan bishops, who were regularly baptized, and received their orders from other bishops, in an unbroken succession from the Apostles. Our Churches are asserted to be unworthy of the name; our sacraments are represented as without virtue, and our people as only "midway" between the favoured members of Episcopalian Churches, "and the heathen, who are without God, without Christ, and without hope in the world." And on a recent occasion, when our title to the very name of a Christian Church was directly questioned in the committee of the Society for propagating Christian Knowledge, neither the Archbishop of Canterbury nor the Bishop of London, though among the most moderate of your prelates, said a word in support of it, but instructed their friends merely to move the previous question. You will not then think it strange, that when no one else will undertake our defence, we should attempt it ourselves; and while we acknowledge willingly your National Church to be a Church of Christ, should state he grounds on which we claim that character to our own Church, and to the rest of the orthodox Presbyterian Churches, which, though they have not diocesan, possess, we are persuaded, scriptural bishops, and enjoy as fully as any churches the means of salvation.

I am aware, that if you were able to establish your position, it would be attended by the most serious and alarming consequences to the great majority of the Protestant Churches; and that they could not too soon either enter your communion, or apply to your Church to furnish them with bishops; for the only alternative, as far as is revealed in Scripture, would be *diocesan Episcopacy, or perdition.* How melancholy would be the feelings which it would awaken in our breasts, respecting the numerous Presbyterians who lived in England in former times, whose Calamys, Pooles, Howes, Henrys, Wattses, and Doddridges could no longer be regarded as Christian ministers, nor the most pious individuals who were connected with their churches, as having had any well founded hope of future happiness, as well as respecting the whole of the learned and excellent individuals among Presbyterians, Methodists, Independents, and Baptists in the present day. How affecting would be the state of the sainted martyrs of the Scottish Church in former ages, and of her Chalmerses, Gordons, and other distinguished clergy, and of her pious people at the present time; as well as of the ministers and members of our Dissenting Churches, all of whom would be labouring under a fearful delusion, as to the validity of their orders, and the efficacy of their privileges; and who would not only be living without the means of grace, but without the smallest prospect, from aught that is revealed in the sacred Scriptures, of their being received when they die into the abodes of blessedness! How painful would be the condition of the Presbyterians in Ireland, the effects of whose labours for the religious and moral regeneration of their country, especially in Ulster, will bear to be compared with those of the clergy, who received their orders from diocesan bishops, in any district of England, but whose Blairs, and Livingstons,* and Lelands, and

---

* Blair and Livingston, with other eminent ministers of the Church of Scotland, laboured for a considerable time in Ireland.

Plunkets,* of former times, as well as their Cookes, Hannahs, Stewarts, and Edgars in the present day, cannot be recognised as Christian ministers; nor can the members of their churches have any thing better to trust in at last, than God's uncovenanted mercy. And how dismal would be the state of the Presbyterians in France, who amounted, at one time, to a third part of the nation, and who numbered among their clergy, Daillé, La Roque, du Moulin, and Blondel, and among the members of their communion, Margaret of Navarre, several princes of the blood, Coligny, du Plessis, and other distinguished individuals; and of the churches of Geneva, Switzerland, Holland, and the North American States, as well as of the Lutherans on the Continent, who have only superintendents, and not diocesan bishops. Surely an opinion which leads to such consequences, and which unchristianizes at once the living and the dead, and takes from them all covenanted hopes of salvation, would require to be sustained by the most convincing reasoning; and it must be due at once to the memory of the one, and to the comfort of the other, to examine the evidence on which you maintain your position. I remain,

Reverend sir,

Yours, &c.

* The father of Lord Plunket, the late Lord Chancellor of Ireland, was a Presbyterian clergyman. See Philip's Specimens of Irish Eloquence, p 357. And Lord Campbell, who succeeded him, was the son of a Scottish Presbyterian minister, and had only Presbyterian baptism ; so that both these Judges, though keepers of the conscience of the Sovereign, according to Dr. Pusey and Mr. Gladstone, could not be Christians, or have any hope of salvation.

LETTER II.

Exclusive claims of Puseyite Episcopalians to the Christian ministry, by no means of recent origin —Saravia not the author of them, but Laud — Account of the principal individuals in the Church of England who have brought them forward at different periods, when they considered her to be in danger —Their doctrines proved to be contrary to her principles, from the Thirty-nine Articles, the writings of the bishops who composed her Formularies, and their immediate successors, their conduct towards Presbyterian Churches, the charter granted by Edward the Sixth to these Churches in London, and the establishment of Presbytery by Elizabeth in Jersey and Guernsey

REVEREND SIR,—I am aware that your views of the spiritual condition of Presbyterian Churches, though startling to those who never heard them before, are by no means new. As Papists are accustomed to deny to your Church the name of a Church, and address the most alarming statements to her members, to induce them, if possible, to join their communion; so some of her more violent and indiscreet defenders have, at different periods, imitated their example, and attempted to terrify the Presbyterians of their day to enter within her pale, telling them that yours was the only Protestant Church in our native country, the ministers of which have authority from Christ to preach the Gospel and administer the sacraments, and in which they can attain any covenanted title to salvation. If we may judge, however, of the measure of success which will attend your labours from the amount of theirs, it will be small indeed; and you will be far more likely to add to the converts to the Church of Rome from the Church of England, than to diocesan Episcopacy from the Presbyterian Churches. I lament to hear that the former has been the case to an appalling extent, and that there is reason to fear it will rapidly increase; for, as O'Connell remarked with great exultation, in a recent debate in the British Parliament, " you and your followers are on your way to Rome."* And I am firmly persuaded, that

* How much is the conduct of Dr. Pusey, as well as his writings, fitted to promote this painful result, when, as he acknowledges, he

if sentiments like yours continue to spread among the clergy of your Church, and are propounded as openly, and if not the smallest cognisance of them in the way of censure is taken by your bishops, and if some who maintain them, as in the case of Dr. Hook, are even promoted to new ecclesiastical honours, it may injure her materially, in the estimation of a number of her most pious members, and may constrain them in a short time to leave her communion.

The first person in your Church, according to Voetius,* who avowed your opinion, was Adrian Saravia, who was at one time a pastor of the Flemish Church, but became a convert to Episcopacy, and who, in a treatise which he published on degrees in the ministry, applied the same language to his former brethren, which is applied to your clergy, in common with the ministers of all other Protestant Churches, by the Church of Rome. It is but fair, however, to acknowledge, that this statement is controverted by Archbishop Whitgift, who says in a letter to Beza, that " his (Saravia's) purpose was wholly undertaken *without the injury or prejudice of any particular Church,* and was designed merely to prove that it was agreeable to Scripture, and should be adopted in England."† And this exposition of his sentiments seems to be confirmed by what is said by Saravia himself, who declares, in his answer to Beza, that he "admitted and excused what was done by the rest of the Reformed Churches, in regard to their polity, and did not blame or condemn them."‡

---

fell on his knees lately at the elevation of the Host in a Popish chapel in Dublin. He says, indeed, that he did not worship the consecrated wafer, but was desirous only to show his respect for it. How he can reconcile this with his remaining a minister of the Church of England, whose homilies speak of the Church of Rome in the language quoted p. 17, or with the apostolic admonition, that "*we should abstain from all appearance of evil,* and do nothing to hurt the conscience of a weak brother," I cannot comprehend

* Politiæ Ecclesiasticæ, pars secunda, p. 837. See, too, Discourse on the Union between Scotland and England, p. 137.

† Strype's Life of Whitgift, pp. 409—424.

‡ " Factum Ecclesiarum Reformatarum accipio et excuso, non incuso nec exprobro." In his letter published by Strype, (Life of Whit-

But though he did not adopt, to their full extent, your intolerant views, they were embraced in part by a few of his cotemporaries, who, according to Sadeel, an early Reformer, contended for the necessity of Episcopal ordination, while they acknowledged the foreign " Reformed Churches to be true Churches of Christ."* They were avowed, however, without any limitation, by Archbishop Laud, who, as far as I can discover, was the first individual in the Church of England that maintained them openly, and who, according to Queen Henrietta, " had the heart of a good Catholic."† And though you have lately robbed him of the honour of giving a name to the party who profess his sentiments, and who are now denominated Puseyites, you ought certainly to resign it, for you, Dr. Hook, Mr. Newman, and Mr. Gladstone, are only his followers. " In July 1604," says Prynne, " hee proceeded batchelour in divinitie. His supposition, when he answered in the divinity schooles for his degree, concerning the efficacie of baptisme, was taken *verbatim* out of Bellarmine, and hee then maintained there could bee no true Church without

---

gift,) p. 424, he says of Presbytery, which he calls " a new mode of governing the Church," "*that it was to be borne with* till another that was better could be obtained."

* " Veras Ecclesias Christi," Treatise de Legitima Ordinatione Ministrorum, p 542, of his works. He represents Dr. Pusey's doctrine as held at that time to its full extent *only by Papists*, and rejected by the whole of the Reformers

† It is remarkable that even Heylin, though an admirer of the Archbishop, and a fierce Anti-Calvinist, says in his life of Laud, p. 252, in reference to the changes in favour of Popery, which took place under his primacy, " The doctrines are altered in many things; as for example, *the Pope not Antichrist*, pictures, free will, &c the thirty-nine articles seeming *patient if not ambitious of some Catholic sense.*" What a faithful representation of the interpretation given of them in the present day, as to many things, by Dr. Pusey, *Archdeacon Wilberforce*, Mr. Gladstone, and many others.

As far as relates to the doctrine of the Articles on the leading points of evangelical belief, the testimony of Bishop Carlton is decisive " I am well assured," says he, in his Examination of Montague, p. 49, " that the learned bishops who were in the Reformation of the Church, in the beginning of Queen Elizabeth's reign, did so much honour St. Augustine, that, in the collecting of the articles and homilies, and other things in that Reformation, *they had an especial respect unto St. Augustine's doctrines.*"

diocesan bishops, for which Dr. Holland (then Doctor of the chaire) openly reprehended him in the schooles for a seditious person, who would unchurch the Reformed Churches beyond the seas, and sow a division between us and them who were brethren, by this novell Popish doctrine."* And when he was elevated to the primacy, he censured Bishop Hall for admitting that the foreign Protestant Churches were Churches of Christ; " a concession," he affirmed, (and you and Mr. Gladstone I have no doubt will agree with him,) " which was more than the cause of Episcopacy would well bear."† It was the doctrine of Bishop Montague, who was at one time Archbishop Laud's chaplain, for he asserts expressly that " ordination by Episcopal hands is so necessary, as that the Church is no true Church without it, and the ministry no true ministry, and ordinarily no salvation to be obtained without it."‡ It was the opinion of Durel, Beveridge and others, in the end of that century, for we are told by the younger Spanheim, who had laboured without success to reconcile them and the Presbyterians, that "he was little solicitous" about what they thought of a proposal which he had made to them for that purpose, " because to such a degree of perverseness had matters been carried by some of them, that they declared that out of the Episcopal communion there was no ordination, nor ministry, nor sacraments, nor Church, nor faith, nor salvation."§ It was held by Dr. Hickes, who used the following extraordinary language respecting the Church of Scotland: " Such a Church I think altogether as unworthy of the name of a Church, as a band of rebels in any country, who have overthrown the constitution of it, would be of the name of a kingdom, state, or republic, because such a pretended Church

* Prynne's Breviate of his Life, p 2
† Breviate, p 399
‡ Montague's Origines Ecclesiasticæ, p. 463—464.
§ " Seu jam Hierarchicis hæc conditio probaretur, seu minus, Spanhemius scapham, scapham dixit, parum sollicitus quid Montacutius, quid Durellus, quid Beveregius," &c. Letter against Van der Wayen, p. 110, note.

is not only a variation from the Catholic Apostolic Church, but a sworn destructive confederacy against it, even the abomination of desolation in the house or kingdom of God, of which their pastors are not ministers, but most malicious enemies,—not pastors, but wolves of the flock."* And without dwelling on the names of Law or Dodwell, in regard to the last of whom, it is surprising that Bishop Burnet should have erred so egregiously, as to say that it was he who gave rise to this conceit,"† I may briefly notice, that it was maintained by Mr. Jones, the projector and patron of the British Critic, who affirms, that it was as impossible for any one to be saved out of the Episcopal Church from future wo, as it would have been for Noah and his family to have been saved from the deluge out of the ark. And it was strenuously defended by the late Archdeacon Daubeny in his Guide to the Church, who, in 1803, gave a remarkable proof of his adherence to your principles, for he refused to obey the orders of his primate to read a prayer on the national fast, because it recognised as true Churches the different Presbyterian Churches, in which act of contumacy he was followed, I believe, by his colleague, Dr. Spry.‡ It is possible, however, that Archbishop Laud and you, with Mr. Percival, Mr. Gladstone, and others of your followers, may be right, and more liberal Episcopalians may be greatly in the wrong, and you may be acting under the influence of the truest kindness when you tell us, that as our ministers did not receive their

* Preface to his Treatise on the Priesthood and the Dignity of the Episcopal Order, p 200. In the same spirit, Wetmore, in his Vindication of the Professors of the Church of England in Connecticut, pp. 29—30, describes Presbyterian Churches as resembling, "in the mystical body of Christ, *excrescences* or *tumours* in the body natural, or perhaps as *fungosities* in an ulcerated tumour, the eating away of which by *whatever means* tends not to the hurt, but to *the soundness and health of the body*"

† History of his own Times, vol. ii p. 603.

‡ With a strange inconsistency, he acknowledged, at the same time, as Christian ministers some foreign missionaries, who had only Lutheran orders. "The legs of the lame," as Solomon remarks, "are not equal."

orders from diocesan bishops, regularly baptized and ordained in an unbroken series from the Apostles, they cannot be considered as Christian pastors, nor can their ministrations have any efficacy, nor can our people have any covenanted title to salvation.

Now, the first observation which I have to offer on this doctrine is, that whether it is true or false, it is not the doctrine of the Church of England.

The best way to ascertain the doctrine of a Church on any subject, is to examine what is said on it in her public formularies, in the writings of the individuals by whom they were drawn up, and of those who succeeded them, and the course she pursued during the best and purest period of her history, when she acted honestly in accordance with her principles. Now, if we try your opinion by any of these tests, it appears to me to be destitute of the least semblance of support, and to be directly opposed to the doctrine of your Church respecting other Protestant Churches. The only things essential to a Christian Church, according to your 19th Article, are, "the pure preaching of God's word, and the due administration of the sacraments, according to Christ's ordinance, in all those things that of necessity are requisite to the same." Now, the experience of centuries furnishes proof which you will not easily answer, that the word may be preached as purely by Presbyterian ministers as by those who have been ordained by diocesan bishops. Even Daubeny speaks with the highest respect of the writings of Doddridge, who never had Episcopal orders; and Archdeacon Wilberforce confesses, that it was by the perusal of one of them, the Rise and Progress, that his own venerable father was led to become pious; and he will not, I presume, venture to deny, that the very same doctrine may *be preached* to their hearers, by Presbyterian ministers, which has been so signally blessed, when it is met with in their writings.* And,

---

* No work published by any Episcopalian divine, during the last century, has been so much honoured in the conversion of sinners, in all countries where Christianity is professed, as that invaluable treatise. Many ministers and members of the Church of England, as

in regard to Presbyterian baptism, Mr. Gladstone at least ought to acknowledge its validity; otherwise his father, who was baptized by a Presbyterian, and was never re-baptized, would evidently be unchristianized, and could have no hope of salvation. Besides, as you acknowledge baptism by midwives, captains of ships at sea, and Popish priests, though some of the latter, as Jewel informs us, have been so ignorant as to use these words, when administering that ordinance, which are not to be found in any language, " Ego te baptizo in nomine Patria, Filia, et Spirita Sancta*," and as the Church of Rome, which you so much admire, according to the 36th and 23d canons of the Canon Law, considers baptism, *even by Pagans*, in case of necessity, as valid, I cannot see on what ground you can question the validity of Presbyterian baptism. It is declared, indeed, in your 23d Article, that " it is not lawful for any man to take upon him the office of public preaching, or ministering the sacraments in the congregation before he be lawfully called." But it is added, " those we ought to judge lawfully called and sent which be chosen and called to that work by those who have public authority given unto them in the congregation to call and send ministers into the Lord's vineyard." Upon which Bishop Burnet remarks, when commenting on the words, "those that are lawfully called and sent," (and his exposition was approved of by Archbishop Tillotson, Bishop Stillingfleet, and other prelates,) " the article does not resolve this into any particular constitution, but leaves the matter open and large for such accidents as had happened, and such as might still happen. *They who drew it up had the state of the different Churches before their eyes that had been differently constituted from their own.*" And says Bingham, your great antiquary, " Episcopal divines have no need to have Episcopal government put into the article (the 19th) as a

well as others, have confessed, that it was the means of awakening their first serious convictions about salvation.
* Defence of his Apology, p. 206.

third note of the Church, though the good men, *the Brownists,* were once for having discipline made a third note of the Church, and so aggrieved for the want of it, that," as you do toward us, *"they unchurched the Church of England."** " In all their disputes with the Papists they never require more than these two notes of the Church, namely, the preaching of the pure word of God, and the due administration of the sacraments, according to Christ's ordinance, as stated in the 19th Article."† Agreeably to which, Hooper remarks, (Declaration of Christ and his Offices, c. 11,) "The commune wealthe of the trew Churche is knowyn by these two markes, the preaching of the Gospele, and the right use of the sacraments." If the language, however, of your formularies is so very general that it may be applied to Presbyterian as well as to Episcopalian Churches, and if they were drawn up in this way, as is acknowledged by these prelates, and that distinguished antiquary, to avoid the smallest appearance of imputation against the validity of the orders of the former Churches, it cannot certainly be the doctrine of your Church that Presbyterian ministers ought not to be considered as Christian ministers, and that their people can have no covenanted hope of salvation.

---

* French Church's Apology for the Church of England, vol. ii. of his works, p 727

† Page 726 The same view of the meaning of the 19th Article is given by Bishop Tomline, who represents Dr. Pusey and Mr Gladstone's sentiments as opposed to the principles of the Church of England, and held only by the Church of Rome. " In like manner," says he, in his Elements of Theology, vol. ii p 325, " we often speak of the Church of England, of Holland, of Geneva, and of the Lutheran Church, and *all these different Churches are parts of the visible Catholic Church.* It is well known that the Church of Rome considers itself as the only Christian Church, but, on the other hand, *we extend the name to any congregation of faithful men in the which the pure word of God is preached, and the sacraments duly ministered according to Christ's ordinance, in all those things that of necessity are requisite to the same* The adherence, therefore, to the fundamental principles of the Gospel is sufficient to constitute a visible Church." And he adds, p. 326, " Upon the same principle we forbear to inquire *what precise additions or defects* in the administration of the sacraments ordained by Christ *annul their efficacy.*"

This view of the principles which I attribute to your Church is confirmed by the fact, that neither Cranmer, nor any of your leading Reformers who drew up the forty-two articles of Edward, nor Jewel, who bore a principal part in reducing them to thirty-nine in the reign of Elizabeth, believed in the divine origin of Episcopacy, but taught expressly, that in the days of the Apostles, bishops and presbyters constituted *only one order*. I shall show afterwards that this was the opinion of Jewel; and it was undeniably that of Cranmer and his fellow Reformers, for Bishop Burnet has preserved a paper subscribed by him, the Archbishop of York, eleven bishops, and many doctors and civilians, in which they say, that "in the New Testament no mention is made of any degrees or distinctions of orders, but only of deacons or ministers, and of priests or bishops." Nor is it any objection to this statement, that it is affirmed in the preface to the Book of Ordination, that " from the Apostles' time there have been three orders, bishops, priests and deacons;" for it is said only that they were *from* or *after* their time, but not *in* their time. But if they admit distinctly that the superiority of bishops to presbyters was a matter of mere expediency, and not of divine institution, will it be believed, for a moment, by any candid individual, that they could intend to teach in your articles the doctrine which you advocate, namely, that Presbyterian ministers, however orthodox and pious, are not Christian ministers, and that their people are only midway between you and heathenism?

And that such cannot be the doctrine which is sanctioned by your formularies will be manifest, I apprehend, if you look into the writings of the men who made them, and give them credit for ordinary honesty and consistency, or into the writings of their successors for seventy years, and attend to their conduct either towards Presbyterian ministers, or Presbyterian churches. If Cranmer, for instance, had held your views, and had intended to introduce them into the Articles, would he have "sent letters," as

Strype informs us, "to Bullinger, Calvin, and Melancthon, disclosing to them his pious design to draw up a book of articles, and *requesting their counsel and furtherance?*" Or would he have appointed *Knox*, along with Grindal, to examine it before it was adopted? Or would he have submitted the Prayer Book to the Genevese Reformer, or said to him, that "he could do nothing more profitable to the Church than to write often to the King?" Or would he have made two of his friends, Bucer and Martyr, the first Protestant Professors of Theology in Oxford and Cambridge?* Would any of the bishops have recommended that the youth should be examined in his catechism after evening prayers? (Strype's Annals, vol. ii. p 91.) Or would his Institutes, as is mentioned by Bayle, "have been placed in the parish churches, that the people might read them, and in each of the universities, that after the students had finished their course of philosophy, those of them who were intended for the ministry might be first of all lectured from that book?" If Edward the Sixth, and his bishops and counsellors, had entertained your views and Mr. Gladstone's, and had considered them as taught in your Articles, would he have granted a charter to the Church of the Germans in London, though they were not Episcopalians, allowing them, among other things, "to exercise their own proper rites and ceremonies, and their own proper peculiar ecclesiastical discipline—that *a Church instructed in truly Christian and apostolical opinions and rites, and grown up under holy ministers, might be preserved?*† If Elizabeth and her prelates, and the enlightened statesmen who directed her counsels, had believed that your sentiments accorded

---

* Strype's Life of Cranmer, pp. 407–413, Council Book and Strype's Cranmer, p 273, Nicholl's Comment on the Book of Common Prayer, Preface, p 5, Gerdesii Hist. Reformationis, tom. iv. p. 365, Strype's Annals, vol ii. p 91. Peter Alexander also, a minister of the Protestant Church of France, and other foreign Protestant clergymen, received prebends from Cranmer.

† Some excellent observations on this charter may be met with in an Essay on the Loyalty of Presbyterians, published in 1713.

PUSEYITE EPISCOPACY. 31

either with Scripture, or with the Articles of your Church, would she have passed an act in the thirteenth year of her reign, as is mentioned by Strype, " by which *the ordinations of the foreign Reformed Churches were declared valid, and those that had no other orders* were made of the same capacity with others to enjoy any place in the ministry within England, *merely on their subscribing the Articles?*"* Would she have interposed in behalf of the Reformed Churches, when the Lutheran princes threatened to persecute them, because they refused to subscribe the Form of Concord, denominating them "Pious Churches," or proposed that they should meet with deputies from the Churches of Scotland, Basil, Embden, Bremen, &c. and draw up a common Confession of Faith, which was to be reviewed by Gualter, and Beza;† or, as is stated by her successor and Dr. Heylin, would she have "established the French Presbyterian Church" in the islands of Jersey and Guernsey?‡ If Archbishop Parker, and the bishops of his day, had concurred in your exposition of the doctrines of your Church, would they have approved of the Second Helvetic Confession? (Strype's Annals, vol. i. p. 488); or would his successor Grindal have applied to the magistrates of Strasburgh, in behalf of the Dutch Church in that city, representing its members as "members of Christ?" or to the Lords of the Council for a contribution to Geneva, "for the relief of that poor town, which had served for a nursery unto God's Church, as well *as for the maintenance and conservation of true religion?*" or would he have sustained the orders of a Scotsman of

* Strype's Annals, vol. ii. p 514.

† Blondel's Actes Authentiques des Eglises Reformées de France, Germanie, Grande Bretagne, Pologne, Hongrie, Pais Bas, touchant la Paix et Charite Fraternelle; edit 1655, pp 61-62. Elizabeth sent an ambassador to a meeting of the deputies of these Churches at Frankfort.

‡ In regard to the Islands of Jersey and Guernsey, see her letter to the baillie and jurats of the former, in Falle's Account of Jersey, p. 123 When a synod of the Churches met, June 28, 1576, and drew up their plan of Church government, the Governors of the island attended and ratified it by their signatures; pp. 124-125.

the name of Morison, "according," as he expressed it, "*to the laudable form and rite of the Reformed (Presbyterian) Church of Scotland?*"* And without quoting at length the sentiments of Jewel;† of Bishop Cox, who, in a letter to Gualter in 1565, speaks of the Church of Geneva as a Church of God, and its ministers as faithful ministers;‡ of Hooker,§ and of Sutclive, who, in his treatise on the Church, maintains, that "that is an orthodox and truly Catholic Church, which, though dispersed throughout England, Scotland, Germany, France, and other countries, is united by a harmonious confession of the Christian faith;" and of Bridges, who says that "the difference of these things, (*i. e.* the manner of orders, offices, rites, and ceremonies,) concerning ecclesiastical government, is not directlye materiall to salvation, neither ought to break the bond of peace and Christian concord,"‖ may I solicit your attention to the opinion of Archbishop Whitgift, who was likely to be as well acquainted with the doctrine of your Articles, as you, or Dr. Hook, or any of your followers?

"The essentiall notes of the Churche," says he, "be these only, the true preaching of the worde of God, and the right administration of the sacramentes, for, as Master Calvine sayth, in his booke against the Anabaptistes, This honour is meete to be given to the worde of God, and to his sacramentes, that wheresoever we see the worde of God truely preached, and God accordyng to the same truely worshipped, and the sacramentes withoute superstition administered, there we may without all controversie conclude the Churche of God to be. The same is the opinion of other godly and learned writers, and the judgment of the Reformed Churches, as appeareth by their Confessions. So that notwithstanding government, or *some kynde* of government, may be a parte

---

* Strype's Grindal, p 271.
† Defence of the Apology, p. 28.
‡ Strype's Annals, vol. 1. Appendix, p 57.
§ Ecclesiastical Polity, book III. p. 152.
‖ Defence of the Government of the Church of England, p. 87.

of the Church, touching the outward forme and perfection of it, yet it is not such a part of *the essence and being, but that it may be the Church of Christ without this or that kind of government,* and therefore the kynde of government is not necessarie unto salvation."* It is true, that after his elevation to the Primacy, he first suspended and then deposed Travers, because he had not received ordination from a diocesan bishop; yet it was not because he regarded Presbyterian orders as invalid *in a religious point of view*, but because he considered Episcopacy as *best adapted to the civil constitution of England*;† for he declared expressly, that "*he did not pinch at any Church that used Presbytery*, so that they had the consent of the civil magistrate;"‡ and that "he did not condemne any Churches where that government was lawfully and without daunger received, but had only regard to whole kingdomes, especially *this realme*, where it could not," he supposed, "but be dangerous,"§ because Elizabeth was an absolute monarch, and would admit no control either in Church or State.

I might show how much your sentiments about the meaning of the Articles differ from those of James the First and his counsellors, for, in 1615, he sent Du Moulin to the Presbyterian Synod of the Isle of France, to urge them to unite with the other Protestant Churches who were sound in the faith, and ready to acknowledge each other as Christian Churches, and to exercise mutual forbearance, in so far as they dif-

* Defense of his Aunswere to Cartwright's Admonition, p. 491.
† See a number of passages in the Defense immediately before p. 658. Notes on Travers' Reasons, Append. to Strype's Whitgift, p. 108.
‡ Defense of the Aunswere, p 633.
§ Defense of the Aunswere, p. 658. In p. 658, 659, he attempts to prove that "there is no one certaine kinde of government in the Churche which must of necessitie be perpetually observed," and in p. 389, that "the externall government of the Church must bee according to the form of government used in the commonwealth," which goes to the opposite extreme of error to the opinion of Dr. Pusey and the Papists.

fered, about ceremonies and Church government.*
And he issued a proclamation at the same time, confirming the establishment of Presbyterianism in Jersey and Guernsey, "after the pious example of his sister Elizabeth, and *for the advancement of the glory of Almighty God, and the edification of his Church.*"†
"He is blind," said Bishop Andrews, though a high Episcopalian, "who does not see churches existing without it, (Episcopalian Church government,) and he must have a heart as hard as iron, who can deny them salvation."‡ "Your praise," said Dr. Carlton in the Synod of Dort to the ministers of the Church of Holland, "is in all the Churches."§ "In doctrine and the profession of the orthodox faith," says Dr. Crakenthorp, "there is no difference between us and the Reformed Churches; and while we agree in this, we can easily forbear with each other as to ceremonies and government."‖ And without quoting at length from the writings of Dr. Abbot, Bishop of Salisbury, who acknowledges that "there lived in the Church of England many reverend and worthy men, which did not reject the Presbytery;"¶ of Dr. Field, who, in his treatise on the Church, employs a whole chapter to prove against Cardinal Bellarmine, a strenuous defender of your opinion, that the Reformed Churches, "whose ministers were ordained only by presbyters, did not cease, on that account, to have any ministerie at all;"**. and of Bishop Davenant, who says, "we

* See the Escrit de M. du Moulin, Envoye de Londres au Synode Provincial de l'Isle de France, in Blondel's Actes Authentiques, p. 72—74.

† He declares them to be "true and lawful Churches," because they were not in England, but in part of the duchy of Normandy, for toleration was then unknown in Britain among the Episcopalians, though it was practised among the Presbyterians in Holland.

‡ Respon. ad Secundam Epist. Molinæi, inter opera, p 35.

§ Brandt's History of the Reformation, vol III. p. 4—6.

‖ Defensio Ecclesiæ Anglicanæ contra de Dominis, p. 254. He says, p. 255, to de Dominis, who had censured the Church of England for endeavouring to effect a union between herself and the other Reformed Churches, "neither you yourself nor any other could have bestowed on her *a finer encomium*"

¶ Eleutheria, p 90.   ** Chap. 39, book 3.

account of them, (the Scottish, Irish, and all other forraigne Churches of the Reformation,) as our brethren in Christ, and doe solemnly protest that we entertain a holy and brotherly communion with them,"* I shall notice only further, the sentiments of Archbishop Usher and Bishop Hall, who were certainly as likely to be acquainted with the true meaning of your Articles, as you, Mr. Newman, Mr. Gladstone, or any other of your followers. "For testifying my communion with these Churches," (those of France and Holland,) said the first of these prelates, "which I do love and honour as *true members of the Church Universal*, I do profess, that with like affection, I should receive the blessed sacrament at the hands of the Dutch ministers, if I were in Holland, as I should do at the hands of the French ministers if I were in Charenton."† And, said the second, "Blessed be God there is no difference *in any essential matter* between the Church of England and her sisters of the Reformation; we accord in every point of Christian doctrine without the least variation; their public Confessions and ours are sufficient conviction to the world of our full and absolute agreement: the only difference is in the forme of outward administration, wherein we are so far agreed, that *we all profess this forme not to be essential to the being of a Church*, (though much importing the well or better being of it, *according to our several apprehensions thereof*,) and that we do all retain a reverent and loving opinion of each other, in our own several ways; not seeing any reason why *so poor a diversity* should work any alienation of affection in us towards one another."‡ I might easily have added many other testimonies from your most eminent writers during the first sixty years of the seventeenth century, but I trust that what has been produced will be considered as sufficient to authorise me to maintain, that there is not a fact more

* Drury's Fides Catholica, p. 41.
† Judgment of the late Archbishop of Armagh on certain points, p 113.
‡ Peace Maker, vol. iii of his Works, p 560.

clearly established in the history of your Church, than that the sentiments which have been expressed by yourself and your followers, respecting the ministers and members of Presbyterian Churches, are in direct opposition to her fundamental principles.

You may tell me, I am aware, with the late Archdeacon Daubeny, that "if I read over the 9th, 10th, and 11th canons, I will find that no meetings, assemblies, or congregations of the King's born subjects, but those of the Established Church, may rightly challenge to themselves the name of true and lawful Churches."* But you must surely know, that these canons were never confirmed by act of Parliament; that they were passed by the Convocation, when the principle of toleration was unknown, and that now, when it is recognised by the law of the land, they are virtually neutralised. The men who made them did not deny that Presbyterian Churches *in other countries* were true and lawful Churches, but maintained merely that they were not so *in England*, because they imagined that the Sovereign might model as he pleased the government of the Church, and the only polity which ought to be established there was that of diocesan Episcopacy, because it was best fitted to promote absolute monarchy. Such, we have seen, were the sentiments of Whitgift, and others of your bishops. Such were the sentiments of Downam, who observes, in the defence of his famous sermon, seven years after the passing of these canons, "the King indeed doth say, that it is granted to every Christian king, prince, and commonwealthe, to prescribe to their subjects the outward form of ecclesiastical regiment which *may seem best to agree with the form of their civil government.*"† Such were the sentiments of Lord Bacon, whom James at one time consulted frequently in regard to the Church. " I for my part," says he, " do confess, that in revolving the Scriptures, I could never find, but that God had left the like liberty to the church government, as he had

* Appendix to his Guide to the Church, p. 270
† Page 8.

done to the civil government, to be varied according to time, and place, and accidents. The substance of doctrine is immutable, and so are the general rules of government; but for rites and ceremonies, and for *the particular hierarchies, policies, and disciplines of Churches*, they be left at large."* And, says James himself, " I protest upon mine honour, I mean it not generally (the name of Puritan,) of all preachers or others that like better the single form of policie of our Church, (the Church of Scotland,) then of the many ceremonies in the Church of England, that are persuaded *their bishops smell of Papal supremacie*, that the surplice, the corner cap, and such like, are *the outward badges of Popish errors.* No, I am so far from being contentious about these things, (which, for my own part, I ever esteemed indifferent,) as I do *equally love and honour* the learned men of either these opinions."† But if such were the sentiments of the King himself, and of some of his principal advisers, and of the leading members of both Houses of Convocation, who made these canons, can you seriously believe it to be the doctrine of these men, or the doctrine of your Church in the present day, that none but clergymen who have received their orders from diocesan bishops, in an unbroken series from the Apostles, are Christian ministers, and that none but the members of Episcopalian Churches have a covenanted title to the blessings of salvation?‡

I remain, Reverend Sir, yours, &c.

* Considerations touching the Pacification of the Church, addressed to King James, vol. iii. of his Works, p 150.

† Basilicon Doron, p. 144 of his Works.

‡ James no doubt endeavoured afterwards to crush the Presbyterians, but it was owing entirely to their refusing to submit to his absolute authority, in religious as well as civil matters, and to the gross flattery which he received from the bishops, while the former spoke to him openly and honestly, when they could not agree to his claims. " I have ever," said Bishop Barlow, (preface to his account of the Hampton Court Conference, p. 2,) " accounted the personal commendation of living princes in men of our sort *a verball symony.*" And yet compare with this remark the adulation which he acknowledges was paid to James at this conference by the Episcopalians, p. 20—62, 83—84. Bancroft fell on his knees and said to him, " I protest my heart melteth for joy that Almighty God, of his singular

LETTER III.

These doctrines condemned in the strongest terms by the most distinguished Protestant Statesmen after the Reformation, Cecil, the Lord President of Queen Elizabeth's Council, Sir Francis Knollys, and Lord Bacon, and denounced as " a Popish conceit," by the leading bishops and clergy. Dissimilarity between the Church of England, beyond whose pale, and that of the Church of Rome, Puseyites deny that there is any hope of salvation, and the Apostolic Church, in the extent of its bishoprics, the civil power exercised by its prelates, the multitude of its ceremonies, and "its want," according to its own acknowledgment, "of a godly discipline"

REVEREND SIR,—I trust that it has been proved in the preceding letter, that so far were your principles from receiving the smallest countenance from the clergy of your Church, for seventy years after the time of the Reformation, they were spoken of generally in terms of the strongest and most decided disapprobation. Nor were these feelings confined to your leading dignitaries, but were expressed by some of the most talented and distinguished among the laity; and, in particular, by some of the most illustrious of Elizabeth's ministers, who constituted the pil-

mercy, hath given us such a king, *as since Christ's time hath never been.*" And said Chancellor Egerton, " I have never seen the king and priest so fully united in one person." Upon which it was observed by Warburton, that " Sancho Panza never made a better speech, nor more to the purpose, during his government." Nay, in the preface to the edition of the works of James, which was published by Bishop Bilson, A. D. 1616, during the life of that monarch, he concludes one of the most fulsome pieces of flattery that was ever written, by raising him in one respect above Solomon ! How justly these praises were bestowed, may be learned from James's " Counterblaste to Tobacco," to which he had a great aversion, and his Treatise on Demonologie, the last of which is represented by the bishop as " a rare piece for many precepts and experiments, both in divinitie and naturall philosophic " The following is a specimen of his wisdom and learning, taken from the titles of some of the chapters of the latter work, and the illustrations are not less worthy of the man who was superior to Solomon " The forme of the conventions of witches, and of their adoring of their master," book ii chap 3. " What are the ways possible, whereby the witches may transport themselves to places farre distant;" chap 4 " *Why there are more women of that craft than men,*" chap 5; and, " What sort of folkes are least or most subject to receive harm by witchcraft," chap. 6, &c.

lars of her political greatness, and whose extensive acquirements, even in theological learning, present a very striking and instructive contrast to those of Mr. Gladstone, as far as we can judge from his writings. So far was Cecil from approving of your sentiments, that he urged his Mistress to attempt that general union among Protestants to which I have already alluded, without any regard to their different forms of ecclesiastical polity. So little did another of her most enlightened counsellors sympathise with your views, that when Archbishop Sandys endeavoured to deprive Whittingham of the deanery of Durham, because he had received only Presbyterian orders, it failed. And when the attempt was renewed, "it again," says Strype, "fell to the ground; the Lord President observing, with some warmth, before the Archbishop and the other members of the Commission, that he could not in conscience agree to deprive him for that, for *it would be ill taken of all the godly and learned at home and abroad, that we should allow,*" as you propose, "*of the Popish massing priests in our ministry, and disallow of ministers made in a Reformed Church.*"* So greatly was Lord Bacon opposed to your opinion, when it was brought forward by some in the days of Laud, that he speaks of it in terms of decided reprobation. " Yea, and some indiscreet persons," says he, "have been bold in open preaching to use dishonourable and derogatory speech and censure of the Churches abroad, and that so far, as some of our men, (as I have heard,) ordained in foreign parts, have been pronounced to be no lawful ministers. Thus we see the beginnings were modest, but the extremes are violent, so as there is almost as great a distance now of either side *from itself,* as was at the first of one from the other."†
And in 1588, when Bancroft, in his sermon at Paul's Cross, advocated only the divine institution of Episcopacy, without unchurching the Presbyterian Churches,

* Strype's Annals, vol. ii p. 523.
† Advertisement touching the Controversies of the Church of England, Works, vol. iv. p. 426.

it excited the astonishment of Sir Francis Knollys, Queen Elizabeth's kinsman, who had never heard such doctrine propounded before; and upon writing to Dr. Reynolds, he received a long and able confutation of it, which I am firmly persuaded you have never seen, and which cannot be too generally perused by the members of your Church in the present day.

Not only, however, was your opinion condemned by the clergy and laity of your Church, at the period referred to, but it was considered as one of the peculiar and most obnoxious tenets of the Church of Rome, by which she was distinguished from *the whole of the Protestant* Churches.

Papists, you know, say of their Church, that it alone is the true Church in which you will meet with the real apostolical succession and the means of salvation. "Nevertheless," says Jewel, "in this they triumph;" and it is the very language which is employed by your followers respecting the Church of England to British Presbyterians, "that they bee the Church; that their Church is Christ's Spouse, the pillar of truth, the arke of Noe, and that without it there is no hope of salvation."* And Professor Nichol Burn, in an address to James the First, gives thanks to God, "because of his infinite gudness, he had granted him knowlege to his aeternal salvation, delivering him out of the thraldome and bondage of that idolatrous Calvinisme, (Presbytery,) with the quhilk, alace, manie, be ane blind zeal, ar fraudfullie deceavit, to the lamentable perdition of their awin saulis, except be earnest repentance spedelie they returne to their spiritual mother, the halie Catholic Kirk."† Now, it is impossible to conceive stronger terms than those in which your Reformers reprobate the idea, that communion either with the Church of Rome, or any other Epis-

* Apology, part 4. chap 9. divis. 2. See, too, part 6. chap. 20. divis 1.

† Disputation concerning the Controversit Headdis of Religion, halden in the realme of Scotland, the zear of God ane thousand five hundred and fourscoir zeirs, &c , by Nicol Burne, p. 2.

copalian Church, is necessary to salvation, or that orders derived from diocesan bishops are necessary, on the part of faithful pastors, to give efficacy to their ministrations, or to entitle their Churches to the honourable character of Christian Churches. "Therefore," says Jewel to Harding the Jesuit, "we neither have bishops without church, nor church without bishops. Neither doth the Church of England this day depend of them whom you often call apostates, as if our Church were no Church without them. Notwithstanding, *if there were not one of them*, (the clergy who had received their orders from diocesan bishops,) nor *of us* (the bishops) *left alive*, yet will not therefore the whole Church of England flee to Lovaine" for orders. And he declares, that in such circumstances *pious laymen might renew the succession*.* "The Pape," observes Whitgift, (and it is remarked by Strype, that his Aunswere to Cartwright may be justly esteemed and applied to as one of the public books of the Church of England,†) "The Pape says, that to be subject to him is of necessitie unto salvation; so do not our archbishops."‡ "*Here is the difference between our adversaries the Papists and us*," says Willet. "They say it is of necessitie to be subject to the Pope, and to bishops and archbishops under him, as necessarily prescribed in the word; but so doe not our bishops and archbishops, which is *a notable difference* between the bishops of the Popish Church and of the Reformed Churches. Let every Church use that forme which best fitteth their state: in external matters every Church is free, not one bound to the prescription of another, so they measure themselves by the rule of the word."§ And,

* Defense of the Apology, p. 129-130, &c. It deserves to be remembered, that Strype says, "it was composed and written by the reverend father as the public confession of the Catholic and Christian faith of all Englishmen, wherein is taught our consent with the German, Helvetian, French, Scotch, Genevan, and other Reformed Churches." Annals, vol 1 p. 251.
† Strype's Whitgift, p. 42.
‡ Defense of his Aunswere, p. 382.
§ Willet's Synopsis Papismi, Appendix to the Fifth General Question.

says Downam to a Puritan who had animadverted on his sermon, " the Popish opinion is farre different from that which I hold; for they hold the order and superiority of bishops to be jure divino, implying thereby a perpetual necessitie thereof. Insomuch that where bishops are not to ordaine they thinke there can be no ministers or priests, and consequently no church. I hold otherwise. Wherefore my opinion being so different from *the Popish conceit,* who seeth not that *the judgment of our divines which is opposed to the doctrine of the Papists is not opposed to mine?"* Nor was the difference less forcibly characterised by Dr. Holland, when he denounced your opinion, as stated by Laud, as "a novell Popish doctrine." If your divines, however, till the days of Downam, considered that opinion as " a Popish conceit," and " a novel Popish doctrine," and the opposite principle as constituting " a *notable* difference" between your Church and the Papists, I trust you will not consider me as wanting in charity, if, under the sanction of such high and venerable authority, I represent you in the character which they would unquestionably have assigned to you, had they been living at present, namely, as a patron of Popery, and to express my astonishment that you and your followers should be allowed to continue in the communion of your Church.

But you may tell me, that though it is a Popish, it is nevertheless a scriptural doctrine, for the Church of which we read, Eph. ii. 20, as having been founded by the Apostles, and out of which there is no salvation, contained in it bishops, priests and deacons, and it is only when a Church resembles the Church as it was then constituted in the orders of its clergy, and its form of government, that it is entitled to be considered as a Church of Christ. You must prove, however, before you deduce this inference, that the Church which is there referred to, and out of which it is declared, in other passages, there is no salvation, is the visible Church possessing in all respects the very form of external government which was at first established. The Church of England at the time of the

Reformation, as I have already showed you, did not think so, nor was it the opinion of any of the Protestant Churches. "There are two kyndes of government," said Whitgift; "the one invisible, the other visible; the one spirituall, the other externall. The invisible and spirituall government of the Church is, when God by his spirite, gyftes and ministerie of his worde, doth governe it by ruling in the hearts and consciences of men, and directing them in all things necessarie unto everlasting life. *This kinde of government indeed is necessarie unto salvation.* The visible and external government is that which is executed by manne, and consisteth of external discipline and visible ceremonies, practised in that Church." And then, after remarking that " the worde necessarie signified eyther that without the which a thing cannot be, or that without the which it cannot so well and conveniently be," he adds, "I confesse, that in a church collected together in one place, and at libertie, government is necessarie *in the second kind of necessitie,* but that *any one kind of government is so necessarie, that without it the Church cannot be saved, I utterlie denie.*"* And he was justified in doing so, for it is not to faith produced *only by the preaching of a diocesan bishop,* or of clergymen ordained by him, that salvation is promised in the Scriptures, but to true faith produced by the preaching of *any pious* ministers who have received their orders through a regular channel. It is not to repentance resulting from the instructions *only of Episcopalian clergymen deriving their orders from diocesan bishops,* that forgiveness is promised through the blood of the cross, (Acts iii. 19; xi. 18;) but to sincere repentance, whoever may be the ministers whose impressive statements and touching appeals, accompanied by the influences of the Holy Spirit, have implanted it in the heart. And it is not to holiness attained *only under the ministry of Episcopalian clergymen,* but of all evangelical pastors, that the Almighty has declared, Heb. xii. 14, that the individual who possesses it shall

---

* Defense of the Aunswere, p. 81.

"see the Lord." But perhaps I am wrong in supposing that you will admit that faith, or repentance, or personal holiness, *can be attained without the pale of Episcopalian Churches,* and that to your other tenets this must be added, (I shall be glad if you disclaim it,) that nothing which can be regarded as spiritually good can result from the labours of Presbyterian ministers.*

But if there be no revealed or covenanted hope of salvation to the members of a church, unless she continue in the state in which the primitive Church was left by the Apostles as to the orders of her clergy, and government, and worship, is there no reason to fear as to their personal salvation to the ministers and members of the Church of England? Does she remain in the state of the Apostolic Church, both as to the offices and distinctions which exist among her ministers? The most eminent individuals who laboured zealously for the purification of the Church, from the earliest ages till the time of the Reformation, would not have thought so, for they have declared it as their opinion, that in the time of the Apostles there were only two orders of ministers in the Church, bishops or presbyters, whose office appeared to them to be the same, and deacons, and that there ought still to be no more. Such was the opinion of the author of the work entitled Aetates Ecclesiæ, which, according to Flaccius Illyricus, was written long before the Reformation.† Such was the opinion of the

---

* I would like to know whether Puseyites believe that the pious conversation of wives, who are Presbyterians, is likely to win their husbands to the faith, and love, and obedience of the Gospel, according to the statement of Peter, in his 1st Epistle, iii. 1, or whether it must be expected to fail, because they have never had Episcopal baptism, and are not in communion with Episcopalian Churches. And I would wish also to be informed, whether they believe the conversation of pious Presbyterians can do no good to others in health or sickness, or when they happen to visit them on their beds of death. I take it for granted that they are persuaded there is no reason to hope that the preaching of the most pious Presbyterian ministers can lead to the conversion of a single sinner.

† " Distinguitur autem juristis ipsa primitiva ecclesia in primam et secundam unde Dist. 93. legimus, &c. The Primitive Church is distinguished by the jurists into the first and second. In the first

celebrated Archbishop of Armagh, the great reformer of his day, usually denominated Ricardus Armacanus, who, though himself a dignified Episcopalian, bears a striking testimony to Presbyterian principles, as characterizing the Apostolic Church, for he observes, that "*in the writings of the Evangelists or Apostles, no difference is to be discovered between bishops and simple priests who are called Presbyters,*whence it follows that their power in all things is the same, and *they are equal from their order.*"* Such, too, was the opinion of Wicklif, the harbinger of the Reformation in England, for one of his principles, which was controverted at great length by Woodford, was, that, "in the time of the Apostle Paul, two orders of clergy were reckoned sufficient for the Church, priests and deacons; nor were there in the days of the Apostles any such distinctions as those of a pope, patriarchs and bishops."† And what, per-

primitive Church, *the office of bishops* and priests, as well as the *names*, was the same But in the second primitive Church, the names and offices began to be distinguished Therefore the names presbyter and bishop were entirely of similar import, and their power was the same, *for the churches were governed by a common council of priests.* Therefore, as there was no difference from the beginning, the prelates ought not to carry themselves too haughtily above the priests."

* " Non invenitur in Scripturis Evangelicis aut Apostolicis aliqua differentia inter episcopos et simplices sacerdotes qui appellantur Presbyteri, &c. Lib. 5. ad Quaest. Armenorum. He flourished in the fourteenth century.

† " Quod tempore Apostoli Pauli sufficiebant ecclesiæ duo ordines clericorum, sacerdos et diaconus, nec fuit tempore Apostolorum distinctio papæ, patriarcharum, episcoporum." Woodford quotes against him a decree, as he terms it, of Clemens Romanus, and adds, " In quibus verbis sicut Clemens distinguit inter presbyterum et diaconum, sic inter episcopum et presbyterum," and prosecutes the argument very fully. See the whole disputation in the Fasciculus Rerum Expet. et Fugiend, published at Cologne, in 1535, by Orthunius Gratius, and republished by Edward Brown, 1600, vol. i. p. 209, from which it is evident that Wicklif must have been a Presbyterian, Henricus de Jota also, or according to others, de Heuta, who taught at Vienna in 1371, and who is highly celebrated by Gerson, Chancellor of Paris, asserts, " that the reservation of causes to the popes and bishops was a matter not of divine but *human appointment*, for *all priests have equally* the power of the keys. Reservationem istam casuum jam papis et episcopis usitatam non divini, sed humani juris

haps, will have more weight with you than the opinion of these reformers, as they appear to have been Presbyterians, even Jewel himself, when he wrote his Apology, does not seem to have thought so; for, says he, "in St. Hierome's time, there were metropolitans, archbishops, archdeacons, and others. But Christ appointed not these distinctions of orders from the beginning."* Here, then, is one point of very great importance, in which there is a striking difference between your Church and the Apostolic Church.

Again does your Church resemble that Church in respect to her ceremonies, guarding against the error which was pointed out by the Redeemer, when he said, "In vain do they worship me, teaching for doctrines," in regard to my service, "the commandments

---

esse. Omnes enim sacerdotes aequale jus clavium habere." Is not this Presbyterianism?

Atto, Bishop of Verceil in Italy, who, according to Ughellus, flourished about the middle of the tenth century, says, in his treatise on the judgment of bishops, published by D'Achery in the eighth vol. of his Spicilegium, "the order of bishops and that of presbyters *were not two different orders in Paul's time*, but were distinguished afterwards."

Francowitz, or Flaccius Illyricus, in his Catalogus Testium Veritatis, fol. 1793, tells us, that Florentinus, when speaking of the heresies of Petrus de Corbaria, and John and Michael Cesanas, of the order of the Minorites, mentions as one of them, that "all priests, of whatever grade, by the institution of Christ, have *equal authority, power and jurisdiction*. Quod sacerdotes omnes, cujuscunque gradus existant, sunt aequalis authoritatis, potestatis et jurisdictionis institutione Christi." They lived in the fourteenth century. The copy of the Catalogus, from which I quote this and some of the other testimonies to Presbyterian principles, belonged to Archbishop Leighton.

Marsilius Patavinus, who lived A. D. 1324, is said, in the Catalogus Testium Veritatis, p. 488, to have maintained this opinion in his treatise, entitled, Defensor Pacis, "that all bishops and priests are equal. Omnes episcopos et sacerdotes esse aequales."

* Defense of the Apology, p 92. "Concerning this work," says Strype, (Annals, vol. ii. p. 490,) "three great princes successively, Queen Elizabeth, King James and King Charles, and four archbishops, were so satisfied with the truth and learning contained in it, that they enjoined it to be chained up and read in all parish churches throughout England and Wales."

Mocket, Archbishop Abbot's chaplain, mentions many more distinctions among the clergy of the Church of England than Bishop Jewel.

of men?" Jewel observes, "The old father S. Augustine, complaineth of the multitude of vain ceremonies, wherewith he even then (beginning of the fifth century) saw men's minds and consciences overcharged."* And yet, according to Hooper and Cecil, you have a greater number of them in the Church of England than were to be found either in the Jewish Church, or in the Christian Church in the days of Augustine. "Further," says the former, "to augment the ceremonies of the Churche, and bring in a new Judaisme and Aaronicall rites, is against this commandment, (the fourth). As the bishopes hath usyd the matter, there be more ceremonies in the Churche of Christ *than were in the Churche of the Jewes*, as it shall easily apere to him that will confer our Churche with the bookes of Moses."† And says the latter to a noble Italian at Rome, whom he wished to convert from Popery, "Yea, as for external discipline, I can assure you, *our Church is more replenished with ecclesiastical rites than was the primitive Church in five hundred years after Christ*. Insomuch as the Church of England is, by the Germans, French, Scots, and others that call themselves reformed, thought to be herein corrupted, for retaining so much of the rites of the Church of Rome."‡ But if this is really the case, (and he could not be mistaken,) it constitutes a very great and serious difference between the worship of your Church and the Apostolic Church.§

* Apology for the Church of England, part 5, chap. iii. divis. 5.
† Declaration of the ten holy commandments.
‡ Strype's Annals, vol. i. p. 533.
§ We are told by A'Lasco, in his Treatise de Ordinatione Ecclesiarum Peregrinarum in Anglia, published A.D. 1555, and dedicated to Sigismund, King of Poland, that Edward the Sixth and his Council were anxious to accomplish a far more extensive reformation of the Church of England than has ever been effected. "When I was called by that King," says he, "and when some laws of the country stood in the way, that it was not possible that the rites of public divine worship *used under Popery* should be immediately purged out, though *it was what the King himself desired;* and while I was earnestly standing up for the churches of the foreigners, at length it was his pleasure that the public rites in the English churches *should be reformed by certain degrees,* as far as it could possibly be got done for the laws of the kingdom. But that strangers, who were not so strict-

You restrict your clergy, in their public services, to forms of prayer which were never employed in the Apostolic Church, though they prevent your ministers from applying to the Spirit, as a Spirit of grace and supplications, to suggest intercessions to them, according to this part of his blessed character, (Romans viii. 26, 27,) which they may present for their people, and though, as Bishop Wilkins remarks, "prayer by book is commonly flat and dead, and has not that life and vigour to engage the affections, as when it proceeds immediately from the soul itself; and set forms do especially expose people to lip service and formality."* And he might have added, that they want

ly obliged by the laws of the country in this matter, should have churches granted them, wherein they might freely perform all things *according to apostolical doctrine and observation* only, without having any regard to the rites of the country, that by this means it would come to pass *that the English churches would be excited to embrace apostolical purity,* with the unanimous consent of all the states of the kingdom.

"The king himself, from his great piety, was both the chief author and defender of this project. For, though *it was almost universally acceptable in the King's Council,* and though the Archbishop of Canterbury himself promoted the thing with all his might, yet there were some who took it ill, and would have showed more reluctance to it, had not the King given them a repulse, both by his authority and the reasons he gave for this design. The churches of strangers being accordingly allowed, upon condition, or rather with a liberty, that all things in them should be ordered according to the doctrine and practice of the Apostles, the care of them, by the authority of the King and Council, was committed to me, and I was commanded to choose such colleagues for myself, as I should judge fittest for that service, that their names might be inserted in the King's patent. Cum ego quoque per regem illum vocatus essem," &c.

Such is the statement of A'Lasco, whom Edward and his counsellors denominated in the patent, "homo propter integritatem et innocentiam vitæ et morum, et singularem eruditionem, valde celebris." He published his book about four years afterwards; and his statement accords with the appointment of thirty two commissioners by Edward, (of whom A'Lasco was one,) to draw up the Reformatio Legum Ecclesiasticarum. That work was stopped, in consequence of the death of the King, and little progress was made in the reformation of the Church under Elizabeth. Many of the bishops, during the reign of that Princess, lamented it greatly, but it gratified the Papists, and is still a source of great satisfaction to them, for one of their bishops declared lately, that " he loved the Church of England, because *she was the least reformed of all the Reformed Churches.*"

* Gift of Prayer, by Bishop Wilkins, p. 9, 10.

that variety which is suited to the ever varying circumstances both of the private Christian, and of the Church at large; and that it is equally uncomfortable to hear the very same prayers repeated annually, for forty, or fifty, or sixty years, as it would be to hear the very same sermons repeated annually for a similar period. Besides the prayer-book you use, and on which you will suffer no alterations, as Edward the Sixth said in his letter to the Kentish rebels, is just "the old Popish service translated into English," which James the First, you know, denominated at one time "an ill-said mass."

In administering baptism, you make the sign of the cross on the forehead of the child, though it was neither made on the forehead of the Saviour at his baptism, nor of any other individual who is mentioned in the New Testament, and though, as Barlow acknowledges, in his account of the conference at Hampton Court, no example of it can be produced before the days of Tertullian, when, as is proved by the author of Ancient Christianity, Sir Peter King, and others, many gross superstitions had been introduced into the Church. And if you tell me that it was adopted at a very early period, I reply, with Bradshaw, "so are many other Popish traditions, (for the mystery of iniquity soon began to work); and if on that ground we are to retain it, *why do we not give the baptised milk and honey?* for this was practised along with the other. Why do we not bring offerings for the dead? for Tertullian, the first of the fathers that ever mentioned the cross, doth establish these and the sign of the cross by one and the self-same warranty. Besides, if upon the fathers' tradition we use the cross, *then must we receive and use it as they have delivered it unto us*, that is, with opinion of virtue and efficacy, not only in the act of blessing ourselves, and *in expelling of devils*, but even in the consecration of the blessed sacrament. For the first, Tertullian is witness, saying, at every passage, at every setting forward, *at every coming in and going out, at putting on of our clothes, shoes*, &c., we stamp our forehead with the sign of the cross."* And surely, if you make the sign of the cross in baptism on the child's forehead, because the fathers did it, you are bound equally to make it on your own forehead, when you put on or off your hat, or coat, or any part of your dress, or your shoes; and for the very same purpose, namely, *to chase away devils;* and I have not yet heard that you have come so far as this in your imitation of the ancient Church. Nor do you use that sign even in baptism as it was employed by the fathers, for, as he further remarks, "it is apparent that Cyprian, Augustine, Chrysostom, and others, in those times, *did consecrate the element (or water)* therewith, and *did not cross the child's forehead*, but referred that unto the bishop's confirmation, so *that our crossing the infant's forehead*, and not the element of baptism, *is a meere novelty*."† In this respect, therefore, you differ both from the apostolic and the ancient Church.

---

* Treatise on Worship and Ceremonies, p. 114.

He adds, "for chasing of devils, Jerome counselleth Demetrius to use the cross," (Epist. ad Demetrium,) "and with often crossing guard thy forehead, that the destroyer of Egypt find no place in thee." Lactantius saith, (lib. 4, cap. 24,) "Christ's followers do by the sign of the cross shut out the unclean spirit." Chrysostom, on Psalm 109, says, "the sign of the cross guardeth the mind, it taketh revenge on the devil, it cureth the diseases of the soul."

† "Neither will that place of Tertullian de Resurrectione Carnis prove the contrary." "The flesh," says he, "is washed, that the soul may be purged; the flesh is *anointed*, that the soul may be consecrated; the flesh is signed, that the soul may be guarded; the flesh is shadowed by the imposition of hands, that the soul may be by the spirit enlightened; the flesh doth feed on the body and blood of Christ, that the soul may be filled and fatted of God. In which words he, joining together diverse ceremonies of the Christians, doth indeed mention the signing of the faithful; but it may be as well referred to confirmation, expressed by imposition of hands, as to baptism, understood by washing of the body, and that on better reason, for *it is more than probable that the sign of the cross was not yet used in baptism*, seeing Justin Martyr, in Defens ad Anton., and Tertullian, de Baptismo et de Corona Militis, do describe the form of baptism used in those times, and yet make no mention of the cross therein, which in all likelihood they would not have omitted if it had been used therein, especially Tertullian, who in that place speaketh of the cross as used out of baptism in the ordinary blessing of themselves."

He says, in his Treatise on Kneeling in the Sacrament, p. 94, of the preceding work, that "Papists themselves call the Church of England, for retaining this and other Popish Ceremonies, Puritan

You lay the stipulations in baptism, not on the parents, who are enjoined by the Almighty to "bring up the children in the nurture and admonition of the Lord," but on god-fathers and god-mothers, who seldom see them, in regard to which even the Episcopalian clergy at Aberdeen confess, "we have no precept or example of it in the Holie Scripture; yea, some of our learned divines affirm that it was instituted by Pope Higinus."*

You represent every one who is baptised as regenerated, or, in the language of your Catechism, as "made thereby a member of Christ, the child of God, and an inheritor of the kingdom of Heaven." And Archdeacon Wilberforce affirms, that "the seed of grace," which was implanted in his father at baptism, was preserved; while his father himself acknowledges, that, till he met with Doddridge's Rise and Progress of Religion, and it was blessed to him by God, he was dead in trespasses and sins. And yet you are informed in Scripture that Simon Magus, though baptised by an Apostle, whose orders surely would be valid, continued " in the gall of bitterness, and the bond of iniquity." And as Frith remarks, "if a Jew or an infidel (as has sometimes been the case) should say that he dyd beleve, and beleved not in deede, and upon his words were baptised in deede, (for no man can judge what his heart is,)"† he could not be in the state described in your Catechism, for it is distinctly stated, that while he who believeth shall be saved, "he who believeth not *shall be damned*."

You receive the communion at an altar like the Papists, and not at a table like Christ and his Apos-

Papistical," and appeals in proof of it to the Concertatio Cathol. Eccles. in Argum.

In the Almanac Spirituel, an old Waldensian Tract, published by Leger, in his Hist. des Eglises Vaudois, p 65, the sign of the cross in baptism is condemned "Le signe de la croix sur l'enfant a la poitrene et au front." And the Churches of the Waldenses were "the cradle" of the Churches of the Reformation.

* Duplies to the Answers of some Reverend Brethren concerning the Covenant, p 97

† See his Myrrour or Looking-Glasse, wherein you may beholde the sacrament of Baptisme described, Works, p. 91.

tles, and the early Christians, and you take it kneeling, though they took it in the posture which was common at meals. This is certainly surprising, since as Peter Martyr, who was to have been one of your first professors of divinity, says, "Kneeling at the sacrament was introduced on account of transubstantiation, and the real presence."* And it is still more extraordinary in a Protestant Church, if it be true, as is mentioned in the notes by Alexander de Hales, that the Pope, when he communicates, does it SITTING, because *the Apostles communicated sitting.* In this respect also you differ widely from the Apostolic Church, and are less scriptural in your worship than the very Pope.†

---

* Per transubstantiationem et realem presentiam invecta est in ecclesiam. Colum. sect 21.

† "At the least," says the author of the Re-examination of the Five Articles of Perth, "kneeling was left free in the days of King Edward the Sixth. The Papists making a stir about want of reverence to the sacrament at the second reviewing of the book of Common Prayer, kneeling was enjoyned upon this reason that the sacraments might not be prophaned, but holden in a holy and reverential estimation. This was done by the directors and contrivers of the book, *partly to pacify the Papists,* partly because their judgment was not cleare in this point."

"That supper had *all sitting in common together,* saith Chrysostom, as he is quoted by that writer, p. 19. Œcumenius hath the like. This is not to eat the Lord's supper, says he. He meaneth that supper which Christ delivered when all his disciples were present. For in that supper the Lord and all his servants *sat* together."

"The two thousand soldiers," he remarks, p. 24, "who were reconciled to the Emperor Mauritius about the year 590, by means of Gregorius, Bishop of Antioch, receaved the sacrament *sitting upon the ground,* as Evagrius reporteth." (Evag. lib. 6, cap. 13.)

"Dr. Lindsay alledgeth *the like done* to the Scottish armie at Bannockburn, in the dayes of King Robert Bruce" (See his Defence, p. 53-54.)

"Balsamon, upon the nineteenth canon of the Concilium Trullanum, saith, the devouter sort, upon Saturday at midnight, *sat* in the kirke, and *did communicate.* Alexander de Hales, in the second part of his tractate concerning the masse, sayth, *the Pope communicateth sitting,* in remembrance that *the Apostles at the last supper communicated sitting.* Si quaeratur quare Dominus Papa sedendo communicat, &c.

"That the Waldenses sat will appear from Balthazar Lydius. And Luther, expounding the epistle upon St. Stephen's day, saith, Christ so instituted the sacrament, that in it *we should sit at* the sacrament. But all things are changed, and *the idle ordinances of men are come*

You bow during the reading of the Gospels at the name Jesus, and not at the name Christ or Immanuel, or any of the other names of the Redeemer, or any of the names of the other persons of the Godhead, justifying your adoration of that particular name, which never appears to have received that external token of homage in the apostolic age, by an erroneous interpretation of Philippians, ii. 10. And yet you are aware that Archbishop Usher, one of your most distinguished prelates denied that the practice could be founded on that passage, and "wondered at some learned men's assertions, that it was the exposition of all the fathers upon it. And as the wise composers of the Liturgy gave no direct injunction for it there, so in Ireland he withstood the putting it into the canons in 1634."* "I think the place to the Philippians," says Bishop Babington, "not well understood, hath and doth deceive them. The place is borrowed from the Prophet Isaiah, and therefore, by conference, evident that the word name signifies power, glory, hon-

in place of divine ordinances. Zuinglius, setting down the forme of celebration used at Berne, Zuricke, Basile, and other neighbour townes, sayth, *sitting* and harkening with silence to the word of the Lord, we eat and drink the sacrament of the supper. We have put down altars," says A'Lasco, " and use a table, because it agreeth better with a supper, and the Apostle hath given the title of a table to denominate the Lord's supper. And again, the terms supper and table of the Lord very familiar with the Apostle Paul, seeme to require sitting rather standing, kneeling or passing by."

"The Bishop of Chester," says Calderwood, in his strictures on the Perth Assembly, p. 19, admits that it is true Christ did administer the sacrament in a kind of *sitting* gesture, and that in the same gesture the Apostles did receive it." Defense, p 248.

"Is it said that we should kneel in this ordinance, because we worship God in it? Then we should do so in praise, and when we swear an oath. God has a right certainly to appoint the gestures which he requires in every act of worship. Is it alleged that it is called a sacrifice, and therefore we should kneel? Upon the same principle, then, we should kneel when we give alms, for it too is called a sacrifice, or when we praise," &c.

"Dionysius Alexandrinus," says Mr. Anderson, in his Answer to the Dialogue between the Curate and the Countryman, p. 57, " is the earliest that Dr. Cave can find, that makes mention even of standing; *but of kneeling, not a syllable to be heard for many hundred years after.*

* Judgment of the late Archbishop of Armagh on certain points, p. 132.

our, and authority, above all powers, glories, honours, and authorities; and bowing the knee signifieth subjection, submission, and obedience of all creatures to his beck, rule and government, for *what materiall knees have things in heaven, hell, &c.?* This knew the ancient father Origen, and therefore, writing on the 14th of the Romans, where these words be, again saith, Non est carnaliter hoc accipiendum. These words are not to be taken carnally, as though things in heaven, as the sun, moon, angels, &c. had knees or tongues, but that all things shall be subject to him."* And says Dr. Fulk, in his Reply to the Rhemists, "it is certain that the bowing of the knee at the sound of the name of Jesus, as it is used in Popery, (and it is the same in your Church, and among the Scottish Episcopalians,) is not *commanded nor prophesied in this place,* (Phil. ii.) but it pertaineth to the subjection of all creatures to the judgment of Christ, when not only Turks and Jews, which now yield no honour to Jesus, but even *the devils themselves* shall be constrained to acknowlege that he is their Judge." And he adds, "Capping or kneeling at the name of Jesus is superstitiously used in Popery, in sitting and not veiling at the name of Christ, Emanuel, God the Father, the Son, and the Holy Ghost, and bowing only at the name of Jesus." And yet such is the practice which is followed by your Church, though, while you bow with the knee when that name is mentioned, *you do not confess with the tongue* that Jesus is Lord; and in this, as well as the multitude of your other ceremonies, of which Cecil speaks, you resemble the Popish but differ very widely from the Apostolic Church.†

* See him on the Creed, p 169.

† It is plain from Bishop Burnet's Sermon before the House of Commons in 1688, and his Letters, p. 46, that a number of the first Protestant bishops were anxious to have many of these ceremonies abolished, but did not succeed. And says Strype, (Annals, vol. 1. p. 162—164.) Parker, Grindal, Cox, Sandys and others, urged a number of arguments to Elizabeth for laying aside altars, and using tables in the communion, as approaching most nearly to the institution of Christ, but she would not listen to them.

Bishop Pilkington, in a letter to the Earl of Leicester, (Append. to Strype's Parker, p. 41,) gives the following account of the reasons

And omitting many other things on which it would be easy to enlarge, does the extent of your bishoprics correspond to that of the bishoprics in the early Church, even admitting that their bishops were diocesan prelates? This, you must be sensible, is a point not only of great, but of paramount importance; for, if you assign to your bishops an amount of duty which it is impossible for them to perform, and not only twenty or thirty, but even a hundred times more than was expected from any of the primitive bishops, you annihilate completely the efficiency of their office, and have bishops only in name. And yet such is the case with almost the whole of your bishoprics. In Philippi alone, where the number of Christians could not be great, we are informed, (Philippians, i. 1,) that "there were several bishops." Bishop Burnet acknowledges that Cenchrea, the seaport of Corinth, formed a bishopric distinct from that of Corinth, and that the little village of Bethany, about a mile from Jerusalem, had a bishop of its own.* And Fuller confesses, that a long time afterwards, "some of the bishops' seats in Palestine were such poor places as they were ashamed to appear in a map. For in that age bishops had their sees at poor and contemptible villages."† The bishopric of Polycarp was so small, that he could be ac-

---

why so many Popish ceremonis have been retained by the Church of England. " They have so long continued," says he, " and pleased Poperie, which is beggerlie patched upp of al sorts of ceremonies, that they culd never be roted out sins, even from many professors of the truth." And said Bishop Parkhurst to Gualter, (Strype's Annals, vol. ii. p. 186,) "Would to God once at last al the English people would in good earnest propound to themselves to follow the Church of Zuric, (Presbyterian) as the most absolute pattern." But how much more happy would it have been for the church of England in the present day, if she had followed the model proposed by Hooper in his Treatise entitled the Declaration of Christ and his Offices. " It is no reproache of the dead man," said he, " but myne opinion unto all the world that the Scripture solely and the Apostelles' Churche is to be folowed, and no man's authoritie, be he Augustine, Tertullian, or other cherubim or seraphim. Unto the rules and canones of Scriptures must man trust, and reforme his errors thereby, or else he shall not reform himself. but rather deform his consciens."

* See his Observations on the 1st and 2d Apostolic Canons, p. 48.
† History of the Holy War, p. 46.

quainted by name with the different individuals who were under his superintendence. "Let your assemblies," said Ignatius to him, "be more frequent;" or as it is rendered by Archbishop Wake, "let them be more full; *inquire after all by name;* despise not the man-servants nor maid-servants; but let not these be puffed up with this circumstance."* And in the extensive diocese of Neocæsarea, in the middle of the third century, there were only *seventeen Christians,* and these probably all residing in the city. In the time of Cyprian, Sage admits that there were only eight presbyters belonging to the Church of Carthage, three of whom, on one occasion, voted for him, and one against him.† In the time of Cornelius, in the third century, there were only forty-six presbyters in the Church of Rome, all of whom, according to Dodwel, did not preach; and even in the fourth century, according to Optatus, it contained little more than forty parishes,‡ or a considerably smaller number than in the Scottish Presbytery of Glasgow, who are under one moderator or president. Victor Uticensis says, that in the fifth century there were nearly as many bishops as there were parishes in one of the provinces of Africa; and Bishop Burnet allows that in the time of St. Augustine there were about five hundred bishops in a very small district.§ And if it be a fact, as is stated by Dr. Hammond, on the authority of Tertullian and Justin Martyr, that the early Christians received the Eucharist from the hand of the bishop, it is evident that his charge could not be large.‖ But

---

* Πυκνοτερον συναγωγαι γινεσθωσαν, &c. "Where he evidently recommends to him to examine, at their usual meetings, into the state of every individual who was under his care, and not merely, as is alleged by Sclater in his Original Draught of the Primitive Church, p 79, "to matriculate them in a register." The latter circumstance, moreover, would have been much less fitted to elate the men and maid servants than the special notice which, on the former supposition, Ignatius exhorted him to take of them at their public meetings.

† Vindication of the Principles of the Cyprianic Age, p 348

‡ Euseb Hist. Eccles. lib 6, cap 43. Optatus contra Parmen. lib 2, 40

§ Conference, p. 348

‖ "Sic et Tertullianus de Cor. Mil. Non de aliorum quam de

while such was the extent of the primitive bishoprics, how different is the size of most of your dioceses! Calderwood remarks, that "the bishopric of Lincoln hath devoured many bishoprics which were in the time of the Saxons, and howbeit it hath been greatly impaired, yet there are twelve hundred and forty-seven parish churches in it at this day."* "The bishoprick of York," too, he says, "hath devoured many lesser bishoprics next adjacent, as Cambden relateth in his Britannia." And the bishopric of London contains a million and a half of souls, all of whom, with their clergy, are placed under the oversight and spiritual jurisdiction of a single individual, which is as great an absurdity is if there were *only a single physician,* however eminent, *to watch over their health, and cure their diseases,* or a single magistrate or judge to administer justice to them, in matters which affected their temporal interests. The same observation applies to many of the other bishoprics, the duties of which are far beyond the powers of the best of your prelates. And as you will not contend that any of them are possessed of a hundred times more mental or physical energy, or learning, or piety, than Polycarp, or Irenæus, or Cyprian, or Cornelius, while they have a hundred times more work, you are bound to admit that this also is a point fraught with the most injurious consequences to religion, in which you have departed very grievously from the more judicious arrangements of the early Church.

præsidentium manu Euchaiistiam sumimus, quod idem sub προεστωτων nomine affirmat Justinus Dissert 3, cap 7, par. 5, et Dissert. 4, cap 17, par. 14." Illud autem a Tertulliano, &c.

* See his English edition of his Altar of Damascus, p. 84, which he afterwards enlarged and published in Latin. My friend, the late Dr. Andrew Thomson of Edinburgh, was in error when he said, in his life of Calderwood in Brewster's Encyclopedia, that the only copy of the English edition in existence was one which belonged to our mutual friend, Dr McCrie, as there is at least another belonging to the University of Glasgow, from which I have taken the above quotation It is a small octodecimo.

The diocese of Lincoln contains still, 1 believe, one thousand and seventy parishes, or as many as there are in the whole of Scotland, and all under the superintendence of one bishop.

58   LETTERS ON

I have only further to remark, that in addition to the numerous and overwhelming duties of their spiritual function, you impose upon them others, as British peers, when they attend in Parliament, and deliberate on important political questions, which must secularise their minds, involve them unnecessarily in civil discussions, and alienate a considerable portion of that time which ought to be devoted entirely to their sacred vocation. And yet nothing can be more contrary to the injunctions of Scripture, which calls upon them to "*give themselves wholly*" to the latter; or to the apostolic canons, the eighth of which declares, "we have already decreed that a bishop or presbyter, or deacon, ought not to interfere in public administrations; but ought to employ himself *entirely in ecclesiastical matters.* Either, therefore, let him be persuaded not to do so, or let him be deposed."* Nothing, too, is more strongly reprobated by your Reformers, though, as Cartwright remarks, "if they had to exercise *both offices, it is to be ascribed to the tyme*,—because the cloudes which Popery had overcast our land with could not be so quickly put to flight."† "They know," says Hooper, "that the primitive Churche had no souch bishops as be now a daie, as examples testifie, until the time of Silvester the First."‡ "Looke upon the Apostles cheffelie, and upon all their successoures for the space of four hundred years, and then thou shalt se good bishoppes, and souch as diligenthe applied that painful office of a bishope to the glorie of God, and honour of the realmes they dwelt in, for *they applied all the witt* they had unto the vocation and ministerie of the Churche. Our bishopes have so mouch witt, they can rule and serve, as they say, in boothe states of the Churche, and also in the civile policie, when one

---
* Επισκοπος η πρεσβυτερος, η διακονος, &c. Consult the notes of Zonaras on this canon. It is mentioned also by Cyprian in his Treatise de Lapsis, p. 278, as one of the sins of his time, which had provoked God to send a persecution on the Church.
† Second Reply to Whitgift, p. 30.
‡ Treatise on the Commandments, p. 182.

of them is more than any man is able to satisfie, let him do all waies his best diligens."* "They are otherwise occupied," says Latimer; "some in King's matters, some of the Privie Councell, some are Lord's of the Parliament. *Is this their duetie? Is this their office?*"† And says Jewel, after stating that "the bishop's charge is to preach, to minister sacraments, to order priests, to excommunicate, absolve, &c., you must remember, M. Harding, that all other privileges, (as Lords of Parliament,) passed unto the clergie *from the Prince, and not from God;* for from the beginning you know it was not so."‡ So sensible, accordingly, were the other Protestant states, at the time of the Reformation, of the incompatibility of such power with the office of the clergy, that they provided against it; and the only prelates of whom I have ever heard, who would have had leisure to exercise it, if it had been lawful, were these bishops among the Scots Episcopalians, who were ordained by Dr. Ross before his death, without any diocese, (for there was none to give them,) and merely to keep up the succession. "Their warmest admirers," says the late Dr. Campbell of Aberdeen, "have denominated them Utopian bishops; and in their farcical consecration by the Doctor and others, they were solemnly made the depositaries of no deposit, commanded *to be diligent in doing no work,* assiduous in teaching and governing no people, and presiding in no church—in short, they were husbands married to no wives "§

If this letter had not already been too far extended, I might notice your want of a godly discipline, which, as Burnet admits, is "owned in the Preface to the Office of Commination," and which, though you have been praying for it annually on Ash Wednesday since the days of Edward the Sixth, you have never yet

* Treatise on the Commandments, p. 184.
† Sermon on the Plough, fol. 12.
‡ Defense of the Apology, p. 550. See, too, the Apology itself, part v. chap 3, divis. 7.
§ Lectures on Ecclesiastical History, vol. 1. p 355.

obtained. I might have adverted to the practice of your bishops in transferring their power of jurisdiction to lay-chancellors, in regard to which, it is remarked by Bishop Bedel, that " it is one of the most essential parts of a bishop's duty to govern his flock, and to inflict spiritual censures on obstinate offenders, and he can no more delegate this power to a layman, than he can delegate a power to baptize and ordain."* And even Whitgift admits that the power of excommunication " was in the beginning joyntly in the bishop, dean and chapter alone;" that afterwards " *through custom*, it was *appropriated to the bishop*, and that it was solely by the authority of the civil lawes" that he was latterly permitted to devolve it on an official or vicar-general, chosen from the laity.† And with respect to the visitations of archdeacons, it is confessed by Bishop Burnet, that "they were an invention of the later ages, in which the bishops, neglecting their duty, cast a great part of their care upon them. Now," he adds, " their visitations are only for form and for fees; and they are a charge upon the clergy; so when this matter is looked into, I hope archdeacons, with many other burdens that lay heavy on the clergy, shall be taken away."‡ It is unnecessary, however, to add to these details; and I shall only further remark, that if, according to your opinion, there must be a resemblance in great and leading points between any Church in the present day and the primitive Church, before the former can be entitled to the name of a Church, and its members have any covenanted hope

* See his Considerations for better establishing the Church of England

† Strype's Whitgift, p 93, and Appendix, p. 33.

‡ History of his OwnTimes, vol ii p 642 He says also, p. 636, " No inconvenience could follow on laying aside surplices, and regulating cathedrals, especially as to the indecent way of singing prayers, and of laymen reading the Litany All bowings to the altar have at least an ill appearance, and are of no use , the excluding parents from being sponsors in baptism, and requiring them to procure others, is extremely inconvenient, and makes that to be a mockery, rather than a solemn sponsion, on too many "

of salvation, it suggests considerations which are fitted to awaken very painful feelings in the ministers and members of the Church of England.

I remain, Reverend Sir,

Yours, &c.

LETTER IV.

Extracts from the Oxford Tracts asserting the doctrines of Puseyite Episcopacy to be the doctrines of Scripture —A contrary opinion avowed by the whole of the Bishops and clergy who were zealous for the spiritual improvement of the Church for five hundred years before the Reformation, by the whole of the Protestant Churches at that memorable period, and by eight thousand Protestant ministers, who subscribed the Articles of Smalkald, which declare that bishops are not superior to presbyters by divine right —Improbability that these distinguished individuals and the whole Protestant Churches were wrong, and Puseyite Episcopalians right

REVEREND SIR,—I have referred, in the conclusion of the preceding letter, to the acknowledgment which has been annually made by your Church for nearly three hundred years, of her want of "a godly discipline." And justly may she do so, for it must be evident to any one who reflects for a moment on the small number of individuals who are entrusted with the superintendence of her ministers and members, and who alone have the power to correct the errors and heresies of the one, and the immoralities of the other, that all which she possesses of this important privilege, so essential to the spiritual prosperity of a Church, is little more than the name. I admit the respectability of many of her bishops, but I would ask any candid and impartial judge, whether *twenty-seven* prelates, or rather *twenty-seven* lay-chancellors, can exercise such an oversight of *seventeen thousand* clergy, as to their principles and conduct, and about *sixteen millions* of laity, or at least the large proportion of them who belong to your communion, as was done by the rulers of the primitive Church over her ministers and members, and as is indispensable to the welfare of every Church? And yet such is the whole amount of superintendence which is provided in your Church for this important end, and which, if Episcopalian church government, as has often been alleged, be far better fitted than Presbyterian polity for preventing schism, and promoting orthodoxy, and unity, and spirituality, ought to render your Church the most sound and united and spiritual Church that is to be met with in Britain.

But how does the actual state of your Church correspond with these anticipations? So far from being free from schism and discord, and remarkable for her unity, is she not torn with dissensions, which are spreading further and further, from day to day, throughout the whole of your cities and towns and parishes? Nor do they relate merely to externals, like those which divide some other Churches, but to the fundamental principles of religious truth and Scriptural Christianity. And in place of the exercise of a godly discipline toward those who are infusing into her some of the worst and most deadly principles of Popery, and who are attempting to overthrow her as a Protestant Church, not a single bishop has put forth his power to expel these heretics, and cut them off from the body whose spiritual health they are seriously injuring. Yes, sir, you are allowed to retain your professorship, though, by your own confession, you prostrated yourself lately in a Popish chapel at the elevation of the host. And Mr. Newman and others retain their livings, though they have been pleading for the mass, and recommending the restoration of auricular confession, and advocating re-union to the Church of Rome. What would the spirits of Cranmer and Latimer say of such conduct, if they were permitted to speak to us? And in what light would it have been viewed by Cecil and Walsingham, who gloried in your Church as the bulwark of Protestantism? But perhaps it does not arise from any want of fidelity on the part of your prelates, but from their want of power, and the utter insufficiency of Episcopalian church government to correct such an evil. How different was the course which was pursued a few years ago by the Church of Scotland towards Mr. Irving and his followers, when, after endeavouring in vain to reclaim them from their heresies, she deposed them from the ministry,* and arrested their errors within the pale of the establishment. Happy would it be for the Church of England and the cause of Protestantism if similar measures were adopted by your bishops; and never was there a time when it was more imperatively the duty of her pious members to labour and pray that the Lord would restore to her a godly and vigorous and salutary discipline.

But whatever may be the apparent defects and imperfections in the constitution and discipline of your National Church, there is one thing you allege of the very highest importance, in which she has a decided advantage over Presbyterian Churches. Her clergy, you affirm, having derived their orders from diocesan bishops, in an uninterrupted series from the Apostles of Christ, must be considered as his ministers, and her ordinances as his ordinances, and her members as his members, children of God, and inheritors of the kingdom of heaven. But the ministers of these Churches having received their orders only from Presbyters, who, in your opinion, had no right to bestow them, cannot be regarded as invested with that sacred and venerable character, nor can their sacraments have any virtue, nor their members any covenanted title to salvation. And so far from acknowledging them as Christian Churches, you represent them as occupying the very same position with the temple of Samaria, which was not recognised by the God of Israel, and denounce their clergy, when they ordain others to the office of the ministry, as involved in the guilt, and

* Presbyterians do not believe in the indelibility of the clerical character, as maintained by the Church of Rome and the Church of England, but think, that if, as is stated, Acts i 25, even *an Apostle* " fell from his office *by transgression*," the same thing may happen to an inferior minister.

likely to be subjected to the doom of Corah, Dathan and Abiram, who wished to extend the powers of the priesthood to the whole of the heads of the families of Israel.

That I may not, however, appear to charge you with sentiments which you do not really entertain, I beg to appeal to the following extracts from the Oxford Tracts, to which I have reason to believe that you are a principal contributor.

"It is not merely that Episcopacy is a better or more scriptural form than Presbyterianism, (true as this may be in itself,) that Episcopalians are right and Presbyterians are wrong, but *because the Presbyterian ministers have assumed a power which was never intrusted to them.* This is a standing condemnation from which they cannot escape, except by artifices of argument, which will serve equally to protect the self authorised teachers of religion."*

"Samaria has set up its rival temple among us.— Had not the Ten Tribes the school of the prophets, and has not Scotland *at least* the Word of God? Yet what would be thought of the Jew who maintained that *Jeroboam and his kingdom were in no guilt?* Consider our Lord's discourse with the woman of Samaria: Ye worship ye know not what; we know what we worship Can we conceive his making light of the difference between Jew and Samaritan?"†

"The parties which are separated from and opposed to *the Church*, may be arrayed into three classes: 1. those who reject the truth; 2. those who teach a part, but not the whole truth; 3. those who teach more than the truth; *i. e.* 1*st*, Socinians, Jews, Deists, Atheists; 2*d*, Presbyterians, Independents, Methodists, Baptists, Quakers; 3*d*, Romanists, Swedenborgians, Southcotians, Irvingites.

"Churchman, whoever thou art, that readest the follies and errors of the *second* and *third* classes, into which the pride of man's heart, and the wiles of Satan, have beguiled so many of those who call upon the name of the Lord Jesus, first, give to God great

---

* Oxford Tracts, No. 7, p. 2. † No. 47, p. 4.

thanks for having preserved you a member of *the one holy Catholic and Apostolic Church*, which teaches the way of God in truth, neither *handling the word of God deceitfully* like the *second* class, nor following cunningly devised fables like the third; and (with reference to the second and third classes, as well as the first,) pray that God would be pleased so *to turn their hearts, and fetch them home to his flock, that they may be saved*, together with his true servants, and *be made one flock under one shepherd*."*

"Here is the difference between such persons as have received their commission *from the bishops*, and those who have not received it, that to the former Christ has promised his presence shall remain; that what they do on earth shall be ratified and made good in heaven. But to those who have not received this commission, our Lord hath given no such promise. A person not commissioned from the Bishop may use the words of baptism, and sprinkle or bathe with water, on earth, but *there is no promise from Christ that such a man shall admit souls into the kingdom of heaven*. A person not commissioned may break bread, pour out wine, and proceed to give the Lord's supper, but *it can afford no comfort to any to receive it at his hands*, because there is no warrant from Christ to lead communicants to suppose, that while he does so here on earth, they will be partakers of the Saviour's heavenly body and blood. And as to the person himself, who takes upon himself without warrant to minister in holy things, he is all the while *treading in the steps of Korah, Dathan and Abiram*, whose awful punishments we read of in the Book of Numbers."†

Now, on this statement, I would offer the following observations:

In the *first* place, it is founded on the assumption, that an order of ministers, denominated bishops, has been instituted by Christ, who are not only distinct from, but superior to, presbyters, and to whom alone he has committed the powers of ordination, confirma-

* No. 35, p. 6. † No. 35, p. 3.

tion and discipline. But this is a position, which, as you question my orders and those of my brethren, I am compelled to controvert, (and you have provoked the discussion,) and the utter groundlessness and fallacy of which I shall endeavour afterwards to establish more fully. I shall remark only in the meantime, that such an order was not discovered in Scripture, as I have already showed you, by Cranmer and others of your leading reformers, for they admitted the validity of Presbyterian ordination. It was not discovered by Usher, one of your greatest theologians, who was surpassed by none in his acquaintance with the writings of the early Christians. " I asked him also his judgment," says Baxter, "about the validity of Presbyterian ordination, *which he asserted*, and told me that the king asked him, at the Isle of Wight, where he found in antiquity that presbyters alone ordained any? And that he answered, I can show your Majesty more, even where presbyters alone successively ordained bishops, and instanced in Hierome's words, Epist. ad Evagrium, of the presbyters of Alexandria choosing and *making their own bishops*, from the days of Mark to Heraclas and Dionysius."* It was not discovered by Willet, whose Synopsis Papismi is said to have been *approved of by the bishops*,† for he represents the vesting of the powers of ordination, confirmation, and government exclusively in bishops, as mere human inventions for their aggrandisement. " To the ecclesiastical policie in the advancing of the dignitie of bishops," says he, " these things (of human appointment) doe pertaine. First of all St. Hierome saith of confirmation committed only to bishops,—Disce hanc observationem, &c. Know that this observation is rather for the honour of their priesthood, *than by the necessitie of any law*." Advers. Luciferian.

"*Secondly*, The Counsell of Aquisgrane, cap. 8, saith, that *the ordination and consecration of ministers* is now reserved to the chief minister only for authoritie sake.

* Baxter's Life by himself, p. 206.   † Acta Regia, p. 289.

"*Fourthly*, The jurisdiction of the Church, which, in time past, Hierome saith, *was committed to the Senate or College of the Presbyters*, was afterward, to avoyd schisme, devolved to the bishop. And of this senate mention is made in the Decrees, Caus. 16, Quæst. 1, cap. 7. As the Romanes had their senate, by whose counsell every matter was dispatched, so we have our senate, the companie of elders.

"*Fifthly*, St. Ambrose saith, 1 Tim. iii., *a bishop and a presbyter have but one ordination*, for they are both in the priesthood. And St. Hierome saith, that in the Church of Alexandria, the presbyters did make choice of one whom they placed in a higher degree, and called him their bishop, like as if an armie should chuse a general, or the deacons should choose an industrious man, whom they make their archdeacon; Hierome ad Evag. So it should seem that *the very election of a bishop in those days*, without any other circumstances, *was his ordination.*"* And so far was Dr. Field, one of the most eminent men of his day, from adopting your opinion, that he says of the fathers, " who made all such ordinations voide as were made by presbyters, that it was to be understood according only to the strictness of the canons *in use in their time, not absolutely in the nature of the thing;* which appears in that they made *all ordinations sine titulo to be voide, all ordinations of bishops ordained by fewer than three bishops* with the Metropolitane, and all ordinations *of presbyters by bishoppes out of their own churches*, without special leave.*"†* It was rejected *by the whole of the Protestant Churches at the time of the Reformation*, almost all of whom united in setting aside diocesan Episcopacy, while the few who retained it, adopted it, not because it was of divine institution, but from

* Page 277.
† Treatise on the Church, book iii. p 158. Consult also chap. 39, where he proves, in opposition to Bellarmine and to Dr. Pusey, that those churches among the reformed, whose ministers were ordained only by presbyters, do not cease, on that account, "*to have any ministerie at all.*"

considerations of expediency. Nor did they abolish it from necessity, as some have asserted, but from principle, for, as Jeremy Taylor acknowledges, they could easily have had bishops if they had wished for them. Such is the statement even of Heylin, one of the most bitter opponents of Presbytery that ever appeared, for, says he, in his answer to Burton, "if, by your divines, you meane the Genevian doctors, Calvin and Beza, Viret and Farellus, Bucan, Ursinus, and those others of forreine Churches whom you esteem the onely orthodox professors, you may affirm it very safely, that the derivation of Episcopall authority from our Saviour Christ *is utterly disclaimed by your divines.* Calvin had never else invented the Presbytery, nor with such violence *obtruded it on all the Reformed Churches;* neither had Beza divided Episcopatum into divinum, human, and Satanicum, as you know he doth."* And such is the statement of Le Blanc, one of the professors at Sedan, who, though he allows that your opinion had crept into the Church of England when he wrote, says, that *" the rest of the reformed, and the divines of the Confession of Augsburgh,* agree in thinking that *there is no difference, by divine institution, between bishops and presbyters;* but as the names are given in Scripture to the same persons, so the office is the same."† This statement is confirmed as to the Reformed Churches, not only by their several Confessions,‡ but by the important fact, which is mentioned

* Pages 64, 65.

† "Ceteri vero reformati, et etiam Augustanæ confessionis theologi communiter sentiunt nullam esse jure divino distinctionem inter episcopum atque presbyterum, sed ut nomina illa in Scriptura sunt synonyma atque invicem permutantur ita quoque rem plane eandem esse; eminentiam autem illam episcoporum supra presbyteros quæ a multis seculis in ecclesia Christiana obtinet, volunt esse tantum juris positivi et ecclesiastici sensimque per gradus in ecclesiam introductam," &c. De Grad. et Distinc Minist. Eccles p 36 His theses are generally acknowledged to be stated and illustrated with grent candour.

‡ The Helvetic Confession says, that all ministers of the Word have equal power and authority, cap. 18. "Data est autem omnibus in ecclesia ministris una et æqualis potestas sive functio. Certe ab initio episcopi vel presbyteri ecclesiam communi opera gubernarunt.

PUSEYITE EPISCOPACY. 69

by Calderwood in his MS. History of the Church of Scotland, namely, that the second Helvetic Confession

Nullus alteri se prætulit, aut sibi ampliorem potestatem dominiumque in episcopos usurpavit." The same is the language of the French Confession, the thirtieth article of which is in these words. "Credimus omnes veros pastores ubicunque locorum collocati fuerunt, eadem et æquali inter se potestate esse præditos sub unico illo capite, summoque et solo universali Episcopo Jesu Christo. And in their Discipline, cap. 1, art. 18, they reject "nomina superioritatis, quemadmodum seniorum synodi, superintendentium, et similia."

The Order of Geneva says, sec 2, "Primum quatuor sint ordines vel species ministrorum quæ Dominus noster ad regimen ecclesiæ suæ ordinariam instituit, nempe pastores, tum doctores, postea seniores, quarto diaconi Propterea si ecclesiam cupimus bene ordinatam et servatam in integro oportet istam observare regiminis formam."

The Belgic Confession says, Art. 31, " Cæterum ubi sint locorum verbi Dei ministri eandem illi atque æqualem omnes habeant tum potestatem, tum autoritatem, ut qui sint æque omnes Christi unici illius episcopi universalis et capitis ecclesiæ ministri "

The first article agreed upon by the National Synod at Embden, in the year 1571, was, "Nulla ecclesia in aliam, nullus minister in alium, nec senior vel diaconus in alios sive seniores, sive diaconos ullam exercebunt dominationem."

The Wirtemburgh Confession says, in the chapter de Ordine, " Docet autem Hieronymus eundem esse episcopum et presbyterum. Quare manifestum est nisi presbyter instituatur in ecclesia ad ministerium docendi, nec presbyteri, nec episcopi, nomen recte usurpare queant " The first Danish Confession, which was drawn up by Taussanus, the head of the Lutherans, and which received the sanction of the State in 1537, and was afterwards translated into Latin by Pontanus, says, " Veri episcopi sive sacerdotes, *qui iidem omnes sunt*, (true bishops or priests, *who are all the same*,) nihil aliud sunt quam verbi divini administri, nec eorum est curare ea quæ ad mundi pompam *vel politiam spectant*. Alterutrum horum aut deserendum aut faciendum." And it is mentioned by Gerdesius, Hist. Evangel. Renovat, vol iii. p. 412, that the King of Denmark, as Duke of Holstein, in 1538, subscribed the Articles of Smalkald, which, as we shall see immediately, declare that *bishops and presbyters are the same* by divine appointment.

And it would seem from what is mentioned by Messenius in his Schondia Illustrata, tom. 5, p. 54, that it was superintendents who were settled after the Reformation in Sweden, as well as Denmark. " Rex Gustavus," says he, "nihil motus, aliis Sueonum tumultibus jam sedatis, nuptiarum molitur celebrationem, illaque cum requireret Archi-Præsulis officium, convocati regni cleri ad 24 Junii diem Stockholmiæ mandat Primatem eligere. Quocirca 4 nominatis candidatis, nimirum, M Magno Stregnensium Episcopo; M. Laurentio Andreæ Doctore, Joanne Upsalensium Decano, et M. Laurentio, ibidem ludimagistro, vota feruntur et colliguntur, pluraque ideo nactus competitor ultimus quod electores Lutherani essent plures, quam

"was allowed and subscrived not only by the Tigurines themselves, and their confederates of Berne, by Scaphusia, Sangallia, Rhetia, Millan, and Viemia, but also Geneva, Savoy, Polonia and Hungaria. In this Confession, superiority of ministers above ministers is called *ane human appointment;* confirmation is judged to be a device of men, which the Kirk may want without dammage; baptisme by women or midwives condemned"[*] And it is confirmed by the famous Articles of Smalkald, which affirm expressly, that, "by divine right, there is no difference between a bishop and a pastor or presbyter, that orders communicated by the latter are valid, *because of divine right*, and that *the power of jurisdiction or government belongs to all pastors or presbyters*, and has been unlawfully and shamefully appropriated to themselves by diocesan bishops."[†] And we know that these articles were subscribed, not only by three Elec-

---

Catholici, ac ejusdem ipsemet professionis foret, Archi-superintendens salutatur.

"Ita electum consequitur ecclesia Upsalensis Archi-superintendentem. Nominatos quoque habuit superintendentes Lincopensis, Scarensis, atque Wexoniensis, non inauguratos Quos propterea velut solennitati, regiarum etiam necessarios nuptiarum, jubet Rex Gustavus, 12. Augusti 1531, suscipere consecrationem non archielectum." Afterwards they assumed the name of bishops.

[*] Vol. ii. p. 25.

[†] In the Article de Episcoporum Potestate et Jurisdictione, after quoting the words of Jerome, in his Epistle to Evagrius, and in other parts of his writings, the Reformers say, (Osiander's Epitome of Church History, tom. 6, pars 1, p. 299,) "Hic docet Hieronymus, distinctos gradus episcoporum et presbyterorum sive pastorum *tantum humana authoritate constitutos esse;* idque res ipsa loquitur, quia officium et mandatum plane idem est, et sola ordinatio *postea* discrimen inter episcopos et pastores fecit Sic enim postea institutum fuit, ut unus episcopus ordinaret ministros verbi in plurimis ecclesiis.

"Quia autem jure divino nullum est discrimen inter episcopum et pastorem, non est dubium ordinationem idoneorum ministrorum a pastore in ecclesia factam jure divino ratam et probatam esse " And they say with regard to jurisdiction, p 301, "Constat jurisdictionem illam communem excommunicandi reos manifestorum criminum *pertinere ad omnes pastores, et eam episcopos tyrannice ad se solos* ad quæstum suum *turpiter explendum attraxisse.*" And they add, p. 302, "Cum igitur hanc jurisdictionem episcopi tyrannice ad se solos transtulerint eaque turpiter abusi sint—certe licet hanc furto et vi ablatam jurisdictionem rursus ipsis adimere et pastoribus ad quos ea de mandato Christi pertinet restituere," &c

tors, forty-five Dukes, Marquesses, Counts, and Barons, the Consuls and Senators of thirty-five cities, but by Luther, Melancthon, Bucer, and Fagius, and about eight thousand other clergymen."* If these things, however, are so, and if neither the founders of your own Protestant Church, nor the most eminent ministers of the other Protestant Churches for many years after the Reformation, who enjoyed so much of the teaching of the Spirit, and studied so successfully the word of God on *other* subjects, could discover the smallest evidence for diocesan Episcopacy, and pronounced it to be entirely a human institution, I would press it most earnestly on your serious consideration, whether it does not furnish at least a very strong presumption that you are likely to be wrong when you maintain, in opposition to their united opinion, with the Church of Rome, that Presbyterian ministers cannot be regarded as Christian ministers, and that their people can have no covenanted title to salvation.

I remain, Reverend sir,

Yours, &c.

LETTER V.

Presumptive evidence that diocesan bishops have not been appointed by God, because the only bishops mentioned in Scripture among the standing ministers of the Church are presbyters, and no passage can be produced specifying the qualifications required in bishops as distinct from presbyters —This inexplicable, if there was to be an order of ministers, denominated bishops superior to presbyters —Presbyter, a name of higher honour than bishop —No minister of an inferior order distinguished by the name of a minister of a superior order —Deacons never called presbyters, but presbyters always represented as bishops —The powers of ordination and government ascribed in Scripture to presbyters —Wickliff held the principles of Presbytery, and maintained that Scripture gave no countenance to diocesan Episcopacy

REVEREND SIR,—But even though I should concede to you, for the sake of argument, that an order of ministers, superior to presbyters, and denominated

* Vincent. Place. Syntagma de Scriptis et Scriptor. Anonymis.

bishops, is sanctioned by Scripture, it remains for you to show that the difference between them is so very great, as to authorise you to unchristianize every Church, the ministers of which have been ordained only by presbyters; and yet, so far are you from being able to prove this, that the contrary seems to be established by two important considerations. In the *first* place, not only are bishops distinguished sometimes by the name of presbyters, but presbyters are denominated bishops, though in one of the principal passages in which they are designated by that name in the original language, our Episcopalian translators have substituted the term " overseers." Thus, in the twentieth chapter of the Acts, we are told, that " from Miletus, Paul sent for the elders or presbyters of the Church, and said to them," according to Wickliff's version, " Take ghe tent to ghou and to al the flok in which the hooli goost hath set ghou bischoppes to reule the Church of God, which he purchased with his blood."* And that it is presbyters who are here represented as bishops is admitted by the Church of England herself, for in the form of ordering of

* I have already produced evidence, that Wickliff held Presbyterian principles with regard to the government of the Church. Flaccius Illyricus, or, as is stated by Czvittinger, in his Specimen Hungariæ Literaturæ, p 153, the celebrated Francowitz, one of the three Centurists of Magdeburgh, who wrote under that name, says, in his Catalogus Testium Veritatis, p 493, that he taught "tantum duos ministrorum ordines debere esse nempe presbyteros et diaconos" And Dr Allix says, p 222, of his Remarks on the Albigenses, " that even Knighton was obliged to acknowledge that one half, yea, the greater part of the people of England owned his doctrine."

I may further appeal to the following decisive testimony by Walsingham, who flourished A D 1440, which puts it beyond a doubt that Wickliff was a Presbyterian " Lollardi," says he, in his History of England, p 339, "per idem tempus in errorem suum plurimos seduxerunt, et tantam præsumpserunt audaciam ut *eorum presbyteri* more pontificum novos circarent presbyteros asserentes (ut frequenter supra retulimus) quemlibet sacerdotem tantam consecutum potestatem ligandi atque solvendi, et *cetera ecclesiastica ministrandi* quantam ipse Papa dat vel dare potest"

" Unum audacter assero," said Wickliff, as quoted by Neal in his History of the Puritans, vol 1 p 3, note, " One thing I boldly assert, that in the primitive Church, or in the time of the Apostle Paul, two orders of clergy were thought sufficient, viz. priest and deacon; and

priests, published in 1549, she appointed this passage to be read to them to point out their duty. But if they are denominated bishops, it seems evidently to follow that they must be little inferior to them, or to speak more correctly, that they must be equal to them; for if you would infer the equality of the Son and the Spirit to the first person in the Godhead, because the same names are given to them which are applied to the Father, I would be glad to know on what principles you can prove that a similar equality must not exist between presbyters and bishops. Nor is it any answer to this to say, as has been often done by Episcopalians, that even Apostles are sometimes denominated presbyters; 1 Pet. v. 1; for though some of the ministers in the primitive Church who were of a superior order were called occasionally by the name of ministers of an inferior grade, because they could discharge their duties, I am not aware of any instance, (and I call upon you to produce one if you are able,) *in which a minister who belonged to an inferior order was designated by the name of a minister of a higher order, to the exercise of whose powers he was completely unequal.* Deacons, for instance, are never represented as presbyters or bishops, and yet presbyters are often denominated bishops. And,

I do also say, that in the time of Paul, *fuit idem presbyter atque episcopus, a priest and a bishop were one and the same.*"

Even Nicol Burne, the Papist, translates the passage referred to in the text, (Acts xx 28,) "Tak tent to zour selfis and the haill flok over the quhilk the Halie Ghaist hes apoyntit zou bischops to governe the kirk of God, quhilk he hes conquesed with his blude;" p. 107, of his Disputation Miles Coverdale renders it, "Take hede, therefore, unto your selves, and to all the flocke among the which the Holy Goost hath set you to be bishoppes to fede the congregacion of God, which he hath purchaced thorou his oune bloude" The Bishops of Gaul and Germany, in their Epistle to Anastasius, quoted by Illyricus or Francowitz, p. 41, of his Catalogus, render it, " posuit episcopos;" and the same version is given by Stephens, Diodati, and even Hooker in his Ecclesiastical Polity, p. 377, book 7, or rather by Dr Gauden, who wrote the last three books of that work. And says the learned Hoornbeck, in his Notes on Usher's Reduced Plan of Episcopacy, p. 51, "Versio Æthiopica pro episcopis habet papis Etenim apud veteres, papa pro episcopo venit, Cypriano Papæ, Augustino Papæ," &c.

74   LETTERS ON

secondly, not only is the name of bishops bestowed upon presbyters, but *the very same qualifications are required from them*, (Tit. 1. 5—9,) for the discharge of their office; and I challenge you to produce any passage of Scripture where a single attainment, intellectual or moral, is demanded from a bishop which is not exacted from a presbyter.* Now, if a presbyter is designated by the name of a bishop, and must have all his qualifications, I would be glad to be informed on what ground you maintain that he is not equal to a bishop, for, as is proved in the notes, the former is even a name implying higher honour. Or if there be any difference, whether it can really be so great as to warrant you to affirm that Churches

* Dr Whitby observes, on Titus i. 7, " Hence, say the Greek and Latin commentators, it is manifest that *the same person* is called a presbyter in the 5th, and a bishop in the 7th verse."

Hoornbeek, in his Notes on Usher, shows that *the term presbyter implies greater honour than that of bishop*, which renders it very strange, if the office of a bishop was intended to be superior to that of a presbyter, that the latter should receive the name expressive of greater dignity. " Neque dubium esse potest," says he, p. 47, "quin ab Judæis nomen presbyterorum ad Christianos, et ex ipsorum politia in ecclesiam defluxerit, prout apud illos semper honoratissimi fuerunt, οἱ πρεσβυτεροι, πρεσβυτεροι των Ιουδαιων, Actor xxv. 15, πρεσβυτεροι του Ισραηλ, Act iv 8, πρεσβυτεροι του λαου, Matt xxi. 23, et alibi. Atque ita apud Judæos *longe dignius nomen* πρεσβυτερον, του Zakan, quam επισκοπου, hetzen, ita perperam in voce episcopi supra presbyteros, gloriantur qui deprimere hos volunt infra episcopum, et coguntur tamen presbyteris in ipso nomine relinquere *monumentum pristinæ atque majoris dignitatis*. Hesychius, Πρεσβυται οἱ εντιμοι honorati, et πρεσβυτερος μειζων φρονιμωτερος, major et prudentior. Inde senioris nomen in alias linguas defluxit ad significandum Dominum, Signor, Seigneur, Sir. De ipsis Chinensibus in præfatione ad Atlantem Sinicum Martinus Martinius inquit, quod tota apud eos honoris ratio a senectute petitur: nos honoris titulos a familiæ dignitate aut muneris amplitudine, illi a sola senectute desumunt, quo seniorem quempiam vocas, eo dignior appellatio est, qua in re tamen suos habent gradus."

It is worthy of remark, that even Hooker, or Bishop Gauden, acknowledges that the bishops referred to in the Epistles to Timothy and Titus were only presbyters "Timothy and Titus," says he, " having *by commission* episcopal authority, were to exercise the same in ordaining *not bishops*, the Apostles themselves yet living, and retaining that power in their own hands, *but presbyters*, such as the Apostles at the first did create in all the Churches. *Bishops by restraint, only James at Jerusalem excepted, were not yet in being.*" Eccles Polity, book 7.

which are governed only by presbyters are not Christian Churches, and that their members are only "midway between you and heathenism."

You may tell me, however, that even admitting the equality, or rather perfect identity, of bishops and presbyters, there were ministers in the Church from the very beginning of a superior order, which was intended to be permanent, and that where these are not to be found in the present day, the Church which wants them cannot be considered as a Christian Church. But I would like to be informed among which of its ministers at that early period you find the individuals who belonged to that order. If it was among the Apostles and the Evangelists, Timothy and Titus, I deny that you are entitled to represent them as belonging to such an order, for I shall endeavour to show you that they were extraordinary officebearers, without any fixed abode or particular charge, who were raised up merely to found and organize the Church. And if I shall succeed in establishing this in a future part of the discussion, it will no more follow, that after they had fulfilled their commission, and had rested from their labours, they were to be succeeded by others with similar powers, than that the same extraordinary powers which had been vested by a king in special commissioners, for organizing the government of a particular country, were to be exercised afterwards by some of its magistrates, when the arrangements were completed. And if it is among its ordinary ministers that you find the individuals who were connected with that order, I will be happy if you will name them. Paul did not discover them in the Church of Ephesus, for he called upon its presbyters to feed and govern, ($\pi o\iota\mu\alpha\iota\nu\epsilon\iota\nu$),* the Church of

* See Mat ii. 6, Rev ii. 27, xii. 15, where our translators render the same word "rule"

While many Episcopalians have acknowledged, that as presbyters are represented as bishops in Scripture, they were the same as bishops, or rather the only bishops among the ordinary ministers, Charles Leslie denied it in the following rambling remarks, which Bishop Russel, it would seem, thought perfectly conclusive, for he has quoted them in the Appendix to his Sermon on the Historical

God, over the which the Holy Ghost "had made them bishops." Peter did not discover them among the

Evidence for Episcopacy, p. 49. "If our opponents will say, (because they have nothing left to say,) that all London, for example, was but one parish, and that the presbyter of every other parish was as much a bishop as the Bishop of London, because the words Επισκοπος and Πρεσβυτερος, bishop and presbyter, are sometimes used in the same sense, they may as well prove that (hrist was but a deacon, because he is called, Rom xv. 8, Διακονος, which we rightly translate a minister." But upon this I remark, that the Redeemer is not called a deacon in that passage, though presbyters are denominated bishops in many parts of the New Testament, nor could he, for he neither served the tables of the poor, nor did he baptise, (John iv 2,) like the deacons in the Episcopalian churches, and consequently the argument fails Besides, the presbyters of the different parishes in England *are never called bishops*, and could not be so designated, which proves no less clearly the groundlessness and capriciousness of the observation, while the presbyters of the New Testament are distinguished by that name, and *the same qualifications are not only required from them as from bishops, but no other bishops are ever spoken of among the standing ministers of the Church.* "Bishop," he adds, "signifies an overseer, and presbyter an ancient man, or elder man; whence our term of alderman And this is as good a foundation to prove that the Apostles were aldermen, in the city acceptation of the word, or that our aldermen are all bishops and apostles, as to prove that presbyters and bishops are all one, from the childish jingle of the words" In reply to which I would only observe, without using that severity of language which it well deserves, that we are at issue, not merely *on the general meaning* of the terms bishop and presbyter, but upon their meaning as applied in Scripture, not to *civil*, but *ecclesiastical* office-bearers, and we consider ourselves as entitled to conclude, from the reasons mentioned above, that presbyters are equal in power to bishops, because they are called bishops, while deacons are equal neither to presbyters nor bishops, because they are never called by these names, just as presbyters are not equal to Apostles, because they are never represented in Scripture as Apostles. The cases, therefore, are evidently not in point, and the argument which appears to have delighted Bishop Russel, as well as his own remarks about Cicero and Hector, whom he makes out to be *two bishops*, is utterly useless It would have been a little more to his purpose if he could have proved, by way of analogy, that *the common councilmen of London*, or any other city, were called *aldermen*, or that *the bailies* of Edinburgh or Glasgow were called *provosts*, (though even that would not settle the question about the meaning of scriptural ecclesiastical terms,) but that illustration, I presume, did not occur either to him or the bishop.

With regard to his observation on the term grace, as applied now to dukes, which was formerly given to kings, it also is not in point, feeble as it is, for, as far as I know, it never was *given* to both *in the same age*, a king being addressed as his majesty, as soon as a duke began to be addressed as his grace And with regard to the ministers to whom he wrote his first Epistle, for the highest order which he mentions among them, ch. v. 1, is that of presbyters." Nor did John discover them even among the angels of the Churches of Lesser Asia, whose name, as Dr. Lightfoot observes, was derived from one of the ministers of the Jewish synagogues, who had no authority beyond his own congregation, and was but ill adapted to be the emblem of a bishop, who had not only authority, but the sole authority, over the ministers and members perhaps of a *thousand* synagogues. Besides, as the seven candlesticks which were seen by that Apostle represented not merely one, but the whole of the congregations of these seven Churches, so it is plain that the seven angels represented not merely seven diocesan bishops, but the whole of the ministers in these different Churches. This is plain from what is said to the angel of the Church of Smyrna, ch. ii. ver. 10; for while he is addressed in the end of that verse as if he were a single person, and is exhorted to "be faithful unto death," and is assured that he will "receive a crown of life," he is addressed in the first part as if he represented *a plurality* of persons; for says the Redeemer to him, "and the devil shall cast *some of you into* prison, that *ye* may be tried, and *ye* shall have tribulation ten days." And it is evident that these persons cannot be the ordinary members of the Church, but the ministers, otherwise the reward would be promised, not to the individuals who were faithful unto death, notwithstanding their sufferings, but to other individuals who did not suffer at all. And as the latter supposition is utterly inadmissible, it is obvious that the angel of the Church of Smyrna must have

---

term Imperator, applied to the general of a Roman army, *when he was in command of it*, and to the Roman emperor, who was chief captain of all the armies of the empire, and whose title always remained while he lived, it will be a better analogy, though not *an argument*, to fix the meaning of the scriptural term bishop, when it is proved from the Bible, that among the standing ministers of the Church, there were to be two orders of bishops—one of a higher grade, like the Roman emperor, and another of a lower, like the generals of armies or of divisions.

represented not merely one minister denominated a bishop, but the whole of the ministers of that early Church, just as the angel whom John saw, ch. xiv. 6, "flying in the midst of heaven, having the everlasting Gospel to preach unto them that dwell on the earth, and to every nation, and kindred, and tongue, and people," did not represent only a single minister, but a number of ministers, who, at the period referred to, were to engage in that work. And the same thing is stated no less distinctly of the angel of the Church of Thyatira, who is addressed in these terms, ii. 24, "But unto you I say, and unto the rest in Thyatira, (as many as have not this doctrine," &c.,) evidently implying that he was not a single individual, but the representative at least of a plurality of persons. And as there is not the slightest allusion to an order of ministers superior to presbyters, among the ordinary and permanent ministers of the Church, in any part of the New Testament, so an incontrovertible proof that no such order was either instituted before the death of John, as has often been affirmed, or was intended to be instituted, is furnished by the fact, that nothing is said of the qualifications which are required in the ministers of that order, to enable those who are to appoint and ordain them to judge whether they are fit for that high office. And this is the more inexplicable, on the supposition that such an order was to be established in the Church, as we have a particular statement of the qualifications of presbyters or parochial bishops, (Tit. i. 5–9,) and even of deacons, (1 Tim. iii. 8–13;) while the office of diocesan bishops, according to Episcopalians, is incomparably more important, inasmuch as they have the sole power of ordination and confirmation, and of the inspection and government of hundreds of congregations; and are far more efficient than Presbyterian ministers or Presbyterian Church courts for preventing schism, and promoting the peace and unity of the Church. I call upon you, then, to produce such a statement of the qualifications which are necessary in the individuals who are to occupy that exalted station; and if, like the whole of the defenders of your ecclesiastical polity for the last two hundred years, you fail to do this, it presents a stiong and unanswerable argument, to prove that the order of diocesan bishops has not been instituted by God.

I might show you, in short, that as presbyters are the highest order of ministers next to the Apostles and Evangelists mentioned in the New Testament, and the only ministers whom it recognises as bishops, so it represents them as exercising the whole of those powers which you appropriate to your prelates. While no instance of ordination is said to have taken place by any of the angels of the Asiatic Churches, whom you allege to have been bishops, we have incontrovertible proof that it was performed by presbyteis. The case, for example, of Paul and Barnabas, recorded Acts xiii. 1–3, is considered by Archbishop Wake, Dr. Hammond and others, as an instance of ordination; and yet it was performed not only by prophets, the second class of extraordinary ministers, (Ephes. iv. 11,) but by teachers or presbyters. And even though it should be admitted that it was not ordination, it was the next thing to it, for they were set apart by prayer and fasting, and the imposition of hands, the usual exercises which accompanied ordination, to a very solemn work, namely, the discharge of their ministry among the Gentiles. And it was they who ordained the Evangelist Timothy, for he is exhorted by Paul, (1 Tim. iv. 14,) "not to neglect the gift that was in him," or, according to the meaning of that expression in a parallel passage, (Ephes. iv. 7, 8, 11,) the office which had been conferred upon him "with the laying on of the hands of the presbytery." Nor does the word translated the presbytery denote, as has been affirmed, the presbyterate or office of the presbyters, for that unquestionably "had no hands," but, according to the uniform meaning of the term, Luke xxii. 66, Acts xxii. 5, &c., a company or assembly of presbyters. Nor were they diocesan bishops as others have asserted, for, as Dr. Forbes, a candid Episcopalian, acknowledges, " the word will not admit of that interpretation, unless you understand by it simple presbyters; and whether the Apostle speaks of Timothy's ordination as a presbyter or as a bishop, it was *presbyters* who composed the presbytery who performed it."* And it is not more difficult to conceive of his having been ordained by presbyters, though he was an Evangelist, than of presbyters having ordained Paul at Antioch, *though he was an Apostle;* or of their having set him apart along with Barnabas, not merely to a temporary mission, but to the great work of preaching the Gospel among the Gentiles.

If it be alleged that Paul took part in the ordination of Timothy, or rather that he alone ordained him, because he exhorts him, (2 Tim. i. 6,) to "stir up the gift of God which was in him by the putting on of his hands," and that the presbytery merely assented or concurred when they laid on their hands, as the preposition μετα seems to signify, I remark, first, that there is no evidence of any other person than the presbytery having taken part in the ordination; for the gift to which the Apostle refers in his second Epistle more probably denotes that extraordinary faith which could remove mountains, (1 Cor. xiii. 2,) or that extraordinary fortitude which triumphed over difficulties, and which, like *other supernatural gifts,* was communicated sometimes by the laying on of his hands; Acts xix. &c. This agrees better with the exhortation to stir up the gift which was in him, if it be understood in that sense, than if it be taken in the other, for we cannot comprehend how he could "stir up" *an office.* And it agrees also better with the words of Paul in the following verse, where he adds, "For God hath not given us the spirit of fear, but of *power,* and of love, and of a sound mind." I call upon you then to prove that the Apostle took any part in the ordination of Timothy; and if you are able to establish this,

* After remarking that the word translated Presbytery signifies "Consessus Presbyterorum," he adds, "sic enim in Novo Testamento passim et apud antiquissimos scriptores ecclesiasticos usurpatur hoc vocabulum. Quod autem nonnulli hoc loco interpretati sunt coetum episcoporum, nisi per episcopos intelligas simplices presbyteros, violenta est interpretatio et sensus insolens," &c.

you will do what has not been done by any of your predecessors. And, 2dly, if he engaged in this transaction, I challenge you to show that he did any thing more than as one of the presbytery. The Apostles, you know, acted occasionally not as extraordinary but as ordinary ministers. They officiated as deacons, when they served the tables of the poor before the office of deacon was instituted. And as they represent themselves sometimes as presbyters, (1 Pet. v. 1,) so they seem to have acted in that character in the Council of Jerusalem, for they assumed no superiority over the presbyters, the latter having come together, as well as the Apostles, " to consider of the matter;" and when the decision was pronounced, " after no small dissension and disputation," it was denominated "the decrees," (Acts xvi. 4,) not only of the Apostles, but of the presbyters. Paul, then, for any thing you can prove to the contrary, if he had any thing to do with the ordination of Timothy, might do it merely as one of the presbytery, in which case it must be evident that your argument fails. And you have no right to allege that he laid on *his* hands *authoritatively*, and the rest of the presbytery *only to express their concurrence*, because Timothy is said to have received his office " with (μετα) the laying on of the hands of the presbytery," while he is represented as receiving *another* gift (2 Tim. 1. 6) " by (δια) the hands of the Apostle." Μετα, you must be sensible, frequently denotes *instrumentality*, as in Acts xiv. 27, and xv. 4, where Paul and Barnabas are said to have declared all things that God had done " *with* them," *i. e.* as his instruments to accomplish them; and such also is the sense in which it appears to be taken in 1 Tim. iv. 14, intimating that the instrumentality by which Timothy received his office from the great King and Head of the Church was " the laying on of the hands of the presbytery," or, as they are denominated by Dr. Forbes, the Consessus Presbyterorum. And no hint is given, that when they laid on their hands one of them did it authoritatively, and the others merely to express their consent, and you cannot produce a single instance where any thing like this was done in the age of the Apostles. I trust, then, I may affirm of the whole of these evasions which have been employed by Episcopalians to set aside the argument from this memorable passage for Presbyterian ordination, that they are utterly groundless; and I would say to you in the words of Whitaker, one of the most learned of your ancient divines, which he addressed to Bellarmine, when he denied like you the validity of our orders, "*this place serveth our purpose mightily*, for we understand from it that Timothy had hands *laid upon him by presbyters*, who at that time *governed the Church by a common council.*"*

It would be easy to show, that agreeably to what is stated by that able writer, the government of the Church was committed to presbyters. It was not a diocesan bishop, but the rulers of the Church of Corinth whom Paul commanded to cast out from their communion the incestuous person, (1 Cor. v.) It was the presbyters of the Church of Ephesus, of whom there appears to have been a number, (and who therefore could not be diocesan prelates, as there could be only one of them in the same city,) whom he exhorts not merely to feed, but govern, $\pi οιμαινειν$, that part of the Church of God; Acts xx. 17—28. Presbyters, as we have seen, sat in the Council of Jerusalem along with the Apostles, and united with them in pronouncing the decision, $δογμα$.† It is of

* Controv. 2, Quaest. 5, cap. v. p. 509.

† The same view of the powers of presbyters is given by Bishop Jewel in the Defence of his Apology, p 527. " Ye say," he observes, "the priests and deacons waited only upon the bishops, but *sentence in council they might give none* This tale were true, M. Harding, if every your word were a gospel. But S. Luke would have told you far otherwise. For, speaking of the first Christian council holden in the Apostles' time, he saith thus, Apostoli et Seniores, &c. The Apostles and Elders met together, to take order touching this matter. And again, in the conclusion, Placuit Apostolis et Senioribus, &c , it seemed good to the Apostles and Elders, together with the whole Church. Here you see the Apostles and Elders give their voice together. Nicephorus saith, Athanasius, being not a bishop, but one of the chief deacons of Alexandria, was not the least part of

them that he says to the Thessalonians, (1st Thess. v. 12, 13,) (for they are represented as ministers who laboured in preaching the word,) "And we beseech you, brethren, to know them which labour among you, and are *over you* in the Lord, and admonish you; and to esteem them very highly in love for their work's sake." It is of the same class of ministers, and not of diocesan bishops, who seldom preach, that he says to the Hebrews, (Hebrews xiii. 7,) " Remember them *which have the rule over you*, which have *spoken unto you the word of God;* whose faith follow, considering the end of their conversation." And it is impossible to conceive a more explicit testimony to their ecclesiastical authority, than that which he gives in his first epistle to Timothy, (v. 17,) where he says, " Let the elders," or presbyters, " that rule well be counted worthy of double honour, especially they who labour in the word and doctrine." And though he says to the Evangelist in the nineteenth verse, "Against an elder" or presbyter "receive not an accusation, but before two or three witnesses," as I shall show you more fully afterwards, he could not intend to exclude the presbyters from judging of the case, or they would not have been *rulers;* or when the Evangelist judged of it along with them, to assign to him a power superior to theirs, or he would have invested him with authority superior to what was claimed by the very Apostles in the Synod of Jerusalem. And it can no more be inferred from what is mentioned in that verse, that he alone was to receive an accusation against a presbyter, and judge of it, when we connect it with what is said in the seventeenth verse, than that he alone was to " give attendance to reading, to exhortation, to doctrine, to preach the word, and be instant in season, out of season, reprove, rebuke, exhort, with all long-suffering and doctrine," &c. because he was enjoined by the Apos-

the Council of Nice, (Niceph. lib. 8, cap. 15.) Tertullian saith, Præsident probati Seniores, &c. The judges in such ecclesiastical assemblies, be the best allowed Elders, having obtained that honour not for money, but by the witness of their brethren," &c.

tle, (1 Tim. iv. 13, 2 Tim. iv. 2,) to attend to the performance of these duties. And though he commanded him, (1 Tim. v. 22,) to "lay hands suddenly on no man," it is evident that it could not be the design of Paul to represent it as a power peculiar to Timothy, and which he was not to exercise along with the presbyters, since he had stated expressly in the preceding chapter, that the Evangelist himself had been ordained by presbyters. Besides, every ordination of a bishop which was performed by Timothy, if he acted merely as a bishop, and made it alone, would have been invalid upon the principles of Episcopalians; for, according to Bishop Beveridge on the second Apostolic Canon, three bishops are indispensable on ordinary occasions, and not less than two can do it in cases of necessity. And if Paul alone ordained Timothy, and did so merely as a bishop, Timothy's ordination, too, *must have been invalid.*

If such, however, are the powers which are assigned to presbyters, it is certainly surprising that you should compare the conduct of Presbyterians, when they ordain their clergy, to that of Korah, Dathan, and Abiram, who assumed the powers of the priests, and taught even the common people to do the same, and insinuate so plainly that they will share in their punishment. I had supposed, that from your situation as Professor of Hebrew, you could not fail to be acquainted with the Hebrew Scriptures, and would have known that these rebels *did not belong to the priesthood* at all, the first of them *being only a Levite,* or an assistant of the priests, and *the two others being of the tribe of Reuben.* And yet they performed the highest functions of the priesthood, and informed the congregation that they too might perform them, and that the sacerdotal office was unnecessary, because "they were all holy," as well as Moses and Aaron. And will you venture to say, after the statements which have been produced from the Sacred Scriptures, that Presbyterian ministers are not ministers, and that they *tell the members of their congregations* that they may preach, baptize, ordain, and bear rule, and do every thing which is performed by their instructors and rulers? Such, sir, was the sin of these ancient transgressors. Will you, Mr. Newman, Mr. Percival, or Mr. Gladstone, say it is ours? It is melancholy to see such charges, which were wont to be heard only from the advocates of Popery in former times, brought forward in the middle of the nineteenth century by the ministers and members of your Protestant Church against their Presbyterian brethren. It is difficult to speak of them in the terms which they deserve; and I owe it to myself, and to the cause which I defend, that I should not attempt it, but pass them over in silence.

I remain, Reverend Sir, yours, &c.

LETTER VI.

Additional evidence that the principal Reformers of the Church of England rejected the divine right of Episcopacy, and pleaded for that form of ecclesiastical polity, chiefly on the ground that they considered it as better adapted to absolute monarchy Testimonies against the divine right of Episcopacy, and acknowledging that Presbyterianism is sanctioned by Scripture, from the writings of Tindal, Barnes, Lambert, Cranmer, Tonstall, Stokesly, Jewel, Redman, Robertson, George Cranmer, Willet, Bedell, and Lord Digby

REVEREND SIR,—If you were able to prove that the Christian ministry is to be found no where except in Episcopalian churches, because they alone have possessed it in an uninterrupted succession through diocesan bishops from the days of the Apostles, and that none but these bishops are able to preserve it, it would be exceedingly alarming to Presbyterian churches. Their ministers, as you allege, would be unworthy of the name; their services would be productive of no spiritual benefit; their sacraments would communicate no grace, and their members could not too soon renounce their fellowship, and apply for admission into your more favoured churches. But before they do so, there are two important points on which you must give them complete satisfaction; 1st, That God has instituted the order of diocesan bishops to preserve the true apostolical succession, and that they alone can do it; and, 2dly, that that succession has never been broken, but exists entire in Episcopalian churches, whether Popish or Protestant, so as to give perfect validity to the acts of its ministers. I propose, accordingly, to examine the evidence in support of these positions, and if it fail as to either, we shall not only be prevented from joining your communion, but it will be impossible to see how any one can do it; for it will follow upon your principles, that there can neither be a Church, nor a Christian minister, nor even a single individual with a revealed or covenanted title to salvation, at present in the world.

You will consider me perhaps as more bold than prudent in attempting to controvert the first of these positions, for Archdeacon Daubeny had said, that "the most famous leaders of the Presbyterians, Blondel and Salmasius, had failed, and he would venture to predict, that no Dissenter" or Presbyterian Churchman, "of learning and character would now choose to enter the field against a Churchman of the same description, on the subject of Church government."*
You will permit me, however, to place in opposition to the first part of his opinion respecting the success of these writers, that of a much more able and competent judge, the celebrated Ernesti, who, in his MS. Lectures on Church History, which were never published, but which, through the kindness of a venerable departed friend, who was one of his students, I have been permitted to peruse, made the following remarks on their two principal works· "Salmasius wrote an admirable book that same year upon bishops and presbyters, under the name of Walo Messalinus, in which he ably replied to Petavius. But afterwards another combatant made his appearance in this con-

* Appendix to his Guide, pp. 18, 19.

troversy, who handled this argument still more elaborately, namely, David Blondel, a Dutch divine, and one most thoroughly conversant in these matters. He published his book at Amsterdam in the year 1646, under the title of an Apology for the Opinion of St. Jerome respecting bishops and presbyters, and *no where is the subject discussed with such ability.* Hammond replied to him in four dissertations, which were published at London in 1651, but *in these he has said nothing to the purpose.*"* And in regard to the latter, I shall briefly observe, that as I write for truth and not for victory, no consideration of a personal nature shall prevent me from inviting a fair, and full, and dispassionate inquiry into a point of such high and paramount importance, as you are disposed to represent it to the Christian Church.

I have stated already, as a negative argument against the institution of the order of diocesan bishops, that no account is delivered in Scripture of the qualifications which are necessary to fit them for their office, which appears to me unaccountable if their office was to be permanent, and not merely temporary, like those of Apostles and Evangelists. And I have referred to the opinion of a number of your Reformers, as well as of many eminent individuals several hundreds of years before the Reformation, who united with the Presbyterians of the present day in declaring their conviction, that bishops had no superiority to presbyters by divine appointment, and that wherever it existed it was a mere human institution. But in addition to these, I beg to subjoin a few extracts from others who occupied a distinguished place among your martyrs and your most learned dignitaries, and who, after studying profoundly the Sacred Scriptures, have left their testimony to this great and leading principle of Presbyterians, that not merely the names of presbyters and bishops are applied indiscriminately to the same individuals, but that there ought to be no

---

* Huic opposuit Hammondus dissertationibus quatuor quae prodierunt Londino 1651. Sed iis nil effecit, &c.

pre-eminence of the one above the other, as far as can be ascertained from the Word of God.

Can any thing, for instance, express this more strongly than the following quotation from the works of Tindal, who is usually denominated the Apostle of your Reformation? "The Apostles," says he, "folowyng and obeying the rule, doctrine and commandment of our Saviour Jesus Christ, their Master, ordeined in his kingdom and congregation *two officers;* one called after the Greeke worde Bishop, in English, an Overseer, *which same* was called Priest after the Greeke, Elder in English, because of his age, discretion and sadnesse, (gravity,) for he was nigh as could be alway an elderly man. And this overseer did put his handes unto the plow of God's worde, and fed Christe's flocke, and tended them onely without looking unto any other businesse in the world." And "another officer they chose, and called him Deacon after the Greeke, a Minister in English, to minister the alms of the people unto the poore and nedy."*

"A byshop," says Barnes, "was instituted to instructe and teach the cytie, and therefore he might have as much underneath him *as hee were able to preach and teach to.*——And if in one place of Scripture they be called Episcopi, in divers other places they be called Presbiteri."†

"As touching priesthood," says the godly Lambert, "in the primitive Church, when vertue bare (as ancient Doctors do deem, and Scripture, in mine opinion, recordeth the same) most roome, *there were no more officers* in the Church of God than bishops and deacons, that is to say, ministers, as witnesseth, *beside Scripture,* full apertly, Hierome, in his Commentaries upon the Epistles of Paul; whereas he saith, that

* Practise of the Popishe Prelates, p 345. of his Works. Consult, too, the section in the following page, entitled, "By what means the Prelates fell from Christ."

This view of the office of the deacons corresponds exactly with what is said of the end for which it was appointed, Acts, vi and with the sentiments of Presbyterians, and differs from those of Episcopalians, who have changed also this part of the institutions of Christ.

† Works, 213—221.

those whom we call priests were all one, and none other but bishops, and *the bishops none other but priests*, men ancient both in age and learning, so near as they could be chosen."* I would like to know if this is not Presbyterianism.

It deserves likewise to be noticed, as is mentioned by Neal, that even in the reign of Edward the Sixth, "*the form of ordaining a priest and a bishop was the same*, there being no express mention, in the words of ordination, whether it was for the one or the other office. And though this," says he, "has been altered of late years, since a distinction of the two orders has been so generally admitted, yet it was not the received doctrine of these times."†

---

* Fox's Monuments, vol. ii p. 336.
† Hist. of the Puritans, vol. i p. 64.

"Of *these two orders only*, that is to say, priests and deacons," says the Necessary Erudition of a Christian Man, "Scripture maketh express mention."

"Even Tonstall and Stokesly," says Sheerwood, in his Answere to Downam, p 21, "latterly writt in their letters to Cardinal Poole. S. Jerome, say they, as well in his Commentary on the Epistle to Titus, as in his Epistle to Evagrius, showeth that those primacyes, long after Christ's ascension, *were made by the device of men* " "And in the margin," he adds, "this note is set, Difference between bishops and priests *how it came in* "

"The bishops and priests," said Cranmer, (Appendix to Burnet's Hist. of the Reform , vol i. p 223,) "were at one time, and were *no two things*, but *both one office* in the beginning of Christ's religion."

"They be of like beginning," said Dr Redmayn, "and at the beginning *were both one*, as St Hierome and other old authors show by the Scripture, *wherefore one made another indifferently.*"

The Bishop of London, and Drs. Robertson and Edgworth, stated it as their opinion, that "they saw no inconvenience, though it were granted that in the primitive Church *the priests made bishops;*" Burnet, vol. i. Append. p. 225. And says Dr. Cox, who acted a conspicuous part both under Edward the Sixth and Elizabeth, " Although by Scripture," (as S. Hierome saith,) "*priests and bishops were one*, and therefore the one not before the other , yet bishops as they be now were after priests, *and therefore made of priests.*" Ibid. p. 224.

I may add, that Stillingfleet makes the following candid statement respecting the opinion of Cranmer, and mentions the ground on which he concurred in consenting that Episcopacy should remain. "Thus we see," says he, (Irenicum, part 2, chap. 8,) "by the testimony chiefly of him who was instrumental in our Reformation, that he owned not Episcopacy *as a distinct order from Presbytery of divine right*, but only as a prudent constitution of *the civil magistrate* for the better governing of the Church."

"But what meant M. Harding heere," says Jewel, "to come in with the difference betweene priests and bishops? Thinketh he that priests and bishops hold only by tradition? Or is it so horrible an heresie, as hee maketh it, to say that by the Scriptures of God a bishop and a priest are all one? Verely, Chrysostome sayth, betweene a bishop and a priest in a manne there is no difference. S. Hierome saith, somewhat in rougher sort, I heare there is one become so peevish, that he setteth deacons before priests that is to say, bishops; whereas *the Apostle plainly teacheth us, that priests and bishops be all one.*"*

And omitting what is stated by Stillingfleet, of the sentiments of Whitgift, Cousins, and Bridges, it would appear from what is said by Mr. George Cranmer, a relation of the Archbishop, that the majority even of your most eminent clergy held Presbyterian principles, or were favourably disposed towards them after the accession of Elizabeth. "It may be remembered," he observes, "that at the first *the greatest part of the learned in the land* were either eagerly affected or favourably inclined that way. The books then written *for the most part* savoured of the disciplinary style : it sounded every where in pulpits, and in common phrases of men's speech · the contrary part began to fear they had taken a wrong course; many which impugned the discipline, (Presbyterian Church government,) yet so impugned it, *not as being the better form of government,* but as *not being so convenient for*

* Defense of his Apology, p. 202

It has been alleged, I am aware, that this account of his sentiments must certainly be incorrect, because he advocated warmly the cause of Episcopacy, in a paper about Metropolitans, which was published under his name, by Whitgift, after his death This quotation however, which is undoubtedly his, and the sentiments of which he never disavowed during his life, as well as other passages equally striking, which might easily have been added, will speak for themselves. And it is not a little surprising, if that paper was his, that he should be classed by Hooker, or rather Bishop Gauden, among those who believed that Episcopacy was a mere human institution, (Eccles. Polity, book 7, p 395,)and that both he and Whitgift should be represented by Willet, who lived after them, (Synopsis, p. 273,) as holding that opinion.

our *State*, in regard of dangerous innovations thereby likely to grow."* And even under the reign of James, the adherents to Presbytery seem to have been very numerous among the best of the laity, for says Downam, "Which things, when I consider how fewe among the people (in comparison) do care for religion, and of those few *how many are* (I am sory to speake it) schismatically, *i. e.* presbyterially disposed, doe make my heart to sorow, and my bowels to yearne in commiseration of them."† And while it was denied by Willet, that "the distinction of bishops and priests is by the commandment and institution of Christ and his Apostles,"‡ it was acknowledged at a still later period by Bishop Bedell, one of the most distinguished prelates who ever adorned your Church, that "bishops and presbyters were precisely the same." When Waddesworth, accordingly, objected to the reformers, "Yea, but in France, Holland and Germany, they have no bishops, Bedell replied, First, what if I should defend they have? Because a bishop and a presbyter are all one, (these Churches had only presbyters,) as S. Jerome maintains, and *proves oute of Holy Scripture*, and the use of Antiquity. Of which judgment, as Medina confesseth, are sundry of the ancient fathers, both Greek and Latin; S Ambrose, Augustine, Sedulius, Primasius, Chrysostome, Theodoret, Oecumenius and Theophylact, which point I have largely treated of in another place against him that undertook Master Alabaster's quarrel."§ And in addition to these testimonies to Presbyterian principles by your martyrs and reformers, and many of your bishops who approved of Episcopacy on the ground only of expediency, I may mention the frank and candid confession of the gallant Lord Digby, a zealous royalist and friend of your Church in the days of Charles the First. "They," said he, "who would reduce the Church to the form of government thereof

* Letter to Hooker, February 1588, prefixed to the Ecclesiastical Polity.
† Preface to his Sermon.
‡ Synopsis Papismi, p. 276. § Bedell's Life, p. 453.

in the primitive times, would be found peeking *towards the Presbytery of Scotland."* Which, he observes to his relative, Sir Kenelm, a bigoted Papist, "for my part I believe in point of government *cometh nearer than either yours or ours of Episcopacy to the first age of Christ's Church."**

If such, however, were the sentiments of these illustrious individuals upon the point in question, and more illustrious individuals never adorned your Church; and if they included, as we have seen, exclusively of those who were formerly mentioned, not merely a few scattered dissentients from the general body, but your holiest martyrs during the reign of Henry, your most distinguished reformers during the reign of Edward, and "the majority of the learned" during the greater part at least of the reign of Elizabeth, as well as Wickliff, and Huss, and the other venerable men who laboured zealously for the purification of the Church for hundreds of years before the Reformation, two important consequences seem necessarily to result from it. In the *first* place, whatever may be the principles of some of your divines in the present day, it is contrary to the doctrine of your early fathers, and of the pillars of your Church, to maintain that Episcopacy is of divine institution; and, 2*dly*, if the arguments which have been adduced in later times, in support of this position, could not satisfy the minds, not only of a Cranmer and a Cox, but of a Jewel, and a Reynolds, and a Pilkington, and a Hooper, it presents a very strong and natural presumption, that they are destitute of the force which you are disposed to ascribe to them.

I am, Reverend Sir,

Yours, &c.

* See his Letter to Sir Kenelm, as quoted by Crofton on Re-ordination, p. 18.

LETTER VII.

The argument for diocesan Episcopacy, from the different orders in the ministry under the Jewish dispensation, examined, and proved to be more favourable to Popery than to Prelacy —As far as it establishes the latter, it furnishes a precedent merely for *a single* bishop in a nation, with far more limited powers than those of any modern bishop —No resemblance between the powers and functions of the Jewish priests and Levites, and those of priests and deacons in Episcopalian Churches —Argument acknowledged to be inconclusive by some of the leading defenders of Episcopacy

REVEREND SIR,—The first of those arguments which have been advanced by the advocates of diocesan Episcopacy in support of their principles, has been derived from the constitution of the Old Testament Church; for as there was a hierarchy under the Jewish, they contend that there ought to be one under the Christian dispensation; "the bishop as supreme governor answering to the high-priest under the law; the presbyters and deacons to the priests and Levites as subordinate ministers in it."* Now, upon this strange analogy, as stated by Daubeny, and Hooker, and Jones, and made the basis of an argument, from mere imagination, for your ecclesiastical system, *without any authority from Scripture*, I would make the following remarks.

In the *first* place, it is relinquished by some of the most enlightened defenders of Episcopacy as completely untenable.

"From these superior and inferior degrees among the priests and Levites under Moses," says Bishop Bilson, "happily *may no necessarie consequent be drawne to force the same to bee observed in the Church of Christ.*" And after stating three reasons for that opinion, he adds, "Lastly, the services about the then sanctuarie and sacrifices, (which none might doe but Levites,) were of divers sorts, and therefore not without great regard, were there divers degrees established amongst them; though to serve God even in the least of them was honourable. Now, in the

* Guide to the Church, p. 34, 35.

Church of Christ, the word and sacraments committed to the pastors and ministers have no different services, *and so require for the service thereof no discrepant offices.*"* And says Willet to Bellarmine, when he made use of this argument, "The high-priest in the law was a figure of Christ, who is the high-priest of the New Testament and chiefe shepheard, 1 Pet. v. 4; and therefore this type being fulfilled in Christ, cannot properly be applied to the external hierarchie of the Church." Besides, "it was untrue that all things were governed onely at the will of the high-priest, for the other priests also were their assistants, and did debate matters in councell with them."†

2*dly*, It is never intimated in Scripture that the ministry under the New was to be modelled after the ministry of the Old Dispensation.

If it had been intended by God that there should be a threefold order in the Christian ministry, corresponding to the orders in the Jewish priesthood, it would certainly be stated in some part of the New Testament, or the names of the ministers of the Jewish orders would have been given to the ministers of the Christian Church. Some Apostle acting in the character of a prelate, or some diocesan bishop would have been called a high-priest, some presbyter a priest, according to the practice of the Church of Rome and of your Church, and some deacon a Levite, as baptism in the opinion of some eminent commentators is denominated circumcision, Coloss. ii. 11—13, because it succeeded that ordinance. I have never, however, met with any intimation of the intention of the Almighty to assimilate the ministry of the New Testament Church to that of the Old, or with any passage where the names of the different orders of the latter are applied to the former, and if you have been more fortunate, I will thank you to mention it. We read, indeed, of a high-priest, and a great High-Priest, under the Gospel dispensation; but he is the great minister

* Treatise on the Perpetuall Government of Christ's Church, p. 12, 13.

† Synopsis Papismi, Appendix to the Fifth General Controversie.

of the Upper Sanctuary, and not any minister of the Church below.* And we are told of a priesthood, a holy priesthood, and a royal priesthood,† and yet it is not composed of presbyters, according to your interpretation and that of the Church of Rome, but of all true believers who offer to God spiritual sacrifices. And though it is mentioned by Paul, (Heb. viii. 5,) that "the ancient priests served unto the example and shadow of heavenly things," yet he does not mean to tell us that they were intended to be a type of the Christian ministry. It may be the tabernacle which is referred to in that passage, as in Heb. ix. 9, as the example and shadow; and the phrase may be translated, "who serve (the tabernacle) the example and shadow of heavenly things," as they are elsewhere represented as serving it, Heb. x. 10. And even though we should adopt another version, and render the clause, "who serve for the example and shadow of the heavenly things," it will not warrant the analogy for which Episcopalians contend; for the heavenly things are not the different orders in the Christian ministry, but, as is elsewhere stated, (Heb. v. 1, 2, ix. 6–12,) the ministry of the Redeemer, our great High-Priest in the heavenly sanctuary, and the effects of his intercession. If not the smallest hint, then, is to be met with in Scripture, that it was the intention of God to model the ministry of the Christian Church after that of the Jewish, it is plain that this argument completely fails. And if, as is mentioned by Semonville, the Jews did not consider it "as absolutely necessary to have recourse for ordination to the Nasci or Prince of the Sanhedrim, but the elders who had received imposition of hands had a right to communicate it to others,"‡ their practice as to the mode of

* Heb. ii 17, iii. 1, iv. 14. See Schmidii Concord. on the word αρχιερευς
† 1 Pet ii. 5–9, Rev. i. 6, &c. See Schmidius on the words ιερευς and ιερατευμα
‡ Les Docteurs Juifs neanmoins remarquent, &c., tom. i. p. 470, des Ceremonies et Coutumes Religieuses

It is asserted by Bishop Gleig, (Anti-Jacobin Review, vol. ix. p. 109,) that "as the Jews were accustomed to a hierarchy, and the conferring orders, and their sentiments respecting the powers vested in elders, resembled more nearly those of Presbyterians than those of the friends of diocesan Episcopacy.

In the *third* place, if the analogy be sanctioned in the New Testament, and the ministry of the Christian is to be assimilated to that of the ancient Church, it will furnish an argument for *the Papacy*, and not for your form of ecclesiastical polity.

You are aware that there was only a single individual in the highest order of the Jewish hierarchy, and that he acted as high-priest to the whole people of Israel. Several high-priests are indeed mentioned occasionally as living at the same time, but, as is remarked by Ravius, they were either those who, though they had held that office, were deposed by the Romans, and retained only the name, or the heads of the twenty-four courses of priests of the second order, who, except as the presidents of these courses, differed only nominally from the common priests.* And as

---

Gentiles to a Pontifex Maximus, and as they saw the worship and discipline of the Church conducted by the three orders of apostles, presbyters and deacons, they could not fail to believe that all these orders were to be permanent, if not expressly taught the contrary by the inspired writers." But they would not require to be told this, if, as will be proved afterwards, the qualifications mentioned in Scripture as necessary for the apostolic office, could not be attained by others after the death of these who first held it. Besides it is a more natural inference, that as the practice of ordination, the most important part of ecclesiastical government, was borrowed from the Jews, and as it was performed among them not only by their Nasci or the President of the Sanhedrim, as the representative of that body, but by any three of their elders, they could not fail to believe, unless they were told the contrary, that the same thing would be done in the Christian Church.

I know that Cyprian and others of the fathers argue for assimilating the orders in the Christian ministry to those in the Jewish. But they traced a resemblance also, as might be easily proved, between it and the officers of an army, and the governors of an empire; and latterly, when the clergy became more ambitious, they assumed the names of exarchs and other political dignitaries, and claimed similar powers.

* "Of all these priests," says Ikenius, in his Antiquitates Hebraicæ p. 106, "the head and chief was denominated the high-priest, and of these, by the law of God, there could be only one at a time, 'Qualis ex lege Dei eodem tempore non nisi unicus erat,'" &c. And says

this office was held only by a single individual, so he acted as high-priest not only to the nation of Israel, as has sometimes been asserted, but to the whole ancient Church, whatever might be its extent. That Church, it is admitted, consisted indeed principally of a single nation; but still it included also the people of the Gibeonites, and many other Gentiles, and their number at some times seems to have been very considerable.* Nay, whatever might be the proselytes who should be converted to the faith of the God of Israel, and however distant their dwellings from the land of Canaan, they were to be members of a Church which had only a single high-priest. If we are to follow, therefore, the model of the Jewish hierarchy, we must adopt a form of ecclesiastical polity different from yours, and from that of all the other Protestant

---

Ravius, in his MS Lectures on that excellent compend, with which I was favoured by the same friend from whom I received Ernesti, " it is most certain that there could be only a single high-priest at a time; nor is it at all inconsistent with this that the writers of the New Testament speak of several who were co-existing at once, as in Luke iii 2, John xviii 13, of Annas and Caiaphas. It is plain from Matthew xxvi. 3, that it was the latter alone who was high-priest; but they were wont also to continue the name to such of the high-priests as had been deprived of that dignity by the Romans, which was the case with Annas, or Ananus, who had been degraded from the honour by Valerius Gratus, of whom it is recorded by Josephus, Antiq. lib 18, cap. 2, sec 2, that after he had been sent by Tiberius into Judea, he changed the high-priests almost every year. Besides these, there are sometimes included among the high-priests those who, in 2 Chron xxxvi 14, are denominated the chiefs or heads of the priests, as is evident from Acts v. 24, where they are called αρχιρεις, while the high-priest receives the name only of ιερευς. Pontificem maximum non nisi unicum fuisse certissimum est," &c. See, too, Carpzovius, p. 99 of his Apparatus Antiquitatum, who says, " Ea tempestate crebra Pontificatus translatio, et mercatura, quam in conferenda hac dignitate agebant Præsides Syriæ, plures efficeret Αρχιερεις, unum officio, cæteros nomine gaudentes " And examine Dr. Mill's Prolegomena, Nos. 1105 and 1184.

The Sagan, it is well known, was only the substitute of the high-priest. There was never more than one of them at a time, and he commonly officiated only when the high-priest was prevented by illness or impurity from discharging his duty. The account given in the Jerusalem Talmud, of the four trifling services in which he acted for the high-priest, is altogether fanciful.

* Esther viii 17, Acts ii. 5-10. Moses Ægyptius in Assurebiah, Derek xiii fol. 137.

Episcopal Churches, whose bishops must be laid aside, and though in some respects similar, different even from Popery, and from every other form of ecclesiastical government which has been witnessed by the world. We would assuredly have a bishop, but there would not be another on the face of the earth; and all the cardinals would be dismissed, all the metropolitans would be discarded, and all the vicars-apostolic, with a single exception, would be done away; for though the high-priest had a deputy, he had no more than one;—and upon that single Supreme Universal Pontiff would devolve the performance of every act of confirmation, ordination and jurisdiction, not only in a particular country, such as England, or France, or Russia, or China, supposing it to be evangelized, but throughout the whole Catholic Church. Such, sir, is the tendency of this boasted analogy between the polity of the Christian and the Old Testament Churches,—an analogy, I confess, which, if you were able to establish it, would be completely subversive of Presbyterian purity, but which would be equally fatal to Episcopal pre-eminence, and even to Popish supremacy, and which would introduce a system not only impracticable in itself, but in a great measure dissimilar to every other government which has existed in the Church.

Such, accordingly, is the light in which it has been viewed by the Papists, who have derived from it, they imagine, an irresistible argument for a universal bishop. "In the synagogue of the Jews," said Costernus, the Jesuit, "in which, as in its first lineaments, the majesty of the Catholic Church was shadowed forth, there was only *one Aaron* with his posterity, who was set over the sacred and spiritual concerns of the people, and that not merely as a teacher, or superintendent of ceremonies, but *as a true prince, with power and authority.*"* And said the Jesuits of Posnania, " We may derive from the Old Testament no feeble argument for

---

* "In Judaeorum nempe synagoga, in qua tanquam primis lineamentis majestas Ecclesiae Catholicae adumbrata fuit, &c. Enchiridion Controversiarum, p. 123

the successor of St. Peter, for as there was under that dispensation only one supreme pontiff in succession, first Aaron, then Eleazar, and then others, why ought there not to be a successor to the high-priest of the New Testament, St. Peter?"* And if they could prove that it would be possible for any individual, assisted by a deputy in case of indisposition, to discharge that office, and that the polity of the Old was appointed to be retained under the New Dispensation, their reasoning would be unanswerable. And such, too, is the light it was regarded in, not only by the Puritans,† but even by Stillingfleet, who candidly acknowledges, that " those who would argue from Aaron's power, must either bring too little or too much from thence;—too little, if we consider his office was typical and ceremonial, and as high-priest, had more immediate respect to God than men, Heb. v. 1, and therefore Eleazar was appointed over the several families during Aaron's lifetime, and under Eleazar, his son Phinehas;—*too much*, if a necessity be urged for the continuance of the same authority in the Church of God, which is the argument of the Papists, deriving the Pope's supremacy from thence."‡

And, in short, I would remark, that though you could obviate these difficulties, and establish this analogy, it would furnish you at most with the mere shadow of an argument, and scarcely even with that in favour of Episcopacy.

As there was only one high-priest for the whole land of Israel, all that you could deduce from it would be merely that there ought to be *one diocesan bishop in every national Church*. Nay, this single high-priest was invested with his office by the inferior

---

* Disputationes, p. 163-164.

† Bradshaw's English Puritanism, p. 40, of his Treatises on Worship and Ceremonies.

‡ Irenicum, p. 174. Carpzovius, who was a Lutheran superintendent, says, p. 66 of his Apparatus, "*Scriptura is ignorant of this threefold typical comparison* between the orders of the Old and of the New Dispensation, for which the author (Goodwin, in his Moses and Aaron) contends, and which has been the fruitful source of the errors of the Papists. Triplicem autem illam quam auctor in medium attulit," &c.

priests,* and latterly by the Sanhedrim;† from which it would evidently follow, that not only ought presbyters, but even the bishops who presided over every country, to be ordained by presbyters. And it does not appear from Scripture that the power of jurisdiction was vested in him exclusively, but he exercised it along with the other priests.‡ And it is observed by Ikenius, that after the return from the Captivity, even when he was president of the Sanhedrim, he was subject to that court,§ and was occasionally judged

* If it be alleged that he might perhaps be consecrated by the Sagan, who probably would be anointed and made nearly equal to the highpriest, upon his being raised to that dignity, it is remarked by Ravius, in his Lectures on Ikenius, that "the office of Sagan, was introduced only during the later and more corrupt times of the Jewish State Patet haud obscure originem muneris sequiori aevo deberi." And it is stated by Carpzovius, that he had no unction as Sagan besides what he possessed as a common priest.

† "The installing the high-priest into his office," says Dr. Lightfoot, vol. i. p. 905, "was by the Sanhedrim, who anointed him, or when the oil failed, (as there was none under the second Temple,) clothed him with the high-priestly garments" And says Ikenius, p. 110, "The high-priest was invested with his office by the great Sanhedrim. Pontifex autem M. a Synedrio M. constituebatur."

‡ The superiority of the sons of Aaron to the different families of the Levites, which is mentioned by Hooker, p. 382, will not prove the contrary, for his sons were only priests *of the second order*. Nor can it be inferred, as he imagines, from the nomination of Amariah, the priest, to be chief over the judges for the cause of the Lord in Jerusalem, 2 Chron. xix. 11; for as Bishop Patrick, in his exposition of the passage, and Carpzovius, in his Antiquities, p 551, observe, he was only the president or moderator of the assembly of priests who were to judge of such matters. Nor can it be deduced from what is asserted by Josephus, when he says, "Priests worship God continually, and the eldest of the stock are governors over the rest. He doth sacrifice unto God before others; he hath care of the laws, judgeth of controversies, correcteth offenders; and whosoever obeyeth him not is convict of impiety against God." In the *first* place, even allowing that he speaks of the high-priest, and not of the eldest priest of each of the families, or of the chief priests of the twenty-four courses, (and the latter seems to be more probable,) the authority which he ascribes to him might be possessed by him merely as president of the Ecclesiastical Sanhedrim. And, 2*dly*, he does not represent that authority as bestowed upon him by God, but says merely that it was POSSESSED by the priests of his day

§ "Plerumque etiam," says he, p. 117, (perhaps in the first part of this remark he is not altogether accurate,) "licet non semper in Synedrio praesidebat, ceterum tamen huic collegio subjectus erat, et ab illo judicabatur" Ravius mentions an instance of this in the case of Simon the Just.

by it; and consequently the bishop would be entitled only to preside in an assembly of his presbyters, and, like the high-priest of the Jews, would be subject to their authority.

And as he would have none of those prerogatives which you claim for your bishops, so there was a variety of privileges which belonged to the high-priest that could not be enjoyed by such a minister under the Gospel dispensation. None but the high-priest was permitted to enter into the presence of God, once a year, in the Holy of Holies, and intercede for the forgiveness of the sins of the people. But you will scarcely, I presume, appropriate such a privilege to any bishop in the present day. He alone applied by Urim and Thummim for supernatural direction in cases of emergency. But it is no longer the prerogative of any minister, whatever may be his rank, to obtain such counsel in a similar way, when a nation or a church is encompassed by difficulties. He was distinguished from the priests of an inferior order by a more copious unction. But there is not the smallest difference, as far as I know, in the imposition of hands on the head of a bishop, from what takes place when they are laid on the head of a presbyter. And though, according to Archbishop Potter, "the proportion of tithes allotted to the high-priest was equal to what three or four thousand Levites lived upon,"* you will scarcely, I suspect, obtain for a bishop, either in your own National Church or in any other, an income equal to that of three or four thousand of your inferior clergy. And yet, if the Christian ministry is to be modelled after the ministry of the ancient Church, you are bound to maintain the resemblance in this, as well as other important particulars. In every point of view, therefore, the analogy fails, and scarcely affords even the shadow of an argument for diocesan Episcopacy.

It would be easy to prove, that as there is a striking dissimilarity between the high-priest of the Jews and the bishops of your Church, so the same remark holds

---

* Discourses of Church Government, p 425.

true respecting their priests and your presbyters, and their Levites and your deacons. Four thousand of the Levites were appointed as porters to guard the gates and passages into the Temple, after they ceased to be required to carry the tabernacle and its utensils; 1 Chron. ix. 17, chap. xxiii. 4, 5. Are any of your deacons employed in this way about your churches or cathedrals? And four thousand were appointed to be singers, and six thousand to be officers and judges. Are occupations like these assigned to any part of that order of your ministers? Besides, as Junius remarks, " as the wants of the poor and the afflicted were provided for in a different way by the law of God *than by the office of the Levites*, it is impossible that deacons" (whose office was instituted to attend to the temporal wants of the poor, and not, as among Episcopalians, to preach and baptize,) " can answer to the Levites of the former dispensation. And as ecclesiastical government was committed by the law to an assembly of priests, and not merely to one highpriest,"* it is obvious that your presbyters do not correspond to their priests.

I am, Reverend Sir, Yours, &c.

LETTER VIII.

The argument of Dr Brett and Bishop Gleig for diocesan Episcopacy from the different orders in the ministry, during our Lord's ministry, inconclusive —The Old Testament Church had not then ceased to exist, nor was the New Testament Church established —Their account of the ministry which was instituted at that time not supported by Scripture, contrary to the representations of it given by the fathers, and so far as it furnishes a pattern of the Gospel ministry, would warrant the appointment of a single bishop over the Universal Church —Archbishop Potter's hypothesis equally unsatisfactory, and would lead to a similar conclusion.

REVEREND SIR,—The next argument in support of your ecclesiastical polity is derived from the alleged

* " Diaconiae usus non fuit in Veteri Testamento quia rebus pauperum et afflictorum alia via lex Dei prospexerat," &c Consult him de Cler., cap. 14, note 13 and 11.

gradation of orders which existed in the Church during the ministry of the Saviour. Your principal writers state it variously, each of them distrusting it in the particular form in which it had been proposed by others. And they had good reason to do so, for in the three different forms in which it has been presented successively, I shall endeavour to show that it is equally inconclusive.

The first of them which I shall notice is that by Dr. Brett, who observes, that "there were three orders of ministers in the Christian Church while Christ was on earth; that is, himself, the head and chief minister or bishop; the twelve Apostles, who were next unto him, answering to the priests or second order; and then the seventy disciples, as an order below the Apostles, and answering to the deacons."* And says the late Bishop Gleig, in an article which he wrote in the Anti-Jacobin Review, " During the time of our Saviour's sojourning upon earth, he was himself the supreme governor of his little flock, and had under him two distinct orders of ministers, the twelve and the seventy. This was exactly according to the model of the Jewish Church, and could not fail to be considered by the Apostles as the model after which they were to frame the Church of Christ."† Now upon this I would remark,

1. That none of the characters which are assigned by these writers to our Lord, his apostles and disciples, are ascribed to them in Scripture.

It is easy, I am sensible, for an ingenious mind to trace a resemblance between the Redeemer, the Apostles and the seventy disciples, and the hierarchy under the Old, and diocesan Episcopacy under the New Dispensation; but none of these characters are ever attributed to them, nor is there the slightest intimation that the alleged gradation which existed at that time in the ministry of the Church was intended to be the model of the Christian ministry. It is a remarkable fact which overturns this hypothesis, that *our Lord is*

* Divine Right of Episcopacy, p. 17, sect 8.
† Anti-Jacobin Review, vol. ix. p. 110.

never represented as a bishop while he sojourned upon earth, and that the only instance in which he was distinguished by that name, (and it is applied to him figuratively,) *was after his ascension to heaven.*[*] Nor did he perform any of the peculiar functions of a bishop. He preached the word; but this is done by presbyters, and very seldom by bishops, who, if, according to this argument, they are appointed to resemble him in regard to their power, bear little resemblance of him in the diligent performance of this important duty. He not only did not baptize, (John iv. 3,) but did not confirm those who were baptized by his disciples, for the only individuals on whom he laid his hands and blessed them, except such as were the objects of his miraculous power, were little children, whom he took up into his arms. He never exercised any ecclesiastical discipline; and though he instituted ordinances, and gave their commission to the Apostles, and afterwards to the seventy, yet it was not as a bishop, but as the head of his Church—sending them forth as his Father sent himself, or as it is elsewhere expressed, (Heb. iv.) as the Son of God who was "over his house," and *distinct from it,* and who had a right to appoint its ministers and institutions. And as such was the character in which he sent forth his Apostles while he was with them on earth, and in which he renewed their commission after he rose from the dead, so it was in it also, and not as a diocesan bishop, that he gave his commission to Paul, (Acts ix., Gal. i. 1,) to the office of an Apostle after he ascended to heaven. Nor are the Apostles represented as corresponding to priests during the life of their Master, or performing any of the peculiar duties of presbyters, for they neither administered the Eucharist, nor took part with him in any act of ecclesiastical discipline. And the seventy are never compared to deacons; and though they preached the word, it was no part of their duty to take charge of the poor, which was the principal, if not the only end for which that office was instituted in the primitive Church;

---

[*] 1 Peter ii. 25.

Acts vi. It is plain, therefore, that the argument founded on this alleged imaginary resemblance between our Lord the King and Head of his Church, and a diocesan bishop, which is revolting to the feelings of a pious mind, and between the Apostles and presbyters, and the seventy disciples and deacons, is utterly worthless; for no such resemblance is mentioned in Scripture, nor are such characters ascribed to them, nor are they represented as intended to furnish a model of the future ministry of the New Testament Church.

The futility of this reasoning will further appear, when it is considered that the Old Testament Church had not then ceased to exist, nor was the New Testament Church established till after the resurrection of the Redeemer.

The truth of this observation is so candidly acknowledged and so clearly demonstrated by a zealous Episcopalian of a former age, that it is unnecessary to trouble you with any additional proof of it. "But how can this prove a solid advantage to him," says Bishop Sage of Principal Rule, "so long as it is impossible for him to make it appear so much as probable, that S Cyprian believed the LXX as making a distinct college from that of the XII, *to have had any standing office in the Christian Church, in which they were to have a constant line of successors?* No intimation, no not the slenderist insinuation of such a belief in any of his writings. On the contrary, it is to be presumed that one of his abilities and diligence in searching the evangelical records could hardly have missed to observe *that which is so obviously observable in them,* I mean that the Christian Church *was not, could not be founded till our Lord was risen,* seeing it was to be founded on his Resurrection. Our martyr (as appears from his reasonings on divers occasions,) seems very well to have known, and very distinctly to have observed, that *the Apostles themselves got not their commission to be governors of the Christian Church till after the Resurrection.* And no wonder, for this their commission is most observably recorded, John xx. 21, 22, 23,—no such thing any where recorded concerning the LXX. Nothing more certain than that commission, which is recorded Luke x. did constitute them only *temporary missioners*, and that for an errand which could not possibly be more than *temporary*. That commission contains in its own bosom clear evidences that it did not install them *in any standing office at all, much less in any standing office in the Christian Church, which was not yet in being* when they got it. Could the commission which is recorded Luke x. any more constitute the LXX *standing officers of the Christian Church,* than the like commission, recorded Matt. x. could constitute the XII such *standing officers?* But it is manifest that the commission recorded Matt. x. did not constitute the XII governors of *the Christian Church,* otherwise what need of a new commission to that purpose after the Resurrection? Presumable therefore it is that S. Cyprian did not at all believe that *the LXX had any successors, office-bearers in the Christian Church,* seeing it is so observable that *they themselves received no commission to be such office-beraers.*"* But if such be the case, it must be absurd in the extreme to talk of the Apostles as succeeding our Lord, and of the presbyters as succeeding the Apostles, and of the deacons as succeeding the seventy disciples in the administration of a Church which was not then in existence; and the absurdity must be increased, if the seventy had only a temporary commission even during the ministry of the Redeemer.

In the third place, the illustrations of this resemblance which are given by the fathers, whose authority is so highly respected by Episcopalians on other subjects, and especially on the constitution of the Christian Church, are in direct opposition to the hypothesis of these writers,

It is remarked by Junius, that the fathers never represent the Christian ministry as modelled after that

* Vindication of the Principles of the Cyprianic Age, p. 235.

of the Church in the days of the Saviour, in consequence of a divine command, but merely because the Church, of its own accord, had resolved to do so. "How then," says he, "you will ask, did they affirm that the latter succeeded the former? By human appointment, and not by any divine institution,—by analogy and imitation, and not from any particular obligation which was binding on the Church."* And as such is the way in which they represent the ministry in the Christian Church as succeeding the ministry in the days of our Lord, so it deserves to be noticed particularly, that in illustrating the succession they leave him entirely out of the parallel, and never intimate that he corresponded to the bishops, the Apostles to the priests or presbyters, and the seventy to the deacons, but assign to the Apostles during the life of Christ the place of bishops, and to the seventy that of presbyters. Such, as is acknowledged by Downam, was the opinion of Cyprian, Ambrose, Jerome, and Augustine; for, says he, "with this distinction of Anacletus those unsuspected fathers agree, who hold that these two degrees of ministers were ordained by Christ, when he appointed twelve Apostles, whose successors are the bishops, and the threescore and twelve disciples, whom the presbyters succeed."† And again he observes, that "it is the judgment of *many of the fathers*, who holde that our Saviour Christ, in ordayning his twelve Apostles, and his seaventy-two disciples, both which sorts he sent to preach the Gospell, instituted the two degrees of the ministerie, bishops answering to the high-priest, and presbyters answerable to the priests."‡ And such also was the opinion of Chrysostom,§ Bede,‖ and many others.

* Quomodo ergo inquies dixerunt hos illis succedere, &c. de Cleric. cap. 14, not. 15
† Defence of his Sermon, booke III. p. 32.
‡ Booke IV. p. 48   His assertion, indeed, is opposed to that of Junius; but it will be found, upon turning to the fathers referred to, that the latter is in the right.
§ See his Homily de Prodit. Judae.
‖ Consult him upon Luke, lib. III. cap. 42.
I am aware that a different view has been given by a few of the

If we attach any weight, then, to the opinion of the fathers, as stated even by Episcopalians, it is plain that the Redeemer cannot be considered as occupying the place merely of a diocesan bishop.

And I would observe, in the last place, that if he were only a bishop, so far as it furnished an argument for an order superior to priests and deacons in the Christian ministry, it would prove by far too much. It would demonstrate, indeed, that there ought to be such an order, but it would be an order which could include only a single individual, and on that individual would devolve not only the duties of ordination and confirmation, but of jurisdiction and discipline throughout the universal Church. But as an argument which leads to such obvious absurdities contains within itself its own refutation, it must be upon very different grounds that you will maintain the cause of diocesan Episcopacy, and persuade us to embrace your favourite doctrine, that where there is no bishop there can be no Church.

It is alleged, however, by Archbishop Potter, that this argument may be proposed in a different way,

fathers of the persons represented by the seventy, who make them correspond to the Chorepiscopi, of whom it is said by Balsamon, upon the 14th canon of the Council of Neocesarea, that "they had privileges superior to those of presbyters, πλειονα και ταυτα παρονομια παρα τους ιερους εχοντες," and by Beveridge, in his notes on the 13th canon of the Council of Ancyra, Bingham in his Antiquities, vol i. p. 173, and Hammond contra Blondel, Dissert. iii. cap. 8. that they were of the Episcopal order, but ordained only by a single bishop, and subject to the bishop of the city in whose diocese they resided Such is the account of the seventy, which is delivered by the Council of Neocesarea, in the canon which I have now quoted, for they tell us that "the Chorepiscopi," or country bishops, "were a type," or exhibited a resemblance of the seventy, "οι δε Χωρεπισκοποι εισι μεν εις τυπον των εβδομηκοντα" And such was the opinion of Balsamon, Zonaras, Aristenus, and Simeon Logothetes, as appears from their annotations upon that canon. The last of these interpretations, indeed, contradicts the first, and shows how little importance ought to be attached to the judgment of the fathers, as to matters relating to the constitution of the Church. According to this view of the Chorepiscopi, *presbyters were not represented among the office-bearers of the Church during our Lord's ministry.* I shall afterwards inquire into the status of the Chorepiscopi.

Even these fathers, I may add, never represent the Redeemer as sustaining the character of a bishop

and that in that way it is unanswerable. Our Lord, says he, was intrusted by his Father with the government of his Church, "and had under him two sorts of ministers; 1. Apostles; and, 2. Disciples."* And after illustrating, as he imagines, in a variety of particulars, the inferiority of the latter to the former,† without attempting to point out to what order the disciples belonged, or what order they were to represent in the future Church, he draws from it merely the general conclusion, that there ought to be a similar gradation in the Christian ministry. But if it prove that there ought to be a gradation, it proves, I apprehend, that there ought to be a corresponding gradation to that which existed during our Lord's ministry; and if this suggestion were to be adopted, it would lead inevitably to a constitution of the Church still more monstrous and absurd than that which I have just noticed. There would be a universal bishop, like our Lord himself, without cardinals, or patriarchs, or metropolitans, or prelates, or any other dignitaries,—a minister corresponding to John the Baptist, belonging to an order which has never yet been defined, and two other orders corresponding to the Apostles and the seventy disciples. And if you consider what he says of the two latter orders during the ministry of the Redeemer, it will confirm my observation. The Apostles, he confesses, (and his statement is correct,) before the night on which their Master was betrayed, *had only the powers of deacons, and yet were of an order superior to that of the seventy!!!* "The plenitude of the apostolick powers," says he, " was not conferred on the Apostles at their first ordination, but given them at three different times.

"First, after a whole night spent in solemn prayer, our Lord chose them to be with him as his constant attendants and ministers, and to preach the Gospel. They had also power to baptize, though that be not expressed in their commission; which is evident from

* Discourse of Church Government, p. 44.
† Ibid. p. 46-50.

St. John's Gospel, where it is said Jesus himself baptized not, but his disciples. All which offices have been generally executed in the Christian Church since our Lord's ascension *by the deacons,* or third order of ministers."*

And though he immediately adds, that "after this they received authority to commemorate our Lord's sacrifice on the cross, when he commanded them at his last supper to do as he had done, that is, to bless the elements of bread and wine in remembrance of him, (Luke xxii. 19,) which raised them to be presbyters," his inference will not follow. The Redeemer in that passage enjoined them not to bless the bread in remembrance of him, but to take it and *eat it,* and not to bless the cup, but to *drink* it; and they were to do this not as presbyters, but as believers; for the same thing is enjoined upon all believers, in the account which is given by the Apostle Paul of the institution of that ordinance, (1 Cor. xi. 23-28;) and not only ministers, but the members of the Church are required to "examine themselves before they eat of that bread, and drink of that cup." The powers of the Apostles, then, were not enlarged on the occasion referred to, and if they had those only of deacons from their first commission, they remained only deacons till before the ascension of their Master; and yet they were superior to the seventy, who must have represented an order of Christian ministers that has never yet existed in any Church. The beau ideal, then, of the orders of the ministry in the Christian Church, according to the model presented by the Church in the days of our Lord, must be a universal bishop, a second minister resembling the Baptist, a third order corresponding to deacons without a single presbyter, and a fourth, *inferior to the deacons,* and corresponding to the seventy, and the powers and end of which no one has ever yet attempted to explain. I am, Reverend Sir,

Yours, &c.

* Page 6L.

PUSEYITE EPISCOPACY. 111

LETTER IX.

The same argument, as stated by Bishop Bilson, Mr Jones, and Bishop Skinner, invalid —Upon their hypothesis there would be no deacons in the Church —No higher powers were possessed at that time by the Apostles than by the Seventy, and the different circumstances mentioned by Archbishop Potter, to prove the superiority of the former, do not establish it —The office of the Seventy seems to have terminated with their mission, or, at farthest, at the death of the Saviour, and consequently they could not be an order in the Christian Church

REVEREND SIR,—The argument for Episcopacy which I have just been considering, as stated by the writers to whom I have already referred, is certainly a failure. But there is still a different form in which it has been proposed by others, who admit that our Lord did not belong to any order, but contend that he bestowed on the Apostles the powers of bishops, and on the disciples those of presbyters, and that similar orders should exist in the Church in the present day. Such was the opinion of Mr. Jones, who says, in his essay on the Church, " our Saviour at first ordained his twelve Apostles, according to the number of the tribes of the Church of Israel. Afterwards he ordained other seventy, according to the number of the elders whom Moses appointed as his assistants. When the Church in Jerusalem was multiplied, seven deacons were ordained by the laying on of the hands of the Apostles— and by these the first Christian Church in Jerusalem was governed and administered."* Such also was the opinion of Bishop Bilson; for " albeit the Son of God," says he, " assembled no Churches whiles he lived on earth—yet lest the house of God should be unfinished, and his harvest ungathered, in his owne person while hee walked heere, he called and authorized from and above the rest certaine workmen and stewards to take the chiefe charge, care and oversight, *after his departure*, of God's building and husbandrie, for which cause he made, when as yet hee was conversant with men, a plain distinction betwixt his dis-

* Page 28–29.

ciples, choosing twelve of them to be his Apostles, and appointing other seventy to goe before him into every citie and every place whither he should come, and to preach the kingdom of God; giving those twelve larger commission, perfecter instruction, higher authoritie, and greater gifts of his Holy Spirit, then the rest of his disciples, which he made labourers also in his harvest, and messengers of his kingdome."* And such, too, was the opinion of Bishop Skinner.† But upon this likewise I would remark,

1. That if we were to adopt this hypothesis, and have only those orders which were in the days of the Redeemer, we would have bishops and presbyters in the Church, but there could not be deacons.

2. It does not appear that the Apostles were possessed of those higher powers as compared to the seventy, while the commission of the latter continued, by which bishops are at present distinguished from presbyters.

It is one of the peculiar prerogatives of bishops to ordain presbyters and all other inferior ministers. But this pre-eminence, we know was not enjoyed by the Apostles over the seventy disciples, for it was from the Lord himself, and not from the Apostles, that the disciples received their commission. "If by imparity," says Stillingfleet, " be meant that the twelve Apostles had a superiority of power and jurisdiction over the seventy disciples, there is not *the least evidence or foundation in reason or Scripture for it.* For the seventy did not derive their power from the Apostles, but immediately from Christ."‡ And says Dr. Whitby, "Whereas some compare the bishops to the Apostles, the seventy to the presbyters of the Church, and thence conclude that divers orders in the ministry were instituted by Christ himself, it must be granted that some of the ancients did believe these two to be divers orders, and that those of the seventy were inferior to the order of the Apostles, and sometimes they make the

* Perpetual Government of the Church, p. 42, 43.
† Primitive Truth and Order Vindicated, p. 121, 122.
‡ Irenicum, p. 217, 218.

comparison here mentioned; but then it must be also granted that this comparison will not strictly hold; for the seventy received not their commission as presbyters do from bishops, but *immediately from the Lord Christ, as well as the Apostles,* and in their first mission were plainly sent the same errand, and *with the same power."** It is another of the prerogatives of bishops that they alone have the power of confirmation. But no instance can be produced in which it was exercised by the Apostles during the life of their Master, and we shall by and by inquire whether they exercised it afterwards. And it is a third prerogative of these dignitaries, that they alone have the chief, if not the only, power of jurisdiction and government. But, as was formerly noticed, the Apostles never appear to have exercised this power during the ministry of the Saviour. Nay, it is acknowledged by Saravia, that " though he promised them the keys of the kingdom of heaven, and the power of binding and loosing, *yet he did not bestow it upon them before his death,* for it belonged to the Aaronic priesthood, which was not to cease till he had put an end to the Levitical sacrifices, and transferred to himself the priesthood and every thing which was connected with it. And hence," he observes, " while the Old Testament Church continued he could not found the New."† But if none of the peculiar powers of bishops was possessed by the twelve any more than the seventy, you can have no right to appeal to the superiority of the Apostles to the seventy disciples, for the superiority of your bishops to the inferior clergy.

In the third place, the office of the seventy seems to have terminated at farthest at the death of the Saviour, and consequently they could not possibly be an order in the Christian Church.

That the first commission, even of the Apostles

* Consult him upon Luke x. 1.

† Praeterea claves regni coelorum potestatemque ligandi se daturum promisit *quam ante mortem suam non dedit, &c.* Defensio, cap. 3, sect. 3. See, too, Potter, ch. iii. p 63, who admits that it was " then only the Apostles received the keys which were first promised to Peter as the foreman of the Apostolick College."

themselves, expired at least with the life of their Master, appears to be beyond a doubt; for, had not this been the case, he would not have delivered to them a new and different commission after he had risen from the dead. And that the same was the case also with the seventy disciples is equally clear, for it is never insinuated that the commission of the latter was to be of longer duration than that of the former, and after they had returned from their mission through the cities of Israel, we hear of them no more. While the commission of the Apostles, however, was renewed and enlarged after the resurrection of the Saviour, no second commission was delivered to the seventy; nor is there the most distant allusion to them, either in the history of the Acts, or in the Apostolical Epistles. Nay, it is stated by Epiphanius, that the first seven deacons were formerly of the seventy; and it is asserted by Balsamon, that they had not the power of remitting sins; for Philip the deacon, who was promoted to be an evangelist, because, "having used that office well, (1 Tim. iii. 13,) he procured for himself a good degree," though he preached at Samaria, (Acts viii.) yet could not lay his hands on the believers.*

* Examine his Annotations on the 14th Canon of the Council of Neocesarea, and Epiphanius, sub finem, tom. prioris, lib 1 p 50

It is maintained, indeed, by Blondel, (Apol. pro Sententia Hieronymi, p. 118,) that Epiphanius must be mistaken, and that the seventy must have retained their ministry after the ascension of the Saviour; but his arguments are unsatisfactory. In the *first* place, he says they are denominated Apostles by a number of the fathers, to whom he refers, p. 113, which would not, he imagines, have been the case, if their office had become extinct before the death of Christ Would not the twelve, however, have been called Apostles, because they were sent forth to preach the Gospel, though they had never received their second commission; and why might not the same name be applied to the seventy, who were sent forth, like the others, two and two, especially as it is acknowledged by Episcopalians that it is given to deacons, who afterwards became Evangelists? 2dly, He argues from the reason for which they were appointed at first, namely, that "the harvest was plenteous, but the labourers few," that as long as there was need for them their office must have continued. "Cum messis inter Judaeos copia," &c. But as no one would have believed that the office of the Apostles remained in the Church, merely because the harvest was plenteous, and the labourers were few, if no evidence could have been produced of their second com-

But if such was the fact, it is plain that they must only have had a temporary ministry, and could not be intended to be a standing order in the Christian Church.

It is affirmed, accordingly, by Bishop Sage, in a preceding extract, that it not only became extinct before the appointment of the deacons, but as soon as they had finished their journey through the cities of Israel. And the same also were the sentiments of Stillingfleet and Whitby, respecting the first commission of the Apostles, as well as that of the seventy disciples. " We observe," says the former, respecting the first commission of the Apostles, "that imployment Christ sent them upon now was only a temporary imployment, confined as to work and place, and not the full apostolicall work. The want of considering and understanding this hath been the ground of very many mistakes among men, when they argue from the occasional precepts here given the Apostles, as from a standing perpetual rule for a gospel ministry. Whereas our Saviour onely suited these instructions to the present case, and the nature and condition of the Apostles' present imployment, which was not to preach the Gospel up and down themselves, but to be *as so many John Baptists*, to call people to the hearing of Christ himself; and therefore, the doctrine they were to preach was the

---

mission, so it is impossible to believe, merely for that reason, that the office of the seventy was to continue, when no evidence can be brought forward of the renewal of their commission. And he contends for it in the *third* place, because it is said by Paul that our Lord, after his resurrection, was seen of James, then of all the Apostles, (1 Cor. xv. 7,) and as his appearance to the twelve is previously mentioned, he thinks " that the Apostles of whom he speaks must be some other ministers, and can have been only the seventy. Haec vero in solos septuaginta viros quadrant," &c. But this is equally inconclusive, for it may be a subsequent appearance which is referred to in that passage, that, for instance, which took place at the ascension of the Redeemer, when all the Apostles were present.

It is remarked by Brokesby, in his History of the Government of the Primitive Church, as quoted by Mr. Dickinson of America, p. 14, of his remarks on a book entitled, A Modest Proof of the Order, &c. that the seventy were sent only " as *forerunners* before the face of Christ, to the places whither he would come *to prepare the people to entertain him.*"

same with his, The kingdome of heaven is at hand. This mission, then, being occasional, limited, and temporary, *can yield no foundation for any thing perpetual to be built upon it.*" And again, he remarks upon the Apostles and seventy, "It seems most probable that both *their missions were only temporary; and after this the seventy remained in the character of private disciples,* till they were sent abroad by a new commission after the resurrection, (but in a different character,) for preaching the Gospel and planting churches. Nothing can be inferred, then, for any necessary standing rule for Church government, from any comparison between the Apostles and the LXX during the life of Christ, because both their missions were temporary and occasional."* And says Dr. Whitby, "it is more material to observe, that as the first mission of the Apostles was only for a season, and ceased at their return, Mat. x. 1; so was this first mission of the seventy, they returning quickly from it; v. 17."† If the commissions, then, both of the Apostles and the seventy disciples were only temporary, and terminated at the period mentioned by these writers, and if the commission of the latter was never renewed, it is evident that it does not furnish even the shadow of an argument for maintaining that there ought to be corresponding standing offices in the Christian Church.

I have only farther to remark, that whatever may have been the duration of the office of the seventy, there is not a circumstance, as far as relates to their commission, in which they were not equal to the Apostles.

Both of them were ordained by Christ himself, (Mat. x. 1; Luke x. 1.) They were sent forth in the same number, or two and two, (Mark vi. 7; Luke x. 1;) were appointed to deliver the same message, (Mat. x. 7; Luke x. ;) were furnished with the same gifts, (Mat.

* Irenicum, p. 211, and 218.
† Exposition of Luke x. 1-19. He endeavours to show that they received a second commission, which he says extended to the Gentiles, but he fails entirely in establishing the latter opinion.

x. 8; Luke x. 17;) were to be exposed to the same dangers, (Mat. x. 16; Luke x. 3;) were to depend on the same support, (Mat. x. 9, 10; Luke x. 4, 7;) were invested with the same authority, (Mat. x. 40; Luke x. 16;) and if their message was disregarded, it was to be followed by the same consequences. But if they were completely on a level not only in some, but in all these respects, and especially in regard to their gifts and authority, it is difficult to conceive on what ground it can be alleged that the seventy were only of an inferior order.

Archbishop Potter, however, labours very strenuously to prove their inferiority; and as he has bestowed more than common pains on his argument, it will be necessary to examine it. " Whereas the Apostles," says he, " were ordained to be *with our Lord,* and accordingly are every where throughout the Gospel reckoned as his constant attendants, both from the time of their ordination till they were sent forth to preach, and again after their return from preaching till his ascension: The seventy were only appointed to preach, and after they returned to our Lord and gave him an account of their success in the execution of that office, they are never once mentioned again."* But this evidently is no proof of the inferiority of the seventy; for the reason why the Apostles were more frequently with their Master, was not that they were of a superior order to the others, but to strengthen their testimony to the resurrection of the Redeemer when their commission was enlarged, and to prepare them for the place which they were destined to occupy in the Christian Church. There were others, too, it should be recollected, besides the eleven, who attended upon the Redeemer from his baptism till his ascension, (Acts i. 21, 22;) and yet no one, I presume, will infer from this circumstance that they were superior to the seventy.

" The seventy," he observes, " were only sent before our Lord's face into the cities and places whither he himself would come, to prepare the people for his

* Discourse of Church Government, p. 47.

reception; whereas the Apostles' commission was in general to preach to all the Jews "* But neither will this demonstrate the inferiority of the seventy, for they were sent forth *towards the end of his* ministry to preach in the cities which he intended to visit, and were directed to travel with such despatch, (Luke x. 4,) as to wait to salute "no man by the way," while the Apostles were sent forth at a much earlier period, and could travel more extensively for a similar purpose among the cities of Israel. Both, as we have seen, were like so many John Baptists, and were appointed to prepare the way of their Master by preaching the same truths, and wherever they came they were to exercise the same powers; and if so, the more extended journeyings of the one, because they were sent forth sooner to *the very same work*, cannot furnish the slightest evidence that they were of a superior order to the others. Timothy and Titus, who you say were bishops, could not itinerate so extensively as the Apostles, and yet there is not an Episcopalian who would consider this as a proof that they were of an inferior order to the latter, when viewed merely as bishops.

"The inauguration of the seventy to their office," says he, "was not so solemn as that of the twelve, before which our Lord not only commanded his disciples to pray to God to send forth labourers into his harvest, but he continued a whole night in prayer by himself."† As he commanded his disciples, however, to pray also before he sent forth the seventy, we have every reason to believe that he himself would pray, (Luke x. 2; Mat. ix. 37, 38.) Besides, no such solemnity was enjoined before the ordination of Matthias to the apostleship, for the Apostles are said to have prayed only at the time that "the Lord would show them which of the two candidates he had chosen;" nor did it precede that of Paul, who, according to the Archbishop's reasoning, *must have been equal only to the seventy, and they and that Apostle must*

---

* Discourse of Church Government, p. 47. † Ibid.

have been inferior to the deacons, for the latter were set apart to their office (Acts vi.) by prayer, as well as the imposition of hands.

When he asserts, that "the twelve only received the commission to commemorate the sacrifice of our Lord on the cross, and to preach the Gospel to all nations,"* the first part of his statement is incorrect; for in the passage to which he refers, as was already noticed, they were commanded only *to observe* and *not to administer* the sacrament of the Supper,—a duty in respect of which they were on an equality with the seventy, and with every Christian. And the last of these powers was bestowed on them by the Redeemer after his resurrection, when he enlarged their commission, and when the seventy, at least in their former character, as their commission was not renewed, were no longer a part of the ministry of the Church.

He argues, that the twelve must have been superior to the seventy, because "twelve thrones were appointed, whereon these twelve men should sit to judge the twelve tribes of Israel." And yet he forgets to show that this promise was fulfilled to them *during the life of their Master*, when they and the seventy were engaged in his service, and not according to its obvious meaning under the Gospel dispensation, when the seventy had ceased to be ministers, and they themselves had been elevated to the principal place in the Christian Church. And he observes, that "the twelve foundations of the new Jerusalem were to contain the names of the twelve Apostles."† But this is a prediction of nothing which was to happen in regard to them during our Lord's ministry, while the seventy were with them, but only of the foundation of the Millennial Church on the very doctrines on which they founded the New Testament Church after the resurrection of the Redeemer, and has not the most distant reference to the point at issue. The very same doctrines might be preached

* Discourse of Church Government, p. 48. † Ibid.

by the seventy while their ministry lasted, and they may still be preached by evangelical ministers. But as the Apostles were invested with the highest of the three extraordinary offices in the New Testament Church, (Eph. iv. 11,) and not only preached these doctrines, but, under the guidance of inspiration, wrote those Epistles which were to be the only infallible rule of faith in regard to these truths throughout future ages, they are represented figuratively, *in consequence of what they did in the New Testament Church*, as having their names engraved in the foundations of the Millennial Church, or, according to others, of the Church in glory.

Nor is he a whit more successful in his last observation, though he seems to consider it as furnishing a very powerful argument for establishing his opinion. "When a vacancy happened," says he, "in the College of Apostles, by the apostasy of Judas, another was, in a most solemn manner, by divine designation, appointed to take his bishoprick. Matthias, the person ordained to succeed Judas, if any credit may be given to Eusebius, was one of the seventy; and Barnabas, Mark, Luke, Sosthenes, and other Evangelists, as also the seven deacons, who were all, undoubtedly, even *after their promotion to these offices*, inferior to the twelve Apostles, if the primitive fathers of the Church may be believed, were also of the seventy."*
If the office of the seventy, as has been repeatedly remarked, after accomplishing its end, had ceased to exist before the death of the Redeemer, it presents an easy and satisfactory solution of these imaginary difficulties. Matthias, who previously was without any office, though he had been one of the seventy, was not only promoted to an office, but to the very highest in the New Testament Church. The same would be the case with Barnabas, Mark, and Sosthenes, when they were appointed evangelists; for if they formerly belonged to the seventy, they were then without an office, and yet were advanced to a superior office. And the same remark applies even to the seven individuals

---

* Discourse of Church Government, pp. 48, 49.

who were ordained to be deacons; for though they had been of the number of the seventy, they also were without an office; and to men who have no office the very lowest is promotion. But upon the hypothesis of the Archbishop, Bishop Bilson and Mr. Jones, this is completely inexplicable; for if the seventy were not only a standing order in the Church, but *the second order*, instead of being *promoted* when they were made deacons, they would have been *degraded*, for deacons belong only to *the third order.* In every point of view, therefore, this boasted argument, in all the forms in which it has been presented by the leading defenders of Episcopacy, utterly fails; and if your ecclesiastical polity can be vindicated only on such grounds as these, it must be revolting alike to every man of Christian feeling and sober sense, to hear you propound the monstrous doctrine, that where it does not exist there can be neither a Christian Church, nor a Christian ministry, nor any covenanted title to the blessings of salvation.*

I am, Reverend Sir, Yours, &c.

LETTER X.

The argument of Archdeacon Daubeny and Bishop Gleig, for the order of bishops, from the extraordinary office assigned to the Apostles in the New Testament Church, proved to be fallacious —It no more follows from what is said in Matthew xxviii 20, that there are to be Apostles till the end of the world, than from what is said in Ephesians iv 11-13, that there are to be New Testament Prophets and Evangelists till that time —That office proved to have ceased as to its peculiar powers with those who were first invested with it, because no one since their death has possessed the qualifications which it required, nor has been called to it in the way in which they were appointed, nor has been instructed by inspiration like them in the truths which he was to deliver, nor could perform miracles —Sutclive, Willet, Barrow and others, deny that bishops succeed Apostles in their peculiar powers

REVEREND SIR,—It is alleged, however, by many of the advocates of diocesan Episcopacy, that whatever

* It deserves to be mentioned, that Willet, in his Synopsis, Appendix to the Fifth General Controv., Quest. 3, refutes this very argument, when it was urged by Cardinal Bellarmine, for the divine right of Episcopacy.

may be thought of the preceding arguments, the superiority of bishops to presbyters and deacons is absolutely indisputable, because they are represented in Scripture as the successors of the Apostles, and as invested with the office, and possessed of all the high and pre-eminent authority which belonged to these ministers in the early Church. Such was the opinion of the late Archdeacon Daubeny, who asserts, that "there was no other difference between the Apostles and bishops but this,—the Apostles being confessedly the first planters of the Gospel, were general and ambulatory bishops, having the care and superintendence of all the Churches, 2 Cor. xi. 28; but *bishops were Apostles* fixed in the jurisdiction of one city or province."* Such also was the opinion of Bishop Gleig, who endeavoured to support it by a lengthened argument in the Anti-Jacobin Review; and such, as will appear in the course of this and the following letter, was the opinion of others of the most zealous defenders of your ecclesiastical polity.

I acknowledge, that if this statement were borne out by fact it would be decisive of the question, and we could not too soon submit to your bishops, and attach ourselves to your communion. But before we can do this we must be convinced of two things;—first, that the apostleship, with all its high and peculiar powers, remains in the Church, and is possessed by your prelates; and next, that if these have ceased, and nothing but its ordinary powers continue, which were exercised by the Apostles in the primitive Church, as was formerly proved, along with presbyters, they may not still be exercised, when the apostleship is extinct as to its peculiar powers, and distinguishing prerogatives, by elders or presbyters.

You imagine that you can produce satisfactory evidence for the perpetual duration of the apostolic office; for our "Saviour," says Bishop Gleig, "when he gave authority to the eleven to convert and baptize the nations, expressly declared that he would be with

* Appendix to his Guide to the Church, p. 63.

them always, even *unto the end of the world.*"* But if you really think so, and are persuaded that your prelates are Apostles, why do you not call them by that name, and speak of the *Apostle* as well as the Bishop of Durham, or Exeter, or Glasgow, or Argyle, or any other diocese in England and Scotland? And if you believe that the apostleship, in its higher powers and peculiar functions, is to continue in the Church, because the Saviour promised to the eleven that he would be with them always till the end of the world, I beg to be informed, whether you believe also that the two next higher orders are to remain along with it and that they exist in the Church in the present day? For you know it is declared by Paul, that the Redeemer "gave" not only "some apostles, but some prophets, and some evangelists, and some pastors and teachers, for the perfecting of the saints, for the work of the ministry, and for the edifying of the body of Christ; till we all come in the unity of the faith, and the acknowledgment (επιγνωσεως) of the Son of God, to a perfect man, to the measure of the stature of the fulness of Christ," (Eph. iv. 11–13,) which will not be attained either by any individual saint, or by the whole mystical body, or Church of Christ collectively, till the end of the world. "These prophets," says Gersom Bucer, "were that order of ministers who, under the supernatural direction of the Spirit, explained the predictions of the Old Testament, and occasionally foretold future events;"† and if we may believe Saravia, the

* Article on Dr. Campbell's Lectures on Church History in the Anti-Jacobin, vol. 9.

† "Prophetae mihi eximii interpretes qui propheticae Scripturae sensum insigni quodam revelationis dono ecclesiae pandebant," &c. Dissertatio de Gubernatione Ecclesiae, p. 2. Nor is it any objection to this, that the interpretations given by one prophet through revelation, 1 Cor. xiv. 30, were allowed to be judged of by other prophets, v. 29–32. Even the private members of the Church of Berea, (Acts xvii. 11,) "searched the Scriptures daily," to ascertain whether the doctrine *of the Apostles* was consistent with the Old Testament, and are praised for doing so, and yet the Apostles were assisted by the same supernatural influence with the prophets. I would only farther remark, that as soon as the canon of the New Testament was completed, and sufficient information was communicated to the Church

friend of Hooker, "were superior to bishops."* And I shall by and by inquire into the office of evangelists. I presume you are convinced that both these offices have long ago been discontinued, and that neither prophets nor evangelists are to be found in your Church, or among the Scottish Episcopalians, though you tell us you have Apostles; and if the former have ceased, though it was announced that they were to continue till the whole Christian Church had attained the stature of a perfect man, I deny that you can infer the perpetual continuance of the apostolic office in its peculiar powers and higher functions, any more than the prophetic, from the promise of the Redeemer, that he would be with the eleven always to the end of the world.

I would remark, farther, that as it is utterly impossible to prove, from that passage, that the apostleship was to continue, so it is evident, from a great variety of considerations which are mentioned in Scripture, that it was an extraordinary office, and has for a long time been extinct.

Every one is aware that an office may be necessary for arranging the affairs and organizing the government of an infant colony, or a disordered province, for the execution of which special powers may be delegated to one or several commissioners; and that as soon as they have accomplished the task which was assigned to them, they are recalled by their sovereign,

---

respecting those ancient predictions which related to the Saviour, this order of ministers was discontinued, as they were no longer necessary.

It would seem, that after they had finished their interpretation of any of the prophecies, they concluded it with an address, for we are told, Acts xv. 32, that "Judas and Silas also being prophets themselves, exhorted the brethren."

* "As the authority of an Apostle," says he, de Minist. Evang. Grad., cap. 1, "was superior to that of an evangelist, and *the authority of a prophet and of an evangelist to that of a bishop* or a presbyter, so the authority of Titus and Timothy, who were presbyters and bishops, was superior to that of the presbyters, who, by the appointment of the Apostle, were ordained by them in every city. Nam quemadmodum major Apostoli authoritas fuit quam Evangelistae," &c. See, too, Hooker's Life by Bishop Gauden.

and their office discontinued. It was so, for instance, on a recent occasion, in the history of our own country, when the late Lord Sydenham was sent to Canada, with special powers to settle the affairs of that distant colony, which have ceased already; and no one would affirm, that because they were vested in him they will be continued to every succeeding governor. And for aught that appears it may have been so in regard to the twelve apostles,* who are represented by Daubeny as " confessedly the first planters of the Gospel," and who may have been furnished with high and extraordinary powers, which have not descended to others, for founding and organizing the Christian Church. And that this was really the case, and though they acted sometimes as ordinary ministers, in which respects they have been succeeded by ordinary ministers, yet, when they acted as Apostles, they sustained a character, and were invested with an office in which they had no successors, will appear, I apprehend, from the following considerations:

Qualifications were required for the office of an Apostle, which have not been possessed by any for many hundred years, and which cannot now be attained, from which it evidently follows that it must no longer exist.

To fit an individual for being invested with this office it was necessary, we are informed, that he should have seen the Saviour, if not before, yet at least after his resurrection. When a successor, accordingly, was appointed to Judas, it was mentioned by Peter as an

---

* " The Apostles and Evangelists," says Calderwood, (Altare Damascenum, p 174,) "exercised the powers of ordination and jurisdiction in the Church, and yet it will not follow that Apostles and Evangelists must remain in the Church till the end of the world. Moses and his successor Joshua led the people of God through the desert, and brought them into the land of Canaan; and yet when the people were settled in that land, *it was not needful that Moses and Joshua should have successors of the same political order.* And, in like manner, the Apostles and Evangelists led the faithful through the wilderness of Paganism, and planted the Churches; and yet it is no more needful that we should choose others to succeed them with the same ecclesiastical authority. Evangelistae et Apostoli potestatem ordinationis et jurisdictionis exercebant," &c.

indispensable prerequisite, that "he should be one of those who had companied with them, (the eleven) all the time that the Lord Jesus went in and out among them;" because, as he adds, he was to be "a witness with them of his resurrection;" Acts i. 21, 22. And when Paul proves his apostleship to the Corinthians, he rests it among other things upon his having *seen the Lord.* "Am I not an Apostle?" says he, 1 Cor. ix. 1, "Am I not free?" *i. e.* as to the matters of which he had been speaking in the preceding chapter, "Have I not seen Christ Jesus our Lord?" But if it was indispensable to this office, that the person who was invested with it should have seen the Lord, and if none of your bishops, nor any other prelates since diocesan Episcopacy was first established, have ever seen him, I cannot see on what ground you can consider them as Apostles, or claim for them that high and paramount authority which belonged to an office that must now be extinct.

If it be objected with Bishop Gleig, that "this could not constitute the essence of the apostleship, because our blessed Lord was seen in the flesh of above five hundred brethren at once after he rose from the dead, though there were then only eleven Apostles,"* I have briefly to remark, that it is not represented as the essence of that office, but only as an *essential qualification* for it. Every one, in other words, who had seen the Redeemer after he rose from the dead, did not, in consequence of it, become an Apostle; but *no one without it* could be made an Apostle. And as there is not at present a diocesan bishop who has seen the Lord, none can either have a right to the name, or be entitled to exercise the powers of an Apostle.

The call of an Apostle, also, to his high office was *external and immediate from the Redeemer himself.*

It was in this way that the eleven were admitted to their office after the resurrection of their master; and it was in a similar way that Matthias was appointed; for we are told that the disciples prayed to the Lord

* Article on Dr. Campbell's Lectures in the Anti-Jacobin, vol. 9.

to show them " which of the two candidates he had chosen; and that by a supernatural influence, exerted on their minds, he directed them to Matthias * And the same, too, was the way in which it was bestowed upon Paul; for when he proves to the Galatians that he was an Apostle, he tells them, (chap. 1. 1,) that he was " an Apostle, not of men, neither *by man*, but by Jesus Christ and God the Father,"—plainly intimating that if he had received his office by the instrumentality of men, and not immediately from the Saviour, he would have been unworthy of the name. But if this be the case, and if none of your bishops, nor any diocesan that ever existed, received his office immediately from Christ, and if all of them obtained it by human instrumentality, they cannot be Apostles, nor be entitled to exercise the peculiar powers of these early ministers, and the office itself must undoubtedly be extinct.

In the third place, an Apostle was instructed by *revelation* in the truths which he delivered, and whether he wrote or preached, it was under the supernatural direction of the Spirit.

It will scarcely be denied that this was the case with the twelve after the effusion of the Spirit on the day of Pentecost, and it is equally plain that it was the case with Paul, for he says to the Galatians, (chap. 1. 11, 12,) " But I certify you, brethren, that the Gospel which was preached of me is not after man. For I neither received it of man, *neither was I taught it*, but by the revelation of Jesus Christ." It was impossible, therefore, that any Apostle could fall into error, whether he preached or wrote, when he was under the supernatural guidance of the Spirit. And though instruction in the truth by means of revelation, and infallible direction in speaking and writing about the doctrines of the Gospel, might be communicated to others who were not Apostles, yet no one could be an Apos-

* " The lot which fell on Matthias," says Spanheim, " was really the voice of God, no less than was that of the division of Canaan, of the scape-goat, &c. De Matthia sorte, id est divina voce, qualiter in distributione terrae, in segregatione hirci," &c. Dissert. 27.

tle without it. If this, however, was another of the privileges of these distinguished ministers, and if none of your bishops have ever advanced the smallest claim to it, and it is possessed by none in the present day, it is impossible to see how they can be considered as Apostles, or can have a right to exercise the powers of that office.*

The power of working miracles to attest his commission seems to have been inseparably connected with the office of an Apostle. Paul accordingly tells the Corinthians, (2 Cor. xii. 12,) that " truly *the signs of an Apostle* had been wrought among them in all patience, *in signs, and wonders, and mighty deeds,* εν σημειοις και τεξασι και δυναμεσι;"† plainly intimating that where such miracles were not performed, the individual could not be considered as an Apostle, and had no right to claim to himself that high character. And the same thing is mentioned elsewhere of the rest of the Apostles. Others, it is true, might possess this power, and might not be Apostles, but no one who wanted it could be included among these ministers. And not only was it requisite that he should possess this power, but that he should have it to a greater extent than any other minister; for none but an Apostle, so far as is mentioned in Scripture, was able to communicate miraculous gifts by the imposition of hands; and " the giving of the Holy Ghost" is represented by Bishop Bilson as " the verie seale of his apostleship."‡ Nor is it any objection to this that Ananias is stated to have put his hands on Saul, (Paul,) Acts ix. 17, and said to him, " The Lord, even Jesus, that appeared to thee in the way hath sent me, that thou mightest receive thy sight, and be filled with the

---

* Origen, when speaking of the twelve Apostles in his 18th Homily on Joshua, tom. 1. p. 370, says, " Assuredly they were wiser than those who now ordain bishops, or presbyters, or deacons. Utique multo sapientiores erant quam ii qui nunc episcopos, vel presbyteros, vel diaconos ordinant," where he evidently distinguishes Apostles from Bishops.

† Compare Acts ii. 22, viii. 13, Rom. xv. 19, Heb. ii. 4, Matthew xii. 38, 39, John ii. 11. xviii. 23.

‡ Acts viii. 14-17, xix. 6. Perpetual Government, p. 85.

Holy Ghost," for the Holy Ghost in his spiritual gifts appears to have been given not by the laying on of the hands of Ananias, but at the baptism of Saul, which is said in the next verse to have taken place *immediately*. But whatever there may be in this, the power of working miracles was indispensable to an Apostle; and as it is not possessed by any of your bishops, or any other bishop in the present day, they cannot have any claim to the name of Apostles, and the office which requires such a supernatural power must unquestionably have ceased.

And, in the last place, the authority of an Apostle was of a much higher order, and his commission more extensive than that of any other minister either in the primitive Church or in the present day.

So far from being restricted to any particular diocese, we are informed that the eleven were empowered by their Master to preach the Gospel, and perform all the other duties of their office, not only " in Judea and Samaria, but among all nations—to every creature, and unto the uttermost parts of the earth;"* so that, in the language of Whitaker, " it may be most truly affirmed that they were bishops of the whole world, and the whole world was their diocese."† And as none of your bishops has such a commission, and as no other bishop has such a diocese, his conclusion is irresistible, that " *they must be mere dabblers in theo-*

* Math. xxviii. 19, Mark xvi. 15, Acts i. 8.

† Possis verissime dicere Apostolos fuisse episcopos totius mundi, mundumque totum fuisse Apostolorum διοικησιν " De Pontif., Quaest. ii. cap 8, sec 41.

" The office of an Apostle," says Jewel, also, in his Exposition of the Second Epistle to the Thessalonians, p 123, " was not to rest in any one certain place, but to passe from country to country, from land to land, and to fill all the world with knowledge of the Gospell, and *therein appeareth the difference between an Apostle and a bishop*—a bishop had the charge of one certaine Church, an Apostle had the charge over all the Churches."

" Paul was not tied to any one citie, or iland, or country. He had authority to preach to all cities and countries, to all lands and ilands, from the east to the west. So did Christ appoint his Apostles.—The whole woi ld was their diocesse and their province.—Therefore, if any of the Apostles should have staid in one place, and have gone no farther, he had offended and done otherwise than Christ commanded."

logy who assert that the apostolic authority still remains in the Church."* And as there are none who can labour wherever they please in such a diocese, so there are none who can lay claim to the same high authority. "That the Apostles," says Bilson, "had a superiour vocation above Prophets, Evangelists, Pastours, Teachers, and even the government and oversight of them, will soone appeare, if we consider what Paul the Apostle writeth of himselfe, and unto them, directing, appointing and limitting as well Prophets as Evangelists, (and therefore much more Pastours and Teachers,) what to do, and how to be conversant in the Church of God."† Where is the man among all your bishops whom prophets or evangelists would acknowledge to be their superior, or who, if any of them were living, could lay upon them his commands, or say with an Apostle, "Thus ordain I in all the Churches?" Or where is the individual who, as he travelled through the world, could summon before him not only the members but the ministers of every Church, and sit in judgment on their conduct? All this, however, was done by the Apostles when they acted in that character, and if no one now would attempt to do it, does it not present a strong and unanswerable argument to prove that he has no right to be considered as an Apostle, and that that office must long ago have ceased in the Church?

So undeniably does this conclusion follow from these premises, that it is admitted by many of your eminent divines, who state it even as a principle which cannot be controverted in their reasonings with the Papists. "Apostles and pastors, or bishops properly so called," says Sutclive, "are so distinguished in Scripture, that it is one thing plainly to be an Apostle, and another to be a pastor or bishop."‡ "His

---

* "Unde intelligi potest quam inconsiderate quidam theologati affirmant apostolicam authoritatem adhuc in Ecclesia remanere." De Pontif Lib. 1, Quaest. 8, cap. 3, not 2

† Perpetual Government, p 45.

‡ De Pontif, lib 2, cap 10, where he proves that Peter was not a bishop "Although the Roman bishops," says he, " succeeded Peter

argument concludeth not," says Willet of Bellarmine, "Apostles were above disciples, *ergo* bishops, &c. unlesse he doe assume thus; but bishops are Apostles, *which is denied by Ignatius*, who, though he were neere to the Apostles' time, being the third bishop of Antioch after Peter, and had seene Christ after his resurrection, yet writing to the Antiochians saith,—I do not command these things as an Apostle."* And omitting what has been said by Whitaker and Lightfoot,† nothing can be more decided than the opinion of Dr. Barrow, or more convincing than his arguments. "It is a rule," says he, "in the canon law, that a personal privilege doth follow the person, and is extinguished with the person. The apostolical office as such was personal and temporary; and therefore, according to nature and design, not successive or communicable to others, in perpetual descendence from them. It was, as such, *in all respects extra-*

in doctrine and the chair, yet they succeeded him not in his apostleship, but the latter bishops in neither. Quare etiam olim Romani episcopi," &c. p. 175, 176.

* Appendix to the Fifth Generall Controversie. Quest. 3, Synopsis, Papismi.

† " Bellarmine," says Whitaker, " seems to say, the Pope succeeds Peter in his apostleship. But none can have apostolic power but he who is properly and truly an Apostle, for the power and office of an Apostle constitute an Apostle. But that the Pope is neither truly nor properly an Apostle, is proved by these arguments whereby Paul proves his apostleship, as that he was not called by men," &c. De Pontif. Roman, lib 4 cap. 25.

"When Paul," says Dr Lightfoot, vol i. p. 788, "reckoneth the several kinds of ministry that Christ Jesus left in the Church at his ascension, Eph. iv. 11, and Cor. xii. 28, there is none that can think them all to be perpetuated, or that they should continue successively in the like order from time to time, for within an hundred years after our Saviour's birth where were either prophets or evangelists, miracles or healings? And if these extraordinary kinds of ministration were ordained but for a time, and for special occasion, and were not to be imitated in the Church unto succeeding times, much more, or at the least as much more were the Apostles, an order much more, at least as much extraordinary as they.

" These things well considered, if there were no more, it will show how improbable and unconsonant the first inference is—that because there was a subordination between the Apostles and Philip, (Acts viii) that therefore the like is to be reputed *betwixt bishops and other ministers, and that bishops in the Church are in the place of the Apostles.*"

ordinary; conferred in a special manner, designed for special purposes, discharged by special aids, endowed with special privileges, as was needful for the propagation of Christianity and founding of churches. To that office it was requisite that the persons should have an immediate assignation and commission from God. It was requisite that an Apostle should be able to attest respecting our Lord's resurrection and ascension. It was needful, also, that an Apostle should be endowed with miraculous gifts and graces, enabling him both to assure his authority and to execute his office. It was also, in St. Chrysostom's opinion, proper to an Apostle that he should be able, according to his discretion, in a certain and conspicuous manner, to impart spiritual gifts. It was also a privilege of an Apostle, by virtue of his commission from Christ, to instruct all nations in the doctrine and law of Christ. Apostles also did govern in an absolute manner according to discretion, as being guided by infallible assistance. It did belong to them to found churches, to constitute pastors, to settle orders, to correct offences, to perform all such acts of sovereign spiritual power, in virtue of the same divine assistance. Now, such an office was not designed to continue by derivation, for it containeth in it divers things which apparently were not *communicable,* and which no man without gross imposture and hypocrisy could challenge to himself. *Neither did the Apostles pretend to communicate it.* They did indeed appoint standing pastors and teachers in each church; they did assume fellow-labourers or assistants in the work of preaching and governance: but they did not constitute Apostles equal to themselves in authority, privilege, or gifts." And he adds in a note, "The Apostles themselves make the apostolate a distinct office from pastors and teachers, which are the standing officers in the Church; Ephes. iv. 11; 1 Cor. xii. 28;" and maintains as the legitimate conclusion from these arguments, that "*the apostolic office did expire with their persons.*"* As Spanheim then said to the pope,

---

* See his Works, vol. i. p. 72–74, Pope's Supremacy.

when he represented himself as an Apostle, "Let him descend now from the Capitol,—let him, as did the Apostles, declare that he has the gift of tongues divinely infused,—let him bring visibly the gifts of the Holy Ghost from heaven,—let him work like the Apostles such illustrious miracles, and then we shall yield that he has apostolic authority;" so I would say to your bishops, and to all other prelates who claim to be Apostles, let them exhibit such proofs of their apostleship as these, and then, but not till then, we will admit them to be Apostles. And till they are able to do this, you must permit me to maintain the opinion of Dr. Barrow, that the apostolate has ceased, and to object to your attempting to found an argument on any of the powers which were vested in these extraordinary and temporary ministers for similar powers to any particular order of ordinary ministers, unless you can prove that they exercised them with ministers of that order in their own day, and consequently, that they were not peculiar to the former, or that the latter are pointed out as their successors. And I am greatly mistaken if you will succeed in accomplishing what has never yet been done, and establish these points in favour of your bishops.

I am, Reverend Sir, Yours, &c.

LETTER XI.

As presbyteries can perform the work of " discipling the nations" by preaching and baptizing till the end of the world, and are the highest order of standing ministers mentioned in the New Testament, they are entitled to be considered as the successors of the Apostles —This acknowledged by Willet —The report that the Apostles divided the world into different parts, and that each of them laboured in one of them as its bishop, proved to be fabulous, though repeated by Bishop Gleig —It cannot be inferred from the application of the name Apostles by the fathers to some of the bishops that the latter succeed the Apostles, for they give it also to presbyters, and even females —Refutation of the argument for Episcopacy from the appointment of James to the Bishopric of Jerusalem —Quotations from spurious writings of the fathers, in support of this fiction, by Bishop Gleig and the present Curate of Derry, exposed

Reverend Sir,—There is none of the statements of Presbyterian writers which has called forth more keen or pointed animadversion on the part of Episcopalians, than that which relates to the temporary duration of the office of the Apostles. "Where," it was asked by the late Bishop Gleig, "is this piece of information to be received? Not surely from Scripture, for our Saviour, when he gave authority to the eleven to convert and baptize the nations, expressly declared that he would be *with them* always, even unto the end of the world. As he knew all things, no man professing to believe the Gospel will presume to say, that he supposed the lives of the eleven and the duration of the world of equal extent. We must therefore conclude that when he said he would be with them, he meant with all who unto the end of the world should hold the commission which he now gave them."* But admitting that it was with their successors, and not with themselves, that the Saviour was to be present till the end of the world, it remains to be proved that their successors were to be Apostles. Now this the bishop never attempted to prove, nor has any thing like argument been produced in support of it by any Episcopalian. I have never heard whether he considered himself as an Apostle; but of this I am certain, that neither he, nor any of his brethren, nor any other bishop for many hundreds of years, has seen the Saviour since he ascended to heaven, nor possessed the other qualifications for the apostleship, nor could perform the signs which are mentioned by Paul as attesting its commission; and consequently whoever are the successors of these early ministers till the end of the world, it cannot be Apostles, or the Scriptures must mislead us. Besides, the work which was committed to them by their Master, when he gave this promise, Matt. xxviii. 19, 20, was that of "discipling the nations," by preaching the word, and admitting them into the Church by baptism; and *though it was begun by Apostles,* who had extraordinary gifts and miraculous powers, *it has been proved by fact,* that it was to be carried

* Review of Dr. Campbell's Lectures in the Anti-Jacobin, vol. 9.

on afterwards by ministers possessed of very different qualifications, and furnished merely with ordinary gifts, till the end of the world. Who these ministers are that were to succeed them, cannot be discovered from this passage, and must be ascertained *from other parts of Scripture.* If you are able to produce satisfactory evidence for the institution of the order of diocesan bishops, and a distinct account of their powers, (which has never yet been done,) you will be entitled to include them among the successors of the Apostles, but not to represent them as Apostles. And if it appear, on the contrary, that presbyters are the highest order of ministers recognised in the New Testament after Apostles, Prophets and Evangelists, and that they have power from their office to preach and baptize, and thus convert the nations, I claim for them the honour of being the successors of these distinguished early ministers. Nor in asserting this claim do I use stronger language than that which has been employed by some of the brightest ornaments of your Church in former times. I might appeal to others, but I shall refer only to Willet. After remarking that "all faithful and godly pastors and ministers are the successors of the Apostles," he thus proceeds: "In respect of their extraordinary calling, miraculous gifts and apostleship, the Apostles properly have no successors, as Master Benbridge, martyr, saith, that *he believed not bishops to be the successors of the Apostles,* for that they bee not called as they were, nor have that grace; Fox,— p. 2046, Art. 6, *That, therefore, which the Apostles were specially appointed unto, is the thing wherein the Apostles were properly succeeded,* but that was *the preaching of the Gospel;* as Saint Paul saith, he was sent to preach, not to baptize. 1 Cor. 1. 17. The promise of succession, we see, is in the preaching of the word, which appertaineth as well *to other pastors and ministers* as unto bishops, as afterwards shall bee declared. Again, seeing in the Apostles' time, episcopus and presbyter, *a bishop and priest, were neither in name or office distinguished,* as Master

Lambert, martyr, (Fox, p. 1111,) proveth by that place of Saint Paul, Tit. i., where the Apostle calleth them *bishops*, v. 7, whom before, v. 5, he had named *presbyters, priests, or elders.* To this agreeth the Councell Aquisgranens, cap 8, collecting thus out of this place, Paulus Apostolus, &c. Paul the Apostle doth affirme the eldeis or presbyters to be true priests or pastors under the name of bishops. It followeth then, that either the Apostles assigned no succession while they lived, neither appointed their successors, or that indifferently *all faithful pastors and preachers of the apostolike faith are the Apostles' successors.*"* Nay, the Church of England recognises presbyters in this character, for she appoints this passage (Mat. xxviii. 20,) to be read to them at their ordination; and the same is the language not only of Irenæus and Jerome, but even of Ignatius, to whose opinion you are accustomed to attach such weight; for if any reliance can be placed on the genuineness of his Epistles, it is presbyters, and not diocesan bishops, (if there were any such ministers in his day,) whom he represents as the successors of the Apostles. Thus, in his Epistle to the Magnesians he speaks of the "bishop, (who he was I shall afterwards inquire,) as presiding in the place of God, and *the presbyters in the place of the Sanhedrim of the Apostles,* των πρεσβυτερων εις τοπον συνεδριου των αποστολων." And in his Epistle to the Trallians he denominates them "*the Sanhedrim* of God, and the συνδεσμον of the Apostles." While I maintain, then, that the office of the Apostles has ceased, I contend that their successors are ordinary ministers, denominated presbyters or pastors and teachers, who are the highest order mentioned in the New Testament, and who are completely equal to the performance of the work of preaching and baptizing, in which they were to have successors, and that with them the Saviour has promised to be present till the end of the world.

It has been mentioned in these letters as one of the circumstances which distinguished the Apostles from

* Synopsis, p. 269.

diocesan prelates, and which proves that their office is extinct, that while the latter are restricted to a particular district, and cannot go beyond it, the former were bishops of the world. But this is contradicted by Bishop Gleig, who observes after Downam,* "not to insist on the reports of antiquity, *that they divided the earth among them;* it will be sufficient on this occasion to appeal to St. Paul, whose testimony, when direct, the greatest zealot for novel opinions will hardly dare to controvert. Now, this Apostle assures us, Romans xv. 20, that he strove to preach the Gospel not where Christ was named, lest he should build on another man's foundation; and as he quotes the authority of Isaiah for his conduct, it is not possible that the other Apostles conducted themselves differently."† But before the Bishop had retailed the fable about the division of the earth among the Apostles, or founded upon it, he ought to have considered whether he could reply to what had been said about it by Stillingfleet. " As for the division of provinces among the Apostles," says the latter, after a long train of most convincing reasoning, " mentioned in ecclesiastical writers, though as to some few they generally agree, as that Thomas went to Parthia, and Andrew to Scythia, John to the Lesser Asia, &c. yet as to the most, they are at a loss where to find their provinses, and *contradict one another* in reference to them, and many of them seem to have their first original from the fable of Dorotheus, Nicephorus, and such writers."‡ And said Ernesti in his MS. Lectures, " There is an opinion that the Apostles agreed among themselves to divide the earth into twelve parts, and to assign one to each Apostle; but it is fabulous, and savours of the traditions of the Jews, who report that Noah divided the earth into three parts, and distributed them to his sons by lot. Our author (one on whom he was commenting,) appeals in support of it to the Ecclesiastical History of Eusebius. Can any one sup-

---

* Defense of his Sermon, book iv. p. 52.
† Anti-Jacobin Review, vol. ix ; Critique on Campbell's Lectures.
‡ Irenicum, p. 237.

pose that Eusebius delivers this? But he produces a passage from the Commentaries of Origen upon Genesis. If men, however, would explain it aright, no such fiction could be deduced from it. He says there, παραδοσις εχει, *i. e* the ancients give out, or there is a report. Now, the term παραδοσις is employed in Scripture, and particularly by Paul, as denoting what is taught or recorded; and part accordingly of the παραδοσις is taken from Scripture; for the account of the place where Peter laboured is borrowed from the inscription of his first Epistle, the account of the labours of Paul from his writings, the account of the ministration of John from the first chapter of the Apocalypse, and the rest from *uncertain and uninspired productions.* Besides the word ειληχεναι has been rendered, 'they divided by lot,' but not very correctly, for it means often what is assigned to us by Providence; and if so translated in this passage, it would signify merely, that *they had received as their lot the different places which were the scenes of their labours,* or, in other words, *were led by Providence to preach in them,* for the propagation of the Gospel. From this misinterpretation, accordingly, has arisen the whole of this fiction; and yet nothing can be more groundless, for Paul taught in the Lesser Asia, in Greece, in Thrace, and in Italy, and *of course could not have been restricted to any particular place.* Very similar to this is another opinion, which maintains that each of the Apostles was confined to a certain place, and which is not only without any foundation in Scripture, but contrary to the notion of an Apostle, who was a universal pastor, while a bishop was the minister only of a particular place. This last opinion is pretended to be drawn from a passage in Paul, where he calls the Churches which he had founded his κανων, 2 Cor. x.;* and says that some had gone beyond their own κανων,† and encroached upon his, *i. e.* when he founded a Church during any of his journeys, he was unwilling that it should be claimed

---

* Rendered by our translators " measure."
† " Measure."

by another, for such is the import of his words, v. 15, not boasting of things without our measure, that is, of other men's labours. This κανων, therefore, could not be any particular portion assigned to Paul, but the Churches of which he had laid the foundation in his journey from Asia to Europe, and the honour of founding which he would not allow should be arrogated by another."*

I would only add farther, that Paul informs us, Rom. i. 5, that "he had received grace and apostleship for obedience to the faith *among all nations*, for the name of Christ." And if this was the end for which he had been invested with his office, can any one believe that he would restrict himself to the superintendence of a particular district, so as that he could neither preach nor exercise jurisdiction beyond it? Besides, though he was the Apostle of the Gentiles, he often preached to the Jews, and addressed to the Christians from that nation in every quarter of the world one of his Epistles. And, in like manner, Peter, though he was the Apostle of the circumcision, was the first of the Apostles who preached to the Gentiles, and must frequently afterwards, if he visited Rome, as Papists assert, have ministered to their churches. And as to the remark of Paul, that "from Jerusalem and round about Illyricum he had fully preached the Gospel of Christ, yea, and had so strived to preach the Gospel, not where Christ was named, lest he should build on another man's foundation," it is not in the least inconsistent with his officiating as an Apostle in every quarter of the world which it was in his power to visit. It is obvious from the facts which have been just now mentioned, and from his addressing an Epistle to the Christians at Rome, though he had never seen them, that an Apostle might both preach the Gospel and write Epistles to Churches which had been collected by others. And his preaching at Rome, after he arrived at that city, as well as in other Christian Churches which had been previously formed, clearly

* "Opinio est Apostolos inter se consensisse de partiendo inter se orbe terrarum," &c.

demonstrates that it was not from any division of provinces which had taken place among the Apostles, but from some other reason, such as that it was more especially the business of an Apostle to plant than to water Churches; and, according to the prediction of Isaiah, quoted by Bishop Gleig, to spread the Gospel as extensively and rapidly as he could, that he refrained usually "from building on another man's foundation."

It is asserted by the Bishop and others of your defenders, that the apostleship could not be peculiar to the twelve and to the Apostle of the Gentiles, because "the words of Paul, Gal 1. 1, inform us, as clearly as language can express any thing, that when he wrote his Epistle to the Galatians, there were in the Church Apostles who had been ordained to their office, δι' ανθρωπου, by the ministry of man. Such we think, was Barnabas, who, though he had been employed in the work of the ministry before St. Paul himself, is never styled an Apostle till after hands were laid upon him at Antioch, by the immediate direction of the Holy Ghost. Such certainly was Epaphroditus, whom St. Paul styles the Apostle of the Philippians, and who, according to the Doctor's man of discernment, Hilary the deacon, was constituted their Apostle by St. Paul himself,* who therefore commands them 'to receive him in the Lord, and to hold him in reputation.' Such likewise were those brethren who were styled, (2 Cor. viii. 23,) αποςολοι εκκλησιων, δοξαι Χριςου, Apostles of the Churches, the glory of Christ. And such undoubtedly were Timothy, Titus, Sosthenes, and Silvanus, whom Paul so frequently associates with himself as his *partners, fellow-helpers and brethren;* and to the two first of whom he assigns such offices at Ephesus and Crete, as, by the confessions of all parties, evince them to have been of an order superior to presbyters. Hence it is that we read of false Apostles, (2 Cor. xi. 13,) and of some who said they were Apostles, and were not, but were found liars, (Rev. ii. 2;) for as

---

* The words of Hilary are, "Erat enim eorum Apostolus ab Apostolo factus"

none of those liars, could possibly pretend to be St. Paul, or any of the twelve, all of whom were dead before that period, we must of necessity infer that they practised their imposition upon their knowledge, that there were then in the Church many true Apostles, the Apostles δι' ανθρωπον, or by the ordination of man."†

Now, I would remark upon this passage, that as it does not contain the slightest proof that the greater part of the individuals to whom it refers were denominated Apostles in the proper sense of the word, or that any one of them is so designated who had not seen the Lord after his resurrection, and who could not exhibit the signs of an Apostle by working miracles, it will not warrant the conclusion, that others who wanted the qualifications for the apostleship, which were before mentioned, were elevated to that high office, and were appointed to be the fellow-labourers and successors of the Apostles. Calderwood imagines that an exception as to the name ought to be made in regard to Barnabas; for he observes, " In what manner he was called to the apostleship does not appear, and yet that he was an Apostle, and of the same rank with Paul, is evident from many circumstances. He is denominated an Apostle, without any limitation of the meaning of the word, Acts xiv. 4–14; and was sent to the Gentiles, with the same authority with Paul; Acts xiii. Others were in their company, and yet Barnabas is mentioned always as the equal of Paul, and not merely as an assistant. The inhabitants of Lystra considered Barnabas as Jupiter, Acts xiv. 12, and Paul as Mercury. He is always distinguished from the other companions of Paul, both during their journey among the Gentiles, and when they went up to the Council at Jerusalem. And the controversy which took place between them, so as that they were obliged to separate, as well as the power of choosing as his assistant John, whose surname was Mark, which was exercised by Barnabas, proves that he was an Apostle, and not an Evan-

* Anti-Jacobin Review, vol. ix.

gelist."* But if he was really an Apostle, there is reason to believe, that as he was one of the seventy disciples, as is acknowledged by Cave† and other Episcopalians, he would see the Redeemer after his resurrection. And we know that he performed miracles; Acts xiv. 1–4, 14. As to the case of Epaphroditus, it is plain, not only from our own and other translations, but from what is acknowledged both by Whitby and Willet, that he is denominated αποςολος, because he was the "messenger" who carried the contributions of the Philippians to Paul. "Concerning the instance of Epaphroditus," says the latter, "he is called their Apostle, *i. e.* messenger, because he brought the benevolence of that church unto Saint Paul; Phil. iv. 18. And so this word *Apostle* is taken both in the civill and canon law, in so much that letters dimissorie,

---

* "Barnabas quo modo vocatus fuerat non constat. Extra ordinem tamen in Apostolorum numerum co-optatus est" Altare Damascenum, p 157

† Historia Literaria, p. 11. Clemens Alexandrinus, in his Stromata, lib ii. p. 300, makes the same statement; "ὁ δε των ἑβδομηκοντα ην και συνεργος του Παυλου" And in p. 273, 274, he called him an Apostle, "Αποστολος Βαρναβας."

It deserves, however, to be mentioned, that Calvin, in his Commentary on Acts xiii. 4, says, "Quum Lucas Barnabam Apostolum cum Paulo vocat nominis significationem longius extendit quam ad primarium ordinem quem instituit Christus in sua Ecclesia · qualiter Paulus Andronicum et Juniam inter Apostolos insignes facit. Proprie autem loquendo evangelistae erant," *i. e.* the name of the Apostle is given to him in a more extended sense than when it is applied to the twelve and Paul He adds, indeed, "Nisi forte quia Paulo additus erat collega Barnabas, utrumque in pari officii gradu statuimus: ita Apostoli titulus vere in ipsum competet," *i e* unless, as he was added as a colleague to Paul, we assign to him the same rank, in which case he may receive the name of an Apostle. Gersom Bucer, however, very properly observes, (Dissert de Gubern Eccles, p. 480,) that the latter remark must be taken in a restricted sense, for, says he, "Calvinus loquitur de illa legatione quam Paulus interveniente Ecclesiae Antiochenae judicio ac moderamine cum Barnaba peragendam susceperat, *non de tota Apostolatus functione*, ad quam immediata prorsus auctoritate Christi e coelo consilium suum expromentis segregatus fuerat." If Barnabas then was an Apostle, in the sense in which Calderwood understands the term, it is plain, from what is stated in the text, that he had some of the principal qualifications for that office. But if he was called by that name, as I am disposed to think, merely because he was sent on the same long and important mission with Paul, then he was not an Apostle in the highest sense of the word, but only an Evangelist.

granted in the cause of appeale, by him from whom the appeale is made, are called (apostoli,) letters of dismissing or sending the cause to him to whom the appeale is made; Decrett. p. 2, Cause 2, Quaest. 6, cap. 24, sext. decret. lib. 2 "* And says the former, "it is noted by Theodoret and others of the fathers, that Epaphroditus, mentioned in this Epistle (that to the Philippians) as their messenger, ch. ii. 15, iv. 18, was also their bishop; though, I confess, the words, τον αποςολον ὑμων, your Apostle, do not prove it."† And while it is evident to any one who peruses the Second Epistle to the Corinthians, that the brethren referred to by Paul, ch. viii. 23, are represented as αποστολοι, as our translators were satisfied, merely because they were messengers;‡ so if we are to infer that there

* Synopsis Papismi, p 274.
† Preface to his Commentary upon the Epistle to the Philippians.
‡ Jeremy Taylor, I am aware, maintains the contrary in his Assertion of Episcopacy, p 19, and observes in proof of it, " They are not called the Apostles of these Churches, to witt, whose almes they carried, but simply εκκλησιων of the Churches, viz of their own, of which they were bishops. For if the title of Apostle had related to their mission from these Churches, it is unimaginable that there should be no terme of relation expressed " But how could it be necessary to distinguish them in that way, when it is said of one of them, v. 19, that he had been chosen of the Churches to travel with Paul and his companions with the grace or contribution which was " administered by the Apostle to the glory of the same Lord, and the declaration of their ready mind?" And as there is no term of relation coupled with εκκλησιων, if we are not guided by what is there mentioned, must not this writer's latter remark strike equally against his own interpretation? 2dly, He says, " It is very cleare, that although they did indeed carry the benevolence of the severall Churches, yet St. Paul, not these Churches, sent them. And we have sent with them our brother." &c. But how this is clear it is difficult to perceive, since it is stated in that verse that these Churches had actually " *chosen him and sent him.*" And certainly, if he was selected for that purpose by these Churches, nothing can be more natural, than that, according to the import of the word which was adopted by our translators, though they were zealous Episcopalians, he should be denominated, *on that account*, their *messenger* or απ,στολος. And 3dly, he remarks, " They are called Apostles of the Churches, not going from Corinth with the money, but before they came thither, from whence they were to be dispacht in legation to Jerusalem [If any enquire of Titus or the brethren, they are the Apostles of the Churches, and the glory of Christ.]" But as other Churches besides that of Corinth were sending to the relief of the saints at Jerusalem, and as these brethren had been appointed by them to carry their contributions before they came

were more Apostles than twelve with Barnabas and Paul, because there were some in the end of the first century " who said that they were Apostles, but were not," it will follow upon the same principle, that there must have been more Messiahs than one, because our Saviour foretold, that after he left the world, " there should arise false Christs and false prophets." Nor will it avail to tell us that Epaphroditus and these brethren are represented by the fathers as apostles and bishops, for they appeal in support of it to Scripture, where no such statements are to be met with. And when we consider that even Barnabas discovers in the three hundred and eighteen male servants who were circumcised by Abraham, a prediction that the Saviour was to die upon a cross,* that Irenaeus affirms

to Corinth, they might very properly be represented as their messengers or ἀπόστολοι, before they either arrived at that place, or left it for Jerusalem.

It is stated in short, by Downam, in his Defence of his Sermon, book iv. p 70, that " Apostoli, used absolutely, is a title of all embassadours sent from God, with authority apostolicall, though, κατ' ἐξοχην, (by way of eminence,) given to Paul and Barnabas, and the twelve Apostles " And he farther maintains, that though when used absolutely, it is a title of all such " embassadours—yet, when used with reference *to particular* churches, it doth signifie *their bishops* And in that sence, Epaphroditus is called the Apostle of the Philippians " But this distinction will not hold, for Paul reminds the Corinthians, (1 Cor ix. 2,) though he had the title of the Apostle, according to this author, κατ' ἐξοχην, " that if he was not an Apostle unto others, yet doubtless *he was to them*," which, according to this observation, would reduce him to be *merely the Bishop of Corinth.* See, too, Causabon, Exercit. 14, p. 313.

* " Learn all things more fully," says he in his Epistle. " Abraham, who first practised circumcision, looking forward through the Spirit to the Son of God, performed this rite, *receiving the mysterious information from three letters* For it says that Abraham circumcised three hundred and eighteen men of his house. What, then, was the instruction which was imparted to him by this? Observe, first, the eighteen, and then the three hundred. The eighteen are denoted by ιη, which point out Jesus And because the cross by which we were to obtain grace resembles T, which marks three hundred, therefore he adds three hundred. *By two letters, therefore he denotes Jesus, and by the third his cross.* He who has implanted within us the engrafted gift of his doctrine knows that *no one has ever learned from me a more certain truth,* but ye are worthy to receive it. Μαθετε ουν τεκνα, περι παντων," &c , p. 29, of Cotelerius's Apostolici Patres How unfortunate that Barnabas did not recollect that *Abraham could not speak Greek!* And how unaccountable that Clemens Alexandrinus,

that the spies who were concealed by Rahab, were the Father, Son, and Holy Ghost,* and that Origen interprets Balaam's ass, on which first the soothsayer rode, and afterwards Christ, as denoting the Church; the five kings of Canaan who were overcome by Joshua as the five senses, and the ten plagues of Egypt as the ten commandments, we will not feel surprised at their finding apostles and bishops in many parts of Scripture where no one else can discover them.† Nay, so vaguely is this term employed by the fathers, that they apply it indiscriminately to the first disciples of the Saviour,‡ to presbyters,§ *and*

and others of the fathers who are cited by Cotelerius in his notes on this passage, should have fallen into the same absurdity.

* "But she received," says he, "the spies who were exploring the whole land, and hid them with her, namely, the Father, the Son, and the Holy Ghost. Suscepit autem speculatores," &c. Lib. 4, cap. 37, p. 268, de Haeresibus.

† "And perhaps," says he, "this ass, that is, the Church, first carried Balaam, but now Christ. Et forte haec asina, id est Ecclesia," &c. 13th Homily on Numbers, tom. 1. p. 249.

"The five kings signify the five bodily senses, sight, hearing, taste, touch and smell. Quinque autem reges," &c. 11th Homily upon Joshua, tom. 1. p 346.

Consult moreover his account of the little ones of the daughter of Zion, in Psalm cxxxvii. 9. Treatise against Celsus, lib. 7, p. 731, of the 2d vol of his works.

Are these the men whose opinions we are to value so highly, and from whom according to Dr. Pusey, Mr. Newman, and Mr. Gladstone, we are to learn the doctrine, or government, or worship of the Christian Church?

‡ "The word Apostle," says Valesius, upon a passage in Eusebius's Eccles Hist., lib 1. cap. 13, p. 33, where it is applied to one of the seventy disciples, " must be understood with greater latitude, in like manner, as particular nations and cities called those persons Apostles from whom they first received the truth of the Gospel. For it is not bestowed merely upon the twelve, but *all their disciples, companions and assistants are in general denominated Apostles.* Sed Apostoli nomen his latius sumitur," &c. The whole of this long note is worthy of attention. See also Jerome on Gal. 1. 1, 2.

§ It is observed by Blondel in his Apologia pro Sentent. Hieronymi, p 85, that "by many of the ancients the seventy disciples," who are represented *as presbyters* by Bishop Gleig and other Episcopalians, "are denominated Apostles, and that *the seven deacons* are distinguished by that name by Caesareus Monachus," Dial. iv. resp. 292. Consult especially Theodoret upon 1 Cor. xii.; and says Origen, in his twenty-seventh Homily upon Numbers, tom. 1. p. 312, "But since our Lord and Saviour chose not only the twelve, but other

146   LETTERS ON

to females, such as the woman of Samaria, Thecla, and many others,* whom you will scarcely acknowledge as diocesan bishops, and yet, as far as we are influenced by their opinion, *all of them were Apostles.*

It is contended, however, by Hooker,† that the Apostles must have been bishops, because the office of Judas, which was conferred upon Matthias, is denominated in our translation of Acts, i. 20, "a bishopric," or, as it is expressed by Bilson,‡ "a bishopship." But even admitting this version, which was the basis of a similar argument to the Papist Furbiti, when he defended Episcopacy against Farel before the Council of Geneva, it will not authorize the conclusion that the Apostles were diocesan bishops, or that the latter are Apostles and their successors. Bishops and presbyters, as is conceded by Downam, *were for a considerable time* convertible expressions,§ and consequently the bishopric which is there attributed to Judas would be equivalent only to *the presbyterate.* Or though we should grant that it was superior, yet as the bishopric of the Apostles was universal and peculiar to themselves, it can furnish no argument for modern diocesan Episcopacy. But it is far from being evident that this translation is correct. The word διακονια occurs in the 17th verse, and

---

seventy-two, therefore we are informed that there were not only twelve fountains, but also seventy-two palm trees; and *they too are denominated Apostles,* as is plain from what is mentioned by Paul; for when speaking of the resurrection of the Saviour, he says that he appeared to the eleven, and afterwards to all the Apostles; in which he shows that there were others who were Apostles besides the twelve. Verum quloniam non solum illos duodecim," &c.

* Chrysostom, Theophylact and Oecumenius think that Junia, who is mentioned in Rom. xvi 7, was a woman, and that she is there called an Apostle. Theophylact, upon John iv. denominates the Samaritan woman αποστολος. And in the account of the martyrdom of Thecla, (Grabe's Spicilegium vol. 1 p 95,) she is distinguished by that name. See, too, Fronto Ducaeus upon Chrysostom, tom. i. p. 90. Women are denominated in Scripture, Rom xvi. 3-12, the helpers and fellow-labourers of the Apostles

† Ecclesiastical Polity, book 7, p 394.
‡ Perpetuall Government, p. 227.
§ Defense of his Sermon, book iii. p 64, and book iv. p. 16.

yet our translators have not rendered it "deaconship" as they ought to have done, on the principle on which they rendered the other word, but "ministry," lest Matthias should have appeared to be only a deacon. And they were equally bound to have rendered επισκοπη " office" or " ministry," and not " bishopric," though, from their leaning towards Episcopacy, they have adopted the latter term, with the view of representing the Apostle as a bishop. Such is the translation of it in the Syriac, Ethiopic, and one of the Arabic versions, where it is rendered " his ministry, ministerium ejus." And such is the version that has been given even by our translators of the passage in the Book of Psalms, which is quoted by Peter, Acts i. 20; for they render the Hebrew word פקדה, to which επισκοπη corresponds in the Septuagint, Ps. cix. 8, by the word *office;* and yet, merely to serve an end, they render the latter term in the Acts by the word " bishopric."*
Nay, they give a similar version of the very same word in Numbers, iv. 16, though the expression in the Septuagint be επισκοπη. And this version agrees better with the authority which was possessed by Judas, whose office, according to Peter, was to be transferred to Matthias, for as was demanded by Farel, " *if Judas was a bishop where was his bishopric?*"† He was only a presbyter, according to Bishop Gleig; and according to Archbishop Potter but a deacon; and nothing, of course, could be more absurd than to represent him as a diocesan bishop. But if the term επισκοπη in the Acts, as in the corresponding passage in the Psalms, be rendered office, and not bishopric, the argument of Hooker, or rather of Bishop

* As it was precisely the office of Doeg, or the unbeliever, who is referred to in Ps. cix 8, that his successor was to take, so the same thing holds true as to the office of Judas, which was bestowed on Matthias, though it might be enlarged in respect of authority to the latter.

† " Si Judas etoit Eveque, ou son Eveche?" Ruchat's Histoire de la Reformation de la Suisse, tom. v. p. 115. The whole of his short but spirited refutation of Episcopacy, which took place before the Council of Geneva, *before Calvin was known in that city,* is deserving of attention.

Gauden, the author of the three spurious books of the Polity, necessarily falls.

If it be maintained with Bilson, that whatever may be the meaning of this passage, "all the fathers with one mouth affirme the Apostles both might bee, and were bishops,"* I answer with Valesius, that when they are so denominated, it is not to be strictly understood.† Nay, it is observed by Whitaker, that *"it almost borders on insanity, to assert that Peter, or any other of the Apostles, was properly a bishop,* for they possessed the very highest ecclesiastical authority, and *the office of a bishop is nothing to that of an apostle."*‡ And says Dr. Barrow, " *The office of an apostle and a bishop are not in their nature well consistent:* For the apostleship is an extraordinary office, charged with the instruction and *government of the whole world.* Episcopacy is an ordinary standing charge *affixed to one place.* Now, he that hath such a general care can hardly discharge such a particular office, and he that is fixed to so particular an attendance, can hardly look well to so general a charge. A disparagement to the apostolical ministry for him (Peter) to take upon him the Bishoprick of Rome, *as if the King should become mayor of London*—as if the Bishop of London should be vicar of Pancrass."§ When the fathers, therefore, speak of the Apostles as bishops, they can mean merely, that wherever they came they exercised the authority which *was latterly assumed by bishops,* but which belonged every where to the apostolic office; and in this sense of their words, the Apostles might exercise that authority in ten, twenty, or fifty places, and *yet they had not as many bishoprics.* Nay, this authority might be exercised

* Perpetuall Government, p 226.

† "The Apostles," says he, in his Notes on Eusebius, Eccles. Hist. book 3, cap. 14, " were extraordinary ministers, and *were not reckoned in the number of bishops.* Apostoli vero extra ordinem erant," &c.

‡ "Hoc enim non multum distat ab insania dicere Petrum fuisse proprie Episcopum, aut reliquos Apostolos. Summam enim ministerii authoritatem habuerunt. Munus Episcopi nihil est ad munus Apostolicum." De Pontif., Quaest 2, cap. 15.

§ Pope's Supremacy, p 120, 121.

by more than one of them at once* in the very same place, as in the case of Paul and Peter at Rome.† And it is an established principle among Episcopalians, that there cannot be more than a single bishop in one city. No argument, accordingly, can be drawn from these expressions of the fathers to prove that the Apostles were diocesan bishops.

But it is asserted by Bishop Gleig, and many of the Episcopalians of former times, that St. James at least must have been a bishop of this description, because " he is expressly said by Hegesippus, (*apud* Euseb. lib. ii. cap. 23,) to have been constituted Bishop of Jerusalem by the Apostles. St. Ignatius, who suffered martyrdom in the year 107, affirms (Epist. ad Trall.) that St. Stephen was deacon to St. James; and Clement of Alexandria, who flourished about the year 192, is quoted by Eusebius, (lib. ii. cap. 1,) as saying, that immediately after the assumption of Christ, Peter, James and John, though they had been highest in favour with their Divine Master, did not contend for the honour of presiding over the Church of Jerusalem, but with the rest of the Apostles chose James the Just to be bishop of that Church. In the fourth century we find Jerome, a man of great learning and research, affirming, (de Script. Eccles.) that immediately after the passion of our Lord, St. James was constituted Bishop of Jerusalem by the Apostles; and St. Cyril, who was himself bishop of that Church in the year 350, and therefore an authentic witness of its records, expressly says, Catech. 16, that St. James was the first bishop of that city."‡

Now, upon this I would remark,

1. That it is exceedingly questionable whether he

---

* Bilson, in his Perpetuall Government, p. 206, affirms, that Peter was Bishop, first of Antioch, and afterwards of Rome, in which he is supported by a number of the fathers; and the author of the Chronicon Alexandrinum, quoted by Cotelerius on the Apostolic Constitutions, lib. 7, cap 46, assigns to him *the see of Jerusalem* before it was committed to James. But upon the principle stated above, he and his brethren must have had many bishoprics.

† Eusebii Eccles Hist. lib. iii. cap. 1, lib. iv. cap. 1.

‡ Anti-Jacobin, vol. 9.

was out of the twelve, or of the seventy disciples. We are informed of a James by Eusebius, (Eccles. Hist. book 1. ch. 12,) " who was one of the seventy, and of the brethren of our Lord." And it is observed by Valesius on the place, that " many of the ancients were of opinion that the James who was the first Bishop of Jerusalem was not one of the twelve, but of the seventy: Thus, Gregory Nyssene, in his second Oration upon the Resurrection of Christ; Clemens, in the second Book of his Constitutions, ch. 59, and in the first Book of his Recognitions, near the end, p. 20; Dorotheus, in his Book upon the Apostles and Disciples of the Lord, and Michael Glycas, in the third part of his Annals." And he adds, " Paul seems to favour this opinion in his Epistle to the Corinthians, for in his enumeration of those to whom the Saviour appeared after he rose from the dead, after mentioning the twelve Apostles, and five hundred others, he subjoins, afterwards he was seen *by James and the other Apostles.* Paul therefore distinguishes James from the twelve Apostles, and in this sense Cyril of Jerusalem (Catech. 4 and 14,) (to whom Bishop Gleig ascribes an opposite opinion erroneously,) understood this passage of St. Paul."* But if James was only one of the seventy, and consequently but a presbyter, it weakens exceedingly the credibility of the story, for there are few, I presume, who will believe that such an inferior minister would be raised to an honour, which, according to the third of the authors quoted by the Bishop, was superior to what was possessed *by the chief of the Apostles.*

But granting, even, that he was an Apostle, I observe, in the second place, that the authorities on which this report is delivered are unworthy of credit.

The first of them is a fragment of Hegesippus, which has been preserved by Eusebius, (Eccles. Hist. book 11. chap. 23,) but which, though often quoted by Epis-

* " Multi quippe ex veteribus Jacobum fratrem Domini," &c. The same, too, was the opinion of the author of the Apostolic Constitutions, lib 6, cap. 12, and lib. 8, cap 4, as well as of Hammond and Bishop Taylor.

copalians, is undeserving of attention. It tells us, indeed, that "he received the government of the Church of Jerusalem *along* with the Apostles;"* but adds at the same time, that "*he alone could enter into the Holy of Holies*," though he was not the high-priest; "that he was buried near the Temple," though the Jews buried only without the gates of their cities;—and that "his tomb was still standing in the second century," though not a stone of Jerusalem was left standing upon another after it was taken by the Romans. If it blunder, however, as to these and other important particulars which are pointed out at length by Scaliger† and Valesius,‡ it must be as unworthy of our belief as to what it says about the former, were it susceptible of the interpretation which has been put upon it by the Bishop. And if its leading authority be overthrown, the others must fall with it.

The second of his quotations is not to be found in the editions of Ignatius by Vossius or Usher, but only in a corrupt edition, which every one who is beyond a sciolist in these matters *knows to be spurious!* But how the Bishop, who has been held out as a man of the highest attainments in professional learning, and who talks so contemptuously of the acquirements of his opponents, could have fallen into this mistake I cannot understand; and can account for it only on the supposition, that he copied it from the works of some of the older Episcopalians, from whom, in common with many of his brethren in the present day, he has often copied his arguments without due examination of his authorities, and being unacquainted with Ignatius, though he refers to him frequently, could not detect the error.§

* It is observed by Salmasius, in his Walo Messalinus, p. 193, that, even allowing this passage to have all the credibility which could be desired, it merely affirms that he received the government of this Church *with*, and not *from*, the Apostles, μετὰ τῶν ἀποστόλων, and that the same also are the readings of Theophanes and Rufinus.

† Animadv. in Eusebii Chronol p. 178.

‡ Examine especially what he says about the contradiction between Hegesippus and Josephus.

§ It is remarkable that Bishop Tomline, who boasted of having examined *more than sixty volumes of the Fathers*, when preparing his

The third of his authorities contains its own refutation, for if Peter, James and John were previously Apostles, and consequently superior to any local bishop, how can it be said that they did not "contend, ἐπιδικαζεσθαι," or, as it is translated by Downam,* " did not arrogate to themselves the honour of being Bishop of Jerusalem, but resigned it to James the Just?" Would not this, as is observed by Dr. Barrow upon another occasion, when contending with the Papists, be like the humility of a sovereign prince, who would not be solicitous about the honour of being made "a justice of the peace?"† or, as it is expressed by Sutclive, would it not be like the lowliness of a king, "who was not ambitious of being created a questor, or any other inferior magistrate?"‡ And if it be urged with Downam that herein James differed from the rest, for to him at the first, before their dispersion, the Church of Jerusalem was assigned, while the others did not receive their provinces till afterwards, "neither did he travaile, as the rest, from one country to another, being not confined to any one province, and whereas they having planted Churches, when they saw their time, committed the same to certain bishops, yet James, abiding all his time at Jerusalem, committed that Church to no other,"§ I answer, it has been proved already that the whole of this story about the division of provinces is fabulous; and even those who believe it cannot inform us when the division took place, Photius affirming that James was ordained by the Saviour,‖ and Nicephorus Callistus that he obtained his diocese, first from the Saviour, and afterwards, as some report, from the Apostles.¶ And if Paul be right when he

Refutation of Calvinism, quotes a passage also from the spurious Ignatius, p. 288. Did he read by deputy?
* Defense of his Sermon, lib. iv p. 60.
† Pope's Supremacy, p. 84.
‡ "Num rex creari solet quaestor," &c. De Pontif. lib. ii. cap 1.
§ Defense of his Sermon, lib. iv. p 57, 58.
‖ Epist. 117, p. 158.
¶ Lib. ii p. 196. Eusebius candidly acknowledges, Eccles. Hist., lib. iv. cap. 5, (though he lived only in the fourth century,) that he had not been able to discover how long James, and a number of the

appeals to his abundant labours and extensive travels, (2 Cor. xi. &c.) as a proof that "he was not a whit behind the very chiefest Apostles;" and if the present honour, as well as future reward of ministers of every order will be proportioned to their labours, (1 Cor. iii. 8, &c.) the second and third of these reasons must be completely nugatory. I shall only add, that as Stillingfleet observes, "the power of James was of the same nature with that of the Apostles themselves. And who," he demands, "*will go about to degrade them so much as to reduce them to the office of ordinary bishops?* James, in all probability, did exercise his apostleship *the most at Jerusalem*, where by the Scriptures we find him resident; and from hence the Church afterwards, because of his not travelling abroad as the other Apostles did, *according to the language of their own times*, fixed the title of bishop upon him."* The latter observation presents a satisfactory

bishops of Jerusalem who succeeded him, were in possession of their sees, and if so, can we depend on the testimony of such writers as affording satisfactory evidence that the alleged apostolical succession was never broken in the course of *eighteen hundred years*?

* Irenicum, p. 321. The passage, moreover, which is quoted by Bishop Gleig from Jerome's Catalogus Scriptorum Ecclesiasticorum, *is not genuine*, for it is observed by Erasmus in his notes upon that work, as well as by Dr. Cave in his account of Jerome, (Hist. Literar., p. 221,) that the lives of James and of Simon the Canaanite, *were added to it by some later author!* Here then we have another very humiliating proof of the Bishop's copying from some preceding writer, and of the inaccuracy with which he was chargeable amidst all his apparent learning. And as to the passage from Epiphanius, it cannot influence a single individual possessed of ordinary powers of reflection, for he tells us in Haeres. Nazaraeorum, that James was accustomed *to wear a plate of gold upon his forehead*,—a fiction like that which is related by Eusebius, (Eccles. Hist. lib. v. cap. 24,) respecting the Apostle John, and which illustrates sufficiently the value of his testimony.

Boyd, also, in his Treatise on Episcopacy and Presbytery, p. 93, (and he makes great pretensions to extensive and accurate investigation into his authorities,) falls into the same blunder with Bishop Gleig, in attributing this part of the "Treatise of Ecclesiastical Writers" to Jerome And he quotes, apparently *with a firm conviction of its truth*, a report mentioned by Chrysostom, of "the Saviour *having ordained*, (I presume with the imposition of hands,) and appointed his brother James the first bishop of Jerusalem," *before he ascended to heaven!* p 92.

and natural reply to the later authorities referred to by the Bishop and other defenders of your ecclesiastical polity; and I trust it will appear from what is stated below, that their scriptural arguments in support of the Episcopacy of James are equally inconclusive.*

It is observed by Downam, that "when the Apostles ceased to travaile in their olde days and rested in some chief citie where they had laboured, they were reputed bishops of that place, though some of them perhaps were not properly bishops."† But if their commission as Apostles still remained to them, as will scarcely be denied, it is impossible to imagine any good reason why even a single individual among them could then be degraded from his office, and *reduced to the rank of a bishop*, merely because, from the infirmities of age, he was less able to travel at large and perform its duties. It is remarked by Bilson, that "though the Apostles were more than bishops, yet they were more also than presbyters; and yet Saint Peter could tell how to speake, when hee called himselfe συμπρεσβυτερος, a presbyter as well as others."‡ He has failed, however, to show that any of the Apostles ever called himself συνεπισκοπος, or *a diocesan bishop, as well as other diocesan bishops;* or that such an order of ministers was appointed, and was included, like all other inferior orders, in the

---

* If James, as is observed by Stillingfleet, exercised his apostleship principally at Jerusalem, for a variety of reasons, and commonly resided there, it will explain the whole of the Scriptures which have been quoted by Episcopalians to prove that he was merely a bishop, without reducing him to that order. "And who knows not," says Augustine, "that *the dignity of an apostle is to be preferred to that of any bishop?* Quis nescit istum Apostolatus principatum cuilibet Episcopatui praeferendum?" (De Baptismo, lib. ii. cap 1.) It will account, in particular, for the way in which he is spoken of, Acts xii. 17, xxi. 18; Gal. ii. 12. And when he said, Acts xv 19, "διο εγω κρινω, wherefore my sentence is," he evidently laid claim to no more power than was exercised by Peter or any other member of the Council, for "the decrees" of the Council are denominated not merely the decrees of James, but "of the Apostles and Elders which were at Jerusalem." Acts xvi. 4.

† Defense of his Sermon, lib iv p. 57.
‡ Perpetuall Government, p. 227.

apostolate, and consequently, it is not an argument in point. And it is stated by the same prelate, that " bishops are fastened to one place, not by the force of their name, but by the order of the Holy Ghost, who sent Apostles to oversee many places, and settled pastors to oversee one. And, therefore, the Apostles were bishops, and more than bishops, even as John was more than a prophet, and yet a prophet."* But it is plain, that if we are to have bishops in the present day, *because the Apostles were bishops, as far as this argument is concerned,* their episcopate must resemble that of the Apostles. The Apostles, however, were not confined to any particular place for the exercise of their authority, but might officiate not only in fifty or a hundred places, but in every quarter of the world. And as no such power could be conceded either to your bishops or to any other, the argument which has been founded on the extraordinary authority conferred on the Apostles, when they founded the Church, for similar power throughout future ages to diocesan bishops, an order of ministers never mentioned in Scripture, totally fails, and you are not entitled to maintain, that where that order does not exist, there can be neither Church, nor ministry, nor any hope of salvation.†

I remain, Reverend sir,

Yours, &c.

* Perpetuall Government, p. 227.

† Even Bellarmine, though a Papist makes the following candid statement of the difference between apostles and bishops. " Bishops," says he, " have no part of the true apostolic authority. *Apostles could preach and found churches in every part of the world*, as appears from the last chapters of Matthew and Mark. Bishops cannot do this. Apostles, as all confess, could write canonical Epistles. Bishops cannot do this. Apostles had the gift of tongues and the power of working miracles This does not belong to bishops. Apostles *had jurisdiction over the whole Church.* This is not possessed by bishops Nullam habent episcopi partem verae Apostolicae auctoritatis," &c. De Pontif. Roman., lib iv. cap. 25.

156

LETTER XII.

Bishop Bilson represents the argument for Episcopacy, from the powers conferred on Timothy and Titus, as "the main erection of the Episcopal cause," and Bishop Hall declares, that if it fails "he will yield the cause, and confess that he has lost his senses"—None of the Fathers during *the first three centuries* represent them as diocesan bishops, and Willet, Stillingfleet, and Bishop Bridges acknowledge them to have been extraordinary ministers, or Evangelists—Nature of the office of Evangelists, as illustrated by Scripture and the writings of the Fathers—Different from that of diocesan bishops, and superior to it—Diocesan bishops never said to have been associated with Evangelists or Apostles in any act of jurisdiction or government, though Presbyters repeatedly took part with them in such acts—No notice of diocesan bishops as an order existing in their days—The argument in every point of view inconclusive

REVEREND SIR,—The next argument in support of diocesan Episcopacy is derived from the powers which are represented as having been committed to Timothy and Titus; and from the terms in which it is mentioned by two of the most eminent and learned of your prelates, it would seem that they attached to it the very highest importance, and considered it as irresistible. " This, indeed," said Bilson, " is *the main erection* of the Episcopal power and function, if our proofes drawn from these ministers stand, or subversion, if your answere be good. For if this faile, wel may bishops claime their authoritie by the custome of the Church; *by any divine precept expressed in the Scriptures* they cannot."* And said Bishop Hall, " I demand what is it that it stood upon, but these two particulars, the especiall power of ordination, and power of the ruling and censuring of presbyters; and if these two be not clear in the charge of the Apostle to these two bishops, one of Crete, the other of Ephesus, I shall yield the cause, and confess to want my senses."† I propose, accordingly, to examine "this main erection of the Episcopal function," the overthrow of which, if I shall succeed in accomplishing it, ought to lead you to abandon that lofty claim of divine

* Perpetuall Government, chap xiv. p. 300.
† Hall's Episcopacy by Divine Right, book 2, p. 26.

right for your ecclesiastical polity which you have built upon it; and if you possess the candour of the last of these prelates, "to yield the cause," though you should not, like him, if you maintain it any longer, "admit that you would want your senses."

This argument, then, (and as I am anxious to do it justice, I have selected the most comprehensive statement of it that I have met with, namely, that by Bishop Downam,) has been proposed in the following terms:

"But we are also," says he, "to show the places *where*, and the *persons whom* the Apostles ordained bishops, and first out of the Scriptures. For by the Epistles of St. Paul to Timothe and Titus, it is apparent that hee had ordained Timothe Bishop of Ephesus, and Titus of Creet; the Epistles themselves being the verie patterns and precedents of the episcopall function. For, as the Apostle had committed unto them episcopall authoritie, both in respect of ordination and jurisdiction, which in the Epistles is pre-supposed, so doth he by those Epistles informe them, and in them all bishops, how to exercise their function. *First*, in respect of ordination, as Tit. i. 5; I left thee in Creet, that thou shouldst ordaine presbyters in every citie, as I appointed thee. 1 Tim. v. 22, Impose hands hastily on no man; neither be partaker of other men's sinnes. *Secondly*, in regard of jurisdiction, not onely over the people, but also over the presbyters; appointing them to be both guides and censurers of their doctrine, as 1 Tim. i. 3, I required thee to continue in Ephesus, that thou shouldest commaund some that they teach no strange doctrine, neither that they attend to fables, &c. 2 Tim. ii. 16; Tit. i. 10–11, iii. 9; and also judges of their person and conversation, as 1 Tim. v. 19, 20, 21, Against a presbyter receive not an accusation, but under two or three witnesses," &c.*

Now, upon this I would remark, in the *first* place, that even admitting their interpretation of the different passages contained in this extract, they have no right

* Sermon on the Function of Bishops, p. 72–74.

to claim similar powers to *ordinary* ministers, like diocesan bishops, in the present day, unless they had proved that Timothy and Titus were only ordinary ministers of the very same order, and were to be succeeded by others till the end of the world. It is this which constitutes the very strength of the argument, and as it has never yet been proved, but only taken for granted, and as I think that the contrary is established by evidence which cannot be controverted, the argument fails. You profess to respect the opinions of the fathers, and I challenge you to produce a single passage from the writings of any of them, during *the first three centuries*, in which they say that they consider them to have been bishops. Dr. Whitby could not do it,* and I have been equally unsuccessful, and I shall wait till I see whether you are more fortunate. Chrysostom, in a passage which is quoted from him by Mocket, Archbishop Abbot's chaplain, acknowledges that they were evangelists.† Such, too, was the opinion of Willet, who says, "It is most like that Timothie had the place and calling of an evangelist, whose office was to *second the Apostles into their ministerie, and to water that which the Apostles had planted.*"‡ "They were but very few," says Stillingfleet, "and those in probability not the ablest, who were left at home to take care of the spoil; the strongest and ablest, like commanders in an army, were not settled in any troop, but went up and down, from this company to that, to order them and draw them forth; and while they were, they had the chief authority among them, but as commanders of the army, and not as officers of the troop. Such were evangelists, who were sent sometimes into this country, to put the churches in order there, sometimes into another; but wherever they were, *they acted as evangelists, and not as fixed officers.* And such were Timothy and Titus, notwithstanding all the opposition made to it, as will appear to any that will take an impartial sur-

* Preface to the Epistle to Titus.
† Tractat. de Politia Anglican.
‡ Append. to the 5th General Controv., Quest. 3.

vey of the arguments on both sides."* And says Bishop Bridges, whom no one will suspect of a leaning to Presbyterianism, "The same Philip is called an Evangelist; so was Timothie; 2 Tim. iv. 5. Such was Titus, Silas, and manie other. *This office also, with the order of the Apostles, is expired, and hath no place.* Likewise, as wee doo plainlie see, that the gifts of healing, of powers or miracles, and of diverse toongs, have long since ceased in the Church; *so the offices of them which were grounded upon these gifts must also cease, and be determined.*"† And what is still more important, such, likewise, is the express declaration of Scripture, for Paul enjoins Timothy, (2 Tim. iv. 5,) to "do the work of an evangelist;" and it is evident that the duties which he prescribes to him are the same with those which were assigned to Titus.

The office of an Evangelist was the third of the three great extraordinary offices which were instituted by the Redeemer, for founding and organizing the primitive Church, and which are represented by Paul, (Eph. iv. 11,) as distinct from that of the ordinary standing ministry, which was to be occupied by pastors and teachers. Those who were invested with the former office, though properly the helpers or assistants of the Apostles, whose function was to cease with that of their masters, approached very nearly to the latter in rank, acted as their substitutes on many occasions, and when executing their commands, seem to have been permitted to exercise almost equal authority. Hence, while they are described by Tertullian as "apostolic men,"‡ and by Jerome as "the sons of the Apostles,"§ Augustine designates them very happily by a most expressive name, signifying literally, "the substitutes of the Apostles, who were almost equal to them."‖ Sometimes, as in the case

* Irenicum, p. 340.
† Defence of the Government of the Church of England, book i. p. 68.
‡ Lib. 4, Advers. Mar. " Viri Apostolici "
§ Filii Apostolorum ; Comment in Iesai. cap. 65.
‖ Suppares Apostolis ; Sermo 146, de Tempore.

of Timothy, they appear to have received an immediate and supernatural call; for Paul refers to "the prophecies which went before respecting him;" intimating, probably, that it was the will of God he should be appointed to his office, as the Holy Ghost said to the prophets and teachers at Antioch, "Separate me Barnabas and Paul for the work whereunto I have called them." We know, too, that they were endowed with the power of working miracles, for it is mentioned, (Acts viii. 6–8,) that "the Samaritans' with one accord gave heed unto those things which Philip (the Evangelist) spake, hearing and seeing the miracles which he did. For unclean spirits, crying with loud voice, came out of many that were possessed with them; and many taken with palsies, and that were lame, were healed. And there was great joy in that city." And we have reason to believe, that the same supernatural gifts which were possessed by him were communicated to the rest of the evangelists; in addition to which, Bilson admits, that in common with the prophets, they "had these two (other) gifts, the revealing of secrets, and discerning of spirits, (though in lesse measure than the Apostles,) which served chiefly to distinguish who were fit or unfit for the service of Christ's Church."* Sometimes, as in the case of Philip, when he preached in Samaria, they came *before* the Apostles, and founded churches, and the Apostles succeeded them, and organized these

* "Nam cum primum ecclesiae plantarentur," says Bilson, in the Latin translation of his Treatise on Church Government, p 125, "etiam illi qui credebant in divinis Scripturis et mysteriis adeo tyrones fuerunt et rudes ut ad populum docendum et regendum nulli fuerint idonei, nisi qui Apostoli, per manuum suarum impositionem variis Spiritus Sancti donis instruerent, et ad illud munus exequendum aptos efficerent; in Samaria recens ad fidem conversa prorsus ad Evangelii praedicationem et ecclesiae gubernationem inermes et inepti fuerunt donec Petrus et Joannes eorum aliquos Spiritus Sancti virtute, per manuum impositionem donantes alios prophetas, alios pastores, alios doctores, mirabiliter effecerant; quemque donis ad functionem necessariis adornantes." So little did he see in this passage, which evidently does not refer to confirmation, to warrant that rite which none of the Apostles or of the ministers of the Apostolic Church ever performed, but which is one of those human inventions that are practised in the Scottish and English Episcopalian Churches.

churches; and as the last writer admits, laid their hands on some of the converts, not to confirm them, as Episcopalians assert, but to communicate to them spiritual gifts, that they might be qualified immediately for becoming the pastors of these churches.* And at other times evangelists came *after* the Apostles; and when the latter had planted, the former, as in the case of Apollos and Titus, " watered and set in order the things which were wanting, ordaining elders in every city." Such is the view which was presented of their office in the New Testament, and it is confirmed by a well-known passage of Eusebius. " At the same time," says he, "flourished Quadratus, who, together with the daughters of Philip, was famous for the gift of prophecy, and besides them, many others who occupy the principal place among the successors of the Apostles. These persons being the venerable disciples of such men, *built up the churches in every place of which the foundation had been laid by the Apostles*, promoting more and more the preaching of the Gospel, and scattering through the world the salutary seed of the kingdom of heaven. For many of the disciples of that period, whose minds were inflamed by the word with the most ardent attachment to the true philosophy, fulfilling the commandment of their Saviour, divided their substance among the poor, and having been sent forth with authority, performed the office of evangelists to those who had never heard the word of faith, being most desirous to preach Christ unto them, and to deliver to them the writings of the divine Gospels. These men having laid the foundations of the faith in some remote places, having ordained also others to be pastors over them, and *having committed to their care the cultivation of what they had themselves begun, hastened to other countries and nations*, being accompanied by the grace and power of God."† It seems impossible, therefore, to deny that the office of evangelists was

* See preceding note.
† " Των δε κατα τουτους διαλαμψαντων και Κοδρατος," &c. Eccles. Hist., lib. iii. cap. 37.

extraordinary and temporary, like that of the Apostles, and not only different from, but greatly superior to that of modern diocesan bishops. And it is certainly contrary to all the acknowledged rules of reasoning to found an argument *on the powers of ministers of a higher order*, (the Suppares Apostolorum,) who were richly endowed with supernatural gifts, and who were able to perform miraculous works, *for similar powers to inferior ministers*, who are destitute of the one, and who cannot perform the other,—ministers too, of an order to which there is no allusion in the Epistles which are addressed to Timothy and Titus, or in any other part of the sacred volume, and who in no sense of the word, when it is used *as a distinctive official title*, can be called evangelists.

I will be told, however, by Bishop Gleig, that "the word ευαγγελιςης, rendered an evangelist, is unquestionably derived from ευαγγελιζω; but that word, says Dr. Campbell, relates to *the first* intimation that is given to a person or people, that is, when the subject may be properly called *news*. Thus, in the Acts, it is frequently used for expressing *the first publication* of the Gospel in a city, or a village, or amongst a particular people. If this be essential to the radical import of the verb, of which, indeed, there can be no doubt, then it follows that an *evangelist*, considered as a distinct character, could only be one, whether apostle, elder, deacon or layman, who *first* carried the glad tidings of the Gospel to an individual or a people. Hence it is that of the seven deacons none is called an evangelist but Philip, because he alone of the whole number is mentioned as having carried the glad tidings of the Gospel beyond the limits of Judea, within which those tidings were first told by Christ and his Apostles. Hence, too, it appears, that those whom St. Paul says Christ, after his resurrection, *gave as evangelists* for the work of the ministry, must have been men miraculously inspired with the knowledge of the Gospel, and impelled by the same heavenly impulse to communicate that knowledge to those to whom it was *news*. But in this sense Timothy and

Titus could not be evangelists to the Churches of Ephesus and Crete, because St. Paul had preached the Gospel in those churches before them, and had even ordained presbyters in the Church of Ephesus."*

Now, upon this I would remark, that according to the principle which is here laid down, (and it is only an old evasion of our reply to the argument for diocesan Episcopacy from the powers committed to Timothy and Titus,) an evangelist was not a distinct office-bearer intrusted with a particular function in the primitive Church, but *any one* who first made known the Gospel in a city or country, whether it was a *woman*, or a *layman*, or a deacon, or a presbyter, or a prophet, or an Apostle. Nay, *the angels must have been evangelists*, when they brought the glad tidings to the shepherds of Bethlehem; and Andrew and Philip, even *before they were baptized*, when they brought them to Peter and Nathanael; and *the Samaritan woman*, when she communicated them to her townsmen. Nothing, however, can be more inconsistent than this with the description which is given of an evangelist, either in Scripture or in the writings of the fathers. In the former, as has been mentioned, he is represented as an extraordinary minister, *with a particular office*, distinct from that of any other minister; for, says Paul, Eph. iv. 11, "he gave *some*, apostles, *some*, prophets, *some*, evanlists, and *some*, pastors and teachers." But how he could be said to have given only *some* to be evangelists, if they did not constitute a separate *order*, and *if every minister of every order* in that early age, and every minister throughout future ages, and even every man, and woman, and child, who first made known these glad tidings to a single individual, was really an evangelist, and performed all that was meant by that word, as Downam and Bishop Gleig and others contend, I cannot comprehend. And how could Saravia blunder so egregiously, as to infer from this passage, that "there were distinct orders among the ministers

* Ninth vol. of the Anti-Jacobin Review.

of the Gospel, the Apostles being prophets, evangelists, teachers and pastors; and the evangelists being prophets, pastors and teachers," &c.* Philip is called an evangelist, not *immediately after he preached the Gospel in Samaria*, but long afterwards, Acts xxi. 8; and not because he was the first who preached the Gospel in that city, but because "having used the office of a deacon well, he obtained for himself a good degree," and was promoted to the office of an evangelist. Besides, as evangelists not only sometimes went before the Apostles, and were the first who preached the Gospel in a place; but as Willet and Eusebius state, sometimes also came *after* them, like Apollos, (1 Cor. iii. 6,) "and seconded them in their ministerie, watering that which they had planted," or organizing the churches which they had founded, and "setting in order the things which were wanting," the latter was a part of the office of an evangelist, which Timothy and Titus could do; and which office, in all its parts, Timothy was expressly enjoined to perform; 2 Tim. iv. 4. This objection, therefore, to the order of extraordinary early ministers, to which we assign these distinguished fellow-labourers of the Apostles, is utterly groundless. And if they are to be ranked among the evangelists, no claim can be urged from the powers which they exercised in their high office for similar powers to diocesan bishops, who are never said to have been associated with them while they lived, either in ordination or jurisdiction, and who are never represented as the ministers who were to succeed them in the exercise of their authority after they left the world.

It is plain also from the fact, that neither Timothy nor Titus was confined to any particular diocese, but was constantly employed in travelling with the Apostles and assisting them in their labours, or in planting or watering different churches, that they were evangelists and not bishops.

* Gradus Ministror. Evangel. consec. ita distinctos fuisse," &c. ad. cap. i. Bez. de divers. grad. Minist. Evangel.

"Episcopacy," says Dr. Barrow, "is an ordinary standing charge, *affixed to one standing place, and requiring a special attendance there.** But evangelists, as is stated by Eusebius, after having founded or organized churches in one place, hastened to another. It is impossible, accordingly, to read what is said of Timothy and Titus in the New Testament, without perceiving that they were evangelists, for they had no more any fixed and settled charge than the Apostles themselves, but were constantly moving from place to place. Thus, it is mentioned respecting Timothy, that as soon as he was ordained to the ministry, (Acts xvi.) he travelled with Paul through Phrygia, Galatia, Asia and Mysia, from which they came to Philippi, and after remaining there for a time he was sent to Corinth, where he preached to that Church, (2 Cor. 1. 19,) and then returned to the Apostle. They went together from Philippi to Thessalonica and Berea; and Paul having proceeded to Athens, Timothy soon followed him, and was by and by despatched again to Thessalonica, to confirm and water the Church in that city. Michaelis thinks that the Apostle wrote his first Epistle to him when he left him at Ephesus, after he himself was obliged to leave it, (Acts xix.) to re-establish order in that Church, to fill the ecclesiastical offices, and to oppose the false teachers;" and he considers it as evident from what is mentioned in the third chapter, that "no bishops had then been appointed among them." This took place when Timothy was young, (1 Tim. iv. 12,) or, according to the opinion of the most eminent critics, when he was about twenty-six or twenty-seven years of age, and several years before the last interview of the Apostle with the presbyters of Ephesus, (Acts xx.) whom he addresses as bishops, v. 28, without representing them as under the Episcopate of Timothy. And as not a word is said of his being the Bishop of Ephesus, or of his being bound to reside there; so his stay there was short, for he accompanied Paul to Jerusalem, followed him to Rome, (Colos. 1. 1,) was imprisoned there, and

* Pope's Supremacy, p. 82.

liberated shortly before the Apostle was liberated, (Heb. xiii. 23,) from which he proceeded very probably to Philippi. And the same observation applies to Titus, whose residence in Crete appears to have been short; for Paul tells him, (ch. iii. 12,) that "when he sent Tychicus or Artemas to him, he wished him to come to him to Nicopolis," and who laboured also among the Churches in Macedonia and Dalmatia, as well as at Rome and Corinth.* If the scene, however, of the labours of these ministers changed so frequently, and if they were constantly moved from place to place at the pleasure of the Apostles, and as Hilary expresses it in his own most apposite language, " had no cathedral seat, evangelizabant sine cathedra," what must we think of this *main erection of diocesan Episcopacy*, since it is evident from these facts that Timothy and Titus were not bishops, but were among the chief of the evangelists?

It has been asserted, I am aware, by Downman, that, " although upon special and extraordinary occasions they were by the Apostles called to other places, as his or the Churches' necessity required; yet Ephesus and Crete were the place of their ordinary residence, where they both lived and died. Paul," says he, " willeth Timothe, (1 Tim. 1. 3,) προσμειναι, permanere, (the word is significant,) to abide still, or to continue at Ephesus; and he left Titus not to redresse things in Creet for a brunt, and so to come away, but that he shuld (Tit. 1. 5,) επιδιωρθωσαι continue in reparasing what should be amisse, and still keep that Church as it were in reparation."† But nothing can be deduced from the term επιδιωρθωσαι which will warrant that statement; for, as is acknowledged by Anselm of Canterbury, it denotes merely that he was to perfect the organizing of the Churches which had been begun by Paul;‡ and the way in which he was to do this was

* 2 Cor. vii. 5, 6; 2 Tim. iv. 10; 2 Cor. vii. 13, 15; viii. 6, 12, 18.
† Sermon, p. 76.
‡ " At ea inquit, quae desunt corrigas, id est, ut *ea quae a me correcta sunt*, et necdum ad plenam veri lineam sunt redacta a te corrigantur, et normam aequalitatis recipiant."

by "ordaining presbyters in every city." And not a word is to be met with about his continuing there *any longer;* and for any thing that is afterwards recorded respecting him, one might as consistently conclude with Aquinas, from 2 Tim. iv. 10, that he was *Bishop of Dalmatia,* as infer from this passage, with modern Episcopalians, that he was *Bishop or Archbishop of Crete.* And as to the term προσμειναι, 1 Tim. i. 3, so far from proving that Timothy was to reside permanently at Ephesus, it does not furnish the smallest ground for that assertion. It signifies in general to remain, but whether for a shorter or longer time, must be ascertained from other circumstances. Sometimes it denotes continuance in a place for a number of days, (Acts xviii. 18;) sometimes for three days, (Math. xv. 3; Mark viii. 2;) and sometimes for scarcely three hours, (Judges iii. 15, Septuagint.) And as such is its general signification, so it is evident that in the passage in question it can denote only a temporary residence; for if Ephesus had been allotted to Timothy as his diocese, Paul would not have *" besought,"* but would have *commanded him* " to remain in it." " How ingenious," says Daillée, " is the passion for the crosier and the mitre, which in a few plain words has discovered such mysteries! For where is the man, who, using only his natural understanding without the fire that affection imparts to it, would have ever found out so many mitres as those of a bishop, and an archbishop,* and a primate in these two expressions, *Paul besought Timothy to remain at Ephesus?* Who, without the aid of an extraordinary passion, could have divined a thing so fine and so marvellous, and could have imagined, that *to entreat a man to abide in a city, was to appoint him the bishop of it,* archbishop of the province, and primate of the whole country? Without exaggeration, the cause of these hierarchical gentlemen must be reduced to great straits when they are obliged to have recourse to such pitiful arguments. As to myself, considering matters coolly, I should have concluded on the con-

---

* Some of the fathers make him an archbishop.

trary, from the Apostle beseeching Timothy to remain at Ephesus, that he could not have been Bishop of Ephesus. For to what purpose would it be to *entreat* a bishop to remain in his diocese? Is not this to beseech a man to continue in a place to which he is tied down? I should not have thought it strange if he had been entreated to leave it, had there been need for his services elsewhere. But to beseech him to stop in a place *of which he had the charge*, and which he could not quit *without displeasing God and neglecting his duty*, to say the truth, is a request which is not a little extraordinary, and which evidently supposes that he had not his duty much at heart, since he needed to be besought to do it. But however that may be, *it is very certain that to beseech a man to remain in a place does not signify that he is constituted the bishop of it.*"* It cannot therefore be inferred from these passages, that either Timothy or Titus was merely a bishop. And when it is recollected, that at the time when some of the fathers began to represent Timothy as Bishop of Ephesus, and say that he was appointed to his see by Paul, they assert that another bishop, named John, was appointed to the same bishopric by the Apostle John, who was Primate of all Asia, in which also others associate Timothy with him,† it increases the absurdity, and shows the desperate state of the cause which depends on such support, and yet the defenders of which are continually boasting that thens are the only Apostolic Churches, out of which you cannot enjoy the Christian ministry, nor a covenanted title to the blessings of salvation.

It will not follow that Timothy was not an evange-

* Sermon 1, sur l'Ep. 1. á Timothee, p 22

† It is said in the Apostolic Constitutions, lib. 7, cap. 46, that "when Timothy was made Bishop of Ephesus by Paul, John was made bishop of it by the Apostle John, της δε Εφεσου Τιμοθεος μεν υπο Παυλου, Ιωαννης δε υπ' εμου Ιωαννου" Cotelerius indeed attempts to show that it means only that John succeeded Timothy, and rejects the idea stated in Metaphraste apud Syrium, and in the martyrdom of Timothy, Codex 254, Bibliothecae Photii, that John the Apostle came after Timothy in the Episcopate of Ephesus and Asia. But he allows that he was Primate of Asia during the bishoprics of Timothy and the other John, and the whole statement appears very ridiculous.

list, as has sometimes been alleged, because he was exhorted (1 Tim. iv. 13,) to "give attendance to reading." Daniel did so, (Dan. ix 2, &c) though he was a prophet; and Paul did so, though he was an Apostle, (2 Tim. iv. 13;) and while I admit that his learning has been frequently overrated,* yet he seems to have been

* It has been asserted by Cave, in his Life of this Apostle, c. 8, p. 428, that he was not only acquainted with Jewish learning, but with the philosophy and the more elegant accomplishments of the Greeks, and that he was thus prepared for being the Apostle of the Gentiles, and for fighting the most learned of the Greeks with their own weapons. And the same was the opinion of Witsius, (Meletem. Leid. in Vita Pauli,) of Pfaffius, (Dissert. de Apostolo Paulo, p 2, 3,) of Windheim, (Dissert. de Paulo, Gentium Apostolo, contra Th. Morganum, Hal 1745,) and of many others. But it is proved by Thalmannus, in an able Dissertation de Eruditione Pauli Apostoli, edit. Lipsiae, 1769, that while he had a very considerable portion of Jewish learning, there is no satisfactory evidence of his high attainments in Grecian literature. His being educated at Tarsus, where, according to Strabo, (Geograph. lib. xiv. p. 463,) there were more celebrated schools of philosophy than at Athens or Alexandria, will not prove it, for, as is observed by that author, p 22, though a Jew in the present day were to be born and educated at Halle, or Leipsic, it would not follow that he must have studied eloquence, or philosophy, or mathematics, under any of the professors in these cities His style furnishes no evidence of it, for this, as is acknowledged even by Cave, (Hist Liter, p. 8,) is pronounced by the ancients to be rough and unadorned; and if it be a little superior to that of his fellow-apostles, it is sufficiently accounted for upon other principles by Thalmannus, p. 45-47 It is not supported by what is said of him by Longinus in the Codex Evangeliorum Bibliothecae Vaticanae, for, as is remarked by Fabricius, Biblioth Graeca, lib. iv cap 31, p. 445, that fragment seems to have been the production of a Christian. And it cannot be established by his quoting, in a few instances, some of the Grecian poets. As is observed by Bengelius, Gnomon ad Tit. i. 12, he never names Aratus, Menander, or Epimenides, and all certainly who have picked up and repeat sentiments from authors, especially when these sentiments have become proverbs, are not to be considered as acquainted with their writings. How many, for instance, of the Romans may have been able to repeat such sentences as these, "Homo sum, humani nihil a me alienum puto," "Mors aequo pulsat pede pauperum tabernas regumque turres," and yet never have perused the writings of Terence or Horace? And, in like manner, says Werenfelsius of Paul, (Dissert. de Stilo Nov. Test tom. 1. Oper. p 315,) " Potuit haec a Graecis conversis accepisse, potuerunt hi versus, certe παροιμίαν redolentes in vulgus noti esse." In short, it was contrary to the rules of the Pharisees that any of their sect should study Grecian literature. (See Josephus, Antiq Jud. 20 9; Talmud in Tract Mesch. Sotah. c. 9, n. 14, and the Gemara, on the place where it is announced, that "whosoever taught his son the philosophy of the Greeks was to be ac-

continually adding to his knowledge, and unquestionably the same thing might be useful to an evangelist.

Nor will it at all affect the title of Timothy to be considered as an evangelist, as Thomas imagines, that he is commanded " not to neglect the gift that was in him, which was given him by prophecy, with the laying on of the hands of the presbytery," for " the clerk of the peace," says he, " might as well make justices, or captains make colonels," as a court of presbyters could make "an evangelist."* Bilson supposes that Timothy was ordained *twice*, first as a presbyter; and if this was done, as is stated, 1 Tim. iv. 14, by a court of presbyters, it proves that presbyters may ordain presbyters; and next as an evangelist, by the Apostle Paul, for he admits that he was an evangelist. "Every one," says he, " by the ancient discipline of Christ's Church, before hee could come from ministring to governing in the Church of God, received thrice, or, at the least, *twice* imposition of hands. The like, if any man list, he may imagine of Timothie, that the good report which the brethren of Lystra and Iconium gave of him unto Paul, whereupon hee would that Timothie should goe foorth, grew upon triall of his faithfull and painfull service in a former and lower vocation, for

---

cursed ") Consult Wagenseil ad 1 c. edit. Surenhus, p 307, Lightfoot, vol ii p. 706; and Wetstein upon Acts vi. 1. Nor is it any objection to this, that Josephus, though a Pharisee, acquired this learning, for it was after he had been carried captive to Rome, and was not under his former restrictions. And not only has this view of the attainments of Paul been taken by Melancthon, (Disput. Orat. in Epist ad Rom.) by Grotius, (Comment on 1 Cor. ii 1,) by J. A. Turretine, (Dissert. Theolog tom. i. sec. 11,) and by Ernesti, (Opusc. Crit. et Phil. p 201;) but, as is proved by Thalmannus, by Origen in his Philocal. c. 15, by Chrysostom, in his 1st and 3d Homilies on the 1st Epistle to the Corinthians, where he says that Paul was unacquainted with Grecian learning, and in his 4th Homily on the 2d Epistle to Timothy, where he observes, " Hebraicam tantum linguam calluisse, Graecam ignorasse ," and by Jerome, Epist ad Algas, qu. 10, and Epist. ad Hedypiam, qu. 11. But though he had not that measure of Grecian learning which has frequently been ascribed to him, he unquestionably had a more than ordinary acquaintance with Jewish learning, for he profited in the knowledge of it, as he tells us, " above his equals;" and he seems to have laboured to increase it, by reading whenever he had an opportunity.

* Answer to James Owen on Ordination, p. 17, 18.

which hee had imposition of hands, and that mooved Paul to take him along with him, and when hee saw his time, to impose hands on him for a greater calling. For it is not credible that Paul would impose hands on him at the first step, to place him in one of the highest degrees, being so young as he was, without good experience of his sober and wise behaviour in some other and former function."* There appears, however, as far as we can judge from what is mentioned in Scripture, to have been only one ordination performed by a court of presbyters, at which, if Paul was present, and took part in it, he must have acted only as a presbyter, and, as Daillée suggests,† officiated as its president. And certainly, if the Apostles sat in the Council of Jerusalem along with the presbyters, and assumed no more authority than they, and issued its decrees in the name of the presbyters as well as their own, why might not Paul act as a presbyter along with other presbyters at the ordination of Timothy? And if an army, as we know, have often made an emperor, though they were greatly his inferiors; and if prophets and teachers, or presbyters, made *Barnabas an Apostle* at Antioch, as Bishop Gleig acknowledges; for " it was after that," he says, "that he was called an Apostle;" it would be exceedingly strange if a court of presbyters, guided by the prophecies which went before respecting Timothy, pointing him out as a fit person for the high office which he was destined to fill, could not ordain him to be an evangelist.

I presume that no one in the present day will maintain that Timothy and Titus were bishops, the first of Ephesus, and the second of Crete, because they are distinguished by these titles in the postscripts of the Epistles which were addressed to them. Dr. Mill admits that these postscripts were added by Eustathius, bishop of Suica, in Egypt, in the middle of *the fifth* century; and Horne confesses, that whoever was the author, he was either grossly ignorant, or grossly inattentive. And

* Perpetuall Government, p. 94.
† Sermon 31, sur l'Epitre 1. à Timothee, p. 296, 297.

it might as consistently be asserted, on the authority of the author of the Scholastic History, that *Timothy was Bishop of Lystra*, because he resided there for some time, and laboured in the Gospel, as that he was Bishop of Ephesus. If it be urged with Downam, that, to prevent us from imagining that what was addressed to these ministers, " was spoken to them as extraordinary persons, (whose authority should die with them,) but to them and their successors to the end of the world, Paul straightway chargeth Timothe, that the commandements and directions which he gave him should be kept inviolable, (1 Tim. vi. 13, 14,) untill the appearing of our Lord Jesus Christ; and therefore, by such as should have the like authority unto the end;"* I reply with Stillingfleet, "this is easily answered; for, first, it is no way certain what this command was which Paul speaks of. Some understand it, of fighting the good fight of faith; others, of the precept of love; others, most probably the sum of all contained in this Epistle; which I confesse implies in it, (as being one great part of the Epistle,) Paul's directing of Timothy for the right discharging of his office. But, granting that the command respects Timothy's office, I answer, secondly, it manifestly appears to be *something personal*, and *not successive*, or at least nothing can be inferred *for the necessity of such a succession* from this place which it was brought for, nothing being more evident than that this command related to Timothy's personal observance of it. And therefore, thirdly, Christ's appearing here is not meant *of his second coming to judgment*, but it only imports the time of Timothy's decease. So Chrysostom, μεχρι τε της τελετης, μεχρι της εξοδου.† So Estius understands it, usque ad exitum vitae,‡ and for that end brings that speech of Augustine, Tunc unicuique veniet dies adventus Domini, cum venerit ei dies, ut talis hic extat, qualis judicandus est illo die.§ And the reason why the time of his

* Sermon p 74.   † "Till the end, till thy departure."
‡ " Till the end of life."
§ " Then the day of the coming of the Lord will arrive to each,

death is set out by the coming of Christ, is ινα μαλλον αυτον διεγειρη, as Chrysostom, and from him Theophylact, observes, to incite him the more both to diligence in his work, and patience under sufferings, from the consideration of Christ's appearance. The plain meaning of the words, then, is the same with that of Rev. ii. 20, Be thou faithful unto death, and I will give thee a crown of life. *Nothing, then, can be hence inferred, as to the necessary succession of some in Timothy's office, whatever it be supposed to be.*"*

And if it be alleged, again, with Downam, that "their being evangelists did not hinder them from being bishops, when ceasing from their travailling about, they were assigned to these particular churches; and that this is proved by the testimony of Zuinglius, who saith (in Ecclesiaste,) that Philip the Evangelist, who had beene one of the deacons, was afterwards Bishop of Caesarea,"† I answer, that if Timothy and Titus were not made bishops *till they had ceased from travelling*, then as, *they travelled frequently after they they had performed what was prescribed to them at Ephesus and in Crete*, they could not, even upon this author's own showing, have been bishops of either of these places. Besides, it is never stated in Scripture that any evangelist in his old age was assigned permanently to any particular place, and reduced to the rank of a diocesan bishop; which, as Dr. Barrow observes, if it were to take place in regard to an Apostle in his old age, "would be such an irregularity, as" if any of your bishops, or of the humbler bishops of the Scottish Episcopalians, who now arrogate to their Church the lofty title of the Reformed Apostolic Catholic Church in Scotland, was in his old age "to *be made a deacon !*"‡

---

when the day shall come to him on which he will be judged as he is in this world," referring probably to the judgment which is spoken of, Heb ix. 27.

* Irenicum, p. 183, 184. Consult, too, Dr. Whitby on the place.
† Defense of his Sermon, p. 96, lib. 4.
‡ Pope's Supremacy, p. 120.

Mark is denominated by some of the latter fathers first Bishop of Alexandria, but it is merely in accommodation to the sentiments

I have only further to remark, with regard to the powers of ordination and jurisdiction, which were committed by Paul to Timothy and Titus, that it will by no means entitle you, though you were able to prove that they alone exercised them in Ephesus and Crete, to claim similar powers to any of your bishops. Both of them were of an order very near to that of the Apostles, appointed for special and temporary purposes, and far superior to diocesan bishops. And it would cetrainly be strange if *the ministers of a lower order*, even admitting *you could show from other passages* that they were instituted by Christ, should exercise powers belonging *to a higher order*, without producing any warrant permitting them to assume them *after that order had ceased*, or any evidence of their having been allowed to exercise them *along with these ministers while that order existed.* And it is still more strange that these powers should be claimed for that lower order, since you have never yet proved from other parts of Scripture, that it was appointed by the Redeemer, either before or after he ascended to heaven. And at the same time I would observe, that it has never yet been demonstrated that Timothy and Titus exercised these powers *by themselves alone*, without allowing presbyters to unite with them in ordination or jurisdiction, or that, when they exercised them along with presbyters, they did it in any higher character than that of presbyters. Paul, indeed, tells Timothy (1 Tim. v. 22,) that he was to "lay hands suddenly on no man;" and Titus, (ch. 1. 5,) that he had "left him in Crete, that he might ordain Presbyters in every city, as he had appointed him." But it no more follows that either of these evangelists was to exercise this power alone in Ephe-

about bishops which prevailed in their own times; for we have undoubted evidence, that after he founded that church, he still retained his office as an evangelist, travelling about and preaching the Gospel, and founding churches in other places It is stated that he did so after this in nearly the whole of Egypt, and in many parts of Africa, by the writer of the Synopsis, ascribed to Athanasius, by the Legend. Aut cap. 57; by the Centur. Magdeburg, Cent. 1. lib. 2, cap. 10, and by Baronius in his Annals, tom 1. p. 695.

sus and Crete, than it would follow from the words of our Lord to Peter, (Mat. xvi. 19,) " I give unto thee the keys of the kingdom of heaven," that the power of which they were the symbol was committed *exclusively to that Apostle.* Theophylact says of the latter, " although it is said only to Peter, I will give *thee*, yet the same was given to all the Apostles." And the same is the language of many others of the fathers, and of all Protestant expositors. Not a single instance of the ordination of a presbyter by *one individual*, whether he was an apostle or evangelist, can be produced from the New Testament; and if it was never done even by an apostle, as far as appears from Scripture, on what ground are we to believe that it was done by either of these evangelists? Besides, if presbyters ordained an apostle at Antioch, as Bishop Gleig admits, and if Timothy was ordained by the laying on of the hands of the presbyteiy, it is plain, as Willet observes, that it " cannot be gathered from these words, lay hands suddenly upon no man, that Timothie had *this sole power in himself,* for the Apostle would not give that to him which he did not take to himselfe, who associated unto him the rest of the presbyterie in the ordaining of Timothie, 1 Tim. iv. 14, but he speaketh to him as the chiefe." Nor would Timothy and Titus find any difficulty in procuring presbyters, to unite with them in ordaining other presbyters, since Paul had preached in Ephesus for more than two years, and had laid his hands (Acts xix.) on twelve men, who not only spoke with tongues, but prophesied, and who having been admitted into the ministry, could take part with Timothy in ordaining others; and Titus would be assisted by Zenas and Apollos, who were with him in Crete, (Tit. iii. 13.) And though the Apostle says to Timothy, (1 Tim. v. 19,) " against a presbyter receive not an accusation, but before two or three witnesses," it will not prove that he alone was to judge of it. For, as Willet again remarks, "though he speak by name to Timothie, directing his speech to him as the chiefe, yet he excludeth not the rest, as the Holy Ghost writing to the angel and chiefe pastors of the seven Churches, Apoc. ii. 3, implyeth the rest of the ministers and Church there, as may appear by the matter of the Epistles, wherein the faults of *the whole Church* are reproved, and their virtues commended." And says Whitaker, " to receive an accusation is to report the evil to the Church, and to bring the culprit to judgment, and publicly to reprove him, which may be done not only by *superiors, but by equals and inferiors.* Thus, in the Roman Republic the knights sat in judgment not only upon plebeians, but upon senators and patricians."* We know, too, that presbyters exercised jurisdiction along with Timothy at Ephesus, for Paul speaks of them (1. Tim. v. 13,) as " worthy of double honour because *they ruled well,* especially if they laboured in the woid and doctrine." And they are represented as exercising the same power among the Thessalonians, (1 Thes v. 12, 13,) and Hebrews, (Hebrews xiii 7) And it is mentioned as one of the qualifications of the bishop or presbyter whom Timothy was to ordain at Ephesus, that he must be "blameless, one that *ruled well* his own house; for if he knows not how *to rule his own house, how should he take care of the Church of God?"* or, as Dr. Hammond paraphrases the woids. " he would be unfit to be *made a governor of the Church of God."* And says Paul to Titus, "a bishop" or presbyter " must be blameless as the steward of God," or, as the same commentator paraphrases it, "as becomes one that hath *the government of God's family* entrusted to him." But if presbyters were associated with evangelists in jurisdiction as well as ordination, (and they would not otherwise be represented as governing the Church,) you have no right to assert that these powers were exeicised *exclusively* by the latter. If presbyters, too, were permitted to share in them then, when that order existed, they must retain them still when that order has ceased, as government must always continue in the Chuich, and *they alone remain,*

* Accusationem admittere, &c. Controv. 4, quaest. 1, cap 2.

while the former have ceased to exercise them along with them. And as you have failed to prove that diocesan bishops existed at that time, in the early Church, or were permitted, like presbyters, to unite with evangelists in ordination or jurisdiction, they can have no right *at least from divine institution* to exercise these powers in the present day; and "the main erection of Episcopacy" having failed, I leave it to candid judges to say, whether you and your followers, instead of telling us that out of your churches there is no salvation, would not act a wiser and more consistent part, if you were to confess with Bilson, "that though bishops may found their claims on the custome of the Church," which I shall by and by examine, "on any divine precept expressed in Scripture they cannot."*

I am, Reverend Sir,

Yours, &c.

* "It is doubtful," says Salmeron, though a Roman Catholic, (Disput 1 on 1 Tim.) "if Timothy was Bishop of Ephesus, for although he preached and ordained some to the ministry there, it does not follow that he was the bishop of that place, for Paul preached there above two years, and absolved the penitents, and *yet he was no bishop*. Add, that now and then the Apostle called him away unto himself, and sent him from Rome to the Hebrews with his Epistle. And in the second Epistle he commands him to come unto him shortly. Timothy was also an evangelist of that order, Eph. iv. He gave some Apostles, some evangelists," &c. So that Dorotheus says in his Synopis, " that *Timothy pieached through all Greece*, but stayed at Ephesus, *not to be bishop*, but that in the constituted Church of Ephesus he might oppose the false Apostles. It appears, therefore, *that he was more than a bishop*, although for a time he preached in that city as a pastor, and ordained some to the ministry. *Hence it is that some call him Bishop of Ephesus.*"

LETTER XIII.

Examination of the argument for diocesan Episcopacy, from the Angels of the seven Asiatic Churches —Refutation of it as stated by Milner, who would restrict the superintendence exercised by bishops to ten or twelve congregations, a plan which would create in England a thousand diocesan bishops —Refutation of it as stated by Bishop Gleig, who represents these Angels as single individuals and prelates —The name Angel borrowed from one of the ministers of the Jewish synagogue, who had no authority over other synagogues, *and was not the sole or chief ruler of his own synagogue —Remarkable blunder of Bishop Russel respecting the Angel of the synagogue and its other officers,* for which he is praised by the Rev Mr Sinclair *—If the Angels of the Churches were single persons, no evidence that they were diocesan bishops —Three arguments to prove that they were not single individuals, but representatives of the whole ministers of the different Churches,* as each of the stars mentioned in Rev i represented the whole of the ministers of each of the Churches, *who shed their united light on the members —Striking remarks of Lord Bacon on the unprecedented powers vested in bishops, and on their being allowed to exercise some of them, without any appeal, by lay-chancellors*

REVEREND SIR,—The last argument in support of diocesan Episcopacy, which has been advanced by the advocates of your ecclesiastical polity, has been taken from the angels of the seven Asiatic Churches. And certainly, if its strength corresponded to the confidence with which it has been stated, at least by some of these writers, it would be perfectly irresistible. And there is none of them who has mentioned it with more of that feeling, as if it could not be controverted, than even the excellent Milner. Having been accustomed to Episcopacy from his earliest days, and imagining that it was indispensable to the order and well-being of the Christian Church, he talks of this argument and of the system which he rests upon it, in the following terms:

"Toward the end of the first century, all the Churches followed the model of the mother Church of Jerusalem, where one of the Apostles was the first bishop. A settled presidency obtained, and the name of angel was first given to the supreme ruler, though that of bishop soon succeeded. That this was the case with the seven Churches of Asia *is certain*. The address of the charges to him in the Book of the Revelation demonstrates his superiority." After which he adds, "Could it be conveniently done, it may perhaps be true, that a reduced Episcopacy, in which the dioceses are of small extent, as those in the primitive Church undoubtedly were, and in which the president residing in the metropolis exercises a superintendency over ten or twelve presbyters of the same city and neighbourhood, would bid the fairest to promote order, peace, and harmony."*

Now, upon this I would remark, that it is certainly surprising he should have believed the fable which has been already refuted, about one of the Apostles having become bishop of Jerusalem; though it must be evident to any one who is at all acquainted with ecclesiastical history, that with all his piety he is sometimes too credulous. Such a descent from the office of an Apostle, whose diocese was the world, Mat. xxviii. 19, to that of a bishop, whose diocese was to be Jerusalem, as Jewel observes, would have been in direct opposition to the command of Christ, and would have been as extraordinary, as Dr. Barrow remarks, as if the King of Great Britain were to become Lord Mayor of London. Besides, it is not supported by any testimony which is worthy of belief, and which could warrant him to employ it as the basis of an argument; and I shall by and by endeavour to show that his other assertion, " that toward the end of the first century all the Churches followed the model of the mother Church of Jerusalem," and had diocesan bishops, is equally unfounded. Writers in the fourth and fifth centuries might call these early ministers bishops, *according to the custom of their own times*, but no historical evidence can be produced of their exercising the powers of your bishops; and as has already been stated, not a father can be mentioned from the first three centuries who even denominates Timothy or Titus a bishop. I would further notice, that as he does not attempt to prove, but merely affirms, that the charges to the angels demonstrate their superiority to the other ministers of the Asiatic

* Vol. L. p. 161, 162.

Churches, I shall pass them over at present, and consider them afterwards as they are referred to by another of the defenders of Episcopacy. And as to the extent of the dioceses which he would assign to bishops in the present day, I would briefly observe, that while none of these angels, admitting them, for the sake of argument, to be diocesan bishops, would have under his care the ministers of ten or twelve of the neighbouring churches, a proposal to reduce the bishoprics of your Church within similar limits, and to oblige your prelates to preach, and to restrict their dioceses to ten or twelve parishes, is a measure of reform, which, though it assimilate them more nearly to the primitive bishops, would call forth feelings of the greatest consternation throughout the whole of your Establishment. Archbishop Usher, you are aware, brought it forward formerly, and it did not succeed, and it is less likely to be accepted if it were to be brought forward at present. In the diocese of Lincoln, in place of one you would have nearly a *hundred* bishops; and throughout the whole of your dioceses they would amount to a *thousand*. Your bishops would cease, as in other Protestant countries, to be spiritual lords, for they would outnumber the peers; or they would sit in the Legislature by a few representatives chosen from among themselves; or, as others might prefer, they would be represented both in the Lords and Commons, (and the privilege might be extended to other Protestant Churches,) by some intelligent and experienced members of your communion, chosen, like the representatives of your three Universities, by your bishops and dignitaries, and a select number of your inferior clergy.* But it

---

* "I have heard," says the author of a pamphlet published in 1641, "that divers abbots voted in Parliament *as anciently as bishops.* Yea this answerer hath informed me that anciently the bishops were assisted in Parliament," before it was divided, "by a number of mitred abbots and priors," p 33. And Sir Edward Coke informs us in his Commentary on Littleton's Institutes, sec 138, that "he found in the Parliament rolls twenty-seven abbots and two priors." In all causes affecting the Church which come before the Supreme Court of Denmark, two bishops are now allowed to sit in that court. In all other causes they are not permitted to judge.

is obviously unnecessary to speculate on these matters, as such a proposal as is thrown out by Mr. Milner will never be entertained. And yet it is upon this ground alone that he pleads for Episcopacy; for, as it exists in your Church with all the overwhelming duties of your dioceses, and the secular duties which devolve on your bishops, the superintendence which they exercise must in a great measure be nominal.

Bishop Gleig however contends, like most Episcopalians, that the angels of these churches were single persons, acting, not as Dr. Campbell of Aberdeen had supposed, as the moderators of the presbyteries belonging to the churches, but in their individual capacity; and he thinks it plain, both from the name bestowed on them, and the duties required from them, that they were diocesan bishops. " Had Dr. Campbell," says he, "taken the trouble to search the Old and New Testaments on this occasion, and to compare Scripture with Scripture, he would very soon have found that the application of the name αγγελος to a person in the ministry or priesthood is by no means peculiar to the mysterious book of the Apocalyse. Thus (Mal. ii. 7,) the Jewish high-priest is by the Seventy called αγγελος Κυριου παντοκρατορος; and St. Paul, in his Epistle to the Galatians, says, "that he was received by them as an angel of God." Now, as the Jewish high-priest, compared with the other priests and Levites, was certainly much more than a mere chairman, and as no man will pretend that in the Churches of Galatia, St. Paul was only the first among his own order, is it not natural to infer that the angels of the seven Churches were likewise something more than mere chairmen or moderators, especially as the charges given to them cannot be reconciled with equity upon the hypothesis advanced by Dr. Campbell? If indeed they were vested with the authority which the Apostle gave to Timothy and Titus over the Churches of Crete and Ephesus; if they had each a right to take cognisance of heretical doctrine, to admonish the heretic, and, in case of pertinacity, to reject him from the communion of the Church; if *they only* had authority to ordain presbyters and deacons in the several cities of Asia; if they were enjoined not to admit any man to the order of deacons till after competent trial, nor to ordain an elder or presbyter till after he had acquitted himself well in the deaconship; if they were authorized to receive accusations against presbyters, and to rebuke them before all when found guilty; if such were the powers of the Asiatic angels of the Churches, and such their duty resulting from those powers, then indeed, but not otherwise, were the orthodox and virtuous angels of the Churches of Pergamos and Thyatira properly reproved for suffering to be taught under their jurisdiction the doctrines of the Nicolaitanes, of Balaam, and of Jezebel."*

But upon this statement of the argument, (and I have selected it as one which was greatly praised soon after it was published, and as one of the most plausible which I have met with,) I would beg to submit the following observations:

No argument can be founded on the term angels as applied to the ministers of these Churches, to show that they were invested with jurisdiction over the rest of the ministers, and the instances to which the bishop refers in proof of this are not in point. It is not of the high-priest, as he alleges, that Malachi says, ch. ii. 7, that " the priest's lips should keep knowledge, and the people should seek the law at his mouth, for he was the messenger" or angel "of the Lord of Hosts," but of *every priest;* and it is astonishing that a man who was lauded for his high professional attainments by his brother prelates, and especially for this article, should not have seen it. Lowth accordingly remarks on the passage, " As it was the priests' duty to understand the meaning of the law, so the people were required to resort to them for instruction in any difficulty that arose concerning the sense of it; see Lev. x. 11, Deut. xxii. 9. For this reason the Levites had *forty-eight* cities allotted to them among the several tribes, that the people might more easily consult them upon every occasion. See Numb. xxxv. 7." Besides,

* Anti-Jacobin Review, vol. ix.

if it had been the high-priest who was meant, it would not have served the bishop's purpose, for *he had no jurisdiction over the other priests;* and though president of the Sanhedrim, he had only his casting vote, and was *even himself subject to their authority.* And when Paul says to the Galatians, ch. iv. 14, that they had "received him" at first "as an angel of God," he surely never intended to tell them that they had received him *as a bishop!* for he was far higher than a bishop, but as *if he had been really a messenger sent to them immediately from the heavenly world,* just as he says, ch. i. 8, "But though we or an angel from heaven (surely not a bishop) preach any other Gospel to you let him be accursed." And certainly it is impossible to see any thing in the term angel itself which is applied to these ministers, or in the corresponding term of stars which is employed respecting them, or in what is said of them in the latter character, (ch. i. 20,) which would lead us to suppose that they were superior to the other ministers of these churches, or had any jurisdiction over them. Every other minister of these Asiatic Churches who preached the Gospel, and who shed spiritual light on the minds of the members, had as good a title to the metaphorical name of an angel who brought the message of reconciliation, and every one of them who communicated that light to the name of a star, as a diocesan bishop; and compared at least to modern prelates, who seldom preach, he had a preferable claim. And I cannot believe that it was prelates alone, whom, as the stars of these churches, the Redeemer held in his right hand to protect and defend them, any more than that it was they alone who were angels or messengers, because *it was to them alone that he had committed the message of salvation.* Such is the view which is given of these terms by some of the more candid Episcopalians, and in particular by Dr. Lightfoot, a man who had few equals in scriptural knowledge and Jewish learning; and if he be right in his account of the source from which the first of these terms was taken and applied to the ministers of Christian churches, it overthrows the argument which has been founded on it, for any thing like superiority on the part of the angels of the Asiatic churches over the rest of the ministers of these churches. " Besides these," (the three rulers of the synagogue,) says he, " there was the public minister of the synagogue, who prayed publicly, and took care about the reading of the law, and sometimes preached, if there were not others to discharge that office. This person was called Sheliach Zibbor, *the angel of the church*, and the Chazan or *bishop* of the congregation. Certainly the signification of the word bishop and angel of the church had been determined with less noise, if recourse had been made to the proper fountains, and men had not vainly disputed about the meaning of words, taken I know not whence The service and worship of the Temple being abolished, as being ceremonial, God transplanted the worship and public adoration of God used in the synagogues, which was moral, into the Christian Church; to wit, the public ministry, public prayers, reading God's word, and preaching, &c. *Hence the names of the ministers of the Gospel were the very same, the angel of the church, and the bishop which belonged to the ministers in the synagogues.*"* As the Sheliach Zibbor, then, or angel, or bishop of the synagogue, *had no authority beyond the single congregation in which he ministered*, and as he exercised that authority along with the rulers of the synagogue, (though he was not the chief ruler,)† it is plain that

---

* Vol. ii. of his Works, p 133.

† Bishop Russel, in his Sermon on the Historical Evidence for Episcopacy, p. 31, attempts to construct an argument for that form of ecclesiastical polity, from the term angel of the churches, but blunders exceedingly respecting the place of the Sheliach Zibbor in the Jewish synagogue, as well as of the other officers. And yet the Rev. Mr. Sinclair, in his Dissertation on Episcopacy, p 43, says that he coincides with him, and that " *on all questions* connected with Jewish antiquity, the Bishop's views must be acknowledged *of the highest authority*" " This mode of phraseology, it deserves to be remarked," says Dr Russel, " is borrowed from the usages of the Jewish synagogue, where the person who presided in divine worship, usually called the ruler of the synagogue, was not unfrequently denominated the angel of the congregation. He had under him, also, two classes of ministers, corresponding to the priest and deacon of the Christian

the application of the name angel to the minister of each of these Asiatic churches, even supposing him to be only a single person acting on his own individual capacity, furnishes no proof that *he had authority over the ministers of other congregations or Christian synagogues*, and much less would it justify any bishop in the present day for being invested with authority over *a hundred or a thousand ministers, and as many congregations.*

As to the censure which is pronounced on some of the angels for suffering false teachers, and their being enjoined to pursue a different course, it remains to be proved, that the acts which they were blamed for not performing, and which they were commanded to perform afterwards, were acts of jurisdiction. And though this should be allowed, it will by no means follow that these angels might not have been the moderators of the presbyteries of these churches, and that letters might not be addressed to them, as in the present day,

---

assemblies; and, in other respects, there are so many points of resemblance, as to remove all doubt that the ecclesiastical model recommended by the Apostles was raised upon the platform of the Levitical establishment."

Now, upon this I beg to remark, in the *first* place, that the synagogue was not a part of the Levitical establishment, but was introduced *afterwards*, so that in the Bishop's argument there is evidently a non-sequitur, there being something in the conclusion which is not in the premises. 2*dly*, It will surprise the reader to learn, after the encomium pronounced on Dr. Russel by Mr. Sinclair, that though there were three rulers in every synagogue, *none of them was ever called the angel of the synagogue*, or its bishop, but they were entirely distinct from that minister, as every one knows who has directed his attention to Hebrew antiquities' See Dr Lightfoot; Godwin's Moses and Aaron, p 71. Horne, in his Introduction, vol. iii p. 242, says, " *Next to* the Αρχισυναγωγος, or ruler of the congregation, was an officer, whose province it was to offer up public prayers to God for the whole congregation hence he is called Sheliach Zibbor, the angel of the church, because, as their messenger, he spoke to God for them." His other duties are described by Dr. Lightfoot, who also represents him as *next to the rulers, or to the chief ruler.* And, in the *third* place, so far were there from being "*two classes of ministers*" under him, corresponding to presbyters and deacons, there was only one, according to Horne, who had the charge of the sacred books, or, according to Lightfoot, (who does not mention that officer,) three deacons, two of whom collected the alms for the poor, and the third distributed them.

as the chairmen or representatives of these presbyteries, expressive either of censure or approbation, which they were to communicate to the presbyters; for, as was long ago remarked by an old writer, "why may not the Senate be saluted in the Consuls, Parliament addressed in the Chancellor, or the House of Commons in an epistle to the Speaker?"* But as I do not consider them as acting in their individual capacity, either as the moderators of their presbyteries, according to Dr. Campbell's hypothesis, or as diocesan bishops, the objection which has been urged against them in the former character, though it had possessed a force of which I conceive it to be destitute, would not apply to my opinion. And as to the assertion of the Bishop, that these angels must have been authorised to ordain presbyters and deacons, it is unnecessary to notice it, as not a word is said in any of the Epistles respecting the exercise of such powers by any of these ministers.

I would farther remark, that "the titles of angels and stars," so far from denoting "single men," as Archbishop Potter maintains,† "which," he thinks, "puts it beyond dispute" that they were bishops, appear to be intended to represent *the whole of the ministers* of these early churches. Such was the opinion of the celebrated Dr. Henry More, who says, "Methinks it is extremely harsh to conceit that these seven stars are merely the seven bishops of any particular churches of Asia, as if the rest were not supported or guided by the hand of Christ; or as if there were but seven in his right hand, but all the rest in his left. Such high representations cannot be appropriated to any seven particular churches whatsover." "And by the angels," he says, "according to the Apocalyptick style, all the angels under their presidency are represented or insinuated."‡ And this opinion is confirmed when we look into the epistles which were addressed to these angels, and into the

---

* Principal Forrester on Episcopacy, p. 73.
† Church Government, p. 147.
‡ Exposition of the Seven Churches, Works, p. 724.

first chapter of the Book of Revelation. Each of these ministers is represented, indeed, in the singular number, as a star and an angel. But each of the seven churches is represented also in the singular number, chap. 1. 20, as *one candlestick* with different branches, shedding light around them, in the cities where they were placed, though as Sclater thinks he has proved in his Original Draught of the Primitive Church, and as Episcopalians in general affirm, it was composed, at least, of several congregations. But if each of the candlesticks represented *the whole of the congregations in the city*, which formed together one Church, why may it not be supposed that with equal propriety *the whole* of their ministers may be described as forming *one star*, the different parts of which, combined in one great luminous body, dispensed those rays of spiritual light which illuminated these congregations, and that *the whole of their ministers* were represented by one angel or messenger, *as they all delivered the same message of salvation to guilty men?* And if there be any difficulty in conceiving that one angel should represent the whole of the ministers of the congregations in each of these cities, as they would amount probably to four or six, we have only to turn to the 14th chapter of this very book, v. 6, where John tells, that "he saw another angel flying in the midst of heaven, having the everlasting Gospel to preach unto them that dwell on the earth, and to every nation, and kindred, and tongue, and people;" which angel represents not merely a single minister, though the term *literally* denotes, like each of the angels of the churches, a single individual, but *thousands of ministers.* Since it is evident, therefore, that each of the angels of the seven churches may *possibly* be intended to represent the whole of the ministers of the congregations which were connected with it; and since it is as *probable* that this was the case, as that each of the candlesticks represented perhaps four or six congregations forming that Church, it is proper that we should examine the epistles themselves, and ascertain whether the angels are to be considered as addressed in their individual capacity as diocesan bishops, or as representing the whole of the ministers of these churches. And that the latter is the character in which we are to view them, will appear, I apprehend, from the following considerations:

In the first place, if the angels are addressed only as single individuals, and not as the representatives of the whole of the ministers of the different churches, then the rest of the ministers are never referred to at all. Now, this certainly would be a strange omission in epistles descriptive of the state of the churches, when you consider their number as contrasted with a single diocesan bishop, and their corresponding influence on the members of the churches for good or evil. In Ephesus, especially, the church seems to have been large from its very commencement, for the value of the magical books burnt by its members is said to have been fifty thousand pieces of silver. And at the time of Paul's last visit to them they had a number of presbyters, whom he calls upon to perform the duty of bishops; (Acts xx 22.) Nor were they the bishops or presbyters of the neighbouring churches, as some have affirmed, for, as Dr. Whitby observes, on Acts xx. 17, this is plainly contrary to the text. And as he farther says, "Chrysostom, St. Jerome, Theodoret, Œcumenius and Theophylact knew nothing of Paul's sending to any other bishops besides those of Ephesus; for otherwise they could not have argued, as they do from this place, that these persons could not be bishops, properly so called, because there could be only one bishop in one city." And if such was the number of the presbyters in that Church at that early period, we have reason to believe that it would be still greater at the time when this epistle in the Book of Revelation was addressed to the angel. If the angel, however, did not represent these numerous presbyters, or the whole of the ministers and was merely a single person like a diocesan bishop, then they are never noticed for good or evil in this Epistle, though their conduct must have had a far more powerful influence than that of the bishop. And this is the more unaccountable, that it is asserted by Episcopalians the people are noticed in two of the Epistles, while not a word is said *in any of them* respecting the presbyters.

2*dly*, If the angel of the Church of Ephesus be addressed as a single person, and not as the representative of the whole of the ministers, is it not farther inexplicable, that *because he alone had left his first love*, the Redeemer threatens, if he did not repent, to extinguish that church, or remove its candlestick out of its place? And this is still more surprising, if Timothy, who according to Pererius and Alcazar, was then alive, was the bishop or angel of that church. But if the angel represented not merely a single prelate, but the whole of the numerous ministers of that church, and if all of them had sunk into that grievous state of spiritual declension which is described in the Epistle, and if the people, as is probable, followed their example, we can perceive a reason for such a denunciation. I infer, therefore, from this circumstance that the angel could not possibly be a single person; but must be addressed as the representative of the whole of the ministers of that early church.

And in the third place, no one can look into the Epistles to the angels of the Churches in Smyrna and Thyatira, without perceiving that they address them sometimes in the singular, and sometimes in the plural, which is incompatible with the idea that the angels were intended to represent *only single persons* like diocesan bishops. Thus, the Redeemer says to the angel of the former Church, "I know *thy* works, and tribulation, and poverty, but thou art rich. Fear none of those things which thou shalt suffer: behold, the devil shall cast *some of you* (ὑμῶν) into prison, that *ye* may be tried; and *ye* shall have tribulation ten days: be *thou* faithful unto the death, and I will give thee a crown of life." And he says to the angel of the Church in Thyatira, "I know *thy* works, and charity, and service, and faith, and *thy* patience, and *thy* works; and the last to be more than the first;" (Rev.

ii. 19) After which he adds, v. 24, but unto *you* I say, (in the plural, ὑμεις) and unto *the rest* in Thyatira, (as many as have not this doctrine, &c) I will put upon *you* none other burden : but that which *ye* have already, hold fast till I come." Now, if after saying to the angel of the Church in Smyrna, v. 10, "Fear none of those things which *thou* shalt suffer," he instantly subjoins, "Behold, the devil shall cast *some of you* into prison, and *ye* shall have tribulation ten days," and if, after addressing the angel of the latter Church in the singular number, he adds soon afterwards, "But *unto you* I say," in the plural, it seems impossible to resist the conclusion, that the angels of these churches must not have been designed to be viewed as *single persons* like diocesan bishops, but as the representatives of *a number of persons*. And as the members of the church or the people are said in the first chapter to be represented by *the candlesticks*, and the ministers by the symbols of the angels and the stars, I cannot see how, without setting aside our Lord's interpretation of these symbols, you can consider the plurality of persons represented by the angel, (for as the pronouns are plural *he must represent a plurality,*) as any other than *the whole of the ministers of these different churches.*

It is alleged by Episcopalians, that when plural pronouns are used in these Epistles after a singular noun or pronoun, it is the people who are referred to by the former. But I would remark, in the *first* place, that even according to this interpretation, the rest of the pastors except the bishop, though by far the most numerous part of the ministry, remain unnoticed; and can we suppose that they would have been overlooked in such particular descriptions of the state of the churches? *2dly*, These Epistles are not addressed to the angels *and churches* of Smyrna and Thyatira, as we would have expected to be the case if this exposition had been correct, but merely to the angels; and no other party is introduced afterwards, and addressed separately. *3dly*, If it be the people who are intended when the plural pronouns are used,

v. 10, without any notice of a change of the persons who were to be addressed, and if it be the bishop alone who is referred to when the singular pronouns are employed in the first and last clauses of that verse, there is an inexplicable *mixing of the persons* who are addressed. And what is still more inexplicable, while the people are told that they are "to suffer, and to be cast into prison," they have no promise addressed to them to animate them under their tribulations, nor the least comfort administered to them, but *it is given exclusively to the bishop*, who alone is told in the last clause, that " if *he* is faithful unto the death," the Redeemer will " give *him* a crown of life." But suppose that *the angel to whom every thing is addressed* in both these Epistles represents not merely a single individual, like a diocesan bishop, but, as the plural pronouns evidently suggest, a number of individuals; and suppose further, that these individuals are not *the members* of either of these churches, who are represented by *the candlesticks*, but the only other persons who remain, namely, the whole of their ministers, and all these difficulties are removed; and you see how all of them could appropriate the promise, and though they were cast into prison, if they were "faithful unto the death," might be cheered by the assurance that they would "receive a crown of life."

So evidently are these views suggested by the Epistles, that they are adopted by Stillingfleet with his usual candour, who scouts the idea that the angels of the churches were diocesan bishops. " If the name angel," says he, "imports no incongruity, though taken only for the Sheliach Zibbor in the Jewish synagogue, the public minister of the synagogue, called the angel of the congregation, what power can be inferred from thence, *any more than such an officer was invested with?* Nay, if in the prophetical style an unity may be set down by way of representation of a multitude, what evidence can be brought from the name, *that by it some one particular person must be understood?* And by this means Timothy may avoid being charged with leaving his first love, which he must of necessity be by those that make him angel of the Church of Ephesus at the time of writing these Epistles. Neither is this any wayes solved by the answer given, that the name angel is representative of the whole Church, and so there is no necessity the angel should be personally guilty of it. For first, it seems strange that the whole diffusive body of the Church should be charged with a crime by the name of the angel, and he that is particularly meant by that name should be free from it. As if a prince should charge the mayor of a corporation as guilty of rebellion, and by it should only mean that *the corporation was guilty*, but the mayor was innocent himself. Secondly, if many things in the Epistles be directed to the angel, but yet so as to concern the whole body, then of necessity the angel must be taken as representative of the body; and then why may not the word angel be taken only by way of representation of the body itself, either of the whole Church, or *which is far more probable, of the consessus or order of presbyters in that Church?"**

If the angels, however, of these early churches represented the whole body of the presbyters, and neither a diocesan bishop, nor the people or members, *the last of whom could scarcely be called angels, for it is not their province to deliver the message, but rather to receive it,* it is easy to perceive how they could perform the different acts of jurisdiction which are ascribed to them by Episcopalians. Presbyters are declared to be worthy of double honour if they rule well, and why might not the presbyters of the Asiatic Churches have attained that honour, by performing acts which were required from the angels of Pergamos and Thyatira? I acknowledge with Forrester, that the expulsion of the individuals from the communion of these churches who taught the heresies, and were guilty of the immoralities which are mentioned in the Epistles, would have been *judicial* acts; but they were acts to which the authority com-

* Irenicum, p. 289, 290.

mitted to presbyters, as was formerly proved, was fully equal.

I have only further to observe, that while I look upon the angels as intended to represent the ministers of these churches, because they alone were to deliver the message of heaven by preaching the Gospel, Dr. Hammond considers them as designed chiefly to represent the people. "Though the angels," says he, "were single persons, yet what is said to them is said not only to their persons, but to the universality of the people under them, whose non-proficiency, or remission of degrees of Christian virtue, especially their falling off from the constancy and courage of their profession, do deserve (and accordingly are threatened with) the removal of their Christian knowledge, that grace, those privileges of a Church which had been allowed them, ch. ii. 5, which is not so properly applied as a punishment of the bishop, as of the people under him. And therefore, in the paraphrase I have generally changed the singular into the plural number, by that means to have it indifferently to the bishop of every church, and the people under him."* The same, too, was the opinion of Willet, who says, in a passage formerly quoted, "the Holy Ghost writing to the angels and chief pastors of the seven Churches, Apoc. ii. 3, implyeth the rest of the ministers and Church there, as may appear by the matter of the Epistles, wherein the faults of the whole Church are reproved, and their virtues commended." And it was the opinion of many of the ancient fathers, who seem never to have imagined that the angels represented only a single individual. Thus, when John says in the first Epistle, "To the angel of the Church of Ephesus," Aretas, Bishop of Cæsarea in Cappadocia, says, "he means the Church in it."† When he exhorts the angel of the Church of Smyrna to "fear none of these things," the author of the Homilies on the Apocalypse, which are bound up with the works

* Consult him on these Epistles.
† Comment. in Apoc. τη εν αυτη εκκλησία λεγει.

of St. Augustine, observes, "he says it to the whole Church."* When he says to the angel of the Church of Pergamos, "I know thy works, and where thou dwellest, even where Satan's seat is," it is remarked by the same writer, "these things under a singular word are said to the whole Church, because Satan dwells everywhere by his body."† I might go over the whole of these little Epistles, and appeal to similar quotations from the fathers in confirmation of my statement, but I consider it as unnecessary. And though I differ from them in their account of the persons represented by the angels of the Churches, they agree with me in this, that these early ministers were not intended to be regarded as single persons, and that you will look to them in vain for the smallest support to your ecclesiastical polity.

Having finished this review of the different arguments for diocesan Episcopacy, which have been adduced from Scripture by its most distinguished advocates, and endeavoured to show, that on whatever you found it, it cannot be on the statements of the word of God, I might conclude this discussion, which has been far more extended than I at first anticipated. But, before I do so, I beg to subjoin a view of the powers which you commit to your bishops, by one of the most enlightened and illustrious men who ever lived in England, and which he pronounces to be as inconsistent with all the principles of good government, as I have attempted to show, that they are destitute of any warrant from the sacred volume.

The individual to whom I allude is the great Lord Bacon, who, in his Considerations touching the pacification of the Church, addressed to James the First, makes the following observations:

"There be *two circumstances* in the administration of bishops, wherein I confess *I could never be satisfied*, the one, the sole exercise of their authority, the other, the deputation of their authority.

"For the first, the bishop *giveth orders alone*, ex-

---

* Augustine, Op. tom. x. Hom. 2, in Apoc. "Omni Ecclesiæ dicit."
† Hom. 2. in Apoc.

communicateth alone, judgeth alone. This seemeth to be a thing almost without example in good government, and therefore not unlikely to have crept in, *in the degenerate and corrupt times.* We see the greatest kings and monarchs have their councils. There is no temporal court in England, of the highest sort, where the authority doth rest *in one person.* The King's Bench, Common Pleas and the Exchequer are benches of a number of judges. The chancellor of England hath an assistance of the twelve Masters of the Chancery. The Master of the Wards hath a council of the court, so hath the Chancellor of the Duchy. In the Exchequer Chamber the Lord Treasurer is joined with the Chancellor and the Barons. The Masters of the Requests are ever more than one. The Justices of Assize are two. The Lords President in the North and in Wales have councils of divers. The Star-Chamber is an assembly of the King's Privy Council, aspersed with the Lords Spiritual and Temporal, so as in courts the principal person hath ever either colleagues or assessors.

"The like is to be found in other well-governed commonwealths abroad, where the jurisdiction is yet more dispersed, as in the Court of Parliament of France, and in other places. No man will deny but the acts which pass the bishop's jurisdiction are of as great importance as those that pass the civil courts: for men's souls are more precious than their bodies or goods; and so are their good names. Bishops have their infirmities, and have no exceptions from that general malediction, which is pronounced against all men living, Væ soli, nam si occideret, &c. Nay, we see that the first warrant in spiritual causes is directed to a number, Dic Ecclesiæ,* which is not so in temporal matters; and we see, that in general causes of Church government, there are as well assemblies of the clergy in councils, as of all the states in Parliament. *Whence should this sole exercise of jurisdic-*

---

* " Tell the Church."

tion come? Surely I do suppose, I think upon good grounds, that *ab initio non fuit ita*,* and that the deans and chapters were councils about the sees and chairs of bishops at the first, and were unto them *a presbytery or consistory;* and intermeddled not only in the disposing of their revenues and endowments, but much more in jurisdiction ecclesiastical. But it is probable that the deans and chapters stuck close to the bishops in matters of profit and the world, and would not lose their hold; but in matters of jurisdiction, which they accounted but trouble and attendance, they suffered the bishops to encroach and usurp; and so the one continueth, and the other is lost. And we see that the Bishop of Rome, fas enim et ab hoste doceri, and no question in that Church the first institutions were excellent, performeth all ecclesiastical jurisdiction as in consistory.

" And whereof consisteth this consistory, but of the parish-priests of Rome, which term themselves cardinals *a cardinibus mundi*, because the bishop pretendeth to be universal over the whole world? And hereof again we see many shadows yet remaining, as that the dean and chapter, *pro forma*, chooseth the bishop, *which is the highest point of jurisdiction:* and that the bishop, when he giveth orders, if there be any ministers casually present, calleth them to join with him in imposition of hands, and some other particulars. And therefore it seemeth to me a thing reasonable and religious, and *according to the first institution*, that the bishops in the greatest causes, and those which require a spiritual discerning, namely, *in ordaining, suspending, or depriving ministers, in excommunication*, being restored to the true and proper use, as shall be afterwards touched, in sentencing the validity of marriages and legitimations, *in judging causes criminous*, as simony, incest, blasphemy and the like, *should not proceed sole and unassisted:* which point, as I understand it, is a reformation that may be planted *sine strepitu*, without any perturbation at all.

* " From the beginning it was not so."

"For the second point, which is the deputation of their authority, I see no perfect nor sure ground for that neither, being somewhat different from the examples and rules of government. The bishop exerciseth his jurisdiction by his chancellor and commissary official," &c. "We see in all laws in the world, *offices of confidence and skill cannot be put over nor exercised by deputy*, except it be especially contained in the original grant; and in that case it is dutiful. And for experience, there never was any Chancellor of England made a deputy; *there was never any judge in any court made a deputy.* The bishop is a judge, and of a high nature. Whence cometh it that he should depute, considering that all trust and confidence, as was said, is personal and inherent, *and cannot, nor ought not to be transposed?* Surely, in this again, ab initio non fuit sic; but it is probable that *bishops when they gave themselves too much to the glory of the world, and became grandees in kingdoms, and great counsellors to princes,* then did they delegate their proper jurisdiction, *as things of too inferior a nature for their greatness,* and then, after the similitude and imitation of kings and counts-palatine, they would have their chancellors and judges."*

I trust that the name of the eminent individual from whom I have taken this quotation, and the weight of his authority, will form my apology for introducing it, notwithstanding its length. And as you still continue to intrust to your bishops those high powers, their title to which you cannot establish from the Sacred Scriptures, and which he demonstrates to be *inconsistent with all the principles of good government,* I leave it to impartial judges to say what we ought to think of the modesty of your pretensions, when, along with your friends of the Church of Rome, and a large proportion of the Scottish Episcopalians, you tell us that yours are the only churches in which there is a Gospel ministry, right ecclesiastical government, sacra-

* Vol. iii. of his Works, p. 150–152, edit. 1765.

ments which have any virtue, and a covenanted title to the blessings of salvation.

I think it unnecessary to advert to the arguments for Episcopacy from mere expediency, as I have engaged in this discussion with a view chiefly to repel the unprovoked attacks of those of its advocates, who, not satisfied with preferring it on other grounds, advance for it the claim of an exclusive title to a divine institution, and imitating the conduct of Papists towards themselves, have ventured to unchurch Presbyterian Churches. But I may briefly notice, that if it be alleged that it is the best and most effectual means for preventing schism, the numerous divisions in the Church of Rome in every age, and the state of your own Church in the present day, prove that it is an expedient which is utterly powerless. Besides, if that be a reason for establishing Episcopacy, it will lead to consequences, of which many who urge it do not appear to be aware. "For," says an old and able writer, "if there be a necessity for setting up *of one bishop over many pastors*, for preventing schisms, then there is as great necessity of setting up *one archbishop over many bishops*, and *one patriarch over many archbishops* and *one Pope over all;* unless men will imagine that there is danger of schism among ministers, but not among bishops. archbishops, and patriarchs, which is contrary to reason, truth, history, and our own experience."*

I am, Reverend Sir, Yours, &c.

* Letter from a Parochial Bishop to a Prelatical Gentleman in Scotland, p. 101.

LETTER XIV.

Apostolical succession —If the Apostles were neither diocesan bishops themselves, nor ordained such bishops, the apostolical succession, as explained and claimed by Puseyite Episcopalians, *never began*—Waving that objection, as far as there was a succession, it was preserved to Presbyterian Churches before the Reformation, as uninterruptedly as to Episcopalian Churches, and since that time it has been preserved as regularly in the former, by Presbyterian ordinations, as in the latter by Episcopal —Unfounded allegation by Spottiswood and others, that the adoption of Presbytery at Geneva orginated in a wish *to assimilate the government of the Church to that of the State,* and that this led to the adoption of that form of ecclesiastical polity in other countries —The contrary proved from the reasoning of Farel with Furbiti, who preceded Calvin, and is considered by many as the modern father or reviver of Presbytery—Eusebius acknowledges that he could not trace the succession in many of the early Churches —Jewel and Stillingfleet confess that it cannot be traced in the Church of Rome, from which many of the ministers of the Church of England have derived their orders

Reverend Sir,—If diocesan Episcopacy, as I trust has been proved in the preceding letters, has failed completely in establishing its claim to a divine institution, it may be considered as unnecessary that I should inquire any further into your boasted privilege of the apostolic succession; for if the Apostles were neither bishops themselves, nor ordained bishops, the series of unbroken Episcopalian ordinations which you represent as the peculiar privilege of your churches, at what ever time it commenced, must be a mere human invention. But waving that strong and insuperable objection to your doctrine of the succession, I am willing to meet you on lower ground, and I shall proceed to examine whether the series of regularly ordained bishops, which, you allege, began in the time of the Apostles, has been preserved uninterrupted in any of these churches till the present day. If the chain which connects either your own bishops, or the bishops of the Episcopal Church in Scotland, with the first in the series, has unfortunately been broken either at the tenth, or fiftieth, or hundredth link, the consequences on your principles must evidently be fatal; for neither of these Churches can be considered any longer as a Christian Church, nor can any of its ministers be Christian ministers, nor can any of its members have any revealed or covenanted title to salvation. And the same, too, would be the state of the Roman Catholic Church, and of every other Church on the face of the earth. The question then to be considered is briefly this, can it be proved that the series, allowing it to have commenced, if not with the Apostles, yet in the apostolic age, (the opposite of which, I apprehend, has been established,) has never been interrupted? or can it be demonstrated on the contrary, that there is not a single Episcopalian Church in which it has not been frequently broken?

I observe in the first place, that in as far as the succession remains uninterrupted, we can claim it for our churches, as much as you are entitled to claim it for yours; for our first reformers when they left the communion of the Church of Rome were possessed of orders which were equally valid with those of your reformers. It was so with Bucer, who was a Popish presbyter before he became a Protestant; and with Farel, who defended Presbytery before the Council of Geneva, against the artful Furbiti, a number of months before Calvin accidentally visited that city,*

* Ruchât says of Farel, in his Histoire de la Reformation de la Suisse, tom. 1. p. 231, that he was "Reformateur d'une bonne partie de la Suisse Romande, d'Aigle, de Morat, de Neuchatel, *de Geneve*, et en partie de Lausanne. And the following is a part of his account of the discussion between the Reformer and Furbiti, who was a doctor of the Sorbonne, before the Council, in January 1534, on the subject of Episcopacy "Furbiti," says he, tom. v. p 114, "voulut prouver la superiorite de l'Eveque par dessus le Pretre, 1*mo*, Parce que Jesus Christ a elu douze Apotres, (Mat x,) qui ont eté Eveques, comme c'il paroit par *Judas*, de qui il est dit, *qu'un autre prenne son Eveche.* (Ruchat adds in a note, that it is quoted by Peter from the 109th Psalm, and one may judge whether David, when he wrote it, *was thinking of bishops.*) 2*do*, Parce que S. Paul dit, Eph. iv. que le Seigneur ai donne les uns pour etre Apotres, les autres pour etre Prophetes, les autres Pasteurs et Docteurs, &c En un Diocesse il n'y a qu'un Eveque, qui a sous plusieurs Pretres, &c.

"Farel, apres avoir releve en passant ce que Furbiti disoit du Pape, et soutenu que Jesus Christ n'a point de Successeur montra que dans les Epitres de S Paul *les mots Eveque et Pretre sont synonimes*, 1*mo*, par l'Epitre a Tite, (c. 1) ou il lui dit qu'il la laissé en Crete, pour y etablir des Pretres πρεσβυτερους, v 5, si quelqu'un soit irreprehensible, &c. 2*do*, Par Act xx. ou S. Paul fit venir les Pretres

PUSEYITE EPISCOPACY.   201

and more than a year and a half before he published
his Institutes,* and who accordingly has been considered by some as having had a preferable claim over
the latter Reformer, to the honourable character of
the modern father, or restorer of Presbytery. And I
may remark in passing, that it is impossible for any
one to look into the arguments employed by Farel, as
they are stated below, or into some of the facts which
are mentioned in the notes, without being struck with
the groundlessness of the assertion of Spottiswood,

d'Ephese, v. 17, et leur dit, Prenez garde a vous et a tout le troupeau
sur lequel le Saint Esprit *vous a etablis eveques*, v. 28. 3*mo*, Par S.
Pierre, qui au commencement du ch. v. de sa premiere Epitre, ne
s'appelle, ni Pape, ni Archeveque, mais *Pretre* avec ou comme les
autres. 4*mo*, Il y avoit plusieurs Eveques dans une ville, comme il
paroit par ceux d'Ephese qui etoient plusieurs, et par le commencement de l'Epitre aux Philippiens ou S. Paul salue *les Eveques et les
Diacres* 5*mo*, Si Jesus Christ a institue 12 Apotres et ensuite 70
disciples, (et non 72,) il n'a point pretendu marquer par la difference
des Eveques et des Pretres *Les noms d'Eveque et de Pretre signifient
la meme dignite*. Le premier marque le soin de inspection, et le
second l'age, signifiant proprement *Ancien*, car il faut qu'il soit
Ancien de moeurs et de Savoir, pour conduire le peuple. 6*mo, Si
Judas etoit Eveque, ou son Eveche?* Mais bien lui convient dit il avec
les Eveques qui au lieu de porter la parole de Dieu portent la bourse,
derobent ce qui doit venir aux pauvres," &c.

It is plain from this, that when Presbytery was established in Geneva, it was not because as Heylin, Spottiswood and other Episcopalians affirm, it resembled the republican government of the state,
but because it appeared to be agreeable to the word of God. Besides,
as the Grand Council of the city, which was composed, according to
Ruchat, of two hundred or two hundred and fifty members, chose all
the members of the Little Council, Petit Conceil, and of the Council
of Sixty, and as the little or lowest council decided in certain matters
without appeal, there was no resemblance in point of fact between the
courts of the state and the Presbyterian courts. And yet how often
have the fictions of Spottiswood been retailed by others.

* Historia Literaria de Johannis Calvini Institutione, tom ii. part 1,
page 453 of the Scrinium Antiquarium of Gerdesius.
It deserves also to be mentioned, that after the celebrated Helvetian
Assembly, which was held for inquiring into the necessity for a Reformation in 1523, and at which, according to Gerdesius, (Histor.
Evangel. Renov. vol. i. p 290,) nine hundred deputies were present,
the magistrates of Geneva and Switzerland published an edict, in
which among other things they condemned organs and all instrumental music. "Sacerdotibus quoque mandatum est ne organis posthac ludant in templis." This paper, says Fusslin, in his Document.
ad Histor. Reform Helvet , tom i. was drawn up with the concurrence
of Zuinglius, Engelhardt and Leo Juda.

that Presbyterian Church government was adopted at Geneva *merely to assimilate the constitution of the Church to that of the State.* It was so with Luther, who was ordained a presbyter of the Church of Rome, and afterwards ordained many presbyters, and who, along with three presbyters, made Amsdorf Bishop of Nuremberg, and, with some other presbyters, made George, Prince of Anhalt, Bishop of Marsburg.* Nor did the Prince imagine that he acted irregularly when he asked the Reformer to ordain him; for, as Seckendorf informs us, he thought he was justified in doing so, by the example of Paul and Barnabas, who were ordained by prophets and teachers at Antioch, and by the opinion of Jerome, who represented bishops and presbyters as equal †

* Melchior Adami Vitae Germanorum Theologorum, p 150, Seckendorf's History of Lutheranism, lib iii p. 392.

† Addit, says Seckendorf, lib. iii p 500, speaking of what is mentioned on this subject by George himself, in a preface to his Sermons, se quidem rogasse Matthiam a Jagow, Episcopum Brandeburgensem, ut ordinationem suam in se susciperet, sed illum eo tempore mortuum esse Itaque Pauli et Barnabae exemplo, quos prophetae et doctores Antiocheni, Actorum, xiii, 1, 2, 3, ordinaverunt, D. Martinum Lutherum piae memoriae, aliosque accersitos fuisse, a quibus solenniter et pie accepto etiam Sacramento, per manuum impositionem ordinatus fuerit, eoque nomine se gratias Deo agere dicit. Subjungit inde ex Hieronymo quae nota sunt, ab ipso tamen egregie deducuntur, de paritate Episcoporum et Presbyterorum.

I may add here, that when a false account of a change of sentiment on the part of Luther and Melancthon was handed about by the Papists in 1539, Seckendorf says, lib iii p 228, Luther and Melancthon never thought that the episcopal office was necessary with all that power and authority as it exists in the Church of Rome, nor did they recognise any essential difference between bishops and presbyters, as is manifest from all their writings which have never been recalled, and especially from the tract on the power and jurisdiction of bishops, composed by Melancthon at Smalkald, in 1537, and subscribed by Luther, and annexed to the articles which they drew up between them. Lutherus et Melancthon nunquam statuerint necessarium esse illud munus Episcopale, &c.

Seckendorf remarks, too, lib. iii. p 240, that in the Ordinatio Ecclesiastica, which was issued by the Elector of Brandenburgh, the ancestor of the present King of Prussia, in 1539, that Prince acknowledges, that at the beginning, as Jerome declares, *there was no difference between the ordination of bishops and presbyters;* and that it was plain from the Acts of the Apostles, and the Epistles to Timothy, that bishops *received it by the imposition of the hands of the college of Presbyters.* Refert ex Hieronymo, et post eum ex aliis Doctoribus,

It was so in regard to the leading Reformers of the Church of Scotland. It was admitted by Winzel, the Popish priest, respecting Knox; for in one of his letters to him he addresses him in the following terms: "As S. Paul ordinatit Timothe and Tite, gevand thaim power and command to ordour utheris, quherin apperes the lauchful ordinatioun of ministeris, zour lauchful ordinatioun be ane of thir two wayis, (he had mentioned another,) we desire zou to shaw sen ze renunce and esteemis that ordinatioun null or erar wickit, (rather wicked,) be the quhilk sum tyme ze war callit Schir John," the title of a Popish priest;* upon which Keith, the Episcopalian historian, remarks, "here is a plain and certain instruction that John Knox had formerly received the ordination of a priest."† And it was acknowledged by Bishop Forbes, an ancient Scottish prelate, with whom none of their present bishops can be compared, either as to learning or *orthodoxy*, so far as we can judge from their writings, for he says to the Papists, of the founders of our Church, "Who *of our first preachers* were not ordinarie churchmen ere they

Scholasticis et Canonistis, praesertim Panormitano in Cap. Quando de Consuetud. nullum fuisse ab initio inter episcopos ot presbyteros ratione ordinationis discrimen," &c.

Melancthon, in his tract de Ordine in Ecclesia, 2d vol. of his Works, p 867, bears the following decided testimony against the divine institution of diocesan Episcopacy. " Sed quaerat aliquis annon etiam gradus diversi sint ac ordo? Respondeo, Est in Ecclesia vera ministerium docendi, sunt doctores ac pastores alicubi, ut scriptum est, alios quidem dedit doctores, alios pastores, ne circumferamur variis ventis doctrinae. Est igitur officium, et sunt gradus donorum. Sed hinc non sequitur jure divino episcopum a presbytero discernendum esse. Imo Hieronymus aperte testatur non esse jure divino diversos gradus episcopi et presbyteri." In other words, he admits that there are different degrees of gifts, but denies that it follows from thence that " there is any difference between a bishop and a presbyter; and says, that according to Jerome, the orders of bishops and presbyters are not distinct from each other by divine right.

* See Strype's Cranmer, pp 100 and 101, where it is given to four Popish priests. Tindal's Practice of the Popish Prelates, p. 343 of his works, and Frith's Aunswer to my Lord of Rochester, p. 59.

Dr. Mackenzie, in his Life of James Tyrie, says, that " in the title of one of that Jesuit's books, in controversy with Knox, he styles him Sir John Knox."

† Appendix to his Church History, vol 1. p. 204.

had their admission to the ministerie by the Reformed Churches of England, Geneva or Germanie? If they were not blindlie miscarried, they might perceave that which they speake and write *of our men* in derision and contumelie, calling them Sir John Knox and Frere John Craig, it verifieth their ordinarie vocation."* As far as the succession then could be kept up by ordinations obtained from the Church of Rome, of which the Scottish Episcopalians say in their Confession of Faith, "we fly the doctrine of the Papistical kirk in participation of the Sacrament, because *their ministers are not the ministers of Christ Jesus,*†" and which is represented in Scripture as "the mother of the spiritual abominations of the earth, out of which the saints are exhorted to come, if they would not be partakers of her plagues, within which the great Antichrist sits in the Temple of God, and exalts himself above all that is called God, and where that wicked one bears rule, whom the Lord is to destroy with the spirit of his mouth, and the brightness of his coming," as far, I say, as the succession could be kept up by ordinations obtained *from such a Church*, it was preserved to us as well as to you; and while it has been maintained among you since that time by bishops, and among us by presbyters, I have only further to add, that if you question the validity of our orders, because we received them only from presbyters, you would be bound, for the same reason, to question the validity of the orders of Barnabas and Timothy, one of whom, as has been proved, was ordained even to the office of an Apostle, and the other to that of an evangelist, by presbyters; and you do so in opposition to the fifty-fifth canon of your own Church, to which you swear obedience, and which, though made in 1603, when the Church of Scotland was Presbyterian, enjoined her clergy at that time, and commands them

---

* Defence of the Calling of the Reformed Churches

† Confession of Faith which they used before the Revolution; and yet it is from these men, whom they deny to be the ministers of Christ, that the present bishops of what they haughtily denominate the Reformed Episcopal Church of Scotland derive *their boasted apostolical succession!*

still to pray for our Church as *a sister Church.** Besides, if you deny the validity of our orders, you must set aside also the validity of our baptisms. And this, as I shall endeavour to show you immediately, will lead to consequences of which you are not aware; for on the very same principle it may be easily demonstrated that you are not a minister, nor Mr. Gladstone a Christian, nor the English and Scottish Episcopalian Churches, Churches of Christ.

In the second place, it is impossible for you or any of your followers to prove that such an uninterrupted apostical succession, as that in which you glory, has been preserved in your Church, or in any other Episcopalian Church which exists upon earth.

Before you can either satisfy your own minds, or demonstrate to others that you have such a succession, you must be able to show *who were the bishops* from the apostolic age from whom your present clergy have derived their orders, and that there was *not so much as one of them for the last eighteen hundred years* whose baptism or ordination was irregular. If, as has already been remarked, the chain which you imagine binds you to the Apostles has happened to be broken by an essential defect in the baptism or orders of any of your bishops, or of those who pre-

---

* "The very canons of the Church of England," says the dissenting gentleman in his answer to Mr. White, p. 227, "to which you have sworn obedience, acknowledge the Church of Scotland to be a sister Church, commanding all its clergy to pray for the Churches of England, Scotland and Ireland, as parts of Christ's Holy Catholic Church, which is dispersed throughout the world."

How different from Dr. Pusey's sentiments about the Church, and those of a number of the present Scottish Episcopalians, were the views of Dr. Forbes, one of their ancient professors of divinity, who, in his Irenicum, defends this position, p. 158, that "a church which retains the orthodox faith, but wants bishops, though it may be defective in its constitution, does not cease to be a true church, nor falls from that ecclesiastical authority which is possessed by churches that are governed by bishops." Presbyterians will deny that it is defective, and will maintain that it resembles more closely the apostolic churches than other churches which have diocesan bishops, an order of ministers whom Christ has not instituted. But still it shows the estimate, that even as an enlightened Episcopalian, he formed of the difference between the two Churches, where the doctrines of the Gospel were faithfully preached.

ceded them, whether they were the fiftieth, or the hundredth, or the two hundredth in the series, it is fatal upon your principles; for it cannot be mended, and we must wait till some Apostle rise from the dead, and begin a new succession, before there can be a church or a minister whose labours can be attended with the smallest benefit to the souls of men on the face of the earth. The first of these qualifications is indispensable, for, as Dr. Hickes observes, "baptism is a fundamental qualification for the priesthood, and the want thereof *must utterly render a man uncapable of being a Christian priest, because it makes him utterly uncapable of being a Christian.*"* And you are sensible that by the canons of the first four General Councils, which are recognised both by your Church and by the Scottish Episcopalians, all baptisms performed by schismatics are considered as invalid, and since the conference at Hampton Court, none but ministers who have been ordained by bishops can legally administer that ordinance.† And the second qualification is no less necessary. Now, I apprehend that you cannot tell who were the persons who baptized those individuals from the days of the Apostles, who were afterwards bishops, (and in the days of Tertullian and afterwards *it was often done by laymen,*) and who were the bishops that ordained the latter till the time of the Reformation. The Jews had a series of genealogical tables from the time of the institution of their priesthood, by turning to which they could know at once who had been high-priest, or priests and Levites, from the days of Aaron. By appealing to these, any one who was descended from a priestly family, upon attaining the age appointed in the law, could demand that he should be put into that office; and by referring to them also, the priests and the people could ascertain whether he had a right to it, and whether his ministrations would be valid.

* Letter to Lawrence, p. 37.
† Both English and Scottish Episcopalians attempt to remedy this defect in different ways when converts join their Churches; but they are always unsatisfactory, unless the individuals are re-baptized.

But you, I presume, have no such record of the predecessors of your bishops, from the apostolic age, nor did they succeed, like the Jewish high-priest, by mere lineal descent, nor can you or the prelates of the Scottish Episcopalians, who are beginning to vaunt of their apostolical succession, though their forefathers, in the nineteenth article of their Confession, deny "*lineal descense*" to be "*a mark of the true kirk*,"* produce any evidence of the regularity of their baptisms, or of the validity of their orders, or tell in many instances which of them was first and which of them was last. Eusebius, the most early of our Church historians, confesses that *he* could not do it; for he says that he was "like a man walking through a desert, with only here and there a light to direct him;" and that he had been able to collect such notices as he had procured "of the successors, not *of all*, but only of *the more illustrious* Apostles."† And if such was his want of light in the *fourth* century, will you, or Mr. Newman, or Mr. Gladstone, throw more light on these matters *in the nineteenth?* And he says in another passage, "Who they were, that imitating these Apostles, (Peter and Paul,) were by them thought worthy to govern the Churches which they planted, is no easy thing to tell, *excepting such as may be collected from Paul's own words.*"‡ On which Stillingfleet remarks, then "what becomes of our unquestionable line of succession of the bishops of several Churches, and the large diagrams made of the apostolical Churches, with every one's name set down in his order, as if the writer had been Clarencieux to the Apostles themselves? Are all the great outcries of apostolical tradition, of personal succession, of unquestionable records, resolved at last into the Scripture itself, by him from whom all these long pedigrees are fetched? Then let succession know its place, and learn to vaile bonnet to the

---

* The article relates to "the notes of the true kirk," of which it says, "they are neither antiquity, title usurped, *lineal descense*, place appointed, *nor multitude of men approving an error.*" It was their Confession of Faith before the Revolution.

† Hist. Eccles. lib. 1. cap. 1.

‡ Lib III. cap. 4.

Scriptures; and withal, let men take heed of overreaching themselves, when they would bring down so large a catalogue of single bishops, from the first and purest times of the Church, for it will be hard to others to believe them, when Eusebius professeth it so hard to find them."*

Dr. Cave admits that "there is a wonderful and almost irreconcileable discrepancy among later as well as ancient ecclesiastical writers in determining the age and succession only of the first Roman bishops."† Bishop Jewel, though he lived *nearly three hundred years before you*, acknowledges in the most explicit terms, that it cannot be determined, for he says to Harding the Jesuit, who denied that your Church had the apostolical succession, "But wherefore telleth us, M. Harding, this long tale of succession? Have these men (the Papists,) their owne succession in so safe record? Who was then the Bishop of Rome next by succession unto Peter? Who was the second? who the third? who the fourth? Irenæus reckoneth them together in this order, Petrus, Linus, Anacletus, Clemens. Epiphanius thus, Petrus, Linus, Cletus, Clemens. Optatus thus, Petrus, Linus, Clemens, Anacletus. Clemens saith that hee himself was next unto Peter, and then must the reckoning goe thus: Petrus, Clemens, Linus, Anacletus. *Heereby it is cleer that of the foure first Bishops of Rome, M. Harding cannot certainly tell us who in order succeeded other.* And thus talking so much of succession, they are not well able to blase their own succession."‡ And says Stillingfleet, who, though he published his Irenicum when he was very young, never retracted any of its leading statements, or refuted its reasoning after he was made a bishop, come we therefore to Rome, and here the succession is " as muddy as the Tiber itself; for here Tertullian, Rufinus, and several others place Clement next to Peter;

---

* Irenic p. 297.

† "Miram ac pene irreconciliabilem discrepantiam," &c. Histor. Literaria, p. 17.

‡ Defense of the Apologie, p. 123.

Irenaeus and Eusebius set Anacletus before him—Epiphanius and Optatus both Anacletus and Cletus—Augustine and Damasus with others, Anacletus, Cletus and Linus all to precede him. What way shall we find to extricate ourselves out of this labyrinth?"* "And as to the British Churches," he says, "that *from the loss of the records we cannot draw down the succession of bishops from the Apostles' time!*" But if these things are so, and if you cannot trace the whole of the bishops in the different Churches through eighteen centuries, and attain decisive and satisfactory evidence that their baptisms and ordinations were regular, you can have no proof that your boasted apostolical succession has been preserved either in your own Church or in the Church of Rome, or among the Scottish Episcopalians, or that there is a single individual on the face of the earth whom you are warranted to recognise as a Christian minister, or who has reason to hope that he has a covenanted title to the blessings of salvation.

Do you object to this reasoning, that upon the same principle I might question the genuineness of the New Testament, and require before it is admitted, " we should be able to trace it from manuscript to manuscript, and (after the invention of the art of printing,) from one edition to another, from the original writers to our own time," and see that no important altera-

* Irenicum, part ii. chap. 6, p 322. He says, too, p 321, "At Antioch, some, as Origen and Eusebius, make Ignatius to succeed Peter Jerome makes him the third bishop, and placeth Evodius before him. Others therefore to solve that, make them cotemporary bishops, the one of the Church of the Jews, the other of the Gentiles, with what congruity to their hypothesis of a single bishop and deacons placed in every city, I know not" See a still more striking view of the difficulties connected with the episcopal succession at Antioch, in Dr. Calamy's Defence of Moderate Non-Conformity, vol. i. p 165—169.

Some have attempted to account for the number of bishops at Rome who received that name near the same time, on the principle that it was given to *the presbyter who presided during the year* in the assembly of presbyters, though he had no pre-eminence as to authority over his brethren, just as the individual among the nine archons or chief rulers at Athens, who presided over them for the year, gave his name to the year, and was called the Archon επωνυμος.

tion has taken place? I answer, that the cases are not parallel, and that this objection which was originally urged by Law, and which has been often since repeated, does not apply. The uneducated Christian is convinced that the New Testament is the word of God, without any such inquiries, from its perfect accordance with the wants of his soul, as a guilty and suffering and immortal creature; and because the more carefully he lives under the influence of its truths, it renders him at once more happy in himself, and more like to his God; and judging from its effects, he never has the slightest doubt of its genuineness.* And it is enough to satisfy a man of learning, that his copy of the New Testament is genuine, when he finds it correspond with *the earliest* manuscripts, and most ancient versions, such as the Syriac and the old Latin, and sees these confirmed as the writings of the Apostles and Evangelists, by the quotations from them in the works of the primitive Christians during the *first five centuries.* And he cares no more for any corrupted copies in *later times,* than Vossius or Usher, who believed, (though I think without sufficient evidence,) in the genuineness of the lesser Epistles of Ignatius, because they contained, as they imagined, the passages which were quoted from them by the

* "Historians inform us," says Fuller in the introduction to his Gospel its own Witness, p. 2, "of a certain valuable medicine, called *Mithridate,* an antidote to poison It is said to have been invented by Mithridates, King of Pontus; that the receipt of it was found in a cabinet, written with his own hand, and was carried to Rome by Pompey, that it was translated into verse by Democrates, a famous physician; and that it was afterwards translated by Galen, from whom we have it. Now, supposing this medicine to be efficacious for its professed purpose, of what account would it be to object to the authenticity of its history? If a modern caviller should take it into his head to allege that the preparation has passed through so many hands, and that there is so much hearsay and uncertainty attending it, that no dependence can be placed upon it, and that it had better be rejected from our materia medica, he would be asked, *has it not been tried, and found to be effectual, and that in a great variety of instances?* Such are Mr. Paine's objections to the Bible, and such is the answer that may be given to him." And such is the way when he applies the New Testament to himself, in which the unlettered Christian is convinced of its genuineness.

early Christians, would have cared for the larger spurious Epistles where these passages are wanting. But it is a very different thing with the apostolical succession, for though it had been preserved uncorrupted during the first five centuries, (and you have no evidence that it was so,) yet if it was vitiated afterwards in the seventh, or eighth, or any other century, it would be utterly destroyed, and could not possibly be restored, except by the mission of an Apostle to commence a new ordination of ministers. And if you tell me with Law, that "it is impossible the succession could be broken, because it has been a received doctrine in every age of the Church, that no ordination was valid but that of bishops; and as there is no possibility of forging orders, or stealing a bishopric in the Church of England in the present day," so it must have been equally impossible in every other Church at every period;* I reply, that facts are stubborn things, and it is an extraordinary mode of reasoning to infer from what was *the doctrine* of the Church, what must also have been *its practice in every instance, from the days of the Apostles*. It has been the doctrine of the Church, for example, in every age, that three bishops could not legally ordain little children to be bishops; and you might maintain on this ground, that *it never happened*, though Bingham informs us that it was actually done, "as the Popes have ordained some at seven."† It has been the doctrine of the Church, that no bishop should obtain ordination through simony, and you might affirm on this ground that *it has never taken place*, though I trust I shall prove to you that it has frequently been the case. And it has likewise been its doctrine, that *bishops who were drunk* could not bestow legal orders on a bishop or presbyter, and you might argue from this circumstance that *no instance of it had occurred*, for it could not occur in the present day in the Church of England. And yet it has been asserted by Pyle in his Strictures on Law, and

* Postscript to his Second Letter to Bishop Hoadly, p. 101.
† History of Lay Baptism, Works, vol. ii. p. 622.

has never been contradicted, that "Novatian, in the third century, procured himself to be ordained a bishop by the hands of three bishops whom he had made drunk for that purpose."* I might easily have added many other instances, in which the practice of the Church in regard to ordination, was directly the reverse of some of her leading doctrines, and it might as consistently be maintained, in opposition to the testimony of the most respectable historians, that they did not occur, as that *there never was an instance since the days of the Apostles, of an individual being made a bishop whose baptism or orders were irregular, because it was the doctrine of the Church that both of them should be in strict accordance with its canons.*

But do you remind me with Bishop Skinner, that the apostolical succession is often mentioned by the fathers as a distinguishing mark of the true Church? For says Tertullian of some of the heretics who existed in his day, " Let them produce the original of their Churches, show the order of their bishops so running down successively from the beginning, as that every first bishop among them shall have had for his author and predecessor some one of the Apostles, or apostolic men who continued with the Apostles." And says Irenaeus of some others, "We can reckon up those who were by the Apostles ordained bishops, and those who were their successors, even to our own time. They never taught nor knew any of the wild opinions of these men."† I might content myself with referring

* Second Letter to a Member of the University of Cambridge, p. 77. The fact is admitted by a friend of Mr Law, who calls himself P. F., and yet in his letter to Pyle, p 40, " because the consecration was performed *in the name of the Holy Trinity* by those *who were duly commissioned* for that purpose," he affirms that it was valid! Would a similar appointment to any civil office in the name of a superior, by persons who were duly commissioned to make it, but who were drunk at the time, be held valid? Upon the same principle it would follow, that if three drunk bishops were to give episcopal orders to an idiot or fatuous person in the name of the Trinity, it would be valid, and he would keep up the apostolical succession!

† Tertullian de Praescript., c 32. Irenaeus adversus Haeres. lib. III. cap. 3.

you to what is said by Bishop Jewel, in answer to the very same objection, when it was urged by Harding for the apostolical succession in the Church of Rome, which that Papist contended was wanting in your Church,* and with merely remarking, that when you reply to his arguments I will reply to yours.† But I would observe further, that they appeal to the succession not to establish your position, that an uninterrupted series of ministers deriving their orders from diocesan bishops, from the days of the Apostles, is essential to the existence of a church, but only to show that their own doctrine, which they asserted was taught by the ministers who succeeded the Apostles in the different churches, till the time in which they themselves lived, was more likely to be true, than that of these heretics. Such was the purpose to which it was applied by Irenaeus, for after mentioning that it would be tedious to go through the successions in all the Churches, he says, "selecting the Church of Rome, and showing them the tradition," or as it is explained in the beginning of the chapter, the doctrine which it has from the Apostles, ("traditionem Apostolorum in toto mundo manifestatam,") and "the faith announced to men by successions of bishops extending to us, we confound them all."‡ And the same also

* Defense of the Apologie, p. 122, 123.

† [Even Laud himself, who is an object of almost idolatrous veneration with Puseyite Episcopalians, however accustomed to extol the succession in his attacks upon the Puritans, was constrained to assume a different language when in controversy with Fisher the Jesuit. He was compelled then to say, "Besides, for succession in the general, I shall say this it is a great happiness where it may be had visible and continued and a great conquest over the mutability of this present world. But I do not find any one of the ancient fathers that makes *local, personal, visible* and *continued succession, a necessary sign or mark of the Church in any one place*" And then to make his testimony still more remarkable, he admits, "most evident it is, that the succession which the fathers meant, is not tied to place or person, but it is tied to the *verity of doctrine.*"]—Am Editor.

‡ "Quoniam valde longum est in hoc tali volumine omnium Ecclesiarum enumerare successiones, maximae et antiquissimae, et omnibus cognitae a gloriosissimis duobus Apostolis Petro et Paulo Romae fundatae et constitutae Ecclesiae eam quam habet ab Apostolis traditionem, et annunciatam hominibus fidem, per successiones Epis-

is the purpose to which it is applied by Tertullian, for while he appeals at one time in proof of the purity of his principles to the doctrines taught by the successors of the Apostles, he appeals in other passages to the Churches themselves, which had their authentic epistles.* Besides, though these fathers speak of the evangelical doctrine, as preserved by a succession of bishops, they never mention a word from which you can infer *that they were diocesan bishops*, and they as frequently represent *the succession as having been kept up by presbyters.* "Wherefore," says Irenaeus, "we ought to obey those presbyters in the Church who have succession, as we have shown, from the Apostles, who with the succession of the Episcopate, received the certain gift of truth, according to the good pleasure of the Father."† And in the following chapter he says, "Such presbyters the Church nourishes concerning whom the prophet says, I will give your princes in peace, and your bishops in righteousness."‡ Nay, Jerome even says, that "*presbyters occupy the place of the Apostles*, (in loco Apostolorum,") and "*succeed the Apostles*, (Apostolico gradui succedere.") Nothing, therefore, can be more just than the remark of Stillingfleet, that " it is the doctrine which they speak of as to succession, and the persons no further than as they are the conveyors of that doctrine; either then it must be proved that *a succession of some persons in apostolical power is necessary for conveying this doctrine to men*, or no argument at all can be inferred from hence, for their succeeding the Apostles in power, because they are said to convey down the apostolical doctrine to succeeding ages."§ I have only further to

coporum pervenientes usque ad nos, indicantes, confundimus omnes eos."

* Age jam qui voles curiositatem melius exercere in negotio salutis tuae percurrere Ecclesias Apostolicas apud quas ipsae adhuc Cathedrae Apostolorum suis locis praesidentur, apud quas ipsae authenticae eorum literae recitantur, sonantes vocem et representantes faciem uniuscujusque. Proxime est tibi Achaia ? habes Corinthum. Si non longe es a Macedonia, habes Philippos, habes Thessalonicenses," &c. De Praescript, cap. 36

† Adv. Haeres., lib. 4, cap. 43.
‡ Ibid. cap. 44.   § Irenicum, p. 305.

observe, that both these fathers lived scarcely a hundred years after the last of the Apostles, and that even if they had been successful in tracing the bishops of the different Churches during *that short period* back to these first ministers of the Gospel, (which is denied, as I have showed you, by Jewel and Stillingfleet,) it by no means follows that you, or Dr. Hook, or any of your followers, can trace your succession *through eighteen hundred years,* and prove that the bishops from whom you have derived your orders, *without a single exception,* were regularly baptized, and regularly ordained.* And yet all this is necessary upon your principles, before it is possible to establish the claim of any minister in the Church of England, or among the Scottish Episcopalians, or even in the Church of Rome, which you so greatly admire, to the honourable character of a Christian minister, or the title of any of the members of these Churches to the blessings of salvation.

I remain, Reverend Sir,

Yours, &c.

---

* Dr. Inett, in his Origines Anglicanae, vol. i. p. 200, says that "the difficulties of succession in the see of Canterbury, betwixt the year 768 and the year 800, were invincible." And in p. 329 he says, that after the death of Dunstan, "Ethelgar, late abbot of the new monastery in Winchester, and at this time Bishop of Winchester, succeeded to the chair of Canterbury the year following; but dying the same year, *our historians are not agreed who succeeded*, some confidently pronouncing in favour of Siricius, others of Elfricus."

In like manner Keith remarks, respecting the diocese of Dunblane, in Scotland, that "the writs of this see have been so neglected, or perhaps wilfully destroyed, that no light can be got from thence to guide us aright *in making up*" *even the list of ancient bishops.*

Sir James Ware, the learned Irish antiquary, acknowledges, in his account of the bishops of Raphoe, that he cannot tell so much as the names of the bishops in some of the Irish sees, and *he leaves whole centuries blank.*

LETTER XV.

The succession destroyed in all those instances in which individuals who had only Presbyterian baptism, and were not rebaptized, joined Episcopalian Churches, and were made presbyters and bishops —Confirmation cannot remedy this defect, because, as Cranmer admits, "it was not instituted by Christ," nor was *the Redeemer himself, or any individual mentioned in the New Testament, confirmed,* and because, as some of the leading English Reformers acknowledged, "it is a domme ceremony," and "*has no promise of grace connected with it*"—Butler, who had only Presbyterian baptism, and was not rebaptized, made a bishop, baptized many, who were afterwards ministers, and made a number of bishops —Secker, who had only the same baptism, made Primate of England, ordained many presbyters, and a number of bishops, and baptized two kings, who for a long time were heads of the Church —Tillotson, though the son of a Baptist, and though there is no evidence that he was ever baptized, or ordained a deacon, made Archbishop of Canterbury —Succession destroyed for more than two hundred years in the important Church of Alexandria, and in the early Church of Scotland, in consequence of the ordinations by the Culdee presbyters —Account of the presbyters of Iona, their evangelical doctrine, their Presbyterian government, and the acknowledgment of their ecclesiastical authority by the Clergy of Scotland

REVEREND SIR,—The charge which I have preferred against you in the previous letter, and which I trust has been established, is apparently uncourteous. I have asserted that you hold, without any thing like proof which you would consider as satisfactory on any other subject, though of far inferior importance, the extraordinary opinion that the apostolical succession has never been interrupted. But the charge which I have to urge against you in the present letter is far more serious, for I affirm that you hold it in opposition to very strong and decisive evidence that it has actually been broken.

You contend that orders which have been obtained from the hands of Presbyterian ministers cannot be valid, because they were received from men who had no right to bestow them, and whom you consider as schismatics. Now, upon the same principle, it is obvious that baptism, when administered by the very same individuals, must be equally invalid, because in your opinion they had no right to give it; and those who have received it, and who have not been rebaptized, cannot be Christians. Nor will it obviate this difficulty to allege, with Archdeacon Daubeny, that what was defective in such baptisms may be supplied in confirmation, when those who have been the subjects of them join your Church. In the *first* place, I see no warrant in Scripture for the rite of confirmation, or the laying on of the hands of a bishop on those who are baptized; and if the Redeemer did not appoint it, I cannot perceive how it can be accompanied by his blessing, or followed by his acceptance, or how it can supply an essential and momentous defect in the mode of administering one of the sacraments of the Church. He himself did not perform it during his personal ministry upon any who were baptized, and surely if the communication of the sanctifying and confirming influences of the Spirit, by the laying on of hands, after an individual has been baptized, be necessary now, before he is admitted to the holy communion, it was no less necessary in the days of the Saviour. And the only two instances mentioned in the New Testament in which the Apostles laid their hands on those who had been baptized, (Acts ch. viii. and xix.) were cases in which miraculous gifts were communicated, which cannot, I presume, be imparted at present to those who are confirmed by any bishop. "After that the bishops had left preachyng," says Tindal, when speaking of this rite, as performed merely by the imposition of hands, without any of the Popish ceremonies, " then fayned they *this domme ceremonie of confirmation,* to have somewhat at the least whereby they might raigne over their dioceses. And as to that they layd against him in the eighth chapter of the Acts, where Peter and John put their hands on the Samaritanes," he "denies that it will establish it. God had made the Apostles a promise, that he woulde with such miracles confirme their preaching and move others to the faith. The Apostles, therefore, beleved and prayed God to fulfill his promise, and God for his truthe's sake even so did."* So decidedly was Cranmer of

* Obedience of a Christian Man, p 152. of his works. See also his Aunswere to Syr Thomas More, p. 276, 277.

the same opinion, though he was obliged to allow this rite to remain, that when he was asked his judgment respecting it, along with "divers bishops and doctors in commission," he gave the following answer to the question, "Whether confirmation be instituted by Christ?"

"There is no place in Scripture that declareth this sacrament to be instituted by Christ.*

"*Secondly,* these acts were done by *a special gift* given to the Apostles for the confirmation of God's word *at that time.*

"*Thirdly, the said special gift doth not now remain with the successors of the Apostles.*"

And said Dr. Edmonds, Master of Peter House in Cambridge, "Confirmation is not a sacrament of the new law instituted by Christ by any expressed word in the Scripture, but *only by the tradition of the fathers.*

"Confirmation hath no promise of any invisible grace by Christ by any expressed word in Holy Scripture.

"*There be no promises of grace made by Christ to them that receive confirmation* "† The same also was the opinion of Jewel, who says, in his Treatise of the Sacraments, p. 264, "Confirmation was not ordained by Christ." And though Bancroft stated, at the Conference at Hampton Court, that he considered it as "founded on Heb. vi. 2, where it is represented as a part of the Apostles' Catechisme,‡ and not so much upon the places in the Acts of the Apostles," as some of the fathers had often showed, yet it is evident that the laying on of hands, which is referred

---

* Cyprian calls confirmation and baptism two sacraments. Epist. 72.

Bishop Bilson, as we have seen, not only admits that it was the extraordinary gifts of the Spirit which were bestowed on the Samaritan converts, (Acts viii.) by the laying on of the hands of the Apostles, and in particular the gift of tongues, but says, that this and these other gifts were imparted to them to qualify them for preaching the Gospel immediately to them who understood these languages. Can bishops bestow any such gifts now on those whom they confirm ?

† Append. to first vol of Strype's Memorials, p. 88, 235-238.

‡ Dr. Barlow's Account of the Conference at Hampton Court, p 32.

to in that passage, denotes rather ordination to the ministry, which, as Archbishop Usher acknowledges, is far more worthy of being described as one of the fundamental principles of the doctrine of Christ than the rite of confirmation.*

And the same is the opinion of your fellow-tractarians, for when speaking of Presbyterians, Independents and Methodists, (Tract 36,) they say, " These three do not receive or teach the truth respecting the doctrine of laying on of hands, which St. Paul classes among the fundamental doctrines of Christianity, (Heb. vi. 2;) and by which the Christian ministry receives its commission and authority to administer the word and sacraments."

And, 2*dly*, even admitting that it may be lawfully performed, though, as is mentioned in an old Waldensian work, " *Christ, the pattern of all his Church, was not confirmed in his own person,*† and it has not been instituted by him, but rests solely on the tradition of the fathers, and no grace has been promised to those who receive it," not an instance can be pointed out *in which it was administered to any one whose baptism was invalid.*‡ On what principle,

---

* Melancthon, in his Apology for the Confession of Augsburgh, tom 1. of his Works, fol. 95, says, in the name of the Lutheran Churches, " Confirmatio et extrema unctio sunt ritus accepti a Patribus." And in the Saxon Confession which he drew up, he says, fol. 129, " ideo non servantur in nostris ecclesiis "

† Sir Samuel Morland's History of the Waldenses, p. 142. Dr. Gilly has been very anxious to show that they were Episcopalians. They not only, however, reject confirmation in the passage quoted above, but add immediately afterwards, that Christ did not require it or unction in baptism. " And, therefore, such a sacrament was introduced to seduce the people, and that by such means they might be drawn more easily *to believe the ceremonies and the necessity of bishops.*"

" It has been inferred," says Dr Jamieson, in his Historical Account of the Culdees, p. 206, " from the language of Bernard, that confirmation was quite in disuse, if at all ever known among the Irish Culdees; for, in his Life of Malachy, he says, that he anew instituted the sacrament of confirmation."

‡ It might be maintained with greater consistency, that the observance of the Lord's Supper, which is a divine institution, would make up, on the part of a Presbyterian who joins an Episcopalian Church, for the want both of confirmation and baptism, than that confirma-

then, baptism, when it has been dispensed by Presbyterians, whom you consider as schismatics, and as having no authority to perform it, can be regarded merely as defective, and not as *a perfect nullity*, like Presbyterian ordination, I am at a loss to understand. You cannot, however, be ignorant, that many who had received only Presbyterian baptism joined your Church soon after the Restoration, and others since that time; nay, that some of them, though they were not rebaptized, have been admitted among your clergy, and have risen to places of power and influence. Two cases especially occurred during the last century, in which young Presbyterians, without being rebaptized, entered your communion, attained your highest ecclesiastical dignities, and contributed to an extent which it is impossible to ascertain to break the succession. One of them was Butler, who, while he was Rector of Stanhope, baptized a number of the members of your Church, some of whom may have become ministers; and who, while he was Bishop, first of Bristol, and afterwards of Durham, ordained many clergymen, and assisted in the consecration of many bishops from whom your present bishops and ministers have descended. If, therefore, the baptisms which he administered, and the orders which he gave

tion, which is a mere human invention, can make up for the want of baptism.

It is admitted by the Oxford Tractarians, (Tract 41, p. 7,) that all that is required from an individual for confirmation is to be able " to say the Creed, the Lord's Prayer, and the Ten Commandments, nothing being said of a change of heart, or spiritual affections." And yet, *upon this mere external profession*, the children receive the imposition of the bishop's hands, "to certify them by this sign of God's favour and gracious goodness towards them," *because they can repeat these things*, after which they are admitted to the communion. How different is the practice of faithful ministers in the Presbyterian Church, where there is no such unauthorised rite as confirmation, to which no grace is promised, but who meet with those young individuals who are candidates for communion for a number of weeks, or even months, before, pray with them, instruct them carefully in the great truths of religion, and in the end of the institution of the sacrament of the Supper, and endeavour to impress them with a sense of the necessity of faith and personal piety to acceptable communion, and who, upon their being encouraged to form a favourable opinion of them as to these points, admit them to that privilege!

to those who afterwards gave orders to others, in many of your dioceses, were invalid, because he himself was unbaptized, what must be the spiritual condition of your Church? The other was his friend and companion, Secker, who, as the son of a Dissenting Presbyterian minister, had only Presbyterian baptism, and was never rebaptized. After joining your Church he was promoted first to be Rector of St. James's, then successively to be Bishop of Bristol and Oxford, and latterly Archbishop of Canterbury and Primate of all England.* But if he himself was not a Christian, and yet baptized not only many of the ordinary members of your Church, but George the Third,† whom he also

---

* " Mr. Thomas Secker, afterwards Archbishop of Canterbury," says the late Rev. Dr. Adam Clarke, vol xii. of his Miscellaneous Works, p. 171, " was the son of a dissenting minister, born in 1693, was baptized after the form of that Church, and studied at three dissenting schools successively until he was nineteen years of age, when he went to the University of Oxford, and afterwards entered the communion of the Church of England. He was in 1732 nominated one of the Chaplains to the King, in 1733, was appointed Rector of St. James's January 5, 1734, he was elevated to the Bishopric of Bristol, to that of Oxford in 1737, in 1750 exchanged a prebend in Durham, and the Rectory of St. James's for the Deanery of St Paul's, and in 1758 he was named and confirmed to the Archbishopric of Canterbury. He officiated at the funeral of King George the Second, and at the proclamation of his present Majesty, whom he had baptized when Rector of St James's, and whom with his Queen he married, and crowned 8th September 1761, and on the 8th September 1762, he baptized the Prince of Wales, and afterwards several of their Majesties' children. We hear nothing of his ever having been rebaptized "

† The same thing happened to Charles the First, whom Episcopalians commonly denominate *the Royal Martyr* for Episcopacy, and yet whom Dr. Pusey, and his followers among the Scottish Episcopalians, cannot consider as a Christian, though they keep the anniversary of his death, for he was baptized by a Scottish Presbyterian minister in the Chapel Royal at Dunfermline, and was never rebaptized. " In the month of December this year, (1600,)" says Wodrow the historian, " Mr David Lindsay baptized the King's son, Charles the First, who was his father's successor, (at Falkland, born November 19,) in Dunfermline, upon Tuesday, the 23d of December 1600, as a book in the Lyon's Office at Edinburgh bears." But how much more extraordinary must have been the situation of the Church of England during the reign of George the Third, when neither that pious and venerable Monarch, the Head of that Church, nor Archbishop Secker, the Primate of the whole kingdom, could be Christians ! And in what a light does it exhibit the conduct of our present gracious Sovereign,

married, and George the Fourth, both of whom were for a long time the heads of that Church, and if, as you must be well aware, he ordained many bishops, priests and deacons, the injury which he must have done to the apostolical succession in the Church of England is absolutely incalculable. As you cannot, therefore, raise him and his illustrious friend, and others of your bishops who had only Presbyterian baptism, from the mansions of the tomb, and get them rebaptized and re-ordained, nor raise up along with them the bishops and clergy whose orders they vitiated, and get the error corrected, not only in the orders of the dead, but in those of the living, I trust that we shall hear no more from you, or Dr. Short, or Mr. Newman, or Mr. Gladstone, of your unbroken succession. And I sincerely hope, that you will inquire anew into the truth of a doctrine which leads unavoidably to these tremendous consequences, and that none of you will in future join in the lofty and presumptuous assertion, which you have already so confidently made, that "yours is the only Church in the realm *which has a right to be quite sure that she is a Church of Christ,* and has the Lord's body to give to his people."

But if the succession has been broken in all those instances in which bishops and presbyters have been baptized by Presbyterians, and have not been rebaptized, you will scarcely deny that it has been still more seriously injured, if any of your prelates have been raised even to the highest dignity in your Church, and yet were never baptized, *either by a*

in inviting her relation, the King of Prussia, who, as he was neither baptized by a bishop, nor by a minister who was ordained by a bishop, cannot, according to Dr. Hook or Mr. Gladstone, be a Christian, to stand as godfather to the young Prince of Wales! The mind revolts at principles which lead to such consequences And yet these are the consequences of the present doctrine of the apostolical succession, which is gaining rapidly numerous converts in the English Universities, and for the propagation of which in the New College of what the Scottish Episcopalians modestly denominate the Reformed Catholic Church of Scotland, the English Society for Propagating *Christian* Knowledge have, through the strenuous advocacy of Mr. Dodesworth, a most zealous Puseyite, supported by Mr. W. Gladstone, voted *a thousand pounds.*

layman, Pesbyterian, or Episcopalian. And yet there is reason to believe that this was the case with Tillotson, who occupied for a long time the See of Canterbury, and the primacy of England. No evidence has been produced, though it has been often demanded, of his having been ordained a deacon, and yet he was permitted to hold the office of a deacon. Nor will it at all appear wonderful, that such irregularities should have been tolerated at that period, when you consider what has taken place almost in our own day. "Even in later and more civilized and enlightened times," says Dr. Whately, "the probability of an irregularity, though very greatly diminished, is yet diminished only, and not *absolutely destroyed. Even in the memory of persons living, there existed a bishop, concerning whom there was so much mystery and uncertainty prevailing, as to when, where, and by whom he had been ordained, that doubts existed in the minds of many persons, whether he had ever been ordained at all.*" I do not, however, refer so much to his want of deacon's orders, and the invalidity of all the baptisms which he administered, nor to the invalidity of his priest's orders, which he received from Sydeself, whose own orders were uncanonical, and who, as he was a Scottish bishop, had no right to confer orders in England, who, we are told by Birch, "ordained all those of the English clergy who came to him, without demanding either oaths (of canonical obedience,) or subscriptions (to articles) of them, *merely for a subsistence, from the fees for the orders granted by him,*—for he was very poor;"—I say I do not refer so much to either of these circumstances, as to his want of baptism. He did not receive that ordinance in his infancy, for his father *was a Baptist;* and though he was often challenged to produce any evidence of his having been baptized afterwards, none was brought forward; and unless it can be furnished by you, or by some of your friends in the present day, or by some of the clergy of the Church of England, we must consider him as unbaptized. But if the man who was so long the Primate of that Church, and who made so many bishops, and priests, and deacons, had not even such baptism as could be obtained from a midwife, I leave it to you to say what must be the value of your own orders, or of the orders of any of the clergy of your Church, who hold your principles, and what must be the virtue of their ministrations, and what the prospects of final salvation to those who hear them.*

But passing from your Church, I would further remark, that the succession must have been injured in all these instances in which bishops and presbyters were not only baptized, but *were ordained by presbyters,* and *were not re-ordained.* Now that this was the case from the earliest ages is beyond a doubt. It was the case in the important See of Alexandria, where, as Usher stated to Charles the First, upon the authority of Jerome and Eutychius, the presbyters for a long time made not only presbyters, but bishops. "For even from Mark the Evangelist," said the first of these writers, "to the Bishops Heraclas and Dionysius, the presbyters always named as bishop one chosen from among themselves, and placed him in a higher degree, in the same manner as if an army should make an emperor, or the deacons should choose from among themselves any one whom they knew to be industrious, and should call him archdeacon."† Upon which Willet, as was noticed formerly,

* "In Mr. Percival's Catalogus," says the author of an exceedingly able article on Scottish Prelacy, in the Presbyterian Review p. 30, note, "there occur the following names, of whose consecration there are no records, and of course no evidence extant, viz William Downham of Chester, in 1561; J. Stanley of Sodor, 1573, J. May of Carlisle, 1577, G Loyd of Sodor, 1600, translated to Chester, 1604, B. Potter, Carlisle, 1628, William Leorster, Sodor, 1633, R. Parr, Sodor, 1635, H Ferne, Chester, 1666, E. Rainbow, Carlisle, 1644, J. Wilkins, Chester, 1668, H. Bridgman, Sodor, 1671, T. Smith, Carlisle, 1684, N Strafford, Chester, 1689 Even the celebrated Pearson of Chester, so well known by his works on the Creed and on Ignatius, has no extant record of his consecration. Nor has Lake, who, in 1684, was translated from Sodor to Bristol, and in the following year to Chichester, and of very necessity, *no man who has received orders through any of these has or can have any evidence that he is in orders at all*"

† "Nam et Alexandriae a Marco Evangelista usque ad Heraclam et Dionysium Episcopos Presbyteri semper unum ex se electum in

remarks, "So it would seeme that the very election of a bishop in those days without any other circumstances was his ordination." And says Stillingfleet, who answers at considerable length the numerous objections urged by Bishop Pearson to this interpretation of the passage, "it appears that by election he means *conferring authority* by the instances he brings to that purpose; as the Roman armies choosing their emperor, who had no other power but what they received by the length of the sword, and the deacons choosing their archdeacon, who had no other power but what was merely conferred by the choice of the college of deacons."* And says Eutychius, who is represented by Ebn Abi Osbae as a "man well acquainted with the sciences and institutions which were in use among the Christians,"† and whose testimony coincides with that of Jerome, "Hananias was the first of the patriarchs who were set over the Church of Alexandria. For Mark the Evangelist appointed along with the Patriarch Hananias twelve presbyters, who should continue along with the Patriarch, so that when the patriarchate became vacant they should choose one of the twelve presbyters, upon whose head the other eleven laying their hands, *should themselves bless him and create him a patriarch;* and then they should choose some distinguished man in his room who was made patriarch, that so there might be always twelve. Nor did this institution respecting the presbyters at Alexandria, that they should create the patriarchs from the twelve presbyters, cease till the time of Alexander, Patriarch of Alexandria, who was of that number

---

excelsiori gradu collocatum Episcopum nominabant, quomodo is exercitus imperatorem faciat, aut diaconi eligant de se quem industrium noverint, et Archidiaconum vocent" Epist. 85, ad Evagrium.

* Irenicum, p. 274.

† "Scientiarum et institutorum quae apud Christianos in usu sunt peritus." Selden represents him as spoken of in terms of high respect by ancient writers And Mosheim says, vol ii p. 414, that ' no author among the Arabians attained higher reputation among the Arabians than he," and refers to Fabricius's Bibliographia Antiquaria, p. 179.

three hundred and eighteen. But he forbade the presbyters afterwards *to create* the patriarch, and decreed that when the patriarch was dead the bishops should assemble, who should ordain the patriarch. Also he decreed, that when the patriarchate was vacant, they should choose either from any quarter, or from these twelve presbyters, or from others, some eminent man of approved probity, and should create him patriarch. And *thus vanished that more ancient institution, according to which the patriarchate was wont to be created by the presbyters*, and there succeeded in its place the decree respecting the creation of the patriarch by the bishops."* And as it is obvious that he could have no inducement to make this statement, but a regard to truth, because, as he himself was a patriarch, it was fitted to lessen the respectability of his order, inasmuch as it showed a deviation from the mode of creating the patriarchs, which had been recommended by the Evangelist; and as it is confirmed by Jerome, who was born only *about eighty years* after the change took place, and who had the best opportunities to become acquainted with the fact, as he lived much in the East, it is perfectly capricious on the part of Episcopalians to question their testimony. Usher, who was one of the most able and learned of their bishops, examined the evidence in former times with the utmost care, and declared himself to be satisfied, and there appears to

* "Hananias fuit Patriarcharum qui Alexandriae praefecti sunt primus. Constituit autem Evangelista Marcus una cum Hanania patriarcha duodecim presbyteros qui nempe cum patriarcha manerent, adeo ut cum vacaret patriarchatus, unum e duodecim presbyteris eligerent, cujus capiti reliqui undecim manus imponentes ipsi benedicerent, et patriarcham crearent; deinde virum aliquem insignem eligerent quem secum presbyterum constituerent loco ejus qui factus est patriarcha, ut ita semper extarent duodecim. Neque desiit Alexandriae institutum hoc de presbyteris, ut scilicet patriarchas crearent ex presbyteris duodecim usque ad tempora Alexandri Patriarchae Alexandrini, qui fuit ex numero illo trecentorum et octodecim," &c. Annals, vol. i. p. 331.

Gibbon says that Jerome's statement "receives a remarkable confirmation from the Patriarch Eutychius, whose testimony he knew not how to reject in spite of all the objections of the learned Pearson."

be no good reason why it ought not to satisfy them now. If they have perfect confidence in the lists of bishops of some of the Churches given by Eusebius, though he lived *nearly three hundred years* after the time when they commenced, nothing but a conviction that it bears so strongly against diocesan Episcopacy, and the apostolical succession, could prompt them to doubt the statement of Jerome, who lived *so much nearer to the event* which he reports, corroborated as it is by another individual who himself presided over the See of Alexandria, and might have access to its records, and who will be acknowledged at least to be an impartial witness. But if the bishops of Alexandria, as Usher affirmed, *for two hundred and fifty years* were made by presbyters, either by election without ordination, or by laying their hands on their heads, and setting them apart to their office, I would like to be informed whether the succession must not have been broken even at the the very beginning, during that long period. And as Alexandria was one of the largest and most populous bishoprics in the early Church, I shall leave it to any candid individual to say, whether he can estimate the amount of the disorder and confusion which may have been introduced into other sections of the Christian Church, by clergymen coming into them, whose orders, upon your principles, must have been irregular and invalid.

Another part of the Church where there was no succession of diocesan bishops for several centuries, was the early Church of Scotland. According to the testimony of all our historians, this part of the island embraced Christianity in the year 203, and no bishop appeared in it till the year 429, or 430, when Palladius was despatched thither by Pope Celestine. Such is the statement of Prosper of Aquitaine, who, according to the late Bishop Skinner, " lived in the time when, and the place where Palladius resided" before he came to Britain; for says he, " two hundred and twenty-seven years before Scotland was converted, or in the year 430, Palladius being ordained by Pope Celestine, was sent to the Scots believing in Christ, as their first bishop, (primus episcopus.) It is confirmed by Bede, though a zealous Episcopalian, who repeats the very words of Prosper.* John of Fordun, a respectable writer, and not, " a dreaming monk, anxious merely for the honour of his order," as Bishop Lloyd calls him, says, that " before the coming of Palladius, the Scots had, as teachers of the faith, and administrators of the sacraments, *only presbyters and monks, following the custom of the primitive Church* † And a similar statement is contained in the Breviary of Aberdeen, where the Scots, before the time of Palladius, are described as " having had for teachers of the faith, and ministers of the sacraments, *presbyters* and monks, following *only the right and custom of the primitive Church.*‡" And says John Mair or Major, of whom Bishop Lesley remarks, that " he was more studious of truth than eloquence,§ in the year of our

* Chron Tempor. p. 26 Hist , lib 1 c 13
† Scotichronicon, lib III. c 8. Sir George Mackenzie, in his Defence of the Royal Line, p. 26, says that "he was a presbyter and not a monk, as St. Asaph calls him "
Dr. Jamieson, in his historical account of the Culdees, p. 97, says, " It is a singular circumstance, that however much later writers have affected to despise the testimony of Fordun with respect to the Culdees, the Canons of St Andrews did not hesitate to avail themselves of it, (I quote the passage, chiefly to show the general respectability of Fordun,) when it was subservient to their credit in the meantime, though at the expense of giving a severe blow to Episcopacy in an early age. As there had been a dispute, at a meeting of Parliament in the reign of James I., with respect to precedency between the priors of St. Andrews and Kelso; the King having heard the arguments on both sides, determined it in favour of the former, on this principle, that he was entitled to priority in rank, whose monastery was prior as to foundation " " We have a proof of this," says Fordun, " from St Columba, who is represented as Arch-Abbot of all Ireland, and who was held in such pre-eminence among the inhabitants, that (and he was only a presbyter) *he is said to have confirmed and consecrated all the Irish bishops of his time.*" (Scotichron. lib, vi c 49) " The whole of this chapter," says Dr Jamieson, " not excepting the passage last mentioned, has been embodied in the Register of St. Andrews."
‡ "Habentes fidei doctores et sacramentorum ministros presbyteros et monachos primitivæ ecclesiæ solummodo sequentes ritum et consuetudinem." In Iulic, fol 24, 25
§ "Veritatis ubique quam eloquentiae studiosior." Hist. Scot. lib, ix. p. 414.

Lord 429, Pope Celestinus consecrated Saint Palladius a bishop, and sent him to Scotland, for the Scots were previously instructed in the faith by priests and monks, *without bishops.*"* Here, then, was another part of the Church, which, according to the united testimony of these writers, all of whom were Episcopalians, was without bishops for more than two hundred years, and which was instructed and governed by presbyters, not according to the form of polity which existed in the days of either Prosper or Bede, but according, as they express it, "to the custom of the primitive Church."†

As the Church of Scotland during that long period had no diocesan bishops, and therefore, upon your

---

* " Anno Domini 429, Sanctum Palladium Caelestinus Papa episcopum consecrat et ad Scotiam mittit   Nam per sacerdotes et monachos sine Episcopis Scoti in fide erudiebantur." Hist. Maj Britanniae, lib ii. cap. 2, fol 23.

† Some have questioned whether Palladius ever visited Scotland. Dr. Jamieson shows that he laboured for a time in that country. ' Fordun," says he, p. 9, " confining the mission of Palladius to the Scots in Britain, says that Eugenius gave him and his companions a place of residence where he asked it. In the MS of Coupar, there is this addition: Apud Fordun, in lie Mearns, *i. e* at Fordun, in the Mearns. This perfectly coincides with the modern account." This parish (Fordun) is remarkable for having been for some time the residence, and probably the burial place of St. Palladius, who was sent by Pope Celestine into Scotland, in the fifth century, to oppose the Pelagian heresy. That Palladius resided, and was probably buried here, appears from several circumstances.   There is a house which still remains in the church-yard, called St. Palladius' *chapel*, where, it is said, the image of the saint was kept, and to which pilgrimages were performed from the most distant parts of Scotland.   There is a well at the corner of the minister's garden, which goes by the name of Paddy's well "

"To this it may be added, that the annual market held at Fordun, is still universally, in that part of the country, called Paldy, or, as vulgarly pronounced, Paddy fair.   This is a strong presumption that a church had been dedicated to him there   as it is a well known fact, that at the Reformation, when the saints' days were abolished, the fairs, which used to succeed the festivals, and were denominated from them, were retained.   Hence, their very name from Lat. Feriae, holidays   Camerarius asserts, on the authority of Polydore Virgil, that the precious reliques of this saint were formerly worshipped at Fordoun," &c.

"According to Sigibert, Palladius was sent to the Scots, A 432. It would appear, that finding his labours unsuccessful in Ireland, he had attempted the conversion of the Picts, for Fordun was in their territory."

principles, could not be a Church, so it is impossible to see how she could attain that character, even after the arrival of Palladius; for as the individuals whom he ordained had been baptized only by presbyters, and consequently were not Christians, nothing which he did could make them Christian ministers. And this was especially the case in regard to those of them whom he raised to the episcopate; for as he had not a single bishop along with him, it was in direct opposition to the whole of the canons, that he himself alone should consecrate bishops. And in addition to these facts, which show that the boasted apostolical succession, so far from being preserved, was not even begun by Palladius, so, though it might be introduced afterwards, (of which there is no satisfactory evidence,) we have reason to believe, that if it was actually begun, it was speedily destroyed after the Culdees arose, and during the whole of the time that they governed the Church. The founder of their institutions was the celebrated Columba, who, according to Dr. Jamieson, was of the blood royal of Ireland, and who, after he became pious, devoted himself to the ministry, and coming over to Scotland with twelve presbyters, established a monastery in Ii or Iona, of which the following account is given by the author of the Scotichronicon, under the year 560. "Columba, presbyter," says he, "came to the Picts, and converted them to the faith of Christ, those, I say, who live near the northern moors; and their king gave them that island, which is commonly called Ii. In it, as it is reported, there are five hides (of land,) on which Columba erected a monastery; and he himself resided there as Abbot, thirty-two years, where he also died, when seventy years of age. This place is still held by his successors. Thenceforth there ought to be always in Ii an abbot, *but no bishop, and to him ought all the Scottish bishops to be subject*, for this reason, that Columba was an abbot, not a bishop."*

---

* "Deincops perpetuum in Ii Abbas erit, non autem Episcopus; atque ei debent esse subditi omnes Scotorum Episcopi, propterea quod Columbanus fuerit Abbas, non Episcopus."

This monastery, it would appear, was speedily followed by the erection of others, which as Dr. Jamieson observes, " may more properly be viewed as colleges, in which the various branches of useful learning were taught, than as monasteries. These societies, therefore, were in fact the seminaries of the Church, both in North Britain and in Ireland. As the presbyters ministered in holy things to those in their vicinity, they were still training up others, and sending forth missionaries, whenever they had a call, or any prospect of success."* Nor was the number of them small; for they had similar institutions, each of them like that of Iona, (to which they all professed subjection,) with an abbot, and twelve presbyters, at Abernethy, Lochleven, Dunkeld, St. Andrews, Brechin, Dumblane, Muthil, Mortlach, Monymusk, Dunfermline, Melrose, Govan, Abercorn, Inchcolm, Tyningham, and Aberlady.† And whether you consider the religious principles taught by Columba and these presbyters, or the authority exercised by them over the Scottish clergy of every order, the facts related respecting them are deeply interesting. " The doctrine of the Culdees, as far as we may judge from that of Columba, was at least comparatively pure. As he was himself much given to the study of the Holy Scriptures," like Luther, "he taught his disciples to confirm their doctrines by testimonies brought from this unpolluted fountain; and declared that only to be the divine counsel which he found there. His followers, as we learn from Bede, would receive those things only, which are contained in the writings of the prophets, evangelists, and apostles.‡ Hence, it has been said that for several generations—with the errors which at that time prevailed in the Church of Rome, they seem not to have been in the least tainted.§

* Page 35. † Ibid. 105–187.
‡ " Tantum ea quae in Propheticis, Evangelicis et Apostolicis Libris discere poterant pietatis et castitatis opera diligenter observantes" Hist. lib. iii. c. 4.
§ Jamieson, p. 29, 30.

"They rejected," says Toland, "auricular confession," which some of your followers so earnestly recommend, "as well *as authoritative absolution;* and confessed to God alone, as believing God alone could forgive sins."* They never practised confirmation, which, though it was never performed after baptism on the Saviour or his Apostles, or any of their disciples who are mentioned in the New Testament, is practised by Episcopalians, who glory in their Churches as the purest Apostolic Churches.†
"In their public worship, they made an honourable mention of holy persons deceased, offering a sacrifice of thanksgiving for their exemplary life and death, but not by way of propitiation for sins. They neither prayed to dead men, nor *for them,*" as the late Bishop Gleig recommended; for they were persuaded, that while we are in the present world, we may help one another, either by our prayers or by our counsels; but when we come before the tribunal of Christ, neither Job, nor Daniel, nor Noah, can intercede for any one, but every one must bear his own burden."‡
"And they were so far," says the same writer, "from pretending to do more good than they were obliged (to do,) much less to superabound in merit for the benefit of others, that they readily denied all merit of their own, and solely hoped for salvation from the mercy of God, through faith in Jesus Christ: which faith, as a living root, was to produce the fruit of good works, without which it were barren or dead, and consequently useless."§ "They paid no respect to holy reliques, or to the mass; but" when they were persecuted for it at St. Andrews, "chose rather to forsake their church and property than desert their principles."‖ And when Boniface was sent from Rome to propagate the principles of his apostate Church, he encountered a noble and magnanimous opposition from Clemens and Samson, two illustrious

* Nazaren., Letter 2, p. 24
† Ibid. p. 22
‡ Nazaren., p 26.
§ Ibid. p. 25, 26.
‖ Jamieson, p. 214.

Culdees, who told him, "that he and those of his party studied to bring men to the subjection of the Pope, and slavery of Rome, withdrawing them from obedience to Christ,—that they were corrupters of Christ's doctrine, establishing a sovereignty in the Bishop of Rome,—and that they had introduced in the Church many tenets, rites and ceremonies, unknown to the ancient and pure times, yea, contrary to them."* In short, their doctrine and worship, in

---

* David Buchanan's Preface to Knox's History.

The following is the account given by Bower, in his History of the Popes, vol. ii p. 523, of the way in which Pope Gregory ordered the missionaries, whom he sent from Rome, to model the worship of the East Saxons "Not satisfied," says he, "with directing Austin not to destroy, but to rescue for the worship of God the profane places where the Pagan Saxons had worshipped their idols, he would have him to treat the more profane usages, rites and ceremonies of the Pagans in the same manner, that is, not to abolish but to sanctify them, by changing the end for which they were instituted, and introduce them thus sanctified into the Christian worship. This he specifies in a particular ceremony, "whereas it is a custom," says he, "among the Saxons, to slay abundance of oxen, and sacrifice them to the devil, *you must not abolish that custom*, but appoint a new festival to be kept either on the day of the consecration of the churches, or on the birth-day of the saints whose reliques are deposited there, and on these days the Saxons may be allowed to make arbours round the temples changed into churches, *to kill their oxen and to feast*, as they did while they were still Pagans; only they shall offer their thanks and praises, not to the devil, but to God." Such was the principle on which many of the Pagan ceremonies were adopted by the Church of Rome; and it was for this reason, more than from the difference of the time at which Easter was observed by them, that the bishops or presbyters sent to England by the Culdees refused to conform to the practices of the Popish clergy among the East Saxons.

"Boniface the Fourth," says Bower, vol. iii. p 1, 2, "availing himself of the partiality of Phocas to his See, asked of him the famous Pantheon, (built by Agrippa in honour of Cybele and all the other gods and goddesses, and thence it took its name,) and having obtained it *he changed it into a church*, substituting the mother of God to the mother of the gods, and the Christian martyrs to the other Pagan deities adored there before, so that only the names of the idols were altered." This took place in A. D. 609. And says Ranke, in his History of the Popes, vol 1. p. 9, " Men saw with surprise a secular building erected by heathens, the Basilica, converted into a Christian temple. The change was most remarkable. The Apsis of the Basilica contained an Augusteum, the images of those Caesars to whom divine honours were paid. The very places which they occupied, received, as we still see in numerous Basilicas, the figures of Christ and his Apostles. The statues of the rulers of the world, who had been

an age of abounding superstition and corruption, were worthy of the purest days of Protestantism; and if I were requested to name the section of the Church which resembled most nearly the Church of the Apostles during the sixth, seventh and eighth centuries, I would say, that with the single exception of the Vaudois, it was the Church of Scotland.

If such, however, was the case, it must be important to ascertain what was the constitution of that early Church, and what were the powers which were exercised by the highest order of its ministers. Now, there is no fact respecting it more fully established than that it was governed by Presbyters. You meet, indeed, occasionally, with a reference in our historians to the Scottish bishops of that age, but the term seems to have been convertible with that of presbyter, the highest dignity of the episcopal office, as Jamieson remarks of a bishop whom the presbyters of Iona first consecrated and then sent to England, " being made to lie in this that he was a preacher.[*]" After observing that the term bishop was used then in a very different sense from that attached to it afterwards, he adds, " Ninian is called a bishop by Bede, and he probably received the title during his life. He says, that the Southern Picts were converted by the preaching of Ninyas, as he gives his name, the most renowned bishop. Ninian receives the same

regarded as gods, vanished, and gave place to the likeness of the Son of Man, the Son of God."

"The feast of the purification of the Virgin Mary," says Bower, vol. ii. p. 227, " commonly known by the name of Candlemass, because candles were blessed, as is still practised in the Church of Rome, at the mass of that day, is thought by some to have been introduced in the room of the Lupercalia, (the feast of Pan)" He adds in a note, " The candles that are blessed on Candlemass-day are thought to be a sure protection against thunder and lightning, and therefore are lighted by timorous persons in stormy weather. But their chief virtue is to frighten the devils and drive them away; and for this reason they are kept burning in the hands of dying persons, so long as they can hold them, and by their beds, from the time they begin to be in agony, till they expire, none of the spirits of darkness daring to appear where they give light." Many other Pagan ceremonies have been adopted by the Church of Rome.

[*] Page 333.

designation from Alcuin, Boece, Leslie, and a variety of writers. Yet he seems to have been no more a bishop than Columba. Nor could Bede use the term in that canonical sense which was become common in his own time; for he afterwards says, 'Pethelm is Bishop of Candida Casa, or Whithern, which, in consequence of the increase of the number of the faithful, has been lately added to the list of episcopal sees, and *had him for its first prelate.'** In the MS. History of Durham, under the year 664, and long after the age of Ninian, it is expressly said, Candida Casa as yet had no bishop. William of Malmesbury, also, in his account of the bishops of this see, although, after Alcuin, he calls Ninian a bishop, using the term in its loose and general sense, says, that toward the end of Bede's life, Pethelm was made the *first* bishop, that is, as Selden explains it, according to the canonical ideas of Episcopacy then generally received throughout Christendom."

He further remarks, " The character of the Irish bishops, in early times, may assist us in judging of the rank of those who were ordained at Iona; especially as Columba, who was not a bishop, but an abbot and presbyter, is designed not only Primate of the Scots and Picts, but Primate of all the Irish bishops.† Till the year 1152, they seem to have been properly Chorepiscopi, or rural bishops. Their number, it is supposed, might amount to above three hundred. They, in the same manner with the Scottish and Pictish bishops, exercised their functions at large, as they had opportunity.‡" " That bishop in Ireland," says Toland, " did, in the fifth or sixth centuries, (for example,) signify a distinct order of men, by whom alone presbyters could be ordained, and without which ordination their ministry were invalid; this I absolutely deny; as I do that those bishops were diocesan bishops, when nothing is plainer, than

---

* " And he was thaere stowe the aereste biscop." Hist. Alfred's Translation, vol xxiv.

† " Omnium Hibernensium Episcoporum Primas."

‡ Jamieson, p. 335.

that most of them had no bishopricks at all in our modern sense; not to speak of those numerous bishops *frequently going out of Ireland, not called to bishopricks abroad, and many of 'em never preferred there.**"

It was mentioned formerly, that the College of Iona was administered by an abbot and twelve presbyters; and it would appear from what is said of it by the venerable Bede, that the ecclesiastical polity of the kingdom of Scotland was at that time Presbyterian. "That island," says he, "is always wont to have for its governor a presbyter abbot, to whose authority both the whole province, and even the bishops themselves, *by an unusual constitution,* ought

* Nazarenus, Lett. 2, p. 37, 38.

Jamieson mentions also, that "the abbots of Hij, because of their great authority and extensive influence, were sometimes called bishops. For this reason, in relation to that monastery, the terms Abbas and Episcopus seem to have been used as synonymous. Hence, Sigibert speaks of Adamannus, the Presbyter and Abbot of the Scots. As the prelacy gained ground, the rage for multiplying bishops, in preceding ages, also increased. On this principle, as would seem, Spottiswood includes both Columba and Adomnan, in his list of the early bishops of Scotland, appended to his history. According to Fordun, Regulus was only an abbot. The Register of St. Andrews, however, makes him a bishop," p 336, 337.

"There seem to have been no regular dioceses in Scotland before the beginning of the twelfth century. The foundation of diocesan Episcopacy was indeed laid in the erection of the bishopric of St. Andrews. In this erection, we may perceive the traces of a plan for changing the whole form of the ecclesiastical government, as it had hitherto been exercised within the Pictish dominions." "He first," says the Register of the Priory at St. Andrews, speaking of Grig, "gave freedom to the Scottish Church, which till that time was in servitude by the constitution and custom of the Picts. This surely refers, says Mr. Pinkerton, to the subjection of the Pictish churches to Hyona, from which they were delivered by erecting St. Andrews into a bishopric;" p 338.

It will by no means follow, as Keith alleges, (Catalogue, Preface, 18,) that the English would not have applied on different occasions to the Culdees for bishops, if the bishops ordained by the latter were not diocesan, and differed essentially from their own. The English were in want of preachers, and would not for a time attach the same importance to a difference in the form of ecclesiastical government. And he might as well have alleged that they would not have applied to them, because, according to the decision of the Church of Rome, with which they were connected, the Scots were schismatical in their mode of observing Easter.

to be subject, after the example of their first teacher, who was not a bishop, but a presbyter and monk."* That subjection was cheerfully yielded to Columba, the first abbot, and, as would seem from the language ascribed to Colman, when he was ordained by the President and the rest of the College, it was given at the same time to the whole of the presbyters And it was enjoined to be rendered to all their successors, not merely by one bishop, as is insinuated by Lloyd, to evade the argument which it furnishes against Episcopacy, but by the whole of the bishops in every part of Scotland, and not only in one diocese, as he would explain the word "province," for there were no dioceses in that country for nearly six centuries after the time of Columba, but as Gillan interprets, "the northern province of the Scots," of which Bede speaks in his third chapter, "the north of Ireland, the Western Scottish islands, and those parts of Britain that were inhabited by the Scots "† He denominates this constitution, "an unusual constitution," and he might justly so describe it; for while the Church of England, and almost every other Church with which he was acquainted, was subject to the authority of diocesan prelates, the whole of the simple scriptural bishops in the country of Scotland, who had no dioceses, were required to be subject to the Abbot of Iona, who was not a prelate, but *only a presbyter, and to his fellow presbyters*, whose original predecessors founded the parent college of the kingdom, where its future clergy were to be educated and ordained.

The power of these presbyters over the clergy of Scotland is further confirmed by what is said by Turgot, Prior of Durham, in his history of that See. "In these days," (A. D. 1108,) says he, "all the right (*totum jus*) of the Culdees, throughout the whole kingdom of Scotland, passed into the Bishopric of St. Andrews."

---

* "Habere autem solet ipsa insula rectorem semper abbatem presbyterum cujus juri omnis provincia, et ipsi etiam Episcopi ordine inusitato, debeant esse subjecti, juxta exemplum primi doctoris illius qui non episcopus, sed presbyter extitit, et monachus." Hist. lib. iii. c 4.

† Remarks, p. 57-79.

"The learned Selden," says Jamieson, "seems justly to view the term *jus*, as denoting the right, which they had long claimed and exercised, of electing and ordaining bishops, without the interference of any others in order to their consecration. Had the writer meant to speak of their temporal rights, or even of the privileges attached to particular priories, he would most probably have used a different term. At any rate, had these been in his eye, he would have spoken of rights in the plural, as referring to the whole extent of their property. But when he speaks of 'the right of the Culdees *throughout the whole kingdom of Scotland*,' it is evident, that he must refer to one distinguishing privilege, belonging to them as a body, by virtue of which their jurisdiction had no limit, save that of the kingdom itself. And what could this be, but the right of choosing, without any *congé d'élire* from the Sovereign, and of ordaining, without any consecration from a superior order of clergy, those who were called *bishops* in a general sense, or *Bishops of Scotland*, as exercising their authority somewhat *in the same unlimited way in which the Culdees exercised theirs?*"*

---

* "The Bishop of St. Asaph conjectures," says he, "that it might be the right of confirming the elections of all the bishops in Scotland This had been done by them, (the Culdees,") he says, "as being the primate's dean and chapter, but was now taken from them, and performed by the primate himself" Here the learned prelate finds himself under the necessity *of conceding to the Culdees a very extraordinary power.* But this power must originally have centered in the Monastery of Iona This monastery, then, must have been to all intents the primacy of Scotland, of the country at least which has now received this name. This power must have belonged to the college, as the chapter, if it must be so. But who was the primate? No bishop, from all that we have seen, but the abbot himself. Thus the Bishop of St. Asaph finds it necessary to admit, however reluctantly, what he elsewhere tries to set aside, the testimony of Bede, with respect to the subjection of "all the province, and even of the bishops themselves, in an unusual manner to this abbot. Even after he has made an ineffectual attempt to show, that the province refered to by the ancient writer could signify only a single diocese, he inadvertently gives up the point in controversy, *making all the bishops in Scotland to be at least so far subject to the Culdees, that they had the right of confirming their elections ,*" p. 341, 342

Lloyd says, (Historical Account, p. 102,) "it appears there was

But what places the matter beyond all dispute is the testimony of Bede in another part of his history, where, after speaking of the settlement of Aidan in England, who had been sent thither by these presbyters, and of his being followed by a number of his countrymen, who preached the word with great zeal, and administered baptism, he mentions that churches were erected, and lands appropriated for establishing monasteries; "for," he says, "they were chiefly monks who came to preach. Bishop Aidan himself was a monk, forasmuch as he was sent from the island

always one (bishop) in his (Columba's) monastery, as Bishop Usher tells us out of the Ulster Annals, Prim. p. 701. Usher's own words in the passage referred to are, 'The Ulster Annals teach us, that even that small island had not only an abbot, but also a bishop.' This is somewhat different from their being always one in his (Columba's) monastery. Usher, however, does not quote the words of the Annals, but immediately subjoins in the same sentence,—' From which (Annals) it may perhaps be worth while to learn the first series of abbots. He then adds a list of ten in succession, giving various notices concerning some of them. Would it not have been fully as natural to have given a list of the pretended bishops if he could have done it? But, although superior to abbot-presbyters, it is not a little singular, that antiquity has thrown a veil over their names."

"Besides the ten abbots of Hii mentioned by Usher, there were, according to the extracts from these Annals, appended by Mr Pinkerton to his Enquiry, during the lapse of about *three centuries*, other nine who are expressly designated abbots, ten called co-arbs, and one denominated 'Heir of Columbcille.' Johnstone, in his Extracts from the same Annals, gives the names of two abbots not appearing in Mr. Pinkerton's. But not another besides Coide is mentioned as bishop;" p. 48, 50.

"In Colgan's List, as given from Innes's MS. Collections, we find twenty-six successors of Columba, in the course of two hundred and sixty-three years, and besides Ceudei, who is evidently the same with Coide, only one of these abbots has the title of bishop. This is Ferganan, surnamed the Briton, the third in this list, the same person with Fergnaus, who also holds the third place in Usher's. But Usher takes no notice of his being a bishop, and Smith, who, in his Chronicle, calls him Fergna, gives him no other designation than that of abbot. His name does not appear in the Extracts from the Annals of Ulster. Smith also mentions Coide under the name of St. Caide or Caidan, but merely as Abbot of Hij."

"To the article respecting Coide, Johnstone affixes the following note 'The Abbots of Iona, Derry and Dunkeld, are frequently styled bishops.' This remark seems to be well founded, from what follows in the Annals, A 723. Faolan McDorbene, Abbot of Iona, was succeeded in the primacy by Killin-fada," p. 51.

which is called Hii, the monastery of which for a long time held the supremacy among almost all the monasteries of the Northern Scots, and those of all the Picts, and *presided in the government of their people;*"* or, according to King Alfred's Anglo-Saxon Version, "it received the principality and exaltation." Here, it is worthy of notice, that it is not only the abbot, but the abbot along with his presbyters, or the

---

* "Monachus ipse Episcopus Aidan, utpote de insula, quae vocatur Hii, destinatus. cujus monasterium in cunctis pene Septentrionalium Scottorum, et omnium Pictorum monasteriis non parvo tempore arcem tenebat, regendisque eorum populis praeerat " Hist. lib iii. cap. 3.

" It has been urged," says Jamieson, p 71, " that we can conclude nothing from this unusual authority against the establishment of Episcopacy in Scotland, because the government of Oxford is vested in the University, exclusively of the bishop who resides there. (Lloyd's Histor. Account, p. 180, 181) But the cases are by no means parallel, for, 1. The government of the whole province was vested in the abbot and college of monks. It has been said, indeed, that the Kings of England might have extended the power of the University of Oxford through the whole diocese, had they pleased, and that it would not have been a suppressing of the order of bishops. But, not to say that such a co-ordinate power would have been extremely galling to the episcopate, it has been proved, that the power of the monastery extended far beyond the limits which Bishop Lloyd has assigned to the pretended diocese of Hii. 2. The power itself is totally different. Although the Bishop of Oxford be subject to the University in civil matters, as well as the other inhabitants of that city, what estimate would he form of the pretensions of that learned body, were they to claim a right of precedence *regendis populis,* in governing all the people of his diocese, and *as a proof of the nature of the government,* the same which Bede gives, of sending forth missionaries to teach, to baptize, and to plant churches ? (Hist , lib. iii. c. 3.) The Bishop, I apprehend, would rather be disposed to view this as a virtual suppressing of the order."

The supposition has been otherwise stated with respect to an university. It has been said, (Life of Sage, p. 52,) " When a bishop is head of a college in any of the universities, (which has frequently happened,) he must be subject to the jurisdiction of the vice-chancellor, though only a priest, and perhaps one of his own clergy. In reply, it has been properly inquired, were the bishops of Lindisfairn no otherwise subject to the Monastery of Icolmkill, than the head of a college in any of the universities, becoming afterwards a bishop, must be subject to the jurisdiction of the vice-chancellor, who may be a priest in his own diocese? The cases must indeed be viewed as totally dissimilar; unless it can be shown that the head of a college may be sent, ordained, and consecrated to be a bishop of any diocese in England, and yet continue subject to the university from which he was sent."

monastery, that is represented as invested with this supremacy over the other monasteries, and as presiding in the ecclesiastical government of the people, both of the Scots and Picts. And accordingly, the passage is thus translated by Stapleton: "The house of religion was no small time the head house of all the monasteries of the Northern Scottes, and of abbyes of all the Redshankes, (the term by which he renders Pictorum,) and had the soveraintie in ruling of their people."* And we have positive evidence of their ordaining bishops, and sending them to England; and if they exercised that power in regard to ministers who were to labour in that country, it furnishes evidence which is fitted to satisfy any unprejudiced mind, that they must have exercised the same power in regard to those ministers who were to officiate in their own country. Bede informs us that Oswald, an English Prince, "sent to the elders of the Scots amongst whom he had been baptized, that they might send him a bishop, by whose doctrine and ministry the nation of Angles which he governed might be instructed in the Christian faith, and receive the sacraments."† The presbyters of Iona accordingly sent him Cormac, whom they ordained to that office; but as his manners were too austere, he failed in conciliating the affections of the people, and was soon obliged to return. Upon his arrival at the monastery, the presbyters met to receive his report; and as the passage which relates to it has been considerably perverted by modern Episcopalians, and has been inaccurately rendered in the version of 1723, I shall give it in the old version of Stapleton, who, though a zealous Papist and Episcopalian, has translated it more faithfully. "He returned," says he, "into his countre, and *in the assemble of the elders,* he

* Bede, Hist. lib. iii. cap. 3.

† "Idem ergo Oswald mox ubi regnum suscepit, desiderans totam cui praeesse coepit gentem fidei Christianae gratia imbui, cujus experimenta permaxima in expugnandis Barbaris jam ceperat misit ad majores natu Scottorum inter quos exulans ipse baptismatis sacramenta, cum his qui secum militibus, consecutus erat, petens ut sibi mitteretur antistes," &c. Hist. lib. iii. c. 3.

made relation, how, that in teaching, he could do the people no good to the which he was sent, for as much as they were folkes that might not be reclaymed, of a hard capacite, and fierce nature. Then *the elders* (as they say) began in counsaile to treat at long what were best to be done."* While they were deliberating about what ought to be done, Aidan (who, for aught that appears, was previously only a monk and not a presbyter) rose and addressed them, and they were so struck with the wisdom which he displayed, and which they had not anticipated, that they resolved to appoint him in the room of Cormac, and ordained him and sent him to King Oswald. "Having heard this," says Bede, "the faces and the eyes of *all who sat there* were turned to him; *they* diligently weighed what he had said, and determined that he was worthy of the episcopal office, and that he should be sent to instruct the unbelieving and illiterate, it being proved that he was supereminently endowed with the gift of discretion, which is the mother of virtues, and *thus ordaining him they sent him* to preach."† The

* "Redierit patriam, atque in conventu Seniorum retulerit, quia nil prodesse docendo genti ad quam missus erat potuisset," &c. Lib. iii. c. 5.

† "Quo audito, omnium qui consedebant ad ipsum ora et oculi conversi, diligenter quid diceret discutiebant, et ipsum esse dignum episcopatu, ipsum ad erudiendos incredulos et indoctos mitti decernunt; qui gratia discretionis, quae virtutum mater est, ante omnia probatur imbutus; sicque illum ordinantes, ad praedicandum miserunt." Hist. lib. iii. c. 5.

Gillan says, "What can be the meaning of his being thought worthy of the office of a bishop, and his being ordained? Certainly he was a presbyter before he was a monk of Hii, and a member of the synod, and spoke and reasoned, and made a great figure in it." (Life of Sage.) But what assurance have we of this? says Jamieson, p. 66. "Bishop Lloyd shows that many monks were laymen. Bede himself admits that of the many who daily came from the country of the Scots into the provinces of the Angles over which Oswald reigned, and entered the monasteries, only some were presbyters. He seems to say, that they all preached, or acted as catechists, but that those only baptized who had received the sacerdotal office. Having observed that they instructed the Angles in regular discipline, he adds, for they were for the most part monks who came to preach. Bishop Aidan himself was a monk, &c. As he had already distinguished those who had the sacerdotal office from such as were merely monks, there is great reason to suppose that he means here to say, that Aidan had been a mere monk before his ordination as bishop."

same persons, it is obvious, ordained and sent him who had ordained and sent his predecessor, and who were met to receive the report of the latter. And these were not, as Bishop Lloyd supposes, (for he merely mentions it as a supposition,) the diocesan bishop of Iona, of whose existence not a shadow of proof can be produced, and the Bishop of Dumblane, and *some* other bishop, of whose presence on the occasion, if there were any such prelates, there is not the slightest notice, but the presbyters of Iona, with their president, the abbot-presbyter, or as the historian denominates them, the seniors of the Scots, (Majores natu Scottorum,) and the assembly of the seniors, (Conventus Seniorum.) And though Gillan insinuates, without producing his authority for it, that they were diocesan bishops, yet these names, Majores Natu, and Seniores, are never applied by Bede to such ministers, while he repeatedly uses them to denote the senior monks in monasteries, who were commonly presbyters. Stapleton accordingly translates the passage in such a way as shows clearly that this is the only just interpretation, for he gives the following version of it: " Al that were at the assemble looking upon Aidan, debated diligently his saying, and concluded that he above the rest was worthy of that charge and bishopricke, and that he should be sent to instruct those unlerned Paynims. For he was *tried* to be chiefely garnished with the grace of discretion, the mother of all vertues. Thus *making him bishop*, they sent him forthe to preach." And that this is what the historian intended to intimate, is further evident from what immediately follows, for says he, " from this island therefore, from the college of these monks, was Aidan sent to the province of the Angles, who were to be initiated into the Christian faith, having received the degree of the episcopate. At which time Segenius presided over this monastery, as abbot and presbyter."*

---

* " Ab hac ergo insula, ab horum collegio monachorum, ad provinciam Anglorum instituendam in Christo, missus est Aidan accepto gradu Episcopatus. Quo tempore eidem monasterio Segenius abbas et presbyter praefuit." Hist. lib. iii. c. 5.

As the episcopate which Aidan received at Iona was conferred upon him by a college of presbyters, with an abbot-presbyter as their president or moderator, so we are told by Bede, that after he died, they ordained Finan to succeed him. "But Finan," says he, "succeeded him in the episcopate, and to this he was appointed from Hii, an island and monastery of the Scots."* And again he says, "Bishop Aidan being dead, Finan in his stead received the degree of the episcopate, being ordained and sent by the Scots,"† *i. e.* obviously the Scottish presbyters in the island of Iona, as is stated in the first passage. They appear also to have ordained Colman, who became Metropolitan of York; for when vindicating his mode of celebrating Easter in the Synod of Straneschalch or Whitby, in 664, he said, "the Easter which I keep I received from my elders [or presbyters,] who sent me hither as bishop, which all our ancestors, men beloved by God, are known to have celebrated in the same manner."‡ It is in vain, therefore, to deny that the power of ordination was exercised by these presbyters; and if it was from them that those ministers who were sent to England derived their orders, it must have been they too who conferred their orders on the clergy of Scotland.

It is mentioned, I am aware, by Bede, that Finan, "seeing the success of Cedd," who had been sent to preach to the East Saxons, "and having called to him two other bishops for the ministry of ordination, made him bishop over the nation of the East Saxons," and that Cedd, "having received the degree of episcopacy, returned to the province, and with greater authority, fulfilled the work which he had begun, erected churches in different places, ordained presbyters and deacons, who might assist him in the word of faith, and the

---

* "Successit vero ei in episcopatum Finan, et ipse illi ab Hii Scottorum insula ac monasterio destinatus." Hist. lib. iii. c. 17.

† "Aidano episcopo ab hac vita sublato, Finan pro illo gradum episcopatus a Scottis ordinatus ac missus acceperat." Ibid. c. 25.

‡ "Pascha, inquit, hoc quod agere soleo a majoribus meis accepi, qui me huc episcopum miserunt," &c. Lib. iii. c. 25.

ministry of baptism."* He might be induced, however, to ordain him in this way, in compliance with the prejudices of the Saxons, who had been previously in connection with the Church of Rome, though for a time they apostatized, and might otherwise have considered his orders as uncanonical. And as bishop Lloyd acknowledges that the bishops who assisted Finan on that occasion were, as Bede says, "Scots," and as they had only like him Presbyterian ordination from the College of Iona, it is plain, that upon your principles the orders which Cedd himself received, and those which he afterwards conferred upon others, were perfectly irregular, and so far from preserving, they must have contributed to destroy the apostolical succession in the Church of England. I shall consider, however, more fully in the following letter, the effects resulting from these Scottish ordinations, and remain,

Reverend Sir,
Yours, &c.

* "Qui ubi prosperatum ei opus evangelii comperit, fecit eum episcopum in gentem Orientalium Saxonum," &c Hist lib. iii. c. 22.

"It ought to be observed that Bede," says Jamieson, p. 90, "when speaking of the episcopate, describes it only by the term gradus, and not by any one expression of difference of office or order. Now, it is well known, that many learned men who have opposed diocesan Episcopacy, have admitted that the term bishop was *very early used in the Church*, as denoting a distinction with respect to *degree*, while the office was held to be essentially the same" In what sense this distinction has been made consult what he says, p 331, 332. And for an answer to the other objections of Episcopalians to the argument for Presbyterian Church Government, from the institutions of Iona, see his able Historical Dissertation.

LETTER XVI.

The succession destroyed in the early Church of England, in consequence of the ordination of its first bishops by Scottish presbyters—Scottish missionaries who were ordained by presbyters, acknowledged by Usher to have christianized the greater part of England—The Presbyterian Culdean Scottish Church, asserted in the twelfth century, before an assembly of English bishops and nobles, to be the Mother Church of the Church of England, and not contradicted—An Archbishop of Canterbury in that century never consecrated, and a Bishop of Norwich consecrated by a presbyter who was an archdeacon—Succession destroyed in the Church of Ireland through the ordination of many of its clergy by the Scottish Culdee presbyters—Eight individuals who never had any orders, Archbishops of Armagh, and Primates of all Ireland.—Succession destroyed among the Scottish Episcopalians, who, according to Dr Pusey, are not a Christian Church—Their first prelates in 1610 never baptized, and their orders irregular—The orders of their next bishops in 1661 uncanonical, and those of the usage bishops, from whom their present bishops derive their orders, pronounced by the college bishops in 1727 to be null and void

REVEREND SIR,—I think I may now assume it as a fact established by the united and uncontradicted testimony of our earliest historians, that the Culdees of Iona were merely presbyters. But if this was really the case, it is attended by consequences of a very serious description to diocesan Episcopacy. It presents to us the purest Church on earth, with the exception of a few handfuls of humble Christians in the valleys of Piedmont, preferring the simple form of Presbytery to your ecclesiastical polity, even in its most modified form; and when we are asked by our opponents, in the haughty spirit of Bancroft and Heylin, where was there a Church governed by presbyters before the days of Calvin, we can point to the early Church of Scotland, which from its very foundation was Presbyterian. And along with the noble example which it exhibits of steadfast adherence to the government and doctrine of the Primitive Church, *while diocesan Episcopacy existed only in Churches which acknowledged the supremacy of the Church of Rome, and were tainted with its corruptions,* or which adopted the superstitions of the Eastern Church, it furnishes an argument against your favourite doctrine of the apostolical succession, which I challenge you to answer. It was they who ordained for several hundreds of years, till the emissaries of Rome obtained the ascendency, the whole of the ministers of the Church of Scotland. And if your position be true, that ordination of bishops, who have themselves been regularly baptized and ordained by those who had power to do it, in an uninterrupted series from the Apostles, be essential to the existence of a Christian Church and a Christian ministry, and a covenanted title to salvation, it evidently follows, that the Church of Scotland, during all that time, even passing by the previous period of her history, could not be a Church; nor did she possess within her pale a single minister or a single individual who could cherish the smallest hope of salvation. And if such was her state during that long period, I would like to be informed how the defect was remedied, and how our Scottish Episcopalians, who are the descendants of these men, notwithstanding their new and lofty pretensions to the apostolical succession, can be in a better condition in the present day.

Not only, however, was the Church of Scotland supplied with ministers ordained by these presbyters, but we have decisive evidence that the greater part of England was planted with churches by zealous and active Christian ministers, who had no other orders except what they received at Iona. It was they, as we have seen, who ordained Cormac, Aidan, and Finan; and, in addition to them, they sent forth many others, who laboured with great and remarkable success. We have a striking testimony to this fact in a speech delivered in A. D. 1176, by Gilbert Murray, then a younger Scottish clerk, and afterwards a bishop, before the Pope's Legate, when the latter attempted to bring the Church of Scotland into subjection to the Archbishop of York, and the kingdom of England. "It is true," said he, "English nation—thou attemptest, in thy wretched ambition and lust of domineering, to bring under thy jurisdiction thy neighbour provinces and nations, more noble, I will not say in multitude, or power, but in lineage, and antiquity; unto whom, if thou wilt consider ancient records, thou shouldst rather have been humbly obedient, or at least, laying aside thy rancour, have reigned together in perpetual love; and now with all wickedness of pride that thou showest, without any reason or law, but in thy ambitious power, thou seekest to oppress *thy mother, the Church of Scotland,* which from the beginning hath been catholique, and free, and *which brought thee, when thou wast straying in the wilderness of heathenism, into the safe-guard of the true faith and way unto life,* even unto Jesus Christ, the author of eternal rest. She did wash thy kings and princes in the laver of holy baptism; she taught thee the commandments of God, and instructed thee in moral duties; she did accept many of thy nobles and others of meaner rank, when they were desirous to learn to read, *and gladly gave them daily entertainment without price, books also to read, and instruction freely;* she did also *appoint, ordain, and consecrate thy bishops and priests; by the space of thirty years and above, she maintained the primacy and pontifical dignity within thee on the north side of Thames,* as Beda witnesseth.

"And now, I pray thee, what recompense renderest thou now unto her that hath bestowed so many benefits on thee? Is it bondage, or such as Judea rendered unto Christ, evil for good? It seemeth no other thing. If thou couldst do as thou wouldst, thou wouldst draw *thy mother,* the Church of Scotland, whom thou shouldst honour with all reverence, into the basest and most wretchedest bondage. Fie, for shame, what is more base?" &c.*

---

* Petrie's Church History, p. 378. He adds, "When Gilbert had so made an end, some English, both prelates and nobles, commend the yong clerk, that he had spoken so boldly for his nation, without flattering, and not abashed at the gravity of such authority; but others, because he spoke contrary unto their minde, said a Scot is naturally violent, and *in naso Scoti piper.* But Roger, Archbishop of York, which principally had moved this business to bring the Church of Scotland unto his See, uttered a groan, and then with a merry countenance laid his hands on Gilbert's head, saying, *Ex tua pharetra non*

"St. Aidan and St. Finan," says Archbishop Usher, "deserve to be honoured by the English nation, with as venerable a remembrance as, I do not say, Wilfrid and Cuthbert, but Austin the monk, and his followers. For, by the ministry of Aidan was the kingdom of Northumberland recovered from Paganism, whereunto belonged then, beside the shire of Northumberland, and the lands beyond it unto Edinburgh Firth, Cumberland also, and Westmoreland, Lancashire, Yorkshire, and the bishopric of Durham; and by the means of Finan, not only was the kingdom of the East Saxons, which contained Essex, Middlesex, and half of Herdfordshire, regained, but also the large kingdom of Mercia converted first unto Christianity; which comprehended under it, Gloucestershire, Herefordshire, Worcestershire, Warwickshire, Leicestershire, Rutlandshire, Northamptonshire, Lincolnshire, Huntingdonshire, Bedfordshire, Buckinghamshire, Shropshire, Nottinghamshire, Cheshire, and the other half of Hertfordshire. *The Scottish that professed no subjection to the Church of Rome, were they that sent preachers for the conversion of these countries, and ordained bishops to govern them,* namely, Aidan, Finan and Colman, successively, for the kingdom of Northumberland; for the East Saxons, Cedd, the brother of Ceadda, the Bishop of York, before mentioned; for the Middle Angles, which inhabited Leicestershire, and the Mercians, Diuma; for the paucity of priests, saith Bede, constrained one bishop to be appointed over two people, and after him Cellach and Trumhere. And these with their followers, notwithstanding their division from the See of Rome, were, for their extraordinary sanctity of life, and painfulness in preaching the Gospel, wherein they went far beyond those of the other side, that afterwards thrust them out, and entered in upon their labours, exceedingly reverenced by all that knew them."* And, says Dr.

exit illa sagitta. This Gilbert was much respected at home after that." He was soon after made Dean of Murray, and Great Chamberlain of Scotland.

* Discourse on the Religion anciently professed by the Irish and British, chap. x.

Jamieson, "it deserves also to be mentioned, that how little soever some now think of Scottish orders, it is evident from the testimony of the most ancient and most respectable historian of South Britain, that by means of Scottish missionaries, or those whom they had instructed or ordained, not only the Northumbrians, but the Middle Angles, the Mercians and East Saxons, all the way to the river Thames, that is, *the inhabitants of by far the greatest part of the country now called England*, were converted to Christianity. It is equally evident, that for some time they acknowledged subjection to the ecclesiastical government of the Scots; and that the only reason why they lost their influence, was, that their missionaries chose rather to give up their charges, than to submit to the prevailing influence of the Church of Rome, to which the Saxons of the West and of Kent had subjected themselves."* But if the Church of Scotland, when she was governed by presbyters, as was asserted by Murray, without any contradiction from the English prelates, was *the Mother Church* of the Church of England, baptized your kings, princes and nobles, and taught them to read, converted the greater part of your countrymen, and ordained your bishops, and if some of her ministers, who conferred on them their orders, for more than thirty years *were invested with the primacy*, you will be bold indeed if you venture to affirm, that there has always been an uninterrupted apostolical succession of diocesan bishops in your National Church. And among all the strange and wonderful things which appear in your own conduct, and that of your followers, in reference to this controversy, it is one of the most extraordinary, to see you unchurching the Church of Scotland, and the whole of the other Presbyterian Churches, because their ministers received their orders from presbyters, *while your own Church*, after all your high and boastful pretensions, *owed its existence, and the very bishops, who began your vaunted apostolical succession, were in-*

---

* Historical Account of the Ancient Culdees, p. 91.

debted for their orders, to men who had been ordained by Scottish presbyters!

It is mentioned, I know, by Bede, that when King Oswy decided in favour of Wilfrid, a zealous partisan of the Church of Rome, in the Synod held at Streoneshalch or Whitby, in 662, to determine the controversy about Easter, "Colman perceiving that his doctrine was rejected, and his sect (as the historian expresses it) despised, left his bishopric at Lindisfarne, and having carried his adherents with him, returned to Scotland." And he further states that after Wilfrid was made a bishop, "he introduced into the churches of the Angles a great many rules of the Catholic observance. Whence it followed, that the Catholic institution daily increasing, all the Scots, who had resided among the Angles, either conformed to these, or returned to their own country."* But still those of them who remained in your Church, after it had been founded by presbyters, and who complied with the Popish rites and canons, and those of the English whom they had baptized and ordained, could not carry on the succession, as the orders of the former, and the baptism and orders of the latter, had been received from men who were ordained by presbyters, and the effects of these fatal and irremediable irregularities must remain in your Church at the present day. So sensible, accordingly, was the Popish party, of the difference between the orders which were obtained from the Culdean presbyters, and those which were conferred by the diocesan bishops of the Church of Rome, that in the fifth canon of the Council of Cealhythe in England, in 816, it is decreed, that "no Scot be permitted to assume to himself the ministerial office in any one's diocese, or that it be lawful to give consent to his touching any thing of holy orders, or to receive from them in baptism, or in the celebration of mass, or that they should give the Eucharist to the people, *because we are uncertain by whom they are*

---

* Hist. iii. 25, 26. "Unde factum est, ut crescente per dies institutione Catholica, Scotti omnes qui inter Anglos morabantur, aut his manus darent, aut suam redirent ad patriam." Ibid. iii. 29.

ordained, if by any one. We know that it is enjoined in the canons, that no bishop (or) presbyter should attempt to intrude upon the parish of another, without the consent of its proper bishop. Much more should the receiving of holy offices from foreign nations be avoided, where they have *no order for metropolitans,* nor *respect for other orders.*"* And in a letter of Richard, Archbishop of Canterbury, written about the year 1170, and published among the works of Peter of Blois, he complains, that "in these days certain false bishops of Ireland, or pretending the barbarism of the Scottish language, although they have received from no one imposition of hands, discharge episcopal functions to the people." And he orders all his clergy, that "they should take care to prohibit the episcopal ministrations of all belonging to a barbarous nation, or of uncertain ordination."† If ministers then, at all these periods, as there is reason to believe, though they had no other orders than those which they received from the Culdee presbyters, baptized many who were afterwards bishops, or priests, or deacons, and even at first ordained your prelates, who ordained others, from whom your present bishops derive their orders, it must be evident to every fair and impartial judge, that the uninterrupted apostolical diocesan succession, which you and Mr. Gladstone represent as essential to the very existence of a Christian Church, is not to be found in the Church of England.

I would notice only further in regard to your

* "Quinto interdictum est ut nullus permittatur de genere Scottorum in alicujus diocesi sibi ministerium usurpare, neque ei consentire liceat ex sacro ordine aliquod attingere, vel ab eis accipere in baptismo, aut in celebratione missarum, vel etiam Eucharistiam populo praebere, quia incertum est nobis, unde et an ab aliquo ordinentur. Scimus quomodo in canonibus praecipitur ut nullus episcoporum (vel) presbyterorum invadere temptaverit alius parochiam nisi cum consensu proprii episcopi. Tanto magis respuendum est ab aliis nationibus sacra ministeria percipere, cum quibus nullus ordo metropolitanis, nec honor aliis habeatur." Spelman Concil t. 1 p. 329.

† Diebus istis quidem pseudoepiscopi Hibernienses aut Scoticae linguae simulantes barbariem, cum a nullo impositionem manus acceperint episcopalia populis ministrant," &c. Pet. Blessensis apud Seld. ut sup. 15.

Church, that the canons of the Synod held at Calcuith, A. D. 787, as Innet remarks, "were subscribed by King Offa, Jambert, Archbishop of Canterbury, and twelve other bishops, some of whose names, and what is more, their Sees, are entirely unknown to our historians."* Selden mentions an Archbishop of Canterbury in the twelth century, who was invested with his office merely by receiving from the King the pastoral staff and ring, without any consecration. "Much stir," says he, "both at Rome and in England, was touching investiture of bishops and abbots *by lay hands*, Anselm, Archprelate of Canterbury, mainly opposing himself against it, whose persuasion so at length wrought with the King, that it was permitted to be discontinued from that time. Notwithstanding this, in the year 1107, by the ring and pastoral staff, per annulum et baculum, (as Matthew Paris tells,) was, by the same Henry, one Rodolph made Archbishop of Canterbury."† And Godwin informs us, that upon the death of Thomas Piercy, the nineteenth Bishop of Norwich, his successor was ordained by the archdeacon, who was only a presbyter. " The fame of his death," says he, flying swiftly beyond the seas, came unto the ears of one Spencer, a gentleman greatly esteemed for his valour and skill in martial affairs, that served the Pope at that time in his wars. Of him with small entreaty, he obtained this dignity for a brother of his, named Henry, a man of his own profession, which of a soldier being made a bishop, came into England, March 16, 1370, and was consecrated in his own church *by the Archdeacon* of Nor-

* Orig. Anglic. vol. i. p. 203.

† " At ab eo tempore (Matthew of Westminster after others reports it,) nunquam per donationem baculi pastoralis vel annuli quisquam de episcopatu vel abbatia per regem vel quemlibet laicum personam investiretur in Anglia," &c. Works, vol. iii. Selden says that even clerks ordained, " and being then capable, without any new ordination of the bishop, of any spiritual function, would take investiture of other churches *without consent or knowledge of the bishop*. Neither was this practice of investitures only in bestowing of parish churches. In monasteries *and bishoprics the like was*." Works, vol. iii c 1124, 1125. *Could baptisms and orders received from them be valid?*

wich."* I might easily specify many similar instances, but I consider it as unnecessary; and I leave it to any one who reflects on these facts to say, whether the succession as transmitted by such bishops and even archdeacons, can be preserved unbroken in the Church of England, or among the Irish or Scottish Episcopalians, many of whose bishops, as I shall immediately show, derived their orders from the prelates of your Church.

If the succession has been interrupted on many occasions in the Church of England, it follows, from the circumstance to which I have just now alluded, as well as from other considerations, that it must have been completely destroyed in the Church of Ireland, and that none of her ministers have a title to the character of Christian ministers, nor any of her members a covenanted right to the blessings of salvation. Independently of what has been said of the state of that Church as governed by presbyters before the arrival of Palladius, (for he visited Ireland before he came to Scotland,) we are informed by Jocelyn, in his Life of St. Patrick, that Columba, who was called Columcille, was the founder of a hundred monasteries in Ireland.† And says Notker Balbulus, who lived in the tenth century, "In Scotland, in the island of Ireland, died St. Columba, surnamed by his own people Columkilli, because he was the institutor, founder, and *governor* of many cells, that is, monasteries *or churches*, whence the abbot of the monastery over which he last presided, (Iona,) and where he rests, in opposition to the custom of the Church, is accounted *the primate of all the Hibernian bishops.*"‡ "On which," says Dr. Jamieson, "by the way we may

---

* Catalogue of the Bishops of England, p 350.

† "Columba, qui Collumcille dicitur, et centum cœnobiorum extitit fundator." Vita S. Patricii, c 89. Messingham, p. 42.

‡ "In Scotia, insula Hibernia, deposito Sancti Columbae cognomento apud suos Columbkilli, eo quod multarum cellarum, id est monasteriorum vel ecclesiarum, institutor, fundator, et rector extiterit, adeo ut abbas monasterii cui novissime praefuit, et ubi requiescit, contra morem ecclesiasticum, primus omnium Hibernensium habeatur episcoporum." Martyrologia apud Messingham, p. 182.

observe, that the claim of superiority on the part of the monastery at Hii was acknowledged, even in Ireland, so late as the tenth century."* But, if Columba was recognised as the Primate of Ireland, and the governor of the hundred churches which he founded, and if, though only a presbyter, he exercised the same powers of ordination in regard to their presbyters or the senior monks, which along with the other presbyters, he exercised at Iona, it must have interrupted at the beginning, and affected afterwards the apostolical succession; and if it was broken at that period, it is impossible to rectify it in the present day. Besides, it is stated in that rare and interesting work, the Monasticum Hibernicum, that "Colman having been a bishop in England, (but having the orders only which he received from the presbyters at Iona,) was no sooner settled at Inisbofinde, (in Ireland,) but that place became a bishoprick; so that St. Colman, who had before been called Bishop of Lindisfarn, was afterwards styled Bishop of Inisbofinde; and the same saint going afterwards to Mayo, that place was likewise a bishoprick, which was united to that of Inisbofinde; so certain is it, that formerly, in the British islands, bishopricks were not regulated and settled, but the bishops were movable, *without being confined to any certain diocese.* This is the reason that in the first ages we find so many bishops in Ireland; for in St. Patrick's days, there were three hundred and fifty at one and the same time, though, as Colgan owns, there were never near so many bishopricks in Ireland. It is very likely, that when the ancient historians speak of so great a number of bishopricks in Ireland, they only meant those abbeys in which *these moving or titular bishops* were abbots; and those houses that were so numerous ceased to be bishopricks

---

* Histor. Account of the Culdees, p. 356.

The following testimony to the influence of the Culdees in Ireland is given by Dr. Sedgwick: "Corruption," says he, " was powerfully retarded by the firmness of the hierarchy and the Culdees. The latter were looked up to as the depositaries of the original national faith, and were most highly respected by the people for their sanctity and learning." Antiquities, p. 94.

the very moment the titular bishops and abbots happened to die, or to shift their monasteries."* But if such was the nature of these bishoprics, (and it is confirmed by what was previously quoted from Toland,) and if Colman and others of the Culdean bishops, who were ordained only by presbyters, went over to Ireland, settled there, and ordained bishops as presbyters, and deacons, they must have contributed still further to destroy the succession, and the injury which they must have done to it is absolutely irretrievable.

And, in short, even though you were able to remove these difficulties, we have decisive evidence that the succession was broken at a still later period. Sir James Ware, in his Prelates of Armagh, says, "St. Bernard, in the Life of St. Malachy, affirms, that Celsus being near to his death, was solicitous that Malachy Morgair, then Bishop of Connor, should succeed him, and sent his staff to him as his successor. Nor was he disappointed, for Malachy succeeded him, though not immediately; for one Maurice, son of Donald, a person of noble birth, for five years, (says the same Bernard,) by secular power, held that church in possession, not as a bishop, but a tyrant, for the ambition of some in power had at that time introduced a diabolical custom of pretending to ecclesiastical sees by hereditary succession, not suffering any bishops but the descendants of their own family. *Nor was this kind of execrable succession of short continuance; for fifteen generations, (or succession of bishops, as Colgan has it,) had succeeded in that manner;* and so far had that evil and adulterate generation confirmed the wicked course, that sometimes *though clerks of their blood might fail, yet bishops never failed.* In fine *eight married men, and without orders,* though scholars, *were predecessors to Celsus,* from whence proceeded that general dissolution of ecclesiastical discipline, (whereof we have spoken largely before,) that contempt of censures, and decay of religion throughout Ireland. Thus Bernard. The names

* Pages 82, 83.

of *these eight married men unordained*, Colgan delivers in the place above cited."* If these eight individuals, however, who were *without orders*, were placed *in succession*, not merely in a humble station of that Church, but *at the very head of it*, or in the Primacy of all Ireland, and ordained bishops, exercised the supreme ecclesiastical authority, and performed confirmation, I would like to be informed, whether you really think the apostolical succession was preserved during that long and disastrous period, under the presidency of men who, though elevated to be Bishops of Armagh, had not even *the order of deacons*. And it is asserted by Dr. Monck Mason, that "the Bishopricks of Dublin, of Waterford and of Limerick were erected by the Danes, and that if we take up the ancient letters of the Irish, which are published in Ussher's Sylloge, we shall find abundant matter to show, that the bishops of those Sees disclaimed all dependence on that of Armagh, and professed obedience immediately to Canterbury."† But if this be the case, then, as it was demonstrated formerly, that the apostolical succession had been broken in many instances in your National Church, and had been interrupted in particular in the See of Canterbury,‡ it

* Bishops of Armagh, p. 9.
† Religion of the Ancient Irish Saints, p 189.
‡ Neale, in his History of the Puritans, vol ii. p. 89, 90, mentions some things which took place at a later period, and which must have affected the succession. "After these," says he, " Mr. Robert Blair came from Scotland to Bangor, (1623,) Mr. Hamilton to Bellywater, and Mr. Livingston to Killinshy, in the County of Down, with Mr. Welsh, Dunbar, and others. Mr. Blair was a zealous Presbyterian, and scrupled episcopal ordination, but the bishop of the diocese compromised the difference, by agreeing that the other Scots presbyters of Mr. Blair's persuasion should join with him, and that such passages in the established form of ordination as Mr. Blair and his brethren disliked should be omitted, or exchanged for others of their own approbation. Thus was Mr. Blair ordained publicly, in the church of Bangor; the Bishop of Raphoe did the same for Mr. Livingston, and *all the Scots who were ordained in Ireland, from this time to the year* 1642, *were ordained after the same manner ;* all of them enjoyed the churches and tithes, though they remained Presbyterian, and used not the Liturgy, nay, the bishops consulted them about affairs of common concernment to the Church, *and some of them were members of the Convocation in* 1634."

evidently follows, that its effects must have extended to these Irish bishoprics, and taken in connection with the preceding remarks, it proves, that upon your principles, the Church of Ireland must long ago have ceased to be a Christian Church.

Nor are the Scottish Episcopalians who have discarded the declaration of their old confession, that "lineal descense is not a mark of the true Church," and are as zealous as yourself for an uninterrupted apostolical diocesan succession, as absolutely indispensable to the very existence of a Church, in a better situation; for, as the succession has frequently been broken among them, it is manifest, upon their own principles, that they cannot be a Church, that they are utterly destitute of the Christian ministry, and that none of them can have a covenanted title to salvation. The succession must have been broken, as I have attempted to show, when for more than two hundred years before the coming of Palladius, their forefathers were governed, as well as instructed, by presbyters "without bishops."* It was interrupted, again, for a much longer period, when the Culdees were in the ascendant, and when the ministers of the Church, till the appointment of the first Popish bishop at St. Andrews, were commonly ordained by presbyters. It was broken among them repeatedly at successive periods, when Episcopacy was attempted to be forced upon Scotland for political purposes by the family of the Stuarts, till they were driven from the throne. Prior, indeed, to the first of these periods, or before the Reformation, Keith acknowledges that it is impossible to trace the lists of the bishops in some of their Sees; for, as was noticed already in one of the

* When Palladius is said to have been "sent to the Scots believing in Christ as their first bishop," Archbishop Usher thinks that the Scots were the Irish, and that it means he was sent to be their primate, for he asserts, that four bishops had previously been sent as bishops to Ireland. But it is now generally admitted, as Professor Killen remarks, that these persons lived *after the time of Palladius*, and Dr. Mason acknowledges that the title of primate was not then known in Ireland. See the able Defence of Presbytery by the Ministers of the General Synod of Ulster, p. 69.

notes, he says of the diocese of Dumblane, "the writs of this See have been so neglected, or perhaps wilfully destroyed, that no light can be got from thence to guide us aright in making up even the list of its ancient bishops." And the same, too, is the state of others, for though you meet with the names of bishops, you have no evidence that their baptisms or orders were regular, and without this the names must go for nothing. Nay, Dr. Jamieson proves that some of those who are mentioned as bishops in Spottiswood's lists were not bishops. And the following is the confession of Mr. Perceval respecting the lists of bishops at the second of these periods. -"It is with regret that I find myself unable to give more particulars of the consecrations in Scotland between 1662 and 1688. A collection of ecclesiastical records belonging to the Church of Scotland, which had been deposited by Bishop Campbell in the Library of Zion College, London, was burnt in the fire which destroyed the House of Parliament, where it had been taken for some purpose of inquiry. These records, I am informed, related to the Archbishopric of Glasgow, (which had under its superintendence three hundred ministers,) and would probably have furnished information of the consecrations in that archbishopric. *It is possible* that the Registers of St. Andrews are still in existence, *though it is not at present known where.*" And yet, it is upon evidence like *this*, or rather upon nothing which they would admit to be satisfactory evidence of any other fact, that the Scottish Episcopalians believe in the preservation of their uninterrupted apostolical diocesan succession.

At the first of the periods to which I have now alluded, or in the year 1610, John Spottiswoode, minister of Calder, Andrew Lamb, minister of Burntisland, and Gavin Hamilton, minister of Hamilton, were, by the command of James the First, ordained at London to the bishoprics of Glasgow, Brechin, and Galloway; but so far was that act from maintaining the succession, that if it had existed previously, it would have been utterly destroyed. In the *first* place, the Bishops of London, Ely, and Bath could not ordain them canonically, for, according to your principles, and those of the Scottish Episcopalians, as they had received only Presbyterian or schismatical baptism, and were not rebaptized, they were not even Christians; and though they became nominally bishops, yet, as they remained unbaptized till the day of their death, all the orders which they conferred upon others, after they were raised to the episcopate, must have been invalid. And, *secondly*, they were not ordained first to be deacons, and then presbyters, before they were made bishops, but their previous ordination as Scottish presbyters, which had been performed by presbyters, was sustained; and as some, though laymen, were in times of great confusion elevated to be prelates without passing through these inferior orders, they were made bishops at once, or *per saltum.** But this, you must be aware, was in direct opposition, to the tenth canon of the Council of Sardica, in the year 347, which enjoins that no one shall be made a bishop till he has first been ordained a deacon, and a presbyter. Nor was the reason which was assigned for it by Bancroft, namely, that the higher office implied the lower, at all satisfactory;† for, upon the same

---

* "A bishoppe," says Dr. Field, in his Treatise on the Church, book III. p. 157, "ordained *per saltum*, that never had the ordination of a presbyter, can neither consecrate and administer the sacrament of the Lord's body, *nor ordaine a presbyter, himselfe being none, nor doe any acte peculiarly pertaining to presbyters.* Whereby, it is most evident that that wherein a bishoppe excelleth a presbyter is not a distinct power or order, but an eminencie and dignity only, specially yeelded to one above all the rest of that same ranke for order sake, and to preserve the unitie and peace of the Church." If this opinion, however, be well founded, (and he was one of the most learned writers on the principles of ecclesiastical polity which the Church of England ever produced,) the conduct of Spottiswoode, Lamb, and Hamilton, in ordaining presbyters after they came from London, on this ground also, must have been illegal, and *the orders of the whole Episcopalian presbyters in Scotland must have been invalid.*

† This was in direct opposition to the doctrine and practice of the Church of England in the days of Archbishop Parker. Consult his account of "the Maner how the Church of England is administered and governed," at the end of Lady Bacon's English Translation of Jewel's Apology, and Strype's Parker, Append. to book II. p. 60. "Amongst us here in England," says he, "no man is called or pre-

principle, you might admit a man to the communion who had neither been baptized nor confirmed; and you might even consecrate him at once to be Archbishop of Canterbury, and Primate of all England, though he had never received the first of these ordinances; or you might raise him to the very Popedom, and make him the visible head of the Universal Church. As this, however, is so obviously absurd, that it would not be tolerated for a moment, what was done in the consecration of Spottiswoode and his brethren, unless you admit the validity of Presbyterian ordination, must have been equally absurd, and could communicate nothing of Episcopal power. Every thing consequently which they did afterwards, when they consecrated bishops, priests and deacons, must have been equally invalid, and the Scottish Episcopalians, whose succession was destroyed by that fatal step, which is now irretrievable, cannot, upon your principles, have any hope of salvation, or be entitled to the character of a Christian Church.

Nor were they extricated from these difficulties at the second of these periods, in 1661, when Sharp, Fairfoul, Leighton and Hamilton were made bishops; for though they were ordained previously to be deacons and presbyters, they were not *rebaptized;* and three of them had only Presbyterian baptism, while the fourth had merely that baptism which a clergyman ordained by one of the Scottish prelates of 1610, whose orders were invalid, was able to perform. If they were not rebaptized, however, they must have remained unbaptized till the day of their death, even though they were consecrated to be bishops; and I leave it to you to say whether any thing which was done by unbaptized prelates could have the smallest efficacy, according to your principles, and whether orders derived from men, who, according to your Catechism, had not even "been made members of Christ, children of God, and inheritors of the king-

ferred to be a bishop, *except he have first received the orders of priesthood,* and he be well hable to instruct al the people in the Holy Scriptures."

dom of heaven," in the way which he has appointed, could keep up in that Church, which is beginning to boast of its uninterrupted apostolical diocesan succession, that important privilege. Besides, Sydserf, the Bishop of Galloway, to which See Hamilton was ordained on the 15th December 1661, in the abbey Church of Westminster, was *then living*, and *was not translated to Orkney* till the 14th November 1662: And as it is contrary to the canons both of the English and Scottish Episcopalians that there should be *two bishops at the same time in one diocese*, the ordination of Hamilton was illegal; and as he was never reordained, every thing which he did must have been irregular, and must have damaged the succession.* It was still further injured, or rather

---

* "The olde canons and auncient fathers," said Archbishop Whitgift to Cartwright, in the Defense of his Answere to the Admonition, "doe testifie, that in one citie there ought to be but one bishop Chrysostome tolde Siricius that one citie must have but one bishop, as we reade, lib. vi. cap.22, of Socrates. Neyther are you able to shewe from Christe's time, that ever there was allowed to be two bishops in one citie."

"Cornelius," says Cyprian, in his 52d, or according to others, his 55th Epistle, "was made bishop by the testimony of the clergy and the suffrages of the people, when no one had been ordained before him, and the Episcopal chair was empty. Whoever after that pretends to be bishop has not the ordination of the Church, whatever he may boast, or assume to himself. *There cannot be a second bishop after the first, and, therefore, whoever is made a bishop after the first, is not a second bishop, but no bishop at all.*"

"The fathers of the Council of Nice, for the same reason," says Bower, in his History of the Popes, vol. ii p 373, "pronounced all whom Meletius of Lycopolis had ordained in Egypt, for Sees *that were not vacant* at the time of their consecration, *to be no bishops*, and at the same time issued a decree, commanding them to be *reordained* before they were admitted to serve as bishops in the Catholic Church." Socrates, lib. i cap. 9, Theodoret, lib i cap 9 "In like manner, the fathers of the Second Oecumenical Council, (that of Constantinople,) would not admit of the ordination of Maximus, the Cynic, though he had been ordained by seven bishops, but unanimously declared *that he was no bishop*, that he never should be a bishop, that *the clerks ordained by him should in no degree whatever be received as true clerks; all that had been done to him, or by him, being absolutely void and null,* because he had intruded himself into a See, that of Constantinople, legally filled by another, by Nectarius." As Hamilton, then, was intruded into the See of Galloway, while it was held by Sydserf, his ordination must have been null and void, the bishops and clerks whom he ordained could not be true bishops or clerks; all that was done to him, or by him, as he was

completely destroyed, when Sharp came from London; for with the assistance of Fairfoul and Hamilton, he consecrated George Haliburton, one of the ministers of Perth, to the See of Dunkeld; Murdoch Mackenzie, minister of Elgin, who had taken the covenant against prelacy *ten times*, or, according to others, *fourteen times*,* to the diocese of Moray; David Strachan, Middleton's minister at Fettercairn, to Brechin; John Paterson, minister at Aberdeen, to Ross; and Robert Wallace, minister of Barnwell, to the diocese of the Isles; without rebaptizing them, or making them deacons and presbyters, though all of them, except Mackenzie, had only Presbyterian baptism and orders. And yet it is from these eight bishops, *who were never baptized*, and who, according to your doctrine, *could not be Christians;* and from a ninth, whose baptism was equally irregular, and who never passed through the previous orders, which were essential to their legal elevation to the episcopate, that the Scottish Episcopalians in the present day derive their orders, the worth of which, if your principles be true, I shall leave you to determine. We know, too, that these prelates admitted a number of the Presbyterian clergy into the communion of that Church, after it was established by the Government, and allowed them to retain their parishes without either rebaptizing or reordaining them, merely upon their agreeing to be collated, and subscribing such a declaration as the following, which was all that Sharp and others required in their dioceses: "Lykas also I, the said Mr. James (Ramsay) doe declair, that I doe owne and submit to the government of the Kirk of Scotland, by archbishops and bishops, as the same is now settled by lawe. In witnes of the premises, I have sub^t the same with my hand at Edinburgh, the   day of September 1662."†

never reordained, must have been invalid, and the injury which he did to the alleged apostolical succession among the Scottish Episcopalians must have been incalculable, and is now irretrievable.

* Wodrow's Church History, vol. i. p. 129, edit. 1829
† MS Register of the Collations and Licences granted by Archbishop Sharp and other bishops, from 1662 till 1675. Both the Collations and Licenses together amount to about two hundred.

And Charles himself, in his Letter to the Privy Council in 1669, states expressly, that "such ministers as shall take collation from the bishop of the diocese, and keep presbyteries and synods, may be warranted to lift their stipends as other ministers of the kingdom." What was the number of the Presbyterian clergy who accepted these terms and conformed to Episcopacy throughout the different dioceses I have not exactly ascertained, but they are represented by the late Bishop Walker of Edinburgh as considerable; and he takes credit to the bishops for receiving them in this way without ordination, though it overthrows the doctrine of an uninterrupted apostolical diocesan succession, which is maintained by you and many Scottish Episcopalians, as absolutely indispensable to the existence of a Church. "The Archdean or archdeacon of St. Andrews, whose name was Waddel, or Weddel," says he, "was a Presbyterian minister before the Restoraration. He readily conformed to the Episcopal Church, but *he would not submit to be episcopally ordained,* which in England would have been indispensable. Well, with all the bigotry with which our poor Church has at every period been accused, *his scruples, and the scruples of many in similar circumstances, were respected,* and *his clerical character was recognised without that episcopal ordination,* which, by Episcopalians universally, is considered as essential."*
Now, if this was really the case, and if some of the individuals afterwards became bishops, and rose to other places of power and honour, and if, as Bishop Burnet declares, "no bishop in Scotland, during his stay in that kingdom, ever did so much as desire any of the presbyters (*i. e.* Presbyterian ministers) to be reordained,"† what must we think of a number of

---

* Sermon in 1831, in behalf of the Gaelic Episcopal Society.

† Bisbop of Sarum's Vindication, p 84, 85.

We have seen already, p. 18, note, that a similar course was pursued by Cranmer towards Peter Alexander, and other foreign Presbyterian ministers, when they were willing to join the Church of England. And, says Bishop Cosins, one of the keenest Episcopalians, in his letter to Cardel, "If at any time a minister so ordained in these French Churches came to incorporate himself in ours, and to

the ministers and members of his Church in the present day, who tell us that an unbroken Episcopalian succession is to be found in their Church, and that the Established Church which is Presbyterian in its government is in a state of schism?

And as the succession is not to be discovered among the Scottish Episcopalians at either of these periods, so it certainly did not commence at the time of the Revolution, when Prelacy was overthrown, and when, a few years afterwards, Dr. Ross ordained two or three bishops *without flocks or dioceses*, merely " to continue the episcopal succession;" or, as Dr. Campbell expresses it, made them " the depositaries of no deposit, commanded them to be diligent in doing no work, vigilant in the oversight of no flock, in teaching and governing no people, and presiding in no church."* This strange proceeding was a flagrant violation of the sixth canon of the Council of Chalcedon, where *six hundred and thirty* bishops were present, which forbids the giving of orders at large, " or without a title," or as it is denominated, " a ministerium vagum." And it was contrary not only to the thirty-third canon of the Church of England, but to the seventh canon of their own Church, in which they say, (and the words are printed in italics,) the candidate for holy orders must "have a particular place or charge assigned to him where he may use or exercise his function," and without it " no person shall be advanced to the order of the priesthood in this Church."

It is plain, therefore, that though the succession had

receive a public charge or cure of souls amongst us in the Church of England, (as I have known some of them to have done of late, and can instance in many other before my time,) our bishops d d not re-ordain him before they admitted him to his charge, as they must have done if his former ordination in France had been void "

* It is remarked in a very able article on Scottish Prelacy in the Presbyterian Review, No. 53, p. 182, that Dr. Campbell in this passage did little more than repeat these words of Optatus, lib. ii. " A son without a father, an apprentice without a master, a scholar without a teacher, a tenant without a house, a guest without a host, a shepherd without a flock, equally absurd was a bishop without people."

remained unbroken till the ordination of these bishops, it must have been completely destroyed, for the orders which they received having been in direct opposition to the whole of these canons, were utterly invalid.

Nor have these evils been remedied at any subsequent period, but if the following statement be borne out by facts, (and it is corroborated certainly by the strongest evidence,) it is impossible to conceive of a religious society, assuming to itself the name of a Christian Church, and according to your principles, *the only Church* (the Roman Catholic excepted) in this part of the island, in a more deplorable state as to the orders of its ministers, the efficacy of its sacraments, and the revealed and covenanted right of its members to the blessings of salvation, than that of the Scottish Episcopalians. In the year 1718, a Mr. Gadderer came from England, representing himself as a bishop, and attempted to introduce among them some important innovations, namely, prayers for the dead, mixing water with wine in the sacramental cup, and praying for the descent of the Holy Spirit upon the bread and the cup, in virtue of which descent, he said, they become *the spiritual and life-giving body and blood,* the priest having, previously to his prayer for the descent, offered up the bread and cup to God the Father, as the symbols of the sacrifice of our Saviour's body and blood, once offered up by him. The College of Bishops resisted these innovations, denominated afterwards the usages, and refused to recognise him. But upon the death of Dr. Ross he prevailed with them to receive him; and in 1727 he persuaded Bishop Cant, who was in his dotage, and bribed Bishop Millar, who too was very old, to assist him in ordaining Rattray and Dunbar, two presbyters, who approved of the usages, and raised them to the episcopate.* Their proceedings were immediately

* Mr. Gadderer, says the author of a short narrative of the Episcopal Church in Scotland, from the year 1718 to 1743, having contracted a familiar acquaintance with Mr Thomas Rattray of Craighall, and Mr. William Dunbar at Cruden, persons as fond as himself of his corrupt doctrines, encouraged them to aspire to the

PUSEYITE EPISCOPACY. 267

condemned by the college, who declared Rattray and Dunbar not to be bishops, and suspended Bishop Millar; but the latter disregarding their sentence, soon afterwards ordained Bishop Keith, another of the Usagers. The college having died out without ordaining any successors, " the present bishops," as the late Bishop Skinner remarks, (Ecc. Hist. vol. ii. p. 468,) " derive their succession *from these three* Usage bishops*, " Rattray, Keith and Dunbar." And in reference to them and to Bishop Millar, I beg to quote, first, the statement of Mr. Sievwright, a re-

episcopate, that a party might be formed in opposition to the college for promoting this doctrine more effectually by their own authority as bishops To facilitate the promotion of these two men no pains was spared ; among others money was offered first to Bishop Ross at Cupar of Fife, upon condition that he would assist in their consecration, and upon his refusing, next to Bishop Millar at Leith, who was prevailed upon to accept the bribe, and accordingly, with the assistance of Bishop Cant in Edinburgh, (both of them old men,) and Mr. Gadderer, consecrated these gentlemen, without the knowledge or consent of the other bishops, six in number, viz. Bishops Alexander Duncan, David Freebairn, James Ross, John Auchterlonie, David Ranken and John Gillan. This happened in 1727, and immediately after, these six suspended Millar upon account of the unworthy part he had acted previous to the irregular consecration of these Usagers. After this there were two different sets of bishops in Scotland, viz. the Usage party, Cant, Millar, Gadderer, Rattray and Dunbar, and the six above-mentioned members of the college The former were indefatigable in undermining the interest of the latter. Mr Keith, another of the Usage party, was consecrated by Millar while he was under suspension. The sentence of suspension against Bishop Millar was issued out in June 1727, and he died under it in October next "

Gadderer's orders were invalid He was ordained at London in 1712 by Dr Hickes, and two Scottish bishops, Falconer and Campbell. The two latter had no authority according to the canons to confer orders in England, and consequently the ordination of Gadderer was schismatical. And with regard to Hickes, who was ordained by White, Lloyd and Turner, three nonjuror bishops, who had been deprived of their Sees, even Mr Perceval says, "Under what plea consecration performed in the province of Canterbury, without consultation or approval of the bishops of the province, whose legitimate institution was never called in question, and without the approval of the now existing metropolitan, can be regarded otherwise than *irregular and schismatical*, I am at a loss to conceive." Papers, vol. ii p. 223

Rattray, who was a man of property, and was anxious to be made a bishop, furnished the bribe which was given to Millar.

spectable Episcopal minister, and next the deed of the college respecting the ordination of Messrs. Rattray and Dunbar, and their sentence suspending Bishop Millar.

"As Messrs. Rattray, Dunbar and Leith," says Mr. Sievwright, "never had regular and canonical orders, (the promotion of *the two first* having been declared most *irregular* and *uncanonical,*) in the judgment of the majority, *six orderly* against *the three disorderly* of the bishops in Scotland at that time, and the promotion of *this last* no less so of consequence, as having been carried on by Bishop Millar and his party, when he the said Bishop Millar was under suspension; and as, for this reason, these men's pretension to the title and jurisdiction of bishops were null and void, according to the express words of the sentence issued out against them by the majority foresaid, *which sentence stands unrepealed to this day*, and attested by the subscriptions of Bishops Duncan, Freebairn, Ross, Auchterlonie, Ranken and Gillan, who denounced it, therefore the pretensions of the successors in office of Messrs Rattray, Dunbar and Keith, whereby they claim the title of bishop and episcopal jurisdiction, as being *by them*, and *them alone,* appointed and promoted to their imaginary episcopate, must be esteemed (upon all church principles) equally void and null; it being impossible that any can communicate more perfect orders, or claims to episcopal jurisdiction, than they themselves possess."[*]

Extract from the original subscribed Deed, above referred to.

"We, the majority of the College of Bishops, conveened at Edinburgh, have thought ourselves obliged in conscience to declare, and by these presents do declare the said election to be null and void, and their

[*] Principles, Political and Religious, by Norman Sievwright, A. M Presbyter of the Communion of the Church of England, as by law established, and Minister to the authorised Episcopal Congregation in Brechin. Edin. 1767, p. 301, 302.

consecrations most irregular and uncanonical, and that the said Dr. Rattray and Mr. Dunbar *are no bishops of this Church*, and ought to claim no power or jurisdiction as such. Wherefor we discharge all the clergy from owning or submitting themselves to them, or giving them any obedience as bishops of this Church, &c.; and appoint this to be intimated. Given at Edinburgh, the 29th of June 1727, and subscribed by us.

    Jo. AUCHTERLONIE, Bishop.
    DA. RANKEN, Bp.
    Jo. GILLAN, Bishop.
    ALEX. DUNCAN, Preses.
    DAVID FREEBAIRN, Bishop.
    JA. Ross, Bpp."

Extract from Sentence of Suspension on Bishop Millar.

"*June* 28, 1727. The College of Bishops being met, &c., find themselves obliged, for recovering the peace and unity of this Church, so miserably violated and broken by him, to suspend, and by these presents do suspend the said Bishop Arthur Millar from the exercise of any part of the episcopal office within this National Church, and particularly within the diocese of Edinburgh, to which we have declared he has no right or title, aye and while he give satisfaction to our reasonable overtures formerly made to him, both by word and writ; and appoint these presents to be intimated to the said Bp. Arthur Millar, and to the presbyters of the diocese of Edinburgh, that none concerned may pretend ignorance."*

I leave these documents, the genuineness of which will scarcely, I presume, be questioned by any one, to speak for themselves, and I would like to know whether you consider the orders of the present bishops of the Scottish Episcopalians, which have been derived from those who had no right to bestow them, as good

---

* Extracted from a MS Collection of Holograph Documents in the possession of the Rev. Thomas M'Crie, Edinburgh.

and valid, and whether you regard their Church as a Christian Church, and its members as having a covenanted title to salvation. You will hardly, I apprehend, venture to do this; and if the orders of their bishops are utterly irregular, and the ministrations of their clergy are consequently destitute of the smallest efficacy, Mr. Doddsworth and Mr. Gladstone, and those of your bishops who are patronising them so zealously against the Scottish Establishment, would confer on them a greater and more important favour, than the grants which they have procured for them from the Society for propagating Christian Knowledge, if they could assist them in recovering the apostolic succession, and could restore them to the character of a Christian Church.

It is scarcely necessary, after facts like these, to inquire whether none of them, though baptized in infancy by Presbyterian Dissenters, or ministers of the Establishment, and never rebaptized, have not afterwards, when admitted into the communion of that Church, been made presbyters and bishops, while, according to your principles, they are not even Christians, and whether instances of the kind are not to be found among her prelates in the present day. Nay, I might further inquire, whether there are not some among her presbyters, who not only have nothing more than Presbyterian baptism, but were Presbyterian elders, and who, though never rebaptized, are permitted to baptize and administer the Eucharist to the members of their congregations, and who, though the orders of her bishops were regular and canonical, would injure the succession. I do not positively affirm that there are such instances, but only inquire whether it is not actually the case; and if it should turn out to be so, it only serves to illustrate the extreme inconsistency and folly of those, who though they no longer venture to repeat the cry of no bishop, no king,*

* It is curious that Infidels and Papists have brought the very same objection against Protestantism in general, which Episcopalians in the days of the Stuarts used to advance against Presbyterianism, namely, that it is unfavourable to *monarchy*. See in proof of this,

repeat another no less revolting to the feelings of every enlightened Christian, no bishop, no church, no ministry, no sacraments, and no hope of salvation.

I am, Reverend Sir,

Yours, &c.

with an excellent refutation of Montesquieu, who recommends Popery as preferable to it in this respect, because the Pope is an ecclesiastical monarch, Froman's Disputatio de Protestantium Religione regali civitatis generi accommodata, tom ii. of his Dissertations, and the Nova Acta Histor. Eccles. Vinar. vol. i. p. 5, where there is an admirable Lettre d'un Patriote sur la tolerance civile des Protestans de France, et sur les avantages qui en resulteroient pour le Royaume, 1756.

The testimony which Lord Bacon bears to the loyalty of Presbyterians in his day, and the injuries which they sustained, is very valuable. "The wrongs of them which are possessed of the government of the Church towards the other," says he, in his Treatise of Church Controversies, vol iv of his Works, p. 427, "may hardly be dissembled and excused. They have charged them as though they denied tribute to Caesar, and withdrew from the civil magistrate the obedience *which they have ever performed, and taught.* They have sorted and coupled them with the family of love, *whose heresies they have laboured to destroy and confute.* They have been swift of credit to receive accusations against them, *from those that have quarrelled with them but for speaking against sin and vice.* Their accusations and inquisitions have been strict, *swearing men to blanks and generalities*, not included within compass of matter certain which the party who is to take the oath may comprehend, which is a thing captious and strainable." "*And as for the easy silencing them in such great scarcity of preachers, it is to punish the people and not them.*"

LETTER XVII.

The Church of Denmark, as its first superintendents were only presbyters, and after the Reformation received imposition of hands only from Bugenhagen, a single Lutheran presbyter, without the succession, and upon the principles of Dr Pusey, not a Christian Church —The same, too, the condition of the Church of Sweden, and of all the foreign Protestant Churches which have only superintendents —Superintendents both among Lutherans and Calvinists, when appointed to their office not ordained anew, but appointed merely the chairmen or moderators of presbyters, by whom they may be deposed —Their Churches, of course, not Christian Churches —Account of the Ancient Scottish superintendents, whose office is misrepresented by Episcopalians —The Church of Prussia not a Church, nor the Protestant Churches of France, Geneva, Switzerland, Holland, America and Scotland —The Presbyterians in Ireland and Great Britain, with the Methodists and Independents, not Churches, and their members without any covenanted title to salvation —The succession destroyed in the Church of Rome —Pagans baptized some who became ministers—laymen ordained to be bishops—bishops often ordained to Sees which were not vacant—This the case with Augustine, Bishop of Hippo

REVEREND SIR,—If the condition of the Churches of England and Ireland, as well of the Scottish Episcopalians, according to your principles, be exceedingly alarming, because they have lost the uninterrupted apostolic succession, the rest of the Protestant Episcopalian Churches are in a similar state, and none of their ministers, any more than yours, can have the smallest confidence in the validity of their orders, nor the holiest of their members any hope of being received into the abodes of blessedness. Such must be the condition of the Church of Denmark, for, as is stated by Gerdesius, Messenius and Des Roches, and acknowledged by King, a zealous Episcopalian, the whole of the bishops were deprived at the Reformation, and were succeeded by ministers under the name of Superintendents, who had previously been only priests or deacons. "But when the Popish bishops," says the first of these writers, "had been vanquished, and expelled from their Sees, the King took care that the very same year there should be ordained in their room seven others, and these evangelical ministers, which was performed by the same Pomeranian. They were enjoined to attend to the churches, and to watch over their affairs, and were called superintendents rather than bishops. The following were those who were thus ordained: Peter Palladius, who was appointed superintendent or bishop of the diocese of Zealand; Francis Wormordus, a Carmelite of Elsineur, and a minister, and Professor of Theology at Malmoe, of the Scanic diocese; George Fiburg, a minister of Copenhagen, of the Fionic diocese; John Vandal, a reader of Hatterslebe, of the Ripensian diocese; Matthias Langius, a Radnensian minister, of the Arhusian diocese; James Scaningius, minister of Fiburgh, of the   diocese; and Peter Thomas, minister of Torn, of the Alburgensian diocese."* And as such was the rank of the first Danish superintendents, prior to their elevation to their new dignity, so the person who ordained them was the celebrated Bugenhagen, who, according to Moreri, was only a presbyter before his conversion to Protestantism,† and who, as is mentioned by Seckendorf,‡ had been appointed by Luther, who, too, was but a presbyter, superintendent of Wittemberg. "Bugenhagen," says Professor Mallet in his History of Denmark, "had orders to choose from the

* "Cum vero ita sedibus suis pulsi motique essent Episcopi Pontificii," &c Introduction in Histor. Evangel. Renovat. tom. iii. p. 111. This account is confirmed by the second of these authors, in his Schondia Illustrata, p. 79, 80, though there is a trivial difference as to some of the names, and the day of ordination. "Immediately after this," says he of Bugenhagen, "he imparted his benediction to the first seven Superintendents of Denmark, namely, Franciscus Vormundus, &c. Inde autem, 14 die Augusti," &c And says Des Roches, in his Histoire de Dannemark, tom v. p. 132, " In place of the seven bishops of Denmark, he consecrated in the Cathedral Church of Copenhagen seven divines, by order of the King and the Senate, under the title of superintendents, though they still retained also that of bishops   A la place des sept Eveques de Dannemarc,—conseccra dans l'Eglise Cathedrale," &c.   "In Denmark," says King in his Miscellanies, p. 183, " at the Reformation, *none of the Popish bishops would embrace it*, but all, because of their errors, were deposed, and then the new superintendents, according to Luther's institution in Germany, were ordained by Dr. Bugenhagen from Wittenberg."
† See his Dictionnaire Historique, tom. ii. p. 361, where he says, " Jean Bugenhagen, ministre Protestante, ne le 24 Juin 1485 à Wollin dans la Pomeranie, enseigna dans son pays, s'y fit prêtre, et y fut considere comme un des plus savans hommes de son temps." After which he gives an account of the way in which he was converted to Lutheranism.
‡ Commentaries, lib. i. sec 45.

Protestant ministers, seven who were most esteemed for their deportment and knowledge. Of these, the most distinguished were Palladius, who had the diocese of Zeland, and Vormordus, who had that of Scania; the last had formerly been a Carmelite at Elsineur, and afterwards a theologian at Malmoe. The ceremony of their consecration was very simple. After the singing of some hymns, Bugenhagen ordained them with imposition of hands, and addressed to them a discourse, pointing out to them the nature of their duties."* And not only did he ordain these superintendents, but, according to Clark,† remained in the country a considerable time, and ordained many ministers. This took place in 1537; and we are informed by Molesworth, that, in 1692, the Church of Denmark was still governed by superintendents. "There are," says he, "six superintendents in Denmark, who take it very kindly to be called Bishops, and my Lord; viz. one in Zealand, one in Funen, and four in Jutland. There are also four in Norway. These have no temporalities, keep no ecclesiastical courts, have no cathedrals with prebends, canons, deans, sub-deans, &c., but are only *primi inter pares*, having the rank above the inferior clergy of their provinces, and the inspection into their doctrine and manners."‡ I may add, that though they are not allowed, like Lords of Parliament, to sit in the Supreme Court of the king-

---

* "Bugenhag eut ordre de choisir parmi les ministres Protestans sept des plus estimes par leur moeurs et par leur savoir," &c. tom. vi. p 366.

He adds, "Apres cela Bugenhag fut charge de dresser un formulaire de foi et de discipline suivant lequel les ecclesiastiques des royaumes, et des duches, et tous ceux a qui l'instruction des fideles etoit confie devoient se regler Elle fut composee en Latin sous le titre *d'Ordonnance Ecclesiastique*, apres avoir ete liee et approuvee par Luther et par les autres Docteurs les plus celebres de l'Universite de Wittemberg, le Roi, le Senat, les etats l'ayant confirmee la firent imprimer en Danois, et l'envoyerent aux Églises de Norvege et de Sleswig, pour qu'elles s'y conformassent, aussi bien que celles de Dannemark, comme elles l'ont toujours fait depuis jusqu'à ce jour." P 367, 368.

† Compare his Lives of the Fathers, p. 253.

‡ Molesworth's Account of Denmark, p. 231.

dom, yet that privilege is conceded to two of them when any matter comes before it which affects the Church. But if such be the source from which the superintendents or bishops of Denmark, and the inferior clergy, have derived their orders for more than three hundred years; and if such be the powers which are entrusted to them by the State, I presume that you, and those Scottish Episcopalians who hold your principles, are prepared to consign the Protestant nation, not only in the present day, but through all those generations which have succeeded the Reformation, to God's uncovenanted mercies, and to say, that, during that long and eventful period, they have been without a church and without a ministry, and that none of them has ever been possessed of a title to the blessings of salvation.

The Swedish Church at the time of the Reformation, as I noticed formerly, is said by Messenius to have had four superintendents, with an arch-superintendent, who, prior to his ordination, was a teacher at Upsal.* He does not mention by whom they were ordained; but if, as is probable, it was by Lutheran presbyters, their orders would labour under the same defects with those of the Danish superintendents. But, independently of this, if those who ordained them derived their orders from Popish bishops, I shall endeavour to show that they could not be valid, because the succession has been broken in that apostate Church. And if I succeed in establishing the latter position, it follows, that upon your principles the Church of Sweden also must cease to be regarded as a Christian Church, and that there is not an individual in that kingdom who can have any hope of salvation.

The situation of those Churches which are governed by superintendents is equally deplorable, for they want the apostolical diocesan succession, and consequently cannot be recognised as Christian Churches. No new ordination takes place when any one is appointed a superintendent. In the tenth regulation

* See note, p. 68-9.

of the Synodus Xanensis, it is said that "his office ought to continue from synod to synod, and that by the decision of the synod he shall either be approved of and retained, or another shall be chosen and appointed."* And though his presidency now is more permanent, yet, as is proved by Parker, on the authority of Zepper, Hemingius and Herbrand, both in the Calvinistic and Lutheran Churches, where such an officer exists, he is only the chairman or moderator of the presbyters, *the primus inter pares*, has no such authority over them as an English prelate has over his presbyters, and may even be judged and deposed by them.†
But if such be the case, how dismal in your opinion must be the state of all those Protestant Churches

* "Munus ejus a synodo ad synodum durare debet. Et juxta sententiam synodi aut is retinendus et approbandus, aut alius eligendus et constituendus erit."

† In his Politeia Ecclesiastica, lib i. cap. 28, p 79, he gives the following very distinct account of the office of the superintendent, from Scultingius, lib. v fol. 14. "Nono, tametsi Lutherani omnes, et Calviniani etiam quidam, ut Zepperus, Pastor Herbonensis, et alii superintendentes constituant, tamen isti adeo inter se dissident, ut nemo alteri velit cedere. Decimo, *inter episcopum et sacerdotem nihil omnino statuunt discriminis.* (They make no difference between the power of a bishop and a presbyter.) Quod ad secundum, authoritatem scilicet in reliquos ministros episcopum Anglicanum habere, inspectorem Germanicum *non item.* Hoc ex Gulielmo Zeppero liquet, qui non obstante superintendentis praesidentia nullam tamen altero majorem authoritatem vel in verbi et sacramentorum ministerio, inque disciplinae ecclesiasticae usu obtinere dicit. Addit etiam de ipso superintendente, (lib. ii. p. 322-324,) quod in disciplinae ipsius ratione aliis subjectus sit, quod illius praesidentiae hoc tantum munus sit quod ecclesiae suae classi operam suam plus aliis ministris omnibus impendere teneatur, quod causas difficiliores ad consistoriorum legitimam cognitionem, et adjudicationem devolvere debeat, quod denique ministri et seniores earum ecclesiarum quibus praeest de eo statuere, de eo judicare, eum punire, imo etiam quemadmodum eligebant primum, *ita etiam deponere et destituere possent.* Id ipsum de Lutheranis superintendentibus dicendum est, (p. 329) Seniores enim agnoscit Nicolaus Hemingius, ita episcopo atque superintendenti suo, nihil aliud relinquit nisi illam in consistorio quam nuper descripsimus praesidentiam, id quod etiam ab ipsius verbis liquet. Ita enim inter caetera habet, qui labore et donis reliquos antecedit, is ab ecclesia praefertur, non ut dominium super caeteros exerceat, sed ut alios regat sapientia et consilio. In testimonio vero Herbrandi ab eodem citato apparet istud adhuc luculentius, disserta enim verba Herbrandi allegat in quibus dicit *superintendentem nullam in caeteros potestatem habere.*"

where superintendents merely preside, and have no greater power than that of a moderator in an assembly of presbyters, and may even be deprived of their office by their fellow-presbyters. And yet this is the condition of the Church of Prussia, where there are no diocesan bishops, though the King is reported, in opposition to the principles of his illustrious ancestor, whose name is affixed to the Articles of Smalkald, to be anxious to have them, but who must apply for them elsewhere than to the prelates of your Church, or of the Scottish Episcopalians, if he would establish a pure apostolical succession. And it is the condition of all those other Churches which resemble it in their form of ecclesiastical polity, none of which, any more than the Church of Prussia, has a single minister whose orders, upon your principles, can be considered as valid, nor a single member who has a covenanted title to the blessings of salvation.*

* The Church of Scotland, for a short time after the Reformation, had a few superintendents, but they differed from those of the continental churches in this, that while the latter was intended to be a permanent class of ministers, and have continued for several hundred years, the Scottish superintendents were intended only to be temporary, and were to cease when the parishes were supplied with pastors. (See First Book of Discipline, where it is said to be "*expedient*" merely, "*at this time.*") Episcopalians have represented them as a kind of bishops. But, says the learned author of the Apologeticall Relation of the particular Sufferings of the faithful Ministers and Professours of the Church of Scotland, since August 1660, p 13, "so cautious were the Reformers, that they would not acknowledge those to be bishops, either in name or thing; for as their work was extraordinary, so they gave them an extraordinary name. They would not suffer *any who had been bishops before in time of Popery to enjoy the place and power of a superintendent*, least the power and place might be abused, and *at length degenerate into the old power of prelates;* but even in those bounds where such lived did appoint others to superintend, as Mr. Pont in Galloway. *They would not divide the bounds of those superintendents according to the prelats' dioceses, but after another manner* They divided the land into ten parts, having respect to the edification and advantage of the poor people. The superintendents were chosen by the consent of the whole bounds which they were to visite. *They were not consecrated*, but only set apart to that worke by preaching and prayer, as is to be seen in the order prefixed to the old Psalme books. *They were tryed and examined by the ministers of these bounds.* They had other ministers conjunct with them when they ordained any. Neither had they sole power of excommunication; for Reformed Churches had power, by

I take it for granted, that you entertain a similar opinion of the spiritual condition of the Church of Scotland, and of the different bodies of our Presbyterian Dissenters, as well as of the Presbyterians in Ireland, the Methodists, Presbyterians, Independents and Baptists in England, and the Presbyterians in France, Geneva, Switzerland, Holland and North America, none of whose ministers, for two hundred years, can be regarded, upon your principles, as Christian ministers, and of none of whose members, however pious, as they are not under the superintendence of diocesan bishops, can there be the smallest hope that they shall be received, when they die, into the abodes of blessedness. But while such are your views of the state of these Churches, there is another Church which you are disposed to consider as presenting a very noble and gratifying contrast to these schismatical Churches, namely, the Church of Rome. That Church, you allege, from which you received the succession, still retains it, and must therefore be a true and apostolical Church. Nay, you talk of it in terms of the highest veneration, as "your Mother Church," and are

the Book of Discipline, to excommunicate the contumacious, and the Tractate of excommunication prefixed to some old Psalme books, sheweth that they might do it *without the advyce of the superintendent. They were subject to the censure of the ministers and elders of the province, who might depose them in some cases.* Their maine work was preaching, for they were to preach at the least thrice every week They had their own particular flocks beside, with which they stayed always, save when they were visiting the bounds committed unto them They might not try any minister thir alone, but were commanded to have the neerest reformed Church, and other learned men conjunct, by an act of the Fourth Nationall Assembly, an. 1562. They might not transport a minister without the consent of the synod, as is clear by act fourth of the First Nationall Assembly, 1562. They might not discusse any impoitant question thir alone, as is clear by act first of the Ninth Nationall Synod, an. 1564 They were at liberty to appeal from them to the Nationall Synod, as is clear by act fifth, Assembly sixth. They were to be subject to the Assembly, as is clear by the fourth Assembly, an. 1562. They never did moderate in General Assemblies, unless they had been chosen by vote Beside, an. 1562, at the Nationall Assembly there were some ministers chosen to assist the five superintendents, (for no moe could be got settled for want of maintainance,) and had equally power with them, and were commanded to give accompt of their diligence unto every Nationall Synod, and *there to lay down their office.*"

anxious to induce your bishops and clergy to return within its pale. Such language, you are aware, would have excited the surprise of your early reformers, who sealed with their blood their attachment to principles, to the importance of which you and your followers seem to be completely insensible, and who have left in their writings the most solemn warnings against that very step which you so strenuously recommend. "O heinous blasphemy, and most detestable injury against Christ," said Cranmer " O wicked abomination in the temple of God! O pride intolerable of Anti-Christ, and most manifest token of the Son of perdition, extolling himself above God, and with Lucifer, exalting his seat and power above the throne of God What man of knowledge, and zeal to God's honour, can with dry eyes see this injury to Christ; and look upon the state of religion, brought in by the Papists, perceiving the true sense of God's word subverted by false glosses of man's devising, the true Christian religion turned into certain hypocritical and superstitious acts, the people praying with their mouths and hearing with their ears they wist not what, and so ignorant in God's word, that they could not discern hypocrisy and superstition from true and sincere religion."* And again he says, "I know how Anti-Christ hath obscured the glory of God, and the true knowledge of his word ; and moved by the duty, office, and place whereunto it hath pleased God to call me, I give warning in his name, unto all that profess Christ, that they flee far from Babylon, if they will save their souls, and to beware of that great harlot, that is to say, the pestiferous See of Rome, that she make you not drunk with her pleasant wine."† "The See of Rome," says Hooper, "is not only a tyranny and pestilence of body and soul, but the nest of all abomination. God give him grace, and all his successors, to leave their abomination, and to come unto the light of God's word. This

* See his Book on the Sacrament, Fathers of the English Church, vol. iii. p 350.
† Fathers of the English Church, p. 332.

beast is preached unto the people, to be a man that cannot err; his authority to be above God and his laws; and to be the prince upon earth of all princes. But God will judge him, as he is a murderer of both body and soul, and punish the princes of this world that uphold his abomination."* "When a man," says Latimer, "is a right Papist, given to monkery, I warrant you he is in this opinion, that with his own works he doth merit remission of sins, and satisfieth the law through and by his own works, and so thinketh himself to be saved everlastingly. This is the opinion of all Papists; and this doctrine was taught in times past, in schools, and in the pulpits. Now, all these that be in such an opinion, they be the enemies of the cross of Christ, of his passion and blood-shedding." "Yea," says he elsewhere, "what fellowship hath Christ with Anti-Christ? *Therefore is it not lawful to bear the yoke with Papists.*"† And says Jewel, "As for us we have forsaken a Church in which we could neither hear the pure word of God, nor administer the sacraments, nor invoke the name of God as we ought,"‡ and of which Gerson complains, that "the multitude of light and foolish ceremonies (in it) had extinguished all that power of the Holy Spirit which should have flourished in us, and all that was truly pious "§ And he adds, "Wherefore, if the Pope does indeed desire we should be reconciled to him, *he ought first to reconcile himself* to God;"‖ which, though you are so desirous to join his communion, has never yet been done. But whether you respect or disregard these warnings, it is necessary to examine whether the apostolical succession has been preserved in that Church; and if I succeed in demonstrating that it has been utterly destroyed, it will follow upon your principles, as well as its

* Fathers of the English Church, vol. v. p. 117.
† Ibid. vol ii p 659, vol. iv. p. 103.
‡ Ibid. vol. vii p. 85.
§ Apology for the Church of England, Fathers of the English Church, vol vii. p. 63.
‖ Ibid. p. 119.

own, that it has long ago ceased to be a Christian Church, and has not, since this happened, had a single bishop, or priest, or deacon who was a Christian minister, nor a single member who could have any hope of salvation. And if that event took place prior to the Reformation, it will furnish another unanswerable argument to show that that succession never even began in your National Church as a Protestant Church, or among the Scottish Episcopalians, or in the Church of Ireland.

Now, I beg to remark, in support of my position, that it would certainly be wonderful if the succession had been preserved in the Church of Rome, when you consider its doctrine respecting baptism. It has acknowledged, at least for many centuries, the validity of that ordinance when administered by *Pagans*, and has declared, that if it has been dispensed in the name of the Father, the Son, and the Spirit, it cannot be repeated "without sacrilege." If baptism, however, when performed by presbyters, because they were not ordained by diocesan bishops, though it has been done in that name, is not valid, you will scarcely, I apprehend, admit its validity when administered by heathens, who were themselves unbaptized, and who avowed their disbelief of the doctrines of the Gospel, and among others the Trinity, though they might pronounce the names of the persons in the Godhead. But if baptism by such persons was invalid, it renders it, I conceive, exceedingly probable that the succession must have been broken in that apostate Church, unless you can prove, that for seven hundred years prior to the Reformation, there was not an individual in any of the numerous and extensive countries which acknowledged its authority, who, though baptized by Pagans, and never re-baptized, was raised to the episcopate.

It is not, however, merely matter of probability, but of absolute certainty, that the succession was destroyed for a number of centuries before the reformation, both in the Western and Eastern Churches; and in confirmation of this assertion, I would solicit your attention to the following facts:

You will scarcely deny, that the orders of laymen, who were promoted at once to the office of bishops were invalid and uncanonical, and yet there were numerous instances in which the succession was broken by such gross irregularities in the Churches of Rome and Constantinople. Cyprian was only a neophyte, or newly baptized, when he was ordained at once to be bishop of Carthage; Ambrose, when he was made bishop of Milan; and Nectarius, when he was appointed to the See of Constantinople. And Eucherius was only a layman when he was made bishop of Lyons; and Philogonius of Antioch was transferred, according to Chrysostom, from a court of justice to a bishop's throne.* Tarasius, though a layman, was consecrated to the see of Constantinople in 784, and made many bishops and presbyters; and Photius, who was in the same state, was made Patriarch in 854. John XIX., while a layman, was raised at once to the Popedom, in 1024, and ordained many both among the higher and lower orders of the clergy. Clement V., in 1308, gave the archbishopric of Mentz to Peter, a physician, who was only a layman, for attending him during his illness, remarking, that "it was fit the cure of souls should be committed to one who was so expert at curing the body." And Amadeus, Duke of Savoy, though a layman, was made Pope in 1439, and consecrated a number of cardinals and bishops while he retained that office, though he resigned it in 1448. It would be easy to specify many more instances, but it is unnecessary. And I have only to ask, whether, believing, as you must, that episcopal orders conferred on those who had been baptized only by Pagans, or bestowed in opposition to the 10th canon of the Council of Sardica, and the decisions of many others of the early councils, on mere laymen, are invalid; and knowing that

* Pontius in Vit. Cypri. Socrat., l. v. c. 8; Sozom. l vii. c 8; Hilary Arelat. in Vit. Honorat. Chrysostom, Homil. 31, de Philog. See Bower's History of the Popes, vol. iv. p 21.

these laymen ordained many bishops, priests and deacons, you are not prepared to admit that the apostolical succession has been lost irrecoverably both in the Western and Eastern Churches? And I have further to inquire, whether it does not follow from these facts, according to your principles and those of the Papists, that in neither of these Churches, any more than in your own, or in any other Church on the face of the earth, is there either at present, or has there been, at least for more than a thousand years, a single minister who was entitled to be considered as a Christian minister, nor a single individual who could have any hope of salvation?

The same thing seems to follow from another important fact, which you cannot controvert, namely, that bishops have frequently been ordained to Sees which were held by others; and consequently the orders which were conferred on them, from the principles laid down in your own canons, and in those of the Scottish Episcopalians, and in the decisions of the early Christian councils, must have been null and void. It was declared by Cyprian, as was stated in a note, p. 262, that "there cannot be a second bishop *after the first,* and therefore whoever is made a bishop after the first is not a second bishop, but *no bishop at all.*" And, on that account, the Council of Nice pronounced those whom Miletius had ordained in Egypt, to Sees that were not vacant, to be "*no bishops.*" Now, we know that many bishops were ordained to Sees, both in the Western and Eastern Churches, which were held by others, just as Hamilton was ordained to the See of Galloway, of which Sydserf was bishop; and therefore their own ordinations, and the orders which they conferred upon others, whether bishops, presbyters, or deacons, and the baptisms administered by the latter, must have been invalid. At the end, for instance, of the very century in which the first Council of Nice was held, Augustine was ordained Bishop of Hippo by the Primate of Numidia, and a number of bishops, while Valerius was living, and had not resigned his See; and he was never re-ordained, and consequently his own orders, and those which he gave, must have been null and void. Nor was it done, either by him or the prelates who ordained him, from a want of respect for the canons of that Council, but, as he himself acknowledges, from their being ignorant of them,* and though he named his successor, and caused him to be elected, he would not suffer him to be ordained while he himself was living † Photius was divested of the priesthood nine years after his consecration to the See of Constantinople, because, as the Council of Metz expresses it, " in the lifetime of their brother Ignatius, Patriarch of that Church, he had intruded himself into it, and entered the sheepfold, not by the door, but like a thief and a robber ;" and yet, in the course of that time, he had made many bishops and presbyters. Pope Silverius, Bishop of Rome, was banished from his See by Belisarius, in 537, but not deposed, and Vigilius was chosen and ordained in his room. His orders, however, were invalid, as there was another bishop to whom the See belonged, and there could not be a second; and as he was not re-ordained upon the death of Silverius, the eighty-one bishops and forty-six presbyters‡ whom he ordained during his pontificate have given a fatal blow to the apostolical succession in the Church of Rome, and in every Church which was connected with it. And as none of your ministers, or of the Scottish Episcopalians, is able to show that he has not derived his orders from some of these prelates, it is evident that, till he is prepared to do so, he can have no assurance that he is a Christian minister. And Eugenius was made Pope and Bishop of Rome in 654, when, as appears from a letter of Martin, his predecessor, the latter had not resigned, so that his ordinations also must have been equally invalid.§ The Anti-Pope Guibert was made Bishop of Rome in 1080, while Gregory VII. held that See; and he claimed that bishopric for twenty

---

* August Ep 110, et 64. Possid. in Vit. Aug. c 8.
† Epist 110.
‡ Bower's History of the Popes, vol. ii p. 374.
§ Ibid. vol. iii. p. 68, 69.

years during the pontificate of Gregory, Victory III. and Urban II., and all the orders which he gave must have been a nullity. From 1159 to 1182 there were in succession four Anti-Popes; and though the ordinations which they made were declared by Alexander III. to be invalid, yet the persons who received them do not appear *to have been re-ordained* upon their submitting to his authority; nor were the individuals whom they baptized rebaptized. And for thirty years more, or from 1378 till 1409, there were two Popes, one residing at Rome, and the other at Avignon, of whom it was remarked by Bower, "that it has never yet been decided *which was the true Pope.*" Both the rival Popes were deposed in 1409, and Alexander V. appointed Pope, who confirmed the ordinations made by the two competitors, provided they were in other respects canonical.* But it is plain, that his decision could not make the orders of those who received them valid without reordination; and as this never took place, the injury which was done to the apostolical succession in the Church of Rome during that long period, by so many irregular and uncanonical ordinations, must evidently be incalculable, and demonstrates that that Church which you so much admire cannot, upon your principles, be a Christian Church, nor its ministers Christian ministers, and that not even one of its members can have any hope of salvation.†

I remain, Reverend Sir, yours, &c.

* Bower's History of the Popes, vol. vii. p. 125.

† It deserves to be noticed, that Formosus, who had been degraded from his bishopric, and reduced to the condition of a layman by John VIII , upon his elevation to the Popedom, ordained Plegmund to be Archbishop of Canterbury, who, as Professor Killen observes, from Innet, (Plea for Presbytery, p. 50,) ordained no less than seven bishops in one day, and held the See for twenty-six years. Formosus, however, was deposed after his death, first by Stephen VII., and then by Sergius, who "deposed likewise all such as had been consecrated and invested by him." The latter act was never revoked by him, and as Plegmund was never reordained, it presents an alarming view of the state of the orders *of the English clergy,* according to Dr. Pusey's principles, and *of the Scottish Episcopalians,* whose bishops, both in 1610 and 1661, received their orders from the English bishops.

LETTER XVIII.

Additional evidence that the succession has been lost in the Church of Rome. —Boys ordained to be Bishops, and striplings made Popes —Atheists and avowed infidels raised to the Popedom —Papal canon, that "if a Pope should carry with him innumerable souls to hell, no man must presume to find fault with him" Simoniacal ordinations declared void by the canons of many Councils, and yet for eight hundred years there were many such ordinations, both in the Western and Eastern Churches —Idiots, and persons, "who, when they read, prayed, or sang, knew not whether they blessed God or blasphemed him," ordained to be bishops —Multitudes of the most immoral individuals, some of whom "drank wine in honour of the devil," made Popes and Bishops

REVEREND SIR,—I appeal further, in support of my position, to the ordination of individuals to the highest and most important functions in the Church, when they were far from an age which could prepare them for being admitted even into the lowest of its orders. John the Tenth, for instance, confirmed the election of Hugh, son of Count Hubert, in 925, to the Archbishopric of Rheims, though he was scarcely five years old; and he was consecrated in a council of bishops at Soissons, when he was only eighteen years of age * John the Twelfth, though destitute of every quality which could fit him for being received even as a member of the Church, was made Bishop of Rome, and Head of the Universal Church, in 956, when he was only eighteen, and retained the Popedom till 963, when he was deposed.† And among other charges brought against him before the Council, and which were not contradicted, "John, Bishop of Narni, and John Cardinal Deacon, attested, that they had seen him ordain a deacon in a stable; and Benedict, deacon, with other deacons and priests, said, that they knew for certain that he had ordained bishops for money, and had, among the rest, ordained a child but *ten years old* Bishop of Todi."‡ Nor were these

* Bower, vol. v. p 94–100.
† Ibid. vol. v p. 104.
‡ Ibid vol. v. p. 108 Bower was Professor of Rhetoric, History and Philosophy in the Universities of Rome, Firmo, and Macerata; and in the latter place, Counsellor to the Inquisition.

solitary instances, for Ratherius, Bishop of Verona in Italy, during the tenth century, is said by Dr. Allix, in his Remarks on the Ancient Churches of Piedmont, (p. 241,) to have written to the Bishop of Parma, "to desire him to confer orders upon children for money no more, as he was wont to do;" and there were many similar ordinations during successive centuries. But if such be the case, I should like to be informed, whether you really believe that the apostolic succession has been preserved in that Church, by orders conferred on boys and striplings, whom none of your bishops would venture to ordain, and whether you, Mr. Newman, Dr. Hook, or Mr Perceval are able to prove that your own orders have not come to you from *the Bishop of Todi*, or *the Archbishop of Rheims*, or some other prelate who was ordained in his boyhood, so as to justify your claims to the honourable character of Christian ministers.

And then, when, along with the consecration of boys and of men who had never been baptized at all, or baptized by Pagans, to the office of bishops, you consider the doctrine which was taught in that Church for many ages, it will certainly be strange if you venture to assert that it has preserved the succession. "The Church," said Melancthon, whom your most distinguished prelates were accustomed to venerate, "*is not bound to the ordinary succession of bishops, but to the Gospel.* When bishops do not teach right doctrine they must be left, for the ordinary succession is of no avail to the Church."* "Of the right use of sacraments," says Bishop Hooper, "it is taught, 1 Cor. xi., Mark xvi., Luke xxiv. and Matt. xxviii., which teach people to know the Church by these signs. The traditions of men, and the succession of bishops teach wrong. Those two false opinions have given unto the succession of bishops power to interpret the Scripture, and power to make such laws in the Church as

* " Dixi supra ecclesiam non esse alligatam ad successionem ordinariam, ut vocant, episcoporum, sed ad evangelium Dum episcopi non recte docent, nihil ad ecclesiam pertinet ordinaria successio, sed necessario relinquendi sunt," tom. i. fol. 231, Operum.

it pleased them. God, for the preservation of his Church, doth give unto certain persons the gift and knowledge to open the Scripture: but that gift is not a power *bound to any order, or succession of bishops, or title of dignity.*"* And said Bilson, "The succession is of no weight, unless truth of doctrine and purity of life be added to it."† I shall immediately inquire whether the bishops and dignitaries of the Romish Church were distinguished by that purity, and I beg to inquire at you and all your followers, as honest, consistent and intelligent members of the Church of England, whether you think that the doctrine of the Church of Rome, and of many of its bishops, not merely on lesser, but on the most momentous points, was agreeable to the doctrine of the Sacred Scriptures? Jewel, in his Apology for the Church of England, points out many monstrous and fatal errors in the Church of Rome; and as it is one of the public books of your Church, as long as you remain in it, you must concur in his statements. And I should like to know whether you believe that any one who held these heresies could preserve the succession. We know, too, that infidels and atheists have been elevated to the highest place in that Church, and I would be glad if you will show how they could maintain the succession, by laying their hands on the heads of others, any more than Satan, if he were to appear upon earth in a human form, could do it by the imposition of his hands. "We remember," says the noble Picus of Mirandula, "another ordained and received for true Pope, who, in the opinion of good men, neither was nor could be true Pope, *as he believed no God,* and exceeded the utmost pitch of infidelity. It is affirmed, he confessed to some of his domestics that *he believed no God even when he sat in the Papal chair.* And I have heard of another Pope, who own-

* Declaration of Christ and his Office, Fathers of the English Church, vol. v. p 177. I quote now from this edition, as I have not retained the copy from which I made the other extracts,

† "Successio nullius ponderis est nisi addatur doctrinae veritas et pura vitae conversatio." Parker de Politeia Ecclesiast. p. 163.

ed to one of his intimates that *he did not believe the immortality of the soul.*"* And yet it is from men like these that you and your followers derive that diocesan apostolical succession in which you so much glory. And we are informed by Jewel, in his Apology for your Church, that "Pope Liberius was an Arian," and undeified his Saviour; that "Pope John thought very lewdly and wickedly of the immortality of the soul, and of the life to come; and that, as Lyranus saith, *many Popes have renounced the Christian faith and become Apostates.*"† The following, too, is the doctrine of the Church of Rome respecting the power of the Popes. "We," says Innocent III., "according to the plenitude of our power, have a right to dispense *with all right;*"‡ upon which Bellarmine remarks, that "should the Pope enjoin vice, and forbid virtue, the Church would sin, if she did not believe virtue to be evil, and vice to be good."§ " Nor was this at all wonderful," says Bower, "for Cardinal Zabarel, who flourished near four hundred years ago, writes, that in his and in the preceding times, the Popes had been persuaded by their flattering divines that they might do whatever they pleased, even such things as were in themselves, and with respect to others, unlawful; and *so could do more than God himself.*"‖ And says one of the Papal canons, " Should a Pope be so wicked as to carry with him innumerable souls to hell, let no man presume to find fault with him, or reprove him, because he who is to judge all men is judged of none."¶ Nay, such was the blasphemy practised in that Church, in which the Papists, according to Jewel, "had left almost nothing

* Theor. IV.
† Apology, p. 91, 92, vol. vii. of the Fathers of the English Church.
‡ Inn. III. Decret Greg. lib. iii. tit, 8, c. 4.
§ Bellarm. de Pontific. Rom. lib. iv. cap. 5.
‖ Zabar. de Schism.
¶ "Si Papas suae, &c. Grat. dist. 40. cap. 6. " Dost thou not know," said Paul the Second to the auditors of the Rota, "that all laws are lodged in our breast. Sentence is given, and all shall obey it. *I am Pope, and have a power to approve or condemn at my pleasure the actions of all other men.*" Platina et Summont. tom. iii. p. 474.

like a Church," that as he elsewhere remarks, "they impudently solicited the Virgin Mary, that she would remember she was a mother; that she would be pleased to command her son, and that she would make use of the authority she had over him."* But if such was the doctrine respecting the power of the Popes which was taught at one time in the Church of Rome, from which you have derived the succession, (and it has never been recalled, as might naturally have been expected, till the present day, for she claims the attributes of infallibility and immutability,) and if such was the blasphemy which she openly tolerated, I ask you whether the imposition of the hands of men, who avowed these sentiments, claimed these powers, and connived at these heaven-daring and revolting sins, could preserve the succession?

Nor is my position less clearly and conclusively established by the numerous instances of the most disgraceful simony which prevailed both in the Western and Eastern Churches. "It has been generally allowed," says Dr. Forbes, "that the lawful succession of true pastors is interrupted and broken by simony, and that every ecclesiastical person who is simoniacally promoted is irregular, and of right alien from the priesthood, suspended and deprived of his office, and lies under an anathema."† "If any bishop, presbyter, or deacon," says the 30th Apostolic Canon, "obtains a dignity by money, let him be deposed; and let him who ordained him be cut off from the communion of the Church, as Simon Magus was by St. Peter." "He who is ordained according to this evil custom," says the Second Council of Nice, (canon 5,) "is alien from God, and excluded wholly from the priesthood." "Neither they who buy, nor they who sell holy orders," says Gregory, "can be priests, because anathema is denounced both against him that gives, and him that receives them." And it is declared by Gelasius, that "the damnation of Simon involves both the

* Apology, p. 56 and 30.
† Instructiones Historico-Theologicae, lib. xvi. cap. 6, sec. 6, p. 781.

receiver and the giver."* The same, also, was the doctrine of the Sixth Council of Constantinople, which decrees, (canons 22, 23,) that "if a bishop or any other of the clergy be ordained for money, both he that ordained him, and he that is ordained, shall be deposed; for grace," say they, "cannot be sold, nor do we bestow the sanctification of the Spirit for money." And if the orders of him who is ordained to be a bishop for money, by the canons both of the Eastern and Western Churches, be void,† it follows on the same principle, that if he should contrive to retain his bishopric, all the orders which he confers afterwards on others, whether bishops, presbyters, or deacons, must also be void, and the apostolical succession must be broken.

And yet how stands the fact in regard to the ordinations in both these Churches, as far as relates to simony? In the year 531, on the death of Boniface II., says Bower, "many aspired to the vacant dignity, sparing neither pains nor money to attain it. For in spite of many laws, both ecclesiastic and civil, simony still reigned without mask or disguise. Votes were publicly bought and sold, and money was offered to the senators themselves."‡ Baronius says of Vigilius, when he was Anti-Pope, that "he was not only a second Lucifer, striving to ascend into heaven, and exalt his throne above the stars, but, by the weight of his enormous sacrileges and heinous crimes, brought down to hell, a schismatic, a simoniac, a murderer, not the successor of Simon Peter, but of Simon Magus, not the vicar of Christ, but an Anti-Christ, an idol set up in the temple of God, a wolf, a thief, and a robber;§ though, when he was elevated to the Popedom, upon

---

* See, too, what is collected by Gratian, canon 1, quaest. 1, as abridged by Francowitz, in his Catalogus Testium, p. 1469.

† The Council of Orleans, in 536, declares, that "if any person, by an execrable ambition, seeks to obtain the priesthood by money, he is to be rejected as a reprobate." A similar decision was pronounced by the Council of Bracara de Braga, in 572; and there is no point in regard to which the Councils of both Churches are more united and determined.

‡ Bower, vol. ii. p. 332. § Baronius, ad an. 538.

the death of Silverius, he makes him a good Catholic. In the end of the sixth century, Gregory the Great wrote a great many letters to the bishops, to the kings and princes, and to all men in power, earnestly entreating them to "assemble councils, and jointly to concert such measures as might put an effectual stop to (simony) an evil that reflected so much disgrace on the ecclesiastical order, and on the holy religion which they taught or professed."* "In the time of this Pope," says Francowitz of the monster Sergius, who lived in the ninth century, "and of his brother, (Benedict,) *bishoprics were disposed of by public sale;*" and in the tenth century, "*no one was provided for or created a bishop* unless he paid for it, or bound himself to do so under the most tremendous penalties."† The same practice continued in the eleventh century, for he says that "they sold bishoprics and other ecclesiastical offices;" and adds, on the authority of Aventinus, that "*most of the bishops and abbots in Germany* had fallen from their dignity through simony, and that three of the Popes, Benedict IX., Silvester III. and Gregory VI. had procured the Popedom by money."‡ And so generally did it prevail throughout the whole Romish Church, that when Leo IX. proposed in a council, which was held at Rome in 1049, that all simoniacal ordinations should be declared null, the majority of the bishops opposed him; for they said, that if such a decree should pass, "*scarce any would be found in some dioceses capable of performing the sacerdotal or episcopal functions.*"§ I have heard, said John, Bishop of Salisbury, in 1159, to Hadrian IV., when he urged him to tell him his mind, that "all things

* Bower, vol ii. p. 480

† Catalogus Testium, 1097 and 1206. See also what is said of John XIII. p. 1277.

‡ Catalogus Testium, 1355, 1356, and 1358 He tells us, p. 1257, that Peter Damianus complained grievously of the simony of his time, and wrote a book against it.

§ Bower, vol. v. p. 167. He states further, that in 1074, most of the German Bishops "had purchased their bishoprics from the emperor or his ministers."

are venal at Rome; that for money you may obtain to-day what you please, but the next day you will get nothing without it. The Roman Pontiff himself is, they say, a burden to all almost insupportable."* And St. Bernard, on the 19th Psalm, observes, that "the offices of ecclesiastical dignity were turned into filthy lucre, and a work of darkness;" and Hugo Flaviacensis, "that all the clergy rather sought their own things than the things of Jesus Christ, and chose rather to adhere to the discipleship of Simon, than to the poverty of Christ."† It was no less prevalent in the thirteenth century, for it is asserted by Matthew Paris, that "it was committed at that time" *in the Church of England,* "without shame;" and it is pointed out by Durandus, as one of the most important steps towards the reformation of the Church, that simony should be repressed, which, says he, "reigns at Rome as if it were no sin."‡ In accordance with which it is mentioned by Wickliff, that, "in the year 1226, a Legate of the Pope, whom he had sent into England, produced a bull to the Parliament, in which it is distinctly admitted, that nothing could be done at Rome without the greatest profusion of money, and the most ample gifts; and that therefore the Church of Rome, the mother of all other Churches, was infamous for its avarice, simony and corruption."§ Alvarus Pelagius, when speaking of the Popes in the fourteenth century, laments that "many of them came into their Sees by simony; of the bishops, that they *conferred orders* for rewards, and were simoniacal, especially in Spain, where *not one of a hundred conferred orders or benefices without simony;* of the presbyters, that they were commonly promoted by simony; and of the Church in general, that her pre-

* Bower, vol. vi p. 109.
† Chron. Verdun, p. 207; Concil. tom. x. p. 375.
‡ Catalogus Testium, p. 1621.
§ See his work de Papae Potestate, as cited by Francowitz, p 1773. The Legate proposed, that to prevent this evil, a certain proportion of the funds of the monasteries and cathedral churches should be given to the Pope, which was refused.

lates did nothing now but by gifts and rewards."*
And while it is mentioned by Sigismund, that "not *a single prelate*" in the fifteenth century, "from Nicholas the Third," *i. e. for three hundred years before,* "*had been free from simony;*" by Alanus Chartier, secretary to King Charles the Seventh, that "he would be silent respecting the simony, and illicit contracts, of the bishops, because he was afraid that by the very recitation of them the heaven itself would be darkened;" and by Hermannus Ried, that "from the greatness of their luxury, their other vices, such as avarice, simony and perfidy, were not considered as sins ;"† it is impossible to read the following account of the conduct of the bishops, delivered by Clemangis, without feelings of the deepest humiliation and regret that such things should have been practised in the Christian Church. "There be very many things," says he, "in our bishops worthy of reprehension, but this least of all to be endured, that for imposition of hands, collation of orders, sacred and inferior, they do not only receive, *but exact and extort money, setting a price upon all orders, which if it be not paid, they will admit no person into orders, though he be never so well qualified, by his manners, life and learning.* The Church is now become a shop of merchandise, or rather of robbery and rapine, *in which all the sacraments are exposed to sale.* Would a man have a bishopric? He must provide his money. Does he desire a prebend, or any other dignity? It is no matter what his life, merit, or conversation be, but the great question is, what money he may have to buy it."‡ It would be easy to produce numerous instances of similar simony, though not to the same extent, in the Eastern Church, where John Talaia was expelled for that crime from the See of Alexandria, in 482, and had many who followed his disgraceful example, but I am unwilling

* Second Book de Planctu Ecclesiae.
† Catalogus Testium, p 1877, 1854, 1853. Examine also what is said by the Bishop of Civita, as it is quoted by Ried, p. 1839.
‡ See his book on Simoniacal Prelates.

to prolong these disgusting details. If it was declared then of old, that those who were guilty of the sin of simony had no part or lot in the power of communicating the extraordinary gifts of the Holy Ghost, by the laying on of hands, and if it follows, as has been determined by the Councils of the Church in every age, that they have no part or lot in receiving the office of the holy ministry, or in conferring it on others, it is plain, that in all cases where individuals were raised to the office of the episcopate by such simoniacal pactions, their orders were void, and consequently the orders which they conferred upon others. And as the instances in which this was done for eight hundred years, not only in the Eastern, but the Western Churches, are said not merely by Protestants, but by ministers and members of the Church of Rome, whose testimony has been produced, to have been incredibly numerous, it is evident that the succession must have been completely broken in both these Churches, and those Episcopalian Churches which were connected with them; and consequently, that, upon your principles, they must long ago have ceased to be Christian Churches, and none of their members can have the smallest hope of being permitted to share in the blessings of salvation.

I have only further to remark, that many who were ordained to the office of bishops were so grossly ignorant, and so notoriously immoral, that it is utterly incomprehensible how they could preserve the succession.

A bishop, you know, is required to be "apt to teach," before he receive his commission; and if he is destitute of this gift notoriously and undeniably to an extreme degree, or if he happen to be an idiot before he is invested with his office, the commission will not avail him, and he cannot give it to others. For as Dr. Whitby observes, in the Appendix to his Sermon on Matthew xii. 7, "it seemeth as absurd to say to an idiot, who lies under a moral incapacity to teach, 'Take thou authority to teach the Gospel,' as to say this to *a deaf and dumb man*, who lies under a natural incapacity to do it, seeing a moral incapacity, whilst it lasts, renders a man as incapable of teaching, as a natural incapacity." Now, the following are the statements of eminent Roman Catholics, respecting the aptness of many who were raised to the episcopate, and who ordained others to teach and preach:

Petrus Blessensis, in the thirteenth century, exclaims thus in his 23d Epistle, "How did this execrable presumption prevail, that unworthy persons should thus grasp at dignity, and the less they deserved such honours, the more earnestly should thrust themselves into them? For now," says, he, "unhappy men do thrust themselves into the pastoral chair by right or wrong. He that hath learned nothing becomes a teacher of others; and though he be like the sounding brass, and tinkling cymbal, usurps the office of a teacher, being an unprofitable trunk and dumb idol."

In the fourteenth century, Marsilius of Padua mentions that "the Pope, in the plenitude of his power rejects and nulls the election of sufficient and approved men to almost all ecclesiastical dignities, though rightly made; and in their stead appoints men ignorant of the Holy Scriptures, *idiots*, unlearned persons, and for the most part men of corrupt minds, and notoriously wicked. Our modern bishops, (which it is a shame to say,) neither know how to preach the word of God to the people, nor to resist the doctrine of the heretics. And as for the rest of the inferior prelates, abbots, priors, and other curates of the Church, I call God to witness, that the numerous multitude of them are both void of sufficient learning and life, so that the most of them know not how to speak congruously, according to the rules of grammar; but yet, out of the fulness of the Pope's power, the greatest dignities are given to such as these." And he says, respecting the cardinals, that "lascivious young men, and ignorant of the Holy Scriptures, are many of them promoted to that dignity."*

Alvarus Pelagius complains of the bishops that

---

* Defensor Pacis, lib. ii. cap. 14, p. 354.

"they conferred benefices on unworthy persons. This," says he, " is so common in our times, that they ordained men whom they knew to be unlearned and unfit, (cap. 3.)—that *being idiots* they suffered themselves to be made bishops; and (cap. 4,) that they promiscuously ordained good and bad."

Nicolaus de Clemangis, in the fifteenth century, in his treatise on Simoniacal Prelates, to which I have already referred, says, "therefore you may see such men admitted to the priesthood, and other holy offices, *who are idiots,* unlearned, and *scarce able to read, though waywardly, and without understanding one syllable after another,* who know no more of Latin than they do of Arabic, and who, when they read, pray, or sing, *know not whether they bless God, or blaspheme him;* men undisciplined, unquiet, gluttons, drunkards, praters, vagabonds, lustful, bred up in luxury, and, in one word, idle and ignorant;" (chap. 1.) And in his book on the corrupt state of the Church, he says that the Pope had stocked the Church with ignorant and wicked men. " Good God," he cries out, " how great a number of expectants from that time, (when he had taken away from the bishops and patrons the power of presenting to benefices,) came in, not from their studies, and the schools, but from the plough and servile arts, to become parish priests, and to obtain other benefices, who knew no more of the Latin than of the Arabic tongue, *who could not read,* and (which it is a shame to speak of) scarce knew A from B, and yet their immorality was greater than their ignorance." And he adds, that " through the avarice, simony and other vices of the cardinals, it came to pass that no man learned in the Scriptures, no honest, just and virtuous persons were advanced to high dignities; but buffoons only, flatterers, ambitious persons, and men corrupted with all vices, that they either wholly were unlearned, or they knew nothing of God's law; that being *youths without beards,* and scarce got from under the ferula, *they obtained a bishopric,* knowing as little of that office as of the mariner's vocation. What should I speak," says he, "of the learning of the priests, when it is visible that *scarce any of them can read?* They know not words, and much less things. He of them that prayeth is a barbarian to himself. If any man is idle and abhors labour, if he loves luxury, he gets now-a-days into the clergy." And Gerson complains "that bishops of good life and doctrine were not chosen any where, but carnal men, and ignorant of spiritual things."

But the most revolting feature in the character of a great majority of the bishops, through a succession of centuries, was not merely their hypocrisy, like that of Judas, which was known only to himself and his blessed Master, for his doctrine was good and his outward demeanour comparatively decent, but their open ungodliness and monstrous immorality. And certainly, if a bishop is required to be blameless in the eyes of men before he receives his commission, can we really suppose that the following individuals, who had *the sole* power of ordaining presbyters, after they were raised to the episcopate, and the principal power in ordaining prelates, if they were raised to the Popedom, had valid orders, or could preserve the succession by the imposition of their impious and polluted hands?

So depraved was the state of the Church of Rome in the year 500, that the following is the description which is given of it by Salvianus, both as to its clergy and laity: "We who are good Catholics, love uncleanliness; they who are heretics, (the Arian Goths,) abhor and detest it; we hate purity, and avoid it; they admire and embrace it."* And so fearful was the declension of religion in the East, that in the year 517, Severus, the Patriarch of Antioch, caused three hundred and fifty monks, who were opposed to the Eutychian doctrines, to be massacred by a band of ruffians whom he had hired for the purpose, and was never called to an account for it, but was permitted to lay his blood-stained hands on the heads of bishops and presbyters.† In 531, Boniface the Second ac-

* Bower, vol. ii. p. 259. † Bower, vol. ii. p. 290.

knowledged, before a great Council of Bishops, and the whole Roman Senate, that he had been guilty of high treason, and notwithstanding, he had been continuing to confer orders.* And during all that century a number of bishops were chargeable with the greatest enormities.

It has been alleged, I am aware, that there was a female Pope of the most dissolute character in the ninth century, who succeeded Leo the Fourth; and it is affirmed by Fox, in his Book of Martyrs, that, "for five hundred years after her time, it was acknowledged as an historical fact of as great notoriety as any other connected with the papal chair."† I am unwilling, however, to found on it, as it does not appear to be supported by sufficient evidence, the earliest writers who relate it having lived two hundred years after the time when it is said to have happened; while Anastasius, who seems to have been in Rome at the death of Leo, and to have been present at the election of his successor, says, that Benedict the Third was chosen in his room, and was brought immediately from the Church of St. Callistus, where they found him at his prayers. Besides, Hincmar, Archbishop of Rheims, informs us in his letters, that some messengers whom he had dispatched to Leo, to procure a grant from him, found that he was dead, but obtained it from Benedict. If there was a female Pope, however, and if she reigned, as is reported, for two years and five months, Hincmar's messengers must have spent all that time in their journey, which is incredible, as they were never prevented from travelling by any obstacle. And the existence of such a Pope was never once referred to by the Patriarchs of the Eastern Church, in all their attempts to resist the claims of superintendence over them by the subsequent Popes, as would certainly have been the case if Pope Joan had been a real character. But while there is no solid foundation for that degrading charge

* Bower, vol. ii. p. 329.
† From what Jewel says in his Apology, p. 43, it would seem that he also believed it.

against the See of Rome, it is liable to others nearly as odious, which rest upon evidence that cannot be controverted, and which demonstrate that the boasted apostolic succession has utterly failed. "This," says Cardinal Baronius, when speaking of the tenth century, "was an iron age, barren of all goodness, a leaden age, abounding with all wickedness, and a dark age, remarkable above all the rest for the scarcity of writers and men of learning." After which he adds, "The abomination of desolation was seen in the temple of the Lord; and in the See of St. Peter, revered by the angels, were placed the most wicked of men, *not Pontiffs, but monsters*. And how hideous was the face of the Roman Church, when filthy and impudent strumpets governed all at Rome, changed Sees at their pleasure, disposed of bishoprics, and intruded their gallants and their bullies into the See of St. Peter, who were written in the catalogues of Roman Pontiffs only to mark time. For who could assert that those intruded by strumpets of this kind, without law, *were legitimate Roman Pontiffs?* No mention was then made of the clergy electing or consenting. The Church was then without a Pope, but not without a head, its spiritual head (Christ) never abandoning it."* And he might justly say so, for in the year 904 Sergius was raised to the Popedom, "who was the slave of every vice, and the most wicked of men;"† and who, as Luitprand relates, had John, who was afterwards Roman Pontiff, and the twelfth of that name, by Marozia, the wife of Guido, a gay and most impudent courtezan,—and during the life both of the father and son, (both of whom ordained bishops and presbyters,) the whole Western Church and the city of Rome was governed by this strumpet."‡ And the same, he informs us, was the power of Theodora, "who obtained the chair of St. Peter to John of Ravenna, with whom she had had a criminal intrigue;"§ and during the time of his primacy, she was the dispenser of the

* Baron, ad ann. 900. † Ibid. ad an. 908.
‡ Luitp. lib. ii. cap 13 § Ibid. lib. ii. c. 13.

dignities and benefices of the Church. In 963, John the Twelfth, to whom I have referred formerly, was condemned by a Roman Council for carrying on scandalous intrigues with four different females, turning the holy palace into a brothel, putting out the eyes of Benedict, his ghostly father, who died of anguish, setting several houses on fire, *drinking wine in honor of the devil*, and when playing at dice, invoking Jupiter, Venus, and the other pagan deities, and all the time he had been conferring orders. In the following century, Gregory the Seventh, denominated Hildebrand, raised himself to the Popedom, *having poisoned, it is stated, no less than six of the Pontiffs* that he might enjoy that honour; and during the whole of his supremacy, ignorance and wickedness overspread the Church. From the beginning, however, of the twelfth century, her situation, if possible, became still more alarming. "*Your court*," says St. Bernard to the Pope, "*receives good men sometimes, but it makes none good: evil men thrive there, good men are ruined.*" And elsewhere he says, "Those bishops to whom the Church of God is now committed are not teachers, but *seducers;* not pastors, but impostors; not prelates, but Pilates."* And yet these impostors and Pilates were the men who ordained other bishops.

In the thirteenth century the clergy are described by the Bishop of Lincoln, in a sermon which he preached even before the Pope himself, as not only "destroying the vineyard of the Lord, and scattering pollution over every land," but as most luxurious, "fornicators above all others, adulterous, incestuous, epicures, and wallowing in every species of iniquity."†
It is asserted also by Rubens, that "they were not only drunk in taverns, but kept them openly, as well as concubines, or tavernwomen;"‡ and his assertion is confirmed by Frederick of Spain and John of Sicily,

* Jewel's Apology, p 43, 64.
† Catalogus Test p. 1592, 1593. He was excommunicated for his sermon.
‡ Catalogus Testium, 1249, 1254.

in a paper which has been preserved by Arnoldi de Villa Nova, and it is accompanied by the statement of some additional circumstances so exceedingly gross, that it is impossible to translate them.* " You have taken," said the Pope in 1274, to Henry, Bishop of Liege " an abbess of the order of St. Benedict for your concubine, and have boasted at a public entertainment of your having had fourteen children in the space of two and twenty months. To some of your children you have given benefices, and *even entrusted them, though under age, with the cure of souls.* The abbess of a monastery in your diocese dying, you annulled the canonical election of another, and named in her room the daughter of a count, whose son has married one of your daughters, and it is said that the new abbess has been brought to bed of a child by you."† And while we are told by Alvarus Pelagius, that in the fourteenth century "idiots were made bishops;" and by Maenard, Count of the Tyrol, that "the prelates were worse than Turks, Saracens, Tartars or Jews,"‡ a picture is presented by Wickliff of the manners of the clergy, which it is impossible to contemplate without loathing and disgust. " So great," says he, in his Treatise on Hypocrisy, " is the corruption of manners in this age, and such its licentiousness, that the priests and monks, besides violating the chastity of married women, *murdered virgins* when they were unwilling to comply with their solicitations. Their sodomy, moreover, was unbounded; and they boasted to those whom they seduced that they were able to pardon them, and would answer for their sins."§ And towards the end of that century, Urban the Sixth, who ordained a number of bishops, besides his other shocking crimes, caused five of his cardinals to be "shut up in sacks, and thrown into the sea, or

* Catalogus Testium, p. 1659, compared with p. 1735.
† Bower, vol. vi. p. 295.
‡ Defensor Pacis, p. 364. Pelagius de Planctu Ecclesiae, lib ii. cap. 3, Catal. Test. p. 1810. It is mentioned that " there were few prelates who were not fornicators, and that they sat in public with their concubines, and sons and daughters."
§ Catal. Test. p. 1814, 1815.

strangled in prison, or beheaded and their bodies to be privately conveyed to his stables, and consumed with quick-lime;" besides whom, it is mentioned by Boxinsegni, the Florentine historian, who wrote soon afterwards, that five eminent prelates were put to death along with them in the same cruel manner.* And John the twenty-third, who was obliged to resign, was accused before the Council of Constance in 1414, (and he did not attempt to repel the charges,) of having been of a wicked disposition from his childhood; lewd, dissolute, a liar, and addicted almost to every vice; of having raised himself to the Pontificate, by causing his predecessor to be poisoned; and of having committed fornication with maids, adultery with wives, incest with his brother's wife, and with nuns," (in some MSS. with 300.) And the memorial concluded with these words: "He is universally looked upon, as will be found on the slightest inquiry, as *the sink of vice, the enemy of all virtue*, the mirror of infamy; and all who know him speak of him as a devil incarnate "† And yet he also gave orders to many bishops and presbyters. And while Innocent the Eighth is represented by Marullus as having left a number of natural children, it is stated by Burchard that Alexander the Sixth, who held the Popedom for more than eleven years, and must have made a number of prelates who ordained others, "was a great lover of women, and that in his time the apostolic palace was turned into a brothel, a more infamous brothel than any other in Rome." And he mentions " an entertainment given in the palace to fifty of the most noted courtezans in the city," and describes a variety of particulars that took place, to which I cannot make even the slightest allusion.‡ If these things, however, were so, (and they were attested by men whose veracity is unquestionable, and who not only had the best opportunities to be acquainted with the facts, but were zealous members of the Church of

* Bower, vol. vii. p. 62, 63.
† Bower, vol. vii. p. 166, 167.   ‡ Ibid. vol. vii. p. 368.

Rome,) I would ask any candid and impartial judge, whether he really thinks that men like these could preserve the succession? Their own orders, as we have seen, were purchased with money, and consequently were void.* And so far from possessing the character of true prophets, and exhibiting their fruits, (Matt. vii. 15-20,) they are described by those who would not misrepresent them, " as murderers, adulterers, sodomites, incestuous persons, Pilates, impostors, the abomination of desolation, sinks of vice, monsters of iniquity, and devils incarnate." Surely orders obtained from such men, by the imposition of their foul and polluted hands, and whose own orders laboured under a fatal defect, could not be valid, and those who received them could not give valid orders to others. And as this happened not merely in a few, but in thousands of instances during a succession of ages, partly in the Eastern, but more frequently and extensively in the Western Church, it follows upon your principles and those of the Papists, that neither of these Churches in the present day, nor any Church connected with them, or descended from them, can be entitled to the character of a Christian Church, nor can any of its members have the smallest hope that he shall be permitted to share in the blessings of salvation.

I remain, Reverend Sir,

Yours, &c.

* This argument for the invalidity of their orders is drawn not merely from one, but the whole of the leading points referred to in this letter.

LETTER XIX.

The Bible the only standard by which we are to regulate our opinions respecting faith and practice, the orders in the ministry, and the rites and ordinances of the Christian Church —This the doctrine of the Bible itself, and of the early Fathers, each of whom rejected the opinions of the other Fathers on every subject when not supported by Scripture, or when contrary to its statements —This the doctrine, too, of Luther, and of the most eminent Reformers of the Church of England —The Fathers not safe guides respecting the meaning of Scripture on other subjects besides Church government.—Numerous instances of the gross misinterpretation of the plainest passages in the writings of Barnabas, Justin Martyr, Irenaeus, Clemens Alexandrinus, Tertullian, Origen, Cyprian, and Jerome. —Numerous instances also of their departing from the doctrine of the Apostles on some of the leading points of evangelical belief, and of their introducing into the Church superstitious rites and idolatrous observances. —This acknowledged by Whitgift and Cox —Presumptive proof which it presents that they might depart as far from the original form of ecclesiastical government which was appointed for the Church

REVEREND SIR,—If I have succeeded, in a previous part of these letters, in proving, according to the opinion of Wickliff, and other distinguished individuals before the Reformation, of your most eminent bishops at that memorable era,* and of the eight thousand

* The present curate of Derry, in his Treatise on Episcopacy and Presbytery, p 43, maintains, that as it is said in the Ordinal, "it is evident unto all men reading Holy Scripture and ancient authors, that from the Apostles' time there hath been three orders of ministers in Christ's Church, bishops, priests, and deacons," the early Reformers of the Church of England believed in the divine institution of Episcopacy. This, however, is an inference which is opposed to their avowed sentiments before quoted, p. 98, 99, where they declare, that "bishops and priests were no two things, but both one thing in the beginning of Christ's religion." Besides, they do not say that these orders existed in the Apostles' time, but *from* or soon after the Apostles' time, according to the opinion of Jerome, in which Tonstal, Stokesley and Dr. Cox (p 98) expressed their concurrence. And though the Reformatio Legum Ecclesiasticarum points out in different sections the duties of bishops, priests and deacons, this was absolutely necessary, since these orders were to be retained in the Church of England, but is no more a proof that they were regarded as of divine institution, than its proposing to introduce a class of men into that Church, like Presbyterian ruling elders, (see cap. viii. 10,) would have been a proof to Mr. Boyd, that these office-bearers were regarded as entitled to lay claim to a similar origin.

He says in regard to Stillingfleet, that he adopted views afterwards different from those which he defended in his Irenicum, and quotes from him, p. 50, these doleful expressions, "Will you not allow one

ministers who subscribed the Articles of the League of Smalkald, as well as the Confessions of the foreign Protestant Churches, that diocesan Episcopacy is not

single person who happened to write about these matters, when he was very young, in twenty years time of the most busy and thoughtful part of his life to see reason to alter his judgment?" Now, certainly we have no right to deny that he was entitled to alter his judgment after he was made a bishop; but, as he did not answer the arguments by which he supported his former opinion, and as no one has since done it, and Mr Boyd has not even attempted it, he must excuse us for bringing them again under his (Mr Boyd's) notice, and that of the other defenders of Episcopacy, and calling upon them to answer them.

He complains that Presbyterians, when quoting the first part of Bishop Bedell's Reply to Waddington, the Papist, in which he admits, that "a bishop and a presbyter are all one, as St. Jerome maintains and proves out of Holy Scripture and all antiquity," leave out the latter part. The latter part, however, relates to a totally different subject; and as the former was adduced merely to show that Bishop Bedell did not consider Episcopacy as of divine right, (and this was clearly his opinion,) it was all that was required, and there was no occasion in settling that point to refer to the other.

He says, p. 45, that when the Reformers of the English Church contended for the identity of bishops and presbyters, it was the old opinion which they entertained as Papists, and which was adopted by many of the ministers of the Church of Rome, in consequence of their believing in transubstantiation. For "it was held inconsistent to allow that the priest could transmute the elements into Deity, and yet be inferior to any in ecclesiastical standing." The same assertion was made long ago by Downam, who says, in the Defence of his Sermons, p. 104, "This new Popish conceipt of confounding bishops and presbyters into one order ariseth from their idol of the masse, and their doctrine of transubstantiation, whereby every priest is as able to make his Maker as the Pope himself." Jerome, however, did not believe in transubstantiation, and wrote eight hundred years before it was introduced into the Church of Rome, and yet he represents it as the doctrine of Scripture that bishops and presbyters are the same. Atto, Bishop of Verceil, who lived two hundred years before transubstantiation was adopted into the creed of that Church, denied the divine right of Episcopacy. The Culdee presbyters, who never embraced that doctrine, ordained presbyters and bishops. Nay, the Councils of Constance and Trent, who were zealous for transubstantiation, instead of holding, as we would naturally have expected, upon Mr. Boyd's hypothesis, the identity of bishops and presbyters, maintained the divine institution of Episcopacy, and pronounced an anathema against all who denied it, while Wickliff, Armacanus, and all who were zealous for the Reformation of the Church asserted, that according to Scripture there was no difference between bishops and presbyters. So contrary to the fact is the account which was long ago given by Downam, and which is repeated by the present curate of Derry, of the circumstances which led the first Reformers to avow

sanctioned by Scripture, but is of mere human origin, I might pass over in silence the argument in support of it, which has been derived from the writings of the early fathers. Though the latter may illustrate the statements of the Bible, on any subject, as far as they correspond with it, they are not to be allowed to usurp its place, nor to add to what it announces a single article of religious belief which we are bound to embrace, or a single precept which we are bound to obey, or a single order in the Christian ministry which we are bound to adopt, or a single branch of the constitution of the Church which we are bound to receive. "The Bible, and the Bible alone," in all these respects, "is the religion of Protestants;" and it alone is "able to make them perfect, and furnish them thoroughly for every good word and every good work." And "to the law and the testimony:" if any thing which is propounded to us on any subject speak not according to their word, "it is because there is no light in it."

And as such is the principle by which we must regulate our opinions, if we believe in the explicit declarations of Scripture respecting its own perfection, and as the only rule of faith and practice, so it is the only principle by which Christians in general, from the earliest ages, have formed their opinions on every part of religious truth. It was the principle, for instance, by which the ancient fathers judged of every thing which was contained in the writings of others of the fathers. "Deare brother," said Augustine to Jerome, (and I choose rather to quote him in the translation of Frith, one of your Martyrs, p. 53 of his works,) I thinke that you will not have your bookes reputed like unto the workes of the Prophetes and Apostles; for I (*the Scripture reserved*) do read all other men's workes on that maner, that I doe not beleve them, *because the author so sayth,* be he never so well learned and holy, *except that he can certifie me by the Scripture,* or cleare reason that he sayth

their belief of the latter opinion, and it is the more reprehensible in him, (Mr. Boyd,) as he ought unquestionably to have known that they appeal in support of it to Scripture.

true. And *even so would I, that other men should read my bookes as I read theirs.*"* And again observes Jewel, in his Defense of his Apology, p. 59, "Joining all the doctours and fathers together, he saith thus, *Ipse mihi pro omnibus, &c.* Instead of all these learned fathers, or rather above them all, Paul the Apostle commeth to my minde. To him I runne; to him I appeale from all maner writers, (doctours and fathers,) that think otherwise." "It is necessary for us," says Origen, "to appeal to the Scriptures, for our senses and interpretations without these witnesses are not entitled to credit."† "There are others," says Jerome, "who have *erred in the faith,* both Greeks and Latins, whose names I need not mention, lest I seem to defend him, (Origen,) not by his own merits, but by the mistakes of others."‡ And in another place he remarks, "I think that Origen ought to be read on account of his erudition, as well as Tertullian, Novatus, Arnobius, Apollinaris, and some ecclesiastical writers, both Greeks and Latins, *that we may choose from them what is good, and avoid what is bad,* according to the injunction of the Apostle, Prove all things, hold fast that which is good."|| It was the principle by which Luther and the foreign Reformers, who were honoured to bear such a distinguished part in discovering, declaring, and vindicating the truth on the most important subjects, judged what they met with in the writings of the fathers. "I follow Augustine," said the first of these great and holy men, "when he agrees with the Scripture, and leave him when he falls short of it, or goes against or beyond it. In matters affecting conscience I regard the word of no man, but of God alone."§ And the same was the principle which guided your Reformers in forming

* Epist. ad Haer. tom. ii. fol. 14.
† Tom. i. p. 628.
‡ "Erraverunt in fide alii," &c. Epist. 65, ad Pam.
|| Epist. 76, ad Tranquil.
§ " Sequor Augustinum ubi cum Scriptura sentit, et relinquo si citra vel contra Scripturam loquitur. In re conscientiarum nullius hominis sed solius Dei amplector." Seckendorf, lib. i p. 283.

their opinion of the writings of the fathers, and which, as stated by Hooper in the following passages, is worthy of the grave and serious consideration of every Episcopalian, when, after failing to establish his particular views of ecclesiastical polity from the Sacred Scriptures, he attempts to prop them by quotations from the fathers. "The water at the fountane hed," says he, "is more halsome and pure then when it is caryd abrode in roten pypes. I had rather folow the shadow of Christ then the body of all generall conselles or doctors sith the death of Christe. The verite of Christe's religion was perfet in Chryste's tyme, and in the tyme of the Apostelles. None sith that time so pure. Saynct Hierome, in Vita Malchi, saith that his time was darkenys in the respect of the Apostelles' tyme." And again he remarks, "Basilius, Ambrose, Epiphanius, Augustine, Bernerd and others, thoughe they stayed themselves in the knowledge of Christ, and erryd not in ony principall article of the faythe, yet they did *inordinatly and more than inoughe extolle the doctrine and tradicion of men*, and after the deathe of the Apostellis, every doctor's tyme was subject unto such ceremonye and mannes' decrees, that was neither profetable nor necessari." After which he adds, " *The Scripture soly, and the Apostelles' Churche is to be folowyd*, and no man's authority. Be he Augustine, Tertullian, or other Cherubim or Seraphim, unto the rules and canones of the Scripture must man trust, and reforme his errores therby, or else he shall not reform himselfe, but rather deform his consciens."*

But while such is the principle by which enlightened Christians in every age have been led to estimate the opinions of the fathers, and while we ought not to receive a single point of religious belief, or rite, or article which relates to the constitution of the Christian Church, though it may have been held in their days, unless it is sanctioned by Scripture, yet I shall wave this circumstance, and consider the argument which

* Declaration of Christ and his Offices, chap. iv.

has been drawn from their writings. And there is certainly none to which some at least of the advocates of diocesan Episcopacy attach greater weight; for they represent them as delivering a united testimony to its existence in the Church from the earliest ages; and from the peculiar advantages which they imagine were possessed by many of the fathers for interpreting aright the statements of Scripture, and the great improbability of their deviating in the least from that form of polity which was approved of by the Apostles, they look upon it as absolutely decisive of the question. Now, upon this boasted argument, which has frequently been urged with the greatest triumph by the friends of Episcopacy, I beg to submit to you the following observations:

In the first place, the superior qualifications of these early writers to interpret correctly the statements of Scripture on the subject in dispute will be best ascertained by examining their expositions of a variety of passages on other subjects. I have referred already to some of them in my eleventh letter, but in addition to these I would select the following: Take, for instance, the Epistle of Barnabas, one of the most ancient of these writers, for it is allowed by Bishop Tomline, Dr. Cave, Archbishop Wake, and Bishop Pearson, that he was the fellow-labourer of the Apostles.* He tells us that "the three young men who were to sprinkle the ashes of the red heifer, (Numb. xix.) denoted Abraham, Isaac and Jacob, because they were great before God; and that the wool was to be put upon wood, because the kingdom of Jesus was to be founded upon wood, or upon the cross;"† that the precept, "thou shalt not eat of the hyena, signifies, thou shalt not be an adulterer, *because that animal every year changes its sex*, and is sometimes *male*, sometimes female; and that the precept, thou shalt not eat of the weazel, suggests that wickedness should

* Preface to Tomline's Elements, vol. i. p 18. Hist. Liter. p. 11, 12. Discourse on the Genuine Epistles of the Apost. Fathers, p. 69, 70. Lect. Secund. in Act.
† Clerici Patres, vol. i. p. 25.

not be committed with the mouth, *because that animal conceives with its mouth.*"* Take Justin Martyr, who considers these expressions respecting Judah, (Gen. xlix. 11,) "He washed his garments in wine, and his clothes in the blood of grapes," as a prediction respecting the death of Christ, and who finds out a reason for the form of the cross on which he was appointed to suffer, in the sails of ships, in the plough, in the shape of our bodies, and in the horn of the unicorn.† Take Irenaeus, who says "that the name Jesus, in Hebrew, is composed of two letters *and a half,* and signifies *the heavens;*" that " the twopence or denarii which were left by the good Samaritan with the host who was to take care of the man who fell among thieves, were the image and superscription of the Father and the Son; and that the unclean animals which did not divide the hoof were those which were destitute of faith, and who did not meditate on the oracles of God."‡ Take Clemens Alexandrinus, who informs us that "the conduct of the Saviour is always straight and agreeable to his nature, as is intimated by the letter *Iota* in the name Jesus; that in these words of the first Psalm, 'He shall be as a tree planted by the rivers of water, which yieldeth its fruit in its season, and whose leaf shall not fail,' there is a reference to the resurrection, $\pi\varrho o\varsigma$ $\tau\eta\nu$ $\alpha\nu\alpha\varsigma\alpha\sigma\iota\nu$ $\eta\nu\iota\xi\alpha\tau o$; that the feet of Christ, which the woman anointed, (Luke vii.) denoted his divine doctrine, which travelled to the uttermost parts of the earth with distinguished glory;" and that marriage is proper, because, when our Lord says, (Mat. xviii.) that "where two or three meet in his name, he will be in the midst of them, it means a man, his wife and his child, $\alpha\nu\delta\varrho\alpha$ $\kappa\alpha\iota$ $\gamma\upsilon\nu\alpha\iota\kappa\alpha$ $\kappa\alpha\iota$ $\tau\varepsilon\kappa\nu o\nu$."§ Take Tertullian, who says that the mark which Ezekiel was to

* I cannot insert what follows, as it is so grossly offensive to every delicate mind.
† Dialog. cum Trypho. p. 40; Second Apol. p. 38; Dial. p. 70.
‡ Lib ii. cap 41, De Haer; lib. iii. cap 19, lib. v. cap. 8.
§ Paedag. lib. i. cap. 9, p. 93, 94; ibid. lib. i. cap. 10, p. 96; ibid. lib. ii. cap. 8, p. 129. Stromata, lib. iii. p 331.

put on the foreheads of the men who sighed and cried in the midst of Jerusalem " was the letter Tau, or the sign of the cross; that the reason why the Israelites overcame the Amalekites, was because Moses lifted up his hands in the form of a cross, and they were commanded by one whose name was Jesus or Joshua; that it is the Saviour who is spoken of, Deut. xxxiii. 17, when it is said, ' His glory is like the firstling of his bullock, and his horns are like the horns of unicorns, and that with them he shall push the people together to the ends of the earth,' because the horns of the bull resemble the two extended arms of the cross; and that by Simeon and Levi, who are mentioned, Gen. xlix. 5, we are to understand the scribes and pharisees who were to persecute Christ."* And omitting the vision of Hermas and other early writings, on which I am unwilling to enlarge, consider out of the many passages which might be selected from Origen what he says of the servants of Isaac, who contended with the Philistines, " whom he affirms to have been Matthew, Mark, Luke and John;" and the proof which is produced by Cyprian to show that the Redeemer is *God's hand* from these words, " Is God's hand weak that it cannot save?" (Is. lix. 1-4.) That the Jews would fasten him to the cross from these passages; " I have spread out my hands all the day unto a rebellious people," (Is. lxv. 2.) " Thy life shall hang in doubt before thine eyes, and thou shalt fear day and night, and shalt have none assurance of thy life," (Deut. xxviii. 66;) and " that they would not understand the Scriptures," because Paul says, (1 Cor. x. 1,) 'I would not that ye should be ignorant how that all our fathers were under the cloud.' "† And reflect only further on what is said by Jerome, can. 3, in Mat. vi. 26, where he maintains very gravely, " that by the fowls of the air, who neither reap nor gather into barns, we are to understand the devils; and that by the lilies of the field, which neither toil

---

* Lib. iii. contra Marcion, p. 813. Lib. advers. Judaeos, p. 169.

† Orig. tom. i. p. 44. Cyprian's Testimonies against the Jews, p. 26, 41, 56.

nor spin, are meant the angels." Are these then the men, I ask now, as I inquired formerly, when I wrote the article from which I have taken a number of these extracts,* (and I might have given a thousand other instances,) " who have interpreted so correctly the word of God; and is it to them that we are to look up with such submission and respect, when they point out to us from Scripture either the articles of our faith," or the particular form of ecclesiastical polity which the blessed Redeemer has appointed to his Church?

It may be alleged, however, that though their interpretation of these passages is extremely absurd, and displays an ignorance of the meaning of the Scriptures which is seldom to be met with in Protestant countries in the present day, yet the errors into which they fell when they delivered these expositions are of inferior moment; and it will by no means follow that they erred as to doctrine, or deviated from that form of ecclesiastical polity which was sanctioned by the Apostles. " As the three authors," says Bishop Russel, " from whose writings I have quoted, were disciples of the Apostles, lived in their society, knew their doctrines and their views in regard to the constitution of the Church, we cannot permit ourselves to imagine that they would sanction a polity which had not the example and approbation of those heavenly teachers to support it. It is universally allowed among the earliest Christian writers, that Ignatius and Polycarp were ordained by the hands of the Apostles; and St. Paul himself informs us, that Clemens was a fellow-labourer with him in the Gospel of Christ. Are we not then entitled to regard the model of ecclesiastical constitution which these holy men adopted, as possessing the full authority and sanction of their inspired masters? Or must we believe, that, under the very eye of those from whom they received their knowledge of the faith—the immediate and personal servants of the Redeemer—those divine commissioners upon

* Review of Bishop Tomline's Refutation of Calvinism in the Edinburgh Christian Instructor, vol. iv. p. 394, 395, which I published many years ago.

whom the foundations of the Church were laid, they deviated from the pattern with which they were thus supplied, and constructed a system according to their own views or convenience?"* And in the following page, he endeavours to show that it is equally improbable that Irenaeus, " who lived about the middle of the second century, and who, as he himself tells us, was acquainted with Polycarp, and heard him preach," would depart from the polity which had been approved by the Apostles; and the same reasoning has been applied to the fathers, even in the days of Cyprian.

I shall by and by inquire into the amount of superiority ascribed to bishops in the writings of these fathers, and if I am not greatly mistaken, it will avail but little for promoting the cause of diocesan Episcopacy. But at present I content myself with meeting the statement of the extreme improbability of their departing in the least from the form of polity which was approved by the Apostles by a similar statement of an equal improbability, that they would depart from the doctrines, and rites, and practices which had received the sanction of these illustrious ministers. And if it shall be found upon inquiry, (and *it is a question of fact*,) that they departed in a short time from a number of the latter, it will appear equally credible, since we are told by Paul that " the mystery of iniquity had begun to work" even in his day, that they might, to a small extent during the first two centuries, deviate from the former.

Now, it is plain that they departed at an early period from *the doctrine* of the Apostles on several important points. When Cecil accordingly wrote to Cox to assist Elizabeth with his advice about the perusal of the fathers, the bishop replied, that " when all is done, the Scripture is that that pearseth. Chrysostom and the Greek fathers favour Pelagius; Bernard sometimes is for monkery; and he trusted her Grace meddled with them but at spare hours."† And

* Historical Evidence of the Apostolical Institution of Episcopacy, p. 27, 28.
† Strype's Annals, vol. i. p. 324.

said Whitgift in his Answer to Cartwright, p. 472, "My comparison of the Church of England with the fathers shall consist in these three points, truth of doctrine, honesty of life, and right use of external things. Touching the fyrst, that is, truth of doctrine, I shall not need much to labour; for I think T. C. and his adherents will not deny, but that the doctrine taught and professed by our bishops at this day *is much more perfect and sounder* than it commonly was *in any age after the Apostles' time.* For the most part of the auncientest bishops were deceyved with that grosse opinion of a thousande yeares after the resurrection, wherein the kingdome of Christe should here remaine upon earth, the fauvorers whereof were called Millenarii. Cyprian and the whole Council of Carthage erred in re-baptization. And Cyprian himself also was greatly overseene in making it a matter so necessarie in the celebration of the Lord's supper, to have water mingled with wyne, which was no doubt at that tyme common to moe than to him. But the other opinion which he confuteth, of usyng water only, is more absurd, and yet it had at that tyme patrones among the bishops." And it is impossible to look into the writings of the fathers without perceiving the unsoundness of many of their opinions. Justin Martyr, for instance, asserts that demons were the offspring of women who had connection with angels; and he asserts, that the spirits of the saints, and even of the ancient prophets who died before the coming of the Saviour, were under the power of these demons; "in potestatem venisse talium virtutum;" and that therefore, when Christ was dying, he commended his spirit to his heavenly Father.* And he believed very firmly in the doctrine of the Millennium, as it was taught by Papias, of which the following account is delivered by Irenaeus, and it is certainly most unlike to what was learned from the Apostles. "The days," said he, " will come, in which there shall grow vineyards, having each 10,000 stocks; and each stock,

* First Apol. p. 7, and Second Apol. p. 15. Dialog. cum Trypho. p. 79, 80; ibid. p. 63.

10,000 branches; each branch, 10,000 shoots; each shoot, 10,000 bunches; each bunch, 10,000 grapes, and each grape squeezed shall yield twenty-five measures of wine; and when any of the saints shall go to pluck a bunch, another bunch will cry out, I am a better, take me, and bless the Lord through me. In like manner, a grain of wheat sown shall bear 10,000 stalks; each stalk, 10,000 grains; and each grain, 10,000 lbs. of the finest flour; and so all other fruits, seeds and herbs in the same proportion. These words Papias, a disciple of St. John, and companion of Polycarp, an ancient man, testifies in writing in his fourth book, and adds, that they are credible to those who believe." Irenaeus asserts that the Saviour lived upon earth " forty or fifty years;" and says that this is not only mentioned in the Scriptures, but *was even reported by the elders who had been acquainted with St. John to have been declared by that Apostle ;* that Enoch, before he was translated, was employed by God *on a mission to the angels ;* " Dei legatione ad Angelos fungebatur;" (and the Commentaries of Cyril, Lyra and Feuardentius, who would understand by the angels the antediluvian giants, are contradicted by the expressions that follow;) and that the souls of the dead depart into an invisible place which is appointed for them by God, and remain there till the resurrection, when they are admitted into heaven.*
Very grievous errors were maintained by Clemens Alexandrinus, one of the best of the fathers. Though he acknowledges in one passage that " we are altogether corrupt by nature," yet it is plain, from what he says elsewhere, that he considered mankind as corrupt only *from practice,* for he asks, " *how the child who has done nothing can have fallen under the curse of Adam ?*" And after asserting, that those who had lived under the law before the coming of Christ would be justified by faith only, and that those who were to be justified from among the Gentiles required not only faith, but as they had followed phi-

---

* Lib. ii. cap. 39 ; lib. iv. cap. 30 , lib. v. cap. 31.

losophy, needed to be converted from idolatry, he remarks, "that the Lord, after he died, went down to Hades, and preached to the Hebrews, that they might obtain that blessing; and that his Apostles, when they died, preached to Socrates and the other virtuous Gentiles, that they might reclaim them from the latter, and prepare them for being justified."* And he affirms even that the Redeemer himself, though he was perfectly holy, was *regenerated* at his baptism; for after referring to the administration of it to him by his forerunner, he adds, " Let us ask, then, the wise, is Christ, who was *regenerated* to-day, perfect? πυθωμεθα ουν των σοφων σημερον αναγεννηθεις ὁ Χριστος ηδη τελειος;" Paedag. lib. 1. cap. 6, p. 68.

In short, while it was the opinion of Origen, that neither the sufferings of the wicked, nor the happiness of the righteous, would properly speaking be eternal, his sentiments about the atonement and many other subjects were in direct opposition to the doctrine of the Apostles. He admits, indeed, the substitution of Christ, but asserts at the same time, that not only apostles and prophets, but *even the celestial angels and glorified saints may be our propitiatory sacrifices for appeasing the Almighty.*† Nay, as is acknowledged by Dr. Cave, he imagined that Christ died not for men only, "*but for angels, and devils,* and *the heavenly bodies.*"‡ And so gene-

* Strom. lib. ii. p. 287; ibid. lib. iii. p. 342; ibid. lib. vi. p. 459, 460, Comp. Strom. lib ii. p. 277.

† Tom. i. p 121, 136, 150. "Sic ergo fortassis, et si quis est angelorum, coelestiumque virtutum, aut si quis justorum hominum, vel etiam sanctorum prophetarum atque apostolorum, qui enixius interveniat pro peccatorum hominum hic pro repropitiatione divina velut aries aut vitulus, aut hircus oblatus esse sacrificium ob purificationem populo impetrandam accipi potest," tom. i. p. 40, 93.

‡ Review of Tomline's Refutation of Calvinism, Christ. Instructor, vol iv. p. 397. Ernesti, though not a Calvinist, makes the following remark in his unpublished MS. Lectures on the doctrine of the fathers: " Videtur existimasse," says he of Justin Martyr, " hominem habere a natura liberum arbitrium, h. e. facultatem eligendi bonum et malum, recte et male agendi, servandi Dei praecepta et violandi. Verum si ex verbis est judicandum *omnes fere doctores ecclesiae hujus criminis rei sunt,* quia omnes fere de libero arbitrio non satis accurate locuti sunt."

ral was this apostasy from the purity of the faith, that, as was remarked again by Whitgift, "*almost all the bishops and learned writers of the Greke Church,* yea and *the Latines also, for the most part* were spotted with the doctrines of free will, of merites, of invocation of sainctes, and such lyke."

Nor did they deviate less from the example of the Apostles, in regard to many rites and religious observances. We have a remarkable instance of this in the time which was selected for the celebration of Easter, the one-half of the Church contending, with Polycarp, that it ought to be kept on the day of the Jewish Passover, and appealing in support of it to the opinion and practice of the Apostle John, and the other, with Anicetus, maintaining that it ought to be kept on a subsequent day, and appealing in proof of it to the opinion and practice of Peter and Paul. It is plain, however, that one of them at least, and most probably both, must have erred as to this matter, for no day seems to have been fixed for it, as far as can be collected from Scripture, in the time of the Apostles. And if they departed in this respect from the example of these early ministers of Christ, though many of them had seen them, and were acquainted with their practice, is it not equally conceivable, that they may have departed from their form of ecclesiastical polity? The Apostles never prayed for the souls of the dead; but it would seem from what is mentioned in the writings of Tertullian, Cyril, and others, that this was the practice of the Church from an early period. "Then," says the last of these authors, "we pray during the celebration of the Eucharist for all who have lived among us, believing that it is a great assistance to those souls for which prayer is made, while that holy and awful sacrifice is presented on the altar."* And in the Greek Liturgy of Chrysostom, they say, especially for our "most holy, immaculate, most

---

* Ειτα και υπερ παντων απλωστων εν ημιν," &c. Tertullian, in his Liber de Corona, p. 341, says, " Oblationes pro defunctis, pro natalitiis annua die facimus." Consult, too, his Treatise de Monogamia, cap. x., and Cyprian's Epistle ad Plebem et Cler. Furnitanorum.

blessed Lady, the mother of God, and ever Virgin Mary." The Apostles never prayed to the saints in in heaven to intercede for them with God; but this seems to have been common in the early Church. Gregory Nazianzen, in his eighteenth oration, speaks of a nun " who supplicated the Virgin Mary to afford aid to a virgin in peril." And Ambrose, in his funeral oration for his friend Satyrus, says that the latter " had asked only of St. Lawrence the Martyr a safe passage."* The Apostles never prayed looking only towards the east. But, says Tertullian, in the name of the Christians of his day, " We pray toward the east,"† because, as he observes in another treatise, (Advers. Valent., p. 284,) " it is a type of Christ,

* " Read," says Bishop Newton in his 23d Dissertation, " the Oration of Basil on the Martyr Mamas."
" Mamas," says the author of Ancient Christianity, vol. ii. p. 174, " a shepherd of Cappadocia, had suffered about the year 275, churches had been built to his honour, and, as it appears, he had come in these provinces to be as much importuned as was St. Lawrence at Milan, or St. Januarius at Naples, being one of the dii majores of the Greek Church; nor was there any sort of aid he would not render to his favoured votaries. In explanation of Basil's allusions, it should be observed, that a principal function of these divinities was to discover lost or stolen goods, in dreams, to those who had occasion to seek such information at their hands.

" Memores estote martyris, quotquot illo per somnia potiti estis, quotquot in hoc loco constituti, adjutorem ipsum ad precandum habuistis, quibuscunque ex nomine advocatus ipsis adfuit operibus: quotquot aberrantes ad viam reduxit, quotquot sanitati restituit, quibuscunque filios jam mortuos ad vitam reductos reddidit, quotquot vitae terminos prorogavit. Collectis in unum his omnibus, ex communi symbolo, martyri encomium construite." Tom. i. p. 595.

" Read," says Bishop Newton, " his Oration on the forty martyrs."
" These," says the author of Ancient Christianity, vol. ii. p. 176, " were so many soldiers, who, at Sebaste, in Armenia, had suffered with great constancy, under Licinius, so late as the year 320. A magnificent church had been erected in honour of them at Cesarea, and in which had been treasured some particles of their inestimable dust, to which the people were accustomed to crowd, under direction of their priests, for obtaining cures and deliverances."

The following are the terms in which Basil apostrophizes these forty martyrs.

" O holy choir! oh! sacred band! oh! unconquerable phalanx! oh! *common guardians of the human family!* kind participants of our cares! helpers of our prayers! most potent advocates (ambassadors!) stars of the world! flowers of the Churches! O sanctum chorum," &c.
† " Nos ad orientis regionem precari," Apol. c. xvi. p. 688.

Christi figuram." The Apostles did not breathe on the faces of those who applied for baptism to exorcize them, or expel the devil from them, before they received that ordinance. But this, as appears from Clemens Alexandrinus and Cyprian, was done to heretics and schismatics by the ancient Church. Nor did they feed those to whom that sacrament was administered with milk and honey, and yet Tertullian tells us that this was the practice of the primitive Church.* Nor did they clothe them with white garments, which they were to wear for a week, saying to them, "receive these white and unspotted garments, which you must produce without spot before the tribunal of our Lord Jesus Christ, that you may have eternal life;" and yet this was done by the early Church. Nor did they anoint them with oil; and yet such, as is mentioned by Tertullian and Cyprian, was the custom which was followed in the first ages of the Church. "As soon," says the former, "as we are baptized we are anointed with the blessed unction—an external carnal unction is poured upon us, but it benefits us spiritually."† And says the latter, "He that is baptized must of necessity be anointed, that having received the chrism or unction, he may be the anointed of God."‡ And they never signed them with the sign of the cross, nor confirmed them by the imposition of hands, except when they communicated miraculous gifts. But both these forms were observed by the primitive Church. "The flesh," says Tertullian, "is signed, that the soul may be fortified." "And when the unction is finished, then hands are imposed, with prayers invoking and inviting the Holy Spirit."§ The Apostles never administered the Eucharist to infants; and yet it would seem that it was done in the days of Cyprian by the ancient Church,

* "Inde suscepti lactis et mellis concordiam praegustamus;" de Corona, p. 431.

† "Egressi de lavacro perungimur," &c ; de Baptismo, p 599.

‡ "Ungi quosque necesse est eam," &c , Epist. 70.

§ De Resurrectione Carnis et de Baptismo, p. 600. Those who were baptized in infancy do not appear to have been signed and confirmed till afterwards.

for he speaks of a deacon who "forced upon a little female infant against her will of the sacrament of the cup; but the Eucharist would not remain in a body and mouth that had been polluted previously with bread and wine, which had been used in the soul-slaughter of perishing Christians."* The Apostles did not take the Eucharist fasting, and yet Augustine informs us in his 118th Epistle, that "it was the custom of Christians over the whole world to partake of it only when fasting (Toto orbe hunc morem tenuisse quo Christiani nisi jejuni Eucharistiam non acciperent.") Nor did they "fast on every Monday through the whole year, or use only dried meat and bread with salt and water at Lent," which Epiphanius (Advers. Haeres. in Epilogo,) says, was "*an apostolic tradition.*"

The Apostles were not in the habit of pouring a little of the Sacramental wine, or dropping a little of the bread, or of their ordinary food, on the ground, or of making the sign of the cross on their foreheads when they put on or off their clothes, or went into the bath, or sat down to meat, or lighted their lamps, or retired to bed, or set out on a journey, and at every successive stage of it. And yet Tertullian informs us that it was the general practice of the Christians of his day, though he confesses that there was no command for it in Scripture, and justifies it, like you, only by tradition.† The Apostles did not enjoin the people to bring the first ripe ears of corn, or the first ripe grapes, and present them on the altar that they might be blessed by the priests, or to lay upon it oil for the lamps of the Temple, or incense to be burnt during the offering of the Eucharist. And yet

* De Lapsis.
† "Calicis aut panis etiam nostri aliquid decuti in terram anxie patimur. Ad omnem progressum, atque promotum, ad omnem aditum et exitum, ad vestitum et calceatum, ad lavacra, ad mensas, ad lumina, ad cubilia, ad sedilia, quacunque nos conversatio exercet, frontem crucis signaculo terimus. Harum et aliarum ejusmodi disciplinarum si legem expostules scripturarum, nullam invenies; traditio tibi praetendetur auctrix, consuetudo confirmatrix, et fides observatrix." Liber de Corona, p. 341.

all this is sanctioned by the third Apostolic Canon, which was made, as is usually alleged by Episcopalians, within the first three centuries.* The Apostles never used such language as the following respecting almsgiving, and yet it was common, not only in the days of Chrysostom, but in a previous age: "Heaven is on sale, and yet we mind it not. Give a crust, and take back paradise; give the least, and receive the greatest; give the perishable, receive the imperishable; give the corruptible, receive the incorruptible."† And, without enlarging farther on this painful subject, I would conclude these details with the following account by the eloquent author of Ancient Christianity, of the corruptions which prevailed from the earliest times in an increasing degree in the ancient Church. "Throughout the east, throughout the west, throughout the African Church, virginity they put first and foremost, then came maceration of the body, tears, psalm-singing, prostrations on the bare earth, humiliations, alms-giving, expiatory labours and sufferings, the kind offices of the saints in heaven, the wonder-working efficacy of the sacraments, the unutterable powers of the clergy, these were the rife and favoured themes of animated sermons, and of prolix treatises; and such was the style, spirit, temper and practice of the Church, from the banks of the Tigris, to the shores of the Atlantic, and from the Scandinavian morasses to the burning sands of the great desert; such, so far as our extant materials give us any information."‡ And again he observes, (and there are few who have read the writings of the fathers with candour and attention, that will not acquiesce in the statement,) "I am bold to express my belief, that if we exclude certain crazed fanatics of our times, the

---

* "Μη εξον δε ιστω προσαγεσθαι τι ετερον εις το θυσιαστηριον η ελαιον εις την λυχνιαν και θυμιαμα τω καιρω της αγιας προσφορας. Ει τις επισκοπος η πρεσβυτερος παρα την του κυριου διαταξιν την επι τη θυσια," &c. Bishop Beveridge, in his Annotations, p. 16, says, "Fructus qui apud Graecos a sacerdote ευλογουνται *benedicuntur* sunt uva, ficus, malagranata, olivae, poma, mala Persica, et pruna." The form of benediction both in the Greek and Latin Church is subjoined.

† Homil. 3, tom. ii. p. 348.   ‡ Ibid. p. 365.

least esteemed community of orthodox Christians among us, whichever that may be, if taken in the mass, and fairly measured against the Church Catholic of *the first two centuries*, would outweigh it decisively in Christian wisdom, in common discretion, in purity of manners, and *in purity of creed.*"*

If these things, however, are so, I leave it to any impartial judge to say, whether it would at all surprise him to discover, upon examining the writings of the fathers, that they had departed by degrees from that particular form of ecclesiastical polity which was approved by the Apostles. They left the doctrines which they had heard from these venerable and holy men, or from the lips of their disciples, and adopted very dangerous and erroneous opinions on some important points of the Christian faith. And they corrupted those simple religious ordinances which these inspired and distinguished ministers of the Redeemer prescribed to the Church for the admission of its members, and the regulation of its worship, and introduced a variety of superstitious rites and unscriptural observances, which constituted the foundation of that monstrous system of will-worship and idolatry which rose at length to such a fearful height in the Church of Rome. And if they deviated so far in both these respects from the principles and practice of the original founders of the Christian Church, it is incumbent on you to show, that they might not deviate as widely in two or three centuries from their form of polity, till they established, in the first place, diocesan Episcopacy, and afterwards the Papacy, in the last of which instances I trust you are not yet prepared to deny that they departed from the Apostles. And till you are able to do this, you can no more infer, from *the early existence* of diocesan Episcopacy, though you could

---

* Page 110. "Those," says this admirable writer, p. 191, "who have known what it is with a hand warm with health, to take within their own the hand of a corpse, know how the chill ascends to the heart and enters the soul. Of this sort is the feeling with which, if the mind be quickened by scriptural piety, it makes its first acquaintance with the body of ancient Christianity."

prove it by the strongest historical evidence, that it received the sanction of these holy men, than you are entitled to infer, from the early existence of these erroneous opinions on subjects of very grave and solemn importance, or of these superstitious rites and idolatrous observances, that the latter were approved by the same individuals, and that the one were to be preached in opposition to what they had expressly stated in their writings, and the others were to be practised throughout future ages in the Christian Church.

I remain, Reverend Sir, Yours, &c.

LETTER XX.

Extraordinary opinion of the Oxford Tractarians, that the Scriptures, though a rule of faith, are not a rule of discipline and practice, and that the latter is to be found in the traditions of the Fathers, along with the Scriptures—This an impeachment of the perfection of the Scriptures in opposition to their own explicit statements, and a mean of virtually adding to the institutions which they prescribe to the Church, in opposition to their express and solemn warnings—The traditions of the Fathers not a safe guide, because those who deliver them were weak, inexperienced, and fallible men, though they lived near to the Apostles, and if the Scriptures, which were written by men who were inspired, are not sufficient to direct us, we can have no assurance that when we are following these traditions we are not embracing error—As much danger of our doing this, and of our making void the institutions of Christ, by our not trusting in the Scriptures exclusively, but adopting what is recommended by the traditions of the Fathers, as there was to the Jews of making void the law of God by following the traditions of the elders, because they lived near to the prophets, instead of trusting exclusively in the writings of the prophets—Eusebius and Socrates condemn some of the traditions of the Fathers, and others of them such as even Puseyites would reject.

REVEREND SIR,—The language which is employed by many of the writers of the Oxford Tracts, respecting the exclusive claims of your National Church (Papists and Scottish Episcopalians excepted) to the honourable character of a Christian Church, is such as is fitted to awaken emotions of no ordinary kind in the minds of Protestants, and would require to be justified by the most powerful arguments. "She is sprung," they affirm, "from the very Church which Christ set up at Jerusalem, and none of the sects (for all others are sects) have this great gift. There is not one of her bishops who cannot trace his right to guide and govern Christ's Church through a long line of predecessors, up to the favoured persons who were consecrated by the laying on of the holy hands of St. Peter and St. Paul. This is a fact which Dissenters from the Church of England do not, and cannot deny. Her ministry is *an appointed condition of the salvation of the elect*" in Britain. They alone have a " warrant which marks them *exclusively* for God's ambassadors," and " they are a perpetual earnest of communion with the Lord at his table to those who come properly prepared to his table. Christ prays *only for those* who believe in him through the word of the Apostles, and their successors, *the bishops*. If men would be disciples or Christians, they must be baptized by apostolical (episcopal) authority in the name of the Holy Trinity. And if they would take and eat Christ's body, they must take and eat the bread and drink of the cup blessed by those who have authority to bless it, in remembrance of him. And in Churches which have not the Episcopal succession, the gracious assistance of the Holy Spirit cannot be so certainly depended upon, as for other sanctifying purposes, so for the guiding the mind to doctrinal truth; nor can they have the same reason to expect the presence of the Saviour."* In short, within those favoured Churches which have diocesan bishops, according to these writers, there is spiritual light, like the physical light in the land of Goshen, which was the abode of the Israelites during one of the plagues, while in other Churches where these guardians of truth and bulwarks against error are not to be seen, like the rest of Egypt at that eventful period, there is " darkness that may be felt."

And what is the ground on which they advance these lofty and intolerant claims in behalf of Episco-

* 4th, 11th, 29th, 30th, 35th, 40th and 57th Tracts.

pacy, at which Cranmer, and Jewel, and Hooker would have blushed, and employ such language respecting other Churches, where the fruits produced both among the old and the young, by the labours of their ministers, will bear to be compared with those of the ministers of Episcopalian Churches? It is partly the different arguments from Scripture which have been already considered, and which will by no means warrant these haughty assumptions and uncharitable conclusions, and partly an argument of a very different kind from the testimony of antiquity, to prove that Episcopacy was approved by the Apostles, which is one of the most extraordinary that I have ever met with in support of that position.

"In the *first* place," says the author of one of the Tracts, "let us suppose, for the sake of argument, that *Episcopacy is in fact not at all mentioned in Scripture, even then it would be our duty to receive it.* Why? Because the first Christians received it. If we wish to get at the truth, no matter how we get at it, *if* we get at it. If it be a fact, that the earliest Christian communities were universally Episcopal, it is a reason for our maintaining Episcopacy, and in proportion to our conviction, it is incumbent on us to maintain it."

"Nor can it be fairly dismissed as a non-essential, an ordinance indifferent and mutable, though formerly existing over Christendom; for who made us judges of essentials and non-essentials? How do we determine them? Does not its universality imply a necessary connection with Christian doctrine? But it may be urged, that we Protestants believe the Scriptures to contain the whole rule of duty. Certainly not: they constitute a rule of *faith,* not a rule of *practice;* a rule of doctrine, not a rule of *conduct* or *discipline.* Where (*e. g.*) are we told in Scripture that gambling is wrong? or again, suicide?" (Tract 45.) "And," says Bishop Russel, "Augustine farther reminds us, that many things which are not to be found in the writings of the Apostles, nor in the councils of later ages, yet because they are observed by the whole Church, are believed to have been delivered and recommended by their authority."* And again, "There are many things which the Universal Church holds, and which for this reason are rightly believed to have been commanded by the Apostles, although they are not found written."† Upon this argument, however, which is adduced repeatedly in others of the Tracts, and on which considerable stress is laid by the writers, I would briefly remark,

1*st*, It is certainly strange for any Protestant to maintain that the Scriptures are a rule of faith, but not of *practice;* a rule of doctrine, but not a rule of *conduct or discipline.* You at least will surely admit that we need an unerring and infallible rule to direct us as to our duty, as well as an infallible rule to guide us as to our faith. And you unquestionably ought to be prepared to acknowledge that we require such a rule in regard to discipline; for if there be only one ministry which Christ has appointed, to which alone he has promised his presence, the existence of which is "a condition of our salvation," and the members of which are the only accredited "ambassadors of heaven;" and if he himself has warned us against following the prescriptions and commandments of men in our religious services, in what a state must we be, if he has not furnished us with a guide on which we can unhesitatingly depend, to point out to us the different orders in that ministry, and those rites and ordinances which he himself has instituted, and which alone he will bless! Now, where is that unerring rule to be found, if it is not contained solely and exclusively in the Holy Scriptures? Every thing which they reveal is guaranteed to the Christian as free from the smallest mixture of error, because it was written by holy men of God, who were moved by the Holy Ghost. But if he is to trust only *in part to them,* and in part

---

* Sermon, p. 44. "Multa quae non inveniuntur in literis corum neque in conciliis posteriorum, et tamen quia per universam custodiuntur ecclesiam, non nisi ab ipsis tradita et commendata creduntur" De Bap. contra Donatistas, lib. ii. c. 7.

† "Sunt multa quae universa tenet ecclesia, et ob hoc ab Apostolis praecepta bene creduntur, quanquam scripta non reperiantur," lib. v. c. 7.

to the writings and *traditions* of the fathers,—weak, uninspired and fallible men,—he can have no assurance that he will be preserved from error, any farther than he follows what is contained in the former, and, for aught that he knows, may be permitted to fall into it, when he follows the latter. Few will deny that it would have been a great imperfection in the Old Testament Scriptures, and an unfailing source of error and superstition to the ancient Jews, if they could not have collected full information from their sacred writings respecting the orders of their priesthood, and their rites and ceremonies, but had to obtain it *in part from the traditions of their elders*, many of whom lived along with the prophets, or at least as near to them as the early fathers did to the Apostles. And will any one deny that it would be an equal imperfection in the New Testament Scriptures, as a rule of discipline, and a similar source of error and superstition to the Christian Church, if they did not present to her complete information respecting the orders in the ministry, and her rites and ordinances, without obliging her to have recourse *to the traditions of the fathers*, or to adopt any thing which is not sanctioned in their pages, though it may have been received universally by the ancient Church? Besides, ninety out of a hundred of ordinary Christians are not able to read the writings of the fathers, and judge for themselves in regard to the ministry, and the rites and ceremonies which existed in the early days of the Church. And though the learned may be assisted by the testimony of these writers in their inquiries into the authenticity and canonical authority of the books of Scripture, yet it is not in this way, but by the internal and experimental evidence for these books, that the former are satisfied in regard to their inspiration. But while they are satisfied in this way as to that momentous point, *there is no internal or experimental evidence by which they can ascertain whether bishops, as an order of ministers, superior to presbyters, have been appointed by Christ;* and when they see how little they preach and labour, that Christ may be formed in the hearts of the thousands and hundreds of thousands who are committed to their care, many of them are led to a very different conclusion. Nor have they any such evidence to convince them that the form of the cross in baptism, and others of your ceremonies, to which I have formerly alluded, were instituted by Christ, or appointed by the Apostles; and consequently, if the Scriptures *in themselves* are not a perfect and infallible rule of practice and discipline, as well as of faith, they are left without the means of forming a judgment, on the correctness of which they can rely with comfort, respecting the ministry, and rites, and ordinances of the Church.

2dly, The Scriptures represent themselves as a *perfect* rule, not only of faith but *practice*, and to affirm that any part of Christian duty, or any thing relating to the constitution or ordinances of the Christian Church, without which our obedience to the will of Christ would be defective and incomplete, was omitted by the Apostles to be inserted in their writings, and must be learned from the fathers, is in direct opposition to some of their most express and explicit statements. " The law of the Lord," says David, "is *perfect*, converting the soul: the testimony of the Lord is sure, making wise the simple. The statutes of the Lord are right, rejoicing the heart: the commandment of the Lord is pure, enlightening the eyes; (Ps. xix. 7, 8.) And again he observes, (Ps. cxix. 105,) "Thy word is a lamp unto my feet, and a light unto my path." And says Paul, in a passage which was quoted in the preceding letter, "All Scripture is given by inspiration of God, and is profitable for doctrine, for reproof, for correction, for instruction in righteousness, that the man of God may be *perfect, thoroughly furnished unto all good works ;*" (2 Tim. iii. 16, 17.) Nay, we are expressly enjoined not to " *add to God's word,*" as a rule of practice; (Deut. iv. 2, 12, 32; Rev. xxii. 19;) as would *virtually* be the case, if we were to receive as a supplement to what was delivered by the Apostles in their different Epistles, some new commandments, or rites, or ceremonies* which they communicated to the fathers, and which have been handed down by tradition. And they may justly claim for themselves the high character of a perfect rule of practice and discipline; for while the words of the fathers are often weak, and foolish, and blended with error, their words "are pure words, as silver tried in a furnace of earth, seven times purified." They set before us a perfect and spotless example in the holy life of the blessed Redeemer, and we have only to consider how he would have acted in any situation in which we happen to be placed, and to walk in his steps. And they set before us also the example of the apostolic Church, perfect *at its institution* in its ministers and ordinances, and call upon us, if we would witness similar results to those which it produced, while we look up by humble and earnest prayer for the influences of the Spirit, to adopt it as our model as to preaching, and government, and worship, and discipline. It does not indeed specify suicide among the sins which it forbids, but it commands us in general to "do *no* murder," and consequently warns us against self murder. And it does not particularize the sin of gambling, but it admonishes us against fraud, and every kind of deceit, and enjoins us to " provide things honest in the sight of all men." But if it exhibit to us a law which is faultless and complete in all its requirements, an example which is spotless, and distinguished by the highest and most transcendent excellence, and a pattern of a church which is perfect, at least as far as relates to its constitution, and ordinances, and discipline; and if it warns us solemnly against adding to its words, it is utterly inconsistent with all these statements to tell us that we may learn from the writings of the fathers some order in the ministry, or

---

* Paul indeed mentions some words of the Redeemer which are not contained in the Gospels, Acts xx. But they do not relate to any new commandment; and though we cannot depend on the fathers, we have perfect confidence in his statement, because he was an inspired man, and was directed by the Spirit to repeat them in the hearing of Luke, that they might be recorded in his History.

some rite or ordinance which was recommended or expressly enjoined by the Apostles, though not the smallest notice of it is to be met with in their Epistles.

3dly, There is not a reformer, either of your own Church or of any Protestant Church with which I am acquainted, who did not hold it to be a fixed and fundamental principle, that we ought to admit nothing as to the Christian ministry, or the rites, and ordinances, and discipline of the Church, which, though supported by tradition, was not sanctioned by Scripture. Your own Reformers wished to act upon it as far as they were permitted, but were unhappily prevented. And there was no Church which acted on it so thoroughly and effectually as the Church of Scotland, which procured for her among many of the foreign Protestant Churches the honourable name of *the best reformed of all the Reformed Churches.**

And, in short, I would remark, that if the general adoption by the ancient Church of any order in the

* I might appeal to many testimonies from the Reformed Churches on the Continent, expressing their respect for the Church of Scotland, but I shall quote only the following from the Harmony of Confessions: " Est Scoticanae Ecclesiae privilegium rarum prae multis in quo etiam ejus nomen apud exteros fuit celebre, quod circiter annos plus minus 54 sine schismate nedum haeresi unitatem cum puritate doctrinae servaverit et retinuerit. Hujus unitatis adminiculum ex Dei misericordia maximum fuit quod paulatim cum doctrina Christi et Apostolorum disciplina sicut ex verbo Dei praescripta est una fuit recepta, et quam proxime fieri potuit secundum eam totum regimen ecclesiasticum fuit administratum. Hac ratione omnia schismatum atque errorum semina, quamprimum pullulare aut se exerere visa sunt, in ipsa quasi herba et partu sunt suffocata et extirpata, *i. e.* It has been the rare privilege of the Church of Scotland above many other churches, for which it is celebrated among strangers, that for about fifty-four years it has preserved and retained unity along with purity of doctrine without schism or heresy. It was a great mean of promoting this unity through the mercy of God, that along with the doctrine of Christ, it embraced also by degrees *the discipline or polity of the Apostles, as it was prescribed in the word of God, according to which*, as nearly as possible, *their whole ecclesiastical government was administered.* In this way all the seeds of schisms and errors, as soon as they appeared to spring and vegetate, were choked and rooted out in the very blade." Such was the testimony which was then borne not only to the doctrine, but the worship and constitution of the Church of Scotland, and the superior efficacy of Presbyterian principles for preventing schism and repressing heresy.

Christian ministry, or rite, or ceremony, prove that it must have received the sanction of the Apostles, though they neither appointed it, nor mentioned it in their writings, it will prove at the same time that all those opinions respecting the doctrines of religion, however unsound, and all those practices, however superstitious, which prevailed generally in the ancient Church from the earliest ages, though not referred to in their Epistles, must have met with their approbation. They must have approved in particular of those heresies about free will, and those gross and extravagant notions about the Millennium, with which, according to Whitgift and Ernesti, the whole of the fathers from Justin Martyr were tainted.* They must have approved also of the practice of praying for the dead, though none of them seems to have observed it; and though they represent the state of those who are departed, after their present course of trial is finished, as immutably fixed, for they tell us that they will be judged *according to their works,* and declare, in the parables of the pounds and the talents, that the rewards of grace which will be bestowed on the righteous will be proportioned to the measure of their religious attainments, and to the amount of their services *while they were living upon earth.* And yet these prayers were offered by the early fathers, not merely for the dead who were truly pious, but in some instances for the unconverted; for the following were the terms in which Ambrose prayed for Valentinian, who, according to the author of Ancient Christianity, died "uninitiated, unregenerate, unjustified, that is, unbaptized; solve, igitur, Pater Sancte, munus servo tuo." And says Dr. Field, whom you quote as a high

---

* "It appears manifestly out of this book of Irenaeus, quoted by you," says Chillingworth, Religion of Protestants, Bishop Patrick's edition, p. 352, "that the doctrine of the Chiliasts was in his judgment apostolick tradition, as also it was esteemed (for ought appears to the contrary) by all the doctors, and saints, and martyrs of or about his time, for all that speak of it, or whose judgments in the point are any way recorded, are for it; and Justin Martyr professeth that *all good and orthodox Christians of his time believed it,* and those that did not he reckons amongst hereticks."

authority when he favours your sentiments, "Epiphanius answers, that though the prayers of the living cutte not off *the whole punishment* of sinne, (from the impenitent,) yet some mercie is obtained for sinners by them, at least *for some mitigation or suspension of their punishment,* of which opinion, as I have showed before, *many other were as well as Epiphanius."* And even when they were offered for the saints, it was not merely to commemorate their virtues, as some have asserted, or to express only a passing wish, as you would insinuate, but according to Cyril, in an extract which was given from him in a former letter, as "a great assistance to them." And they must have approved likewise of prayers *to* the dead, though no such intercessions were ever offered by them, as far as appears from their writings, while they remained upon earth, and though they must have been aware that the saints in the other world, unless they were omniscient and omnipresent, could not hear them. Nor were these prayers merely apostrophes, as you are desirous to represent them;* for,

* "The addresses in the fourth century being rather apostrophes to the blessed saints who were at the moment before the minds of those who used them, than systematic requests for their intercession." Letter from Dr. Pusey to Dr. Jelf, on the Aiticles treated in Tract 90, p. 119.

Would Dr. Pusey have the goodness to say whether the following expressions, used by Ephrem, the Syrian, to the Virgin, are only an apostrophe? "Be present with me now and always, O Virgin, Mother of God, Mother of Mercy, beneficent and kind.

"O Virgin, Lady, Mother of God, who didst carry Christ our Saviour and Lord in thy womb, *I repose in thee all my hope, and I trust in thee who art* higher than all heavenly powers."

"Adesto mihi nunc et semper, O Virgo, Dei Genetrix, mater misericordiae, benigna et clemens.

"Virgo, Domina Dei Genetrix, quae Salvatorem Christum et Dominum nostrum in utero portasti, in te spem meam omnem repono, et in te confido, quae sublimior es omnibus coelestibus potestatibus." (De Sanct. Dei Gen. Virgin. M. Laud)

Bishop Ridley, immediately before he suffered, seems to have imagined that departed saints might pray for the living. "Brother Bradford," says he in a letter to that martyr, February, 1555, "so long as I shall understand that thou art in thy journey, by God's grace, I shall call upon our heavenly Father, for Christ's sake, to see thee safely home; *and then,* good brother, *speak you, and pray for the remnant that are to suffer for Christ's sake, according to that thou shalt know more clearly.*" See his Life by Ridley, p. 572.

as I stated formerly, they applied to them to assist them in recovering stolen goods, and to protect them at sea, and to deliver them from the licentious, as in the case of the nun who prayed to the Virgin to rescue her from Cyprian, when before his conversion he attempted to seduce her. And so great was the confidence which they had in the prayers of departed saints, that the following are the terms in which they were mentioned by Nazianzen: "I am persuaded," says he, in his 19th oration, when speaking of a martyr, "that *our father's intercession now avails us more than his teaching did while present with us in the body*, now that he has got near to God, has shaken off the fetters of the body, and freed from the mud of earth approaches naked the naked and most pure mind." I might extend these observations to other superstitious rites and practices which prevailed very generally in the early Church, and which neither you nor Bishop Russel would be disposed to maintain were approved by the Apostles. But if you admit that the errors in regard to doctrine, and the superstitious practices to which I have just now alluded, cannot be considered as having obtained their sanction, though they prevailed so generally in the early Church, you have no right to draw a different conclusion respecting diocesan Episcopacy, or any of the rites and ceremonies of your Church, though you could prove that they existed from the earliest times, and were as generally adopted, unless you could demonstrate at the same time that they are mentioned in the Scriptures as having been instituted by the Redeemer, and as possessing the high and authoritative sanction of these illustrious ministers of the only King and Head of the Church.

I have only farther to observe, that in rejecting any order in the Christian ministry, or any religious rite which rests merely on tradition, however early, and is not sanctioned by Scripture, *we are only following the example of the fathers*, who acted upon this principle, and rejected opinions and religious customs which were common in their day, though they rested on traditions which were asserted to have come down from the age of the Apostles, but were not supported by Scripture. Eusebius, for instance, gives that very reason for condemning the doctrine which was taught by Papias respecting the Millennium, and which was adopted as generally by the early fathers, as, according to your statement, even diocesan episcopacy, namely, that it rested only *on unwritten tradition*, from the days of John, and had received his approbation. "Moreover," says he, "the same writer alleges something as from *unwritten tradition*, viz. some strange parables and doctrines of our Saviour, and some other fabulous things; and amongst the rest, he says, that after the resurrection there shall be a thousand years, wherein Christ shall reign on earth bodily. But he appears to me, through a misunderstanding of the Apostle's discourse, to have taken what was spoken mysteriously in a different sense from the true meaning. For he was of a very weak judgment, as appears from his writings. He was, notwithstanding, the author of this opinion to most of the ecclesiastical writers who succeeded him, for Irenæus and those who favoured his opinion looked only to his antiquity."* Irenæus, too, as he is quoted by the same historian, says, respecting the controversy about the time of keeping Easter, that "this difference did not arise first in his age, but *long before, in the time of their fathers*, who, as is probable, being negligent in their government, delivered to their posterity a custom which had crept in only through simplicity and ignorance."† And, says Socrates, the historian, "neither the more ancient nor later fathers, who were disposed to follow these Jewish rites, had any cause to raise so great contention for the keeping of Easter and such holy days, the observation of which is not enjoined in the Gospel," (I trust that you and the rest of the Tractarians, as well as the Scottish Episcopalians, will mark this,) "was altogether legal," *i. e.* ceremonial. "They did not consider that after

---

* Lib. III. cap. 39, "Και αλλα δι ο αυτος," &c.   † Lib. v cap. 24

the Jewish religion was changed into that of the Christians, the strict observation of the law of Moses, and the shadows of future things, were entirely abolished, which may be thus most surely evinced. For by no law of Christ is it granted to Christians to observe Jewish customs. Yea, the Apostle expressly forbade it, not only setting aside circumcision, but admonishing them that about feast days there should be no contention. And in the Epistle to the Hebrews, confirming the same declaration, he says, "the priesthood being changed, there is also a change of the law." After which he adds, when accounting for the appointment of such holy days as you observe in your Church, without any authority from Scripture, "surely the Apostles and Evangelists never imposed a yoke upon those that became obedient to the doctrine of faith, but Easter and other holy days were left to the choice and equity of those who in such days had received the benefits. *Wherefore, seeing men love holy days because they bring them some respite from their labours,* different individuals in different places, following their particular inclinations, according to a certain custom, *celebrated the memory of our Saviour's passion. For neither our Saviour nor his Apostles by any law ordained that it should be observed;* neither did the Gospel nor the Apostles threaten us with a mulct, punishment, or curse, as the law of Moses was wont to do the Jews."* And yet

---

* Lib. v. cap. 22. "It is not," says Bishop Russel in his Sermon, p. 40, "the keeping of those fasts and festivals which commemorate the great events of our holy religion, that constitutes the real difference between Episcopalians and other Christians, for in many parts of the Continent they observe the principal festivals and fasts of the Church, as regularly as do the Episcopalians among whom we live." But even Socrates, as we see, declares that there is no warrant for such festivals in Scripture, nor any law appointing them And the ancestors of the Continental Protestants condemned them, though, with a strange inconsistency, as James the Sixth remarked, even at Geneva they retained "Yule and Pasche." "In a National Synod," says the author of the Re-examination of the Five Articles of Perth, p. 208, "holden at Dort, anno 1578, of the Belgick, Almaine and French Churches, we have these words. 'Optandum foret nostros sex diebus laborare, *et diem solum dominicum celebrare.*' Among the articles agreed upon and concluded, concerning ecclesiastical policie in the

the keeping of Easter on one day was asserted by Polycarp and the Eastern Church, as was formerly noticed, to be supported by a tradition respecting the opinion and practice of the Apostle John; and the keeping of it on a different day, as was done by the Romish Church, was supported by a tradition res-

Palatinat, anno 1602, we have this following. "Omnes feriae per annum et festi dies tollendi e medio. *All the festivall dayes through the year are to be abolished*" Bucer, howbeit, not one of the precisest reformers, upon Matthew ii hath these words, as I find him cited by Amesius in his Fresh Suit, p. 360, "I would to God that every holy day besides the Lord's day were abolished. That zeal which brought them first in was without all warrant or example of the Scripture, and onely followed naturall reason to drive out the holy dayes of the Pagans, as it were to drive out one nail with another."

"Farellus and Viret," it is elsewhere remarked, "removed all holy dayes out of the Kirk of Geneva, as Calvin testifies, (Epist 118.) The same decree which banished Farellus and Calvin out of Geneva brought in other holy dayes They were all again abrogate except the Sabbath day. Howsoever, after came in the keeping of Pasche, and the Nativity. Calvin was so far from liking of holy dayes, that he was slandered of intention to abolish the Lord's day. Yea, Luther himselfe, in his book de Bonis Operibus, set forth anno 1520, wished that *there were no feast days among Christians but the Lord's day.* And in his booke to the Nobilitie of Germanie, he saith, Consultum esse, &c. it were expedient *that all feast days were abrogate*, the Lord's day only retained. Howsoever forraigne divines in their epistles and councils speak sometimes sparingly against holy dayes, when their advice was sought of Kirks newly risen out of Popery, and greatly distressed; they never advised a Kirk to resume them when they were removed, neither had they leisure to consider narrowly the corruption of every error that prevailed in their time, the work of reformation was so painful to them."

And the following are the terms in which Bishop Hooper reprobates all such festivals, though neither Cranmer nor he could get them abolished in the Church of England. "It is against this commandment," (the fourth,) says he, "to kepe or dedicate ony fast to ony sainct, of what holinis soever he be. Therefore saith the law, ye shall celebrate the fest unto the Lord; Exod xxiii. This honor shuld be gyven only unto God. *In the Old Testament was no fest ever dedicated to ony sainct, neither in the New* It happened *after the deth of the Apostelles*, as it is written in Euseb. Eccles. Hist. lib. iv. cap. 15, and *better auctorite have they not* that be the auctors of these holy dayes, the which the Consel of Lugd hath geven us They have not above two hundred and seventy three yers in aige, and *is the levyn of the Pope*" Such is the Bishop's account of the origin of Bishop Russel's holy days, for which he praises the Church of England and the Scottish Episcopalians. Declaration of the Ten Holy Commandments, p. 115.

pecting the opinion and practice of Peter and Paul, handed down from the time of these Apostles. But if the fathers themselves, for whom you profess such deference, rejected opinions and religious rites which rested merely on unwritten traditions, however early, and however general, but which were not sanctioned by Scripture, we are only following the example which they have set us, when we reject the claims of diocesan Episcopacy, and all your rites, even though you should be able to show that they existed generally in the Christian Church from the earliest ages, and were recommended by traditions extending backwards to the very days of the Apostles, unless you can prove that they are recommended or appointed in the Word of God.*

I remain, Reverend Sir,

Yours, &c.

---

* Even Cyprian uses the following language respecting a tradition, of which he disapproved "Unde est ista traditio? Utrumne de dominica et evangelica auctoritate descendens, an de Apostolorum mandatis atque Epistolis veniens?" Epist. 74, ad Pompon. p. 192. And says Whitaker of the whole of the early fathers, (and he was one of the most learned and distinguished theologians that ever filled the high situation of Professor of Divinity in the University of Cambridge,) "We may warrantably reject all human testimonies, and insist upon some clear Scripture testimony *For this is the constant sense of all the Catholic fathers*, that nothing is to be received or approved in religion which is not supported by the testimony of Scripture, and which cannot be proved and confirmed out of these sacred writings. *And very deservedly, since the Scripture is an absolute and sufficient rule of truth.*" Treatise against Bellarmine, Controv. ii. quaest. 5, cap. 6. p. 506.

LETTER XXI.

If the reasoning employed in the two preceding letters be well founded, it will not follow that diocesan Episcopacy received the approbation of the Apostles, though it could be proved that it existed in the age next to the apostolic, unless it could be demonstrated that they had expressed their approbation of it in their writings,—but it cannot be proved that it existed in that early age —The mere catalogues of bishops, to which Episcopalians appeal, will not establish this, unless they can show that these bishops had the same powers which belong exclusively to their prelates — This, however, they have never yet done, and Jerome declares, that even toward the end of the fourth century the power of ordination alone distinguished a bishop from a presbyter —In his Commentary on Titus, and his Epistle to Evagrius, he represents bishops and presbyters as the same, not only in name, but in authority, and diocesan Episcopacy as a mere human institution, introduced by the Church to prevent schism —He describes it further as adopted *by degrees, as divisions arose in different Churches or nations,* by a decree of each of the Churches, and not of any general council, and as having commenced, not at the time of the schism in the Church of Corinth, referred to by Paul in his first Epistle to that Church, but after the writing of the third Epistle of John, and the death of the Apostles —This represented as the opinion of Jerome, as stated in his writings, by Luther, Melancthon, Calvin and the most eminent foreign Reformers, by the Wirtemburg Confession and the Articles of Smalkald, and by Jewel, Willet, Whitaker, and many other learned and distinguished divines of the Church of England.

REVEREND SIR,—I have endeavoured to show, in the preceding letter, that though you could succeed in proving diocesan Episcopacy to have existed in the Church in the very age next to the Apostles, and that it had been regarded subsequently as an apostolic institution, we would be justified in refusing to it that high character, unless it could be demonstrated that it was sanctioned by Scripture. And I have attempted to prove that it has no such sanction, presbyters being the highest order of office-bearers among the standing ministers of the Christian Church, who are represented as bishops, and no one being ever called by that name who was a diocesan bishop. Nay, not only are presbyters denominated bishops, and the same qualifications required from them that are necessary in bishops, but, as the celebrated Armacanus remarks, when Paul enumerates the different orders, he mentions *no middle order* between the presbyter-bishop and the deacon. "It is evident," says he, after quoting the words of the Apostle to Timothy about bishops and deacons in his first Epistle, that "between the episcopal," or presbyter episcopal " order, and that of the deacon, there is *no middle order*, since if there were any, we cannot doubt that that illustrious Doctor, who, as he tells the Galatians, ch. i., received his Gospel from Christ himself, would have instructed his beloved disciple Timothy respecting it, and would have given him rules in regard to it, as he gave him respecting the higher and lower orders,"* Such an omission is altogether inexplicable, on the supposition that presbyters, who are represented as bishops, were inferior to them, and were to constitute only *a middle order*. And if you can account for it, and for the want of the slightest notice of the qualifications which are required in such bishops, that those who aspire to that high office may know whether they are fit for it, and those to whom they apply for ordination may know whether they ought to grant it, you will have the honour of performing what has never yet been accomplished by any of the former defenders of Episcopacy, from the time of Epiphanius till the present day.

I am aware that the present curate of Derry, one of the most zealous though not the most intelligent and judicious advocates of your ecclesiastical polity, objects to our reasoning, when we infer the equality, if not the perfect identity, of presbyters and bishops; because presbyters are distinguished by the name of bishops, just as we infer the equality of the Son to the Father in the ever-blessed Godhead, because the highest names characteristic of divinity which are bestowed on the first are applied to the second person in the Trinity. "The man," says he, "who would rest his cause (the proof of the divinity of the Son) upon it," *i. e.* the application to him of these names, " would be subjected to a logical defeat, for he would

* "Constat quod inter ordinem episcopalem et inter ordinem diaconatus non est ordo medius, quoniam si quis esset, non dubium, quin iste Doctor maximus, qui suum Evangelium recepit a Christo, ut ipse scribit ad Gal. i., suum dilectum discipulum Timotheum de isto ordine instruxisset, et ei regulam dedisset, sicut de superiori et inferiori regulas dedit." Ric. Armacan. lib. ii. quaest. Armen. cap. v. fol. 84.

be at once open to the reply, that if Christ be God, because he is called God, magistrates and princes are, for a similar reason, gods; that if Christ be God, because styled God, Baal and Ashtaroth are, for a similar reason, gods."* Now, I would ask this writer, who is equally rash in his remarks on some of the leading doctrines of theology, as in some of his arguments in defence of Episcopacy, where he finds the highest names which are applied to the Supreme and Eternal God given to angels, or magistrates and princes, or to Baal and Ashtaroth? Any of them may be called θεος but I challenge him to produce *a single passage* where he is called ὁ θεος, a name which even Socinians and Arians admit is peculiar to the Supreme God. And yet that name is bestowed on the blessed Redeemer by God the Father, (Hebrews i. 8,) by the Apostle Paul, (Romans ix. 5,) and by the Apostle Thomas, (John xx. 28,) as well as in other passages. And any of them may be distinguished by other inferior names, which are applied occasionally to the persons in the Godhead. But I call upon him to point out a single passage where they are called *Jehovah*, that incommunicable name, which is represented by the Psalmist as peculiar to him who is " the most high over all the earth," (Ps. lxxxiii. 18,) or, as it is expressed by Dr. Waterland, who, in his masterly writings on the divinity of the Saviour, will be acknowledged by most to have thought as closely and argued as ably as the curate of Derry, " which is a word of *absolute* signification, and is the incommunicable name of the one true God."† And yet we know that that name is given to the Redeemer by God the Father, (compare Ps. cii. 12, 26, with Hebrews i. 8, 10, 12,) and by the Apostle John, (compare Isaiah vi. 1-3, 10, with John xii. 37, 39, 41,) as well as in other passages. The argument, therefore, for the supreme and eternal divinity of the Son, from his being represented by these names, is perfectly conclusive; and if we are

* See his Episcopacy and Presbytery, p. 24.
† Defence of some Queries relating to Dr. Clark's Scheme of the Trinity, p. 57.

right in inferring, in opposition to Mr. Boyd, his equality to the Father from his receiving these names, as was maintained by Bishop Bull, Dr. Waterland, and Bishop Horsley, we are justified in inferring the equality of presbyters to scriptural bishops, because they are represented as bishops. And as no other bishops, or standing ministers, *under any other name*, are mentioned in the New Testament, we are warranted further in drawing the conclusion, that, as far as is revealed in the sacred volume, they are *the highest order of Christian ministers* appointed by the Redeemer, and *the only bishops*.

You will tell me, however, that diocesan bishops existed universally in the Christian Church from the earliest ages, and that for fifteen hundred years Episcopacy was regarded as an apostolic institution. Such I am sensible was the statement of Bancroft, Chillingworth, and Leslie, in former times; and such is the statement which has been made recently in almost every page of the Oxford Tracts, and in terms of the boldest and most confident assertion, as if it did not admit of a single doubt, or of the smallest contradiction. I propose, accordingly, in concluding these letters, to inquire into the fact; while, if it should even correspond to the statement, since the Apostles themselves have never told us that they sanctioned it, I would object to the inference, that diocesan Episcopacy was a divine institution.

Now, in examining this statement, I beg to premise, that it will not be enough to convince me of its accuracy, though you should bring forward lists of different individuals in after times denominated bishops, who occupied the Sees in the various quarters of the Christian Church from the very age which was next to the Apostles till the present day. It will not satisfy me that they were diocesan bishops, to tell me merely that *they had the names of bishops;* but I must have more precise, and distinct, and full information from unexceptionable witnesses *as to the extent of their powers*, and must see that they were the same as to ecclesiastical matters which are possessed by your bishops, and which are exercised by the prelates among the Scottish Episcopalians. I must see that they were not merely the moderators or chairmen of the councils of presbyters in the different churches, who were only the *primi inter pares*, the first among equals, chosen annually like the Αϱχοντες Επωννμοι at Athens, each of whom was denominated in his turn the Archon for the year, and presided over the rest; which, according to some, as was formerly mentioned, is the only principle on which you can explain the apparently contradictory accounts given by the fathers of the order of succession among the first four bishops of the Church of Rome. And I must see that even afterwards, when a change was introduced, they were not merely standing moderators with the name of bishops, because they summoned when they thought fit the councils of the presbyters to meet and deliberate about the affairs of the Church, and possessing only the powers of the annual moderators. All this must be ascertained; and it must be proved that the authority committed to the bishops was far more extensive than was vested in these moderators with the designation of bishops, and was equal to that which has been conferred upon your prelates, before the argument, brought from the lists of bishops in the different Churches, can have the smallest weight to convince me of the fact asserted in your statement, and that of other Episcopalians, namely, that diocesan Episcopacy existed universally in the Christian Church from the earliest ages. Now, I request to know, whether you or Mr. Boyd can give me this information? He has furnished *the names* of the bishops of two of the Asiatic Churches,* and said very properly, that "it was surely unnecessary to pursue that line of proof any further;" and as he produced nothing more as a proof, it was unquestionably right that he should stop. Will he have the goodness to accompany it in the next edition, or in some future publication, with a well-attested account of the extent of the powers which were entrusted to these ministers?

* Episcopacy and Presbytery, p. 114-117

I feel it to be the more necessary to obtain this information, because it was common with the fathers, as was proved formerly in one of these letters, to represent the Apostles as the bishops of Churches in which they had laboured for a time, though they sustained a much higher and more important character, and to ascribe to their successors the very same powers which were exercised by these distinguished early ministers; and the same language is used in the fourth and fifth centuries respecting Timothy, and Titus, and others of the Evangelists. It is plain, however, that any list of bishops in one of these Churches which begins either with an Apostle or an Evangelist, commences with an error, and is consequently vitiated; for being a minister of a greatly superior order, he could not sink into a bishop. And as his name ought never to have been placed on the list of these ordinary ministers, so it is not enough to present to me a catalogue of those who succeeded him, but you must furnish me with a distinct and well-authenticated account of the extent of their powers; and you are not to take for granted, that because they were bishops, they were invested with the same amount of spiritual authority over other ministers which he could exercise in virtue of his high and extraordinary office, while he was engaged in founding and organizing these Churches. Besides, Bishop Burnet admits that "the names of bishop and presbyter are not only used for the same thing in Scripture, but are also used promiscuously by the writers of the two first centuries."* And it is evident from the writings of Irenaeus, and of others of the fathers, that his observation is just, and that Bishop Russel is mistaken when he affirms,† that "immediately after the demise of the Apostles, the term Bishop was applied (appropriated) to their successors in the government of the Church," or diocesan prelates. So far was this from being the case that Irenaeus represents presbyters as preserving the very succession from the Apostles *in the episcopate,* and as

* Conference, p. 310. † Sermon, p. 30.

the bishops whom it was foretold by the prophets that God would give to the Church. "Wherefore," says he, in his Fourth Book against Heresies, c. 43, "we ought to hear those presbyters who are in the Church, who have the succession from the Apostles, and who, *with the succession of the episcopate,* have received the gift of the truth according to the pleasure of the Father."* And he says, in the following chapter, "*Such presbyters* the Church nourishes, of whom also the prophet says, I will give thee thy princes or rulers in peace, and *thy bishops* in righteousness.† But if presbyters were the ministers who preserved the succession in the episcopate from the Apostles to the days of Irenaeus, and who were then considered as the bishops whom God had promised to give to the Church, how is this consistent with their being no longer bishops, nor the bishops predicted by the prophets, and subordinate to a higher order of ministers, who long before that time had become the only bishops? And, in short, it is indispensable that you should furnish us with this information about the powers of the bishops, whose names are in the lists of the early Churches, that we may see whether they were really distinct from presbyters, and if so, how far they were superior; for it would appear from what is mentioned by Jerome, that even in the fourth century they were greatly inferior, in respect to their authority, not only to your prelates, but even to those of the Scottish Episcopalians. Your bishops possess the exclusive power of administering confirmation, exercising jurisdiction, and conferring orders, but it was not so with the bishops, nearly three hundred years after the death of the Apostles; for, says that father, and he was not contradicted by Epiphanius, or any of his contemporaries,) "*what does a bishop perform,* (ordination

---

* "Quapropter eis qui in Ecclesia sunt presbyteris obaudire oportet, his qui successionem habent ab Apostolis, sicut ostendimus, qui cum episcopatus successione charisma veritatis certum secundum placitum Patris acceperunt."

† "Tales presbyteros nutrit ecclesia, de quibus et propheta ait, Et dabo principes tuos in pace, et episcopos tuos in justitia."

excepted,) which a presbyter cannot do?"* But if the bishops who lived at such a distance from the Apostles were distinguished from presbyters only as to the power of ordination, and not as to the powers of confirmation or jurisdiction, which are possessed exclusively as well as the former by modern bishops, it presents a very strong additional reason why, along with the names in the list of bishops in the second century, you should furnish us with an exact account of their powers, that we may see whether at that time they differed from presbyters even as to the power of ordination, which, in the days of Jerome, appears to have been their only peculiar privilege.

Jerome, however, who is acknowledged universally to have been the most learned of the Latin fathers, and whose veracity, I believe, has never been questioned, makes another statement of far greater importance respecting diocesan Episcopacy, namely, that even in the comparatively limited form in which it existed in his time, it was not appointed by Christ, nor sanctioned by the Apostles; and while he represents it as a mere human institution, mentions the circumstances which led to its introduction. But as I write only to ascertain what is truth, and not for victory, and as I would be sorry to impute to him a single sentiment which he did not really hold, or to deduce from his words a single inference in favour of my principles which they do not fairly warrant, I take the liberty to select from his writings the following passages:

"Let us attend carefully," says he in his Commentary on Titus, "to the words of the Apostle, (Titus, i. 5,) that thou shouldst ordain presbyters in every city, as I have appointed thee. Pointing out afterwards what sort of presbyters should be ordained, he says, if any be blameless, the husband of one wife, &c.; after which he adds, for a bishop must be blameless, as the steward of God. A presbyter, therefore, *is the same as a bishop;* and before, through the in-

* "Quid enim facit excepta ordinatione episcopus quod presbyter non faciat?"

stigation of the devil, there were different parties in religion, and it was said among different people (or states,) I am of Paul, I of Apollos, and I of Cephas, *the Churches were governed by the common council of presbyters.* But afterwards, when every one thought that those whom he had baptized belonged to himself, and not to Christ, it was determined throughout the whole world, that one chosen from the presbyters should be placed over the rest, to whom the care of the whole Church should belong, and the seeds of schisms should be taken away.

"If any one should think that this is merely my opinion, and not the doctrine of the Scriptures, let him read again the words of the Apostles to the Philippians, 'Paul and Timotheus, the servants of Jesus Christ, to all the saints in Christ Jesus which are at Philippi, with the bishops and deacons, grace to you and peace,' &c. Philippi is a single city of Macedonia; and certainly in one city there could not be several bishops, as they are now denominated, or of the kind that now exist. But because at that time they called the same persons bishops who were presbyters, he has spoken indifferently of bishops as of presbyters.

"If this should still appear doubtful to any one, unless it be confirmed by another testimony, it is written in the Acts of the Apostles, that when the Apostle had come to Miletus, he sent to Ephesus, and called the presbyters of the same Church, to whom afterwards he said among other things, Take heed to yourselves, and to all the flock in which the Holy Spirit hath placed you bishops, to feed the Church of God, which he has purchased with his blood. Observe carefully, that when calling the presbyters of that one city Ephesus, he afterwards denominated *the same persons bishops.* If any one is willing to receive that Epistle to the Hebrews, which is ascribed to Paul, there also the care of the Church is divided among a plurality of rulers; for says he, Obey them who have the rule over you, and be subject to them, for they watch for your souls, as those who must give an account, &c. And the Apostle Peter, who received his name from the firmness of his faith, speaks in the same way in his Epistle, saying, the presbyters who are among you, I beseech, who am your fellow presbyter, and a witness of the sufferings of Christ, &c. The object for which we state these things, is to show that among the ancients, *presbyters and bishops were the same; but that by little and little,* that the plants of dissensions might be plucked up, the whole care of the Church was committed to one. As the presbyters, therefore, know that they are subject by *the custom* of the Church to him who is placed over them, so let bishops know that they are greater than presbyters, more by custom than by any real appointment of the Lord; and that they ought to govern the Church *along with the presbyters,* imitating Moses, who, when he alone was to preside over the people of Israel, chose seventy, with whom he might judge the people."*

Again, he says in his Epistle to Evagrius, " I hear that a certain individual has discovered such madness, as to place deacons above presbyters, *that is, bishops;* for when the Apostle plainly teaches that presbyters are the same persons who are also bishops. who can endure that a minister who waits only on the tables of the poor, and widows, should in his pride exalt himself above those at whose prayers the body and blood of Christ are made? Hear a testimony in proof of this." After which he quotes the different passages referred to in his Commentary on Titus, and then adds, " Do these testimonies of such men appear to you of little weight? Let the evangelical trumpet sound in your ears, the son of thunder whom Jesus loved, who drank copiously the streams of doctrine from the breast of the Saviour. The Presbyter to the elect Lady and her children, whom I love in the truth; and in another Epistle, The Presbyter to the well beloved Gaius, whom I love in the truth. And that one was *afterwards* chosen, who was placed (or presided over,

* " Diligenter Apostoli verba attendamus dicentis, ut constituas per civitates presbyteros sicut ego tibi disposui qui qualis presbyter debeat ordinari," &c.

praeponeretur,) the rest, was a remedy which was adopted against schism, lest every one drawing the Church to his party should break it in pieces. For also at Alexandria, from Mark, the Evangelist, to the Bishops Heraclas and Dionysius, (or, according to Blondel,* till A. D 246,) "the presbyters always named as bishop one chosen from among themselves, and placed him in a higher degree, in the same manner as if an army should make an emperor, or the deacons should choose from among themselves an industrious man, and call him Archdeacon." After which he remarks respecting the terms, presbyters and bishops, which he had said were applied to the same persons, that "the one was a name expressive of age, the other of dignity; whence, when directions are delivered to Titus and Timothy about the ordination of the bishop and the deacon, the Apostle is entirely silent about presbyters, because the presbyter is comprehended in the bishop."† Now, upon the account which is given in these passages of the rise of Episcopacy by this early father, who lived so near to the Apostles, and of whom Augustine says, that "no man knew any thing which was unknown to Jerome," and Erasmus testifies that he was " without controversy the most learned of all Christians, and the prince of divines," I would make the following observations :

In the *first* place, it is a gratuitous and unworthy insinuation of Mr. Boyd, for which he has not produced a particle of evidence, that Jerome was induced to deliver this statement, because " his expectations in life were disappointed, and that disappointment vented itself in the acerbities which mark his writings ; or that there was that in the haughtiness or the worldliness of the bishops of his time which excited his displeasure."‡ No such acerbities appear in these passages, but they express his calm and deliberate opinion as to the origin of Episcopacy ; and if, under

* Apologia pro Sententia Hieronymi, p. 7.
† " Audio quendam in tantam erupisse vaecordiam ut diaconos presbyteris, *id est, Episcopis* anteferret," &c.
‡ Episcopacy and Presbytery, p. 123.

the influence of these feelings, he could deliver a testimony respecting a matter of such moment, which he knew to be false, so far from being worthy of being represented by Bishop Hurd as "the most esteemed, as well as the ablest of the fathers," he would be deserving of contempt.

2dly, It was the general opinion, not only of the most eminent individuals who laboured for the spiritual improvement of the Church before the Reformation, but of the leading Protestants at that memorable period, and for ages afterwards, that the doctrine taught in these passages, is, that bishops are not superior to presbyters by divine appointment, and that the elevation of the former above the latter is a device of men, and not an institution of God. I may refer in proof of this to Laurentius Valla, a noble Roman, and distinguished divine, who, according to Dr. Cave, flourished A. D. 1440, who, in his Commentary on Acts xv. after quoting Acts xx. 28, says, "As to this, that the same persons were presbyters who are here said to be bishops, I need not employ many words, since it is proved by Jerome on Titus."* It was the view of their meaning taken by Luther, who says in his Disputation at Leipsic, (tom. 1. of his works,) "that Jerome makes bishops equal among themselves, and presbyters equal to bishops, and that any inequality which took place afterwards arose from custom and expediency."† It was the view of their meaning which was entertained by Melancthon, for, says he, "Jerome plainly testifies that a bishop and a presbyter are not different grades" or orders "by divine right;"‡ by Calvin, who, after remarking that diocesan Episcopacy "was an arrangement introduced by human agreement," adds, "Thus Jerome, on the Epistle to Titus,

* "De hoc quod iidem fuerunt presbyteri qui episcopi, non est pluribus agendum, quod ab Hieronymo super Epistola ad Titum probatur."

† "Hieronymus non modo episcopos aequat inter se, sed et presbyteros episcopis comparat. Patet itaque re ipsa aequales episcopos inter se et presbyteros, solo usu et ecclesiae causa, alium alii praeferendum."

‡ Tract. de Ordine, tom ii. Oper. p. 867. "Imo Hieronymus aperte testatur, non esse jure divino diversos gradus episcopum et presbyterum."

says, a presbyter is the same as a bishop;" by Bullinger, (Decad 3, Sermo 3); by Zanchius on the Fourth Commandment; by Danaeus, (in Augustini de Haeres., Haer. 53); Chemnitz, (Examen Concil. Trident. Pars 2, de Sacrament. ord.); Junius, (Controv. 5 lib. 1, cap. 15,) and many others. Nay, it was the view taken of them in all the Confessions of the Churches of the Reformation. Thus the Wirtemburgh Confession, in the chapter on Order, says, "Jerome teaches that a bishop and presbyter are the same."* And you cannot fail to recollect, that in the quotations which were produced from the Articles of Smalkald, in a former letter, and which were subscribed by so many thousands of the foreign Reformers, the very same view is given of their import. " Jerome," say they, " teaches that there is no difference between bishops and presbyters, but that *all pastors are also bishops.* And he alleges that text of Paul, (Titus 1. 5,) ' Therefore left I thee in Crete, that thou shouldst ordain presbyters in every city."† And again, " Here Jerome teaches that the different degrees of bishops and presbyters were established solely by human authority, and this is evident from the thing itself, for the office and the directions respecting those who are to be appointed to it are the same."‡ Nay, such was the view which was entertained of their meaning by many of the most learned and able divines of your own Church. I shall prove immediately that it was held by Dr. Whitaker, who replies triumphantly to the very same objections against this interpretation of these passages, when urged by Bishop Russel, the curate of Derry, and other modern Episcopalians, when they were adduced formerly by Sanders the Papist, a most zealous defender

---

* " Docet autem Hieronymus eundem esse et presbyterum "
† " Ideoque Hieronymus claris verbis inquit inter episcopos et presbyteros non esse discrimen, sed omnes pastores et episcopos esse. Et allegat textum Pauli, Tit. i.," &c.
‡ " Hic docet Hieronymus distinctos gradus episcoporum et presbyterorum sive pastorum *tantum humana authoritate constitutos esse;* idque res ipsa loquitur, quia officium et mandatum plane idem est. Quia autem *jure divino nullum est discrimen inter episcopum et pastorem,* non est dubium, ordinationem ideo eorum ministrorum a pastore in ecclesia sua factum, jure divino ratam et probatam esse."

of the exclusive claims and divine institution of diocesan Episcopacy. And I apprehend that it is plain from the following quotation from the Synopsis of Willet, that a similar view of the meaning of Jerome was adopted by himself, and by Jewel and Whitgift. "Amongst the rest," says he, " S. Hierome thus writeth: Apostolum perspicue docere, &c. The Apostle teacheth evidently *that bishops and priests were the same:* yet he holdeth this distinction to be necessary for the government of the Church, Quod unus postea electus, est, &c. That one afterwards was chosen to be set over the rest, it was done to bee a remedie against schisme. To this opinion of S. Jerome subscribeth Bishop Jewel in the place before quoted,*

---

* The testimony of Willet, whose book, as I showed, was approved by the bishops, establishes the accuracy of the statement which was given in a former letter of the sentiments of Jewel respecting the origin of Episcopacy, which he regarded, (as was proved) only as a human institution, and furnishes an answer to what is urged to the contrary by Mr. Boyd, (Episcopacy and Presbytery, p. 51.)—"I reply," says the latter writer, "in the *first* place, by saying, that these" (they had been quoted by the authors of the Plea for Presbytery, and are the same nearly as I have referred to) "are not Jewel's words. They are part of a quotation taken from St. Jerome, and given in the quotation imputed to Jewel, as any person who has read even the first clause of that father's epistle to Evangelus (Evagrius!) could not have failed of knowing." Willet was aware of this as well as Mr. Boyd, and yet he affirms, from the manner in which Jewel not only quotes, but *applies* the words of Jerome, that he was of the same opinion with that father. And certainly the writer who quotes with approbation the words of another must be considered as adopting them. I presume Mr. Boyd does this, when he quotes in this way the authors to whom he appeals in different parts of his work. "In the *second* place, all that Jewel says is, that it is no heresy to say, that by the Scriptures of God, bishops and priests are all one. And does this prove the Bishop of Salisbury an advocate for Presbytery?" No, certainly; for Jewel, like Jerome, thought that Episcopacy might be adopted on the principle of expediency, though not as a divine institution. And he admits, like Jerome, not as Mr. Boyd would insinuate, that a bishop and a Presbyter are represented in Scripture *as all one*, because they belong to *one order*,—the one occupying its higher grade, and the other its lower,—but as one *in degree* as well as *order*, or, as he expresses it in another passage, which he quotes with approbation from Jerome, *one thing;* and this is farther confirmed by his representing them as at first ruling the Church *with equal power.* "Againe," he observes, (Defense of the Apologie, p. 100,) "Jerome saith, therefore a priest and a bishop *are one thing*, and before that

and another most reverend prelate of our Church, (Whitgift,) in these words: "I know these names be confounded in the Scriptures, but I speak according

by the inflaming of the divell parts were taken in religion, and these words were uttered among the people, I hold of Paul, &c., the Churches were governed of the common advice of the priests " Besides, when Harding, as Jewel informs us, p. 196, affirmed, that "they which denied the distinction of a bishop and a priest were condemned of heresie," and appealed in proof of it to the condemnation of the sentiments of Arius by Epiphanius, lib. III. cap. 75, he charged them with denying any distinction between them to the same extent to which it was denied by Arius. Now, we know that Arius denied any distinction between them, not only as to order, but *as to degree.* And Jewel observes, on the margin, with regard to Harding's charge, that "this was an untruth, for hereby both S. Paul and S. Hierome, and other good men, are condemned of heresie," plainly showing that he considered them as teaching that, by divine appointment, bishops and presbyters are not only of one order, but of the same degree. As to the two quotations from the Defense, and the passage produced by Mr. Boyd from the Apology, where Jewel says, "We believe that in the Church there are various orders of ministers, some deacons, others priests, others bishops, to whom the instruction of the people, and the care and administration of religion, is intrusted," it contains no contradiction to the statement, that, like Jerome, he considered bishops and presbyters the same as to order and degree by divine right, for he thought also, like him, that it was agreeable to Scripture to adopt a superior order to presbyters on the principle of expediency. And as he acknowledges, in another part of the Apology, that they had retained some rites which were not instituted by God, they might be disposed to retain diocesan bishops though not appointed by him. And as to the other passage of the Apology referred to by Mr. Boyd, where Jewel says, "We have approached, as much as possibly we could, the Church of the Apostles, and ancient Catholic bishops and fathers," it is evident from the following sentence, which Mr. Boyd ought to have quoted, but which he has taken care to suppress, that the bishop is speaking only of their approaching that Church in regard to *doctrine and worship,* and never alludes to the orders among the clergy. So much for Mr. Boyd's allegation of frauds practised against Bishop Jewel.

I may add, that the celebrated Dr. Reynolds, of whom Bishop Hall said, that "his memory and reading were near a miracle," and Crackenthorp, that "to name him was to commend virtue itself," confirms this view of the sentiments of Jewel, in opposition to Mr. Boyd; for, says he, in his letter to Sir Francis Knollys, "which untruth, (that Augustine charged Arius with heresy, for asserting that, according to Scripture, bishops and presbyters are the same,) it may appeare by this, that our learned countryman, of good memory, Bishop Jewel, (Defense of the Apology, part 2, cap. 9, divis 1, p 198,) when Harding, to convince the same opinion of heresie, alleadged the same witnesses, he cyting to the contrary Chrysostome, Jerome, &c., knit up his answer with these words: All these and other moe holy fathers,

to the manner and custome of the Church ever since the Apostles' time;" Defens. Answer. Admonit. p. 383.* But if such was the view of the meaning of these passages which was adopted by these eminent and venerable individuals, some of whom continued to adhere to Episcopacy on the ground of expediency, though not of divine right, does it not furnish a strong presumptive argument, whether you reflect on their number, or learning, or piety, that it must be the true interpretation; and if this be really the case, and if the testimony of Jerome respecting the origin of prelacy, and the time when it was introduced, be worthy of credit, does it not subvert completely all its claims to the character, which so many of its injudicious friends are so anxious to claim for it, of an apostolic institution?

As it is still, however, possible, though not very probable, that this interpretation may be wrong, and as we ought to judge for ourselves, I shall examine very shortly the leading statements contained in these quotations, and the principal objections which were urged against it formerly by some Popish controversialists, when they advocated the cause of diocesan Episcopacy, and which have been repeated of late by some of its defenders among Protestant Episcopalians.

Now, upon looking into these passages, I apprehend, that it will appear to an impartial reader, who has no theory to establish, that the following points, bearing very strongly on the question about Episcopacy, are asserted by Jerome, who, according to Bingham, "may be allowed," on many subjects, "to speak the sense of the ancients."

---

together with the Apostle S. Paul, for thus saying, by Harding's advice must be held for heretikes." And Hooker, in his Ecclesiastical Polity, book vii. p 395, when speaking of those who believed that "*the Apostles did neither by word or deed appoint it,*" (diocesan Episcopacy,) mentions among them, on the margin, Jewel, in his Defens. Apol part 2, cap. 9, and Dr. Fulk, in his Answer to the Rhemish version of the Testament, Tit. 1. 5. Surely Dr. Reynolds and Hooker will satisfy Mr. Boyd and his friends on this point.

* Page 273.

1st, That bishops do not belong to a different order from presbyters by divine right, or even to a higher grade in the same order; "because the Apostle, when pointing out *what kind of presbyter* ought to be ordained, says, that *a bishop* ought to be blameless, plainly showing that a presbyter is *the same with a bishop*, (idem est ergo presbyter qui et episcopus:") that "it was not merely his private opinion, but the doctrine of Scripture, that a bishop and a presbyter *are one*, (episcopum et presbyterum unum esse;) that the same persons who are called presbyters *are afterwards denominated bishops,* (presbyteros vocans postea eosdem episcopos dixerit;) and that Paul, when writing about the ordination of bishops and deacons, *is entirely silent about presbyters*, because they are comprehended under bishops, (de presbyteris omnino reticetur, quia in episcopo et presbyter continetur.") It is evident, therefore, that in his opinion bishops had in no respect any superiority to presbyters by divine right, and that not the smallest sanction of that superiority is to be met with in Scripture.

2dly, That while presbyters and bishops continued the same, as the Lord had appointed, no one possessed any pre-eminence as to power beyond another, and "*the churches were governed by a common council of presbyters*" (Communi concilio presbyterorum ecclesiae gubernabantur.)

3dly, That when bishops were placed above presbyters, it was to prevent schisms, and they were raised to their superiority *only by the custom of the Church*, and *not by any divine direction*, (ut dissensionum plantaria evellerentur ad unum omnem solicitudinem esse delatam, *episcopi noverint se magis consuetudine* quam *dispositionis dominicae veritate presbyteris esse majores*.)

4thly, That this change took place when dissensions arose among different people or states where Christian Churches had been planted, and "one said, I am of Paul, another, I of Apollos, another, I of Cephas, and another, I of Christ;" to remedy which, "it was resolved or determined over the whole world, that one should be set over the other presbyters, to whom the whole care of every separate church should be committed. (In toto orbe decretum est, ut unus de presbyteris electus superponeretur caeteris, ad quem omnis ecclesiae cura pertineret, et schismatum semina tollerentur.")

5*thly*, He does not affirm, as has often been alleged by many Episcopalians, both Protestant and Popish, that this elevation of one of the presbyters above the rest of his brethren took place *at once throughout the early Church*, when the schism referred to by the Apostle Paul in his first Epistle to the Corinthians arose in that Church. Had this been the case, an extraordinary spectacle would unquestionably have been exhibited to future ages, namely, the inspired and accredited ministers of Christ, the twelve Apostles, along with Paul, allowing the Church at its own pleasure to alter that constitution which they had prepared for it under the guidance of the Spirit, and to provide a remedy against the progress of schism which he had not suggested; and their conduct would have excited still greater surprise, as they have never made the most distant allusion to it, or expressed the smallest approbation of it in any of their Epistles. Besides, had it been introduced at that time and received their sanction, Jerome would never have represented it as originating merely *in custom*, (consuetudine ecclesiae,) and not in divine appointment, (dispositio dominica); for the approbation of the Apostles, acting under the direction of the Holy Spirit, would certainly have invested it with that high character. He makes no such statement, however, in either of these passages, but asserts distinctly, that as bishops and presbyters were originally the same, both as to order and power, by the appointment of the Saviour, so they continued the same *long after the schism which took place at Corinth*, and *even during the whole of the time referred to in the latest of the apostolic writings;* quoting in proof of this the Epistle to the Hebrews, the First Epistle of Peter, and the Second and Third Epistles of John.* And so far from declaring that this elevation of one of the council of presbyters took place *at once throughout the whole Christian*

* When Sanders, the Papist, asserted that bishops had been appointed by the Church, after the schism at Corinth, with the approbation of the Apostles, though not under their direction, and appealed in proof of it to the testimony of Jerome, Whitaker replied in the following terms: "Respondeo Sanderum plane aut non intelligere, aut non attendere quid Hieronymus velit. Etiamsi enim Apostolis vivis aliqui dixerunt, ego Pauli sum, ego Cephae, ego Apollo, et Hieron. scribit, *antequam* diceretur ego sum Pauli, &c., tamen Hieronymus non sensit ab Apostolis eum ordinem mutatum esse, sed postea ecclesiae judicio. Id Hieronymus significat cum ait, mox, in toto orbe, decretum est ut unus ex presbyteris electus superponeretur caeteris. Num hoc ab Apostolis factum decretum est? Hieronymus ipse respondeat. Sicut presbyteri (inquit) sciunt, se *ex ecclesiae consuetudine* episcopo sibi praeposito esse subjectos. Ex ecclesiae consuetudine Hieronymus ait, non Apostolorum decreto; tum subnectit, ita episcopi noverint se presbyteris majores consuetudine magis quam dominicae dispositionis veritate. At si illum ordinem Apostoli mutavissent, et presbyteris episcopos praefecissent, et communi presbyterorum consilio ecclesias posthac regi vetuissent, *ea sane dominica dispositio fuisset, utpote a Christi Apostolis profecta*, nisi forte quae Apostoli decreverant ea consuetudini non dispositioni dominicae ascribenda sint. Sed vivis Apostolis nihil est in illo ordine mutatum. Nam illa ad Corinthios scripta epistola est, quum Paulus in Macedoniam ageret; at post hoc tempus Titum reliquit in Creta, ut presbyteros oppidatim constitueret; Tit. i. 5. Si mutandum ordinem Apostolus putasset, non praecepisset constitui in singulis oppidis presbyteros, nec Hieronymus ex Paulo; Philip. i 1 ; 1 Tim iii. 2, Tit. i. 5, 7; ex Petro, 1 Pet. v. 1 ; ex Actis, Act. xx. 17, 28 , ex Joanne, 2 Joh. i. et 3 Joh. i., testimonia attulisset, quibus presbyterum eundem esse cum episcopo demonstraret. Paulus Epistolas suas ad Philippenses, ad Timotheum, ad Titum, et Petrus suam, et Joannes suas scripserunt postquam illud Corinthi natum schisma est; et Lucas etiam presbyteros Ephesinos post illud schisma a Paulo Miletum accersitos esse scribit Cum Hieronymus his potissimum locis fretus, (Epist. ad Evagr) contendat *presbyterum parem esse episcopo per omnia*, non potuit esse tam immemor sui ut putaret ab apostolis eam rationem mutatam esse. Sic alibi cum Scripturae testimonia adduxisset quibus episcopum et presbyterum non differre evinceret, subjicit *postea* unum electum, qui caeteris praeponeretur. Si *postea* electus unus est qui presbyteris superior esset, non ergo Apostoli, sed *ecclesiastica quaedam consuetudo aut constitutio differentiam illam introduxit.*" Controv. 4, Quaest. 1, cap. 3, sect 29. Such is the answer which was given to this Papist in the beginning of the seventeenth century, by this learned professor of divinity, when he brought forward the very same objections to our view of the sentiments of Jerome which are advanced by some of the advocates of Episcopacy in the present day.

Church, in consequence of the decree of some general council, as Bishop Russel and Mr. Boyd insinuate that we represent Jerome as asserting, "though there is not in the writings of any of the fathers, nor of any other author, ecclesiastical or civil, the slightest reference to any such canon or institute,"* we consider him as stating directly the contrary. He describes the progress of the schisms *as gradual,* for he says that they extended *"from people to people,"* or through different countries, ("in populis,") when every one thought that those whom he had baptized belonged to himself, and not to Christ. And he mentions expressly that the adoption of the remedy was *equally gradual,* or, according to his own words, *"by little and little,"* (paulatim); and that it was not in consequence of a decree of any general council, but of a resolution or determination of each of the Churches throughout the whole world, (toto orbe decretum,) as the schisms spread, to try the expedient for checking them which had been employed by others. He does not specify the particular time at which it was first tried, but it is plain that it must have been after the apostolic age. He tell us, indeed, that it was "when every one said I am of Paul, or I am of Apollos, or I of Cephas;" but he does not state that it was *when* this was said *at Corinth,* but when it was said among different people or in different countries; and he uses the very same expressions to describe the conduct of schismatics in the ages which followed, and even in his own day; for, says he, "we do not all speak the same thing, one saying I am of Paul, another, I am of Apollos, and another, I of Cephas, and destroy the unity of the Spirit," &c.† And as it will not follow from his applying the expressions which were used by the first schismatics at Corinth to the schismatics who lived after the apostolic age, that he designed to tell us, in opposition to

* Sermon, p. 35.
† "Quando non id ipsum idem loquimur, et alius dicit ego Pauli, ego Apollo, ego Cephae, dividimus Spiritus unitatem, et eam in partes et membra discerpimus," in Ephes. lib 2. cap. 4.

the whole of his previous reasoning, that it was at the first of these periods, and not at the last, that this change was made, so it cannot be inferred, as has been done by Episcopalians from his saying to Evagrius, that "what Aaron, and his sons, and the Levites were in the Temple, the bishops, and presbyters, and deacons might claim to be in the Church,"* he intended to represent bishops as superior to presbyters by divine appointment. He had been endeavouring previously, through the whole Epistle, to show, that as presbyters were equal to bishops, by the appointment of Christ, the conduct of deacons, who exalted themselves above the former, was presumptuous and sinful. And as we cannot believe that *he would subvert in the end* what he had been labouring to establish in *the rest of* the Epistle, he must have designed merely to affirm, that he might check the ambition of the insolent deacon, that the same superiority which was possessed by Aaron and his sons over the Levites under the Old Dispensation, ought to be possessed by presbyters and bishops, whom he had proved to be not only equal, but the very same, under the New Dispensation. And he denominates the latter apostolic traditions, from the numerous passages which he had brought in proof of the equality and identity of presbyters and bishops, and their superiority to deacons, from the writings of the Apostles.

He tells us, in short, as was already noticed, that even in the middle, or rather towards the end of the fourth century, the only thing in which a bishop was superior to a presbyter, was the power of ordination. But if this was really the case, and if bishops afterwards acquired the two additional powers of jurisdiction and confirmation, as they now possess them, not by divine right, but by assuming them to themselves, and the clergy consenting from whatever motives, it confirms the truth of his previous statement with regard to ordination, which he says they did not origi-

* "Et ut sciamus traditiones Apostolicas sumptas de Veteri Testamento, quod Aaron et filii ejus atque Levitae in Templo fuerunt, hoc sibi episcopi, et presbyteri, et diaconi vindicent in Ecclesia."

nally possess, and to which they had no more a title by divine right than to these other powers, but received it only by the deed of the Church, and not by the appointment of the Lord. It is likely that they attained the two latter powers by little and little, so as not to excite the jealousy of the clergy; and the extent to which they exercised their power in regard to ordination, and to presiding among the presbyters, might be so very small as not to awaken any such feelings in the ministers of the Church, and it might be only by degrees that it reached the height at which it arrived afterwards in the days of Jerome. If such, however, was the amount of their power when it was first conferred on them, it furnishes an answer to the extravagant and declamatory observations of Mr. Boyd, who expresses his astonishment, that "while this transaction (the introduction of diocesan Episcopacy) was going on, whether originating in one ambitious individual, or the example of some wonderfully influential Church,—of which individual or of which Church there is no mention in history,—no note of alarm is sounded, no summons to resistance issued, no remonstrance heard from east to west, calling upon Christians to protect the constitution of the Christian Zion from impending injury and destruction."* When the bishops assumed the two last of these powers, and when archbishops, partriarchs and primates arose in the Church, he will certainly allow that a very great change took place in its constitution, whether originating in a few ambitious individuals, or in any other cause, "of which individuals, and of which cause, there is no mention in history; nor does it appear that any note of alarm was sounded, any summons to resistance issued, or any remonstrance neard from east to west, calling upon Christians to withstand these changes." But if the latter innovations passed unopposed, and were quietly acquiesced in, and generally adopted, though nothing is recorded of the individuals who introduced them, or of the way in which they were effected, I would like to be in-

* Episcopacy and Presbytery, p. 156, 157.

formed whether the same thing might not happen, when, according to Jerome, the power of ordination and a perpetual presidency in the councils of the presbyters were bestowed upon bishops by the deed of the Church.

I have only further to remark on the statement of Jerome, that in the only instance which he mentions of the appointment of bishops, after they were first introduced, that of the bishops of Alexandria, he represents them as made by presbyters, just as the Roman army by its own deed made their emperor, and the deacons made their archdeacon. He does not say whether they ordained them, though this is asserted afterwards by Eutychius. And it is evident that if they were ordained, they alone must have performed it; for before diocesan bishops were adopted by the Church, who did not receive their office by any divine appointment, but by a mere human arrangement, there could be none but presbyters to consecrate those who were raised to the episcopate, not only in the Church of Alexandria, but in all the Churches. But if, according to Jerome, it was presbyters alone who began the succession, and ordained the first diocesan bishops in all the Churches, from whom the whole of the bishops of the present day, and the whole of their clergy, have derived their orders, the succession has been vitiated at its very commencement, and cannot be rectified; and if Presbyterian orders have no validity, there cannot, upon your principles, be a Church, or a minister, or a single individual who has any revealed and covenanted title to salvation on the face of the earth.

The sum, then, of Jerome's observations seems to be this: He affirms it to be a fact, that while the original constitution of the Church remained, and presbyters were equal to bishops, the Church was governed by a common council of Presbyters; that when that constitution was altered by the introduction of diocesan bishops, it was not by divine appointment, but by a mere human arrangement; that when one presbyter was elevated above his brethren, and promoted to the episcopate, it was an expedient to repress schism; that it was introduced by little and little, as dissensions spread among the Churches in different countries, and not all at once,* and was adopted ultimately by every Church, in consequence entirely of its own resolution, (decretum;) that even towards the end of the fourth century, bishops were distinguished from presbyters only by the power of ordaining ministers, and that when bishops were first made they were not only chosen, but made by presbyters. Now, if these be really *facts*, and not merely *opinions*, and we must hold them to be so, unless Episcopalians can show that the testimony of Jerome, "the most esteemed of the fathers," was contradicted by his contemporaries, and by those who succeeded him, (and this has never yet been attempted,) they prove incontestably that Presbyterianism is the original constitution of the Church, as it was settled by the Apostles, and account for the introduction of diocesan Episcopacy; that the latter is an innovation, and a mere human institution; and that Churches which are at present governed by presbyters are far more likely to be free from schisms than other Churches, unless the inventions of men are superior to the polity which has been approved by God, because they resemble more nearly the model which he has presented to them in the Sacred Scriptures.

I remain, Reverend Sir,

Yours, &c.

* It never entered into the minds of Presbyterians to represent Jerome as saying that bishops were adopted *at once through the whole world*. Important changes, either in the civil constitutions of nations, or in the creation of a new order of ministers in Churches, and changes, too, exactly resembling each other, were never known to take place to that extent simultaneously, and could not by any possibility so take place, nor does Jerome say that it happened in the instance of which he speaks, but quite the contrary. Besides, he describes the pre-eminence conferred at first on one of the presbyters above his brethren as so very small that it would awaken no jealousy, and says that it was increased gradually.

LETTER XXII.

While the constitution of the Church, as settled by the Apostles, is acknowledged by Jerome to have been Presbyterian, he seems to have approved of a modified Episcopacy as a human arrangement for the prevention of schism —This remedy acknowledged by Gratian to have increased, in place of repressing the evil —Invalidity of the objection to Presbyterian principles, that they were held by Arius, who denied the divinity of Christ, inasmuch, as though he might err on the latter point, it would not follow that he erred on every other, for he agreed in many things with Episcopalians, and especially with those of them who condemned prayers for the dead —Hilary, Augustine and Chrysostom admit the identity of presbyters and bishops —Clemens Romanus mentions only two orders of ministers, and never refers to diocesan bishops —No reference to them in the Epistle of Polycarp —The short Epistles of Ignatius proved to be corrupted, so that no dependence can be placed on their statements respecting the orders in the ministry, and even admitting them to be genuine, no such powers are ascribed in them to bishops as are possessed by modern diocesan bishops

REVEREND SIR,—The quotations which have been produced from the writings of Jerome prove incontestably, that in the opinion of that distinguished early father the constitution of the Church, as it was settled by the Apostles, was strictly Presbyterian; and they contain also his testimony to the important fact, (and from his nearness to the period when the change took place, and the absence of every thing like an opposite testimony, it is entitled unquestionably to the utmost credit,) that when Episcopacy was introduced, it was a mere human institution for preventing schism. But it is only fair to remark, that he approved of that arrangement; for he says in another part of his writings, "The safety of the Church depends on the dignity of the highest priest, on whom, if a certain extraordinary and superior authority above all be not conferred, there will be as many dissensions as there are priests."* He appears to me to have erred in that opinion; for human institutions are certainly less fitted to prevent schisms, and promote at once purity of doctrine, and peace and harmony,

* "Ecclesiae salus in summi sacerdotis dignitate pendet, cui si non exsors quaedam, et ab omnibus eminens datur potestas, tot in Ecclesiis efficientur schismata, quot sacerdotes." Dial. ad Lucifer.

than the *form of government which the Redeemer himself has appointed for his Church.* And it is far more likely that a number of faithful Presbyterian ministers, residing near each other among their several parishes, will watch over one another, and repress the first beginnings of evil, meeting as they do once a month, or once every two months, in their Presbyteries, and once every six months in their Synods, to which complaints may be carried by any single minister, if the rest fail to perform their duty, and once a year in their General Assembly, to whom even the Synod is responsible; it is far more likely, I say, that they will repress the first beginnings of evil, than a single individual denominated a bishop, who, though equally faithful, has to superintend perhaps four or five hundred, or perhaps a thousand ministers and congregations, and who is responsible to no Synod or General Assembly. And accordingly, as was observed by Orthuinus Gratius, the very remedy soon increased the evil; for, "as Origen acquaints us, the Christians," even then, " were divided into so many factions, that they had no name common to them but that of Christian, and *they agreed in nothing else but that name;* and as Socrates informs us, they were derided publicly in the theatres by the people for their dissensions and sects; and when, as Constantine the Great said, *there were so many contentions and controversies in the Church, that this very single calamity seemed to exceed the miseries of the former times (of persecution);* when Theophilus, Epiphanius, Chrysostom, Augustine, Ruffinus, and St. Jerome, all of them Christians, all fathers, and all Catholics, contested with each other with most violent and implacable animosity; when, as Nazianzen saith, *the members of the same body consumed one another.*"* But still, though Jerome erred in that opinion, for these were the schisms which prevailed in the Church after the introduction of Episcopacy, yet it was undeniably his opinion, and that of the fathers of his day, who agreed with him in thinking

---

* Bishop Jewel, Apology of the Church of England, p. 36.

that presbyters and bishops were originally equal, and who corroborated also his testimony, that the Church was then governed by a council of presbyters. "And therefore," says Stillingfleet, "some have well observed the difference between the opinions of Jerome and Arius. For, as to the matter itself, I believe, upon the strictest inquiry, Medina's judgment will prove true, that Jerome, Austin, Ambrose, Sedulius, Primasius, Chrysostom, Theodoret, Theophylact, were all of Arius' judgment as to the identity of both name and order of bishops and presbyters in the primitive Church; but here lay the difference. Arius from hence proceeded to separation from bishops and their churches, *because they were bishops.* And Blondel well observes, that the main ground why Arius was condemned, was for unnecessary separation from the Church of Sebastia, and those bishops too who agreed with him in other things, as Eustathius the bishop did; whereas, had his mere opinion about bishops been the ground of his being condemned, there can be no reason assigned why this heresie, if it were then thought so, was not mentioned either by Socrates, Theodoret, Sozomen or Evagrius, before whose time he lived, when yet they mention the Eustathiani, who were contemporaries with him. Jerome, therefore, was not ranked with Arius, because, though he held the same opinion as to bishops and presbyters, yet he was far from the consequence of Arius, that all bishops were to be separated from."*

Having mentioned Arius, who is often thrown up to us as the first who maintained the identity of bishops and presbyters, and who erred at the same time so greatly in denying the supreme divinity of the Saviour, I would briefly remark, that many have entertained doubts of his having really embraced that fearful heresy. It is unnecessary for me, however, to enter on that question, as the last of these opinions surely has no connection with the first; and no one will contend that because he was wrong in his sentiments on one great point, he was wrong, for instance, in his

* Irenicum, p. 276, 277.

views of the inspiration of the Scriptures, or of the difference between virtue and vice, and of the doctrines of a supreme overruling providence, and of a future judgment; and that we ought to reject the latter as well as the former because he held them. Arius entertained the very same opinion of the identity of bishops and presbyters with Jerome and others of the orthodox fathers, to whom I shall refer immediately, and defended it with much ability, even according to the statement of Epiphanius, by the very same arguments; while the very first of the arguments of Epiphanius for diocesan bishops is a begging of the question, and the rest are so weak, that most Episcopalians would be ashamed of them. Arius denied also, that under the New Testament Dispensation we are bound to observe the fasts of the Church and other festivals which are kept by your own and other Episcopalian Churches, and reasoned very forcibly in support of his position. Epiphanius maintained the opposite opinion, and argued in proof of it from Paul's going up to Jerusalem at the time of Pentecost, and from his conforming to other Jewish rites, which if at all conclusive, would have justified the Church in the days of that father, and in succeeding ages, in circumcising as well as baptizing the children of Jewish converts, because Paul circumcised as well as baptized Timothy, and in keeping the new moons, as well as other Jewish holy days. And Arius contended against prayers for the dead; for, said he, "if prayers can assist those who have departed this life, no one in future will need to live piously, or to do good, but he will require only to attach to himself some friends in whatever way he chooses, and prevail with them by money or entreaties to intercede with God for him, that he may sustain no disadvantage from his evil conduct, and may be delivered from the punishment of his aggravated offences." While Epiphanius boldly vindicated the practice to an extent to which I presume you would scarcely follow him, declaring, that "they prayed not only for the righteous, but for sinners, to whom they implored mercy from the Lord;"* and that "their prayers were useful to them, though they could not extinguish all their faults."† Now, as no consistent Protestant Episcopalian would hesitate for a moment to condemn the practice of praying for the dead, because Arius was one of the first who ventured to oppose it, so no Presbyterian will hesitate in the least, or feel at all ashamed to adopt his views respecting presbyters and bishops, or fasts and festivals in honour of the martyrs, when they are supported by Scripture, though you should establish by evidence which cannot be controverted, that he entertained unsound and unscriptural sentiments respecting the divinity of Christ.‡

---

* " Nam et justorum pariter et peccatorum mentionem facimus; peccatorum quidem ut iis a Domino misericordiam imploremus."

† "Caeterum quae pro mortuis concipiuntur preces iis utiles sunt, tametsi non omnes culpas extinguant"

‡ " The argument," says Dr Reynolds in his letter to Sir Francis Knollys, "which he (Dr Bancroft, who had represented Augustine as charging Arius with heresy, for asserting that, according to Scripture, bishops and presbyters are the same,) bringeth to prove it are partely overweake, partly untrue, overweake, that, p. 18, 19 and 69, he beginneth with, out of Epiphanius, untrue, that he adjoyneth of the general consent of the Church. For though Epiphanius do say that Aerius his assertion is full of folly, yet he disproveth not the reason which Aerius stood on out of the Scriptures, nay, he dealeth so in seeking to disprove it, that Bellarmine the Jesuit, (tom 1. cont. 5, lib. 1, cap 15,) though desirous to make the best of Epiphanius, whose opinion herein he mainteyneth against the Protestants, yet is forced to confesse that Epiphanius his answer is not at all the wisest, nor any way can fit the text."

" As for the general consent of the whole Church, which D. Bancroft saith, condemned that opinion of Arius, for an heresy, and himself for an heretike, because he persisted in it, that is a large speach: but *what proof hath he that the whole Church did so?* It appeareth, he saith, in Epiphanius. It doeth not, and the contrary appeareth by S. Jerome, and sondry others, who lived, some in the same time, some after Epiphanius, even S. Austin himself, though D Bancroft cite him as bearing witness thereof likewise. I grant S Austin, in his book of Heresies, ascribeth this to Aerius for one, that he sayd, Presbyterum ab Episcopo nulla differentia debere discerni · But it is one thing to say, there ought to be no difference betwixt them, (which Aerius saying, condemned the Churches' order, yea, made a schisme therein, and so is censured by S Austin, counting it an heresie as in Epiphanius he took it recorded, himself, as he witnesseth, (de Heres. ad quod vult Deum in praefatione,) not knowing how far the name of heresie should be stretched,) another thing to say that *by the word of*

I have said, that a number of the early fathers in the age of Jerome adopted his views of presbyters and bishops; and among these I would refer only to the following:

"In the bishop," says Hilary, "are all orders, because he is the first priest, that is, the prince of priests, and a prophet and evangelist. The things which were written by the Apostle do not correspond in all respects with the ordination which is now in the Church, because they were written at the beginning, or first age of the Church. For he calls Timothy, who had been ordained a presbyter by himself, a bishop, because at first presbyters were denominated bishops, so that one dying, the next succeeded him. In fine, in Egypt, the presbyters (according to some) confirm, (consignant,) or (according to others) ordain. But, because the following presbyters were found to be unworthy of the first place, the plan was changed, a council ordaining,

God there is no difference betwixt them, but by the order and custome of the Church, which S. Austin (Ep. 19,) *saith in effect himselfe; so far was he from witnessing this to be heresy, by the general consent of the whole Church* Which untruth, how wrongfully it is fathered on him and on Epiphanius, (who yet are all the witnesses that D. Bancroft hath produced for the proofe thereof, or *can for ought that I know,*) it may appear by this, that our learned countryman of good memory, Bishop Jewel, (Defense of the Apology, part ii cap. 9, divis. 1, p. 198,) when Harding, to convince the same opinion of heresie, alledged the same witnesses, by cyting to the contrary Chrysostome, Jerome, Austen, and Ambrose, knit up his answer with these words; All these, and other more holy fathers, together with the Apostle S. Paul, for thus saying by Harding's advice, must be held for heretikes. And Michael Medina, (de Sacrif Nom. Orig. et Confirm., lib. i. cap. 5,) a man of great account in the Counsell of Trent, more ingenuous herein than many other Papists, affirmeth not only the former ancient writers alleadged by Bishop Jewel, but also another Jerome, Theodoret, Primasius, Sedulius, and Theophilact were of the same mind, touching this matter, with Aerius. With whom agree likewise Œcumenius, (in 1 Tim. iii.,) and Anselmus, Archbishop of Canterbury, (in Epist. ad Tit;) and another Anselmus, (Collect, Can. lib. vii. cap. 87 et 127;) and Gregorie, (Policar, lib ii tit. 19 and 39;) and Gratian, (Can. legimus, dist. 39, cap. Olimp.;) and after them how many, it being once enrolled in the canon law for sound and Catholike doctrine, and thereupon publikely taught by learned men, (Author. Gloss. in cap. dist citat, &c;) all which do bear witnes against D. Bancroft, of the point in question, that it was not condemned for an heresie, by the general consent of the whole Church," &c. See the letter at large, which is worthy of a careful perusal.

that not priority of order, but merit, should guide them in the appointment of a bishop, which was to be made by the judgment of many priests, lest one who was unworthy of it should rashly usurp the office, to the offence of many."* And again, he remarks on 1 Tim. iii, "After the bishop, he gives directions about the ordination of the deacon. Why? because *there is only one ordination of a bishop and a presbyter*, for each of them is a priest; but the bishop is the first, so that every bishop is a presbyter, not every presbyter a bishop; for he is a bishop, who is the first among the presbyters. In fine, he mentions that Timothy had been ordained a bishop, but, because he had no other before him, he was a bishop."† But, if he state expressly that presbyters were at first denominated bishops; that the individual who afterwards received that name by way of eminence was only the first presbyter, and succeeded to his situation at first by seniority of order, and subsequently by the votes of his fellow presbyters; that his ordination, and that of the other presbyters, was the same, and he received no new consecration when he was made a bishop, and that in Egypt, when the bishop was absent, presbyters either confirmed or ordained, I leave it to any impartial judge to say whether he must not have considered the constitution of the primitive Church to have been strictly Presbyterian.

In like manner, the author of the Questions on the Old and New Testament, which are bound up with the works of St. Augustine, but which Blondel thinks were written by Hilary, the deacon, says, "Paul shows that a presbyter is meant when he speaks of a bishop, for he points out to Timothy, whom he had made a presbyter, what kind of a person he should ordain a bishop. For what is a bishop but the first presbyter; that is, the highest priest? In fine, he speaks of them

---

* " In episcopo omnes ordines sunt, quia primus sacerdos est, hoc est, princeps est sacerdotum, et propheta, et evangelista," &c.

† " Post episcopum diaconi ordinationem subjicit. Quare, nisi quia episcopi et presbyteri una ordinatio est, uterque enim sacerdos est, sed episcopus primus est," &c.

as his fellow-presbyters and fellow-priests. Does a bishop call the deacons his fellow-ministers? No, assuredly, for they are greatly his inferiors. In Alexandria and all Egypt, if a bishop be wanting, a priest *consecrates or ordains.* That there is a great distance between a deacon and a priest is evident from the Acts of the Apostles"* But if, as this writer declares, Paul meant bishops when he spake of presbyters, if the bishop was only the first presbyter, and if presbyters ordained when the bishop was absent; and if, as he further asserts, (Quest. 46,) no one could act in the room of a minister who held any office, if he was not possessed of power to execute that office, it is plain that he must have regarded bishops and presbyters as nearly the same, and that his sentiments must have been similar to those of Jerome.

"Although," says Augustine to Jerome, "according to the names of honour which *custom* has now introduced into the Church, the office of a bishop is higher than that of a presbyter, yet in many things Augustine is inferior to Jerome,"† where he represents the superiority of the former to the latter as originating merely in custom. "If it is asked," says Primasius, Bishop of Adrumetum, who was a disciple of Augustine, "why the Apostle, in 1 Tim. iii. made no mention of presbyters, but comprehended them under the name of bishops; it was," he replies, "because they are the second and nearly the same degree, as he shows when writing to the Philippians; for he addresses his Epistle to the bishops and deacons, though one city could not have a plurality of bishops.‡" And, says Chrysostom, in his 11th Homily, "omitting the order of the presbyters he passes to the deacons. And

---

* "Presbyterum autem intelligi episcopum probat Paulus Apostolus quando Timotheum quem ordinavit presbyterum instruit qualem debeat creare episcopum. Quid est enim episcopus *nisi primus presbyter*? Nam in Alexandria et per totam Ægyptum, si desit episcopus, consecrat presbyter," &c.

† "Quanquam secundum honorum vocabula quae jam ecclesiae usus obtinuit episcopatus presbyterio major sit," &c. Epist. 19. ad Hieron.

‡ "Quaeritur cur de presbyteris nullam fecerit mentionem, sed eos in episcoporum nomine comprehenderit: quia secundus, *imo pene unus est gradus*, sicut ad Philippenses," &c.

why so ? Because there is not much difference between bishops and presbyters; for presbyters are ordained for the instruction and government of the Church; and the same things which he said to bishops apply to presbyters; for in ordination alone they are superior to presbyters, and appear to be above them."*

But admitting that these writers agree with Jerome, and the difference between them, if there be any, is extremely small, let us consider very shortly what is said on this subject by the early fathers. And here I must repeat a former remark, that it will not avail the cause of Episcopacy, though we should meet *with the names* of bishops, priests and deacons, unless it be distinctly stated, that *the powers which were possessed by the primitive bishops correspond to those which are claimed at present by diocesan bishops.*

The first of these is Clemens Romanus, whose first Epistle to the Corinthians is perhaps the purest production of Christian antiquity, though his argument for the resurrection from that of the Phoenix is so weak and contemptible, that we would scarcely have expected it to have been used by a man who was entitled to the high character which is ascribed to him by Episcopalians."† It deserves, however, to be

---

* " Το των πρεσβυτερων ταγμα αφεις," &c. Homily on 1 Tim. iii. 1 Theodoret, too, says, " The Apostle calls a presbyter a bishop, as we showed when we expounded the Epistle to the Philippians, which may be also learned from this place; for, after the precepts proper to bishops, he describes the things that agree to deacons. But, as I said, *of old they called the same men both bishops and presbyters.*"

† " Let us consider," says he, " that wonderful type of the resurrection, which is seen in the Eastern countries, that is to say, in Arabia. There is a certain bird, called a Phœnix: of this *there is never but one at a time*, and that lives five hundred years; and when the time of its dissolution draws near, that it must die, it makes itself a nest of frankincense, and myrrh, and other spices; into which, when its time is fulfilled, it enters and dies. But its flesh, putrefying, breeds a certain worm, which, being nourished with the juice of the dead bird, brings forth feathers, and when it is grown to a perfect state, it takes up the nest in which the bones of its parent lie, and carries it from Arabia into Egypt, to a city called Heliopolis · and flying in open day, in the sight of all men, *lays it upon the altar of the sun*, and so returns from whence it came. The priests then search into the records of the time, and find *that it re-*

noticed, that it is neither addressed to a bishop, but to the Church of Corinth; nor is there the slightest notice of him in any part of the Epistle, but he speaks always of their rulers, (ἡγουμενοι) and presbyters, (πρεσβυτεροι,) though Archbishop Wake, in order to keep the latter out of view, translates the term, "such as were aged." And says Stillingfleet, "Had Episcopacy been instituted on the occasion of the schism at Corinth," (as many Episcopalians contend,) "certainly of all places we should the soonest have heard of a bishop at Corinth for the remedying of it; and yet almost of all places, these heralds that derive the succession of bishops from the Apostles' times are the most plunged whom to fix on at Corinth. And they that can find any one single bishop at Corinth at the time when Clemens wrote his Epistle to them, (about another schism as great as the former, *which certainly had not been according to their opinion, if a bishop had been there before,*) must have better eyes and judgment than the deservedly admired Grotius, (and he was a great friend of Episcopacy,) who brings this, in his Epistle to Bignonius, as an argument of the undoubted antiquity of that Epistle, that Clement no where mentions that singular authority of bishops, *which, by Church customs,* after the death of Mark at Alexandria, and *by its example in other places, began to be introduced,* but Clement clearly shows, as did the Apostle Paul, that then, by the common council of the presbyters, who, both by Paul and Clement, are called bishops, the Churches were governed."* Nay, when he speaks of the persons against whom the schismatics had risen up, he represents them as the presbyters, and never makes the smallest allusion to a diocesan bishop. "It is a shame, my beloved," says he, "yea, a very great shame, and unworthy of your Christian profession, to hear that the most firm and ancient Church of the Corinthians should,

turned precisely at the end of five hundred years." And yet Clement, who retails this fable, and reasons from it, *is the best of all the fathers.*

* Irenicum, p. 279, 280.

by one or two persons, be led into a sedition against its priests," as Archbishop Wake renders it, or, according to the original, "its presbyters, (πρεσβυτερους.") And it is the same persons to whom he endeavours to bring them into subjection. "Who is there among you that is generous? Let him say, if this sedition, this contention, and these schisms be on my account, I am ready to depart, to go whithersoever ye please, and to do whatsoever ye command me; only let the flock of Christ be in peace, with the (elders, Archbishop Wake,) *presbyters that are set over it*, (καθεςαμενων πρεσβυτερων") And yet Clement is one of the writers to whom Bishop Russel, Mr. Boyd, and other Episcopalians are accustomed to appeal, as proving that the Church was then governed by diocesan bishops.

Clement indeed says, that "the Apostles knew, by our Lord Jesus Christ, that contention would arise on account of the name of the episcopate. And therefore, having a perfect foreknowledge of this, they appointed persons, and then gave directions how, when they should die, other chosen and approved men should succeed in their ministry." And he tells us in another passage, that the Apostles, "preaching through countries and cities, appointed the first fruits of their ministry bishops and deacons (Archbishop Wake, ministers,) over such as should believe, after they had proved them by the Spirit. Nor was this any thing new, since long before it was written concerning bishops and deacons. For thus saith the Scripture in a certain place, I will appoint their bishops in righteousness, and their deacons in faith." Now, the first observation which is suggested by these passages is this, that he mentions only *two*, and not *three* orders of ministers as appointed for the Church. And it is impossible to escape from this remark, by saying with Mr. Boyd, that the Apostles were still living, and that they occupied the place of the first order; for it is evident, from the first quotation, that he enumerates the orders of ministers who were to govern and instruct the Church *after their death*.

And it is further evident, that the highest of these two orders, or the bishops, were the presbyters, of whom he had been speaking throughout the whole Epistle as set over the Church of Corinth, as well as other Churches, and in reference to whom he says at the conclusion, "Do ye therefore, who laid the foundation of this sedition, submit yourselves unto your *presbyters*, bending the knees of your hearts." Milner accordingly admits this; for, says he, "At first indeed, and for some time, church governors were only of two ranks, presbyters and deacons. The Church of Corinth continued long in this state, *as far as one may judge from Clement's Epistle*"* And says Faber, "Here we may observe no more than two orders are specified, the word bishops being plainly used as equipollent to the word presbyters; and all possibility of misapprehension is avoided by the circumstance of Clement's affirmation, that the appointment of these *two* orders was foretold in prophecy which announced the appointment of exactly *two descriptions of spiritual officers*. Had the Church in Clement's time universally acknowledged and believed that three distinct orders of clergy had been appointed, that father never could have asserted such a form of polity to be foretold in a prophecy which announced the appointment of no more than two sorts of officers, described as being overseers and ministers"† And it agrees exactly with the interpretation of the prophecy given by Irenaeus, in a passage before quoted, where he observes, "Such *presbyters* the Church nourishes, of whom the prophet says, I will give thee thy princes or rulers in peace, and *thy bishops* in righteousness" And though, as Bishop Russel remarks, "Clement reminds them, that, in the Jewish Church, the high-priest had his proper services to perform; that to the priests their particular place was appointed; and that the Levites also had their allotted ministry to discharge;" it can no more be inferred that he intended to assert that there ought to be as

* Church History, vol i. p. 161.
† Consult him on the Vallenses and Albigenses, p. 558.

many orders in the Christian ministry as in the Jewish, than it could be alleged that he meant to teach us that there ought to be as many orders in it as there were gradations of rank *in an army;* because, when enforcing subjection, he says in another passage, "all are not generals, nor colonels, nor captains, nor inferior officers, but every one in his respective rank does what is commanded him by the king, and those who have the authority over him."

And though he says that "the Apostles knew by our Lord Jesus Christ that there should contentions arise upon account of the episcopate," yet it is plain, from the conclusion of the paragraph, that it means merely the over-sight or superintendence of a congregation; for he represents it as an oversight or episcopacy which could be performed by presbyters. " It would be no small sin in us," says he, " should we cast off those from the episcopate," or, as it is translated by Archbishop Wake in the notes, " bishopric, who holily, and without blame, *fulfil the duties of it.*" After which he adds, showing that he is speaking of presbyters, " Blessed are those *presbyters,* (πρεσβυτεροι,) who, having finished their course before these times, have obtained a fruitful and perfect dissolution, for they have no fear lest any one should turn them out of the place *which is now appointed for them.*" Not a particle of evidence, then, can be produced from Clement for diocesan Episcopacy.*

---

* When Clement says that the Apostles, foreseeing there would be contentions about the episcopate, appointed fit persons to succeed them, Dr. Hammond, in his Power of the Keys, c. iii. p. 413, and Dr. Arden, in his Discourse on the passage, translate the word, επινομην, *list,* and render the phrase thus, " They left a list of other chosen and approved men to succeed them in their ministry." "They set down," says Hammond, a list or continuation of successors ," which version the Tractarians in their notes on this passage seem to favour. It would be truly satisfactory if any of the Tractarians, or any other Episcopalian, could mention a single father who had seen the list, and examined the names in it, and ascertained whether it fixed their successors for the following century, or the first six centuries, or till the end of the world, and whether it included their successors in all the Churches. And it would be still more satisfactory, if he could tell where it was now to be found. If it could only be discovered, how invaluable would it be to the Christian Church! It would settle

The next document which is quoted by Bishop Russel in proof of the existence of three Episcopal orders, is the Epistle of Polycarp to the Philippians. But he has omitted to tell us in what part of it he found them, and I have been unable to discover it. *Polycarp does not represent himself as a bishop,* and for aught that appears, he might have been only the senior presbyter or moderator of the Church of Smyrna. He makes no allusion to a diocesan bishop at Philippi, or to any vacancy in that see, or to any bishop in any other diocese. And though he points out the duties of deacons and presbyters, he does not give the smallest hint of a superior order, nor make any reference to the duties belonging to it. And as Archbishop Wake fixes the date of this Epistle "at the end of the year of our Lord 116, or in the beginning of 117," (Preliminary Discourse, p. 119,) *the silence of Polycarp* respecting the Episcopal order, so far from supporting the assertion of Bishop Russel, furnishes a strong presumptive proof that it had not at that time been introduced into the Church.

The third, however, and the principal authority to which Episcopalians appeal for the existence of these orders at that early period, are the short Epistles of Ignatius, which were written, according to Bishop Russel, in the year 110, or in 116.* But before any argument can be founded on them in support of their principles, two things must be proved; 1*st*, not only that they were written by Ignatius, but that they are so free from interpolation, as that we can depend on them as the uncorrupted writings of Ignatius; and, 2*dly*, that if they are genuine, as when they issued from the pen of the Martyr, they present such a view

at once, by ocular demonstration, all dispute about the apostolic succession; for we would require only to look into it, to see whether the bishops who had come after them in all the Churches for 1800 years, were the very individuals whom the Apostles, before they died, put down in their list. And there would be no need for the sovereign to issue a conge d'elire in future to any dean and chapter to elect a new bishop, for they would require only to examine some certified copy of the list, and see who came next. It is difficult to write with any thing like patience of such absurdities.

* Sermon, p. 28.

of the powers of bishops as is inconsistent with Presbytery, and confirm the powers which are claimed and exercised by diocesan bishops. Now, I deny that they can establish either of these positions, though, from the length to which this discussion has already extended, I am prevented from entering so fully into the subject as I had originally intended.

I am aware, that when Calvin and the Centurists of Magdeburgh rejected these Epistles, it was the long Epistles, and not those which were discovered by Usher and Vossius, and therefore I do not found on their opinion with regard to the latter. But I would remind Episcopalians, that Whitgift, and Bilson, and others of their bishops, contended as zealously for the genuineness of the former, though it is now abandoned by every one as utterly untenable, as they themselves contend for that of the short Epistles. Salmasius and Blondel deny the genuineness of the latter, and were ably supported not only by Daillé, but by La Roque, the suppression of whose second dissertation, through the influence of the Episcopalians of his day, was acknowledged by his son, as is mentioned by Mr Jamieson in his Examination of the Fundamentals of the Hierarchy.* Dr. Owen, too, of whom the Rev. Mr. Sinclair says that he was respectable for his piety, as well as erudition,† so far from entertaining an opposite opinion, as he supposes,

---

* "La Roque, in favour of his deceased friend, (Daillé,) undertook the patrociny of this hero; and except fame be altogether false, has fortunately defended his judgment. These observations were again assaulted by the famous Beveridge, to whom our author, preparing an answer which *we have by us, almost perfected, through the importunity of some friends, was suddenly turned another way.* Thus he, and who these friends were we are informed by another author, a man of the Episcopal persuasion, and therefore may the better be believed in this matter, viz. Jos. Walker, translator of La Roque's History of the Eucharist, who, describing the life of La Roque, which he prefixes to his translation, tells us, that at the request of some persons *favouring Episcopacy*, he did not finish this second piece." Jamieson's Fundamentals of the Hierarchy examined, p. 112.

† Dissertations vindicating the Church of England, p. 57, note —It is evident that Mr. Sinclair is not acquainted with the writings of Dr Owen, which contain a view of his sentiments respecting these Epistles.

says, that "these Epistles seemed to him to be like the children that the Jews had by their strange wives, Neh. xiii., who spake partly in the language of Ashdod, and partly in the language of the Jews."* Mosheim says, "So considerable a degree of obscurity hangs over the question respecting the authenticity of not only a part, but the whole of the Epistles ascribed to Ignatius, as to render it altogether a case of much intricacy and doubt." And again, he remarks, "to ascertain with precision the exact extent to which they may be considered genuine appears to me to be beyond the reach of all human penetration."† Dr. Neander represents them as "interpolated by some one who was prejudiced in favour of the Hierarchy;" (Church History, vol. i. p. 190.) And Ernesti declares in his MS. Lectures, that "though he sat down to the perusal of them under an impression that they were genuine, he was forced, while reading them, to come to the conclusion, that it was scarcely credible that an apostolical man, such as Ignatius was, could have written them as they now are "‡ And that this conclusion was just will appear, I think, from the following considerations:

1. Passages are quoted from them by some of the fathers which are not now to be found in them. Jerome, for instance, says, (Dial. 3, contra Pelag.) "Ignatius, an apostolical man and martyr, writes boldly, that the Lord chose as Apostles men who were sinners above all others." It was indeed a bold saying, but it does not occur in any of the Epistles; and if they have undergone some changes, and have some things left out, why might they not undergo others, and have some things put in?

---

* Preface of his Treatise on the Perseverance of the Saints, p. 13. "The foysted passages," says he, p. 10, " in many places are so evident, that no man who is not resolved to say any thing, without care of proof or truth, can once appeare in any defensative of them."

† Commentary by Vindal, vol i. p 276, 278.

‡ "Ernesti vero se etsi ad lectionem harum epistolarum cum opinione esse genuinas accesserit, tamen inter legendum cognovisse profitetur, vix credibile virum apostolicum, qualis fuerit Ignatius, sic scripsisse," &c.

2. Many weak and foolish things occur in them, as Ernesti observes, "and scarcely worthy of an apostolical man. You meet with numerous passages about the dignity and prerogatives of bishops and presbyters; and the constant song of almost all the Epistles is this, "Honour the bishop, and you will honour God the Father; honour the presbyters, and you will honour the Son; honour the deacons, and you will honour the Holy Spirit. Such a comparison of the ministers of the Church with the Sacred Trinity is unquestionably unworthy of an apostolical man."* And it is impossible, I think, to look into these Epistles, without perceiving that his observations are well founded. In the first of them, for example, the duties of the Church of Ephesus to the bishop, (and it extends to little more than *eight pages*,) are dwelt on *more frequently* than the duties of the members of the Church to its ministers *in the whole New Testament.* In the second, (the Epistle to the Magnesians,) which extends to five pages, the bishop is brought forward six times; in the third, (the Epistle to the Trallians,) which is scarcely five pages, seven times; in the fifth, (to the Philadelphians,) which is little more than four pages, five times; in the sixth, (to the Church of Smyrna,) three times; and once in very strong terms in the short Epistle to Polycarp. And compare the language in which the Scriptures point out the degree of respect, and the other duties which are due from Christians to their ministers, with that which is used in these Epistles to express the respect which was considered to be due especially to bishops. "We beseech you brethren," said Paul to the Thessalonians, (1 Thess. v. 12, 13,) "to know them which are over you in the Lord, and admonish you; and to esteem them very highly in love for their work's sake." "Let the presbyters

---

* "Multa jejuna et viro apostolico vix digna Multa enim in iis reperiuntur loca de dignitate et praerogativa episcoporum et presbyterorum, et continua fere omnium epistolarum cantilena est, honora Episcopum, et honorabis Deum Patrem; honora presbyteros, et honorabis Filium; honora diaconos, et honorabis Spiritum Sanctum. Talis vero comparatio ministrorum ecclesiae cum S S. Trinitate profecto est indigna viro apostolico."

that rule well," said he to Timothy, (1 Tim. v. 17,) "be counted worthy of double honour," (or, as appears from the following verse, maintenance, τιμη, where it is required,) "especially they who labour in the word and doctrine." And said he to the Hebrews, (xiii. 17,) "Obey them that have the rule over you, and submit yourselves; for they watch for your souls, as they that must give account." But the following are the terms in which the dignity of the bishop is represented in these Epistles, and in which they point out the honour which was due to him:

"I beseech you, by Jesus Christ, to love your bishop, and that you would all strive to be like unto him. It becomes you to run together, *according to the will of your bishop*, as also ye do. For your famous presbytery (worthy of God) is fitted as exactly to the bishop as the strings are to the harp. *You are joined to him as the Church is to Jesus Christ*, and Jesus Christ to the Father. *The more that any one sees his bishop silent, the more let him revere him." " It is therefore evident that we ought to look upon the bishop even as we would do upon the Lord himself!"* Epistle to the Ephesians.

"I exhort you that ye study to do all things in a divine concord: *your bishop presiding in the place of God;* your presbyters in the place of the Council (or Sanhedrim) of the Apostles; and your deacons, most dear to me, being entrusted with the ministry of Jesus Christ, who was with the Father before all ages, and appeared in the end to us. It will behove you, with all sincerity, to obey your bishop in honour of him, whose pleasure it is that ye should do so. As therefore the Lord Jesus Christ did nothing without the Father being united to him, so neither do ye any thing without your bishop and presbyters. Study to be confirmed in the doctrine of our Lord, and of his Apostles, that so ye may prosper together with your most worthy bishop, and the well-wrought spiritual crown of your presbytery, and your deacons, which are according to God." Epistle to the Magnesians.

" Whereas *ye are subject to your bishop as to Jesus*

Christ, ye appear to me to live not after the manner of men, but according to Jesus Christ, who died for us, that so believing in his death, ye might escape death. It is therefore necessary, that as ye do, so without your bishop you should do nothing; also be subject to your presbyters, as to the Apostles of Jesus Christ, our hope. In like manner, let all reverence the deacons as Jesus Christ and *the bishop as the Father*, and the presbyters as the Sanhedrim of God, and College of the Apostles. Without these there is no Church. I have received, and now have with me, the pattern of your love *in your bishop, whose very look is instructive,* and whose mildness powerful, whom I am persuaded *the very Atheists themselves cannot but reverence.* It becomes every one of you, especially the presbyters, *to refresh the bishop, to the honour of the Father, of Jesus Christ, and of the Apostles.*" Epistle to the Trallians.

"The bishop is fitted to the commands, as the harp to the strings. *As many as are of God and of Jesus Christ are also with their bishop.* Although some would have deceived me according to the flesh, yet the Spirit, being from God, is not deceived; for it knows both whence it comes, and whether it goes, and reproves the secrets of the heart. I cried while I was among you, I spake with a loud voice, *Attend to the bishop,* and to the presbytery, and to the deacons. Now, some supposed that I spake this as foreseeing the division that should come among you. But he is my witness for whose sake I am in bonds, that I knew nothing from any man; but *the Spirit spake, saying on this wise, Do nothing without the bishop!* The Lord forgives all that repent, if they return to the unity of God, and *to the council of the bishop.*" Epistle to the Philadelphians.

"*See that ye all follow your bishop as Jesus Christ the Father;* and the presbytery, as the Apostles; and reverence the deacons, as the command of God. Wheresoever the bishop shall appear, there let the people also be; as where Jesus Christ is, there is the Catholic Church. It is a good thing to have a due regard both to God and to the bishop; he that honours the bishop shall be honoured by God; but he that does any thing without his knowledge, ministers unto the devil." Epistle to the Smyrneans.

"*Hearken unto the bishop, that God also may hearken unto you. My soul be security for them that submit to their bishop, with their presbyters and deacons. And may my portion be together with theirs in God.*" Epistle to Polycarp.

Now, I would ask any candid and impartial individual, whether language like this is employed in the New Testament respecting even an Apostle or Evangelist, or whether honour like this was claimed to the highest of the ministers of the Gospel in that early age from the members of the Church? Did any of them declare that he was moved by the Spirit to cry with a loud voice, " Attend to the bishop, and to the presbyters, and to the deacons?" Or say that he would be security for those who did so? Or call upon them *to look upon a bishop even as they would do upon the Lord himself?* I would inquire farther, whether any thing like it is to be met with, not only in the Epistle of Clement, but in any of the remains of Christian antiquity for hundreds of years after the death of Christ, even when heresies abounded, and when it might have been considered as advisable to increase the influence of orthodox bishops? And if he shall answer in the negative, I would submit it to his calm and deliberate judgment, whether it does not furnish a very strong and decisive proof, that these celebrated Epistles, to which Episcopalians appeal for one of their strongest arguments, but which are completely without a parallel among the early fathers, must have been interpolated by some one in a subsequent age, who was desirous to exalt the authority of the bishops?

3. These Epistles contain some exceedingly erroneous opinions, which I can scarcely believe would have been held by Ignatius. He affirms distinctly, that even the holy angels require to believe in the blood of Christ, that they may be saved from condemnation.

"Let no man deceive himself," says he, in his Epistle to the Church of Smyrna: "both the things which are in heaven, and the glorious angels and princes, whether visible or invisible, if they believe not in the blood of Christ, it shall be to them to condemnation." And yet Paul declares in his Epistle to the Hebrews, that the Redeemer "took not on him the nature of angels," or rather, "laid not hold of them" to save them from misery, "but he laid hold on the seed of Abraham." He says also to the Church of Tralles, "My soul be your expiation not only now, but when I shall have attained unto God, for I am yet under danger." And he says to the Ephesians, "*My soul be for yours*, and I myself the expiatory offering for your Church of Ephesus, so famous throughout the world." But in what sense he could represent himself as an expiation to God, after he had been received into heaven, for men upon earth, without being chargeable with blasphemy, I cannot comprehend. And in opposition to the original institution of marriage, the example of some of the Apostles, and the declaration of Paul, that "marriage is honourable in all," he approves of celibacy. "If any man," says he, in his Epistle to Polycarp, "can remain in a virgin state, to the honour of the flesh of Christ, let him remain without boasting; but if he boast, he is undone. And if he desire to be more taken notice of than the bishop, he is corrupted." As we have no evidence, however, that this doctrine was introduced at so early a period into the Christian Church, I consider it as presenting a strong presumption that the Epistle must have been interpolated, and indeed the whole of it is pronounced by Usher to be spurious.

I have only farther to remark, in the language of Ernesti, that "there are Latin words in these Epistles which no Greek writer in the first and second century used, but which began to be used by Greek writers in the seventh and eighth centuries. For instance, δεσεϱτωϱ, for which all the writers of those times used αποσαλης, as is done in the New Testament; αxxεπλα, σεποσελα, and others which are found in no Greek writer of that age."* And when Dr. Hammond had replied to this objection, that "many more Latin words occur in the New Testament than are used in these Epistles," Dr. Owen answered, that "there is scarce one but it is expressive of some Roman office, custom, money, order, or the like: words which pass as proper names from one country and language to another, or are indeed *of a pure Greek original*, or at least were in common use in that age, neither of which can be spoken of the words above mentioned used in the Epistles." And he adds, "I would indeed gladly see a fair, candid, and ingenuous defence of the style and

* "Vocabula Latina quae sec. 1. et 2. nemo Graecus scriptorum usurpavit, sed quae demum a scriptoribus Graecis, sec 7 et 8 usurpari coepta sunt, v. c. δεσερτωρ, pro quo scriptores horum temporum omnes dicunt αποσαλης, ut etiam dicitur in N T. ακκεπλα, σεποσελα, et alia, quae apud nullum scriptorem Graecum hujus aevi reperiuntur"

He gives the following brief and candid account of the different writers who have taken opposite sides in the controversy about these Epistles.

"Extitit vero etiam authentiae harum epistolarum defensor, Pearsonius, Episcopus Cestrensis, qui vindicias earum edidit, imprimis contra Blondellum. Verum etsi hic liber bene est scriptus, tamen rationes ejus non sufficiunt. Accessit etiam Hammondus in dissertationibus tam supra laudatis quas imprimis Blondello opposuit. Oudinus in Comment. de Script Eccles, tom 1 p 86, quo etiam inde a pagina 89 usque ad 142 contra authentiam harum epistolarum disputat. Etiam La Roque opusculum de hac re scripsit, contra quem Bullus scripsit in defensione fidei Nicenae." (He happens to omit Bishop Beveridge) "Quod autem ad controversiam ipsam attinet non potest negari plerosque viros doctos hac in controversia cupidius esse versatos. Nam *Episcopalium multum intererat authentiam harum epistolarum defendere, ut dignitatem suam atque auctoritatem retinerent.* Presbyteriani cupiditate abrepti saepe argumentis earum authentiam oppugnabant quae valere non possent, quam ob rem utraque pars in hac disputatione modum excessit. Sed aliam quoque ob causam nonnulli coeperunt authentium harum epistolarum simpliciter negare, nempe, quia in iis insunt diserta testimonia divinitatis Jesu Christi. Sociniani vero et Ariani divinitatem Christi negant, ideoque has epistolas simpliciter rejiciunt; imprimis cum Zwickerus unus ex eorum familia contendisset dogma de divinitate Christi esse novum, tribus prioribus seculis ignotum, et in Concilio Nicaeno inventum. Verum ideo nonnulli de orthodoxis nimis cupide authentiam epistolarum Ignatii defenderunt, nec tam incommoda quam potius utilitatem hujus defensionis spectarunt, in quo vehementer errant. *Nam tali in re defendenda neque utilitas neque incommoda spectari debent, sed ut veritas rei postulat, judicandum est.*"

manner of writing used in these Epistles, departing so eminently from any that was customary in the writings of the men of those daies; for truly, notwithstanding any thing that hitherto I have been able to obtaine for help in this kind, I am enforced to incline to Vedelius his answers to all the particular instances given of this nature, (barbarisms, rhyming expressions, &c.) this and that place is corrupted: this is from Clemens's Constitutions, this from this or that tradition; which also would much better free these Epistles from the word σιγης, used in the sense whereunto it was applied by the Valentinians, long after the death of Ignatius, than any other apologie, I have as yet seen, for the securing of its abode in them."* But if, as appears from this and the preceding considerations, there is reason to believe that these Epistles have been corrupted, it destroys at once every thing like an argument, which could be brought from their statements, even though they had been the most precise and explicit, for diocesan Episcopacy.

And, in short, I would remark, that even though we should waive the whole of these objections, and admit that these Epistles were perfectly genuine, the power which they ascribe to those early bishops by no means corresponds to that which is possessed in the present day by diocesan bishops. Not a word is mentioned about confirmation or ordination; and all that is said of their ecclesiastical authority might be affirmed of them as the moderators or standing presidents of the presbyteries of the Churches. The Bishop of the Magnesians is represented, indeed, in Archbishop Wake's translation, as the governor of that Church; but the word *governor* is not in the original. If the members of the Churches of Philadelphia and Smyrna are exhorted to have "a due regard to the bishop, and to refresh him, and attend to him," they are admonished "to attend also to the presbyters and to the deacons." If the Trallians are urged to reverence the bishop as God the Father, they are told

* Preface of his Treatise on the Perseverance of the Saints, p. 11.

also to reverence the presbyters as the Sanhedrim of God, and the College of the Apostles, his highest ministers. If the members of the Church of Smyrna are warned to "follow the bishop as Jesus Christ, the Father," they are directed to " follow the presbyters as the Apostles." If the Ephesians are required to be subject to the bishop, the same subjection is demanded "to the presbytery." And if they are commanded to " obey the bishop," they are enjoined to yield similar obedience to " the presbytery with entire affection." If Sotio, the deacon of the Magnesians, is represented as " subject unto his bishop as the grace of God," he is said to be " subject to the presbyters as to the law of Jesus Christ." If the Trallians are described as "subject to the bishop as to Jesus Christ," they are exhorted to be " subject also to the presbyters as to the Apostles of Jesus Christ;" and again, as they were to be " subject to their bishop as to the command of God, so likewise to the presbyters." And while the members of the Church of Smyrna are admonished in the Epistle to Polycarp to " submit to their bishop," the same submission is required to the presbyters.* The ecclesiastical court of these Churches is uniformly described by *a reference to the Sanhedrim*, for it is expressly denominated " the Sanhedrim of God;" and as the high-priest was merely the president of the ancient Sanhedrim, so the bishop in these Churches seems to have occupied only a similar place in the presbytery; and though nothing was to be done without his orders, as the head and representative of that body, yet no passage in the Epistles ascribes to him the smallest portion of power beyond what he might possess as the president or moderator of the council of presbyters.

And though he tells the Church of Tralles that they were to "do nothing without their bishop," and the Church of Smyrna, that " it was not lawful without the bishop, either to baptize, or to celebrate the

* If the bishop is said to preside over the Magnesians in the place of God, the presbyters are represented in the very same paragraph as " presiding over them."

holy communion," or, as others render the word, " to make a love-feast," and says to them, " Let no man do any thing of what belongs to the Church separately from the bishop," yet he uses similar language in regard to the presbyters. Thus, in his Epistle to the Trallians, he says, " He that is without, that is, that does any thing without the bishop, and presbyters, and deacons, is not pure in his conscience." And he says to the Magnesians, " Neither do ye any thing without your bishop and presbyters." "I exhort you that you study to do all things in a divine concord; your bishop presiding in the place of God; your presbyters in the place of the Council," or " Senate of the Apostles."—" Let there be nothing that may be able to make a division among you; but be ye united to your bishop, and those who preside over you, to be your pattern and direction on the way to immortality." In every point of view, therefore, the argument brought from the Epistles of Ignatius for diocesan Episcopacy appears to me to fail; and it is to a much later period in the history of the Church that you must look for a precedent for those extraordinary powers which you claim for your bishops.

I would only further remark, that the primacy which is ascribed to the Ignatian bishop is perfectly consistent with the strictest equality between him and the presbyters, as in the case not only of the president of the Sanhedrim, which is referred to in these Epistles, but of the presidents of other courts; for, as Cicero remarks in one of his orations, " when many are equal in dignity, one only can occupy the first place."*
And it is acknowledged by Whitaker, that "there may be primacy where there is no dominion, no pre-eminence in power, no prerogative of jurisdiction or authority."† And while the Ignatian bishop is represented as teaching or preaching, which, according to

* " Quum multi pares dignitate sint, unus tamen primum locum solus potest obtinere." Pro Murena.
† "Primatum esse posse ubi nullus sit dominatus, nullum imperium, nulla omnino jurisdictionis aut juris praerogativa." Controv. 4, quaest. 2, cap. 10.

Hooper, (Declaration of Christ and his offices, chap. III.) "is *the chiefest part* of the bishope's office, and most diligently and streightly commandid by God," though seldom performed by your bishops, the extent of his charge bore no proportion to that of the prelates in your National Church. It would appear that though there might be several congregations in Ephesus, yet they met with the bishop at the celebration of the communion, and received it along with him. "Let no man," says he to that Church, "deceive himself; if a man be not within the altar, he is deprived of the *bread* of God. For if the prayer of one or two be of such force as we are told, how much more powerful shall that of the bishop and the whole Church be. He therefore that does not come together into the same place with it, is proud, and has already condemned himself." And in the 20th paragraph he represents them as "breaking one and the same bread, which is the medicine of immortality," along with the bishop and the presbyters. In like manner he describes the Magnesians as "coming together into the same place" with the bishop and presbyters, "having one common prayer, one supplication, one mind, one hope, in charity and in joy undefiled." And he says to the Church in Philadelphia, " Wherefore let it be your endeavour to partake all of the same holy Eucharist, for there is but one flesh of our Lord Jesus Christ, and one cup in the unity of his blood; one altar; as also there is one bishop, together with his presbytery, and the deacons, my fellow-servants; that so, whatever ye do, ye may do it according to the will of God." Does this resemble the charge of a modern bishop? Could the whole of the communicants in the diocese of London, or Lincoln, or Durham, or even Edinburgh or Glasgow, meet with their respective bishops and presbyters, and participate together in one place of the holy Eucharist? And amidst all that you say of the superior advantages which are possessed by the members of Episcopalian Churches, is it not evident from this fact, that they are in a very different state as to episcopal superintendence from the primitive Churches, even in the age which succeeded that of the Apostles?

I remain, Reverend Sir, Yours, &c.

LETTER XXIII.

No allusion to the powers of diocesan bishops in the writings of Hermas — Nor any notice of such ministers, or of the sign of the cross in baptism, or of confirmation, by Justin Martyr —No reference to them by Irenaeus, who speaks of the ministers who maintained a succession of sound doctrine from the time of the Apostles in the different Churches, alternately as presbyters and bishops —The Churches of Gaul describe him as a presbyter, nine years after he was a Bishop of Lyons, in the Epistle which they sent with him to the Bishop of Rome, considering it as the most honourable name which they could give him —Irenaeus represents Polycarp as a presbyter —No such powers as those of diocesan bishops ascribed to bishops in the writings of Clemens of Alexandria, or Tertullian, or Origen —Examination of the writings of Cyprian, whose language respecting the dignity of bishops, is frequently extravagant —Proofs of his erring grievously on other subjects, so that it would not be wonderful if he had erred also on this —Evidence, however, even from his Epistles and other writings of the early Christians, that presbyters both in his day, and for some time afterwards, could not only ordain, but sit in councils and even preside in them —Passages in Cyprian's writings which furnish more plausible arguments, not only for bishops, but for a Pope, than any which are to be found in the preceding Fathers

Reverend Sir,—The references which occur in the writings of Hermas, usually denominated the Shepherd, to the orders in the ministry, are so vague and general, that it is scarcely worth while to notice them. In his second vision he represents the old woman who appeared to him as inquiring whether "he had sent her book to the elders of the Church," and enjoining him to " write two books, and send one to Clement, (who is commonly understood to be Clemens Romanus,) and one to Grapte. For Clement was to send it to foreign cities, because it was permitted him so to do; and Grapte was to admonish the widows and orphans; but he (Hermas) was to read in that city, (supposed by some to mean Rome,) with the elders of the Church;" from which it would seem that the presbyters or elders were the chief ministers of the Church. And though he says in his third vision, that "the square and white stones" were, as he informs us, "the

Apostles, and bishops, and doctors, and ministers;" yet it is evident that the term doctor applies to the bishops, and refers to another part of their duty; for in his ninth similitude he mentions only two orders of ministers, bishops and deacons, as placed over the Church, as its ordinary ministers, and consequently he would contradict himself if the term doctors in his third vision represented presbyters as distinct from bishops. "As concerning the tenth mountain," says he in that similitude, "in which were trees that covered the cattle, they are such as have believed, certain bishops, that is, persons set over the Churches, (praesides ecclesiarum,) and then such as are set over the services, (praesides ministeriorum,) who have protected the poor and widows." And while he never elsewhere, as far as I have discovered, speaks of Apostles, and bishops, and doctors, and ministers, he repeatedly speaks of Apostles and doctors, meaning evidently the order of ministers, who were distinct from deacons. Thus, in similitude 4, sect. 16, it is said, " The forty stones are the Apostles of the preaching of the Son of God." In the following section they are said to mean "the Apostles and doctors of the preaching of the name of the Son of God." And in section 25, he speaks of those who "believed the Apostles, and certain doctors who sincerely preached the word." But his writings throughout are so destitute of precision, and so feeble and puerile, that it is impossible to derive from them any distinct information respecting the orders in the ministry in the early Church.

The next of the fathers was Justin Martyr, whose celebrated Apology for the primitive Christians, presented to Antoninus Pius, according to Page, Basnage, and Lardner, in 139, and to Blondel, in 150, contains the following account of the ministers and worship of the Christian Church: "We bring him who is convinced, and who embraces our principles, to the place where the brethren, so called, are assembled for common prayers, both for themselves, the illuminated (baptized) individual, and all others every where;

which prayers we offer with earnest desires that we may be accepted, and may be saved with an everlasting salvation. Prayers being ended, we salute one another with a holy kiss. Bread, and a cup of water and wine, are then brought to the president of the brethren, (προεςωτι;) and he receiving them, gives praise and thanks to the Father of all things, through the name of the Son and the Holy Spirit, and he continues long in giving thanks that we are thought worthy of these blessings. The president having given thanks, and the whole people having expressed their approbation, those who are called among us deacons, (διακονοι,) give to those who are present bread and wine mixed with water, after they have been consecrated with thanksgiving, and carry them to those who are absent. This food is called among us the Eucharist, of which no one is permitted to participate, unless he believes those things to be true which have been taught by us, and has been washed in the laver that is for the remission of sins and regeneration, and so lives as Christ has prescribed."*

And again, he observes, " Upon Sunday, all those who reside in cities and in the country meet together, and the writings of the apostles and prophets are read. And the reader having finished, the president addresses them, and exhorts them to the practice of those things which are comely. We then rise and unite in prayer. And, as we have mentioned, when it is finished, bread and wine mixed with water are brought, and the president gives thanks, &c. Those who are wealthy, and willing, contribute as they are severally disposed; and it is deposited in the hands of the president, who assists orphans, widows, those who are in want from sickness or any other cause, those who are in bonds, and strangers who come from other places."†

If this, however, was a faithful description of the constitution and services of the primitive Church in

* " Επειτα προσφερεται τω προεστωτι," &c.
† " Τη του ηλιου λεγομενη ημερα παντων κατα πολεις η αγρους μενοντων επι το αυτο," &c.

the days of Justin, it does not present the faintest resemblance of diocesan Episcopacy, either in the orders of its clergy, or its rites and ceremonies. The highest of its ministers was the president of a congregation which met for worship *in one place*, either in the cities or in the country, and not a word is mentioned of *his ruling over presbyters*, or of his being of a superior order. Nor is there the slightest reference to the sign of the cross in baptism, or to the rite of confirmation, as administered by the hands of any minister before those who had been baptized were admitted to the Eucharist. It follows, of course, that this celebrated Apology, though presented publicly to the Roman Emperor, and capable of being detected as to all its omissions, kept back an important part of the truth; or diocesan bishops, and these rites and ceremonies, did not then exist. Or, at all events, it is obvious, that to whomsoever you appeal in support of that order, and these unwarrantable additions to the divine institutions, it cannot be to Justin.

Nor is the testimony of Irenaeus, the Bishop of Lyons, whose work against heresies, according to Baronius, was written in the year 180, and according to Blondel, in 185, at all more favourable to diocesan Episcopacy. He speaks, indeed, in some passages of the orthodox doctrine having been preserved in the different Churches by a succession of orthodox bishops from the time of the Apostles; but he never says that *they were invested with the powers of diocesan bishops,* nor mentions even a single instance in which any of them exercised them. And yet, till this is proved, no argument can be deduced in support of Episcopacy from his denominating them bishops. Besides, while he says in one place that the faith was preserved by succession of bishops, he tells us in another that it was preserved *by successions of presbyters;* plainly intimating, as was formerly observed, that he considered presbyters as bishops, and that he looked upon the presbyter, who was called bishop by way of eminence, as nothing more, as Hilary says, than the president or moderator of the council of presbyters, or the first among his equals. Thus, while he says, (book iii. ch. 3,) "We can enumerate those *who were constituted bishops* by the Apostles in the Churches, and *their successors, even to us*, who taught no such thing,"* he says, (book iii ch. 2,) " When we challenge them (the heretics) to that apostolical tradition which is preserved in the Churches through *the succession of the presbyters*, they oppose the tradition, pretending that they are wiser than *not only the presbyters*, but the Apostles also."† While he says, (book iv. ch. 53,) " True knowledge is the doctrine of the Apostles, according to *the succession of bishops*, to whom they delivered the Church in every place, which doctrine has reached us, preserved in its most full delivery," he says in the 43d chapter, " *Obey those presbyters in the Church who have succession, as we have shown, from the Apostles*, who, with the succession of the episcopate, received the gift of truth, according to the good pleasure of the Father."‡ While he says, (book v. ch. 20,) " These are far later than the bishops, to whom the Apostles delivered the Churches; and this we have carefully made manifest in the third book;"§ he says, (book iv ch. 44,) " We ought therefore to adhere *to those presbyters* who keep the Apostles' doctrine, and together with the order of the presbyterate, (cum oidine presbyterii,) show forth sound speech. *Such presbyters* the Church nourishes; and of *such* the prophet says, I will give them princes in peace, and *bishops* in righteousness." While in his 3d book, ch. 3, he says, " The Apostles, founding and instructing that Church, (the Church of Rome,) delivered to Linus the

---

* " Et habemus annumerare eos qui ab Apostolis instituti sunt episcopi," &c.

† "Cum autem ad eam iterum traditionem, quae est ab Apostolis, quae per successiones presbyterorum in ecclesiis custoditur provocamus eos," &c.

‡ " Quapropter eis qui in ecclesia sunt presbyteris obaudire oportet, his qui successionem habent ab Apostolis, sicut ostendimus, qui cum episcopatus successione, charisma veritatis certum," &c.

§ " Omnes enim ii valde posteriores sunt quam episcopi, quibus Apostoli tradiderunt ecclesias."

episcopate; Anacletus succeeded him; after him Clemens obtained the episcopate from the Apostles; to Clement succeeded Evaristus; to him, Alexander; then Xystus; and after him Telesphorus; then Hyginus; after him Pius; then Anicetus: and when Soter had succeeded Anicetus, then Eleutherius had the episcopate in the twelfth place;" in his Epistle to Victor, Bishop of Rome, he represents the whole of them, as well as Victor himself, as presbyters. "*Those presbyters*, (in the Church of Rome,) before Soter," says he, "who governed the Church which thou now governest, I mean Anicetus, Pius, Hyginus, Telesphorus, and Xystus, they did not observe it, (*i. e.* the day on which Victor observed Easter) And *those presbyters who preceded you*, though they did not observe it themselves, yet sent the Eucharist to those (presbyters) of other Churches who did observe it. And when blessed Polycarp, in the days of Anicetus, came to Rome, he did not much persuade Anicetus to observe it, as he (*i. e.* Anicetus) declared that the custom *of the presbyters who were his predecessors* should be retained."* Unless, therefore, you maintain that Irenaeus did not know how to express his sentiments, and that his language is destitute of every thing like precision, I consider it to be plain, from a comparison of those passages, that he looked upon the bishops who succeeded the Apostles in the different Churches, till the age in which he wrote, *merely as presbyters;* or if there was any difference between them and the rest of the presbyters, it was that merely of those who were the moderators or presidents of the councils of presbyters in the several Churches.

And this was not the opinion of Irenaeus only, but of the Churches of Gaul; for when they sent him, nine years after he was bishop of Lyons, to Eleutherius of Rome, and gave him a recommendatory letter to that Prelate, the highest title which they bestowed on him was that of "*a presbyter of the Church*, πρεσβυτερον εκκλησιας;" and the terms in which the presbyters

---

* Euseb Hist Eccles., lib. v. cap. 24.

spoke of him were, that he was "their brother and colleague."* Upon which Stillingfleet remarks, "that it seems very improbable, that when they were commending one to the bishop of another Church, they should make use of the lowest name of honour, then appropriated to subject presbyters, which instead of commending, were a great debasing of him, if they had looked on a superior order above those presbyters as of divine institution, and thought there had been so great a distance between a bishop and subject presbyters as we are made to believe there was: which is, as if the master of a college in one university should be sent by the fellows of his society to the heads of the other, and should, in his commendatory letters to them, be styled a senior fellow of that house. Would not any one that read this imagine that there was no difference between a senior fellow and a master, but only a primacy of order; *that he was the first of the number without any power over the rest?* This was the case of Irenaeus. He is supposed to be Bishop of the Church of Lyons,—he is sent by the Church of Lyons on a message to the Bishop of Rome, when, notwithstanding his being a bishop, they call him *presbyter of that Church*, (when there were other presbyters who were not bishops;) what could any one imagine by the reading of it, but that the bishop was nothing else but their senior presbyter, or one that had *a primacy of order among*, but no divine right to *a power of jurisdiction over his fellow presbyters?*"† And the same, too, were the views which were entertained by Irenaeus of the rank of Polycarp, whom Episcopalians represent as a diocesan bishop; for after telling Florinus, whose heretical opinion he had been condemning, "this doctrine, *such as were presbyters before us*, (πρεσβυτεροι προ εμου,) and disciples of the Apostles, never delivered unto thee;" and after referring to Polycarp, he adds, "I am able to testify before God, that if *that holy and apostolical presbyter* (αποστολικος πρεσβυτερος) had heard

---

* Euseb. Hist. Eccles., lib iv. cap 5, who quotes the Epistle.
† Irenicum, p. 311, 312.

any such thing, he would at once have reclaimed and stopped his ears, and after his manner cried out, Good God! to what times hast thou reserved me?"* But if the highest rank which he assigns to Polycarp was that of a presbyter, and if the highest title which was given to himself by the presbyters of Lyons, in their commendatory letter to the Bishop of Rome, was the name of "a presbyter of their Church, and their brother and colleague," you will appeal in vain to him or to them to show that at that time diocesan bishops, or an order of ministers superior to presbyters, existed in the Church.

The reference to the different orders in the ministry in the writings of Clement of Alexandria, which were published either in the end of the second or in the beginning of the third century, are so few and indistinct, that it is difficult to ascertain his opinion. You meet, indeed, with one passage, (Stromata, lib. vi.) where he mentions the three names of bishops, presbyters and deacons; and with another in his Paedagogus, (lib. iii. cap. 12, p. 194,) where he puts presbyters before bishops, and says, "very many commands relative to particular persons are written in the sacred books, some to presbyters, some to bishops, some to deacons, and some to widows." But he never points out the difference between bishops and presbyters, nor represents the former as possessing exclusively the powers of ordination, confirmation, and government, like modern bishops, nor says even a word from which it can be inferred that they were any thing but the standing moderators or presidents of the councils of presbyters. On the contrary, he represents himself, though he was only a presbyter, and all who were pastors, as governing the Churches; for, says he, (Paedag. lib. i. p. 120.) "If *we who bear rule over the Churches* are shepherds or pastors after the image of the Good Shepherd," &c. And in the eleventh chapter of the same book, (p. 182,) he tells us that presbyters gave imposition of hands, whether for confirmation or mere bene-

* Euseb. Hist. Eccles. lib. v. cap 20.

diction does not appear; for, says he, "On whom does the presbyter lay his hand, (τινι γαρ πρεσβυτερος επιτιθησι χειρα, &c.) whom does he bless?" He says, (Strom. lib iii) that Paul declares it "to be necessary, that those should be appointed bishops, who, from ruling their own house, were prepared for ruling the whole Church;" but he never specifies the extent of their powers; and though he speaks, (Strom. lib. vi.) of "a presbyter, who, though a righteous man, had not attained the chief seat on earth, (προκαθεδρια,") yet there is no evidence that it was any thing but the seat of the president, or moderator of the presbyters. Nay, as far as we can discover his sentiments, he appears to have thought there were only two orders, presbyters or bishops, and deacons. Thus, in the third book of his Stromata, after quoting the words of Paul in 1 Tim. v. 14, 15, he adds, "But he must be the husband of one wife only, whether he be a presbyter, or deacon, or layman, if he would use matrimony without blame." And in book seventh, he says, "Of that service of God, about which men are employed, one is that which makes them better, (βελτιωτικη); the other, that which is ministerial, (υπερετικη) *Presbyters maintain that form of service in the Church which makes men better;* deacons that form which is ministerial. In both these ministries the angels, as well as he who is endowed with knowledge, serve God, according to the dispensation of earthly things." Nor is it any objection to this, that he says in the sixth book of his Stromata, as Episcopalians have often asserted, "Now, in the Church here, the progressions (προκοπας) of bishops, presbyters, deacons, I think are imitations of the angelical glory, and of that dispensation which the Scriptures declare they look for who have lived according to the Gospel in the perfection of righteousness, walking in the steps of the Apostle. These men, the Apostle writes, being taken up into the clouds, shall first serve as deacons, and shall then be admitted among the presbyters, according to the progression in glory." If he considered the progressions among the ministers of the

Church in the present world, as imitations of *the two degrees of glory* which shall be bestowed upon the angels in heaven, corresponding either to the higher services which they rendered to men upon earth, (as he says, book vii.) resembling those of presbyters, or to the lower services, resembling those of deacons, then it is plain that he must have looked upon these progressions among the ministers of the Church in this world as extending merely to *the two offices* of presbyters and deacons, the discharge of which led to the performance of these two kinds of service, which were copied by the angels. And as he does not speak of *a third kind of service*, or that of diocesan bishops, something like to which was rendered by the angels, it is evident that he could not intend to represent these prelates *as a third order or progression in the Church on earth*. And this is confirmed by the fact, that he describes the faithful ministers of the Gospel, after they are caught up together in the clouds, as minis tering first only as deacons in the heavenly temple and then promoted to be presbyters, after which they never rise to any higher order; for *if he regarded presbyters as the principal order in the Church in heaven*, he must undoubtedly have looked upon them, as far as we can judge, *as the principal order in the Church on earth.*

Little occurs in the writings of Tertullian bearing on the question. In his work against the heretics, he appeals to the successions of bishops in the different churches, from the age of the Apostles till his own day, in proof of the truth of the doctrine which was taught in the orthodox churches; but *he does not specify the powers which were exercised by these bishops*, so as to enable us to judge whether they were of a superior order to presbyters. And the following is the account which he gives of the rulers of the Church in the end of the second century: " In the Church," says he, in his Apology for the Christians, (and I quote his words, as they are translated by Usher in his Reduced Scheme of Episcopacy, that I may not be suspected of giving a turn to the passage to favour my own views,) "are used exhortations, chastisements and divine censure; for judgment is given with great advice, as among those who are certain they are in the sight of God; and in it is the chiefest foreshowing of the judgment which is to come, if any man have so offended that he is banished from the communion of prayer, and of the assembly, and of all holy fellowship. The presidents that bear rule therein are certain approved elders" or presbyters, " who have obtained this honour, not by reward, but by good report;"* " who were no other," says the Archbishop, "as he intimates elsewhere, (de Corona Militis, cap. 3,) but those from whose hands they used to receive the sacrament of the Eucharist." But if these presidents were seniors or presbyters, who were pastors of churches, and administered the communion to their members, and if he never mentions any order above them, though he denominates their moderator or chairman " the chief priest," who first had authority to baptize *for the honour of the Church*, and after him the presbyters and deacons, (de Baptismo, cap. 17,) you will look in vain also to him for support to the cause of diocesan Episcopacy.

The view which is presented of the orders in the ministry in the writings of Origen, who flourished towards the middle of the third century, are by no means clear. Sometimes he speaks as if there were only two orders, that of the presbyters or priest, and that of the deacons, whom he compares to the Levites. Thus, in his second Homily on Numbers, (tom. ii. p. 203,) he says, " Let a man walk according to his order. Do you think that those who are appointed to the office of the priesthood, and who glory in the order of the priesthood, walk according to their order, and do all things which are worthy of that order? And in like manner, do you think that the deacons walk according to the order of their ministry? Whence, then, is it that you often hear men speaking ill of them, and saying, See what a bishop, or what a presbyter, or what a deacon! Are not these things

* Apology, cap. 39.

said, when a priest or a minister of God is seen to behave in a way which is contrary to his order, and to perform any thing unworthy of the priestly or levitical order?"* where he evidently represents priests or presbyters and bishops as belonging to the same order. And he says again in his fourth Homily on Joshua, (tom. 1. p. 327,) "The priestly and levitical order is that which stands near the ark of the testimony of the Lord, in which the law of God is carried; and they enlighten the people respecting the commands of God, as the prophet says, Thy word is a lamp to my feet, and a light to my paths. This light is kindled by the priests and Levites."† And yet he mentions in other passages bishops, presbyters and deacons, as in his sixth Homily on Isaiah, (tom 1. p. 635,) where he says, "No deacon, or presbyter, or bishop, taking a linen cloth, washes the feet of those who come to him."‡ And he refers to them else-

---

* "Homo ergo secundum ordinem suum incedat. Putasne qui sacerdotio funguntur, et in sacerdotali ordine gloriantur," &c.

† "Sacerdotalis et Leviticus ordo est qui assistit arcae testamenti Domini, in qua lex Dei portatur," &c

‡ "Nemo enim quibuscunque venientibus assumens linteum, diaconus, vel presbyter, sive episcopus lavat pedes."

He says indeed, in his fifth Homily on Ezekiel, tom 1. p. 715, "Those who are connected with the Church, and who have tasted of the word of God and transgress it, deserve to be punished; but it ought to be according to their different degrees in the Church. He who presides over the Church, and sins, must be visited with heavier punishment. A catechumen deserves more clemency than one of the faithful, a laic than a deacon, and a deacon than a presbyter Omnes enim qui in ecclesia peccatores sunt, qui sermonem Dei gustaverunt, merentur quidem supplicia," &c. But still the language is general, and conveys no definite idea of the powers of the president, and does not even enable us to judge whether he was more than the president, if not of a congregation, at least of a council of presbyters

He says, too, when interpreting the word "ἡγουμενος, chief, in Luke xxii. 26," so I think he may be termed, who, "in the Church, is called bishop." But what the powers of that minister were he does not say; and sometimes he represents even a whole church as meeting in a private house. Thus, he says of Gaius, in his Commentary on Romans xvi. 23, that he was "a hospitable man, who not only received Paul and other Christians to share of his kindness, but afforded *to the whole Church* a place of meeting in his house Ecclesiae universae in domo sua conventiculum ipse praebuerit." He says, too, " If Jesus Christ, the Son of God, is subject to Joseph and Mary, shall not I be subject to the bishop, who of God is ordained to be my

where in his eleventh Homily on Jeremiah, (tom. i. p. 679,) and eighth on Ezekiel, p. 726; as well as in his Homilies on Matt. xv. 19, (tom. ii. p. 29 and 88.) But whether bishops differed from presbyters any further than the first among equals, *primi inter pares*, and what was the extent of their powers, if they were of a superior order, I have not been able to ascertain.

I intended to have examined at considerable length the different statements respecting the office of bishops which are to be met with in the writings of Cyprian, Bishop of Carthage, who flourished from A. D. 248 to A. D. 260; but as my remarks on the works of the preceding fathers have exceeded the limits within which I had hoped to restrict them, I must do it at

father? Shall not I be subject to the presbyter, who by the divine appointment is set over me?" But it is evident from what he says in his third book against Celsus, who had represented the Christians as excluding from their communion all learned and prudent men, that he understood by a bishop, a pastor or teacher. "It is evident," says he, " that Paul, in his account of those whom he calls bishops, describing what manner of man a bishop ought to be, requires that *he must be a teacher*, saying, that *a bishop must be able to convince the gainsayers*, to the end that by his wisdom he may stop the mouths of vain talkers and seducers. And as he prefers in his choice of a bishop one who is the husband of one wife, before him who has married a second time, and one who is blameless before him that is faulty, and a vigilant man before him that is not so, and a sober man before one who is not sober, and a modest man before a less modest, so he wills that a bishop duly constituted be apt to teach, and able to convince the gainsayers." And though he says, "there is a debt peculiar to widows maintained by the Church, a debt peculiar to deacons, and another peculiar to presbyters, but of all these peculiar debts, that which is due by the bishop is the greatest. It is exacted by the Saviour of the whole Church, and the bishop must smart severely for it if it is not paid," yet Jamieson, in his Cyprianus Isotimus, remarks upon it, p 410, " as if Origen could not judge, that he to whom the Church had committed the chief care of affairs was to account to God for more than were others. Might not the ancients think that the archdeacon was accountable for more than were the rest? Did they therefore believe that he, as contradistinguished from other deacons, was of divine institution? Now, that there was pretty early an archdeacon, who had a power over the other deacons, appears plain from Hierome's Epistle to Evagrius; and this he never doubted to be either lawful or expedient." To what extent, however, the power of the bishop was superior to that of the presbyters, or the power of the archdeacon to that of the deacons, does not appear.

26

present more briefly. And here I would observe, that the terms in which he speaks of it are certainly more lofty than those which were employed by any of his predecessors; for even Milner, who, I think, delineates his character too favourably, and extenuates his faults, is forced to acknowledge, that " there are some expressions savouring of haughtiness and asperity to be found in his writings; and that the episcopal authority, through the gradual growth of superstition, was naturally advancing to *an excess of dignity.*"* He speaks, for instance, of the episcopal office as "the lofty summit of the priesthood;† (though no such expressions are applied in Scripture even to the office of an Apostle;) of the vigour of the episcopate, and the sublime and divine power of governing the Church;"‡ of " the honour of the bishop,§ and of the honour of his priesthood and chair;"‖ and he orders a deacon who had offended his bishop to "honour him, and with full humility or prostration, to make satisfaction to him;"¶ while the Roman clergy, in their letter to Cyprian, say that it was time that the lapsed, *" by rendering the honour which was due to the priest of God, should obtain for themselves the divine mercy."*** Nay, he represents bishops as the successors of the Apostles,†† and says, that "through the courses of times and successions the ordination of

---

* Milner's Church History, vol. i p. 457.

† "Sacerdotii sublime fastigium." Epist. 52

‡ "Actum est de episcopatus vigore, et de Ecclesiæ gubernandæ sublimi et divina potestate." Epist 55.

§ "Nec honorem episcopi cogitantes" Epist. 11.

‖ "Nec episcopo honorem sacerdotii sui et cathedræ reservantes." Epist. 12.

¶ "Honorem sacerdotis agnoscere, et episcopo præposito suo plena humilitate satisfacere " Epist. 65.

** "De honore debito in Dei sacerdotem eliciant in se divinam misericordiam" Epist 30 In his fifty eighth Epistle, he represents presbyters as united with the bishop in the honour of the priesthood, but what their portion of it was he does not say. " Qui cum episcopo presbyteri sacerdotali honore conjuncti."

†† " Hæc enim," he observes to Cornelius in his forty-second Epistle, " vel maxime frater et laboramus, et laborare debemus, ut unitatem a Domino et per Apostolos nobis successoribus traditam, quantum possumus, obtinere curemus."

bishops, and the order of the Church, descends to us, so that the Church *is constituted upon the bishops,* and every act of the Church is regulated by the same rulers; that the Church is constituted on the bishop and clergy, and all who stand steadfast in their Christian profession;"* that " the bishop is in the Church, and the Church in the bishop; and that if any one is not in the bishop, he is not in the Church."† And while such is the place which is assigned to bishops, he tells us at the same time that the Church is founded on the Apostle Peter, and has only one ruler; and makes use of expressions, on which the Papists found very plausible arguments for the supremacy of the Pope, as the successor of Peter, and the one universal bishop, of which there is no example in the earlier fathers. Thus, in his seventieth Epistle, he says, " There is one Church founded by Christ the Lord, the origin and principle of unity, upon Peter."‡ And again, in his seventy-third Epistle, " The Church, which is one, is, by the declaration of the Lord, founded also upon one who received its keys."§ Justly, therefore, might Whitaker say of Episcopacy, which had been adopted as a preventive of schism, (and Heylin observes, that he was a zealous defender of your Church against Cartwright,) that " the remedy was well nigh worse than the disease itself; for, as at the first, one presbyter was set over the rest of the presbyters, and made a bishop; so afterwards, one bishop was set over the rest of the bishops. Thus, that custom hatched the Pope with his monarchy, and by degrees brought him into the Church." Nor will these extravagant expressions about the power

* " Inde per temporum et successionum vices episcoporum ordinatio, et Ecclesiæ ratio decurrit, ut Ecclesia super episcopos constituatur, et omnis actus Ecclesiæ per eosdem præpositos gubernetur. Ecclesia in episcopo et clero, et in omnibus stantibus sit constituta." Epist 27.

† " Episcopum in Ecclesia esse, et Ecclesiam in episcopo, et si quis cum episcopo non sit, in Ecclesia non esse " Epist. 69.

‡ " Una Ecclesia a Christo Domino super Petrum origine unitatis et ratione fundata."

§ " Quæ una est, et supra unum qui et claves ejus accepit, Domini voce fundata est."

and dignity of bishops appear at all wonderful, when you consider what erroneous sentiments he expressed on other subjects, and what corruptions he sanctioned in the early Church. He states it, for instance, to have been his own opinion, and that of a council of sixty-six bishops, at which he was present, that the baptism of infants was essential to their salvation; for, says he, " as the Son of man came not to destroy the souls of men, but to save them, as far as depends on us, if it (salvation) can be procured for them, (infants,) no soul ought to be lost."* He thought, that while the blood of Christ obtained for men the pardon of the sins which they had committed before baptism, almsgiving procured for them the forgiveness of those sins which they committed after baptism, and delivered them from eternal death. " Almsgiving," says he, (and this is overlooked by Milner, in his laudatory account of Cyprian,) " frees from death; not that death, our liability to which the blood of Christ once abolished, and from which the grace of baptism and of our Redeemer has rescued us, but from that which has crept upon us afterwards through our sins."† He approved of unction after baptism; for, says he in his seventieth Epistle, " it is necessary that he who is baptized should be anointed, that having received chrism, he may become by unction the anointed of God, and have the grace of Christ in himself."‡ He represents those who were baptized as brought *afterwards* to the bishop, that they might receive, through the laying on of his hands, the Holy Ghost, and *might be perfected* by his making on them the sign of the cross.§ He thought that the cup in

* " Quantum in nobis est, si fieri potest, nulla anima est perdenda." Epist. 59.

† " Eleemosyna a morte liberat, et non utique ab illa morte quam semel Christi sanguis extinxit, et aqua nos salutaris baptismi, et Redemptoris nostri gratia liberavit, sed ab ea, quæ per delicta post modum serpsit." Epist 52.

‡ " Ungi quoque necesse est eum qui baptizatus sit ut accepto chrismate, id est, unctione, esse unctus Dei, et habere in se gratiam Christi possit."

§ " Quod nunc quoque apud nos geritur, ut qui in ecclesia baptizantur præpositis ecclesiæ offerantur, et per nostram orationem ac

the Eucharist should contain wine and water; for, says he, "the cup of the Lord is not water only, or wine only, but both must be mingled, just as it is not the Lord's body, if it is flour only, or water only, but both must be united into one substance, and become one solid piece of bread."* And he sanctioned the practice of praying for the dead; for he says, in his sixty-sixth Epistle, that "it had been determined by the bishops, his predecessors, that if any one appointed a clergyman to act as a tutor for managing his secular affairs after his death, no offering should be made for him when he died, nor *any sacrifice for his repose.*"† If he was capable, however, of teaching such errors, and countenancing and recommending such corruptions, it is certainly not more surprising that he should have deviated so far from the doctrine of Scripture, and from the whole of the fathers who lived before him, in his pompous expressions about the dignity of bishops.

Still, however, it deserves to be mentioned, that whatever may be the lofty and unwarrantable claims which he advances occasionally in regard to the honour and authority of bishops, there is not a power which is possessed by the latter, that he or his correspondents do not acknowledge at other times might be exercised by presbyters. Thus he not only tells his clergy in his sixth Epistle, that from the very beginning of his episcopate he had resolved to do nothing from his own private opinion without their council and the consent of his people;‡ but in his fifth, which was written to them during his banishment, "he re-

manus impositionem Spiritum Sanctum consequantur, et signaculo Dominico *consummentur.*" Epist 73.

* "Calix Domini non est aqua sola, aut vinum solum, nisi utrumque sibi misceatur, quomodo nec corpus Domini potest esse farina sola, aut aqua sola, nisi utriumque adunatum fuerit, et copulatum, et panis unius compage solidatum." Epist. 63.

† "Ac si quis hoc fecisset non offerretur pro eo, nec sacrificium *pro dormitione ejus celebraretur*, neque enim apud altare Dei meretur nominari in sacerdotum prece qui ab altari sacerdotes et ministros voluit avocare."

‡ "Quando a primordio episcopatus mei statuerim nihil sine consilio vestro, et sine consensu plebis meae privata sententia gerere."

quests them to perform their own duty *and his*, that nothing which related *either to discipline* or diligence might be wanting."* In his seventeenth Epistle, he says, that he would not "prejudge the case of the lapsed, nor assume to himself the sole power of deciding respecting it, but would wait till he returned;"† and in his fifteenth, he mentions with approbation the presbyters and deacons of the Church of Rome who had exercised discipline, and displayed, as he expresses it, "the energy of the priesthood in restraining some who had rashly communicated with the lapsed."‡ In his thirty-third Epistle, he tells his presbyters that he was "always accustomed to consult them before he conferred orders," and apologizes to them for not doing it in the case of Aurelius, whom he had appointed to be a reader.§ And in his fourteenth, he says to them, that "trusting in their affection as well as religion, of which he had sufficient evidence, he both exhorted and commanded them by that letter, that those of them whose presence there might be least invidious, and attended with least danger, might perform his part in managing those things which the administration of religion required."‖ And in like manner, the presbyters of the Church of Rome who appear to have been without a bishop, say to the presbyters of the Church of Carthage, during Cyprian's exile, that "it was incumbent on us, (*i. e.* on both,) who seem to be set over the flock, to keep it in place

---

* " Peto vos pro fide et religione vestra fungamini illic et vestris partibus et meis, ut nihil vel ad disciplinam vel ad diligentiam desit "

† " Quae res cum omnium nostrum consilium et sententiam spectet, praejudicare ego et soli mihi rem communem vindicare non audeo," &c.

‡ " Presbyteris et diaconibus non defuit sacerdotii vigor ut quidam minus disciplinae memores, et temeraria festinatione præcipites, qui cum lapsis communicare jam coeperant comprimerentur."

§ " In ordinationibus clericis, fratres carissimi solemus vos ante consulere, et mores et merita singulorum communi consilio ponderare "

‖ " Fretus ergo et dilectione et religione vestra, quam satis novi, his literis et hortor et mando, ut vos quorum minime illic invidiosa, et non adeo periculosa praesentia est, vice mea fungamini circa gerenda ea quae administratio religiosa deposcit."

of the pastor or shepherd."* And says Firmilian, the Bishop of Caesarea, an intimate friend and correspondent of Cyprian, who could not fail to be acquainted with the powers which were at that time vested in presbyters, " All power and grace are established in the Church where elders (or presbyters) preside, who possess the power of baptizing and confirming, as well as of ordaining."† But if the presbyters of Carthage could perform not only their own duties, but *those of Cyprian*, during his long continued exile ;‡ and if it be stated by so distinguished a prelate as Firmilian, that presbyters in general possessed the powers of ordination and confirmation and were entitled to exercise them, it neutralises in a great measure the pompous descriptions of the episcopal dignity which are given by Cyprian; and it not only proves that the powers of presbyters at that early period were of a superior kind to those of presbyters in Episcopalian Churches in the present day, but makes it extremely probable, that when he speaks of the

* " Et incumbit nobis, qui videmur praepositi esse, et vice pastoris custodire gregem," &c

† "Omnis potestas et gratia in ecclesia constituta sit, ubi praesident majores natu, qui et baptizandi et manum imponendi, et *ordinandi possident potestatem.*" Upon which Rigaltius remarks, "Seniores et vere πρεσβυτεροι qui et baptizandi et manum imponendi *et ordinandi possident potestatem*, ordine sic ab ecclesia constituta. Sed quare hic non fit mentio offerendi, nisi quod tacite trium illorum potestate includitur ?"

‡ " If there be no Church without a bishop," says Stillingfleet, (Irenicum, p 376,) "where was the Church of Rome, when, from the martyrdome of Fabian, and the banishment of Lucius, the Church was governed only by the clergy? So the Church of Carthage, when Cyprian was banished; the Church of the East, when Meletius of Antioch, Eusebius Samosatenus, Pelagius of Laodicea, and the rest of the orthodox bishops were banished for ten years' space, and Flavianus and Diodorus, two presbyters, ruled the Church of Antioch the mean while. The Church of Carthage was twenty-four years without a bishop, in the time of Hunerick, King of the Vandals; and when it was offered them that they might have a bishop, upon admitting the Arians to the free exercise of their religion among them, their answer was upon those terms, Ecclesia Episcopum non delectatur habere; and Balsamon, speaking of the Christian Churches in the East, determines it neither safe nor necessary in their present state to have bishops set up over them " The whole of these Churches for that long period were governed by presbyters.

Church as established in the bishop, he regarded him merely as the president or chairman, and on some occasions, (if he alone ordained, like the president of the Sanhedrim,) as the representative of the presbyters.*

I cannot proceed further at present with this part of the subject, but shall only remark, that though bishops, after this, made gradual encroachments on the privileges of presbyters, the latter were allowed, even in the fourth century, to ordain priests and deacons, with the consent of their prelates, and bishops were enjoined to do nothing without consulting their presbyters. Thus, it is decreed in the thirteenth canon of the Council of Ancyra, held in the beginning of the fourth century, that " it be not lawful for chorepiscopi to ordain priests or deacons, nor for city presbyters in another parish, without the permission of the bishop;"† evidently implying, that if he gave them leave they might confer orders. Origen, though only a presbyter, is said to have been chosen to preside at a synod, held at Philadelphia, A. D. 327; and Malchion, a presbyter of Antioch, presided in the second council held in that city, A. D. 269, in which Paul of Samosata was condemned.‡ Thirty presbyters sat in judgment along with three hundred bishops, in the year 295, on Marcellinus, Bishop of Rome, who had apostatized and burnt in-

* The Rev Mr Sinclair remarks, after Sage, (Dissertation on Episcopacy, p. 82,) that " we read," in Cyprian's Epistles, " of bishops having a primacy, an absolute, arbitrary, sovereign jurisdiction, for which they are accountable to none but to our Lord Jesus Christ, who singly and solely has the power of preferring bishops to the government of his Church, and of calling them to account for the administration of it." But any one who is acquainted with the writings of this father will perceive that it is one of those pieces of rhodomontade about the power of bishops, in which he frequently indulges. Cyprian was aware that the Lord Jesus Christ called bishops to account, even in the present world, before councils or synods, which were composed not only of bishops, but presbyters, and in which, as will be immediately proved, the latter occasionally presided, and caused them, when their opinions were heretical, or their conduct schismatical or immoral, to be censured, and even deposed. Instances of this are mentioned in his Epistles

† "Χωρεπισκοπους μη εξειναι," &c.

‡ Letter from a Parochial Bishop to a Prelatical Gentleman, p. 39.

cense in the temple of Isis and Vesta, and pronounced sentence upon him.* Thirty-six presbyters subscribed

* "Hic Marcellinus convictus est, quod thurificasset in templo Isidis et Vestae, per Gaium et Innocentium diaconos, et Urbanum, Castorium et Juvenalem, presbyteros et per alios testes. Et tandem in Synodo 300 episcoporum et 30 presbyterorum caput cinere convolutum habens, Marcellinus, Episcopus urbis Romae, voce clara clamans dixit, Peccavi coram vobis, et non possum esse in ordine sacerdotum, quoniam avarus me corrupit auro. Et subscripserunt in ejus damnationem, et damnaverunt eum extra civitatem dicentes, quia ore suo condemnatus est, et ore suo anathematizatus, accepit maranatha." See Carranza's Summa Conciliorum.

"Marsilius Patavinus," says Jessop, in his Remarks on Episcopacy, p 55, "disputing concerning the order of priesthood, or of a presbyter, (for they are all one,) and the power of the keyes to bind and loose, observeth out of the forementioned father, (Jerome,) the Church hath these keyes in the presbyters and bishops, and gives this reason why Hierome, speaking of this power of the keyes, doth mention presbyters before the bishops, *because this authoritie belongs to a presbyter, as a presbyter primarily and properly* Praeponens in hoc presbyteros quoniam authoritas haec debetur presbytero, in quantum presbyter, primo, et secundum quod ipsum.

"Bartholomaeus Brixniensis and Joannes Semeca," says he, p. 56, "both glossators of the common law, doe maintaine and prove even out of it, that by right presbyters may excommunicate, though the bishops, *by custom and prescription*, have taken the power out of their hands Ecclesiarum praelati de jure communi possunt excommunicare, licet episcopi jam praescripserint contra multos praelatos. Gloss in caus. 2, ques. 1, cap 11 verbo Excommunicat.

Not only have bishops taken away this power from presbyters, but if the following account of the way in which they exercise it in the Church of England be true, it is impossible to think of it without the deepest regret. "If there be any thing," says Bishop Crofts, in his Naked Truth, p. 58, "in the office of a bishop to be challenged peculiar to themselves, certainly it should be this, (excommunication), yet this is in a manner quite relinquished to their chancellors, laymen who have no more capacity to sentence or absolve a sinner, than to dissolve the heavens or the earth. And this pretended power of the chancellor *is sometimes purchased with a sum of money*. Their money perish with them ! Good God, *what a horrid abuse is this of the divine authority?* But this notorious transgression is excused, as they think, by this, that a minister, called the bishop's surrogate, but who is indeed the chancellor's servant, chosen, called and placed there by him to be his crier in the court, no better, that when he hath examined, heard and sentenced the cause, then the minister forsooth pronounces the sentence. Just as if the rector of a parish church should exclude any of his congregation, and lock him out of the church; then comes the clerk, shows and fingers the keys, that all may take notice that he is excluded. And by this his authority, the chancellor takes upon him to sentence not only laymen, but clergymen also brought into his court for any delinquency ; and in the court of Arches *sentences even bishops themselves.*"

the canons of the Council of Elliberia, which related to excommunication, and not merely to doctrine; and twelve presbyters subscribed the canons of the Council of Arles, concerning the suspension of bishops. Nay, even the imperial law seems to intimate, that presbyters might excommunicate as well as bishops. "We charge," it says, "all bishops and priests, that they separate no man from the communion before they show the cause, &c. And he that presumes to excommunicate, let him be put from the communion." Nov. Constitut. 125, c. 11. And though the Fourth Council of Carthage decreed, in their 35th canon, that "the bishop, when he was in the church, and sitting in the presbytery, should be placed on a higher seat," yet they required him "when he was in the house to acknowledge himself the colleague of the presbyters;" enjoining him, in their 22d canon, "to ordain no one without the advice of his clergy, and the consent of his fellow-citizens;"* and that "he should hear the cause of no one without the presence of his clergy, otherwise his sentence should be void."† Attempts, indeed, were soon made to circumscribe the powers of presbyters, and to increase the dignity and authority of bishops, and to depress the power of the bishops of smaller sees, and subject them to the bishops of cities and to metropolitans. Thus it was decreed in the 6th canon of the Council of Sardica, that "no bishops should be settled for the future in villages and country places, *lest the name and authority of a bishop should fall into contempt;*"‡ by the Council

* "Ut episcopus sine consilio clericorum suorum clericos non ordinet, ita ut civium conniventiam et testimonium quaerat."

† "Ut episcopus nullius causam audiat absque praesentia clericorum suorum; alioquin irrita erit sententia episcopi nisi clericorum praesentia confirmetur."

‡ So rapidly did corruption spread, that the Council of Carthage say, in their twenty-fourth canon, that "their fathers had deservedly granted the pre-eminence *to the episcopal throne in Rome,* because it was *the imperial city;* και γαρ τω θρονω της πρεσβυτερας, &c. And Augustine, in his Quaestiones ex utroque mixtim, cap. 101, tom. iv. says, that for the same reason, the deacons of the Church of Rome were to have *the pre-eminence above the deacons of the churches of all other cities.*" "Idcirco honorabiliores habitos fuisse quam apud

of Laodicea, (canon 57,) that "those bishops who were ordained in such places already, should do nothing without the knowledge of the bishops of cities;" and by the Council of Nice, A. D. 326, "that in every province there should be some one bishop reckoned chief and supreme, who should be called a Metropolitan, without whose knowledge and consent (it was further determined by the Council of Antioch, A. D. 341,) the bishops of inferior cities should not ordain any bishop, nor do any thing of moment." Having deviated thus far from the arrangements of the Redeemer respecting the office-bearers of his Church as they are revealed in Scripture, patriarchs followed, and by and by they were succeeded by one supreme universal bishop.

It has been asserted, I am sensible, that the ordination of Ischyras, who had received orders from Colluthus, a presbyter of Alexandria, which were pronounced invalid by the Council of Alexandria, proves, that presbyters were considered at that period as having no power to ordain. But it will be evident to any one who looks into the facts as they are stated by Blondel,* that it was for other reasons than his having been ordained by a presbyter, that the orders of Ischyras were declared to be uncanonical. The ordination took place in another diocese than that to which Colluthus belonged, and where he had no right, according to the canons, to ordain any one. Colluthus, too, was in a state of schism, which alone would have vitiated these orders. Ischyras had no title, and orders conferred where there was no title were declared to be void. And Colluthus is alleged to have been made a bishop by Meletius, who also was in a state of schism; for the

caeteras Ecclesias, propter magnificentiam urbis Romanae, quae caput esse videbatur omnium civitatum" How different was this from the equality which, according to Jerome, ought to exist among all the ministers of the Church who are of the same order, and in particular among bishops. "Ubicunque," says he, in his Epistle to Evagrius, "fuerit episcopus sive Romae, sive Eugubii, sive Constantinopolis, sive Regii, sive Alexandriae, sive Tanis, ejusdem meriti, ejusdemque sacerdotii esse, potentiam divitiarum, et paupertatis humilitatem vel sublimiorem, vel inferiorem episcopum non facere."

* Apology, p. 317, 327.

clergy of Mareotis, when speaking of the ordination of Ischyras, say, that it was performed "by Colluthus the presbyter, making a show of being a bishop."*
No argument, therefore, can be brought from the case of Colluthus, a schismatical presbyter assuming the character of a bishop, and ordaining another without a title, in a diocese with which he had no connexion, to show that presbyters, who were living in communion with the Church, could not give valid orders, with the permission of the bishop, within their own diocese, to such as were not schismatics, and who had a title.

I remain, Reverend Sir,   Yours, &c.

LETTER XXIV.

Reply to the argument for Episcopacy, that there was always imparity among the orders in the ministry under the preceding dispensations, and there ought still to be imparity under the New Testament Dispensation—This proved to be a begging of the question, and that we must learn from the Scriptures themselves whether imparity was to continue among the ministers of the Gospel—Dr Raynolds acknowledges, that "those who had been most zealous for the Reformation of the Church for five hundred years before that event," did not believe in the divine institution of Episcopacy—Dr Raynolds and Hooker admit this to have been the doctrine of the Waldensian Churches, and of Huss and his followers, who had no minister superior to presbyters—This proved to be the highest order of their ministers by the testimony of their own pastors, and other authorities—Calvin and Beza, according to Dr Raynolds, Hooker, and Heylin, denied the divine right of Episcopacy, and this confirmed by their writings—The rest of the leading foreign Reformers rejected it, though Melancthon would have submitted to bishops, and even a Pope, for the sake of peace—Zanchius unfairly claimed by Episcopalians as approving of the powers possessed by their bishops—The foreign Protestant Churches without bishops, not from necessity, as Episcopalians allege, but from principle—This proved by Jeremy Taylor.

REVEREND SIR,—Having finished the examination of the different arguments for diocesan Episcopacy and the apostolical succession, which have been advanced by its advocates from Scripture and antiquity, I might close this discussion, which has been already too pro-

* "Ὑπὸ Κολλούθου τοῦ πρεσβυτέρου φαντασθέντος ἐπισκοπήν.

tracted; but before I do so, I must advert very briefly to one or two topics on which they are accustomed to expatiate, and by which they endeavour to evade the force of our reasoning. They tell us, for instance, that there has always been imparity among the ministers of religion, for under the Mosaic Dispensation the high-priest was superior to the priests and Levites; the Redeemer, while he was on earth, was superior to the twelve and the seventy disciples; and under the Gospel Dispensation, the Apostles were superior to the rest of the ministers of the early Church. But upon the principles of Presbyterians this imparity is destroyed, the different individuals in the standing ministry in the New Testament Church being placed, by their form of ecclesiastical polity, on a footing of equality. Upon this, however, I remark, that since they appeal to Scripture for the model of the constitution of the Christian Church, they are bound to follow it; and the only point which we are called to determine, is simply this, whether the Gospel ministry, as it is represented in its pages, is characterized by the principle of imparity or parity. It is not enough to tell us that there was imparity among the ministers of the Old Testament Church, but they must prove that they were to be the pattern of the evangelical ministry; and if they succeed in doing this, it will immediately follow that there is not a single Episcopalian Church, whether Protestant or Popish, on the face of the earth, as was formerly demonstrated, which resembles that Church in the orders of its ministry. Nor is it enough to refer to the superiority of our Lord, while he ministered upon earth, to the twelve and the seventy, for the Old Testament Church had not ceased to exist, nor had the New Testament Church been begun; and consequently any imparity which they may discover between him, and the Apostles and the disciples, prior to his resurrection, furnishes no warrant for a similar imparity among the ministers of the Church under the present dispensation. All therefore that remains is the apostolic age; and unless they can prove that there was imparity, not only at that time among the ministers of the Church, but that it was appointed to continue till the end of the world, they have no right to maintain that there ought to be imparity at present among the ministers of the Gospel. It is the prerogative of Christ, the only King and Head of his Church, to fix the arrangements respecting the Christian ministry; and we are neither to add to it a single order which he has not appointed, because we are desirous to preserve a similar imparity to what existed among the ministers of the Old Testament Church, nor to take from it any order which he has instituted, because we are partial to parity. There was certainly imparity among the ministers of the Church in the apostolic age; but it remains yet to be proved that it extended any further than between those of them who were extraordinary, and who were destined to cease after they had founded and organized the early Church, such as Apostles, prophets and evangelists; and those of them who were ordinary, and who were destined to continue throughout future ages, namely, pastors and teachers; Eph. iv. 11, 13. If the imparity, however, which existed in that age consisted only of the inferiority of pastors and teachers to Apostles, prophets and evangelists, and of the inferiority of the last of these three extraordinary orders to the two former, and of both prophets and evangelists to the Apostles; and if no evidence can be produced, (and I challenge you to do it, for it has never yet been done,) of the appointment of an order of ordinary ministers superior to presbyters, you have no right to introduce a principle of imparity, which Christ has not sanctioned, into the Christian priesthood, and I am entitled to maintain that a principle directly and expressly the reverse ought to characterize the ministry of the New Testament Church.

It has been alleged, too, that the famous Waldensian Churches, as well as the followers of Huss, believed in the divine institution of Episcopacy, and that this was the light in which it was viewed also by Luther, Melancthon, Calvin and Beza, and the other foreign Reformers, who were prevented only by necessity from having bishops, as they had neither funds to support them, nor could they procure for them regular episcopal ordination. Nothing, however, can be more contrary to fact than the first part of this statement, if the testimony either of Hooker or Dr. Raynolds is entitled to any credit. The former mentions "them of Walden," or the Waldenses, among those who thought that "*the Apostles did neither by word or deed appoint" Episcopacy.** And says the latter, "wherto may be added, that they also who have laboured about the reforming of the Church *these five hundred years* have taught, that all pastors, be they entitled bishops or priests, *have equall authority and power by God's word.* First, the Waldenses, (Aeneas Sylv. Hist. Boh. cap. 35, et Pigh. Hierarch. Eccles., lib. ii. cap. 10;) next, Marsilius Patavinus, (Defens. Pacis, pars 2, cap. 15;) then Wickliffe and his schollers, (Thom. Walden. Doct. Fidei, tom. 1. lib 2, cap. 60;) afterwards Husse, (Aeneas Sylv. loco citato;) last of all, Luther, Calvine, Brentius, Bullinger, Musculus, and others, who might be reckoned perticularly, in great number, sith as here with us; both Bishops Jewel, (loco citato,) and Pilkington, in the Treatise of Burning Paule's Church; and the Queen's Professors of Divinity in our universities, (D. Humphrey in Camp. et in Duraeum Jesuitas, pars 2, et rat. 3, et D. Whitaker, ad rat. Campiani, &c.) and other learned men, M. Bradford, Lambert, and others, M. Fox, Acts, &c , D. Fulke against Bristow, and Answer to the Rhemists, (tit. 1. 5,) do consent therein: *so in forreine nations all whom I have read treating of this matter,* and many moe, (no doubt,) whom I have not read."† And this account of the Waldenses is confirmed, not only by Mr. Acland, who acknowledges that Episcopacy, which he considers as "the ornament of your Establishment, is no longer preserved among the Vaudois," but by Alphonsus de Castro, who says, that "after many years

---
* Ecclesiast Polity, book vii. p. 395.
† Letter to Sir Francis Knollys.

the Waldenses revived this erroneous opinion, that there is no difference among priests."* And in the year 1530, when George Mauzel and Peter Latomus, two of their ministers, were sent to inquire into the doctrines of the Reformation, after stating to Œcolampadius that "they were the teachers of a poor people, who had existed for more than four hundred years, or, as their ancestors told them, from the days of the Apostles,"† they inquired whether there ought "to be degrees of dignity among the ministers of the Gospel, such as the episcopate, the presbyterate, and the office of the deacon," and at the same time added, that "*they* did not use these degrees, having only presbyters;"‡ which agrees exactly with a still more early testimony recorded by Perrin, (ch xiii p 25,) in which they say, "We hold that no person ought to presume to take that honour, (the office of the ministry,) but he who is called of God, as Aaron; feeding the flock of God, not for filthy lucre's sake, or *as having superiority over the clergy*, but as being an example to them in word, in conversation, in charity, in faith, and in chastity." And with regard to Huss, I have only briefly to mention, that the fourth of the articles, on account of which de Caussis accused him

* "Hunc eundem errorem post multos annos, ab inferis suscitarunt Waldenses dicentes nullum esse inter sacerdotes discrimen."

† "Quandoquidem ut rem semel capias sumus qualescunque doctores cujusdam plebis indigae et pusillae quae jam plusquam quadringentis annis, imo ut frequenter nostrates narrant, a tempore Apostolorum, non tamen ut facile judicarunt quique pii, citra Christi ingentem favorem commorata est." Sculteti Annales Evangelii Renovati, p. 161.

‡ "Primo an inter verbi Dei ministros debeant ordinari dignitatum gradus, ut puta episcopatus, presbyterii et diaconatus. His tamen gradibus inter nos non utimur."

Speaking of the ordination of their candidates for the ministry, they say, "Consumpto autem hoc tempore, Eucharistiae sacramento impositioneque manuum discipuli praedicti suscipiuntur in presbyterii et praedicationis officium, et hoc modo instructi ac edocti ad evangelizandum bini emittuntur. Verumtamen talis mos observatur ut omnino qui prius susceptus fuerit sequentem semper honore, dignitate et administratione praecedat eique magister constituatur" Sculteti Annales Evangelii Renovati, p. 161, in Von der Hardt's Historia Literaria. See, too, Ruchat's Histoire de la Reformation de la Suisse, tom. iii. p. 258, and Gerdesius's Hist. Evang. Renov., vol. ii. p. 402.

to the Pope, and he was afterwards condemned by the Council of Constance, was that he represented "all presbyters as having equal power; and asserted that the reservation of causes to the Pope and the bishops, and the ordination and consecration of the clergy, had been introduced through the avarice and ambition of their superiors."* And while Aeneas Sylvius asserts, in general terms, that both Huss and Jerome of Prague " had embraced the doctrine of the Waldenses," (Catalog. Test. fol. 1833,) it is acknowledged by Heylin, that their followers "had fallen upon a way of ordaining ministers among themselves, without having recourse to the bishop, or any such officer, as a superintendent;" and it appears from their Formularies, that the excommunication of a minister was a power which was exercised only by a synod. " Excommunicatio ministri non nisi toto synodo competit." (Ratio Unitatis Fratrum.)

Nor is the view which is given by Dr. Raynolds, of the sentiments of the leading foreign Reformers, less just, though Whitgift, Bancroft, Bishop Hall and others, represent them as admitting the divine right of Episcopacy. Luther, Melancthon, and the whole of the divines who subscribed the articles of Smalkald, declare expressly, that according to Scripture there is no difference as to power or dignity between bishops and presbyters; and the same opinion, as was formerly proved, is distinctly avowed in their writings,

* " Quarto circa ecclesiam errat, quod *omnes presbyteros pares dicit esse potestatis, ordinationem et clericorum consecrationem* dicit propter cupiditatem vel ambitionem superiorum adinventas." Historica Narratio de Fratrum Orthodoxorum Ecclesiis in Bohemia, &c. of Camerarius, p. 174. And in an Epistola Elenchtica Anonymi Theologi in Concilio Constantiensi, addressed to de Misa, one of the followers of Huss, and published by Von der Hardt, in his Magnum Constantiense Concilium, tom. iii , he refers to the disciples of the Reformer as holding that opinion, and attempts to refute it. " Sic illi maxime peccant qui detrahunt Papae dicentes, quod non Papa sit major sacerdos, sed frater cum aliis sacerdotibus, quia Apostoli vocabant se invicem fratres. Et sic illi errant, sicut quidam haeretici de secta Graecorum qui errabant dicentes, quod Papa non sit majoris auctoritatis quam simplex sacerdos. And so they err, as certain heretics of the sect of the Greeks erred, who affirmed that *the Pope had no more authority than a simple priest.*"

and was never retracted. Melancthon, indeed, who was too ready to give up even great principles for the sake of peace, inserted a liberal statement about bishops in the Confession of Augsburg; and from a desire to conciliate the Papists, expressed the willingness of the Lutherans to submit to them to a certain extent, if they would only be subject to Christ, and not tyrannize over their brethren.* But, as Mr. Hickman remarks, "he complains repeatedly how much he was blamed for it by his brethren."† And we know that under the influence of these feelings, he declared his willingness not only to have diocesan bishops, *but even a Pope*, (though we never hear of it from Episcopalians;) and thought it might be useful, because it would unite all nations in the faith, if he would only take care that sound doctrine should be preached throughout the Church. When he subscribed, accordingly, the Articles of Smalkald, which were drawn up by Luther, we are told by Osiander, (Epitom. Hist. Eccles. p. 285,) that he did it in the following terms: " I, Philip Melancthon, approve of the preceding articles as pious and Christian. And in regard to the Pope, if he would admit the Gospel, I think that for the common peace of Christians, who are under him, or who shall in future be under him, we could allow him that superiority which he possesses over bishops, as a mere human arrangement."‡

* In the conference between the Papists and Protestants, which took place at Augsburg, in 1530, Sleidan says, that "as far as related to the power and jurisdiction of bishops, the Saxons, including Melancthon, were disposed to make large concessions, but the Landgrave of Hesse, the inhabitants of Luneburg, and others, did not approve of it. Sed neque Luntgravius, neque Luneburgici, neque Noribergenses probabant," &c. Upon which Osiander remarks, (Epitome Hist. Eccles. cent. xvi p. 185,) "Melancthon seems to have been inclined to make some concessions to bishops as to jurisdiction, for he hoped, if this were done, that they would be less unfavourable to the pure doctrine of the Gospel; but Philip did not consider that the wolf might change his hair, but not his disposition. Sed non cogitabat Philippus," &c.

† "Certum est Melancthonem episcopis in Augustana confessione aliquid concessisse quo nomine quantum a fratribus incusatus fuerit ipse non in uno loco conqueritur." Apologia pro Ejectis in Anglia Ministris, p. 122

‡ " Ego Philippus Melancthon suprapositos articulos approbo, ut

In his tract, however, upon order, which was written many years after the Augsburg Confession, as well as in his exposition of the 118th Psalm, and others of his works, he denies in the most pointed and explicit terms the divine institution of Episcopacy; and, as Seckendorf informs us, both Luther and he retained that opinion till the day of their death. And the view which is presented by Dr. Raynolds of the sentiments both of Calvin and Beza is equally correct; for though, in consequence of repeated and earnest applications from the English prelates, and from the respect which they entertained for the English Government, as the principal protector of the Protestants, they expressed themselves favourably on different occasions respecting orthodox bishops, yet we have incontestable evidence that they did not look upon Episcopacy as founded upon divine appointment, but regarded it merely as a human institution. Such, for instance, is the statement of Hooker respecting Calvin, for in a passage before quoted, he includes him among those who did not think that " the Apostles appointed it either by word or deed;" and he was as likely to be acquainted with the opinion of the Reformer as any Episcopalian in the present day. Such, too, was the statement of Heylin, who wrote long after his time, and after the publication of the whole of Calvin's works; for he says to Burton, in a passage before referred to, "if by your divines you meane the Genevian doctors, Calvin and Beza, Viret and Farellus, Bucan, Ursinus, and those other of forreine Churches, whom you esteem the only orthodox professors, you may affirm it very safely, that *the derivation of episcopal authority from our Lord Christ is utterly disclaimed by your divines.* Calvin had never else invented the presbytery, nor with such violence *obtruded it on all the Reformed Churches;* neither had Beza divided episcopatum into divinum,

pios et Christianos. De Pontifice autem statuo, Si Evangelion admitteret, posse ei propter pacem, et communem tranquillitatem Christianorum, qui jam sub ipso sunt, et in posterum sub ipso erunt superioritatem in episcopos quam alioqui habet jure humano etiam a nobis permitti." See, too, Geidesii Hist. Evang. Renovat. vol. iv. p. 123.

humanum, and Satanicum, as you know he doth." And such, as is evident from the writings of Calvin, was undeniably his opinion. Thus, after remarking, in his Exposition of Philippians, I. 1, that "the term bishop was common to all the ministers of the word," he adds, that "from the corrupt signification of the word, (when it was appropriated to one,) this evil ensued, that under the pretence of this new designation, one has usurped authority over the others, as if all the presbyters had not been colleagues called to the same function." "It was therefore a very wicked deed," says he in his Institutes, "that one man having got the power into his own hand which was common to the whole college (of presbyters,) paved the way to tyrannical domination, snatched from the Church her own right, *and abolished the presbytery, which had been ordained by the spirit of Christ.*"* And in his Commentary on the 20th chapter of the Acts, which was written shortly before his death, he says, "Concerning the word bishop, it is observable that *Paul gives this title to all the presbyters of Ephesus;* from which we may infer, *that according to Scripture, presbyters differed in no respect from bishops,* but that *it arose from corruption,* and a departure from primitive purity, that those who held the first seats in particular congregations *began to be called bishops.* I say that it arose from corruption,—not that it is an evil for some one in each college of pastors to be distinguished above the rest, but because *it is intolerable presumption that men, in perverting the titles of Scripture to their own honour, do not hesitate to alter the meaning of the Holy Spirit.*"†

* Lib. iv. cap 11, sec. 7.

† When one of the presbyters was elevated above the rest, he says in the same work, lib. iv cap. 2, that it originated in an arrangement by the Church, and not in a divine appointment, " pro temporum necessitate humano consensu inductum " And Whitaker observes, Controv. iv. quaest. 1, cap. 2, " Dat quidem Calvinus fuisse olim in singulis ecclesiis episcopos singulos, in provinciis archiepiscopos et patriarchas, sed nullum his Calvinus aut episcopis aut archiepiscopis principatum vel dominatum in reliquos fratres tribuit " How much is this opposed to the representations of Calvin's sentiments, which are made by modern Episcopalians !

It is plain, not only from the testimony of Heylin, that similar sentiments were held by Beza, but from Whitgift's letter to him in 1593, in which he reminds him that "the same year, (1572,) he writ to Mr. Knox against the degree of bishops, *however they professed the Gospel,* that *the bishops brought forth the Papacy,* that they were bishops falsely so called, and were the relicts of Popery;"* as well as from the part which he took in drawing up the second Helvetic Confession, the declaration of which respecting the identity of bishops and presbyters is exceedingly explicit. And that this account of his views is strictly true, whatever Mr. Sinclair or modern Episcopalians may allege to the contrary, is undeniable. It is placed beyond a doubt, by what Bancroft says in his Survey of the pretended holy discipline, p. 39, where he tells us, (and if the Reformer had changed his opinion, it would have been known to that keen and haughty prelate, and he would have turned it to his advantage,) that Beza, in his account of the three kinds of bishops, asserts, that "all bishops, other than such *as have an equality amongst them,* and such as he alloweth and requireth that *every minister should be,* must of necessity be packing." And says Beza to Knox, "I wish you, dear Knox, (Epist. 77,) and the other brethren, to bear this also in mind, which is even now passing before our very eyes, that *as the bishops begat the Papacy,* so the pseudo bishops, *the relicts of the Papacy,* will bring infidelity into the world. This pestilence let all avoid who wish the safety of the Church; and since you have succeeded in banishing it from Scotland, *never, I pray you, admit it again;* however it may flatter you *with the specious pretext of promoting unity,* which deceived many of the ancients, even the best of them."†

---

* Strype's Whitgift, p 408.

† I quote his words from Professor Killen's translation of them, (Plea for Presbytery, p. 64,) as I happen to have no opportunity at present to examine them in the original.

Even in the most favourable statement which he makes about Episcopacy, he speaks of it as a mere human institution. "Tyrannidis non insimulasse episcopos veram Christi religionem profitentes et docentes, atque *in hoc humano gradu* ita se gerentes, ut eo ad aedi-

Nor were the sentiments of others of the Continental Reformers less express and decided. Zepper, in his Treatise on Ecclesiastical Polity, represents the following as the only form of Episcopacy which existed in the early Church. "Before," says he, "the tyranny of the Roman Pontiff arose in the Church, they chose, by the suffrages of all, one of the ministers distinguished by his age, learning, zeal, piety, experience, and other spiritual gifts, who being received, according to the rule of the divine word, as a more noble member of the Churches, by a synod of ministers, and the pious magistrate, without assuming any primacy, superiority, and dominion over his colleagues and brethren, or claiming any exemption from the order or office of the ministry or the laws, undertook the superintendence or principal care of these Churches."* "That no one," says Conringius, "should be allowed to teach or perform the offices of religion, unless he has been ordained by bishops, is enjoined by no divine law."† " As long," says Damaeus, " as the apostolic constitution continued in the Church, the presbyters that laboured in the word and doctrine did not differ at all from bishops But after that, by the ambition of those who presided over other presbyters, and took to themselves the name of bishops, the apostolical form and discipline was abol-

ficationem ovium sibi commissarum uterentur." De Minist. Evangel. Grad cap. 23.

The Oxford Tractarians admit (Tract. 4, p 7,) that Beza called the Presbyterian polity, which he considered as " the system handed down from the Apostles, *a divine episcopate.*"

* "Ante Pontificis Romani tyrannidem fuisse in Ecclesia, quod unum quendam ministrum aetate, eruditione, zelo, pietate, experientia, aliisque donis spiritualibus praestantiorem communibus suffragiis elegerunt, qui secundum verbi divini normam, et leges illi consentaneas a synodo ministrorum atque magistratu pio, tanquam nobiliori ecclesiarum membro, unanimo consensu et approbatione receptus sine primatus cujusdam, superioritatis et dominii in collegas et confratres usurpatione, aut e communi ministerii ordine, officio, aut legibus exceptione, atque immunitate, primariam ecclesiarum illarum curam humeris suis sustineret" Lib. ii cap 14.

† "Quod nemini porro docere religiosa sacra liceat, nisi in id ab episcopis fuerit ordinatus, non praefecto ulla est divina lege institutum." Apologia pro Reformatione Evangelica, published by Gerdesius in his Scrinium Antiquarium, tom. vi. pars 2, p. 694.

ished, then the bishops began to be distinguished even from these presbyters that preached the word, and to these bishops, contrary to God's word, the whole dignity was ascribed, nothing thereof almost being left to the presbyters; which thing, and the ambition of the bishops, did in time ruin the whole Church, as the matter itself appears in the Papacy. And *so the apostolic episcopate was abolished, and a human Episcopacy began, from* which sprang the Satanic Episcopacy, as it is now in the Papacy."*
" Upon the same account," says Chamier, " we may likewise say, that equality among pastors is better in a certain respect, to wit, for avoiding the tyranny of a few over the rest of their brethren, yea, of one over all. And how great an evil tyranny is, and how wide a door has been opened to it from the ambition of this presidency, experience has long since more than sufficiently proved. There is none who doubts that this custom (of investing one with the presidency) was introduced by good men, and with a good design; would to God not rather from carnal prudence, than by the direction of the Spirit."† And without quoting at length the opinion of the professors of Leyden, who say, (Disput. 42,) that " bishops are called such, not with relation to any supposed subordinate bishops or presbyters, but to the Church committed to their care, in which respect alone they have that title in Scripture, and *not upon account of any prerogative or authority which one minister has over another;*" of Saumur, who say, that " pastors being in the beginning constituted by the Apostles, governed the Church by common suffrages, (communibus suffragiis, communi solicitudine et cura;" (Thes. 7, de divers. Minist. Grad.;) of Walleus, who declares, that " in all the Scriptures there is no mention of such eminency and power of bishop over pastors;" (de Funct. Eccl.;) and of Arnoldus, who says, on Acts xx. 17, that "bishops and presbyters are not names of different gifts in the Church, *but of one and the same office;*"

---

* Controv. 5, lib. 1. cap. 14.
† Pan.trat., tom. ii. lib. ix. cap. 14.

I shall notice only further the sentiments of Zanchius, who is often referred to by Episcopalians as a great admirer and zealous patron of their ecclesiastical polity. But it is certainly surprising, if this was really the case, that, as is stated by Maresius, Zanchius should have declared " he could not but love the zeal of those who hated the very names of bishop and archbishop, being afraid that with these names the ancient ambition and tyranny, with the ruin of the Church, would return."* And the Reformer himself, in his exposition of the fourth commandment, gives the following account of the extent to which he could acknowledge the power of bishops, which differs not only from that which they possess under every form of diocesan Episcopacy in the present day, but under every form of it which has existed in the Church for the last fourteen hundred years. " In course of time," says he, " not long after the Apostles, a practice obtained by which one from among many pastors, presbyters and bishops was set over the rest, not as a lord, but as a guide or director to the rest of the seniors, (or rulers,) to whom especially the care of the whole of any particular church was committed, while the rest were his coadjutors and colleagues. This practice was adopted, as Jerome declares, that schisms and dissensions might be prevented, and the Churches might be preserved in a better state; therefore this institution and practice of pious antiquity cannot be condemned, *provided the bishop does not claim greater authority to himself than the other ministers possess, as Jerome rightly advises*."† But

* Exam. Prim. Quaest Theolog., p. 65. I quote the words merely to bear witness to his opinion, without approving of his feelings about the names.

† "Successu temporis non ita multo post apostolos obtinuit consuetudo, ut ex multis pastoribus, seu presbyteris et episcopis, unus praeficeretur reliquis omnibus, non tanquam dominus, sed ut rector reliquis senatoribus, cui imprimis commendata esset cura totius alicujus ecclesiae; reliqui illius essent co-adjutores et collegae. Constitutionem hanc factam esse ut tollerentur schismata et dissensiones, ut Hieronymus testatur, meliusque servarentur ecclesiae : idcirco damnari hanc piae vetustatis ordinationem et consuetudinem non posse, modo plus sibi auctoritatis non usurpet episcopus, quam reliqui habent ministri, ut recte monet Hieronymus."

where is the bishop, either in your Church, or among the Scottish Episcopalians, or in the Church of Rome, or in any of the other Episcopalian Churches, who assumes no more power in ordination or jurisdiction than he concedes to his presbyters? And if, as you are well aware, there is not a prelate on the face of the earth who is content with the measure of ecclesiastical authority which Zanchius would give him, is it fair in Mr. Sinclair, in his Dissertations on Episcopacy, or any other advocate of your ecclesiastical polity, after the example of Bishop Prideaux, *to claim for it the sanction of this venerable Reformer?*

I consider it unnecessary to prosecute this inquiry into the opinions of these Reformers to a greater extent, as it will be evident, I apprehend, from the preceding quotations, as well as from the confessions of their Churches, that you will appeal to them in vain in support of the claims of diocesan Episcopacy. Some of them, after proving, by the most convincing arguments, that it was not instituted by God, but was an arrangement of the Church in the early ages, may have expressed a wish, that where it had long existed, and was associated with protestantism, it might still be preserved; and if any one would prefer a form of polity devised by men to that form of government which is delivered in the Scriptures, it would be wrong to deny him all the asssistance in maintaining Episcopacy which he can derive from their testimony. Nothing, for instance, can be more precise and direct, than the declaration of the sentiments of Blondel respecting the perfect identity of bishops and presbyters, according to the statement of Scripture. Thus he says in his Apology, "If we will listen to Jerome, according to Scripture and the ancients, a presbyter is the same as a bishop; a bishop and a presbyter are one thing; the same persons are called presbyters and bishops." Again, "Whoever, when intending to prove what kind of person ought to be ordained a presbyter, describes him as bishop, decides purposely that a presbyter is the same as a bishop. But the

Apostle does so in his Epistle to Titus. Therefore the Apostle, on purpose, decides that a presbyter is the same as a bishop. Whoever is called upon to feed the flock, and to perform the duty of a bishop, is really a bishop, and has a title to the name. But presbyters (Peter being witness) are required to do so. A presbyter, therefore, (Peter being witness,) is really a bishop, and is entitled to the name. Whatever was the government of the church at Philippi, Ephesus, Jerusalem, in Pontus, &c. during the age of the Apostles, was the form of government every where among Christians of all nations. But the government in each of these churches, during the whole age of the Apostles, was such, that the brethren in it were subject to a plurality of bishops and rulers, who governed it in common. Therefore the government of the Church among Christians of all nations was such, that the brethren in each church were subject to a plurality of bishops and rulers acting together, who governed it in common."* I could easily quote many similar passages from other parts of his Apology, and show it to have been his opinion, that even when bishops were first introduced, the only pre-eminence which they possessed was that of constant moderators, and that they had nothing like the powers of modern bishops. I am aware, however, that it was reported by Du Moulin, that Blondel "concluded his Apology

---

* "Si Hieronymum audiamus, idem est presbyter, qui et episcopus; episcopus et presbyter unum sunt, iidem presbyteri et episcopi dicuntur. Quisquis qualis presbyter debeat ordinari probaturus, episcopum describit, eundem presbyterum qui et episcopus sit ex professo statuit. Apostolus Epistola ad Titum qualis presbyter ordinari debeat probaturus episcopum describit. Ergo Apostolus Epistola ad Titum eundem presbyterum et qui episcopus sit, ex professo statuit. Cujuscunque est pascere gregem Dei et episcopum agere, is est veri nominis episcopus. Atqui presbyteri cujuscunque (Petro teste) est pascere gregem Dei et episcopum agere, &c. Qualecunque ecclesiae inter Philippenses, Ephesios, Hierosolymitas, Ponticos, &c. toto Apostolorum seculo regimen fuit, tale inter Christianos omnes ubivis gentium fuit. Atqui tale ecclesiae inter Philippenses, Ephesios, Hierosolymitas, Ponticos, &c. *toto Apostolorum seculo* regimen fuit, ut pluribus una episcopis, praepositis, &c. subjiceretur fraternitas, *qui eam in commune regerent.* Ergo tale inter Christianos omnes ubivis gentium regimen fuit, &c. Apology, p. 3 and 4. See, too, his third, fourth, and fifth Observations, p. 7, besides many other passages.

with words to this purpose. "By all that we have said to assert the rights of the presbyter, we do not intend to invalidate the ancient and apostolical constitution (he calls sometimes what is ancient, apostolical) of episcopal pre-eminence. But we believe, that wheresoever it is established conformably to the ancient canons, it must be carefully preserved; and wheresoever by some heat of contention, or otherwise, it has been put down, or violated, it ought to be reverently restored." It is alleged, however, that he was prevailed with by some of the agents of the Westminster Assembly to erase them; and upon Du Moulin's stating this to Blondel's brother in London, and requesting him to write to Mr. D. Blondel, and inquire whether it was true, "he did not fail" to do so; "and then," says he, "in three or four weeks after, he showed me a letter from him, wherein he remembered his love to me, and acknowledged that that relation was true." Now, upon this extraordinary statement, which is quoted continually by the advocates of Episcopacy, I remark, in the *first* place, that it is certainly very wonderful this letter was never published, which would have removed completely all doubt upon the subject; and as this never was the case, though Durel and others brought forward every letter from the foreign divines which favoured them in the least, it appears to me unaccountable. Besides, though Mr. John Blondel was living in London, not a single individual has ever been mentioned, even by any Episcopalian, as having seen this letter, but Du Moulin himself, whose zeal for Episcopacy was of no ordinary kind, and who would be one of the very last, if there was really such a letter containing these words, to keep it a secret; and, 2*dly*, admitting that there was actually such a letter, though the world has never seen it, all that it would amount to would be merely this, to stultify Blondel, and demonstrate his inconsistency, but not to answer his powerful and irresistible reasoning. I have showed you that he considered presbyters and bishops to be perfectly the same in name and power during the whole apostolic age, and declared that every Christian Church was governed at that time by a common council of presbyters, who were bishops. And as you cannot suppose that he believed in *two apostolic constitutions existing at once*, it is plain, that when he represents primitive Episcopacy by that name, he could intend only to tell us that it was ancient, according to a frequent use of that expression. Episcopacy, however, as described by him, when it was first introduced, was very different from yours, or that of the Scottish Episcopalians; and if he was really chargeable with such gross inconsistency as that which is imputed to him by modern Episcopalians, I shall leave it to you, or Bishop Russel, or Mr. Sinclair, to estimate the respect which is due to his opinion, and allow you, without a grudge, all the assistance which it can render to your cause.

Nothing, too, can be more groundless than the report which was formerly circulated by Episcopalians, and which has been repeated of late by some of the most eminent and influential of your prelates, that it was necessity alone, and not choice or principle, which prevented the Protestant Churches on the Continent from having diocesan bishops. So far was this from being the case, that it is not only affirmed, but proved by testimony which cannot be set aside, to have been directly the reverse. "M. du Plessis," says Jeremy Taylor, in his Episcopacy asserted, p. 191, "a man of honour and great learning, attests, that at the first Reformation, there were many archbishops and cardinals in Germany, France and Italy, &c. that joined in the Reformation, *whom they might, but did not employ in their ordinations. And, therefore, what necessity can be pretended in this case, I would fain learn,* that I may make their defence. For the Dutch Church, let the celebrated Gisbert Voet be heard. Nos, says he, qui ordine illo episcoporum caremus, neque etiam indigemus, ab Anglicanis, aut Germanis ordinationem in forma petere semper potuimus; neque illi negarent. De Desp. Caus. Papatus, lib. ii. sect. 1, p. 110. He says, *they could have had episcopal or-*

dinations if they would, but thought they needed it not, and therefore would hardly have taken it kindly of any one, that would have pleaded for them that they would have had it, (as the present Bishop of London says,) *if they could.* For the French Church let Peter du Moulin's letter to Bishop Andrews be considered; where, excusing himself for not making the difference between bishops and presbyters to be of divine appointment, he pleads, that *if he had laid the difference on that foundation, the French Churches would have silenced him;* which doth not argue that concern among them for bishops, as would be requisite before such a plea from necessity were allowed them. And I have been credibly informed, that the French King was so earnest with them to admit bishops among them, that they durst not desire an English bishop to preach there, though they admitted him to communicate." Nor would there have been the smallest difficulty in procuring funds for the maintenance of bishops, either in France, where at one time a great number both of the nobility and gentry were Protestants; or in Holland, where it would have been the form of polity adopted by the State; or in Saxony, Prussia, or Hesse Cassel, as well as other countries, where it would have been supported by the Sovereign; so that on what ground it can be alleged, as is done at present by some of the zealous friends of Episcopacy, who are anxious to extend it among these Protestant Churches, that *it was necessity alone* which prevented them from establishing it, I am at a loss to understand. And my surprise is increased, when I see it declared in the 18th chapter of the Helvetic, the thirtieth Article of the French, and the thirty-first Article of the Belgic Confession, that according to the Scriptures all the ministers of the word "have equal power and authority, (una et aequalis potestas et functio, eadem et aequali inter se potestate praeditos, eandem et aequalem tum potestatem, tum autoritatem omnes, habeant;") in the first Article of the National Synod at Embden, that "no minister is to exercise any authority over another;" in the Wirtemburg Confession, that "a bishop and a presbyter are the same;" in the first Danish Confession, that "true bishops or priests are all the same;" and in the Articles of Smalkald, that "by divine right there is no difference between a bishop and a pastor or presbyter, and therefore there is no doubt that the ordination of fit ministers by pastors is ratified and approved by divine authority;" my surprise, I say, is increased, on the supposition that they were honest and upright men, that they would have introduced these statements into their public Formularies, or suffered them to remain, if nothing but necessity kept them from adopting diocesan bishops.

I have only further to add, that as you have introduced one order into the Christian ministry, or that of bishops, for which you have never yet produced any warrant from Scripture, so you have changed entirely another order, or that of deacons. In the primitive Church they were instituted to serve the tables of the poor, (Acts vi.,) and no other office was ever assigned to them, though Philip, having executed the office of a deacon well, obtained for himself "a good degree," and was promoted to be an Evangelist. But in your Church, and that of the Scottish Episcopalians, they are allowed not only to preach, but to baptize, and are relieved, I believe, from the care of the poor. But this, as Dr. Whitby candidly acknowledges, is a deviation from the practice of the Apostolic Church, and an innovation on its constitution. "The ancients," says he, in his sermon on Mat. xii. 7, "were so far from believing this, that they expressly forbade all deacons to baptize, and introduce this as a prohibition laid on them on this very account, that *baptism was an office belonging only to the priesthood.*" "A deacon," say the Apostolic Constitutions, "doth not baptize, or offer." And again, "it is not lawful for a deacon to offer sacrifice, or to baptize." And again, "we permit only a presbyter to teach, to offer, and to baptize." See this fully proved by Cotelerius, in his notes on the word ἱερατευσαι, p. 206, 207, where he introduceth an old author saying, that if baptism, in case of necessity, be performed by the minor clergy, we expect the event, that what is wanting either should be supplied by us, or reserved to be supplied by our Lord. *The baptism, therefore, of deacons, which is now commonly in use among us, can only be of human institution. It was permitted only in the third century,* from which time till the Reformation even laymen were allowed to baptize in cases of necessity; and if any thing be wanting to that baptism in those cases, we have like reason to believe it will be supplied by our Lord."* What reason the doctor could have for entertaining that belief, when the ordinance of baptism is performed by a deacon, either in your Church or among the Scottish Episcopalians, while no power to administer it is given to him in Scripture, I cannot conceive; and if he exercise a power not contained in the commission bestowed on him by the only Head of the Church, it suggests unquestionably very serious considerations to the members of all Episcopalian Churches, when they apply to him for baptism to their infant children. How you will be able to remedy that defect, I cannot tell. " We permit none of the clergy to baptize," say the Apostolic Constitutions, "but only bishops and presbyters." But *you* permit those who have no right to do it to administer that ordinance. The Russians formerly, as is mentioned by Reuss, used to re-baptize all who joined their communion;† and when the daughter of Christian the Fourth of Denmark, who had been betrothed to the Grand Duke in 1643, refused to be re-baptized, the marriage was broken off. But what will you do in the case of these individuals who were baptized by deacons in their early days, and who

---

* "Their deacons," says Archbishop Whately, of the churches in the time of the Apostles, "appear to have had an office considerably different from those of our Church."—*Essays on the Kingdom of Christ*, p. 131.

† "Olim," says he in his Dissertatio Historico-Theologica de Ecclesia Ruthenica, p. 335, "ne baptisma quidem extra suam et Graecorum ecclesiam susceptum legitimum et validum arrogantissime opinati sunt," &c.

have never been re-baptized? I trust that Bishop Russel, instead of repeating those trite objections to what he is pleased to denominate the office of lay-presbyters, which have been frequently answered, will direct his attention to this perplexing question, and point out the way in which baptisms received by innumerable individuals from the hands of men, who, as Jerome remarks, " were only the ministers of the tables," and who had no right to perform them, may be most effectually remedied.

There are several other topics of considerable moment, to which I was desirous to advert, but I must close this discussion. I hope that nothing which has been said in these Letters will be construed by any one as implying a doubt that I do not look upon your Church as a Christian Church, or that I am insensible to the great and important services which, especially at the period of the memorable Revolution, along with the Church to which I have the honour to belong, she rendered to the cause of our common Protestantism. I have noticed her defects, but I have far greater pleasure in acknowledging her worth; and while you compare myself and the other ministers of the Church of Scotland, as well as the ministers of the other Presbyterian Churches in our native land, to the priests of Samaria, I concede most willingly to your sound and pious bishops and clergy the honourable character of ministers of Christ. But how, upon your principles, you can claim that honourable character to yourself, or grant it to any other minister of your Church, or consider her as a Church, or cherish any sure and certain hope of the salvation of a single individual within her pale, or of a single individual in the Church of Rome, or of any individual on the face of the earth, I cannot perceive May she not only seek, but attain that more thorough and important Reformation which was intended by Edward, and longed for by Cranmer, and of which there is an admirable outline in the Reformatio Legum, which was drawn up by that great and illustrious prelate, and the other commissioners who were appointed by that young and enlightened Prince. Would to God that her Professors of Theology could adopt in some measure the language of Dr. Prideaux, when he said to James the First, a few years before his death, "Within the last nine years Oxford has sent forth seventy-three Doctors in Divinity, and more than one hundred and eighty-three Batchelours in that sacred science. I, as your Majesty's Professor of Divinity, had the honour of being concerned in conferring these degrees; and I can confidently affirm, that all these two hundred and fifty-three divines, and more, are warm detesters of Popery, remote from favouring Arminianism," though I have no wish they should add, "strong disapprovers of Puritanism,"[*] if by that term be meant Presbyterianism. May purity of doctrine distinguish her ministrations, and a spirit of piety and Christian benevolence extend its influence throughout all her parishes; that Ephraim may no more vex Judah, nor Judah vex Ephraim; and that while the ministers of Episcopalian and Presbyterian Churches differ from each other on certain points, it

[*] "Intra proxime elapsum novennium, obstetricante pro modulo meo qualicunque professoris tui conatu," &c.

If the directions contained in the Reformatio Legum Ecclesiasticarum, prepared by Cranmer, Ridley, Knox, and the rest of the thirty-two commissioners of King Edward, were followed out, the clergy of the Church of England would, like the Scottish Presbyterian ministers, have ruling elders, or as they call them, lay elders, to assist them in exercising a kind and prudent oversight of their parishioners. Would not this be a benefit? But what would Bishop Russel say of it, after the note in the Appendix to his Sermon on Lay Presbyters?

Besides what Cranmer proposed in the Reformatio Legum, Strype informs us, that when the monasteries were proposed to be dissolved, "the Archbishop is said to have counselled and pressed the King to it, but for other ends than the former had in view, viz. that out of the revenues of these monasteries the King might found more bishoprics; and that dioceses being reduced into less compass, the diocesans might the better discharge their office, according to Scripture and primitive rules."— *Life of Cranmer*, p. 35.

may be with feelings of mutual kindness and forbearance, and it may still be said,

"See how these Christians love one another."

I remain, Reverend Sir,

Yours, &c.

THE END